Volcanoes

VOL

CANOES

GORDON A. MACDONALD

University of Hawaii

PRENTICE-HALL, INC., ENGLEWOOD CLIFFS, NEW JERSEY

VOLCANOES
Gordon A. Macdonald

© 1972 by PRENTICE-HALL, INC.
Englewood Cliffs, New Jersey

10 9 8 7 6 5 4 3 2
ISBN: 0-13-942219-6

Library of Congress Catalog Card Number 78–37404
Printed in the United States of America

Prentice-Hall International, Inc., London
Prentice-Hall of Australia, Pty. Ltd., Sydney
Prentice-Hall of Canada, Ltd., Toronto
Prentice-Hall of India Private Limited, New Delhi
Prentice-Hall of Japan, Inc., Tokyo

Contents

v

Preface

There is nothing in all of nature that arouses more interest and more terror in mankind than a great volcanic eruption. And likewise there is nothing that arouses more superstitious veneration or more aesthetic delight than a volcanic mountain. The beautiful green-clad symmetry of Mayon, the cold sparkling glory of Shishaldin, the colossal power of the broad rounded outline of Mauna Loa, the breathtaking majesty of Fuji standing serenely with its snow-clad head in the clouds above the lake-dotted green of the surrounding countryside—all are never-to-be-forgotten sights that call up in man a fundamental reaction of awe and delight. For untold centuries Fuji has stood to the Japanese people as a symbol of loveliness and exalted power, venerated no less today for its beauty than it was formerly out of superstition. The slow, inexorable advance of a destroying lava flow on a village lying in its path; or the inky midday blackness of a great explosive eruption, shot through with brilliant lightning and the jarring crash of thunder, and accompanied by the trembling of the ground beneath and the choking stench of sulfur fumes; these are experiences to give pause to even the most experienced and callous of observers!

Volcanoes are many things. They are ruthless destroyers of human lives and property. But they are also benefactors, on whose past action depends the fertility of agricultural countrysides, and the very existence of the land itself. A large proportion of the land surface of the globe (not to mention the vast preponderance of the deep-ocean floors) is made up of volcanic rocks, which have yielded a large part of the earth's mineral wealth. Through the eons of geologic time, the gases of the atmosphere and the water of oceans, lakes, and rivers, have been liberated onto the earth's surface by volcanoes; and thus it is perhaps not stretching fact too far to say that the existence of life on earth also depends on past volcanic action. And finally, to the earth scientist volcanoes are windows that provide our only direct glimpse, albeit a very slight one, of our last earthly frontier—the unknown interior of our globe!

The term *volcano* is a multiple one even in technical definition. A volcano is defined as a place or opening from which molten rock or gas, and generally both, issue from the earth's interior onto its surface. But a volcano is also defined as the hill or mountain built up around the opening by accumulation of the rock material poured or thrown out. The behavior of erupting volcanoes shows wide variations, depending both on the nature of the material being erupted and on the surrounding environment.

These, then, are the many-sided objects that we will be examining in the following pages. The book has been prepared primarily for students of geology who have already had an introduction to the subject, including some petrology. I have tried, however, to write it in such a way that it can be read also by the interested non-geologist. To that end, I have avoided specialized geological terms insofar as it appeared practical, and have defined the ones that are used. Most of the technical terms directly related to volcanology must, of course, be introduced and defined in a book dealing with volcanoes on a level that is at all technical. Because the variations in volcanic activity are closely dependent on the kind of molten rock (magma) involved, it is necessary to designate the magma type, and this is most concisely done by giving the name of the rock that results from consolidation of the magma. The rock names and other petrologic terms used in the text are defined in the appendix on igneous rock classification.

Volcanology, the science of volcanoes, has three principal aspects: descriptive, interpretive, and humanistic. This book is largely descriptive. Interpretive volcanology depends heavily on physical chemistry and rather advanced petrology, an adequate treatment of which is beyond the scope of this book. Proper interpretation also depends on description. Before we can interpret volcanoes and volcanic activity in terms of the physical chemistry of magmas we must know in some detail the physical makeup, structure, and behavior of volcanoes. Several good books deal with the petrologic aspects of volcanism, and others along similar lines are in preparation, but there is today no book in English to which the student can turn for an adequate description of volcanoes and their activity. I hope that the present book will fill this gap. Petrology and petrologic interpretations have been avoided, except on the very elementary level necessary to understand the relationship of different types of volcanoes to different varieties of magma.

The glimpse of the earth's interior, mentioned on an earlier page, that volcanoes provide through the petrologic interpretation of the materials they bring to the surface, is still highly speculative and is not dealt with here.

Even with the many pictures included in this book it has not been feasible to try to illustrate all vocanic features. The reader seeking more illustrative material will find a large collection of photographs of volcanic landforms in Green and Short (1971).

The humanistic aspects of volcanology are already important, and will become much more so in the future. Many volcanic districts are heavily populated, and the risk of volcanic catastrophe is ever present in them. The solution cannot be to move the people out of these districts. They are heavily populated because they are highly fertile, and as our world population grows and the need for food increases, we cannot afford to abandon rich agricultural areas. We must accept the volcanic risk, but we must also do our best to minimize it. To do so we must be able to recognize the different types of volcanoes and their degrees of maturity, and know the types of eruption that are likely to be associated with each. The type of eruption to be expected depends upon recognition of the type of volcano involved and its history. Prediction of the course of an eruption depends on a knowledge of the behavior of the sorts of flows, or other types of activity, that type of eruption is likely to produce; and this in turn leans largely on descriptions of previous activity, at the same volcano or elsewhere. Prediction of the time of an eruption depends partly on physical measurements, but the interpretation of these depends on knowledge of the habitual behavior of the volcano or other similar volcanoes. We cannot predict without knowing what to expect; we cannot take alleviative actions without knowing how the activity is likely to behave. Thus descriptive volcanology is basic to humanistic, as well as to interpretive, volcanology. The last chapter of the book is the only extended discussion of the humanistic aspects of volcanology that I know of in English.

The study of volcanoes has its aspects of high adventure. In an effort to convey some of the drama and excitement of volcanic eruptions, and also to give some insight on the human problems they create, I have written the first chapter in the form of a diary of two different eruptions in which I have been involved. Words can convey only feeble portraits of the actual events, and they give a very inadequate feeling of the satisfaction that comes from trying to help, with whatever success, people who are in trouble. But perhaps they will convey enough of the idea to interest students, and inspire some of them to enter a field still in its infancy, but which in the future certainly will be as important as it is satisfying.

Finally, perhaps the best excuse for writing a book dealing with the descriptive and humanistic aspects of volcanology, with comparatively little attention to interpretation in terms of magma chemistry and physics, is that these are the aspects in which I am most interested.

It is impossible to go into great detail in a book of this sort. The various subjects are covered adequately, I think, but certainly not exhaustively.

If as I hope, some of my readers find they want to go further into some or all of the subjects, they will find a good starting point in the lists of suggested additional reading at the end of each chapter. These, in turn, will suggest still other readings; and I want to emphasize the fascination and vital importance of original field work. In the words of the great pioneer volcanologist, Desmarest, "Go and see for yourself!" The volcanoes themselves are the ultimate source of all our knowledge of volcanoes.

It has been a long time since any man started out "from scratch" and progressed entirely on his own in the pursuit of any branch of knowledge. I am sure he must have lived longer ago even than the cave man! Perforce, we build on the work of those who went before us and incorporate into our own the work and thought of our contemporaries. Everything in the following pages is dependent to some degree, and generally to a very large degree, on the work of others. I think that my own research may have contributed something worthwhile to science; but in a general compendium of this sort my principal contribution must be my evaluation, on the basis of my own experience, of the work of others.

I am grateful to all of my colleagues, past and present, who have aided me with their writings, and to my contemporaries with whom I have worked in the field and laboratory and with whom I have spent many hours in discussion and debate of the habits and whimsies of volcanoes. They are far too many for me to mention them all individually. Professor Willard H. Parsons has been very helpful in his critical reading of the manuscript and his suggestions for strengthening originally weak points in it.

To four persons I owe special tribute: Prof. Howel Williams, of the University of California, who first awakened my interest in volcanoes and whose brilliant work has been a constant inspiration; Dr. Thomas A. Jaggar, whose twin devotions to volcanoes and to human welfare have greatly shaped my own interests; Prof. Alfred Rittmann, whose broad knowledge of active volcanoes has led to especially stimulating discussions; and most of all to my wife, Ruth, who has shared the joys and hardships of field and office, whose unfailing encouragement has kept me going at times when I might otherwise have faltered, and whose keen insight has helped me out of many a tight spot. To all of them, a fond thank you!

G.A.M.

Volcanoes

1

Narrative of Two Eruptions

A pale fringe of dawn was just beginning to lighten the eastern horizon as the Philippine Navy tug came to anchor off the town of Mambajao, on Camiguin Island. For some time the black outline of the island had been visible off the port side, and now in the increasing light its silhouette grew more and more distinct. A few lights marked the position of the town. To its left rose the humpy outline of Mt. Mambajao, and to the right the even humpier mass of Hibokhibok. Gradually the green forest-clad slopes of the mountains appeared, and the town itself, with its wharf projecting like a beckoning finger toward us. At the summit of Hibokhibok, a steep-sided irregular peak was sharply outlined against the pale sky, and drifting off to the left was a dove-colored plume of "smoke," which was beginning to turn pink in the first refracted rays of sunlight (Plate 1-1). As though not content with a single appearance, the lovely scene repeated itself, upside down, in reflection on the oily rippled water!

Thinking back to that morning in September, 1953, it is hard for me to realize that all this beauty is covered in my notebook by the terse words, "Fume cloud drifting southwestward from Hibokhibok summit dome." And at the time it was hard to visualize the grim events that were the cause of our being there.

The ship's crew served us coffee and doughnuts, and the small boat

PLATE 1-1. Hibokhibok Volcano, seen from the ship off Mambajao in September 1953. A faint cloud of fume is drifting away from the dome built in the crater at the summit of the mountain between 1948 and 1953. U. S. Geological Survey photo by G. A. Macdonald.

took us ashore. We were a party of about 30 scientists, mostly geologists, from the just-concluded Pacific Science Congress in Manila. We were there as guests of the Philippine government to see the results of a great volcanic eruption.

Hibokhibok had been known to be an active volcano, but its last eruption had been in 1871–1875, and with the passage of two or three generations men tend to forget. To be sure, a small gas vent had appeared in the crater at the summit of the mountain in 1897, and another in 1902, but these caused no one any trouble and even formed a small deposit of sulfur that for a short time was mined commercially. The people in Mambajao and the other villages scattered around the foot of the mountain were not apprehensive.

Nothing more happened until 1948, when frequent earthquakes began to be felt. These became very numerous in late August, and on September 1 an explosion sent a boiling cauliflower-like cloud upward several thousand feet from the summit crater. Avalanches of red-hot ash and streams of mud swept down the northern slope of the mountain (Fig. 1-1), devastating an area of nearly 3 square miles and destroying part of one village. A lava flow spread over part of the upper southeastern slope, but did no important damage. Early in 1949, a mass of viscous lava, known to volcanologists as a volcanic dome, started to accumulate in the summit crater. It gradually grew to a height of several hundred feet, accompanied from time to time by small explosions and glowing avalanches (Plate 1-2). On Sep-

2

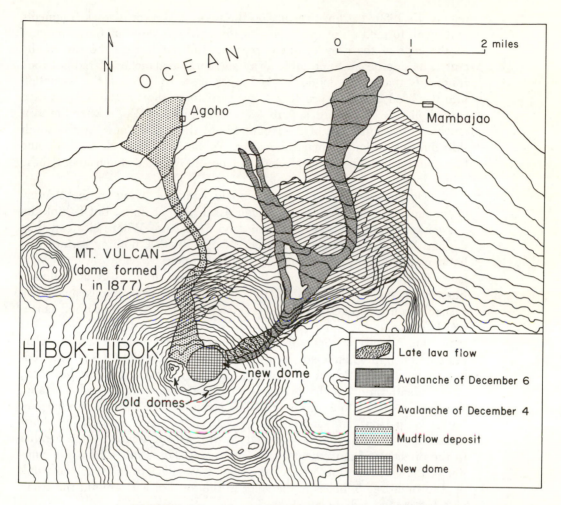

FIGURE 1-1. Map of Hibokhibok Volcano, Camiguin Island, Philippines, showing the summit dome, the course of the glowing avalanche of December 1951, and the location of the village of Mambajao. The lines are form lines, not contours. (After Macdonald and Alcaraz, 1956.)

PLATE 1-2. Small glowing avalanche, and the ash cloud rising from it, on the flank of Hibokhibok Volcano, Philippines, on July 17, 1949. Photo by L. F. Abad, Philippine Bureau of Mines.

tember 15, 1950, a stronger explosion threw out a shower of rock fragments that again formed a hot avalanche on the northern slope of the mountain. As the edge of the growing dome reached and overlapped the rim of the crater, its side began to crumble away and form avalanches of red-hot rock fragments that slithered down the upper eastern slope of the mountain into the head of a valley that ran eastward for a short distance, and then turned sharply northward toward Mambajao (Plate 1-2). Neither the avalanche on the north side of the mountain nor the smaller ones on the south side did any serious damage, however. To be sure, they destroyed some forest and a little agricultural land, but no one worried much about these minor losses.

Do you wonder why people would continue living in the shadow of the mountain under such circumstances? I have at times, but I think the answer is obvious. This is their home and their land. Where else can they go, and how else can they make their living? Besides, nothing serious had happened yet, and perhaps nothing would happen!

But then, on December 4, 1951, came catastrophe. A great explosion burst from the eastern base of the dome, and a tremendous avalanche rushed down the valley on the eastern slope of Hibokhibok, turned northward following the valley, and spread out at the northeast base of the mountain. No one who saw it close up lived to tell about it, but an alert photographer in Mambajao recorded it in pictures (Plate 1-3). The red-hot avalanche, enveloped in writhing clouds of stifling gas and hot dust, swept silently and lethally over the villages just north of Mambajao and, in a few moments, took the lives of 500 persons. Houses were burned and bodies of persons and animals were charred and mummified. The blast accompanying the avalanche knocked down trees and aligned them parallel to the direction of movement of the avalanche. Three miles from the summit of the mountain the force of the blast was sufficient to wrap the trunk of a coconut tree 5 inches in diameter in the form of a U around the trunk of a big mango tree (Plate 1-4).

PLATE 1-3. Ash cloud rising from a glowing avalanche on the flank of Hibokhibok Volcano, Philippines, with part of the town of Mambajao in the foreground, December 4, 1951. The avalanche killed about 500 persons in the outskirts of Mambajao. Photo by Hibok-Hibok Studio, Mambajao.

A similar avalanche rushed down the same general route early in the morning of December 6, and its path was visible in the predawn darkness as a dull red streak (with a temperature of about 700°C) down the mountainside. Later, examining the deposit left by it, we saw a great block of rock from the dome, 25 feet across, that had been rafted down for 1½ miles on the top of the avalanche. Local people told us that the block had sat quietly for half an hour, and then torn itself apart in an explosion that embedded rock fragments in coconut trees 60 feet away! The embedded fragments were still there. We also saw, at the very tip of the deposit, a coconut tree that had been engulfed in the cloud of dust, though the avalanche itself had stopped before getting to it. The side of the tree toward the volcano was charred to a height of 15 feet, clearly marking the depth of the dust cloud, but the side away from the volcano was still fresh and green. The accumulation of ash—dust from the settling of the cloud—was only about half an inch thick around the base of the tree. The heat from this rather diffuse dust cloud had charred the side of the tree trunk instantaneously. Small wonder that no living thing in the path of the avalanche survived! And if the avalanche had spread half a mile farther north, into Mambajao, the loss of human lives would have reached several thousand instead of 500! Not knowing what was coming next, the Philippine government had evacuated all of the villages around the base of the volcano and most of Mambajao, and moved the people to the nearby island of Mindanao.

The disaster had also resulted in the establishment of a national Commission on Volcanology to study Philippine volcanoes and advise the government on volcanic risks. Our party spent the day examining the effects

PLATE 1-4. Coconut tree uprooted and bent around the base of another tree by the glowing avalanche of December 6, 1951, at Hibokhibok Volcano. Photo by Torquato Reyes.

of the eruption under the able guidance of Arturo Alcaraz, the chief geologist of the Commission on Volcanology, his assistant, Gregorio Andal, and the local observer for the Commission, Gene Omahoy. That evening some of the people still living in Mambajao came to us and asked if the volcanologists in the party would speak to them and tell them about their volcano. We agreed, and after a late dinner we took our places on the balcony of Gene Omahoy's house, overlooking the street. The scene was dramatic in the extreme. The street was filled with people, their faces lighted by a dozen flickering torches. We lined the balcony—Gene and Art Alcaraz and Greg Andal of their own country; Jim Healy, in charge of volcanological work in New Zealand; George de Neve, head of the Volcanological Survey of Indonesia; Howel Williams, University of California, the leading American volcanologist; and I. Gene introduced us, and each of us spoke in turn, de Neve in Indonesian, Alcaraz and Andal in Tagalog (the national language of the Philippines), and the rest in English. Gene also translated for each of us, including the other Philippino speakers, for these people were Visayan and proudly refused to admit they understood much of either English or Tagalog. We noticed, though, that they laughed heartily at jokes before they were translated! The purpose of the meeting was serious enough. Their friends and relatives who had been moved to Mindanao wanted to return. Not only was Camiguin Island their home, where their land was, but it is free of the malaria that is rampant on Mindanao. No wonder they wanted to come back! But by government edict they could not come back so long as the volcano remained dangerous. We reassured our audience as best we could, but none of us knew enough about the local volcanic situation to speak with any confidence at that stage.

We left that night to return to Manila, but Alcaraz, Andal, and I promised to return soon to try to find out if it was indeed yet safe for the people to come home to Hibokhibok. I had been loaned by the U. S. Geological Survey to the government of the Philippines to help the new Commission on Volcanology get started in its program of installing seismographs and watching and interpreting the volcanoes.

We were back in early December, and after some preliminary work around the base, we prepared to climb the mountain. As long as the dome at the summit continued to grow, the volcano was dangerous. Gene Omahoy made careful observations on it every day with a telescope and had not been able to detect much change in it for several months, but only a close inspection would give the final answer. If the dome had stopped growing and had become reasonably stable, only a reasonable risk would be involved in allowing the people to come home. There was, of course, always the possibility that the dome would resume its growth but careful watch would be kept for any sign of that.

We were joined in our ascent of the mountain by a couple of local men to help with our equipment, and by Father Arthur Shea, S.J. Father Shea, from New York State, had been with the Philippine guerrillas through the war and had been parish priest at Mambajao at the time of the catastrophe in December, 1951. His personal efforts in the behalf of his suffering parishioners had been tremendous. We knew he was very popular with the people and that his work was appreciated, but we didn't find out to what degree until later! Father Shea had done a lot of climbing on Hibokhibok and, although he had been transferred to Mindanao, he was still intensely interested in the volcano and in the people. He wanted to climb the mountain with us to see the situation for himself, and we were delighted to have his excellent companionship.

Climb it we did, examining the avalanche valley on the south side of the mountain for any signs of recent avalanches. The great rock flows of 2 years earlier had filled the lower part of the valley to a depth of more than 400 feet, but there were no signs of recent movements. Finally, about 11 A.M. we began the ascent of the dome itself, separating into smaller parties to gather more information. The dome was shrouded in clouds, and we couldn't see far. Father Shea and I ate lunch at the summit. The dome was steaming heavily (Plate 1-5), but aside from occasional tumbling

PLATE 1-5. The craggy summit of the dome built on Hibokhibok Volcano between 1948 and 1951, as it appeared in January 1954. U. S. Geological Survey photo by G. A. Macdonald.

rocks there was no sign of further movement. The dome had stopped growing and had become reasonably well stabilized. It was safe for the people to come home.

Our party reassembled, and as a final check we circled the northern base of the dome. Our work done, we were returning along the path we had followed a short time before when our own disaster overtook us. It was the sort of accident that had a million-in-one chance of happening. One of the many rolling rocks we had been seeing and hearing all day broke loose near the top of the dome and came bounding down, headed straight for Father Shea. The chance of it coming directly toward him was almost vanishingly small, and even if it did, it would be seen coming and almost anywhere he could have dodged it; but as fate would have it, he was at that moment crossing a narrow and difficult ledge where dodging was impossible. The rock, weighing a couple of hundred pounds and traveling with tremendous speed, struck him squarely, knocked him into the air, and fractured his pelvis.

We moved him the short distance to the crater floor, away from the base of the dome and the danger of any other falling rocks, but we dared not attempt to take him farther. Instead, we immediately sent one of the local men to Mambajao for aid, and made Father Shea as comfortable as circumstances would permit in the lee of a big boulder, with our jackets and shirts over him and a big fire reflecting its heat off the boulder to keep him warm in his state of shock. We had not intended to spend the night on the mountain and had no other equipment; and even in the tropics, in the swirling mists of the mountaintop the night was cold and miserable. He suffered intensely but without a word of complaint. And we suffered with him, in sympathy and anxiety.

Before daylight our messenger returned to tell us that help was already on the way, and before long we could hear people coming. Word had spread fast, and everyone was eager to come to the aid of their padre. Nearly everything else was abandoned. Up the mountain they came, men, women, and children, dozens of them, cutting a broad trail, bringing food and blankets and a basket stretcher, and ropes to lower the stretcher over the difficult steep places. Then down again they came with the stretcher, slowly and carefully, so that the trip would be no worse for the injured man than it had to be. Father Shea spent months in the hospital, but eventually made a good recovery, and in his indomitable way returned to climbing mountains in the little time he could spare from tending his new parishes.

As a result of our report and recommendations, the people were allowed to return to their homes around the base of Hibokhibok. They were warned, however, not to live in the bottoms of the valleys close to the streams. As is commonly the case after big eruptions, the upper slopes of the mountain were covered with sandy ash and dust, which is easily transformed into mud by heavy rains. Mud formed in that way flows downslope and, gathering velocity, rushes down the stream courses burying anything immovable in its path and sweeping with it anything movable. Two or three persons who disregarded the admonition and chose to live close to the streams were killed during the next couple of years by mud-flows. Except for them, however, the people have been safe, and happy to be home again.

The contrast between the explosive violence of volcanoes such as Hibokhibok and the gentle lava effusions of Hawaiian volcanoes is amazing. At the beginning of 1955 I was back at the Hawaiian Volcano Observatory, on the rim of the crater of Kilauea Volcano, finishing my part of the report on the short eruption that Kilauea had staged in the crater at the end of May, 1954, and trying to catch up on things left over from my work in the Philippines. Things had been rather quiet for the last few months, and I was grateful for it, though the very quietness might have made me uneasy. Things seldom are quiet long at the Volcano Observatory, and that year was no exception! In mid-January, Dr. Jerry Eaton, the Observatory's seismologist, told me that the number of earthquakes was increasing on the east flank of Kilauea mountain. There are always some earthquakes, but an increase in their frequency indicates an abnormal amount of shifting of the rocks that make up the mountain. It does not, however, tell us what sort of shifting. The mountaintop may be rising, pushed up by liquid lava squeezed into the lower part of the volcano, and this may lead to an eruption; or it may be sinking as the liquid drains away from beneath it. The sort of movement has to be ascertained from other sorts of measurements; but the earthquakes showed clearly enough that some sort of movement was going on along the system of cracks, known as the east rift zone, that extends eastward from Kilauea Crater (Fig. 1-2).

Because the source of the earthquakes indicates to us where the movement of the rocks is taking place, we had been anxious to improve the accuracy of our locations of earthquake origins and had been increasing the number of seismograph stations operated by the Observatory. (The Hawaiian Observatory was soon to have the closest spaced net of seismograph stations in the world.) Just a few months before we had established a new station at the town of Pahoa, on the east slope of Kilauea, and now the records from it, combined with those from other stations, told Dr. Eaton that the quakes were originating on the east rift zone about 20 miles east of Kilauea Crater. Were we about to see another eruption? We weren't too excited yet, because the volcano had fooled us before. Sometimes it gave every indication of building up toward an eruption, and then things quieted down again without one. We would wait and see what happened.

During January the number of earthquakes recorded at the Pahoa station averaged 6 per day. Between February 1 and 23 the average increased to 15 per day, most of them originating within a few miles of the station. On February 24 about 100 earthquakes were recorded, and on February 25 the number increased to 300. Harold Warner, who lived on a ranch situated directly on the rift zone 5 miles east of Pahoa, informed us that Mrs. Warner was feeling quakes every few minutes, that many of

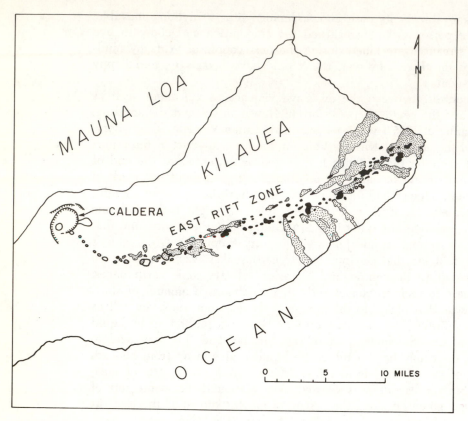

FIGURE 1-2. Map of Kilauea Volcano, Hawaii, showing the location of the crater (caldera) and east rift zone, with historic lava flows (dotted), spatter cones (solid black), and pit craters (open circles).

them were accompanied by rumbling and booming noises resembling blasting, and that the ranch dogs were behaving peculiarly, digging in the ground and snuffling excitedly in the diggings as though they were pursuing some burrowing animal, although there were no other signs that any such animals existed. Were the dogs able to smell volcanic gases that were leaking through the rocks to the surface? We also sniffed in the holes, but we could smell nothing except damp earth, and one can smell a very small trace of sulfur gases! We still do not know what was bothering the dogs, but we do know of at least one other instance in which dogs behaved in a similar way before a volcanic outbreak.

On February 26 the Pahoa seismograph recorded 600 earthquakes. For several days the heavy pendulums of the seismograph had been slowly shifting the positions to which they returned when they were at rest. This shift of the pendulums was caused by the ground at the station tilting northward as a result of a rising of the ground surface along the rift zone south of the station.

There was every indication that an eruption was coming and that the outbreak would be in the vicinity of the Warner ranch. But I couldn't forget that in 1924 a very similar series of earthquakes, accompanied by a sinking of the ground of as much as 14 feet, had taken place in the nearby Kapoho area without any eruption that was ever seen (one may have taken place in deep water miles offshore), and I was reluctant to alarm the people unnecessarily. Eaton and I spent Sunday, February 27, examining the ground and recording with a portable seismograph in the vicinity of the Warner ranch, while the Pahoa instrument recorded 700 quakes. By that night there was no longer any doubt in our minds that an eruption was imminent, but I didn't think it would come quite as soon as it did! At the end of every month we issued a bulletin to the press telling the public what was going on at the volcanoes. Usually it was a pretty routine affair, but this time I would have something really interesting to say. I would predict the coming eruption! But Pele, the goddess of our Hawaiian volcanoes, is impatient, and perhaps intolerant of human vanities. She wouldn't wait for my announcement!

The eruption started at eight o'clock the next morning on the rift zone only a few hundred feet east of the Warner ranch. Cracks opened across a road and up over the side of a hill built by an ancient prehistoric eruption, and from the cracks spurted fountains of liquid lava from a few feet to 60 feet high. Escaping gas blew some of the lava to bits and threw the still-liquid gobs into the air. These fell back around the bases of the fountains, froze, and piled up to build low cone-shaped hills. During the day some of the hills grew to a height of 20 or 30 feet, but most of the lava poured out as fluid streams that flowed off down the gentle slopes toward the sea. By midafternoon activity at the first vents had become weaker, but a new group of lava fountains had started northeast of the first ones.

The area of the first outbreak on February 28 was almost unpopulated. The Warner ranch was uphill from it and temporarily safe, and no other habitations were close by. Farther east, however, lay the village of Kapoho, almost in line with the opening cracks (Fig. 1-3). If, as appeared likely, the eruption shifted in that direction, Kapoho would be in grave danger. In midafternoon we met with the Civil Defense administrator for that district and suggested that Kapoho should be evacuated. By evening of that first day the evacuation was already well advanced, with private and National Guard trucks moving people and their possessions to areas of safety. Some went to stay with friends, others to an evacuation center set up by the Red Cross at the Pahoa School.

By next morning only one additional small outbreak had occurred. Fountains in the area of the first outbreak continued to play to heights of 50 to 75 feet all morning, but suddenly, just after noon, they started to shrink, and in 5 minutes they had entirely disappeared. Immediately, clouds of steam started to rush forth carrying showers of sandy ash. The lava appeared to have retreated to below the level of the water table and

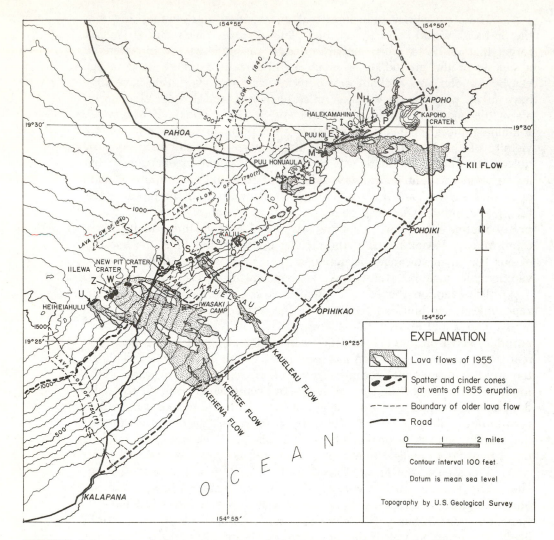

FIGURE 1-3. Map of the eastern part of the Puna District, Island of Hawaii, showing the vents and lava flows of the 1955 eruption of Kilauea Volcano. (After Macdonald, 1959.)

groundwater pouring into the red-hot fissures was being rapidly transformed into steam.

On the morning of March 2 only wisps of steam were drifting gently out of the vents, and people were beginning to say the eruption was over. Had we evacuated Kapoho needlessly? Far from it! A glance at the seismograph told us that the eruption was not over. Earthquakes had nearly ceased after the opening of the vents early on February 28, but on the night of March 1 they started again in great numbers, most of them from origins closer to Kapoho than those that had preceded the first outbreak. It didn't take long to find where they were coming from. A bus that had brought a load of people up the hill from Kapoho about seven o'clock in the morning started back down at about eight. Suddenly, less than 2 miles from Kapoho, the driver saw an open crack across the road ahead of him. He stopped. Within a few minutes the crack was a foot wide, and the ground surface on the side toward Kapoho was starting to sink. By eleven o'clock the crack was 2 feet wide, and the Kapoho side had sunk 18 inches. More cracks were opening farther east. Burt Loucks, our instrument maker, and I set up a movie camera and photographed cracks as they widened across a canefield road while we awaited the further developments we were sure were coming. Sure enough, at 2:15 P.M. we spotted white "smoke" rising above the top of the sugarcane about 50 feet from our position on the road, and this was quickly followed by bits of red-hot cinder. A new outbreak had commenced.

This was followed during the next 24 hours by seven other outbreaks from points closer and closer to Kapoho, and from each vent lava poured out, burning the sugarcane and destroying some of the best agricultural land on the island. The main lava flow headed eastward, forming a field nearly a mile wide and 2½ miles long, but to our relief it headed well south of Kapoho (Fig. 1-3). Finally, at 7 P.M. on March 3, still another outbreak took place at the west edge of Kapoho. The erupting cracks lengthened slowly eastward, and it appeared that the village was doomed. Fortunately, the village was completely evacuated except for a police detail and the volcanologists, and when the crack opened right through the middle of the village itself, even we moved out. Eruption of lava continued to spread farther and farther along the crack into the edge of the village; but then, suddenly, it stopped. The western edge of the village was destroyed; but the Kapoho vents were short lived, and a low ridge built by a prehistoric eruption deflected the lava flow northward away from the main part of the village. It was to survive for another 5 years, when it was annihilated by another eruption.

The lava fountains at the vents we had watched opening on March 2 grew taller and taller until the largest of them reached a height of nearly 1,000 feet—great jets of molten rock, shot skyward by the liquid pressure of the lava itself and the force of the expanding gas, looking like streams of water shot from a garden hose, red to dull black in daylight but glowing liquid gold at night. Near them the ground trembled as though from the passing of a heavy freight train, and half a mile away the heat was so intense that cameras got too hot to hold and we had frequently to step behind a tree or a rock to cool off! At times the roar of falling lava fragments and escaping gas was deafening, but for the most part the fountains were surprisingly quiet. A dull plopping of liquid blobs striking the ground mingled with a crashing and rattling resembling more than anything else the noise of a busy restaurant with careless waiters dropping dishes and silverware on the floor. A peculiar sort of sound for a volcano?

It is the usual one of lava fountains and easily explained. The thousands of shreds of lava thrown out of the edge of the fountain chill in the air to glass, and when they strike the ground, they shatter like so many glasses and plates striking the floor.

During the night of March 4 the rate of lava outpouring was more than 580,000 cubic yards per hour, but through March 5 and 6 the lava outflow and the size of the fountains steadily decreased. By the morning of March 7 all activity had ceased. Once again the cessation of surface activity suggested that the eruption might be over, but earthquakes told us otherwise. A new series of earthquakes had started on March 5, and Dr. Eaton found that this time they were coming from points on the rift zone west of the road from Pahoa to Kalapana, several miles west of the place of the original outbreak (Fig. 1-3). Lava flows from vents in this new area might destroy villages along the shoreline and farther inland south of Kapoho; or if the villages were not destroyed, they might be isolated by lava flows crossing the roads and their people cut off from sources of food and medical aid. For these reasons the Civil Defense authorities advised people to evacuate all the villages south of Kapoho. It was the first time in Hawaiian history that large-scale evacuations had been necessary, because it was the first time that eruptions had invaded areas in which there was much population. Evacuation of Kapoho was necessary again in 1960, and we must expect it to happen more and more frequently in the future as more people occupy more of the land on the flanks of the volcanoes.

For a week we waited for the new outbreaks. Finally, on March 12, cracks opened in the Pahoa–Kalapana road, and that night lava broke out a mile east of the road (at point Q in Fig. 1-3). March 13 was a great Sunday for us. The villages were evacuated, for the moment no one was in danger, and we were free to spend the whole day watching something never witnessed by scientists before that eruption—the very beginning and the whole sequence of development of new volcanic vents, seen at close range! We saw not one, but several. First two different vents opened in cleared land planted to cucumbers just east of the road, and then in the afternoon one opened directly across the paved road itself (Plate 1-6). How lucky can a volcanologist be? I actually set up my camera tripod astride of the opening fissures and took movies of the whole sequence of events! One thing only marred the day's success (and we didn't know that until afterward). I shot a whole 100-foot roll of movies with the camera set up only about 15 feet from the place where lava first issued, recording (I thought) the expansion of the bulb of lava and the gradual development of the lava fountain. When the film came back from the processing laboratory, it was completely blank. It had never been exposed. The film had gone through the camera, and the lens cap was not on the camera—a still photo of the camera setup shows that. One of my Hawaiian friends says that Pele, goddess of the volcano, stood in front of the camera blocking the view, though I have always suspected more mundane intervention.

PLATE 1-6. Molten lava pushing up through a crack that opened across a highway during the 1955 eruption of Kilauea Volcano, Hawaii. This is the top of a growing dike. A lava fountain later developed at this place, and built the spatter cone shown in Plate 1-7. U. S. Geological Survey photo by G. A. Macdonald.

But the day was far from lost. We had some good movies, we had still pictures, and, by far the most important, we had our notes and our memories of the formation of new volcanic vents.

At the end of the day I sat down on the ground and summarized my notes describing the formation of the vents in the cucumber patch. I have quoted them in earlier reports, but I can't do better than to quote them again.

> First, hairline cracks opened in the ground, gradually widening to 2 or 3 inches. Then from the crack there poured out a cloud of white choking sulfur fume. This was followed a few minutes later by the ejection of scattered tiny fragments of red-hot lava, and then the appearance at the surface of a small bulb of viscous molten lava. The bulb gradually swelled to a diameter of 1 to 1.5 feet, and started to spread laterally to form a lava flow. From the top of the bulb there developed a fountain of molten lava which gradually built around itself a cone of solidified spatter (Plate 1-7). (Macdonald and Eaton, 1955, p. 6.)

There is no particular point in giving a detailed account of the rest of the 1955 eruption. It can be found in the official reports. (See list of

15

suggested additional reading.) A whole series of new outbreaks took place during the next 2 weeks along the rift zone for 4 miles west of the Pahoa–Kalapana road (Plates 1-8 to 1-12), and three big lava flows spread from them down slope and into the ocean (Fig. 1-3). At times the flows moved with great rapidity, and made men move even faster to keep out of their way. One evening just after a new outburst, Richard Lyman, the manager of the estate on which most of the destruction was taking place, came in and with mock seriousness informed us that he had been driving 30 miles an hour down a canefield road to escape from in front of an advancing lava flow, and an operator on a D-8 bulldozer had been trying to pass him!

One thing I want to mention in particular, because it illustrates one of the good effects of volcanic eruptions. Just to the lee of one of the principal vents was a patch of banana trees, and pumice and cinder from the vent rained down on the plants for weeks. The leaves hung in limp brown shreds, and we felt sure the plants had been killed. Poor farmer! But a month after the end of the eruption I went by the patch on my way to study the vent. The plants were not only alive, but beautifully healthy. Ah, I thought, they are hardier than we realized, and the farmer must have fertilized them to help them make such a fine comeback! He assured me he had done no such thing. The prosperity of the plants was due to

PLATE 1-7.   Spatter cone being built on a road during the eruption of 1955 on the east flank of Kilauea Volcano. The cone is approximately 20 feet high. U. S. Geological Survey photo by G. A. Macdonald.

PLATE 1-8. Lava fountain starting to build a spatter cone, at a vent on the east rift zone of Kilauea Volcano, March 14, 1955. The fountain is approximately 150 feet high. U. S. Geological Survey photo by G. A. Macdonald.

PLATE 1-9. Spatter cone being built during the 1955 eruption of Kilauea Volcano. The cone is approximately 1.5 feet high. U. S. Geological Survey photo by G. A. Macdonald.

PLATE 1-10. Lava fountain 250 feet high building a big spatter cone during the 1955 eruption of Kilauea Volcano. U. S. Geological Survey photo by G. A. Macdonald.

PLATE 1-11. Cinder-and-spatter cone, about 100 feet high, being built by a lava fountain during the 1955 eruption of Kilauea Volcano. A pahoehoe lava flow is in the foreground. U. S. Geological Survey photo by G. A. Macdonald.

PLATE 1-12.   Lava river, 12 feet wide, near one of the vents of the 1955 eruption of Kilauea Volcano. The speed of this river, flowing down a 30-degree slope, was estimated to be at least 35 miles an hour. U. S. Geological Survey photo by G. A. Macdonald.

two properties of the volcanic ash and cinder that I knew well but hadn't realized would work so quickly and effectively. The ash not only held water for the use of the plants through dry periods, but it contained mineral substances that the plants need for food, locked up in glass that was readily broken down and the food elements released by weathering. The bananas had indeed been fertilized and mulched, but not by the hand of man.

Not all the results of the eruption were so felicitous! The activity finally came to an end on May 26. All of one village had been destroyed, and part of another. Still worse, lava flows had covered some 3,900 acres of arable land, much of it actually under cultivation. Such land is not permanently lost. In tropical climates it becomes arable surprisingly rapidly. Through specially developed methods, several hundred acres of the 1955 lava flows were again growing crops successfully before 1960. But the land is lost to sugarcane or other crops that require deep soil for many decades or centuries. On the credit side of the ledger, no lives had been lost and no one seriously injured. And we had gained a vast amount of volcanological information.

These accounts of the eruptions of Hibokhibok and Kilauea have been chosen to start this book on volcanoes not only because of their dramatic qualities, but also because they illustrate well two sorts of great volcanic eruptions and their effects on the people living in the vicinity. They show both similarities and differences. Everywhere volcanic action shows certain basic similarities, so that principles developed through the study of one volcano can, to some extent, be applied to other volcanoes. The differences are generally of degree rather than kind. The accounts of the two eruptions bring out also some of the reasons we are studying volcanoes and illustrate the sort of practical use we are trying to make of our knowledge. Some aspects of volcano studies are immediately or potentially of great practical value—recognizing areas and degrees of risk, warning of impending danger, the saving of lives and property, and the utilization of volcanic energy, as in the electricity-generating plants now being operated on volcanic steam in several parts of the world. But in addition to these "humanistic" aspects there are others that for the moment, at least, are of purely intellectual or aesthetic value. Men have an intense compulsion to know and understand their environment, and volcanoes would be studied even though no practical considerations were involved.

SUGGESTED ADDITIONAL READING

The full titles and references to the following will be found in the list of literature cited at the end of the book.
Alcaraz, Abad, and Quema, 1952; Macdonald and Alcaraz, 1956; Macdonald and Eaton, 1955; Macdonald, 1959; Macdonald and Eaton, 1964.

2

Some Definitions

Definitions are boring but necessary. Every science has its own special vocabulary—a sort of shorthand in which thoughts can be expressed in a few words instead of the many that would otherwise be necessary. Most of the technical terms of volcanology will be defined, either formally or by implication, as we come to them; but a few should be defined immediately before we go further.

Just what is a volcano? The commonest popular concept seems to be that of a "smoking mountain." I am reminded of the definition said to have been given by a high-school girl in an examination: "A volcano is a cone-shaped mountain, and at the top you can see the creator smoking." The definition is fun, but fallacious! It is also quite inadequate. The "smoke" is, for the most part, not smoke at all, but steam and other gas, often loaded with pulverized rock. A new vent, spouting liquid lava and gas, that has not yet had time to build a mountain or even a small hill is nevertheless certainly a volcano! And even long after volcanic activity has ceased and "smoke" has stopped coming from the crater, and the crater itself has been partly or entirely obliterated by erosion, the mountains built by volcanic eruptions are still very generally called volcanoes. Furthermore, as we shall see later, that man is possessed of more than human wisdom who can be sure that one of these seemingly dead mountains will not suddenly return to life! We must try again for a suitable definition!

The dual nature of volcanoes has already been pointed out in the preface. *A volcano is both the place or opening from which molten rock or gas, and generally both, issues from the earth's interior onto the surface, and the hill or mountain built up around the opening by accumulation of the rock materials.*

The rock material may be simply fragments of older near-surface rocks thrown out by the escaping gas, or it may be new rock brought up from depth. The new rock may be solid when it is thrown out, or it may be in a liquid (molten) state. The molten rock, whether it is still within the earth or has been ejected onto the surface, is called *magma*. New rock material, whether liquid or solid, when it has been ejected onto the surface is called *lava*. Thus, a stream of liquid rock on the earth's surface is both magma and lava. Both the streams of liquid on the surface and the rock that results from solidification of the streams are called *lava flows*. This is a troublesome ambiguity sometimes resolved by referring to the solid material as *lava rock*.

Rock that is formed by the freezing of magma is known as *igneous* ("fire-formed") rock. The rocks resulting from consolidation of magma after it has been poured out onto the surface are called *extrusive* igneous rocks. However, some magma does not reach the surface, but instead solidifies beneath the surface to form *intrusive* igneous rocks. All the rocks formed in direct relationship to volcanic activity, whether they are extrusive or intrusive, are *volcanic rocks*.

Not all igneous rocks are volcanic. Some have been formed at great depth below the surface and, so far as we can see, without any direct association with volcanic activity. These are called *plutonic* igneous rocks (after Pluto, the Roman god of the underworld). They include many of the great bodies of granite that form in the deep cores of mountain ranges. (Other granites are, strictly speaking, not igneous rocks at all, but are formed by processes of recrystallization without having become liquid.) Plutonic rocks will not concern us in this book. Except that fragments of them are occasionally thrown out by accident during explosions, or simply torn loose and rafted upward by magma rising through them, they are not a part of volcanic activity, although no doubt plutonic magmas have sometimes broken through to produce volcanic activity on the surface. Intrusive igneous rocks that are demonstrably related genetically to overlying volcanoes, and which usually have solidified at relatively shallow levels within the earth, are referred to as *subvolcanic rocks*.

The issuing of gas and rock material onto the earth's surface is volcanic *eruption* or *extrusion*. Eruptions resulting from the direct action of magma or magmatic gas are *magmatic eruptions*. Those resulting from secondary steam generated by heating of water external to the magma may be called *hydroeruptions*. When the water is groundwater (as opposed to surface water), the eruption is *phreatic* (after the Greek word for a well).

Many hydroeruptions throw out only solid fragments of surrounding older rocks. Others, however, throw out liquid clots of magma mixed with the solid fragments; in still other cases, the material thrown out is almost wholly a shower or spray of liquid clots or droplets. These, in which the material ejected is partly or wholly magmatic but the explosion is largely the result of secondary steam, may be termed *hydromagmatic* or *phreato-magmatic* eruptions.

Materials thrown out in fragmentary form, whether in a liquid or a solid condition, and whether by magmatic or hydroexplosions, are called *pyroclastic* ("fire-broken") materials. When they eventually become cemented into solid masses, they are *pyroclastic rocks.* The terms "pyroclastic materials" and "pyroclastic rocks" are long and awkward, especially when they are frequently repeated, and the Icelandic volcanologist, S. Thorarinsson, has recently suggested that they be replaced by the term *tephra.* The term did not originate with Thorarinsson. It was used by Aristotle, but for centuries it had been forgotten. *Tephra* is rapidly coming back into use as a synonym for "pyroclastic materials" in general. Both lava flows and tephra are further classified in various ways, as will be described in later chapters.

The opening from which volcanic material issues onto the surface is the *vent,* and the channelway that brings the material up from depth is the *conduit* (Fig. 2-1). Volcanoes usually are thought to be fed from a

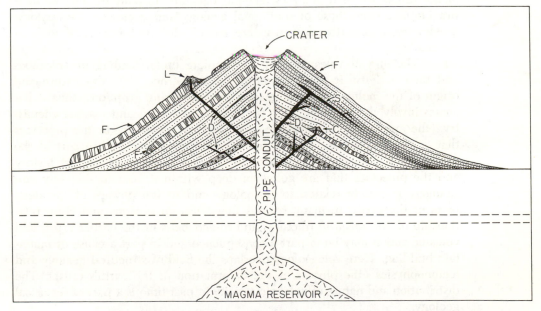

FIGURE 2-1. Diagram of a typical composite volcano, showing the cone, crater, central pipe conduit, magma reservoir, dikes (D), a dike conduit feeding a lateral cone (L) and lava flow (F), a buried cinder cone (C), and a sill (S). Tephra layers are dotted, breccia layers are marked with small triangles, and lava flows (F) are irregularly cross-hatched.

body of magma accumulated at comparatively shallow depth in a chamber or body (perhaps passing gradationally outward into the rocks that form its walls) that is known as the *magma reservoir*. The source of the magma, whether it is at the same place as the reservoir or some place else, is sometimes called the *magmatic hearth*. Some conduits are more or less cylindrical, and these may be referred to as volcanic *pipes*. Filled with solidified material and later exposed at the surface by erosion, they become volcanic *necks*. Other conduits are long narrow cracks or fissures; these, filled with volcanic rock, are *dikes*.

Eruptions from many separate vents may build broad flat topographic surfaces known simply as volcanic *plains* or *plateaus*, depending on whether they are at low or high altitude. Either single eruptions, or repeated eruptions at the same vent, commonly build hills or mountains more or less conical in shape and known as volcanic *cones*. The top of the cone usually is truncated and indented with a bowl-shaped or funnel-shaped depression called a *crater*. Craters may also occur independently of any cone. The forms of craters and cones will be discussed later. *Calderas* are unusually large craters, by definition more than a mile in diameter.

Volcanology is the science of volcanoes. In the broad sense, it is a part of geology—the science of the earth. It makes strong use, however, of the techniques of geophysics and geochemistry—subjects that also are broadly a part of geology, but that are commonly separated from it because of the difference in techniques, general background, and training of their practitioners from those of traditional geology and geologists. Seismology, gravimetry, and earth magnetism are among the most important tools of volcanology.

The aim of volcanology is a complete understanding of volcanoes and their activity. It must, therefore, be concerned with the nature and origin of the molten rock and gases liberated during eruptions; thus it becomes involved with petrology (the science of rocks) and magma chemistry (the application of chemistry and physical chemistry to the processes that go on in magmas). The ultimate causes of volcanism are part of the evolution of the earth as a planet and are consequences of its past history and the processes that are going on deep within it, and in this way volcanology is closely related to cosmology and to the physics of the deep parts of the earth. In many regions there was an obvious and close relationship of volcanism to fractures and folded belts in the earth's crust, and volcanic action may be in part a consequence and in part a cause of mountain building. Here volcanology overlaps the field of structural geology and tectonophysics (the physics of the deformation of the earth's crust). The distribution and nature of volcanic activity in past time is a part of historical geology.

As we have already seen, volcanoes may have a profound effect upon people. One of the most important goals of the volcanologist is the prediction of volcanic activity, partly as a test of his own knowledge, but, of more direct importance, to help avoid or ameliorate human disaster. More than simply to predict, we are hoping to learn to control volcanic phenomena, to lessen or prevent destruction, and ultimately to make use of the tremendous stores of volcanic energy. In the control and utilization of volcanoes, the volcanologist must work closely with engineers and physicists. In his relationships with people during volcanic disasters, the volcanologist must make use of sociology and psychology. His very presence at such times can give people calmness and confidence, thereby avoiding many foolish, and even disastrous, individual and mass reactions that might otherwise take place. Frank Perret's presence in an observation station high on the side of Mt. Pelée during the 1929 eruption sustained the people of the city of St. Pierre and avoided their panic-stricken flight from the city. If "the doctor" could sit calmly in the path of eruption, why need they, who were much farther away, abandon their homes? If there was danger, Perret would warn them! One of my colleagues (an engineer) and I once brought out a group of people who had been trapped by sulfurous volcanic fumes simply by having them cover their faces with wet cloths while they walked through it. It was a small thing, but we knew it could be done, and our presence gave them the confidence to do it.

Volcanology is a many-sided subject! It is also both an old and a new subject. Some of the lore on which it is based dates back at least to the Romans. On the other hand, it is only within the last 150 years that it could be graced by the designation *science*, and for only a small fraction of even that time can it be called an interpretive science. Its development is closely tied to the general intellectual advance of Western civilization, and a few pages can profitably be spent in sketching its particular part in that advance. Today, volcanology is of great importance in parts of the Orient, and indeed Japanese volcanologists are among the leaders in the science, but their science has been absorbed from the Occident rather than developed through the civilization of the East. I shall, therefore, confine myself to the evolution of volcanology in Europe.

3

The Growth of Volcanology

Primitive man is very much a slave to his natural environment. Both his physical actions and his thoughts are largely controlled and guided by it. Indeed, the advance of civilization is in large part a gradual development of control over environment and ability to make use of its components, so that to some extent the situation is reversed and environment becomes the servant of man. Today we make extensive use of our environment. We use the mineral wealth it provides; we harness streams and the wind; we control the evolutionary processes of the animals and plants we have pressed into our service; we have conquered the natural barriers of mountain ranges, rivers, and oceans, and travel over the waters and through the air. We even bend the fundamental structure of matter to our own purposes. We still cannot control such forces of nature as great storms, earthquakes, and volcanic eruptions; but we are progressing toward the point where we can predict and avoid them and make some use of their tremendous energy. Someday we may be able to control them. All this increasing triumph over environment results from increasing knowledge of the things of which it is made. Primitive man cowered before the elements of nature and attributed to each a vindictive spirit bent on hurting him unless it was propitiated. Not until this animistic approach was displaced by a realization that such things as earthquakes, volcanoes, and the wind are governed by physical laws and not by their own caprice could real advances in knowledge be made.

In all volcanic lands primitive people have feared volcanoes and paid homage to the spirits they supposed controlled them. Considering the great releases of energy in big eruptions, the towering, menacing black column of ash-laden gas that rises miles into the air and turns into clouds that spread laterally over the countryside and transform day into night, the brilliant flashes of lightning and deafening cracks of thunder from the cloud, the rain of ash that buries the land, and the fiery streams of lava that come down the mountainside destroying everything in their paths, it could hardly have been otherwise! Explanations of these fearful phenomena took different forms. In the lowest societies it was simply that the spirit of the volcano was angry. To the Polynesians, volcanoes were under the control of the demigoddess Pele, who often appeared in human form, sometimes young and beautiful, but usually as an ugly old woman. It was best to be very nice to her! The story is told of a young chief in the eastern part of the island of Hawaii who was sliding down hill on his bone-runnered sled one day, when a strange old woman appeared and asked if she could borrow the sled for a ride. He refused and curtly told her to get her own sled. He should have been more circumspect! She soon came back with another sled and challenged him to a race. He accepted the challenge and beat her. She leaped angrily from the sled and stamped on the ground. Immediately, the ground split open, smoke started to rise, and hot rocks flew into the air. Finally, the rather stupid chief realized who she was! He ran for his life toward the seashore, and Pele pursued him, throwing showers of hot rocks after him. At the shore he stole a canoe and finally escaped. The truth of the story can be demonstrated, or so the old people said. Even today, one can still see the hill where the chief was sliding and the long row of spatter conelets built by the hot rocks that Pele hurled after him! Obviously, the story is a dramatization of an actual volcanic eruption.

There was no moral attached to the Hawaiian legend, other than the obvious implication that one should be nice to all strangers, particularly old women. In some parts of the world, however, the tales took the form of a contest between good and evil. A legend of the Indians of Oregon tells of a conflict between the bad god of fire, whose home was on Mt. Mazama, the big mountain where Crater Lake is now, and the good god of snow, who dwelt on Mt. Shasta. The good god finally triumphed, but during the battle the top of Mt. Mazama was destroyed. Again, this is probably an allegorical account of the actual eruption that destroyed the mountaintop and formed the basin of Crater Lake—an eruption known to have been witnessed by earlier Indians about 4,000 B.C. In Peru, other Indians told how the bad spirit that occupied El Misti, the beautiful but once-destructive volcano that rises above the present city of Arequipa, was punished by the Sun God, who plunged the evil one's head into a flow of molten lava and then blocked the crater of the volcano with ice. Will the plug hold? Modern inhabitants of Arequipa may well show some concern over the question!

In more sophisticated societies the explanations were more complex. The early Greeks believed that earthquakes resulted from the restless stirrings of giants buried by Zeus beneath the mountains, or from the mountain-rending activities of Poseidon, the god of the oceans. Their concern about volcanoes was limited, because the mainland of Greece is not a volcanic country; but they were aware that volcanoes existed in the islands to the south and east and in Asia Minor, and they attributed their eruptions to the blowing out of the breath of the same buried giants. As the limits of travel expanded and Greek knowledge of volcanoes in other parts of the Mediterranean world increased, and as their theology evolved, the story changed. Hephaestus, the lame and ugly son of Hera, became the god of fire. He had been literally cast out of Olympus by Zeus, who became angry with him for trying to defend his mother from Zeus' charges of infidelity. Landing on the island of Lemnos, he took up his abode there. He eventually regained the grace of Olympus and became the artisan god, who presided over the manufacture of armor and other metal work. His forge was beneath one or another volcano, commonly Thera (the present island of Santorin).

The Greek gods were taken over by the Romans, who adapted them and their attributes to their own pantheon and added embellishments. As late as the first century B.C. we find Virgil attributing an eruption of Etna to the impatient threshing about of Encelade, one of the Titans, imprisoned under the mountain by Jupiter. Hephaestus, under the new name of Vulcan, was the Roman god of metal working, who manufactured the armor of the gods and the thunderbolts of Jupiter. His forge was sometimes placed beneath Etna Volcano, but more commonly beneath the island of Vulcano, an active volcanic island in the Tyrrhenian Sea which has lent its name to all the other volcanoes of the world.

Greek and Roman thought soon went beyond these deistic explanations of nature. However, Greek thought in particular remained for the most part quite impractical in most matters of science. The philosophers speculated at length on natural phenomena, but their speculations were based hardly at all on actual study of nature. Thales (sixth century B.C.) attributed earthquakes to a shuddering of the disk-like body of the earth floating upon the universal waters, Democritus (ca. 400 B.C.) attributed the trembling to the movement of water or air through passages within the earth, and Anaxagoras (ca. 450 B.C.) to air seeking to escape upward through fissures in the under side of the earth. Plato (ca. 427–347 B.C.) believed in caverns and channelways within the earth in which streams of the elemental substances in the universe—earth, air, fire, and water—were moving about. The largest of the subterranean chasms was Tartarus, into which all the streams converged. To explain volcanoes he envisioned a great stream of fire, Pyriphlegathon, from which, and other lesser streams, fiery springs issued at the surface of the earth; this fire, together with entrapped superheated air, produced lava flows and other volcanic manifestations.

Roman influence introduced a little more attention to the realities of nature, but among Roman philosophers the emphasis was still on speculation rather than investigation. Empedocles (492–432 B.C.), who resided in the Greek colony on Sicily, was unusual in his attempts to acquire some factual basis for his speculations. He became particularly interested in volcanoes and spent the last several years of his life living near the summit of Etna, observing and contemplating the volcano. He is said to have lost his life in the crater. Empedocles believed that the center of the earth was molten and that volcanoes were formed where the molten material came to the surface. Unfortunately, most of his writings have been lost! Strabo (ca. 63 B.C.–30 A.D.), a Greek geographer who traveled widely but made his headquarters in Rome, described a volcanic eruption in 196 B.C. that built a new island between Thera and Therasia. He believed that oceanic islands in general had been formed by "fires" of subterranean origin. Although Vesuvius had been inactive through all of Roman history, he recognized it as a volcanic mountain. Strabo suggested that volcanic eruptions acted as safety valves for pent-up subterranean vapors, and that in regions where small eruptions were frequent, the danger of big eruptions and earthquakes was lessened—an idea that persists to our own day.

Seneca (2 B.C.–65 A.D.) regarded volcanoes as vents through which molten material issued onto the earth's surface from local subterranean reservoirs, an idea that in a general way much resembles our own! He gave a list of the principal volcanoes known in his time, including Etna, Santorin, Vulcano, and Stromboli, but notably not Vesuvius. Perhaps he was unwilling to list a mountain as a volcano unless he knew of a record of it having actually erupted.

The tremendous compendium on natural history prepared by Pliny the Elder (born in 23 A.D.) lists much information on volcanoes, but also much misinformation. As in other fields of natural history, he allowed himself to be carried away by his enthusiasm and was very uncritical in his recording of supposed facts. He did, however, have an intense intellectual curiosity and an instinct for investigation of natural phenomena that led to his death in the catastrophic eruption of Vesuvius in 79 A.D. The story was told in two fascinating letters addressed to Tacitus by his nephew, Pliny the Younger, that are often referred to as the first actual documents in volcanology. It is recounted briefly in Chapter 10 of this book.

In the acquisition of knowledge about volcanoes, as in other fields of learning, the decay and fall of the Roman Empire brought an end to progress. Actually, although a few of the Roman ideas sound surprisingly modern, the sum of knowledge gained had been very little! The famous paleontologist, Karl A. von Zittel, in his monumental *History of Geology and Paleontology* (1899), points out that on the whole the heritage of geological knowledge passed on to us by the ancients is very meager. And all through the Middle Ages knowledge remained frozen. The scholastics were interested not in the acquisition of new knowledge but in the passing on of the old writings that had been made sacred by church sanction, by no means always the most advanced of their kind even in the ancient world.

One of the commonest popular ideas during the Middle Ages was that volcanoes were gateways to hell or the prisons of the damned. One such was Hekla, in Iceland, where the noises that sometimes issued from the volcano were thought to be the moans and screams of tormented souls. Even in the late fifteenth century, Mt. Etna was said to be the place of confinement of the unfortunate Anne Boleyn!

It was not until the Renaissance, beginning in the late fourteenth century, that the attitude toward learning began to change, and men began to turn for knowledge to nature rather than to books; and as we all know from our study of history, the new attitude was fraught with the danger of accusation of heresy and its attendant drastic reprisal. As late as 1600, Giordano Bruno was burned for heresy. Among his scientific contributions was the recognition of the common location of volcanoes in close proximity to the ocean. He suggested that volcanic activity might be due to interaction between the ocean water and the hot interior of the earth. (The downward increase of temperature in the earth had already been recognized in the German mines.) The idea was to persist among some geologists into the early years of the twentieth century. In a sense it was not new with Bruno, although he may have developed it independently. It was a common belief among the Romans that the water swallowed by the whirlpool of Charybdis was regurgitated as steam from Mt. Etna.

Athanasius Kircher (1602–1680) considered volcanoes as the surface manifestations of subterranean places of combustion, thus foreshadowing ideas later taught by the famous Werner and others.

Martin Lister (1638–1711), a British physician, but not the famous pioneer of antisepsis, suggested that mixtures of sulfur with sand or other materials exposed to air became heated and exploded, resulting in volcanic eruptions; and, in 1700, J. Lemery became one of the first "experimental geologists" by putting Lister's hypothesis to a test. He showed that a mixture of sulfur, iron filings, and water buried in earth gets warm and finally takes fire spontaneously, bursting open its cover and giving off flames and smoke. Superficially, the heat, explosion, and choking sulfur fumes bore strong resemblance to a volcanic eruption!

Like Strabo long before him, the Italian abbot Antonio Lazzaro Moro (1687–1740) was greatly impressed by the formation of a new island near Santorin in 1707. The sea floor, covered with oysters, was heaved up out of the water to the accompaniment of numerous earthquakes; then volcanic eruption commenced and buried the new island with cinder. Moro had been convinced by the evidence of fossils in the rocks that, as Leonardo da Vinci and Nicolaus Steno had pointed out, great parts of the dry land had once been under the sea. He suggested that all mountains, all islands, and indeed all continents, had been elevated from beneath the ocean by volcanic forces, as had the small island near Santorin.

Sir William Hamilton, the British ambassador to the court of Naples, became fascinated with Vesuvius. In a series of letters to the president of the Royal Society of London, later (1774) published in a well-illustrated volume, he gave an account of Vesuvius and its eruptions. It can be considered as the first modern work in volcanology.

To that time the only rocks recognized as of volcanic origin were those obviously and closely connected with volcanoes, and (with the exception of the recognition by Strabo of the volcanic nature of Vesuvius) the only mountains recognized as volcanoes were those that had actually erupted in historic times. Soon afterward came two great advances: Giovanni Arduino (1713–1795) recognized in northern Italy volcanic rocks of ancient age, interstratified with sedimentary rocks of marine origin, and attributed them to repeated eruptions of long-gone volcanoes alternating with inundations of the area beneath the sea. Still farther from any known volcanic area, Jean Etienne Guettard (1715–1786), who prepared the first geological maps of parts of France and England, in 1752 recognized the since-famous Chaine des Puys, in the Auvergne region of central France, to be a row of extinct volcanoes. These contributions may seem rather unimportant, but actually the step of extending into past time the processes of the present, a step being taken by students of other types of rock also, was a very important one. It was the emergence of the principle of *uniformitarianism*—one of the basic principles of modern geology, which insists that the rocks and landscapes we see around us have been formed not by special cataclysms of the past but by the ordinary familiar processes that we see going on around us today. The principle was eventually firmly established by James Hutton and succinctly set forth by the brilliant English geologist, Charles Lyell, in the words, "The present is the key to the past."

Guettard declared volcanoes to be vents connecting the earth's surface with a central zone of "fire" within the earth.

As usual, once the pioneers had broken the barrier, others were quick to follow. Guettard had been deceived by the six-sided columns in the basalt (dark lava rock) layers of the Auvergne—columns of a sort found in many layers of volcanic rock and that we now know to be the result of shrinkage of the rock on cooling. Guettard believed that they were huge crystals formed like many others with which he was familiar by precipitation from water solution. Soon afterward the Auvergne region was again studied by Nicolas Desmarest, who pointed out (1771) the similarity of the columnar basalt to lavas of the active Italian volcanoes and maintained that it too had solidified from a molten condition. He recognized the similarity of form of the hills of the Auvergne region to those of more recent volcanoes, and, furthermore, that the Auvergne volcanoes were of various ages and had been eroded to varying degrees.

Guy S. Tancrède de Dolomieu, for whom the magnesium-bearing limestone, dolomite, and the Dolomite Alps are named, studied the volcanoes of the Roman region, the Lipari Islands, and Mt. Etna, and concurred in Desmarest's conclusion of the igneous origin of basalt, though he regarded it as formed mainly in submarine eruptions. Through a detailed study of the materials ejected by volcanoes, he demonstrated that there is a complete gradation in the texture of igneous rocks from coarse grained to very fine grained and glassy. He believed that there was a combustible substance in lavas, possibly sulfur, that exerted an expansive force and thereby both caused the bubbly structure of lava flows and forced the lava to rise upward to the surface. It was the first recognition of the great importance of gas in magmas. Lazzaro Spallanzani attempted unsuccessfully to test Dolomieu's hypotheses in the laboratory.

In 1780, Girard Soulavie also studied the Auvergne region, and the volcanic districts of Vivarais, Velay, and Provence, farther south, and likewise took a strong stand for the igneous origin of basalt. About the same time, Ignaz von Born recognized the Kammerbuhl, and Baron von Dietrich recognized the Kaiserstuhl, in Germany, as extinct volcanoes.

At about this same time, there enters on the scene one of the most influential figures in the whole history of geology. Abraham Gottlob Werner, professor of mineralogy in the School of Mines at Freiberg, Germany, developed a "universal theory" of the composition and structure of the earth. Werner wrote little, but through his brilliant lectures and magnetic personality he inspired enthusiastic students to spread his doctrines throughout Europe. For a generation his ideas held sway almost undisputed. To be sure, there were always some who disagreed with him, but their voices were lost in the general acclamation of Wernerism. Werner taught that the rocks of the earth were arranged in a regular succession of five great divisions, those of the lower two and part of those of the third having been formed by precipitation from solution in a once-universal ocean. These included such rocks as granite and schists (now known to have crystallized from a molten condition or to have been formed from earlier rocks of other types by recrystallization under intense heat and pressure). Later, said Werner, came rocks formed by erosion of the older rocks and transportation and deposition of the eroded debris (what we now call sedimentary rocks). Finally, as the last of the five divisions, Werner recognized volcanic rocks, including both lava flows and fragmental products. Basalt, however, was included (in spite of the demonstration of its igneous origin by Desmarest, Dolomieu, and Soulavie) among the rocks supposed to have been formed by crystallization from water solution. Werner supposed that the cause of volcanic action was the burning of buried coal beds, which supplied the heat to bring about the melting of older rocks. In turn, the heat necessary to ignite the coal was supplied by reaction of iron pyrite and percolating water. These ideas on the cause of volcanism were not new. They had been advanced by Kircher and others in the preceding century and were supported by Georges Louis Leclerc Buffon in his famous *Historie Naturelle,* published in 1769. Actually, Werner was far less important as an originator of ideas than for his tremendous influence in spreading them. In fairness, it should be pointed out that although his basic concepts of geology (geognosy, he would have called it) have not stood the test of time, much of his work in mineralogy and the relationships of ore-bearing veins was good and of fundamental importance.

Werner's conclusions on basalt were immediately challenged by J. K. W. Voigt, one of his own students, who insisted that the basalt studied by Werner in the Scheibenberg area was a lava flow of volcanic origin.

Voigt's dissension was of little avail against the powerful influence of Werner, but other voices were soon to be added. In Scotland, James Hutton had evolved his own *Theory of the Earth* (1788) as a result of a lifetime of careful observation of the rocks and landscape and analysis of what he saw in them. Hutton's work, as ably set forth by his friend and disciple, John Playfair, in his *Illustration of the Huttonian Theory* (1802), is generally regarded as the foundation of modern geology. His contributions are far too numerous to list them all here, but among them was the recognition that thin sheets (dikes) of granite and similar rocks cut through rocks that Werner considered to be the younger. This was, of course, an impossibility, and Hutton concluded that the granite and related rocks that formed the dikes must have been younger than the surrounding rocks, and that they originated by solidification of molten material that had risen into fissures in the surrounding older rocks. Hutton and his followers in this area of the origin of granite from a melt formed deep in the earth became known as the Plutonist school (after the Roman god of the underworld, Pluto); whereas Werner's school, which attributed granite to chemical precipitation from the ocean, became known as the Neptunists. Hutton recognized many of the rocks of old geologic units, including basalt, to be of volcanic origin, again in opposition to Werner's ideas.

James Hall, another friend of Hutton's, demonstrated by remelting rocks in the laboratory the correctness of Hutton's view that fine-grained surficial lava flows and coarser grained intrusive rocks had alike solidified from igneous fusion, and that the difference in grain size resulted from the different rapidities with which the rocks cooled.

The conflict between Neptunists and Plutonists was a violent one, and that it eventually was decided in favor of Plutonism was due largely to the work of Werner's own students. Driven by the enthusiasm Werner inspired in them, they went far and wide into the field; and though they were intensely loyal to Werner they nevertheless slowly came to realize that some of his ideas were untenable. The change came largely from more observations of the rocks in vastly broader regions. Werner had worked only in one small area, and his misconceptions can be traced largely to a too-narrow provincialism. Two of Werner's students must be counted among the greatest geologists of all time. Alexander von Humboldt (1769–1859) is chiefly renowned for his great work *The Cosmos* (1847), but more important to volcanology is his description of the volcanoes of Central and South America and his account of the eruption of Jorullo Volcano, Mexico, in 1759. His work gave the first adequate picture of the widespread distribution of volcanoes, and Jorullo is still renowned as one of the very few "new" volcanoes, the very beginning of which has been observed by man. Still more important was the work of Leopold von Buch (1774–1852). At first he was one of the strongest advocates of Neptunism, but in 1798 he spent 5 months with von Humboldt in the region around Naples and saw many lava flows that closely resembled the basalt Werner said was formed by precipitation from water. Doubts began to stir, but his intense loyalty to Werner was an obstacle difficult to surmount. He compromised with the idea that older beds of water-formed basalt had been remelted at depth by the heat of burning coal and the melt poured out to form the lava flows.

In 1802 von Buch visited the Auvergne region, and apparently without knowledge of the earlier work of Guettard, Desmarest, and Soulavie, he reached the conclusion that the Chaine des Puys is a row of volcanoes. Furthermore, he saw that the volcanoes rested directly on granite; and if Werner was right in claiming that granite was a part of the lowest and oldest geologic unit, that which nothing else could be lower, where could be the coal that had burned to bring about the volcanism? His belief in the tenets of Werner was still further strained! In 1815 he visited the Canary Islands and recognized their volcanic origin, and in 1817 he saw the magnificent displays of columnar basalt on the island of Staffa, Scotland, and at Giant's Causeway in northern Ireland. The evidence was too strong! He finally was convinced of the igneous origin of basalt. He went even further and attributed the upheaval of the mountain range of the Alps to the subsurface intrusion of molten rocks! The conversion of this, its staunchest advocate, together with two other of Werner's foremost students, d'Aubuisson de Voisins and von Humboldt, was the final blow that brought about the downfall of Neptunism.

Von Buch's experiences in the Auvergne and Canary Islands led him, in 1819, to set forth his theory of "craters of elevation." True volcanoes formed by the ejection of materials from depth onto the earth's surface did exist, but they were all small. Great volcanic cones, such as the Mont Dore in central France, or Vesuvius itself, had been formed not by piling up of materials around a vent from which they issued onto the surface, but by bulging upward of formerly horizontal layers due to the expansive force of molten material beneath—approximately the same process that he now felt had elevated the Alps. (The general picture rather resembled our present idea of laccoliths—masses of molten material that are intruded under layers of sedimentary rocks and arch them up into a dome-shaped structure.) The upheaved beds sloped upward in all directions to a central summit crater formed by pulling apart of the ends of the beds. Sometimes the molten material broke through to the surface and formed a small true volcano, generally in the summit crater. The reasons for von Buch's conclusion were primarily two: he had found in the crater of La Palma, in the Canary Islands, coarse-grained granitic rocks that according to Neptunian concepts must belong to the "primary," or lowest, system, and therefore must have been elevated above their proper position to bring them to where he found them, high up in the volcanic structure; and the sides of the mountain sloped outward at angles that he believed were too steep for lava flows to have solidified on them.

Von Buch's theory of craters of elevation did not go long unchallenged. Some students of volcanoes, such as Élie de Beaumont in France, and Charles Daubeny, professor of chemistry and mineralogy at Oxford, were convinced by his arguments; but others promptly set out to disprove them. The most vehement opponents of the theory were two Englishmen, George Poulett-Scrope and Charles Lyell, and a Frenchman, Constant Prévost. Lyell, who was just starting out on his brilliant career, was to become one of the foremost geologists of all time; but in the more restricted field of volcanology Scrope's contributions were even more important. In fact, it is generally considered to have laid the first firm foundation for modern volcanology. Scrope studied at Cambridge under the famous pioneer geologist Adam Sedgwick. As a student, in 1816 he had already studied Vesuvius and the nearby Phlegraean Fields, and in 1818 to 1822 he extended his work to Etna, Stromboli, and the older volcanoes near Rome. In 1821 he made a thorough and careful study of the Auvergne region, and in 1823 he studied the volcanic districts of the Eifel and the Rhineland. In 1825 he published the outcome of his general studies under the title of *Considerations on Volcanoes*, and in 1827 his *Memoir on the Geology of Central France*. His geological map of the Auvergne was far in advance of the general mapping of his time and is still useful today. Scrope attacked the theory of craters of elevation by pointing out that all the layers of rock exposed in the crater walls of volcanic cones were materials ejected from the vent itself, and that the cones did not show the patterns of cracking and distension that they should have shown were they pushed up by pressure from beneath. (Today we recognize that there actually are some signs of upward pressure and distension of the cones, as believed by von Buch, but that these are relatively minor; we are forced to agree with Scrope's general contentions. The word "forced" is used advisedly, because geologists are always delighted to find grounds for disagreeing with each other.)

With the publication of his superb *Principles of Geology* in 1830, Lyell added his voice to that of Scrope. In 1831 a new volcanic island, Graham Island or Ile Julia, appeared in the Mediterranean Sea southwest of Sicily, and Prévost was named a member of the French expedition sent to study it. On his way home he also studied Etna, Stromboli, Vesuvius, and the Phlegraean Fields. On his return to Paris he announced that not one of the volcanic areas he had visited contained a single crater of elevation. Under the influence of Élie de Beaumont, hardly a member of the French Academy of Sciences was willing to agree with him! The battle went on, and it was not until 1857, when Scrope presented two forceful summaries of the evidence against it to the Geological Society of London, that the craters of elevation theory was finally laid to rest.

Actually, Scrope went a little too far in his advocacy of his theory of the formation of volcanic cones purely by the accumulation of ejected materials. There are in the Auvergne, as well as in many other regions, hills of massive lava that have formed by the gradual expansion of a mass of viscous lava being inflated from below by the squeezing of additional liquid into their interiors (volcanic domes, see Chapter 6). These he erroneously attributed instead to the piling up of successive viscous lava flows one on top of another. Already, in 1789, Count Reynaud de Montlosier had published an *Essay of the Volcanoes of the Auvergne* in which he recognized that some of the hills were formed as a single protrusion of viscous lava that congealed in the form of a steep-sided dome.

One of the most important features of Scrope's theory of volcanic action was his belief in the importance of the gas contained in the molten rock. The expansion of the gas caused volcanic explosions; the abundance of the gas influenced the viscosity of the molten lava, and this in turn governed the character of the eruption; the expansive force of the gas caused the magma to rise from depth to the surface; the temporary exhaustion of gas brought about the quiet periods between eruptions. In many respects the ideas sound quite modern. Indeed, Scrope could easily have been the author of the words written many decades later by F. A. Perret: "Gas is the active agent, and the magma is its vehicle!"

Once on the sound foundation provided by Scrope and Lyell, volcanology progressed rapidly and on the factual basis of field observations and their interpretation, rather than deductions from theory and pure flights of fancy. It is impossible to mention here all the many enthusiastic workers who have contributed to its growth! Charles Darwin's superb work on oceanic islands during the famous voyage of the Beagle, James Dwight Dana's studies in the Hawaiian Islands and other places visited by the United States Exploring Expedition in the early 1840s, F. Junghuhn's careful descriptions of the volcanoes of Indonesia, A. Stübel's study of the volcanoes of Ecuador and Colombia, the investigations of the great eruption of Krakatoa in 1883 by R. D. M. Verbeek and J. W. Judd, the superb study of Santorin Volcano by F. Fouqué, and a host of others, all left their important marks. Not only recent volcanoes but also ancient ones contributed to the growing mass of knowledge. Special mention may be made of the studies of the basal parts of old eroded volcanoes in Scotland begun in 1861 by Archibald Geikie and pursued ever since by Geikie and his many associates and successors—Edward Forbes, Judd, A. Harker, G. W. Tyrrell, C. T. Clough, J. W. Gregory, E. B. Bailey, and J. E. Richey, to mention only a few of the most important. The results of the work are described in Chapter 15.

Like most sciences, volcanology has advanced in surges, dependent in part on the development of new techniques of studying volcanoes and partly on stimulation of interest by great volcanic eruptions. The outbreak of Krakatoa, mentioned above, was one example of the latter. The 1902 eruptions of Mt. Pelée and Soufrière volcanoes in the Lesser Antilles, and the tragic destruction of the city of St. Pierre by Mt. Pelée, brought forth several reports, including two of basic importance: a monograph by Alfred Lacroix on the volcano Pelée and the eruption, containing detailed accounts of the growth of the dome and spine at the summit of the mountain (see Chapter 6), and the first accounts of the murderous "glowing clouds" (Chapter 8); and one by Tempest Anderson and J. W. Flett on the eruption of Soufrière. Perhaps even more important—it inspired two of the twentieth-century's greatest volcanologists to devote their lives to that profession.

Thomas A. Jaggar, professor of geology at Massachusetts Institute of Technology, was already interested in volcanoes, but he divided that interest with igneous petrology and experimental geology. He had been doing extensive laboratory experiments on the processes of erosion and deposition of sediments. When the news of the disasters on the islands of Martinique and St. Vincent reached Washington, the United States Government organized a relief expedition and dispatched it to the scene with food, clothing, and medical aid aboard the cruiser *Dixie*. Jaggar and several other American scientists were aboard. His experiences as a member of the expedition tipped the balance in favor of volcanoes, and for the rest of his career Jaggar's work was almost wholly devoted to active volcanoes and the aspects of geophysics that are closely related to them. He took time out to invent the first amphibian automobile, the forerunner of the military "duck" of World War II, as an easier means of travel between the islands of the Aleutian chain, where he was studying the volcanoes.

Frank A. Perret was an electrical engineer and inventor who had worked with Thomas Edison, but overwork had broken his health and his doctor had suggested a rest cure, including travel. He arrived in Martinique, as a tourist, a couple of years after the eruption of Mt. Pelée, and was so impressed by the destruction of St. Pierre and the power and grandeur of the eruptive manifestations that he decided to abandon his well-established career and devote himself to the study of volcanoes. His background did little to prepare him for it. He had no training in geology or chemistry, and his training in physics had no relation to geophysics. Realizing this, he went in 1904 to Vesuvius and offered his services, unpaid, to R. V. Matteucci, who was then the director of the Vesuvius Observatory. Perret's brilliance enabled him to learn very quickly, though in all his later work one detects occasional gaps in geological knowledge. He also had luck on his side! In 1906 came a tremendous eruption of Vesuvius, which he studied in detail with Matteucci. His report on the eruption, published many years later by the Carnegie Institution of Washington, is one of the classics of volcanology. He went on to work at many other volcanoes, and in 1929 returned to the scene of his first enthrallment to study another eruption of Mt. Pelée and add highly important information to our growing knowledge of volcanic domes and glowing avalanches.

We cannot leave the history of volcanology without some account of the establishment and operation of volcano observatories. An observatory for the continuous study and recording of the activity of Vesuvius was established on the slope of the mountain above the site of Herculaneum in 1847. It has survived, through many vicissitudes, until the present time; and its directors have included such well-known volcanologists as L. Palmieri, R. V. Matteucci, G. Mercalli, and A. Malladra. For the most part, however, the study of volcanoes continued to be of an expeditionary character. Brief visits were paid to volcanoes to map them geologically and to collect their products for study in distant laboratories, or to examine the results of specific eruptions. It was rare that a trained scientist was on the ground to study the eruption while it was in progress. Furthermore, the feeling grew increasingly strong among volcanologists that eruption was only a part of the picture of volcanic activity, and that much information, perhaps of equal importance, was to be gained between eruptions. The latter is especially true of the development of means for predicting eruptions and thereby saving lives and property. Prediction must be done during the period before the eruption begins! Increasingly, it was felt that what was needed was continuous observation of volcanoes.

One of the strongest advocates of continuous study was T. A. Jaggar. In 1909 the Whitney Fund became available to the Massachusetts Institute of Technology, donated by the Whitney Estate for the study of earthquakes and related phenomena with a view to reducing human sufferings from those causes. An observatory for the study of an active volcano and its related earthquakes seemed the best use of the money, and Jaggar and a colleague, R. A. Daly of Harvard University, set out to locate the best site for it. Both Daly and Jaggar visited Kilauea Volcano in Hawaii in 1909, and Jaggar went on to examine possible sites in Japan and at the same time to consult with Japanese volcanologists and seismologists regarding instruments and methods in use in Japan. During the trip he formed a lifetime friendship with a famous Japanese seismologist, F. Omori. Kilauea was chosen as the site of the Observatory because of the constancy of its activity and its gentleness, which allowed investigators to work with active lavas at close range.

The Hawaiian Volcano Observatory was formally established in 1911, and Jaggar made arrangements with the Geophysical Laboratory of the Carnegie Institution of Washington to initiate the scientific work by making temperature measurements in the lake of molten lava in Halemaumau Crater at Kilauea. The instruments (electrical thermometers) were prepared in Washington, and a gas chemist, E. S. Shepherd, was delegated to take them to Hawaii and supervise their operation. But at the last minute Jaggar found that his teaching commitments at the Massachusetts Institute of Technology (where he was chairman of the Geology Department) would not allow him to leave. It was a great disappointment! But rather than postpone the beginning of the work, he made arrangements for Frank Perret to accompany Shepherd in his place. To Perret went the responsibility, and the honor, of starting the work of the Hawaiian Volcano Observatory. In the summer of 1911 he built a field station on the floor of Kilauea Crater, close to the edge of the inner crater of Halemaumau, he and Shepherd made the temperature measurements (see Chapter 4) and collected a sample of molten lava from the lake, and for several weeks Perret kept a record of the behavior of the lake. But then the work was stopped by their return to Washington.

It was not until the spring of 1912 that Jaggar was able to go to Hawaii and begin the continuous observations he so much desired, and even then it was not smooth sailing. The money available from the Whitney Fund was insufficient to finance the operation, let alone to erect a suitable observatory building. But with the enthusiastic aid of L. A. Thurston, editor of the *Honolulu Advertiser* and longtime devotee of the volcano, Jaggar established the Hawaiian Volcano Research Association, composed of local business and professional men interested in the activity of the volcano, and the Association provided the additional money needed to operate the Observatory. The Chamber of Commerce of the city of Hilo raised the money to pay for an Observatory building on the rim of Kilauea Crater. The great scientific adventure was begun! But once under way, the sailing was still far from smooth! After 5 years the Whitney funds expired, and for a time Jaggar financed the work with money he made by raising pigs—at the same time keeping his volcano observations going without interruption. He had been joined in 1912 by H. O. Wood, who took charge of the seismological program. (Wood later established the world-renowned southern California network of seismograph stations of the California Institute of Technology.) It was a great relief when the operation of the Observatory was taken over, in 1919, by the U. S. Weather Bureau, which at that time was under the mandate of Congress to keep a record of earthquakes in the United States. Being part of a big government bureau gave a new promise of permanence to the operation, but the Volcano Research Association continued its active interest and aid.

The Hawaiian Volcano Observatory has now completed more than half a century of continuous recording of the activity of the Hawaiian volcanoes, successively under the auspices of the Massachusetts Institute of Technology, the U. S. Weather Bureau, the National Park Service, and the U.S. Geological Survey. The tremendous mass of information that it has produced has more than justified the faith of its founder! Jaggar remained its director until 1941, when he was succeeded by his former assistant, R. H. Finch. I, in turn, succeeded Finch in 1951, and since 1956 the Observatory has been under a succession of Geological Survey scientists. We confidently expect that it will continue to operate fruitfully for many years to come.

The success of the Vesuvian and Hawaiian observatories led to the establishment of others. In 1921 the government of the Netherlands East Indies established a Volcanological Survey, which in turn established observatories, manned for the most part by Indonesian observers, at several of the Javanese volcanoes. For a quarter of a century the Survey turned out a series of reports containing a tremendous amount of information on Indonesian volcanoes. Interrupted by World War II, the work was resumed after the war. It is continuing under the government of Indonesia, but unfortunately it has not produced much in the way of published results.

In Japan, also, several observatories have been established. That at Mt. Asama has been operating since 1934 under the very able direction of T. Minakami of the University of Tokyo's Earthquake Research Institute. Others have been established in recent years at Oshima and Aso volcanoes and at several other places, partly under the Earthquake Research Institute and partly under the Japan Meteorological Agency. Volcano research is probably more active in Japan than anywhere else in the world.

The USSR is maintaining a very active program of research on the volcanoes of Kamchatka, with permanent observatories and seismograph stations. New Zealand has an active volcanological program, with a field station in the famous hot-spring area of Rotorua. France is maintaining observatories for the study of the volcanoes of the Lesser Antilles; and Belgium recently, with the concurrence of the Congolese government, has been operating an observatory at the foot of Nyamlagira Volcano, just north of Lake Kivu in central Africa. The Philippine government is maintaining observatories at Taal Volcano, where several thousand lives were lost in 1911, and at Hibokhibok under its Commission on Volcanology.

The Australian government, in 1938, established a volcano observatory at Rabaul on New Britain Island. Its operation had to be discontinued during World War II. N. H. Fisher, who was in charge of the observatory at that time, has told me that on the eve of the Japanese invasion he and his assistant decided that they might as well be bombed by the volcano as by the Japanese and climbed to the very rim of the active crater of Matupi Volcano to make a final observation of the activity in the crater. Starting to lean against a big boulder on the crater rim to take a rest, he had the inspiration to spit on it first. When the spit sizzled and bounced from the heat of the boulder, he decided to look for another resting place! The observatory has been reequipped since the war and is again in operation, and observations are being carried on at other volcanoes in Australian territory.

The U.S. Geological Survey established an observatory in 1926 at Mineral near Lassen Peak in California. Its operation was discontinued by the Survey during the depression of the 1930s, but the seismograph station has been continued in operation by the National Park Service; and a second station equipped with a seismograph of low sensitivity suitable for display to visitors, loaned by the Geological Survey's Hawaiian Observatory, is operated at Manzanita Lake. The Cascade Range as a whole is badly in need of additional surveillance. Another seismograph station is being operated at Mt. Rainier by the University of Washington. A program of volcano studies in the Aleutian Islands was carried on for several years by the Geological Survey, but has been discontinued—we hope only temporarily.

One of the most interesting and promising recent developments has been the establishment of an International Center of Volcanology in Catania, Italy, supported by the Italian and Belgian governments. Volcanologists from several countries are working there under the general supervision of the famous volcanologist Alfred Rittmann. There is also a current move to establish an observatory for the continuous observation and study of Mt. Etna—observations that will pick up where Empedocles left off more than 2,000 years ago!

The past century and a half has been largely a period of data gathering. Volcanoes have been studied and described in great detail. Much information has been gathered on the composition and physical properties of volcanic rocks, both solid and molten, and on the physical and geological relationships of volcanoes. But comparatively little progress has been made in understanding the fundamental processes of volcanic activity. This has been partly because interpretation must await knowledge of such basic facts as we have been gathering; but it is partly also because volcanology is a complex science dependent on the development of other sciences, particularly physical chemistry, geochemistry, and geophysics. We are only now beginning to get an understanding of such things as the behavior of melts and solutions at very high temperatures and pressures and other similar fundamental knowledge necessary to an understanding of volcanoes. Fact gathering must continue, of course, but volcanology is now entering an interpretive period, and one that promises to be increasingly fascinating to the workers taking part in it.

SUGGESTED ADDITIONAL READING

Fenton and Fenton, 1952; Geikie, 1897; Sapper, 1927, p. 1–200; Tazieff, 1961; Williams, 1941; Zittel, 1901, p. 1–11, 46–145, 186–323.

4

Volcanic Rocks and Magmas

Some of the rock fragments and gas ejected by volcanoes are of surface origin. Water in near-surface rocks may be converted into steam by volcanic heat, and the expansion of the steam may bring about explosions of considerable violence. These explosions, and also explosions of gases of deeper origin, may throw out fragments of the solid, and often much older, rocks that surround the vent but that have no other relation to volcanic activity. Both of these phenomena will be discussed in later chapters, but for the present we are concerned with things more fundamentally volcanic in nature. By far the greater bulk of the products of volcanoes is the result of the rise of molten material and gas from the depths of the earth.

The gas released by volcanoes is dissipated in the atmosphere, but the molten material solidifies to rock and remains as a record of the volcanic activity. By studying the rocks we can tell a great deal about the eruption that produced them. Conversely, the different types of volcanic rock differ considerably in their physical properties when they are in the molten state, and to these differences are attributable most of the differences among eruptions. If we know what kind of rock is erupted by a particular volcano, we can foretell to a considerable extent what sort of eruption is likely to take place at it. Thus, to understand properly the similarities and differences

PLATE 4-1. Cloud of fume rising from the vent of an eruption on the flank of Mauna Loa, Hawaii, in April 1942, seen from a distance of 14 miles. The cloud consists largely of steam, with lesser amounts of sulfur and carbon gases. Photo by United States Department of the Interior, National Park Service.

between eruptions, we should have some knowledge of the different kinds of volcanic rock.

The molten rock, or *magma*, consists primarily of a mass of completely or partly molten silicates (combinations of other chemical elements with silicon and oxygen) containing volatile materials either dissolved in the melt or as bubbles of gas. When the magma solidifies, the silicates (plus minor amounts of oxides) remain as a solid rock, but most of the gas escapes (Plate 4-1). The mineral and chemical composition of the rock can be determined with the microscope and by chemical analysis, but the amount and nature of the gas are much more difficult to determine. Both the silicate and the volatile portions affect the physical properties of the magma and, thereby, the nature of the volcanic eruption. The rocks can be classified on the bases of mineral and chemical composition. Complicated and detailed classifications have been made, but for the present purpose a very simple classification will suffice. Such a classification is given in

Appendix 2, and it is suggested that the reader not familiar with rock names consult Appendix 2 before reading further.

The nature of the magmatic gases is discussed in the next section, and the average chemical compositions of common types of volcanic rocks are given in Table A2-2. The rest of this chapter is devoted to the physical properties of magmas and their effects on the character of volcanic eruptions.

Magmatic Gases

Measurement of the amount of gas in magma and determination of its composition are very difficult problems that have not been satisfactorily solved. Measurements on magma below the earth's surface are as yet impossible. Laboratory measurements have been made on artificial magmas, including remelted natural rocks, and the amount of gas that can be dissolved in them at various temperatures and pressures has been determined; but there is no assurance that natural magmas deep in the earth are saturated —that is, that they contain all of the gas they are capable of holding in solution. Indeed, the evidence suggests that many of them do not. Direct measurement of the amount of gas in magmas erupting at the surface is also impossible because of the very difficult physical conditions, particularly the high temperatures, that are encountered in trying to work close to the vent during eruptions. Moreover, movement of the viscous lava is liable to damage instruments thrust into it, and the strongly corrosive liquid attacks most metals violently. It is, of course, comparatively easy to determine the amount and nature of the gas trapped in igneous rocks after the magma has frozen. The amount of water in very fresh volcanic rocks is generally only 0.1 to 0.2 per cent by weight (it may be as low as 0.02 per cent), and other gases are far less abundant. But this is only part of the gas that the magma originally contained, and in most instances it is only a small part.

The amount of gas that can be dissolved in a magma depends on the composition of the rest of the magma and on the temperature and pressure. The solubility increases with increasing pressure and decreases with increasing temperature. Thus, at a temperature of 900°C, a dacite magma is capable of dissolving about 0.6 per cent (by weight) of water at a pressure of 69 bars (1 atmosphere equals 1.013 bars), equivalent to a depth of less than 700 feet below the surface of the earth, but at a pressure of 1 bar (approximately atmospheric pressure at sea level) only about 0.1 per cent. Similarly, a rhyolite magma can contain nearly 10 per cent of water at 900°C and 5,000 bars, but only about 0.5 per cent at 1 bar (Goranson, 1931) (see Fig. 4-1). More recent figures (Hamilton et al., 1964) show that andesite magma can contain 4.5 per cent of water at 1,000 bars and 10.1 per cent at 5,300 bars, whereas basalt magma can contain only 3.1 per cent at 1,000 bars and 9.4 per cent at 6,000 bars. Because of the much greater solubility of volatiles in magma at high pressures, it is probable that nearly all magmas contain

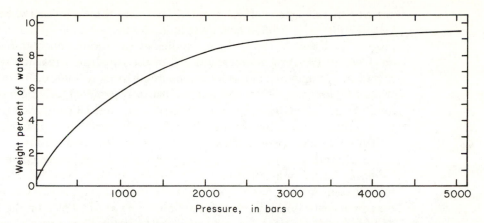

FIGURE 4-1. Solubility of water in rhyolite magma (molten Stone Mountain granite) at 900°C and various pressures. The scale on the upper edge of the diagram indicates the depth in the earth corresponding to the pressures shown along the lower edge. (After R. W. Goranson, 1931.)

more gas at depth than they can continue to hold in solution when they reach the surface, and this is confirmed by the fact that nearly all erupting magmas are separating excess gas as bubbles in the liquid.

Only rarely are conditions suitable to make even a well-based estimate of the amount of gas released during a volcanic eruption. The gas makes an enormous cloud; however, not only does the gas expand greatly when it escapes into the atmosphere, but it becomes mixed with a large amount of air; so the size of the cloud is very misleading in judging the amount of gas. In eruptions in which lava pours out freely at the surface, the actual proportion by weight of gas to lava is generally small. During several eruptions of Hawaiian volcanoes, the amount of gas, including that retained as bubbles and still dissolved in the lava as well as the cloud that streamed off into the atmosphere, ranged from about 0.5 to a little more than 1 per cent of the total weight of the magma that reached the surface. On the basis of the volume of vesicles (gas-bubble holes) as related to experimentally determined solubility of water in magma, Moore (1970) concludes that basalt magmas of different compositions erupted in the deep ocean contain on eruption from 0.25 to 0.9 per cent water.

According to Fries (1953), the water liberated as steam during the eruption of Paricutin Volcano, Mexico, in the year 1945, amounted to about 15,000 short tons a day, or approximately 1.1 per cent of the total weight of the erupted magma. Rittmann has calculated that the gas liberated during a 4-day eruption of Vesuvius in June, 1929, was more than 2 billion cubic yards, but reduced to weight proportion this was only about 0.6 per cent of the extruded lava. Combined with the gas frozen into the solidified lava (0.61 per cent), this makes a total of only about 1.2 per cent of the magma that reached the surface. Verhoogen (1939) estimated the gas liberated during the 1938 eruption of Nyamlagira Volcano in central Africa to be 0.7

per cent of the weight of the erupted lava, and this combined with the gas locked up in the solidified lava gives a gas content of only 0.9 per cent of the magma as it rose to the surface. Studies of the radon concentration in the gas from Surtsey Volcano, Iceland, led to the conclusion that the water dissolved in the magma cannot have amounted to more than 0.75 per cent by weight (Björnsson, 1968), and water constituted from 60 to 90 per cent of the total gas in the analyzed samples (Sigvaldason and Elísson, 1968).

The above examples are all mafic magmas (rich in magnesium and iron and relatively poor in silicon), and it is possible that acid magmas (rich in silicon and relatively poor in magnesium and iron) may contain a considerably larger proportion of gas, but there are few estimates that appear to be based on reasonably good data. H. Arsandaux (1934) has estimated that during the 1929 eruption of dacitic magma at Mt. Pelée on the island of Martinique, the water liberated amounted to about 2.5 per cent of the weight of the erupted magma.

There are other examples in which the gas is released from the magma below the earth's surface. Little or no material other than gas and fragments of older rocks may reach the surface. In that case, of course, it is impossible to make any estimate of the gas content of the magma. It has been estimated that during the great eruption of Vesuvius in 1906, the weight of the gas that rushed out with tremendous violence for many hours exceeded that of the erupted lava. But how much magma had lost its gas below the surface? And how much of the gas was not derived from the magma at all?

Large amounts of steam liberated in some eruptions clearly come in large part or entirely from the boiling of groundwater in the rocks adjacent to the volcanic conduit. Carbon dioxide may also come in part or wholly from the calcining of limestones by magmatic heat, or it may be released by alteration of carbonate minerals in the limestone to silicates. Almost surely, both of these processes contributed to the great gas column that rose from Vesuvius in 1906. Limestones are known to be in contact with the Vesuvius magma at depth and to have been partly changed to silicate minerals. Fragments of the altered limestone thrown out onto the flanks of the mountain are well known for the fine suites of "contact metamorphic" minerals they contain. Water-bearing sedimentary rocks also underlie the volcano. The amount of water (steam) and carbon dioxide from these sources during the 1906 eruption cannot be determined, but it may well account for most of the gas discharged. Similarly, in other eruptions of Vesuvius and of other volcanoes, gases of nonmagmatic origin may play an important part.

Every collection of volcanic gases that has ever been made from the vents of active volcanoes or from live lava flows has been to some degree contaminated with air. Partly, the air is simply sucked into the collecting apparatus along with the volcanic gases, but partly it is probably of deeper-seated origin. The open spaces in the upper parts of volcanic cones are filled with air, and the air in adjacent rocks is heated by the rising magma and rises with it, and to some degree is incorporated into it. Also, air-saturated rock fragments are engulfed by the magma, and the air from them is released into the surrounding liquid. Atmospheric contamination appears unavoidable, and to arrive at a true picture of the composition of magmatic gases we must find some way to circumvent it. The best approach seems to be to make use of the inert gases in the atmosphere—those that do not enter into reactions with other things in the magma. The composition of the atmosphere is known very accurately. Along with the abundant nitrogen and oxygen, it contains small amounts of such inert gases as argon. If we determine the amount of argon in collections of volcanic gas, and assume that all the argon has been derived from atmospheric contamination (which certainly is not entirely true), we can calculate the amount of other atmospheric gases that are present. These are then subtracted from the whole, and the remainder represents the gas of nonatmospheric origin. Unfortunately, however, there still remains the possibility of additional contamination resulting from the introduction of water and carbon dioxide, and possibly other things, from near-surface wall rocks. It is hoped that eventually the amount of such contamination can be detected by determining the relative abundance of isotopes of elements in the gases. This work is still in its infancy, and no worthwhile results on the isotopic composition of eruption gases have yet appeared, though they have supplied some indication of the amount of magmatic water that is reaching the surface in hot springs (see Chapter 13).

Several different methods have been used for the collection and analysis of volcanic gases. The earliest method is that of capturing a sample of gas from erupting lava in some sort of container and bringing it back to the laboratory for analysis. The best collections by that method have been made at Kilauea Volcano in Hawaii. Previous to 1924, the Halemaumau Crater at Kilauea contained an almost permanent lake of molten basaltic lava a quarter of a mile wide, sometimes overflowing the crater rim and sometimes hundreds of feet below it. Explosive action was very weak, taking the form of gentle lava fountains only a few feet high, and for long periods the surface of the lake was covered with a tough black crust a few inches thick. When the lake was at a high level, it was possible to go out onto the crust with little danger and little discomfort except from the choking sulfurous gas that seeped out of the molten lava. In May, 1912, A. L. Day and E. S. Shepherd of the Geophysical Laboratory of the Carnegie Institution of Washington went out onto the lake wearing gas masks and collected samples of gas as nearly as possible directly as it issued from the lava. Their method was simple. A small lava fountain had built a cone of solidified spatter on the crust of the lake and had closed in the top, forming a hollow dome with cracks in the sides through which flames and gas were escaping. Into the glowing interior of the dome they inserted the end of a pipe. Most of the pipe was lined with glass to prevent reaction of the gas with the metal, but 1 foot of the iron pipe that protruded into the dome lacked the glass lining. Gas accumulating in the dome was drawn back through the pipe by means of a hand-operated pump, through a series of glass tubes. First, gas was pumped through the system until it was reasonably certain that it had displaced all the air, and then the tubes were filled with gas from the dome. Nearly all the steam in the gas condensed to liquid water in the first few tubes. Then valves in the tubes were closed and the tubes removed and shipped to Washington, D.C., where the gas was later chemically analyzed by Shepherd. The dome collapsed soon afterward, and no other chance to collect came until December when another similar sample was taken. That time, however, an opening near the base of the dome allowed air to enter, and it was found that the gases in the collection tubes had been completely oxidized. The composition of the gases collected in May, minus the water, averaged 55.4 per cent CO_2, 4.3 per cent CO, 7.7 per cent H_2, 29.6 per cent N_2, and 2.9 per cent SO_2. The proportion of water could not be determined, because the water collected in the tubes included that from the large volume of gas pumped through the tubes to flush out the air. It was obvious, however, that a large amount of water was present.

Besides the determination of the relative amounts of the different gases in the sample tubes when they reached Washington, this work had two immediate important results. A little argon was present in all of the samples, indicating clearly that contamination by air had taken place; but also the ratio of nitrogen to argon in the samples was less than in air, suggesting that some of the atmospheric nitrogen had been used up by reactions with the volcanic gases. Indeed, reaction with air had been apparent in the field, since the gases were seen to be burning in the upper part of the dome. These reactions indicated a source of heat that might contribute to the high temperature of the lava.

Another important finding was the large amount of water in the samples. Including the water collected in the condensation tubes, the various samples averaged nearly 70 per cent water. This finding was important because, despite the fact that students of volcanoes had traditionally believed volcanic gases to consist largely of water, A. Brun, a Swiss geochemist, had claimed that volcanic gases were essentially anhydrous!

Brun's evidence consisted largely of the facts that the white cloud of gas drifting away from the volcano does not evaporate and disappear, as does the cloud from an exhausting steam boiler, and water does not condense from the cloud where it blows across cold rocks to the lee of the vent. This latter is indeed often a striking fact. Several times I have stood in the thin outer edges of the gas cloud during cold weather, even at temperatures below freezing at the summit of Mauna Loa, and no water has condensed on my spectacles or on other cold objects, as it would from an ordinary cloud of steam; and others have had the same experience. Could Brun be right, that the cloud was essentially without steam? Day and Shepherd's results showed clearly and conclusively that the water was actually there. The lack of condensation was due to the fact that the cloud was not saturated. Its apparent denseness was caused by the presence of finely divided sulfur particles, and its failure to condense on cold objects was partly the result of the "drying" effect of sulfur gases—the combination of some of the water with sulfur dioxide and trioxide in the gas cloud. Perret has pointed out that the degree of visibility of the cloud of water vapor given off is strongly dependent also on the state of saturation of the atmosphere. There is no question that water is the principal constituent of the gases in most collections made during volcanic eruptions, but how much of it is resurgent, derived from near surface rocks, and how much is the result of surface oxidation of deep-seated hydrogen? It is worth recalling that during the submarine eruption of Santorin Volcano in 1866, where the escaping gases were protected from immediate contact with the atmosphere, Fouqué (1879, p. 226) found them to contain a large proportion (up to 30 per cent) of hydrogen. Unfortunately, these pioneer analyses are questionable. Gases collected during the eruption of Surtsey Volcano in 1963–1966 contained up to 4.7 mole per cent of hydrogen and averaged nearly 3 per cent (Sigvaldason and Elísson, 1968).

The Kilauea collections of 1912, although they were the best to that date, still were unsatisfactory. The amount of atmospheric contamination was very large, and, furthermore, the iron pipe had reacted with the gases and produced some degree of change in their composition. (Reactions of this sort may have been responsible for the large amount of hydrogen in the analyzed samples.) Better collections were needed. In 1917, Shepherd again found an opportunity to make collections on the surface of the lava lake, and still more extensive collections were made by T. A. Jaggar in 1919. This time the collecting vessels were glass tubes with long thin tips from which the air had been pumped out with a vacuum pump. Shepherd and Jaggar took these vacuum tubes out onto the crust that had formed on the lava lake. The ends of the tubes were thrust into the openings from which gas was issuing and the thin sealed tips were broken off, allowing the gas to enter and fill the tube. The tip was then sealed again, either by bringing it in contact with the orange-hot lava beneath the crust or with a gasoline blowtorch. The tubes were again shipped to Washington for analysis of the gas by Shepherd.

These samples of 1917 and 1919 are still among the best ever collected from an erupting volcano. The average of the 10 best samples is given in column 1 of Table 4-1. Even in these samples, however, there was a large amount of atmospheric contamination, and, worse still, it was apparent that there had been considerable reaction between the gases in the tube between the time they were collected and when they were analyzed. The reaction was to be expected. A mixture of gases that can exist together in equilibrium in one physical environment becomes unstable when introduced into a different environment, and reaction occurs. The composition found in the tubes in Washington did not represent the combination of gases as it existed in the magma in Halemaumau Crater, and still less did it resemble that in the magma under high pressure deep in the earth. How was this difficulty to be overcome? For many years there was no answer.

The old methods of gas analysis were very complicated and tedious, and the results often were not highly accurate. This, together with the

TABLE 4-1. Compositions of volcanic gases (*In volume percent*)

	1	2	3	4	5	6	7	8	9
CO_2	21.4	46.2	40.9	4.6	10.1	2.1	15.3	10.4	25.9
CO	0.8	0.7	2.4	0.3	2.0	0.6	1.4	8.3	*
H_2	0.9	0.03	0.8	2.8	0.2	0.4	4.4	1.1	—
SO_2	11.5	14.3	4.4	4.1	—	0.01	—	—	0.0
S_2	0.7	0.0	—	—	0.5	0.9	0.2	1.3	—
SO_3	1.8	38.8	—	—	—	—	—	—	—
Cl_2	0.1	0.0	—	—	0.4	0.3	0.2	0.4	—
F_2	0.0	0.0	—	—	3.3	1.5	0.0	0.0	—
HCl	—	—	—	0.6	—	—	—	—	—
N + rare gases	10.1	16.6	8.3	4.5	0.9	0.6	5.2	7.2	11.1
H_2O	52.7	71.4	43.2	83.1	82.5	93.7	73.2	71.3	63.0

* Included with N.

1. Kilauea, Hawaii; average of the best 10 collections of gas from Halemaumau lava lake in 1917–1919 (Jaggar, 1940).
2. Mauna Loa, Hawaii; average of two samples collected from molten lava in 1926 (Shepherd, 1938).
3. Nyiragongo, Congo; the single "excellent" analysis of gas from the lava lake in 1959 for which water was determined (Chaigneau, Tazieff, and Fabre, 1960).
4. Surtsey, Iceland; average of 11 analyses of samples taken between Oct. 15, 1964, and March 31, 1967 (Sigvaldason and Elísson, 1968).
5. Mt. Pelée, West Indies; gas extracted from lava (hypersthene andesite) of the spine formed in 1902 (Shepherd and Merwin, 1927).
6. Lassen Peak, California; gas extracted from lava (dacite) erupted in 1915 (Shepherd, 1925).
7. Mauna Loa, Hawaii; gas extracted from pumice (basalt) of the 1926 eruption (Shepherd, 1938).
8. Niuafo'ou; gas extracted from lava (basalt) of the 1929 eruption (Shepherd, 1938).
9. Kozu-shima, Japan; gas extracted from rhyolite lava (Iwasaki, Katsura, and Sakato, 1955).

problem of how to overcome the reaction of the gases in the collection tube, was very frustrating. Shepherd ended a lifetime of work with the statement that there had never been an analysis of volcanic gas made that was worth the paper the report was printed on! His defeatism was exaggerated, but not wholly without grounds.

Finally, in recent years there has come an improvement. New methods of analysis, particularly chromatographic ones, have made gas analyses easier and more accurate, and new techniques of collection have been devised. One of these, adapted by Elskens, Tazieff, and Tonani (1964) from colorimetric methods of fume analysis used in industrial plants, analyzes the gas in the field within a few seconds of the time of collection, thus largely avoiding the reactions in the collecting tube. The results are believed to be accurate to within a few per cent. Another method, devised by J. J. Naughton of the University of Hawaii, utilizes a vacuum tube similar to that used by Jaggar, but draws the gas in through an absorption column. The different components of the gas are held in different parts of the column and kept from contact with each other, thus avoiding reactions between them until the collection can be analyzed by precise methods in the laboratory. These methods promise to give much improved results.

Still another method of determining the compositions of gases from an erupting volcano is the making of spectrograms—records obtained by directing a spectrograph at volcanic flames. At high temperatures each element gives off light radiation of particular characteristic wavelengths, and these are separated by the spectrograph and recorded on photographic plates. Early attempts were made with this technique during the 1938 eruption of Nyamlagira Volcano by J. Verhoogen (1939). Among other spectral lines shown on Verhoogen's plates were lines that were at first interpreted as very high energy lines of nitrogen, which would have required for their generation more energy than was available from the heat of the burning gases. However, this anomaly has been solved by Delsemme (1960), who has shown that the lines in question were caused by copper chloride. At Kilauea, also, recent work by K. J. Murata has demonstrated the presence of copper, apparently carried in the magmatic gases as a volatile copper chloride.

Among the results of the new techniques of rapid analysis of the gases in the field, by Elskens, Tazieff, and Tonani, is the demonstration of considerable variation in the composition of the gas over intervals of a few minutes. On Stromboli in 1963, 26 analyses were made of the gas being liberated at one of the eruptive vents over a period of 2 hours. One analysis showed 51 per cent water, nine showed between 47 and 30 per cent, thirteen showed between 25 and 3 per cent, and three contained no water at all. The average water content was about 22 per cent. On Etna in 1966, of ten determinations over a period of 11 minutes, five contained more than 50 per cent water, three less than 50 per cent, and two contained none. In 1969, eleven determinations of Etna gases over a period of 5.3 minutes all showed between 3 and 36 per cent water. In all the determinations, carbon dioxide was at least as abundant as water, and probably much more abundant (Tazieff, 1969). As striking as the variability of the abundance of water in these analyses is the small amount of water present in many of them—a result that differs greatly from the findings of most other analyses.

An approach quite different from the collection of gases being released by erupting volcanoes is the extraction from volcanic rocks of the gases trapped in them when they solidified. The rocks are crushed in a vacuum, and the gases thus obtained are analyzed by standard methods.

In Table 4-1 are given the compositions of volcanic gas collected directly from still-fluid lavas (columns 1–4) and extracted from solidified rocks in the laboratory (columns 5–9). Other collections of gas analyses have been published by Chamberlin (1908), Shepherd (1938), and White and Waring (1963). Compositions of fumarole gases are given in Table 13-1.

All these techniques are contributing to a slowly growing mass of more and more accurate information on the composition of the gases held in the magma when it reaches the surface. Furthermore, thermodynamic studies of the gases are beginning to indicate the composition the gases must have had under high pressure and temperature at depth in the earth, and to explain some of the facts observed at the surface. Thus, for a long time volcanologists have been aware of the fact that the clouds poured out during eruptions contain large amounts of sulfur dioxide (the same choking gas given off by the burning of a sulfur fumigating candle), whereas the gas liberated after eruptions has the rotten-egg odor of hydrogen sulfide. This is easily explained by thermodynamic relations. At low temperature the predominant sulfur gas in an equilibrium mixture of hydrogen, oxygen, carbon, and sulfur in the proportions found in the eruption gases at Kilauea is hydrogen sulfide (Fig. 4-2), whereas at a temperature of 1200°C, sulfur dioxide is nearly as abundant as hydrogen sulfide and much more conspicuous because of its very pungent odor and choking quality. It is not appropriate to attempt a discussion of the thermodynamics of volcanic gases here, but those interested can find a discussion of these and other relationships in papers by Ellis (1957), Heald, Naughton, and Barnes (1963), and Verhoogen (1949).

It may be noted in Table 4-1 that in the gases of Kilauea Volcano chlorine is present only in very small amounts, although it was found in fumarolic gases from the cone of the 1959 eruption (Murata, et al., 1964), and fluorine is absent. In contrast, chlorine, and particularly fluorine, are much more abundant in the gases of Vesuvius, Lassen Peak, and Mt. Pelée. This difference appears to be characteristic of the volcanoes of oceanic and continental environments, the gases of continental volcanoes nearly always being notably richer in fluorine and chlorine than those of oceanic volcanoes. For example, during the eruption of Katmai Volcano in Alaska in 1912, chlorine was liberated in such abundance that it is reported that clothes hung on clotheslines as far away as Chicago were rotted by the gas drifting through the atmosphere and combining with water to form hydrochloric acid. E. G. Zies (1929) has calculated that gas vents in the ash flow formed at that time in the Valley of Ten Thousand Smokes just west of Mt. Katmai, during the height of their activity, previous to 1920, were giving off 1.25 million tons of hydrochloric acid and 200,000 tons of hydrofluoric acid per year.

Before leaving the subject of volcanic gases, it may be worth mentioning the occurrence of flames from burning gas during eruptions. Although volcanoes were once thought to be the result of combustion of coal or other substances, we now recognize that flames are a very minor feature of eruptions. Small flames are occasionally seen over erupting vents and over openings in lava tubes where gases are escaping, and waving banners of flame 20 to 30 feet long have been observed above lava fountains in Halemaumau Crater at Kilauea Volcano. The weakness of the light source and the distance from which they must be observed have made it impossible thus far to get positive identifications of the burning gases, but the very pale blue color of the flame suggests that it is hydrogen. Flames are often seen moving along the surface of an aa lava flow, above tree trunks submerged in the moving lava, and issuing from cracks in older rocks close to a flow and from

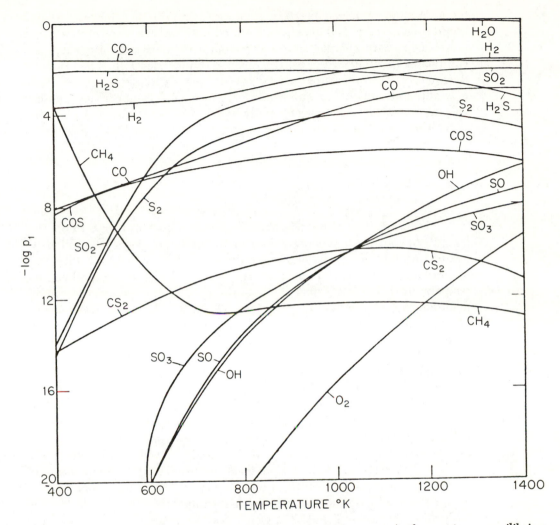

FIGURE 4-2. Concentration (partial pressure) of gases in an equilibrium mixture with the atomic ratios hydrogen 275.5, oxygen 142.2, carbon 2.680, sulfur 1.000, at different temperatures and one atmosphere pressure. The larger the number of the -log value in the scale on the left, the lower the concentration of the gas. (After Heald, Naughton, and Barnes, 1963.)

the edge of the flow itself. They appear largely to be burning methane formed by destructive distillation of plant material buried by the hot flow. Occasionally these hydrocarbon gases, moving outward through lava tubes and other openings in the older underlying lavas and gradually mixing with air, explode with sufficient violence to blast craters 5 to 15 feet across and as much as 5 feet deep at distances as great as 100 feet from the edge of the active flow.

Another aspect of gas in magmas is worthy of attention. Most of the minerals that crystallize first as the magma cools contain no volatile materials, and, consequently, the volatiles are left dissolved in the remaining liquid portion. As crystallization continues, the volatiles in the residual liquid become more and more concentrated until finally the saturation point is reached and the volatiles start to come out of solution and form a separate gas phase. In other words, the remaining liquid starts to boil. The gas liberated by this process of "second boiling" may increase in pressure until it is able to burst the confining roof of the magma chamber and cause a volcanic explosion. The efficacy of the process to bring about large explosions is in doubt, but it should not be ignored as a possibility.

Temperature of Magmas

Determination of the temperature of molten rock as it rises to the surface of the earth can be approached in two different ways. Natural rocks can be remelted in the laboratory and the melts then cooled until they start to crystallize and until they eventually become entirely crystalline, the temperature being measured at various stages. Or measurements can be made directly on erupting magmas in the field. The latter are fraught with physical difficulties: high working temperatures, often higher than the worker can bear without the protection of some sort of shield or asbestos suit; choking fumes that may necessitate the use of a gas mask; and the rough treatment that the viscous moving magma inflicts on any instrument thrust into it.

Hawaiian basaltic lavas remelted in the laboratory start to crystallize when the temperature of the melt is lowered to a level varying from about 1240 to 1190°C, depending on the chemical composition of the lava, and they become entirely crystallized at 1090 to 1065°C (Yoder and Tilley, 1962, p. 382). This does not, however, indicate the true eruption temperature of the original magma that cooled to form the lava. The original magma contained dissolved gas, but the lava remelted in the laboratory has lost essentially all of its gas; and since it is well known that the presence of volatiles in solution lowers the temperature at which solidification takes place, the temperature of the natural magma when it became solid almost certainly was somewhat lower than that at which the remelted lava becomes entirely solid in the laboratory. This supposition is borne out by laboratory experiments in which the melted lava was cooled under high pressures of water vapor, driving some of the water into solution in the melt. With a water-vapor pressure of 1,000 bars, remelted Hawaiian basalts start to crystallize at temperatures ranging from 1170 to 1160°C, and crystallization is not complete until the temperature drops to a level ranging from 960 to 930°C. Thus, the presence of even a moderate amount of water in solution lowers the temperature of total consolidation roughly 130°C. Higher pressures of water vapor result in still greater reduction of consolidation temperatures. The same phenomenon appears to be demonstrated in nature by the fact that temperatures of lava measured with optical pyrometers during eruptions of

Kilauea Volcano range from 25 to 120°C lower than those inferred on theoretical grounds from the composition of the glass in the lava (Wright, Kinoshita, and Peck, 1968).

Actual field measurements of temperature are usually made with one of two general types of instruments. The one least subject to error is the thermocouple—a pair of wires of different composition welded together at both ends. When one end is immersed in hot material, an electrical current is generated in the circuit, its strength depending on the difference in temperature between the hot and cold ends of the pair of wires. An ammeter is connected into the circuit near the cold end, and the amount of current can be read on the meter. If the temperature of the "cold junction" is known (it is usually kept at 0°C by immersing the junction in ice water), and the current-generating capacity of the pair of wires has been determined, the temperature of the "hot junction" can be calculated.

In violently exposive eruptions it is, of course, impossible to approach close enough to the vent to measure the temperature of the erupting magma with a thermocouple. Thermocouples have been used a few times to measure the temperature of lava flows, but one must approach very close in order to thrust the end of the instrument into the lava, and if the lava is very viscous it becomes very difficult to thrust it in at all. Furthermore, movement of the viscous liquid is likely to damage the instrument and freezing of the lava is likely to make it impossible to get the instrument out again. In 1911, two very expensive "resistance thermometers" were tried by E. S. Shepherd and F. A. Perret at the lava lake in Halemaumau Crater, Kilauea. When both failed, they fell back on a thermocouple, which in turn gave them only a single brief reading before it was torn loose from its cable and swallowed by the lava. Since the most satisfactory thermocouples for this use are made of platinum and its alloys, such losses cannot be repeated frequently! More commonly chromel–alumel thermocouples are used, but these also are expensive, more subject to corrosion by the lava and gases than the platinum ones, and the physical difficulties of using them are the same.

In recent years a series of excellent temperature measurements has been made by the U.S. Geological Survey with thermocouples inserted into the molten lava through holes drilled in the solidified crust of lava lakes in three different craters on Kilauea Volcano. In the lake in Alae Crater the maximum temperature was found to be about 1140°C (2084°F), and the temperature of half-solidified material at the base of the crust was 1067°C (Peck, Moore, and Kojima, 1964). The latter temperature is a little lower than that at a comparable degree of crystallization in the laboratory.

The instrument most commonly used to measure temperatures at volcanoes is the optical pyrometer. This consists essentially of a telescope in which a wire filament is mounted in such a way that it is visible in the telescope field at the same time as the glowing object, the temperature of which is being measured. Passing electrical current through the filament causes it to glow, its color changing from dull to bright red, orange, yellow, and white as the strength of the current is increased. At some point the color of the filament is exactly the same as that of the glowing object, and viewed against the object the filament completely disappears. The amount of current necessary to bring this about can be measured in one of several ways and the temperature of the object calculated, or on some instruments the temperature can be read directly from a calibrated dial. There are several drawbacks to this instrument. Under most conditions the color of the glowing object is not an exact indicator of the temperature, and a correction (for "absorption" or "emissivity") must be applied to the reading to get the correct temperature—but in the case of lavas the correction is seldom, if ever, accurately known. Moreover, any haze or smoke in the air absorbs some of the radiation to which the apparent color of the glowing object is due and results in a temperature reading that is too low. Even when no haze is apparent, the reading may be affected in this way. In making measurements of this sort on the lava lake of Halemaumau in 1952, we found that viewing the lava through a quarter of a mile of seemingly clear air resulted in an apparent temperature that was approximately 50°C lower than that obtained by closer readings. But perhaps the greatest shortcoming of all is the fact that one views only the outer surface of the hot object—a surface that is always somewhat cooler than the inside. Frequently, part of the front of a lava flow will break off and tumble down revealing the very hot interior part of the flow, but even when the telescope is already sighted and waiting, the newly exposed surface has generally started to darken before the current can be adjusted to make a reading. In spite of these drawbacks, measurements with optical pyrometers are usually the best we have.

Some estimate of the temperature can be made simply from the color of the glowing object as viewed with the unaided eye. This principle has long been familiar to blacksmiths and operators of steel furnaces, who formerly used it as an indication of the correct temperature to heat the steel. (Some sort of pyrometer is now generally used.) Following is a list of the colors commonly used and the approximate temperatures they indicate when the object is seen at night or in rather dark surroundings:

White	1150°C and up
Golden yellow	1090°C
Orange	900°C
Bright cherry red	700°C
Dull red	550–625°C
Lowest visible red	475°C

The color can be used to estimate temperature only when the line of sight to the object is clear. If a yellow-hot lava fountain is viewed through a brownish fume cloud, the color is, of course, changed, and the apparent temperature will be too low.

Where a hot vent or lava flow can be approached closely, its temperature can be estimated from the kindling temperatures of various familiar materials, or the melting temperatures of metals. If a stick bursts into flame when it is thrust into an opening in the crust of a lava flow, the temperature of the lava must be above the kindling temperature of the wood. If the lava will melt lead, but not copper, its temperature must be between the melting temperatures of those two metals. Some examples of temperatures usable in this way are

	°C	°F
Kindling temperatures		
Paper	184	364
Dry wood	ca. 246	ca. 475
Melting temperatures		
Tin	232	449
Pewter	295	563
Solder	183–250	361–482
Lead	327	621
Zinc	419	787
Aluminum	660	1220
Silver	960	1761
Copper	1083	1981

Table 4-2 lists some of the better determinations of temperatures of erupting magmas. Most of them are from Hawaii, because the gentleness of Hawaiian eruptions makes it possible to work with the lavas at close range. All but one of the measurements in the table are on basic magmas, because the eruptions of more siliceous magmas are generally so violent that investigators are kept too far away to make good measurements. The measurements made by Jaggar in the lava lake at Kilauea in 1917 were made by a method different from the standard methods described above. At intervals in a steel pipe he fastened groups of Seger cones—little conical mounds of ceramic carefully made to soften and melt at certain temperatures. The pipe was thrust into the lava lake. Then it was withdrawn and broken open, and the cone in each group that had just started to melt was ascertained. This indicated the approximate temperature of the level in the lake to which that particular group of cones had been immersed. The temperature at the surface of the lake was 140°C higher than that at a depth of 3 feet (Fig. 4-3). This was ascribed by Jaggar to heating caused by burning of the gases at the surface of the lake. At places where gases were escaping and burning just above the lake surface, the temperature reached 1350°C. In view of later work it appears probable that the temperature of 1170°C at the bottom of the lake was close to the actual temperature of the magma as it rose from depth.

In 1966, Tanguy and Biquand (1967) measured the temperature at various depths in a small lava flow close to its vent on Etna using a chromel–alumel thermocouple. The measurements were as follows:

Depth in flow (inches)	Temperature (°C)
Surface	920
4	1030
8	1035
12	1045
16	1045

TABLE 4-2. Temperatures of erupting magmas

Volcano	Date	Temperature (°C)[1]	Name of investigator	Remarks
Kilauea, Hawaii	1909	1000	Daly	Surface of lava lake in Halemaumau
	1911	1000	Shepherd	Surface of lava lake in Halemaumau
	1917	1000	Jaggar	Surface of lava lake in Halemaumau
	1917	860	Jaggar	3 feet below surface of lava lake
	1917	1170	Jaggar	Bottom of lake (depth 40 feet)
	1952	1095–1130	Macdonald	Lava fountains in Halemaumau
	1955	1080–1100	Macdonald and Eaton	Lava fountains at vents, flank eruption
	1959	1120–1190	Eaton and Murata	Lava fountain at vent in Kilauea Iki
	1960	1050–1130	Eaton and Murata	Lava fountain, flank eruption
	1963	1140	Peck, Moore, and Kojima	Lava fountains and lake in Alae Crater
Mauna Loa, Hawaii	1950	1070	Macdonald	Lava fountain at vent
Vesuvius	1913	1200	Perret	Flowing lava
	1916–1918	1015–1040	Perret	Flowing lava
	1929	1150	Rittmann	Lava fountain at vent
Etna	1910	900–1000	Perret	Lava flows at vent
	1966	880–1050	Tanguy and Biquand	Lava flows near vents
	1910–1957	940–1150	Cucuzza-Silvestri	Lava issuing from vents
Paricutin	1943	1135	Bullard	Lava flow at vent
Klyuchevskaya	1938	865	Popkov	Lava flow $\frac{1}{2}$ mile from vent
	1938	690	Popkov	Lava flow $1\frac{1}{2}$ miles from vent
Stromboli	1901	1150	Brun	Lava flow close to vent
Oshima	1950	1060	Murauchi	Lava flow near vent
	1951	1125	Minakami	Lava flow near vent
Nyamlagira	1938	1040–1075	Verhoogen	Lava at vents
Nyiragongo	1948–1959	987–1080	Tazieff	Fountains in lava lake
Santa Maria	1940	725	Zies	Dacite dome (determined with optical pyrometer from distance of several miles)

[1] To convert °C to °F, the familiar scale used in most household operations, multiply by $\frac{9}{5}$ and add 32. Thus, the lava fountain at Kilauea in 1955 had a temperature of about 1100°C, equal to 2012°F.

Some cases have been observed in which the fronts of lava flows at a considerable distance from the vents were as hot as, or even hotter than, the lava in the vents. Thus, at Kilauea in 1955 measurements on the fronts of advancing aa flows gave temperatures as high as 1025°C, whereas the readings on the fountains in the vents averaged only 1030°C. This maintenance of temperature despite loss of heat during flowage seems

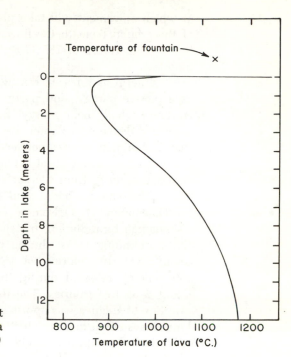

FIGURE 4-3. Temperatures at different depths in the Halemaumau lava lake at Kilauea Volcano in 1917. (After T. A. Jaggar, 1917b.)

probably to have resulted from heating of the lava by burning of gas generated from vegetation buried by the flow. Many instances of generation of methane and other hydrocarbon gases by destructive distillation of vegetation buried by lava flows have been observed. Commonly, the burning gases are visible as flames on the top and along the sides of the flow, and sometimes the gases explode with sufficient violence to blast holes several feet across and a foot or more deep in the lava or in older rock near the edge of the flow.

The lowest temperature at which lava flows can continue to move is difficult to ascertain. In 1938 two Russian volcanologists, V. F. Popkov and I. Z. Ivanoff, succeeded in inserting a thermocouple into a lava stream from Biliukai, a parasitic cone on the lower slope of Klyuchevskaya Volcano, and making temperature readings while they rode along on the top of the flow, which was moving at a rate of 1 to 1.5 miles per hour. A steel rod was pushed down into the viscous lava and the thermocouple was inserted into the resulting hole with its tip approximately 16 inches below the surface. The galvanometer reading stabilized at a temperature of about 860°C (Popkov, 1946). However, the temperature may have been higher at a greater depth. In 1949 a temperature of 745°C was measured in a deep crack in a lava flow of Mauna Loa. The flow was barely moving, but the underlying ground surface had a slope of less than one degree. At Paricutin also, the lowest temperature observed on flows still in motion was about 750°C. Since the temperature affects the movement of the lava through its effect on viscosity (see next section), the lowest temperature at which movement will take place depends on the steepness of the slope of the ground beneath the flow. Thus, in 1955 a Kilauea flow with an internal temperature of 785°C resting on a gentle slope was completely immobile.

Energy is released during a volcanic eruption partly as heat, partly as explosive energy, and partly in earthquakes. In Hawaiian eruptions it is almost wholly heat energy. R. A. Daly calculated that in 1909 the lava lake in Halemaumau Crater was giving off heat at a rate probably greater than 230 million calories per second. According to Bonnet (1960), the heat lost from the lava lake at Nyiragongo during 1959 due to radiation and conduction away from the surface by convecting air was on the order of 222 million calories per second (a value surprisingly close to Daly's figure for Halemaumau). Delsemme (1960a) calculates the total heat output of Nyiragongo by radiation, transport outward by gases, and conduction into the surrounding rocks, during the month of August 1959, to have been about 2.3×10^8 calories per second. Verhoogen (1948) estimates that the total energy released during the 1938–1940 eruption of Nyamlagira was about 2×10^{18} calories. The total heat energy given off during the 1952 eruption of Kilauea was approximately 4.3×10^{16} calories. In work equivalent, this is equal to 1.8×10^{24} ergs. (Translated into electrical energy, this is equivalent to approximately one fifteenth of the total power consumption of the United States for the year 1960, or about two fifths of the power production of the whole United States for the period of the eruption.)

The total amount of energy released in some other volcanic eruptions, as calculated by the Japanese volcanologist, I. Yokoyama, and others, is given in Table 4-3. Comparison with these figures shows that in terms of total energy release, the 1952 eruption of Kilauea was a moderately big

TABLE 4-3.   Total energy released in volcanic eruptions [1]

Volcano	Year	Energy released (ergs)	Volcano	Year	Energy released (ergs)
Tambora	1815	8.4×10^{26}	Pematang Bata	1933	4.5×10^{22}
Sakurajima	1914	4.6×10^{25}	Una-Una	1898	1.8×10^{22}
Bezymianny	1955–1966	2.2×10^{25}	Mihara	1954	1.3×10^{22}
Krakatoa	1883	ca. 1×10^{25}	Adatarasan	1900	6.4×10^{21}
Asama	1783	8.8×10^{24}	Asama	1938	4.0×10^{21}
Fuji	1707	7.1×10^{24}	Mihara	1912	6.3×10^{20}
Sakurajima	1946	2.1×10^{24}	Tokachidake	1926	2.8×10^{20}
Torishima	1939	9.7×10^{23}	Kusatsu-Shirane	1932	1.6×10^{18}
Komagatake	1929	5.6×10^{23}	Kilauea	1952	1.8×10^{24}
Miyakeshima	1940	4.8×10^{23}	Showa Sin-San	1944	1.4×10^{20}
Bandaisan	1888	ca. 1×10^{23}	Capelinhos	1957	4×10^{24}
			Arenal	1968	1×10^{22}

[1] After Yokoyama (1957) with additions.

eruption, in spite of the fact that there were no great explosions. In the same terms, the big eruptions of Mauna Loa in 1859 and 1950, which liberated at least five times as much lava as did Kilauea in 1952, were of the same order of magnitude as the giant explosive eruption of Krakatoa in 1883, although in the Hawaiian eruptions explosion was practically absent.

Viscosity of Erupting Magmas

By viscosity is meant the "stickiness" or resistance of a substance to flow. It is the inverse of fluidity. Liquids of low viscosity, or high fluidity, flow readily; those of high viscosity flow only very slowly and with difficulty, and their behavior approaches that of solids. Indeed, solids also flow, though in general much less readily than liquids. A liquid of low viscosity, such as water, poured out on a table top, quickly spreads into a broad thin sheet. A liquid of higher viscosity, such as cold molasses, poured out in a similar way, spreads slowly and never attains as thin and widespread a sheet as does the water; and still more viscous substances, such as cold tar or shoemaker's wax, remain standing for a time as a steep-sided lump on the table, but over a period of a few days or weeks gradually flatten and spread out.

Magma reaching the surface and lava flowing out from vents are much more viscous than most liquids with which we are familiar. Sometimes lava appears to be very fluid, and one often hears it said that such a lava "flowed like water." Actually, the most fluid lava I know of had a viscosity about 100,000 times that of water (the water at room temperature, the lava at 1100°C or more). The false appearance of great fluidity results from the high density of the lava, which causes it to assume the flow characteristics of a liquid of much lower density and viscosity. From this "low" viscosity, lava ranges to very high viscosity and, in fact, grades insensibly into a solid condition.

The viscosity of magma depends on several factors, including the chemical composition of the magma, the amount and condition of the gas in it, the amount of solid load being carried by it, and its temperature. In general, the more silicon a magma contains in proportion to the bases (iron, magnesium, calcium, etc.), the higher is its viscosity. The fact has been known for a long time, but only quite recently have X-ray studies of silicate melts supplied us with the apparent reason. The fundamental unit of combination of silicon in silicate melts, as well as in minerals, is the silica tetrahedron—a single atom of silicon with four atoms of oxygen tied to it in a tetrahedral pattern (Fig. 4-4A). The four oxygen atoms have eight negative bonds (valences), and since the silicon atom has only four positive ones, there are four negative bonds left over. These are partly taken up by atoms of the bases, but if there are not enough of the basic atoms to use up all the bonds, some of the bonds join instead to other

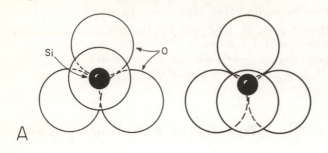

A

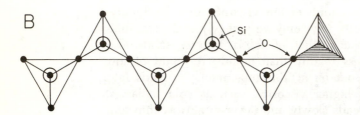

B

FIGURE 4-4. Diagrams of (A) top and side view of the silica tetrahedron, and (B) a single chain of silica tetrahedra.

silica tetrahedra. In this way, chains and networks (polymers) of the tetrahedra (Fig. 4-4B) are established extending throughout the liquid. If an extensive network is present, it tends to restrict the change of shape of the liquid—that is, it restricts its freedom to flow. With a large proportion of bases, however, bonding of one tetrahedron to another is less extensive, the liquid consists more nearly of a series of independent units without interconnecting bonds, and flow is easier. Thus rhyolite lavas, rich in silicon in proportion to bases (see Table A2-2), are generally very viscous, whereas iron- and magnesium-rich basalts are much more fluid.

The presence of solid fragments (either phenocrysts or fragments of foreign origin) in magma increases its effective viscosity simply by increasing the frictional resistance to flow. The effects of gas are more complex. Gas dissolved in magma decreases its viscosity. On the other hand, gas present as bubbles in the lava may decrease its effective viscosity if they are not too abundant; but if they are very abundant, they increase the viscosity. We are all familiar with the fact that a solution of soap in water will flow much like ordinary water, but if it is whipped up to a foam, one can set a mass of soapsuds on a table top and have it remain there without flowing appreciably until the bubbles have burst. In this way, a layer of froth formed on the surface of lava in a volcanic crater may have enough toughness and viscosity to retard the outward flow of the lava, or to restrain the escape of gas from beneath it, until the pressure builds up enough to cause a minor explosion.

Second to composition, the most important determiner of viscosity is temperature. The higher the temperature of a magma, the lower its viscosity. This is particularly evident in the behavior of lava flows. As they flow away from the vent, they lose heat by radiation and conduction into the air above and the ground beneath, and the viscosity steadily increases. Thus, lava in a flow from Mauna Loa was found to be more than twice as viscous 12 miles down the mountainside as it was when it issued from the vent. The fact is well illustrated in Table 4-4. On Etna, Walker (1967) found the viscosity of a small flow to increase about 375 fold (from 0.4×10^5 to 1.5×10^7 poises) in a distance of only about 1,500 feet. He also found that on the flanks of Etna the viscosity at which flow movement virtually ceases is usually between 10^9 and 10^{11} poises, depending on the angle of slope.

Some field determinations of the viscosity of natural lavas and viscosities of a few rocks remelted in the laboratory are listed in Table 4-4. Most of the field figures were obtained by calculating the viscosity from the observed rate of flow of the lava in a channel with approximately known slope and size. Uncertainties in the latter are great enough so that the figures should be taken to indicate only the order of magnitude of the viscosity. Measurements on the Hekla flow were made by T. Einarsson (1949) with a "penetrometer." A dull-pointed rod was thrust against the liquid in the flow front with an approximately determined force, and the rate at which it sank into the liquid was measured. This was then compared with similar results obtained in the laboratory on materials of known viscosity. Similar experiments have been tried in Hawaii, but the rate of penetration is greatly affected by the tough skin that quickly forms on the liquid surface as a result of chilling when the instrument touches it, if such a skin was not there already because of chilling against the air. The effect of the skin appears to be so great as to make the penetrometer measurements of little value, though they do, in general, agree with the results of other measurements. Attempts made by Jaggar to obtain the viscosity from the rate at which liquid entered a small hole in a steel cylinder immersed in the Halemaumau lava lake were largely unsuccessful because the freezing lava tended to clog the hole.

Recently, successful measurements were made in a lava lake in Makaopuhi Crater at Kilauea, using a rotation viscometer. A blade was rotated in the liquid lava below a drill hole through the crust of the lake, and the frequency of rotation under a constant turning force was recorded. The viscosities measured ranged from 500 poises in completely liquid lava at 1200° C to 8×10^3 poises in a mixture of crystals and liquid at 1130° C (Shaw et al., 1968). Measurements on remelted lava in the laboratory gave values nearly the same as the field measurements (Shaw, 1969). The viscosities are nearly the same as those estimated from rates of movement of lava flows of Mauna Loa and Kilauea (Table 4-4), but the temperatures measured with a thermocouple in the drill hole are considerably higher than those measured with an optical pyrometer on the lava flows at comparable viscosities. The temperatures from optical pyrometry may have been too low, or the viscosities in the flows may have been lowered appreciably by dissolved volatiles which had escaped from the lava in the lake during the several months that had elapsed between the formation of the lake and the date of the measurements.

TABLE 4-4. Typical viscosities of magmas

Volcano	Date	Composition of Magma	Temperature of magma (°C)	Viscosity of magma (poises)	Published source
Oshima, Japan	1951	Basalt	1125	5.6×10^3	
	1951	Basalt	1108	1.8×10^4	Minakami and
	1951	Basalt	1083	7.1×10^4	Sakuma, 1953
	1951	Basalt	1038	2.3×10^5	
Capelinhos, Azores	1957– 1958	Basalt	—	3×10^4– 5×10^6	Machado, Parsons, Richards, and Mulford, 1962
Mauna Loa, Hawaii	1950	Basalt	1070	4×10^3	
	1950	Basalt	940	7×10^3	Macdonald, 1954
	1950	Basalt	940	1×10^4	
Kilauea, Hawaii	1952	Basalt	—	2×10^4	
	1955	Basalt	1100	2×10^3	Macdonald and
	1955	Basalt	1050	2.5×10^3	Eaton, 1964
	1955	Basalt	950	1×10^4	
Gituro, Congo	1948	Basalt	1040	3.4×10^4	Tazieff, 1951
Vesuvius	1936	Tephrite	—	7.6×10^4	Imbo, 1959
Etna, Sicily	1957	Basaltic andesite	1100– 1120	3.6×10^4	Tazieff, in Rittmann, 1963a, p. 434
	1966	Basaltic andesite	—	0.4×10^5	
	1966	Basaltic andesite	—	1.5×10^7	Walker, 1967
	1966	Basaltic andesite	1020	7.3×10^4– 2.9×10^5	
	1966	Basaltic andesite	1010	5.1×10^4– 3.8×10^5	Tanguy and Biquand, 1967
	1966	Basaltic andesite	—	1.2×10^5– 7.4×10^5	
Hekla, Iceland	1947	Andesite	—	$10^5 - 10^7$	Einarsson, 1949
Trident, Alaska	1953	Dacite	—	6.9×10^{10}	Friedman, Long, and Smith, 1963
		Rhyolite	800	1×10^{12}	Barth, 1962
		"Andesine basalt"	1150	8×10^4	
Lavas remelted in the laboratory		"Andesine basalt"	1200	3×10^4	
		"Andesine basalt"	1300	2.6×10^2	
		Olivine basalt	1150	9×10^2	Goranson, 1934
		Olivine basalt	1200	5×10^2	
		Olivine basalt	1300	2×10^2	

SUGGESTED ADDITIONAL READING

Basharina, 1965; Cucuzza-Silvestri, 1968; Ellis, 1957; Elskens, Tazieff, and Tonani, 1964; Heald, Naughton, and Barnes, 1963; Jaggar, 1940; Macdonald, 1963; Naughton, Heald, and Barnes, 1963; Peck, Moore, and Kojima, 1964; Walker, 1967; Wentworth, Carson, and Finch, 1945; White and Waring, 1961; Zies, 1941.

5

Lava Flows

The external forms and internal structures of lava flows are the result of the physical properties of the magma described in Chapter 4 and the external environment in which the flow takes place. The principal physical property involved is viscosity, but, as we have seen, this is influenced by both the chemical composition and the temperature of the magma. The variables in the external environment include the steepness of the slope down which the flow is moving and the presence or absence of water and ice. The rate of supply of magma to the flow in relation to the velocity with which it moves away from the vent also is important.

Lavas of low viscosity may spread to great distances from their vents if the supply of liquid is great enough, and if the slope of the surface beneath the flow is appreciable the flow is thin. Fluid lava flows in Hawaii extend for more than 35 miles from their vents, with an average thickness of only about 15 feet. Some Icelandic flows can be traced for more than 80 miles. In the Columbia River region of the northwestern United States, several flows are known to extend for more than 100 miles, and one has been traced over an area of about 100 by 200 miles. At most places this latter flow ranges between 100 and 150 feet thick. The ground beneath many of the Columbia River flows was almost horizontal, and the spreading of the lava was due largely to the outpouring of more and more liquid from the vent, in the same way that a pool of molasses poured on a flat table top will spread farther and farther as more liquid is added to the middle of it. The surface of the liquid tends to become horizontal, no matter what the topography of the ground surface over which it is spreading.

Lavas with greater viscosity spread out less readily, forming thicker flows that extend less far from the vents, the supply of liquid being equal. Such flows may be several hundred feet thick, even on steep slopes. Still more viscous lavas spread out even less and may pile up over their vents to form steep-sided hills known as *volcanic domes* (Chapter 6); and very viscous lava may protrude upward without spreading at all, forming *plug domes* or *spines*.

Because siliceous magmas are usually more viscous than basic ones, siliceous lava flows tend to be thicker and shorter. Andesite flows are generally stubbier than basalt flows, and dacite and rhyolite flows are stubbier yet. Most domes and spines are dacite or rhyolite. Although trachyte may contain nearly as much silicon as rhyolite, and more than dacite, it is commonly less viscous. This may be partly because of a larger amount of gas dissolved in the magma, but more important probably is the fact that trachyte magma contains less free silica—that is, silica that is not tied up with bases, in this case particularly with the alkalies—and hence has less polymeric bonding of the silica tetrahedra in the liquid. At any rate, although trachyte and phonolite do at times form short thick flows and domes, in general flows of these rocks tend to be thinner and broader than those of dacite and rhyolite, and may even show pahoehoe structures such as are usually formed on basalt.

Some flows, of any composition, are very small. Individual flows only a few square feet in area and a few inches thick are known. Others are very large. The most voluminous flows are of basaltic composition. Some historic flows of the Hawaiian volcanoes are more than 30 miles long, and some have volumes of more than 600 million cubic yards (0.11 cubic mile). Some Icelandic flows are even bigger. The one that issued from the Laki fissure in 1783 had a volume of approximately 2.8 cubic miles. It is the largest flow known to have occurred in historic time, but some prehistoric flows are even bigger. According to G. Kjartansson, the Great Thjórsá flow has a length of about 78 miles, an area of 275 square miles, and a volume of 3.2 cubic miles. Even this is small compared to some of the flows of the Columbia River region, where recent drilling for water and for damsite testing has made possible tracing of individual flows over broad areas. According to J. H. Mackin (1960), the Roza flow in eastern Washington extends over an area of about 20,000 square miles and has a volume on the order of 600 cubic miles!

Running a close second to basaltic flows in volume are the great rhyolite "ash flows" (see Chapter 8). Some of these in Nevada are reported to cover areas of as much as 7,000 square miles and have volumes on the order of 250 cubic miles.

Both basaltic lava flows and rhyolitic ash flows are thin in comparison with their extent because of their fluidity. Hawaiian basalt flows average about 12 to 15 feet thick where they ran freely down the mountainsides, though they are sometimes much thicker where they accumulated in pools in craters or other depressions. The Thjórsá flow averages about 60 feet in thickness, and flows of the Columbia River region generally range between 30 and 200 feet. The rhyolitic ash flows of Nevada range from about 20 to 250 feet in thickness. In comparison, dacitic and rhyolitic lava flows are much thicker in proportion to their length. Rhyolite flows at Mono Craters in California are roughly a mile long and more than 700 feet thick. The Ring Creek dacite flow in British Columbia is reported by W. H. Mathews to be some 11 miles long and more than 800 feet thick.

Lava flows extruded on dry land include the three general types known as pahoehoe, aa, and block lava. Magmas of the same composition, extruded under water or in marshy areas where they come in contact with abundant water, form pillow lavas and hyaloclastite flows. Gas-rich siliceous magmas reaching the surface with appropriate temperature and viscosity tear themselves apart into a spray of hot glass fragments suspended in gas, and form ash flows. Each type of flow and its most characteristic structures are discussed below. Some minor structures are omitted, because of limitations of space, but discussions of them will be found in the papers listed at the end of the chapter.

Some lava flows are formed by a single gush of liquid spreading as a single unit. Usually, however, there are repeated gushes of liquid during a single eruption, and in any one place the accumulation of lava during an eruption may consist of several superimposed layers formed by several successive gushes. These individual layers are known as *flow units,* and commonly the whole accumulation formed during the same eruption is referred to as one lava flow. In the following discussions of flow types, we are referring to individual flow units, not to compound lava flows, unless it is specifically so stated.

Vesicles and Amygdules

Magma may be wholly liquid, but commonly it contains suspended solid fragments, and probably always it contains at least some gas. The gas may be present as discrete bubbles like those we see rising in a recently opened bottle of soda water; or it may be dissolved in the liquid and invisible as is the gas in the bottle of soda water before the cap is removed. The solid fragments in the magma may be bits of the surrounding rocks torn loose and engulfed in the rising liquid; or they may be crystals formed within the liquid by the separation of some of the mineral matter dissolved in it, in the same way that crystal grains form in a saturated solution of sugar in water when the solution cools or some of the water evaporates.

Each of the different states of matter—liquid, solid, and gas—is known to chemists as a phase. A magma may consist of a single phase, liquid, with any potential solid or gas that it contains held in it in solution, so that only liquid is visible even under the highest magnification; it may consist of two phases—liquid with suspended solid fragments, or liquid containing bubbles of gas; or it may consist of all three phases—liquid, solid, and gas. At great depth most magmas must consist of liquid alone or of liquid containing some solid material; but on reaching the surface most magmas contain all three phases. Obviously, then, some changes must take place during the upward movement of the magma. The changes in the magma are in turn due to changes in the physical environment. At depth the hot, molten magma is under great pressure resulting from the weight of the overlying rocks (and perhaps in some instances also from squeezing of the magma by the compressional forces in the earth's crust that crush rocks together to form mountain ranges). Even if the liquid mass extends all the way to the surface, its lower part is under a pressure equal to the weight of the liquid above it. As the liquid rises toward the surface, the pressure decreases. At the same time the temperature of the surrounding rocks becomes less, and the magma loses heat by conduction and radiation into its surroundings.

The most conspicuous effect of the change in pressure is a decrease in the solubility of gas in the magma. As the magma rises, less and less gas can be held in solution in it. At depth most magmas probably are capable of holding in solution more gas than is actually present, and for that reason no gas exists as a separate gas phase. But as the solubility of gas becomes less with decreasing pressure, a point is reached at which the magma can no longer hold all the gas in solution, and some of it starts to form bubbles scattered through the liquid. At first the bubbles are very tiny, but as the magma rises, they increase in size. The lessening pressure allows them to expand; also, as more and more of them form, they occasionally come in contact with each other and unite.

Because they are lighter than the surrounding liquid, the bubbles tend to rise in it. If the magma is stationary, in time all the gas bubbles may rise to its top and escape. However, because the liquid is very viscous, the bubbles rise slowly, and if the magma is rising toward the surface, the rate of rise of the bubbles may be very little faster than that of the surrounding liquid. Commonly, the magma reaches the surface as a mixture of liquid and gas bubbles. Poured out on the surface, the liquid cools and solidifies. If the solidification is very slow, all the gas bubbles may escape, leaving the solidified rock dense; but if cooling is rapid, the liquid freezes with the gas bubbles still in it. This produces a rock that is full of bubble holes, resembling swiss cheese. The bubble holes are called *vesicles*, and the rock is said to be *vesicular* (Plate 5-1). Thin lava flows and the top and bottom of thick flows cool quickly, and the rock is generally vesicular. But because rock is a poor conductor of heat, the frozen top and bottom of a thick flow serve as insulators and the central part cools slowly. Commonly, the center of a thick flow has cooled and solidified slowly enough to allow most of the gas to escape, and the resulting rock is dense; thus, there is produced a flow that has a dense center but vesicular top and bottom. Some degree of vesicular structure is found in nearly all extrusive igneous rocks and many shallow-seated intrusive rocks, and is perhaps their most characteristic feature.

The vesicles may be nearly perfect spheres, but more commonly they are stretched out by flowage of the surrounding liquid as it solidified, forming ellipsoidal or almond-shaped openings, or openings that are so twisted and distorted that they defy description (Plate 5-1).

Gases and hot solutions moving through the rock just after it has solidified, and warm or cold groundwater circulating through it for eons thereafter, both carry dissolved mineral matter and may deposit it in the vesicles. Sometimes there results a thin shell of mineral lining the vesicle from which beautifully formed crystal ends may project into the central opening. At other times the vesicles are completely filled, forming masses known as *amygdules* (from the resemblance in shape of many of them to almonds). A rock containing amygdules is said to be *amygdaloidal*, and particularly in older literature such rocks are sometimes called *amygdaloids*. The "amygdaloids" of Michigan, containing amygdules of native copper, are well known both as beautiful mineral specimens and because of their great economic value.

Other gas cavities, sometimes containing more or less concentric shells of mineral matter that in cross section resemble the petals of a flower,

PLATE 5-1. Cross sections of the massive portions of an aa lava flow (left), and a pahoehoe flow (right), showing the characteristic forms of the vesicles. Both flows are on Mauna Loa, Hawaii. Hawaii Institute of Geophysics photo by G. A. Macdonald.

are known as *lithophysae* ("stone lilies," singular: lithophysa). Lithophysae, which occur also in consolidated ash-flow deposits, commonly contain minerals formed by deposition from the gas phase of the magma, such as sanidine, tridymite, and fayalite. Lithophysae, and other spheroidal and less regular openings, may be partly or wholly filled with opal or chalcedony, sometimes beautifully banded, and surrounded by a thick spheroidal shell that breaks free from the surrounding rock. Mineral collectors often call these "thunder eggs."

The fillings of amygdules and thunder eggs are often banded concentrically as a result of deposition of mineral matter parallel to the walls of the cavity. At other times, however, the bands cut sharply across the amygdule or lithophysa. The bands were then formed parallel to the surface of liquid that only partly filled the cavity. Since the liquid surface must have been horizontal, any inclination of the banding indicates that the beds have been tilted since the cavity fillings were formed and supplies a measure of the tilting. Thus, lavas in eastern Iceland contain amygdules in which the inclined banding shows that the rocks have been tilted several degrees toward the broad sunken trough that runs through central Iceland.

Pahoehoe

The Hawaiian words pahoehoe and aa are now used all over the world to designate two of the common types of lava flows. When they were first introduced into scientific literature by C. E. Dutton in 1884, they met with strong opposition on the part of some writers, who objected to the use of such "barbarous" terms. Despite such disapproval, most geologists quickly adopted them.

To the Hawaiians, the terms referred only to the surface character of the lava. Pahoehoe has a smooth crust, often disposed in a series of rolling hillocks and hollows (Plate 5-2). The most spectacular feature of pahoehoe surface is the occurrence of some areas in which the crust is wrinkled and twisted into forms resembling folds in heavy cloth and

PLATE 5-2. Tumulus on the surface of a pahoehoe lava flow, Kilauea Volcano, Hawaii. Hawaii Institute of Geophysics photo by G. A. Macdonald.

PLATE 5-3. Ropy pahoehoe surface, on the 1920 lava flow of Kilauea, Hawaii. Hawaii Institute of Geophysics photo by G. A. Macdonald.

parts of coils of rope (Plate 5-3). These forms result from the dragging and twisting of the thin, hot, still-plastic crust of the flow by movement of the liquid lava underneath, or sometimes by the sliding of the crust where it has been heaved up into a hillock. In a narrow stream of lava, frictional resistance results in the edges of the stream moving less rapidly than the middle, and where ropy structure has formed on the crust of such a stream, the "ropes" are bent into curves that are convex in the direction toward which the stream was moving. The ropy and festooned crust was quickly seized on by writers, particularly of textbooks, as the characteristic surface of pahoehoe; and the direction of curvature of the ropes was cited as a tool to be used in determining the direction of the advance of flows in ancient geological formations where the location of the vent from which the flow issued is no longer apparent. The bending does indeed generally indicate the direction of movement at the particular place where the ropy structure is found, but this may be only an eddy or other local movement, and the curvature of the ropes can be used only with a good deal of caution to determine the direction of the advance of the flow as a whole. Also, ropy structure usually is present only on part of the flow surface. Broad expanses of pahoehoe, and almost the entire surfaces of some flows, are entirely devoid of it.

In broad view, the surfaces of most pahoehoe flows are rolling or undulating (Plate 5-8). In detail, many of them are covered with a lace-like network of threads a few hundredths of an inch in diameter, usually arranged in a more or less parallel pattern. This "filamented" pahoehoe surface usually results from the escape of myriads of small bubbles of gas, each carrying upward a tiny tail of liquid that falls back onto the surface and is drawn out parallel to the direction of movement of the flow. At other places it is formed by a "combing" action where the semi-liquid lava is issuing from beneath the rough edge of a slightly older crust or much older rock at the side of the vent.

In pahoehoe the gas bubbles were still expanding and, consequently, tending to take a spheroidal or inverted drop shape at the time the lava froze to immobility. Consequently, the vesicles are spheroidal or drawn out into almond shape, or sometimes formed of a cluster of such rounded shapes (Plate 5-1). A thin tough skin, often less than a hundredth of an inch thick, forms quickly on the surface of the lava when it is exposed to air, and the first gas released from the lava tends to rise and form a layer of very abundant bubbles just beneath the skin. As a result, the skin often is nearly detached from the underlying mass. Men and animals walking across the flow crush the skin to powder, and looking down on recent flows (such as some of those to be seen in Hawaii Volcanoes National Park), one can often see dull-looking paths extending across the glistening flow surface. The gas bubbles separated from the magma as it continues to cool also tend to rise in the flow. In thick flows that remain liquid for a considerable period, this may result in a concentration of the vesicles in the upper part of the flow; but thin flows cool too quickly to allow much movement of the bubbles and commonly are quite uniformly vesicular throughout.

Ordinarily, the upper few inches of a pahoehoe flow quickly cool to a semisolid state, but the crust thus formed remains somewhat plastic. It is this crust that may become wrinkled and twisted to form the ropy structure. It is possible to cross a flow on this plastic crust while the flow itself is still moving. The crust sags and bends under one's weight, like "rubber" ice on a partly frozen pond, but does not break. Similarly, one can jump on the top of small "toes" along the edge of an active pahoehoe flow and cause the liquid lava to spurt from the end of the toe, without breaking through the top, as long as the toe remains filled with liquid. (But it should be noted that some toes are hollow, and those can be dangerous, because they may collapse under a man's weight and allow his feet to go down into their very hot interiors.) The crust of a lava flow, like other rock, is a poor conductor of heat, and the part of the flow beneath the crust may remain hot and liquid for long periods. Flows only a few feet thick probably always solidify within a few days after they stop moving, but the interior of thick flows may remain liquid for weeks, months, or years. In December, 1959, a pool of pahoehoe 300 feet thick was formed in Kilauea Iki Crater in Hawaii, and 7 months later we put a diamond-drill hole into it. We went from solid crust into liquid lava at a depth of only $18\frac{1}{2}$ feet. Occasional loud explosive reports and sharp jolts marked the opening of cracks (joints) in the crust as it cooled and shrank, and at first this made us rather uneasy when we thought of the fact that

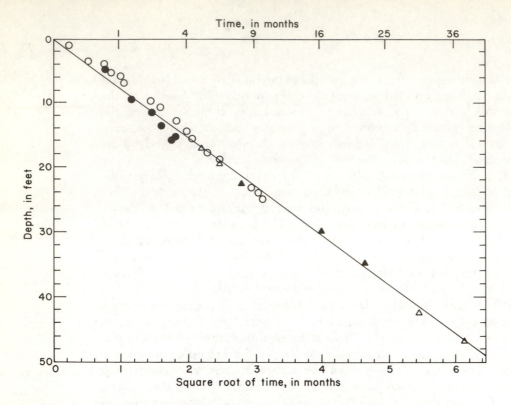

FIGURE 5-1. Graph showing the rate of thickening of the crust on Alae and Kilauea Iki lava lakes, Kilauea Volcano, Hawaii. Solid circles represent the base of the crust and open circles show the 1067°C isotherm at Alae Crater, solid triangles show the base of the crust and open triangles the 1065° isotherm at Kilauea Iki Crater. The two temperatures are those at the base of the crust in the two lakes. The thickness of the crust is proportional to the square root of the length of time elapsed since the end of the eruption. (After Peck, Moore, and Kojima, 1964, with data added from Peck, Wright, and Moore, 1966.)

liquid lava at a temperature of more than 1000°C was such a short way below us! The drilling has been continued from time to time by the U.S. Geological Survey, and in the summer of 1964 the crust was approximately 65 feet thick (Fig. 5-1).

Beneath the crust the liquid interior remains mobile, and so long as new liquid is added from the vent it continues to flow. In very thick flows, such as those of the Columbia River region, or flows that are advancing over rather flat and featureless terrain, the spreading of the liquid may be essentially uniform in all its parts. However, in thinner flows such as those of Hawaii, the movement of the liquid is nonuniform. Because of irregularities in the underlying surface, the localized nature of the feeding of liquid into the mass, and other irregularities that develop within the flow itself, the movement of the liquid is faster along certain paths within the flow. The loss of heat results in freezing of the less active parts of the flow, and it is only along the paths of most rapid movement, where new heat is constantly being brought in, that the interior of the flow remains fully mobile. Thus, there develop pipe-like zones of liquid

74

PLATE 5-4. Small lava tube in a pahoehoe flow of Hualalai Volcano, Hawaii. Note the concentric structure resulting from the partial filling of the tube as the surrounding lava congealed. U. S. Geological Survey photo by G. A. Macdonald.

movement within the much less mobile body of the flow, and it is through these roofed-over pipes that most of the movement of liquid lava to feed the advancing flow margin takes place. When the supply of magma from the vent is cut off at the end of the eruption or by some blocking of the pipe itself, the liquid remaining in the downslope portion of the pipe may drain away leaving a partly or wholly open tube where it had been (Plate 5-4). It is in this way that the lava tubes familiar to visitors to many volcanic areas are formed. Familiar examples are the Subway Cave north of Lassen Volcanic National Park, the Lava Caves near Bend in Oregon, and the Thurston Tube in Hawaii Volcanoes National Park. Caves of this sort in the Lava Beds region of northeastern California supplied innumerable hiding places for Captain Jack and his Indian warriors during the Modoc wars. Some lava tubes can be followed for distances of more than a mile. Most of them are only a few feet in diameter, but some reach as much as 50 feet.

Lava tubes generally have arched roofs (Plate 5-5), but their floors may be quite flat, formed by the surface of the last liquid lava to move through them. Occasionally, the last lava is enough more viscous to form aa instead of pahoehoe, and the floor of the pahoehoe tube is then covered with a layer of clinkery aa.

PLATE 5-5. Postal Rift tube, a lava tube about 10 feet in diameter in Kilauea Caldera, Hawaii. Photo by United States Department of the Interior, National Park Service.

In many instances the lava does not drain out at the end of the eruption, and the former feeding pipe remains nearly or entirely full. This is particularly common in flows such as those of flood basalts on lava plateaus or plains (Chapter 11) that advanced over nearly horizontal surfaces. Gradual consolidation of the flowing lava results in the deposition of successive layers on the walls of the pipe, and when cross sections are later exposed by erosion or highway construction, the former pipes are marked by concentric circular or oval rings of lava differing somewhat in vesicularity, color, or both. In three dimensions, these bodies are nearly horizontal solid cylinders. Like open tubes, they are usually only a few inches to a few feet in diameter; but more rarely, as in some of the thick flows of the Columbia River lavas in Oregon and Washington, they have diameters of several tens of feet. Lutton (1969) has described very large cylindrical structures of this sort that differ from the surrounding lava principally in being denser, presumably because they remained fluid longer and lost a large proportion of their gas before they solidified. In the vicinity of the consolidated feeding pipe, the lava is a single massive flow unit as much as 200 feet thick, whereas the lava at a little distance from the pipe is vesicular and divided into several thinner flow units.

Because of the viscosity of the liquid and the confining effect of the tough crust, the margin of a spreading pahoehoe flow does not taper down to a thin edge but rises steeply above the adjacent ground surface (Plate 5-7). In the case of thick uniformly moving flows or rather narrow thin flows, the entire front may advance as a unit. Friction against the ground delays the advance of the basal part of the flow, so the upper part over-rides the lower and the movement resembles that of the front end of an endless track on a tractor. Commonly, however, the main feeding tubes within the flow branch as they near the margin, like the distributaries of a great river, and some parts of the margin advance faster than others. Constant addition of liquid behind it causes the margin to swell, and the plastic crust is stretched until at some point it can stretch no more. There it ruptures and allows a stream of liquid to escape and push a short way ahead of the adjacent margin. Generally, these minor streams, only a few inches to a few feet across, advance only a few feet before their outside becomes chilled and loses its mobility. Thus, there is formed at the edge of the flow a finger-like projection, commonly referred to as a pahoehoe "toe" (Plate 5-6). The process repeats itself over and over again, other toes forming on each side, and still others filling in the spaces between the earlier ones (Plate 5-7). The margins of many pahoehoe flows advance in this way by the protrusion of one toe after another.

Only a few special features of the surfaces of pahoehoe flows will be discussed here, and those only briefly. More detail can be found elsewhere (Wentworth and Macdonald, 1953; Macdonald, 1965). The crust of a pahoehoe flow quickly becomes fractured, partly by shrinkage on cooling and partly because of distortion by the movement of the liquid beneath it. Liquid lava from below moves upward into the cracks driven

PLATE 5-6.   Pahoehoe toe, about 1 foot across, issuing from beneath up-heaved ropy crust during the 1955 eruption of Kilauea Volcano. U. S. Geological Survey photo by G. A. Macdonald.

PLATE 5-7.   Pahoehoe surface and toe, 1920 lava flow of Kilauea, Hawaii. The toe is approximately 9 inches in diameter. Hawaii Institute of Geophysics photo by G. A. Macdonald.

PLATE 5-8. Pressure ridges on the surface of the 1940 lava flow in Mokuaweoweo Caldera, Mauna Loa, Hawaii, formed by thrusting of the crust of the pahoehoe flow from the right against the caldera wall, which lies just left of the picture. U. S. Geological Survey photo by G. A. Macdonald.

by hydrostatic pressure resulting largely from the weight of the crust itself. This forms "auto-intrusive" dikes cutting the crust, and some of them reach the surface. There the lava may be squeezed up either into an elongate bulb-like structure with a rounded top that tends to spread over the adjacent lava surface or into a sharp-pointed wedge that projects a few inches to a few feet into the air. These were called *squeeze-ups* by R. L. Nichols, who originally described them on the McCarty's basalt flow in New Mexico. The term has stuck and is in general use.

In places the crust of the flow has been heaved up into elongate ridges or shorter dome-like forms. The former are called *pressure ridges* (Plate 5-8) and are the result of the flow crust being pushed against some obstacle by the continued movement of the crust behind it. The elevation of the crust into an elongate fold (anticline) is aided by the hydrostatic pressure of the liquid beneath it. Some pressure ridges are as much as half a mile long and 50 feet high. In some, the continued movement has resulted in overturning of the fold with a gentle slope of the surface on the side toward the source of the lava and a steep slope on the side away from it, and occasionally the folded crust breaks and slides forward over the steep side of the fold forming a thrust fault. Generally, the crust in the fold is much broken, and the ridge consists largely of a heap of variously oriented blocks. Large pressure ridges were watched forming in the summit crater during the 1940 eruption of Mauna Loa.

The shorter dome-shaped structures (Plates 5-2 and 5-9) are called *tumuli,* because they were thought (by the famous American geologist, R. A. Daly) to resemble ancient burial mounds. Most are oval in ground plan, but some are nearly circular. They range in size to 150 feet or more in length and commonly to 25 or 30 feet in height. The surface of a tumulus

PLATE 5-9. Tumulus, with driblets, on the 1919 lava flow in Kilauea Caldera, Hawaii. The mound is about 8 feet high. U. S. Geological Survey photo by G. A. Macdonald.

PLATE 5-10. Tumulus covered with "entrail pahoehoe," which has dribbled out of cracks in the upheaved crust of the lava flow on which the mound is located; Kilauea Volcano, Hawaii. Hawaii Institute of Geophysics photo by G. A. Macdonald.

is the same as that of the surrounding lava flow. The uparched crust generally is cracked open, and lava often rises in the cracks to form squeeze-ups or small flows that dribble down the side of the dome (Plates 5-9 and 5-10). Where they have not been filled with lava from below, the gaping cracks often are excellent places to study the internal structure of the flow. Tumuli are formed in much the same way as pressure ridges, and, in fact, there is a complete gradation from one to the other. Only rarely are tumuli hollow, and then it is generally clear that they were once filled with liquid lava that later drained away. They are not blisters, formed by big gas bubbles. True blisters do occur, and some structures resembling tumuli have been claimed to be blisters, but no structures more than a few feet across have been proved to have formed as a result of gas expansion. Not uncommonly, gas-charged spattering lava escapes through cracks in tumuli and builds *hornitos* ("driblet spires") (Plates 5-11 and 5-12), which are merely conelets of welded spatter (Chapter 7). The congealed spatter may gradually arch across to seal the top of the conelet.

Sometimes the crust of a pahoehoe flow is broken up into slabs by the drag of the lava flowing beneath it, and the slabs are tilted up and pushed together like the floes in an ice-jammed river. Commonly, the lava beneath the tilted slabs has the characteristic spiny surface of aa, and apparently the condition is caused by an increase in the viscosity of the

PLATE 5-11. Driblet spire on the floor of Kilauea Caldera in 1911. The spire is about 4 feet high. Photo by F. A. Perret. From Perret, 1950. Courtesy of Carnegie Institution.

PLATE 5-12. A rootless spatter cone (hornito), in Lava Beds National Monument, California, formed of welded spatter. Hawaii Institute of Geophysics photo by G. A. Macdonald.

liquid flowing beneath the crust. In a sense, this *slab pahoehoe* constitutes a gradation into aa, but the slabs are all typical pahoehoe crust, smooth or ropy on one side and on the other covered with bumps and icicle-like projections resulting from liquid lava dripping from the bottom of the crust.

Similar *stalactites* are often found hanging from the roof of a lava tube (Plate 5-13). They may resemble icicles, or they may be long pencil-like rods often covered with rounded drops resembling bunches of grapes. They are formed by the freezing of molten lava dripping from the roof of the tube. Sometimes this is liquid left by a rapid lowering of the lava level in the tube, but commonly it is formed by fusion of the solid roof of the tube by the heat of gases burning in the air between the tube roof and the surface of the liquid stream in the tube. Liquid dripping from the stalactites onto the floor of the tube solidifies and builds up little mounds called lava *stalagmites*.

Lava tree molds (often called simply "lava trees") are formed where fluid lava surrounds the trunk of a tree and is chilled against it (Plate 5-14), resulting in a cylinder of solidified lava encasing the tree. The tree is, of course, burned and when the charcoal is removed, a well-like opening is left. (In many instances the intense heat of the surrounding lava seems to result in complete combustion of the wood, leaving only a little light feathery ash; at other times whatever charcoal remained is later removed by rotting and the action of organisms, wind, and perhaps running water.)

PLATE 5-13. Lava stalactites, from the roof of a lava tube in Kilauea Caldera, Hawaii. Photo by F. A. Perret. From Perret, 1950. Courtesy of Carnegie Institution.

PLATE 5-14. Lava tree mold, with the charred stub of the tree projecting from it, on the 1923 lava flow of Kilauea Volcano. Photo by United States Department of the Interior, National Park Service.

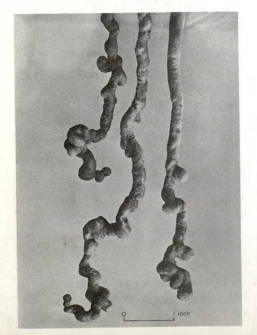

The size of the well depends on the size of the tree trunk. Often, the form of the trunk and branches, and even details of the bark, are quite perfectly preserved. In forming, the charcoal on the outer part of the trunk often develops a pattern of shrinkage cracks, and the liquid lava invades these cracks and preserves the pattern (Plate 5-15). Almost paper-thin septa of lava may project two or three inches into the charcoal! The very great fluidity that would permit the lava to move into such narrow cracks probably results partly from the heat generated by the burning wood. The 1868 lava in Kilauea Iki Crater, Hawaii, was so fluid that it molded the under sides of fern fronds in such perfection that the pattern of the spores could be seen and used to identify the species of fern! In many instances the level of the flow surface subsides during later stages of the eruption as the supply of lava from the vent decreases, and the cylinder of lava solidified around the former tree trunk is left standing above the flow top (Plate 5-16). Many of these "lava trees" are 10 or 12 feet high, and during the 1962 eruption in Aloi Crater at Kilauea, some 25 feet high were formed.

Tree molds are occasionally found in aa, but are much commoner in pahoehoe.

PLATE 5-16. Lava tree mold, formed by a pahoehoe flow of Kilauea Volcano in 1965. The base of the column is approximately 1 foot in diameter. Hawaii Institute of Geophysics photo by G. A. Macdonald.

PLATE 5-15. Lava cast of charcoal on the inner surface of a tree mold. The charcoal shrank, forming a rectangular pattern of cracks, which were filled by very hot very fluid lava. Photo by F. A. Perret. From Perret, 1950. Courtesy of Carnegie Institution.

PLATE 5-17. Clinkery surface of a prehistoric aa lava flow of Mauna Loa, Hawaii. The crag in the center is 30 inches high. U. S. Geological Survey photo by G. A. Macdonald.

Aa

To the Hawaiians, aa was the sort of lava characterized by an exceedingly rough rubbly surface, in contrast to the rather smooth surface of pahoehoe (Plate 5-17). In most places the surface of an aa flow consists of a layer of angular jagged fragments, each fragment covered with tiny sharp spines. The fragmental material is known as *clinker* (or sometimes as "slag"). It is difficult to convey with words an adequate idea of the roughness of this clinker. It must be seen to be realized (Plate 5-18)! When we were mapping the active Hawaiian volcanoes, we had to cross and recross miles of aa. The loose fragments rolled under our feet and we fell frequently. Repeated lacerations of our hands soon taught us to wear gloves, and the uppers of heavy work boots were cut to ribbons in a week of hiking.

The fragmentation of the surface of aa flows results from disruption of the very viscous crust by movement of the flow beneath it, but the

PLATE 5-18. Fragments of aa clinker, showing their very irregular and spinose forms. The fragment on the right is 8 inches across. U. S. Geological Survey photo by G. A. Macdonald.

spinose surfaces of the fragments have another origin. The blocks are
not simply angular fragments of a disrupted crust. To a minor extent
the spiny projections result from pulling apart of fragments that were still
"tacky" and tended to stick together, but most of the spines have a different character. Furthermore, they sometimes form on flow surfaces that have
not been disrupted and where there has been no pulling apart of blocks.
So far as I know, the actual process of formation of the spines has been
witnessed only once. In 1920, R. H. Finch was studying the development
of the Mauna Iki lava flow on the flank of Kilauea volcano. At lunch
time he found a comfortable place to sit on the surface of the flow itself,
and it was not long until he realized that the landscape was moving
slowly by him. He was on a moving part of the flow! He finished his lunch
at leisure, enjoying his ride, and as he went he watched a nearby part
of the flow where the lava crust remained unbroken. All over it little
spines were growing, as Finch put it, much like tiny plants sprouting from
the ground. What can be the cause of these sprouts? They are not the
result of growing crystals or chains of crystals: most of them are largely
glassy. Possibly they are the result of the formation of polymers in the
glass, perhaps linkages of silica tetrahedra similar to the structure we
believe may be the cause of the greater viscosity of silica-rich magmas.

Movement of the flow top causes the fragments to grind together,
breaking them, rubbing off the corners, and producing a variable amount
of sandy or dusty rock powder that settles between the larger fragments.

The streams of molten lava that feed aa flows usually do not freeze
over like those of pahoehoe, and consequently lava tubes are seldom found
in aa. Writing in 1950, I stated that tubes were absent in aa, but since
then we have found a very few of them. For the most part, however, the
feeding rivers are open to the sky (Plates 5-19 and 5-20). Close to the
vent the surface of the stream may be smooth orange-hot lava quickly
becoming covered with a thin lead-gray glassy skin. Soon, however, the

PLATE 5-19. Feeding river of
the lava flow of Mauna Loa, October 6, 1919. The surface of the
river has not yet formed a crust.
Note the standing waves in the
river. Hawaiian Volcano Observatory photo by T. A. Jaggar.

PLATE 5-20. The lava river of the southernmost lava flow of 1950 entering the ocean on the west side of Mauna Loa, June 3, 1950. The very small amount of steam being formed is believed to result from the development of a thin layer of steam that acts as an insulator between the surface of the molten lava and the overlying water. Aloha Airlines photo by Jack Matsumoto.

characteristic spiny surface begins to appear. Overflows spread lava a few feet on either side of the river. Close to the vent the overflows may congeal as pahoehoe, overlying the aa, but more commonly they also are aa. Repeated overflows gradually build up natural levees, resembling those of rivers like the Mississippi, and in time the surface of the river may stand several feet above the surface of the flow on either side of it. The main feeding rivers are generally between 10 and 25 feet, rarely as much as 50 feet, in width; and they generally run more or less along the middle line of the flow, which may be half a mile or more wide. They consist of two portions: an upper part of fluid liquid in which viscosities as low as 1×10^4 poises have been estimated, and which may flow down slopes of 20 to 30° with speeds as great as 35 miles an hour; and a lower more viscous part that is flowing much more slowly. At times the supply of liquid decreases and the upper part drains away, so that the lower part is visible. The depth of the upper part is generally between 2 and 8 feet in flows with a total thickness of about 15 feet. At the end of the eruption, the upper part and some of the lower part commonly drain away leaving an empty channel. These trough-like aa channels (Plate 5-20) may serve at a later date as the channels of water streams, and thereby exert an important affect on the development of the pattern of stream erosion.

The rest of the flow surface is covered with the typical spinose rubble (Plates 5-17 and 5-21). For a time, however, the river retains a fluid connection with the flow margins, even when the latter appear to have become stationary. As a surge of liquid from the vents travels down the river, one can often see the margins of the flow swell up a little, and sometimes this swelling amounts to a foot or more. As the surge passes and the level of liquid in the river drops, the flow margin settles down again.

Toward the distal end of the flow, the feeding river gradually disappears. Apparently, the liquid is dispersed through innumerable vaguely defined distributaries into the fluid interior of the flow and thereby brought to the advancing flow margin. The speed of advance of aa flows varies greatly. On steep slopes they have been known to move at a rate of several miles an hour. The first flow of the 1950 eruption of Mauna Loa, Hawaii, took less than an hour to cover the last 2 miles to the sea. On slopes of 2 or 3° they may roll ahead at a rate of 1,000 feet an hour (Plate 5-22). Most, however, advance much more slowly—a few tens of feet per hour or per day (See Plate 16-1)—and the most viscous of them creep along at a rate that is hardly perceptible.

The process of advance of an aa flow is easiest seen on a slow-moving flow. Such a flow was the last big one of the 1950 eruption of Mauna Loa, where it was creeping across a nearly flat bench near the sea, 16 miles from the vent from which it issued. The rate of advance was only about 30 to 40 feet an hour. The flow front, 50 feet high and half a mile broad, was a steep bank of reddish-brown to black clinkery

PLATE 5-21. Accretionary lava ball on the surface of a prehistoric aa lava flow of Mauna Loa, Hawaii. U. S. Geological Survey photo by G. A. Macdonald.

PLATE 5-22. Aa lava flow 50 feet thick advancing about 1,000 feet an hour across a coastal flat on Mauna Loa in June 1950. The bright spots are places where fragments of the clinker cover had just been detached from the front of the flow and rolled downward. A cloud of dust rises from the flow front. U. S. Geological Survey photo by G. A. Macdonald.

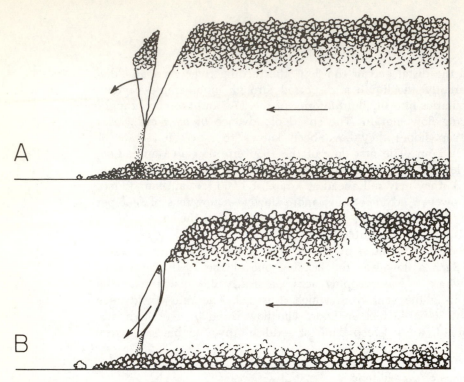

FIGURE 5-2. Diagrams of advancing aa flow fronts, showing (A) a block tilting forward away from a crack separating it from the massive center of the flow; and (B) a block sliding downward and forward on a separation plane. Showers of incandescent sand are coming from the lower edge of the separating block. The arrows show the directions of flow movement and movement of the blocks.

rock partly buried by a heap of clinkery fragments that was accumulating at its base. For short periods it was quite motionless and appeared dead, except for small amounts of sulfurous fume and the peculiar odor of hot iron, resembling that of a foundry, that characterizes active basaltic lava flows. An incessant grating and cracking noise resulted from the shrinking and shifting of the blocks on the flow surface and an occasional boulder tumbling down the flow front. At night myriads of red "eyes" glared out through holes in the dark cooler cover. During such quiet times, the amount of heat radiating from the flow was so small that it was possible to go right up to the flow front, and even climb part way up it.

As in pahoehoe flows, the lower part advanced less rapidly than the upper; as a result, the front grew gradually steeper until eventually it became unstable at some point and a chunk of the dark clinkery rock began to separate from the mass of the flow behind it. Sometimes the block leaned slowly forward as the crack behind it grew wider, until finally it tore free and tumbled down the slope. At other times it started to slide slowly forward and downward along a foreward-sloping surface that separated it from the lava behind it (Fig. 5-2). From the brightly glowing edge of the separation plane little streams of red-hot sand trickled down, formed apparently by the crushing and granulation of the incandescent lava. Eventually, the separation of the block became complete, and it also tumbled down the steep flow front. The surface left on the lava mass by the blocks separating from it glowed a bright orange-red with a temperature estimated to be about 900°C. The blocks also, where they broke open as they tumbled down, were brightly incandescent on the inside, but when the glowing surface was exposed to the air, it cooled quickly and became darker, and within less than a minute most of them had become completely black. Yet when a corner of such a block was knocked off with a hammer, the inside often was still cherry red a quarter of an inch below the surface. This illustrates well the low heat conductivity of the lava.

The process of collapse was repeated over and over again all along the flow front, fragments rolling down to add to the bank of loose material (talus) at its foot. At the same time the middle and upper parts of the flow crept almost imperceptibly forward. The main mass of the flow was a very viscous paste-like material, so viscous that it was impossible to push anything into it, but still sufficiently fluid to flow. As it oozed forward it carried along on its back a cover of clinkery blocks, and at the same time it buried the fragments that had been accumulating at the foot of the flow front. A pall of reddish-brown dust hovered over the advancing flow.

At the front of a faster-moving flow (Plate 5-23), the process is essentially the same, but the forward movement of the pasty layer is more nearly continuous along the whole flow front. The upper clinker layer is carried forward by the advance of the liquid portion beneath it, and there is a continual tumbling of fragments down the flow front, which advances over its own debris. Again, the motion resembles that of the front end of an endless track on a tractor. The faster advance of the flow may be caused simply by a steeper slope supplying a larger gravitative force to cause the liquid to move, or it may be the result of lower viscosity of the liquid. During the eruption of Kilauea in 1955, aa flows moved across a very gentle slope at a speed of about 1,000 feet an hour. It was possible to push the end of a small pole into the glowing lava of the flow front. (The heat from burning of the surface of the pole no doubt helped counteract the chilling of the lava caused by contact with the pole, and helped eliminate the "skin effect" that usually confronts one when he tries to push a cool object into hot lava.) The viscosity was probably about 1×10^7 poises. Fragments tumbling down the

PLATE 5-23. Aa lava flow advancing across cleared land during the eruption of 1955, Kilauea Volcano. The flow front is approximately 10 feet high, and was advancing 1,000 feet an hour. U. S. Geological Survey photo by G. A. Macdonald.

flow front sometimes broke up, but in many instances the smaller fragments thus formed were still sufficiently plastic to gradually flatten out a little under their own weight. This is an interesting example of the different behavior of a substance under different speeds of deformation. Subjected to a sudden stress by the impact of falling, the blocks fractured; but later, under the continuing small stress of gravity, they flowed.

Jostling of the blocks in the flow top as they are moved along results in abrasion and the formation of a certain amount of fine debris of sand and gravel size that settles down among the larger fragments. In most aa flows the proportion of this fine debris is quite small, but in some, and particularly in block lava flows, it may become quite large. Both the larger blocks and the fine debris may remain loose, or they may become stuck together by welding of their glassy surfaces in the heat of the flow.

The result of the above-described process of flow advance is a lava flow that consists of three parts. A central layer of massive rock, formed by solidification of the central pasty part of the moving flow, has layers of fragmental clinker both above and below it. The lower clinker layer is generally thinner than the upper, and in places it is absent. Locally, patches of clinker may be found within the central massive portion, and rather rarely the flow may consist of clinker all the way through. The proportion of clinker in the flow generally is between 15 and 65 per cent. The clinker fragments may remain loose, or they may be partly stuck together by welding of their glassy surfaces while the flow was still hot or by later deposition of cement between them by circulating ground water.

Some aa flows lack the basal clinker layer. Flows of this sort have been reported, for instance, by A. C. Waters in the Columbia River region. No flow of this sort has been observed in formation. Such flows are generally thick, and it has been suggested that the heat remaining in the flow after it came to rest was great enough to remelt the basal clinker fragments and cause them to loose their identity. This appears very unlikely, however, because the flows are not always thick, because even in thick flows one would expect to find at least some remnants of incompletely remelted fragments at the base, and because other structures such as pipe vesicles have persisted at the base of the flow without showing any loss of sharpness due to remelting. The absence of the lower clinker must mean that the mechanism of flow advance was somewhat different than that observed in Hawaii. Specifically, it must be that the upper portion does not advance faster than the lower, so that clinker from the top does not tumble down the advancing flow front. The very slow advance of these flows over nearly horizontal surfaces must result in a slow oozing forward of the entire mass, at least from the central pasty part upward, as a single unit at essentially the same speed, so that the top does not overrun the central portion.

The central part of a congealed aa flow is generally somewhat vesicular. The vesicles tend to differ in shape from those of pahoehoe. In aa the gas bubbles had stopped expanding before the flow stopped moving, so the bubble holes were twisted and distorted by the movement of the

PLATE 5-24. Accretionary lava ball on an aa lava flow of Mauna Loa, Hawaii, showing the internal structure of the ball. Hawaii Institute of Geophysics photo by G. A. Macdonald.

liquid around them. Aa vesicles are typically highly irregular as compared to the fairly regular spheroids and groups of spheroids in pahoehoe (Plate 5-1). The difference is not wholly consistent. Sometimes some fairly regular vesicles are found in aa, and, more rarely, pahoehoe vesicles are considerably distorted. However, the difference is consistent enough to give a fairly reliable indication of the type of flow in cases where the more dependable surface characteristics cannot be seen.

Fairly regular spheroidal balls are present on the clinkery tops of some aa flows or embedded in the clinker (Plate 5-21), and on some flows they are very abundant. They are formed by the rolling up of solid fragments, either clinker or chunks derived from the walls of the flow channels, in the viscous lava of the moving flow. As they roll, they grow in size in the same manner as snowballs rolling downhill in soft, sticky snow. They are sometimes called by the French term, *bombes en roulement,* but since they are not bombs in the ordinary sense of fragments thrown out by explosion (Chapter 7), a better term for them is *accretionary lava balls.* They range in diameter from a few inches to about 10 feet. Broken open they reveal the core around which they grew (Plate 5-24), and sometimes show a spiral structure.

Where lava flows cross wet ground, steam is generated and bubbles of steam may rise into the lava. This may result in lines of vesicles or roughly cylindrical groups of vesicles extending up into the lava for several feet. They may also form small tubes, usually less than half an inch in diameter, that project upward several inches to a couple of feet from the base of the flow. These are known as *pipe vesicles.* The upper ends of pipe vesicles and vesicle cylinders commonly are bent in the direction of movement of the flow (Fig. 5-3). Where the lower skin of the flow is tough, the steam may burst upward into the lava explosively, creating an irregularly cylindrical opening called a *spiracle.* These range in size up to 25 or 30 feet in diameter. Generally, they terminate within the body of the flow, but in the Pedregal lava flow on the outskirts of Mexico City some of them pass entirely through the flow and are more than 100 feet high. Mud from the underlying ground surface often is blown up into the spiracle by the explosion. Spiracles and vesicle cylinders are found in all types of flows but are commonest in aa.

Actually, there is every gradation in structure from aa into pahoehoe

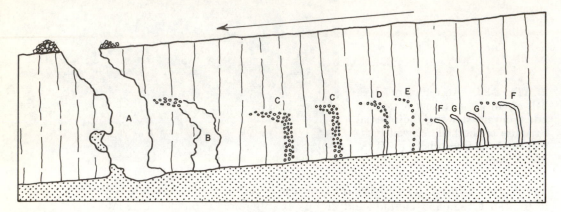

FIGURE 5-3. Diagrammatic cross section of a lava flow showing (A) a spiracle that blasted through to the surface, with some of the underlying sedimentary material blown up into the spiracle; (B) a spiracle passing into a vesicle cylinder; (C) vesicle cylinders; (D) a pipe vesicle passing into a small vesicle cylinder; (E) a vesicle train; (F) pipe vesicles passing into vesicle trains; and (G) pipe vesicles. (C) to (G) are exaggerated in size in comparison with (A) and (B). The arrows show the direction of flow.

on one hand and into block lava on the other. Most flows can be assigned without question to one type or another, but some partake of some characteristics of each.

Many of the Yakima basalt flows in the southeastern part of Washington and adjacent parts of Oregon and Idaho, which have generally been referred to as aa, do not fit the descriptions of typical aa, nor of either pahoehoe or block lava. The upper portions of the flows are fragmental, but the fragments are not spinose; neither are they the fairly regular and smooth-sided fragments of block lava. (See the following section.) They range from angular to rounded and from dense to highly vesicular. Many have the regular vesicle forms of pahoehoe, and some are so vesicular that they resemble pyroclastic cinder (Chapter 7). Occasional fragments of smooth or ropy pahoehoe crust can be found. The material between the larger fragments is sandy and silty pulverized rock debris and is generally much decomposed by weathering.

The fragmental portions range from a few per cent to more than 50 per cent of the thickness of the flows, but most commonly are between 20 and 35 per cent. Some of the flows consist essentially of two portions: the upper fragmental part, and a lower massive part that is often crudely to moderately columnar jointed, with columns several feet across. Sometimes there is a small amount of fragmental material at the base, but commonly the massive lava rests directly on the preflow surface. Other, generally thicker, flows consist of three parts: a lower zone of coarse, fairly regular, nearly vertical columns, a middle zone of smaller columns often with very variable orientations, and the upper fragmental zone. In these flows the lower and middle zones are the colonnade and entablature of typical columnar-jointed flows (see p. 99), and the fragmental zone replaces the "upper colonnade."

The lower portions of the flows are generally moderately to very dense, but they often contain nearly horizontally oriented elongate vesicles 1 to 3 inches long, and sometimes more than 6 inches. The vesicles are generally irregular, but sometimes they are nearly spherical, or spheroids stretched in the direction of flow. Rarely, nearly spherical vesicles up to a foot across are found with walls that are botryoidal (resembling in form a bunch of grapes) or kidney shaped, sometimes with small ridges of lava projecting into the opening.

Pahoehoe is a more "primitive" form than aa. This is demonstrated by two facts. In pahoehoe the gas is still actively coming out of solution and expanding when the flow congeals, whereas in aa it has stopped expanding. Even more conclusive is the fact that many flows issue from the vent as pahoehoe but change to aa during their progress downslope. The reverse change, from aa to pahoehoe, does not occur. The change of pahoehoe to aa has been shown to be a function of both the viscosity of the magma and the amount of mechanical stirring to which it is subjected. The more viscous the magma and the more stirring it receives, the more likely it is to form aa. It is a common observation that pahoehoe flows change to aa when they go down a steep slope. Also, violent lava fountaining is likely to result in aa issuing directly from the cone at the vent, whereas lava issuing gently forms pahoehoe. The latter is probably responsible for the erroneous statement sometimes met with that aa lava is richer in gas than pahoehoe. The common change of pahoehoe to aa downslope appears to result largely from an increase in viscosity due to cooling, loss of gas, and increasing degree of crystallization. Both the cooling and the increase of viscosity are demonstrated by measurements on flows (Table 4-6).

Block Lava

The name "block lava" is sometimes applied to all lava flows that are covered with angular fragments, and in that sense it includes aa. The term is more useful, however, if it is restricted to a type in which the fragments lack the characteristic spininess of aa, and it is used here in this more restricted sense. Block lava flows (Plate 5-25) resemble aa in their general structure and in their mechanics of movement. They differ from aa in that the fragments that make up the top of the flow have more regular forms and smoother faces. Instead of the exceedingly irregular and jaggedly spinose fragments of aa, those of block lava are angular blocks, often approaching cubes in form, and the tiny sharp spines are almost absent (Plate 5-26).

PLATE 5-25. Margin of a block lava flow in the Modoc Plateau, on highway 89 in northeastern California. U. S. Geological Survey photo by G. A. Macdonald.

PLATE 5-26. Close view of the front of a flow of block lava, showing the forms of the blocks, on highway 89 in northeastern California. (Compare Plate 5-18.) U. S. Geological Survey photo by G. A. Macdonald.

There are gradations from one type of lava to the other, and some spiny fragments are found in some block lava flows just as some smooth blocks are found in aa; but, in general, the two types are quite distinct.

The lava that forms block flows is more viscous than that forming aa. The angular blocks are formed by breaking up of the partly to wholly congealed upper part of the flow as the still-mobile part beneath it continues to move. The flows are, on the average, thicker than those of aa. Most of them are between 25 and 100 feet thick, and some of them reach several hundred feet.

The fragmental material commonly makes up a greater proportion of a block lava flow than it does of aa, and it may in places constitute the whole thickness of the flow; but a massive central layer usually is present. As already mentioned, finer crushed debris commonly is much more abundant in block lava than it is in most aa. Both the massive part of the flow and the fragments are usually more glassy than the corresponding parts of aa flows. Block lava tends to be less vesicular than aa, but the vesicles usually have the same irregular form.

The surfaces of block lava flows generally are very irregular with many hummocks and hollows, often 10 or 15 feet deep and sometimes much deeper. Some of these are disposed irregularly without any apparent pattern. Some, however, form wavelike ridges extending across the flow at approximately right angles to its direction of motion. The ridges may be only a few feet high, but not uncommonly the height from the ridge crest to the bottom of the adjoining trough is several tens of feet. The ridges appear to result from irregular outflow of lava from the vent, each greater surge causing the adjacent flow top to rise and resulting in a ridge that moves on down with the advancing flow. The center of the flow moves faster than the edges, causing the ridges to become bent with their convexity down stream. The fact that the ridges often extend completely across the flow indicates that the entire flow advanced as a unit. Concentration of movement in a narrow central river appears to be less pronounced in block lava than in aa.

Block lava flows generally move very slowly, seldom advancing more than a few tens of feet a day, and often only a few feet.

Describing the advance of a block lava flow from Hekla volcano, Iceland, in 1947, T. Einarsson (1949, p. 6) writes:

> At most places on the lava front the flowing plastic lava was now hidden under a thick slide of cold blocks. The movement of the flow was . . . seen only by the nearly continual fall of blocks down the scree-covered front, which caused thick clouds of dust to rise. . . . The general movement of the lava front was very slow, being hardly perceptible over a period of several hours.

Block lava flows may be basaltic in composition, but typically they are more siliceous. The greater richness in silica correlates with the greater viscosity. There is also a marked correlation with the type of geological environment. The flows associated with the big volcanic cones of continental mountain-building belts (regions of compression) are generally block lavas. (But in some such regions, if not in most, the building of the big cones was preceded by the formation of widespread and thick accumulations of flows that did not build cones and were mostly of pahoehoe or pillow-basalt type.) The flows of midocean "shield" volcanoes and of the basaltic plains and plateaus (regions of distension rather than compression) are typically basaltic pahoehoe and aa.

The rather high viscosity of the fluid portion of block lava flows results in a greater amount of internal shearing than in aa. The movement of the base of the flow is retarded by friction against the underlying ground, and the moving liquid higher up tends to separate into a series of sheets slipping over each other like a series of cards in a deck when the deck is bent. The same sort of motion (laminar flow) is present in aa and pahoehoe flows, but the separation into sheets shearing over each other is less pronounced. The movement of the sheets is predominantly nearly parallel to the underlying surface, and in solidified flows the shear surfaces are visible as planes of separation (joints) essentially parallel to the top and bottom of the flow. The sheets may be very thin. Sometimes they are only a fraction of an inch thick, and then the lava resembles the platy sedimentary rock, shale. Toward

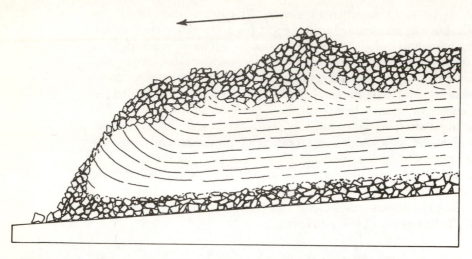

FIGURE 5-4. Diagrammatic cross section of the front of a block lava flow showing platy jointing. The arrow indicates the direction of movement of the flow.

the front of the flow, especially when it is becoming so viscous that it has almost stopped moving, the shear planes may bend sharply upward (Fig. 5-4). This is seen in many old flows that have been cut into by erosion. It appears to result from congealing of the front of the flow to the point that it is easier for the lava just behind it to move upward than to push the front forward. Local conditions may create a similar situation at other places in the flow, and local upward movement of the lava, upheaving the surface, is the cause of many of the small hills that dot the tops of block lava flows. This upthrust of portions of the flow on shear planes over the portion directly in front of them has been called *ramping,* and each of the shear planes is referred to as a ramp.

In extremely viscous flows, such as those of rhyolite, the upward bending of flow planes and shear planes may be present throughout the flow from source to terminus. In such flows, the flow laminae ("foliation") may be very pronounced, individual laminae ranging from a millimeter to several meters in thickness, though they are most commonly less than 2 centimeters. Alternating laminae are distinguished by differences in color or texture, particularly by different degrees of vesicularity. Bands of dense glass may alternate with bands that are as vesicular as pumice as a result of the drawing out into thin sheets by flowage of respectively gas-poor and gas-rich portions of an inhomogeneous magma. Other bands are rich in lithophysae or in spherulites, also apparently as a result of the greater abundance of volatiles in them. The same sort of variation may explain the greater degree of crystallinity of microlite-rich laminae that alternate with others that are almost completely glassy.

Christiansen and Lipman (1966) have made a detailed study of the lamination in a rhyolite flow, up to 800 feet thick, near Beatty in southwestern Nevada. In the lower part of the flow the laminae are essentially

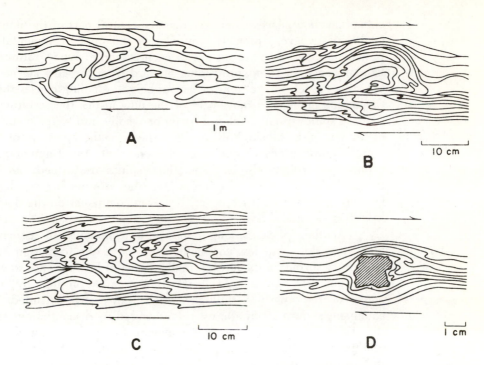

FIGURE 5-5. Contorted lamination resulting from shear in a viscous flow of rhyolite in Nevada. (From Christiansen and Lipman, 1966.)

parallel to the bottom and lateral margins, but in the upper part they curve steeply upward in the direction of advance of the flow. Some pass upward into spines on the flow surface. Also, in the upper part the laminae commonly are much distorted, owing to the resistance to motion offered by the forward portion of the flow. Commonly, the laminae have been folded into anticline-like and syncline-like forms ("antiforms" and "synforms") the limbs of which may be much crumpled, and which are commonly overturned in the direction of advance of the flow. In many the upper limb of the anticline has been thrust forward over the adjacent syncline (Fig. 5-5A), and in some the continued motion has resulted in shearing off of the anticline, forming a low-angle thrust fault (Fig. 5-5B). Somewhat similar distortion of the laminae is found around inclusions of foreign rock in the flow, where the adjacent laminae have been crumpled by rotation of the inclusion (Fig. 5-5D). Differential slippage of one lamina over another during the last stages of movement of the flow is indicated by small grooves and ridges on the surface of one lamina formed by the dragging over it of phenocrysts projecting from the next lamina.

Another result of extreme viscosity during the last stages of movement of some flows is the formation of curved cracks nearly normal to the surface of the flow and convex upstream. These are formed by pulling away of the lava from the part of the flow farther up the valley. They are akin to the curved crevasses found in valley glaciers.

Cross sections of block lava flows exposed by erosion or in highway cuts often show places where the massive central part of the flow (the congealed pasty layer) projects upward into the upper fragmental part. The projection may reach the surface or even extend above it, forming a tower-like eminence, or *spine*, protruding upward from the flow surface. Some of the spines reach several tens of feet in height. Cooling causes the spines to shrink and crack, and movement of the flow jostles the resulting blocks so that the spines usually collapse partly or wholly into heaps of blocks. Some of the numerous blocky hills on the surfaces of the flows are of this origin. Upward protrusions of the massive layer into the fragmental part are common in aa flows also, and sometimes spines are formed; but because of the prevailing lower viscosity of aa lava, they are much rarer than in block lava flows. As we shall see, spines are even commoner on the domes formed by still more viscous lava.

Another phenomenon, found quite commonly in association with block lava flows but less commonly with aa, is the formation at the front and on the surface of the flow of small tongues of lava that are so viscous that they retain the grooved and ridged outline imposed on them by the irregular edges of the aperture through which they were extruded. They also commonly show a series of cross ridges caused by discontinuous extrusion of the viscous liquid. The process is analogous to the squeezing of very viscous toothpaste out through a jagged break in the tube, and the tongues have been dubbed "toothpaste lava."

The parts of lava flows that consist of aggregations of angular blocks are known as *flow breccias*. ("Breccia" is a general geological term used to designate any mass of angular fragments.) Various degrees of brecciation of a flow may result from shattering of the very viscous lava by stresses set up by flowage. Lava flows shattered in this way are said to be *autobrecciated*. Some flow breccias are simply the fragmental parts of block lava or aa. The fragments may be loose, or they may be bound together by welding of their edges or by cement deposited long after the flow was formed. Sometimes the larger blocks are embedded in the finer debris resulting from their attrition during movement of the flow. At other times they are enclosed in the same sort of rock that makes up the massive part of the flow and that must have been formed by solidification of liquid lava. In part, the blocks have settled into underlying liquid, and in part the liquid has moved upward or laterally into the fragmental part of the flow. It is rare that the process can actually be observed, but one such case is recorded by Einarsson (1949, p. 41), again at a flow from Hekla. The flow was moderately fluid with a front only 6 to 10 feet high advancing at a rate of 3 feet a minute over a very gentle slope. The bulging pasty mass was creeping forward under a load of blocky debris. "The plastic lava appeared at the base of the front. It was covered by a thick cover of blocks . . . [which] moved with the lava, sank into it, and when they tumbled near the front one could see the plastic lava being squeezed out from their base."

Where lava flows come in contact with water, they may be shattered by steam explosions yet still retain the general form of the flow. The breccias formed in this way are composed of fragments that resemble the lava in the unbrecciated parts of the flow, although they are commonly somewhat more glassy. The surfaces of the blocks sometimes are quite smooth fractures, but others are rough or slaggy, and sometimes blocks are partly welded together. The surfaces of the blocks often are reddened by oxidation. The breccias may contain irregular or lenticular masses of less shattered lava and grade into ordinary massive parts of the lava flow. Gradations may be either upward or downward. On Mt. Rainier in Washington, the brecciation is believed to have resulted from extrusion of the lava onto snow or ice or from contact with the resulting melt water. "The breccias that grade upward into lava flows were formed by steam explosions at the base of lava as it moved down slopes mantled with mud and melting snow and ice. Lava that burrowed beneath melting ice or mud, on the other hand, has breccia on its top" (Fiske, Hopson, and Waters, 1963, p. 74).

Lava flows in eastern Siberia that contain very numerous angular to lenticular inclusions of other rock, sometimes genetically related to the enclosing lava and sometimes considerably older, have been called "tuff lavas." They are discussed in Chapter 8.

Very thick and relatively short block lava flows, formed by lava that was extruded in a very viscous condition, have been termed "coulées" (Putnam, 1938); but the name *coulée* has long been used by the French for lava flows in general, and it seems undesirable to give it this restricted meaning in English. These flows may be several hundred feet thick and only a fraction of a mile in length with very steep, largely scree-covered margins (Plate 5-27). Dacite flows on the northern flank of Mt. Mazama at Crater Lake, Oregon, are as much as 2 miles long and 1,200 feet thick. Flows of this sort show all of the general characteristics of block lava flows, both in structure and in mechanics of movement, although the proportion of massive lava to

PLATE 5-27. Thick lava flows on the west side of the Mono Craters, California. Two of the domes built over vents are visible on the skyline. Hawaii Institute of Geophysics photo by G. A. Macdonald.

breccia is commonly much greater than in thinner flows. Their surfaces usually are very irregular with block-covered hillocks 5 to 50 feet high, and very commonly with curved ridges that are convex downstream (Plates 5-28 and 5-29). Spines are common on them, and they show every gradation into the volcanic domes described in Chapter 6.

Joints in Lava Flows

All lava flows are broken into blocks by fractures known as *joints*. Joints have several different origins. Some are formed by distortion of the rock during folding or warping, or by shearing stresses, as a result of deformation of the earth's crust long after the formation of the flow. However, only those directly related to the formation of the flow concern us here.

The joints that form parallel to the top and bottom of the flow due to shearing during formation of the flow have already been mentioned. They are the result of the tendency of the lava to continue moving after the fluidity becomes too low to allow true flowage.

As the lava cools it shrinks, and this results in tensional stresses within it. These in turn cause the rock to fissure. Some of the joints thus formed are at approximately right angles to the cooling surface, which is usually the

top or bottom of the flow but may be the side of the flow, as for example where it rests against the wall of a former valley filled by the lava. Other joints are at approximately right angles to these first-mentioned joints. In most flows, particularly thin ones, the joints normal to the flow surface are at roughly right angles to each other, and, with the joints of the other set, tend to form blocks that are roughly rectangular parallelepipeds approaching cubes in form. In other flows, particularly thick slowly cooled ones, the joints normal to the flow surface tend to develop in three directions at roughly 60° to each other and form multisided blocks that are cut off by the joints parallel to the flow surface. Jointing of this sort may attain a high degree of perfection, breaking the flow into a series of regularly formed columns. The columns tend to be hexagonal, but range from four- to eight-sided, and five- and seven-sided columns are nearly as common as six-sided ones (at some localities they are commoner). The horizontal joints divide the columns into a series of segments. Often the horizontal joints are curved, and when they are closely spaced, the columns may resemble a stack of thick saucers, or concavo-convex lenses, piled one on another. The saucers may be stacked either right side up or upside down. Some imaginative geologist has written that, rather than stacks of saucers, the columns resemble stacks of dutch cheeses.

Columnar jointing is very well developed in many of the thick widespread "plateau basalt" flows. It is, for example, well displayed in the Columbia River region. Another well-known locality is the Devil's Postpile in the Sierra Nevada of California (Plate 5-30), and possibly best known of all is the Giant's Causeway in northern Ireland. Columnar-jointed basalt flows often show a separation into three principal zones parallel to the flow surface. Above a thin basal zone with poorly developed inconspicuous jointing comes a thick zone with very well developed vertical columns, 2 to as much as 60 feet thick, known as the *lower colonnade*. Next upward comes another thick zone in which the columns are much narrower and commonly have much variety of orientation, sometimes forming fan-like, rosette-like, or chevron-like structures. This zone is known, using another architectural

PLATE 5-30. Columnar jointing in a basalt lava flow, Devil's Postpile, California. The columns average about 18 inches across. Photo by the Department of the Interior, National Park Service.

term, as the *entablature*. At the top of the flow comes a thinner zone, the *upper colonnade,* in which the columns are again thick but much less perfectly developed. In some flows the colonnade is thin or absent, and the entablature may consist of as many as six separate tiers of pillars.

Columnar jointing is found in all types of lava flows, including ash flows. It is also very conspicuous in many dikes, where it is developed normal to the dike walls. In a vertical dike exposed by erosion, the columns may resemble cut and stacked firewood. Columnar joints are well developed in other types of intrusive bodies also and along the margins of volcanic necks (the filled feeding pipes of volcanoes, later exposed by erosion). Since they form at right angles to the outer (cooling) surface of the body, they may help us determine the original shape of the body when its outer margins are covered or have been destroyed by erosion. Unfortunately, the joint pattern is not always sufficiently diagnostic to identify the body with certainty. The magnificently columnar Devil's Tower in Wyoming is probably a laccolith, but may be a volcanic neck.

Pillow Lavas

Some lava flows consist of masses of more or less ellipsoidal bodies from less than a foot to several feet across that are distinctly separated from each other (Plate 5-31). The form of these "ellipsoids" has been variously described as mattress-like, sack-like, ball-like, balloon-like, and bun-shaped, but the usual description is pillow-shaped. The rocks are generally referred to as *pillow lavas*. As the descriptions suggest, the "pillows" are generally flattened, with rounded tops. Where a pile of them has been formed, the bottoms of the pillows conform in shape to the rounded tops of those beneath them, so that in vertical cross section they show lobes projecting downward between the intersecting curved tops of the underlying pillows

PLATE 5-31. Pillow lavas, Waimea Canyon, Kauai Island, Hawaii. Note the radial structure. U. S. Geological Survey photo by D. A. Davis.

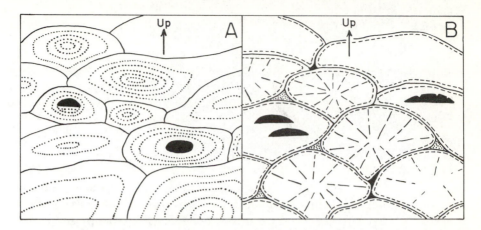

FIGURE 5-6. Diagrammatic cross section of a mass of pahoehoe toes (A) and pillow lava (B), showing characteristic structures. The dashed lines represent the inner margin of the glassy skin on the pillows, the stippled areas represent sedimentary material filling interstices between the pillows, and the black areas are open spaces. (From Macdonald, 1967.)

(Fig. 5-6). In cross section they also usually show a distinctly radial structure (Plates 5-31 and 5-32) resulting from crudely developed columnar joints and from the radial elongation of vesicles. Each pillow is enclosed in a thin skin of glass. Both the glassy surface and the joint columns extending inward from the surface indicate rapid cooling of each individual pillow, and the conformity of their lower surfaces to the tops of those below them indicate that they accumulated by settling one on top of another while they were still sufficiently plastic to mold themselves to the underlying surface. Angular spaces often remain between the pillows, however, and these are commonly filled with angular glassy sand-sized fragments of lava or with mud or other sedimentary material (Plate 5-32). Often the sedimentary material can be seen to have been squeezed up between the pillows from an underlying bed that was covered by the lava (Plate 5-33). The sedimentary material must have been water-saturated and very plastic. It often contains fossils, sometimes of marine and sometimes of freshwater organisms. Layers of water-laid sedimentary rocks often alternate with layers of pillow lava.

PLATE 5-32. Pillow lava, with marl in the interstices between the pillows, at Acicastello, near the base of Mount Etna, Sicily. The ballpoint pen gives the scale. Hawaii Institute of Geophysics photo by G. A. Macdonald.

PLATE 5-33. Pillow lava resting on diatomite deposited in a former lake, on highway 89 near Lake Britton, California. U. S. Geological Survey photo by G. A. Macdonald.

The evidence of rapid chilling and close association with water-deposited sediments indicates clearly that pillow lavas were formed either beneath water or by extrusion over very wet swampy surfaces.

Until very recently we did not have a single well-authenticated observation of the actual formation of pillow lavas—probably because they are usually formed under water, where observation is difficult. An oft-cited description is by Tempest Anderson, who observed the lava flow of Matavanu Volcano reaching the shoreline on Savaii Island, Samoa, in 1910. However, Anderson's text indicates that the ellipsoidal masses he observed were forming above sea level, and his photograph shows them to be ordinary pahoehoe toes. In 1859, W. L. Green watched the lava flow of Mauna Loa in Hawaii entering the sea, and described blebs of pahoehoe breaking free and dripping down a low sea cliff into the water. Almost surely these were pillows in the making, but we cannot be certain. J. G. Moore (1970) has recently found well-formed pillows on the submerged portion of the nearby lava flow of 1801, but the offshore portion of the 1859 flow is covered with gravel and corals, and any pillows that may be there are hidden. In April 1971 a team of divers, including J. G. Moore, explored the active under-water front of a small lava flow that had been pouring over a low cliff at the south coast of Kilauea Volcano for about 6 weeks. Moore (in an Event Report of the Smithsonian Institution's Center for Short-lived Phenomena) states: "The flow is advancing under water as a wall of rubble which is some 300 to 500 feet seaward of the new sea cliff. The front of the rubble wall is at the angle of repose of about 45°, and the base of it is covering over the old ocean floor to a depth of about 100 feet. Tongues of lava, circular in cross section, extend down the front . . . of this rubble slope. Some of these are as long as 200 feet and they are 3 to 4 feet in diameter, generally. Budding off of them are typical pillows." The account resembles pillow lava-hyaloclastite assemblages described in the next section.

In spite of the paucity of actual observations, there is little question that most or all true pillow lavas are formed either under water or in a very wet environment.

In cross section, pillows are mimicked by heaps of pahoehoe toes. Although the latter apparently can form under water, they commonly are formed on dry land and therefore cannot be relied upon as indicators of the environment in which they were formed, as can pillows. They commonly are more vesicular and often are partly hollow, since they represent cross sections of small pahoehoe tubes. (Occasionally, pillows also may be hollow.) The pahoehoe toes usually lack the radial structure characteristic of pillows; they have instead a concentric structure resulting from deposition of successive layers of lava on the walls of the tube and from a concentric arrangement of rows of vesicles (Fig. 5-6).

In older geological formations, the occasional hollow pillows are useful in indicating the original attitude of the beds that contain them. When it comes to rest, the upper surface of the liquid in the incompletely filled pillow assumes a horizontal position, and any deviation from this indicates a disturbance of the pillow since its formation. Conversely, if the internal lava surfaces in the pillows in inclined beds are horizontal, the inclination of the beds must be original.

Most pillow lavas are basalt, or a variety of basalt known as spilite, in which sodium is considerably more abundant than in ordinary basalt. It has been suggested that this extra sodium was absorbed from seawater into which the lava was extruded, but the evidence is far from conclusive and many petrologists do not accept it. Fragments of pillows dredged from the deep ocean on the flanks of the Hawaiian volcanoes are basalts with only a normal amount of sodium (Moore, 1965). It nevertheless is noteworthy that many of the basic lavas that accumulate to great thicknesses in sinking marine troughs (geosynclines) are spilites, and that many of them are pillow lavas. Pillow lavas of other compositions, ranging from rocks more mafic than ordinary basalt to trachyte, have also been described. B. V. Ivanov has given an account of formation of pillows by dacitic andesite lava, believed to have been unusually fluid because of an unusually high content of volatile materials, flowing into snow on the flanks of Karymskiy Volcano, Kamchatka, in the winter of 1962.

Pillows appear always to form from pahoehoe-type flows. The exact mechanism by which they form is still not known, though it appears almost certain that they passed through a stage in which the individual blebs of lava that were to develop into pillows were suspended in water or water-saturated mud like the drops of liquid in a liquid–gas emulsion(resembling an exceedingly coarse insect spray). Just how they got into this "emulsified" condition is less clear. The giant drops of liquid lava plunging from the sea cliff into the water during the 1859 eruption on Hawaii may very probably have developed into pillows on the sea floor. Elsewhere, evidence indicates that lava flows advanced into or beneath water with steep fronts, and that blebs of lava (pahoehoe toes) repeatedly broke off from the upper part of the face and tumbled down it to form pillows lying on the bottom part of the face or on the sea floor or lake floor in front of it.

Bailey, Irwin, and Jones (1964, p. 51) have suggested that pillow lavas may form from blebs of fluid lava ejected upward into the water by lava fountains, much as showers of similar blebs are thrown into the air by subaerial eruptions, and that the blebs sink to the bottom to form accumulations of pillows. This mechanism might well account for thick local accumulations of pillows but does not appear adequate to explain widespread layers of pillow lava only a few tens of feet thick.

In many places pillow lavas are of considerable importance in indicating the conditions under which they were formed in past geologic time and the changes that have occurred since then. For instance, on the southern end of the island of Guam there is a succession of pillow lavas more than 1,000 feet thick now exposed above sea level. Because these pillow lavas must have been formed under water, the island must have risen relative to sea level more than 1,000 feet since the lavas were formed. The same is true of other islands around the edge of the Pacific basin; but with very minor local exceptions that can be explained by extrusion of lava into swamps, pillow lavas are absent on the islands of the central Pacific. Thus, there is indicated a fundamental difference in the behavior of the islands of the central Pacific and those around its edges. Movement of the islands around the edge of the basin has been both upward and downward, but that of the center of the basin must have been very predominantly downward.

Hyaloclastite Flows

The fine glassy lava debris that is sometimes found between the pillows in pillow lavas has already been mentioned. It is formed by a flaking off, or decrepitation, of the surface of the lava as a result of its sudden chilling in water. The same sort of thing may take place on a much larger scale, and extensive flows consist partly or largely of glassy sand formed by decrepitation in water. These masses were formerly thought to be tuffs—consolidated masses of volcanic ash formed by explosive eruption (see Chapter 7)—but their origin by disintegration of lava in water is now clearly established. It has recently been suggested by the Swiss volcanologist, Alfred Rittmann, that they be called *hyaloclastites* (literally "broken glass rocks").

The shape of most of the fragments in hyaloclastite differs from that of most of the fragments in volcanic ash. The latter are formed by the blowing apart of rock froth by expanding gas bubbles, and consequently the fragments have many curved surfaces that were once the edges of bubble holes. In contrast, the hyaloclastite fragments tend to be flat plates or angular chips with only occasional curved surfaces of disrupted vesicles (Fig. 5-7). The original glass of hyaloclastite has commonly been altered by oxidation and absorption of water into a yellowish-brown waxy-looking substance known as palagonite. Apparently, the alteration can take place either in water or subaerially.

Hyaloclastite commonly forms massive deposits with little or no trace of bedding. If the exposures are extensive enough, it can usually be seen to grade downward or laterally into ordinary lava, or often into pillow lava. Apparently, the formation of hyaloclastite on the top of the flow tends to

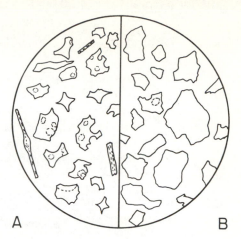

FIGURE 5-7. Sketch showing characteristic outlines of fragments in (A) glassy basaltic ash, and (B) hyaloclastite, under the microscope. The diameter of the field is 2 mm. (A) is from Hawaii, (B) is from Sicily.

A

B

protect the lava beneath it from contact with the water. Pillows and fragments of pillows often are scattered through the finer debris (Plate 5-34). Sometimes the hyaloclastite shows distinct bedding, and sometimes it is clear that the loose sandy material on the advancing flow front has been reworked by waves and currents in the water and redeposited in beds with the structures typical of sedimentary rocks. R. E. Fuller has described flows of the Columbia River lavas that advanced into lakes and were granulated by contact with the water, forming beds of sandy debris that sloped forward into the lake like the foreset beds of a delta (Fig. 5-8). Blebs of lava dropping into the water rolled or drooled down the bank of sand to form long sack-like pillows, and occasionally sheets of lava trickled down without changing to pillows. These can be traced upslope into the base of the lava flow that gradually advanced over the growing mass of hyaloclastite.

Many flows of hyaloclastite formed in the ocean or in lakes, but in Iceland they have had a different, and very intriguing, origin. During the glacial period much of the island was covered by ice, but volcanic activity continued. Lavas erupting beneath the glaciers melted the ice and formed great subglacial pockets of water and steam. The lavas were chilled and granulated to hyaloclastite, and the glassy fragments were altered to palagonite. Pillows are scattered through the sandy debris, and the hyaloclastite passes laterally into pillow lavas ("ball breccias"). Thus originated thick and extensive deposits known as "moberg," or the "Palagonite Formation." Where the lava was erupted from fissures, long narrow ridges of "moberg" were built; but where eruption was from a pipe-like vent, the cavity beneath

PLATE 5-34. Pillows in hyaloclastite, in the Columbia River lavas in northern Oregon. U. S. Geological Survey photo by G. A. Macdonald.

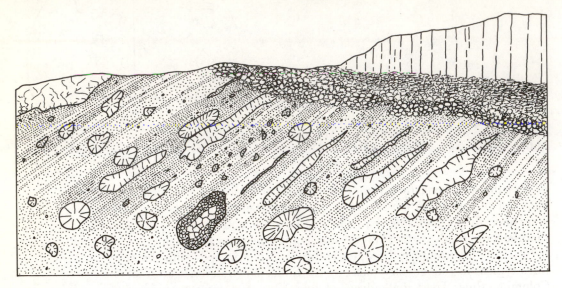

FIGURE 5-8.   Cross section of a hyaloclastite flow formed in a lake in the
Columbia River Plain of Oregon, showing bedding of the hyaloclastite and
elongated pillows.

the ice was more nearly circular in plan, and the hyaloclastite and pillow
lava accumulated in a roundish mass that had very steep sides because it was
confined by the walls of ice. At some places the ice was finally melted all the
way to the top, and a lake was formed temporarily within the glacier.
Similar lakes, either beneath the ice or extending all the way to the surface,
are formed today by subglacial eruptions, and from time to time they are
drained by the water bursting out under the ice (forming the "glacier
bursts" described later). Lava erupted into the drained lake basin formed
a cap of normal lava flows on top of the mass of hyaloclasite. Later, when
the ice melted away, these lava-capped mounds of hyaloclastite formed
flat-topped "table mountains." Very similar table mountains, formed in
essentially the same way, have been described by W. H. Mathews in British
Columbia and given the Indian name "tuyas."

In eastern Iceland one example has been described of hyaloclastite
and associated pillow lavas that were formed by a lava flow that flowed
down the axis of a valley beneath a valley glacier. The flow traveled at least
12 miles, and probably 20 miles, melting its way through the bottom of the
ice. Liquid lava traveling through a central conduit in the flow in places
escaped upward and sideways through fractures in the lava shell and formed
pillows and hyaloclastite where it came in contact with the melt water
(Walker and Blake, 1966).

Fragments of lava dredged from the deep ocean commonly have a
thick glassy rind that is partly or wholly altered to palagonite. They also
exhibit various degrees of brecciation, and, like the masses described in the
preceding paragraphs, also are frequently referred to as hyaloclastites. In

many, if not in most, the fragmentation of the glass appears to have resulted from shrinkage on cooling, producing a large number of polygonal blocks a fraction of an inch to a few inches across. Alteration to palagonite has proceeded inward from the fractures bounding the blocks, commonly leaving more or less rounded residual fresh or little-altered cores. Many of the "hyaloclastites" dredged from the Mid-Atlantic Ridge and from seamounts in other parts of the world appear to be of this nature.

SUGGESTED ADDITIONAL READING

Baker and Harris, 1963; Bullard, 1947; Christiansen and Lipman, 1966; Einarsson, 1949; Krauskopf, 1948; Loney, 1968; Macdonald, 1953, 1967; Putnam, 1938; Tomkeieff, 1940; Walker and Blake, 1966; Washington, 1922; Waters, 1960; Wentworth and Macdonald, 1953.

6

Volcanic Domes

Lava that is very viscous flows with such difficulty that it tends to pile up, forming a steep-sided hill directly over and around the vent (Plate 6-1). Such hills are known as *domes,* or *tholoids.* The term dome is used in geology also for other types of structures, particularly that resulting from the up-bending of sedimentary strata into a form resembling an overturned bowl (such as the once-famous Teapot Dome in Wyoming). It has also been used for broad dome-shaped volcanic mountains built of successive lava flows, such as the great turtle-backed mountains of Hawaii. These, called by R. A. Daly (1911, 1968) "exogenous lava domes," are now generally known as shield volcanoes (see Chapter 11). In volcanology, the term dome is now usually reserved for the steep-sided heaps of viscous lava formed over vents, and context generally serves to distinguish these from the domes of sedi-mentary strata. If any uncertainty of meaning exists, the accumulations of viscous lava may be referred to as *volcanic domes, bulbous domes,* or *cumulo-domes.*

Some domes result from the bodily upheaval of the filling of the upper part of a pipe-like volcanic conduit, the semisolid to solid material being pushed up like a cork from the neck of a bottle. These are true *plug domes,* also known as *belonites.* However, by far the greater number of domes result from actual outpourings of very viscous lava. The heap may grow by addi-

PLATE 6-1. Obsidian dome south of South Sister, in the Cascade Range of Oregon. Note the jagged summit, and the taluses of crumble breccia. Photo by G. A. Macdonald.

tion of lava either internally or externally. Some domes form by extrusion of viscous lava through an opening near their crest, the growth taking place by the piling up of one short flow over another. More commonly, however, new lava being squeezed up through the vent simply distends the mass above it, so that the growth is somewhat like that of an expanding balloon. But the amount of stretching that the cooling outer part of the growing dome can sustain without rupturing is limited. The shell of the dome is literally torn open, and lava oozes out through the ruptures forming flows that trickle for varying distances down the side of the dome. Most domes form in this last manner, by a combination of internal and external growth, but the internal accession of lava usually greatly predominates.

The degree to which the edges of a growing dome spread out from the margin of the vent depends on the viscosity of the liquid. Some spread very little. Others spread out to several times their height, and they grade into the short, thick lava flows described on an earlier page. Occasionally, part of a growing dome breaks away and forms a short lava flow (Fig. 6-1).

In ground plan most domes are more or less circular, or very short ovals. More rarely, they are elongate as a result of extrusion of lava through

FIGURE 6-1. Schematic cross sections of domes, showing flow lines and brecciated margins (stippled). The arrows indicate the direction of lava movement. (A) Dome built on a nearly horizontal surface. (B) The top of the dome has sagged due to drainage of magma back into the vent and to slight spreading of the dome. (C) Dome built on a sloping surface. (D) Summit of the dome broken by faults due to down-slope movement of the main mass of the dome. (Modified after van Bemmelen, 1949 and 1970.)

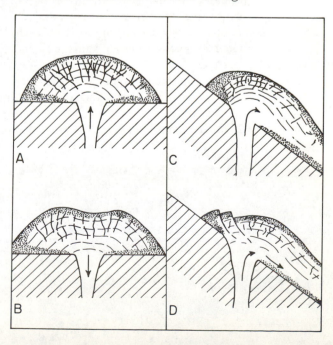

PLATE 6-2. Chaos Crags, a series of dacite domes just north of Lassen Peak, California. The left-hand dome partly buried a slightly earlier ash cone. Crater Peak and Burney Mountain, composite volcanoes in the Cascade Range, lie in the background. U. S. Geological Survey photo by G. A. Macdonald.

a long fissure vent. The mass of rhyolite in Pinnacles National Monument, California, has been described as an elongate dome some 6 miles long and a mile or so wide. However, extrusion of the mass took place mostly at certain points along the fissure, where the outflow was more abundant than elsewhere, so that in a sense the mass can be considered as a row of coalescing domes rather than a single long dome. Where extrusion is even more concentrated at certain centers, there results a row of clearly separated and independent domes, sometimes with overlapping bases. The domes in such a row may grow simultaneously, but more commonly extrusion progresses from point to point along the fissure, and the domes in the row grow successively rather than simultaneously. Rows of domes of this sort are seen, for instance, at the summit of Mt. Merapi in Java, at the Chaos Crags just north of Mt. Lassen in California (Plate 6-2), and on the Snaefells Peninsula in Iceland. At this latter locality domes of pale colored rhyolite are strikingly contrasted with black flows of basalt. This close relationship of rhyolite and basalt was recognized in the 1840s by R. W. von Bunsen, the famous German chemist known to every student of chemistry as the inventor of the Bunsen burner.

The size of domes varies greatly. Some have been described that are only a few yards across and a few feet high. Lassen Peak in California, one of the largest domes on record, is more than a mile across at the base and 2,000 feet high (Plate 6-3). Most domes are broader than they are high.

PLATE 6-3. Lassen Peak, from the west, showing the small lava flow that spilled westward out of the crater in the top of the dome in 1915. The sides of the dome are mantled with crumble breccia and tephra. U. S. Geological Survey photo by G. A. Macdonald.

As might be expected from the viscous character of the lava that forms them, most domes are of acid composition. Commonest are domes of rhyolite, dacite, and trachyte. Domes of andesite are far less common, and domes of basalt are rare.

The classic example of the actual observation of the growth of domes took place in 1866 at Santorin Volcano in the islands southeast of Greece. The activity was described in detail by F. Fouqué (1879), from his own observations and those of others. On February 4 a new island appeared in the submerged crater (caldera) of Santorin amid clouds of steam and boiling water. It consisted of a heap of lava blocks bearing on its surface debris from the bay floor, including dried mud, mollusk shells, and fragments of a sunken boat. The surface was so cool that the pieces of wood were not ignited, and it was possible to land on the island and walk across it, though at night the bright orange glow of incandescent lava was visible through cracks in the broken crust of the dome. The island continued to grow, and by February 7 it was 200 feet across and 100 feet high. Fouqué tells us that the growth of the heap was silent without any explosion or earthquake shocks. The expansion was from within outward, the blocks on the surface seeming to move constantly outward from the center toward the periphery. The lower slopes were covered with loose cooled blocks.

On February 15 a second dome appeared from the sea alongside the first one. Its growth was very similar, except that there were occasional mild explosions that threw up showers of cinder (see Chapter 7). In late February explosions blew away part of the top of the first dome, scattering blocks over it and the adjacent younger dome, but the first dome continued to grow. From his observation point on the surface of the growing dome, Fouqué could hear all around him the incessant cracking of the cooling and shrinking rock and a rattling resembling that of falling fragments of porcelain caused by the tumbling down of loosened blocks of glassy rock. Banks of loose rock fragments were being formed by the accumulation of the fallen blocks around the edge of the dome. Still a third dome appeared on March 10 and, by March 13, had joined itself to the second dome. Activity continued until October, 1870, by which time the first dome was a truncated cone with a nearly flat irregular top 400 feet above sea level with sides consisting of talus slopes of loose angular blocks.

The banks of loose rock fragments observed by Fouqué surrounding the domes of Santorin are very characteristic features of most domes. They are the result of fracturing of the crust of the dome by stretching as the dome expands and the stresses set up in the rock as it contracts on cooling. The resulting angular blocks are pushed and jostled by the movement of the growing dome, and on the edges of the dome many of them break free and roll down to come to rest against the base (Plate 6-1). The heap of fragments formed in this way is known as a *crumble breccia*. The breccia commonly extends far up the sides of the dome, sometimes practically to its summit, giving the dome a conical form (Plates 6-4A and 6-4B) even though the central massive portion of the dome is more nearly a vertical-sided

PLATE 6-4A. The fuming dome of Didicas Volcano, north of Luzon Island, Philippines, June 17, 1952. Note the craggy summit of the dome and the long banks of crumble breccia. Official photograph, U. S. Navy.

PLATE 6-4B. The dome of Goriachaia Sopka, Shimushir Island, Kuriles, with the prehistoric composite cone of Milne Volcano in the background. Note the long banks of crumble breccia nearly burying the solid core of the dome. Photo by G. S. Gorshkov, Kamchatka Volcano Station, U.S.S.R.

cylinder. Crumble breccia commonly is quite massive, but it sometimes shows a suggestion of bedding parallel to the surface of the heap. The appearance of bedding may result wholly from the crude parallel orientation of elongate fragments. More rarely there is a crude stratification in which layers formed predominantly of small fragments alternate with others in which larger fragments are more abundant. Occasionally, layers of ash are found, which accumulates on the surface of the growing mass of fragments due to explosions during the dome growth.

Even better studied than the Santorin domes were the domes that grew in the crater of Mt. Pelée on the island of Martinique in 1902 and 1929. The growth of the dome of 1902 was observed by several American and British volcanologists, but by far the most complete study was by the French volcanologist, A. Lacroix. The eruption is described in Chapter 8, and only a few features of the dome will be mentioned here. The dome probably started to grow early in May. On May 21 it was seen by T. A. Jaggar to be a rounded heap of boulders not more than 400 feet high separated from the crater walls by a deep moat. The dome continued to grow through June, and early in July Jaggar observed a new feature.

> On the summit of the cone [dome] was seen a most extraordinary monolith, shaped like the dorsal fin of a shark, with a steep and almost overhanging escarpment on the east, while the western aspect of the spine was curved and smooth in profile. The field glass showed jagged surfaces on the steeper eastern side, and long smooth striated slopes on the western. Other horn-like projections from the cone could be discerned with difficulty on its slopes lower down. (Jaggar, 1904, p. 36.)

Projections of this sort are very common on volcanic domes (Plate 6-5), and are known as *spines*.

Many domes fairly bristle with spines of all sizes, from a few feet to hundreds of feet high. The spines are formed by the squeezing out of viscous magma from within through ruptures in the solid to semisolid shell of the dome, the magma solidifying as it is extruded like wire being squeezed out through a die. Some spines continue to be extruded for only a few hours, but others continue to grow for many months. The largest spine on record was formed later during the same eruption of Mt. Pelée. After a period of growth of about 9 months, it had reached a height of nearly 1,000 feet above the top of the dome. It repeatedly crumbled away during its growth, and Lacroix has estimated that without this loss of material it would have had an ultimate height of 2,800 feet!

Commonly, spines are angular in cross section during early stages of their growth, becoming more and more rounded as time goes on due to wearing away of the sides of the aperture through which they are being extruded. Like the earlier spine described by Jaggar, the great spine of Pelée had one nearly vertical straight face and on the opposite side a curved face that was polished and striated by upward movement through the solid carapace of the dome (Fig. 6-2). The "shark-fin" or horn-like form has been observed on many other spines, including one that developed on a dome at Bogoslof Island north of the Aleutians in 1906. Like most spines, the great spine of Pelée was short lived. By September, 1903, it had crumbled down to a heap of blocks. The destruction was due partly to collapse resulting from undermining of the spine by explosions around its base, and partly to strains set up in cooling. The block-littered surface of the dome is partly the result of the disintegration of spines.

The speed of growth of domes varies greatly. The dome of Mt. Pelée reached a maximum rate of rise of as much as 78 feet per day in August, 1903. By September, 1903, its height was approximately 1,000 feet, and its diameter at the base was about 3,000 feet. It had attained a volume of approximately 120 million cubic yards in 17 months of growth. Howel Williams (1932, p. 142) has estimated that even the huge dome of Lassen Peak may have been built within about 5 years.

Thus, volcanic domes rise under a continuously shifting cover of blocks, formed by breaking up of the crust due to movement, the collapse of

PLATE 6-5. Metcalf Dome, on Bogoslof Volcano, Alaska, in August 1907. Note the spiny central mass of the dome and the growing embankments of crumble breccia. Photo by T. A. Jaggar, Massachusetts Institute of Technology.

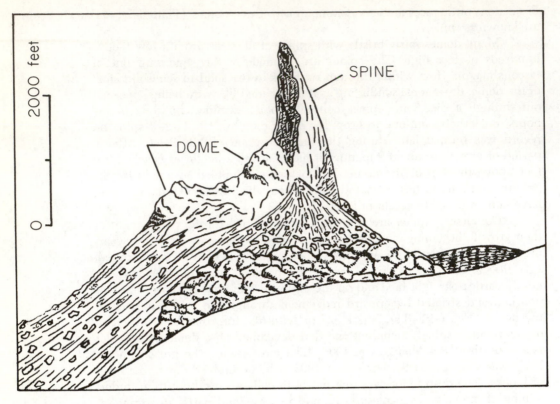

FIGURE 6-2. Sketch of the dome and great spine of Mt. Pelée during April 1903. (Redrawn after Lacroix, 1904.)

spines, and occasional explosive disruption of the dome surface. Blocks tumble down the sides and form growing banks that gradually encroach on the dome and in the end may nearly bury it. Magma welling up between the blocks may weld them together into a solid mass of breccia, and occasionally thin lava flows are interbedded with the layers of debris.

Explosions on the dome at Santorin have already been mentioned. They are quite common on other domes also. Some of them take place at the summit of the dome and may blast out a crater in it. Previous to the eruption of 1914, the dome of Lassen Peak had at its summit a crater about 200 feet long, 75 feet wide, and 50 feet deep, blasted out by an explosion. It is possible, however, that the explosion was considerably later than the formation of the dome. The dome of Ko-Usu at Usu Volcano in Japan also has a summit crater 200 feet across and 100 feet deep. At Cross Hill on Ascension Island, a dome of trachyte rose into the crater of an older basaltic cinder cone, and at a later date a channelway was burst through the dome and its surface was buried by basaltic cinder and ash.

Possibly the commonest explosions occur around the base of the dome and around spines on the dome. The surfaces of separation between the dome and the surrounding rocks, and between the spine and the crust of the dome, constitute zones of weakness that allow gases to escape from below and within the dome. In studying the dome that formed at Santorin in 1925 (named Fouqué Kameni after the pioneer student of domes), H. S. Washington observed jets of gas issuing around the base of the dome like the spikes of a crown, and to these he gave the name "coronet explosions." Explosions of this sort often cause the collapse of a spine above them and undermine the side of the dome, allowing it also to collapse and add to the mass of crumble breccia. Some 300 to 600 years ago, explosions at the base of the Chaos Crags domes (Plate 6-2) just north of Lassen Peak resulted in collapse of part of the domes, forming great rock avalanches that rushed 3½ miles down the valley and as much as 300 feet up the opposite mountain slope. The blocky deposit left by the avalanches is known as the Chaos Jumbles.

Some domes have an internal structure consisting of a series of concentric layers like the shells of an onion (Fig. 6-3A). These appear to result from gradual expansion from within of a mass of somewhat non-homogeneous magma. Much more commonly, however, domes are either essentially structureless except for the gradual inward passage from a much-brecciated outer part to a massive interior, or show a divergent structure, fan-like in cross section with the ribs of the fan radiating upward from the vent. The structure is shown by aligned phenocrysts and layers of varying

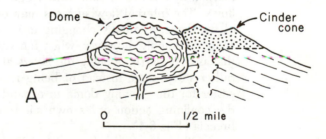

A

0   1/2 mile

FIGURE 6-3. (A) Cross section of the dacite dome of Raker Peak, Lassen Volcanic National Park, California, showing concentric structure in the dome. (After Williams, 1932; originally published by the University of California Press; reprinted by permission of The Regents of the University of California.) (B) Cross section of the lower edge of the Novarupta dome, Valley of Ten Thousand Smokes, Alaska, showing fan structure in the shattered rock of the dome. (After Fenner, 1923.)

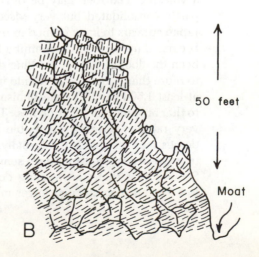

50 feet

Moat

B

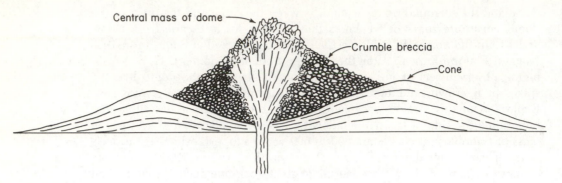

Central mass of dome

Crumble breccia

Cone

FIGURE 6-4. Cross section of a typical endogenous dome, showing steep
fan structure developed within the confining wall of crumble breccia.

composition or vesicularity drawn out by differential flowage (in the same
way a drop of ink is drawn out into a long colored streak in flowing water),
and by joints resulting from shearing of the magma when it had become too
viscous to flow. The fan structure is, of course, simply a two-dimensional
cross section of a series of nested cones with their points downward. The
cone-shaped joints are sometimes expressed on the upper surface of the
dome by concentric fractures from which, while the dome is active, issue
jets of vapor and occasional explosions. The surface of the dome is often
marked by a series of concentric ridges resembling the ridges on block lava
flows. The internal flow surfaces may be nearly horizontal around the base
of the dome, gradually changing to verticality near the center (Fig. 6-3B).
More commonly, however, when fan structure is present it resembles a fan
that is only partly opened, the layers at the outer edge sloping inward at a
rather steep angle instead of being nearly horizontal. It appears that it is
easier for the growing dome to expand upward than sideways, because of
the confining action of its own shell and the increasing heap of crumble
breccia (Fig. 6-4).

Plug domes are formed by the pushing up of a cylindrical mass of
rock that occupied the crater or the upper portion of the feeding conduit of
a volcano. The rock may be old and long consolidated, or it may be only
partly consolidated but very viscous. The O-Usu dome at Usu Volcano in
Japan appears to have formed in that way, being pushed up nearly 1,000 feet.
It carried upward on its summit a layer of sand and gravel that had formerly
been the floor of the crater. Plug domes range in size from a few tens of feet
to more than a quarter of a mile in horizontal diameter, and in height up to
at least 1,500 feet. The mechanism of their formation is essentially identical
to that of spines on other domes. The edges of plug domes generally crumble
very rapidly, forming a crumble breccia. Like other types of domes, plug
domes may be massive internally, or may show onion-like structure or an
upward-diverging structure resembling in cross section a nearly closed fan.
Some domes that start as plug domes later change into ordinary domes as
less viscous magma from lower in the conduit reaches the surface.

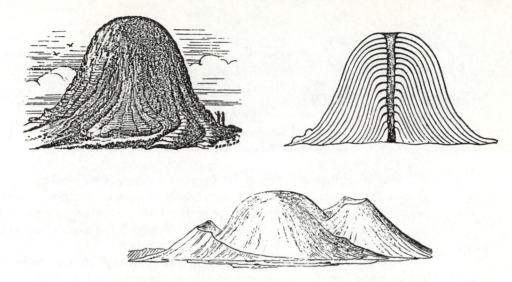

FIGURE 6-5. (A) A small exogenous dome (mammelon) on the summit of Bourbon Volcano, near Madagascar. (After Bory de St. Vincent.) (B) Hypothetical cross section of the dome shown in (A). (C) Sketch of the Grand Sarcoui dome, lying between the cinder cones of Puy de la Goutte and Little Sarcoui in the Auvergne region of central France. (From Scrope, 1862.)

Domes that form by repeated overflows of very viscous lava from a vent in their summit are known as *exogenous* domes, in contrast to *endogenous* domes formed by expansion from within. They are comparatively rare. Small ones, 80 to 100 feet high, were seen forming on Bourbon Volcano in the Indian Ocean by the pioneer geologist, Bory de St. Vincent, early in the nineteenth century (Fig. 6-5A and B). A much larger example is the Grand Sarcoui dome in the Auvergne region of central France. This bell-shaped mass is 800 feet high with a basal diameter of 2,500 feet and sides that in places slope as steeply as 80° (Fig. 6-5C). Of the formation of such domes as the Grand Sarcoui, Scrope (1862, p. 133) writes:

> One layer of the pasty mass may be supposed to have overlapped another as it welled up from the vent, so as to form . . . a series of rudely concentric beds dipping outwardly on all sides . . . . The small hummocks . . . upon the summit of the volcano Bourbon which Bory de St. Vincent watched in the act of formation by the welling-up of highly viscous matter at a white heat, and its consolidation as it guttered down the outside of the hill it had itself raised in irregular coatings may . . . be looked upon as types of the mode of production of the larger trachytic domes and hummocks likewise.

Williams (1932, p. 116) points out the smoothness of these exogenous domes as compared to the endogenous domes (described on an earlier page), but suggests that many of them may have originated through the

PLATE 6-6. Panum Crater, a rhyolite obsidian dome in the crater of a pumice cone at the north end of the Mono Craters, California. Mono Lake and the Sierra Nevada are in the background. Hawaii Institute of Geophysics photo by G. A. Macdonald.

burying of endogenous domes by lava outwellings at the summit of the dome. This is supported at the Grand Sarcoui by the occurrence in quarries on its flank of breccia that he regards as the crumble breccia of the earlier endogenous dome. Probably few, if any, large domes are wholly exogenous.

Domes may grow in the craters of older cones (Plate 6-6) or on their flanks, and a few develop independently of older volcanic edifices.

Occasionally, domes do not quite break through to the surface of the earth, but instead heave up the overlying beds of older rock. These are actually shallow intrusive bodies of the sort known as *laccoliths* (Chapter 15). In the San Francisco Mts. of Arizona, laccoliths of this sort finally ruptured their covers and produced surficial lava flows. At other times, when the magma finally breaks through, it forms a typical dome on the surface. A good example is furnished by the 1943 eruption of Usu Volcano near the southern end of Hokkaido Island in Japan.

Usu is situated at the southern edge of Lake Toya, which occupies a broad sunken crater or caldera (see Chapter 12). It had erupted in 1910, but for more than 30 years it had lain quiet. Then, in late 1943, earthquakes began to be felt near its eastern base. Japan was at war, and no large-scale scientific expedition could be put in the field, but scientists from several institutions paid it occasional visits. Most remarkable, however, was the record kept by a village postmaster, Masao Mimatsu. The volcano was visible from his postoffice window, and throughout the eruption he kept track of the growth of the new volcanic structure by means of notes accompanying a series of more than 120 sketches made on the paper covering of the window. A detailed report on the eruption, making use of the information gathered by Mimatsu as well as much more, was issued after the war by Japan's present dean of volcanologists, Prof. Takeshi Minakami, and his associates (1951).

The first earthquake of the preeruption series was felt on December 28, 1943, and it was followed by many more during the next few days. By the end of January 1, 1944, more than 500 earthquakes had been counted at Toya Hot Springs, and no doubt far more of them were too small to be felt. Quakes continued in increasing number and intensity. At first they were felt most strongly at the northwestern base of the mountain, but after January 6 they were strongest at the eastern base. Past the eastern base of Usu the Sobetsu River flows southward, and parallel to it ran irrigation canals, roads, and the railroad. Late in January the ground surface near the south base of the volcano began to rise. Cracks appeared in the roads and the banks of the canals, and the water began to flow less rapidly through the canals. Wells and springs in the rising area dried up, while those in nearby areas flowed more abundantly. By early April the rising area was roughly circular and about 2.4 miles across, and its central part had gone up 53 feet. Then the center of the uplift suddenly shifted half a mile northward with its summit very close to the village of Fukaba. In mid-June more than 100 severe earthquakes were being felt each day in Fukaba, and on June 22 the number reached 250. The ground surface had by then gone up about 150 feet. The villagers of Fukaba were very literally being taken for a ride!

Then, at about 8:30 A.M. on June 23, a column of "smoke" was seen rising quietly from a cornfield. The "smoke" appears to have been a cloud of steam. The outflow of steam on June 23 increased gradually in strength, and at 10 A.M. an explosion hurled out mud and sand and blocks of rock, creating a crater about 150 feet across. A stream of mud flowed out of the crater and formed a steaming pool in a nearby hollow. More explosions occurred every few seconds for several hours. Then, after a few hours of quiet, steam again began to rise, followed by another series of explosions. Similar series of explosions continued at short intervals through the next 3 months, some of the explosions throwing blocks of rock half a mile into the air. Other craters formed near the first one.

On July 2 a violent explosion hurled out about 2 million long tons of debris, mostly dust (ash) resulting from the pulverization of older rocks. The falling ash did much damage to forests and cultivated fields. Another big explosion occurred on July 3, and the villagers of Fukaba finally abandoned their homes.

By late September seven separate craters had been formed in a group 2,000 feet west of Fukaba, the earliest craters being partly buried by the material thrown out from the later ones. Avalanches of ash rushed down the mountain slope but were not hot enough to set wooden houses on fire. By late October the upheaved area formed a dome-shaped mountain half a mile across. Its flat top was formed wholly of old rocks, but the old ground surface had been lifted 460 to 560 feet above its former level. A similar dome-shaped upheaval formed during the eruption of 1910 had been named Sin-zan, or "roof mountain," and this new one was now called Showa Sin-zan—"New Roof Mountain." The Sobetsu River had been dammed by the rising ground and had formed a lake half a mile long. But in spite of the upheaval and the numerous explosions, no new lava had appeared. The explosions were all of the type known as *phreatic*—steam explosions formed by heating of the groundwater in rocks near the surface.

At last, early in November, a smaller upheaval began to poke up from the top of the larger one just to one side of the group of explosion craters. This new hill was formed of new incandescent lava with such high viscosity (10^{24} poises) that it was almost solid. It gradually grew

PLATE 6-7. Dome of Showa Sin-Zan, Usu Volcano, Hokkaido, Japan. Photo by T. Minakami, Earthquake Research Institute, University of Tokyo.

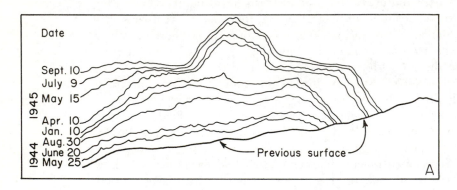

FIGURE 6-6. (A) Successive profiles of the Showa Sin-zan dome at Usu Volcano, Japan, from the north. (After Minakami, Ishikawa, and Yagi, 1951.) (B) Sketch of the Showa Sin-zan dome, seen from the north, October 15, 1948. (Drawn from a photograph in Minakami, Ishikawa, and Yagi, 1951.)

120

in height and diameter, but it carried up on its top a cap of older rock, including stream gravel that had once laid on the nearly level surface west of Fukaba village. The temperature of the new rock was at least 1,000°C, and the heat baked the clay of the old rocks in the cap to natural brick. Growth of the small dome (Plate 6-7) finally came to an end about October 1, 1945, with its summit about 330 feet above the top of the New Roof Mountain and nearly 1,000 feet above the original level of the ground.

The events of the eruption can be explained by intrusion of very viscous magma at a shallow depth beneath the nearly level plain at the eastern base of Mt. Usu. The intrusion bowed up the layers of older rock above it and elevated their surface into the domical New Roof Mountain. Water in the older rocks was heated by the heat of the magma and transformed into steam, which burst out at the surface in phreatic explosions, throwing out fragments of the old rocks. Water pouring from the craters formed by the explosions carried with it partly decomposed old rock material to form flows of mud, and steam clouds laden with hot powdered rock rolled down the slope as hot avalanches. Finally, at a point near the top of the upheaval, the magma broke through to the surface and slowly protruded upward, carrying older rock on its surface, to form a small steep-sided volcanic dome.

The changes in profile of the growing structure are well seen in Mimatsu's sketches (Fig. 6-6A), and the general form of the structure is shown in Fig. 6-6B.

SUGGESTED ADDITIONAL READING

Jaggar, 1904; Jaggar, 1908; Lacroix, 1904, p. 110–162; Minakami, Ishikawa, and Yagi, 1951; Perret, 1935, p. 106–120; Williams, 1929; Williams, 1932.

7

Products of Explosion

Fragments of rock thrown out by volcanic explosions are called *ejecta* (singular: ejectum), and accumulations of such fragments are known as *pyroclastic* ("fire-broken") *rocks*. Long ago, Aristotle used the term *tephra* for this material, and the term has recently been revived by the Icelandic volcanologist, Sigurdur Thorarinsson (1951). Its brevity makes it preferable to the cumbersome phrases "pyroclastic rocks" or "pyroclastic materials," especially where their frequent repetition is necessary.

Volcanic explosions range in intensity from the weak spattering that commonly accompanies the eruption of very fluid basaltic lava to cataclysmic blasts that throw debris many miles up into the atmosphere. The usual concept of an explosion is a sudden violent outburst of very short duration—essentially a single brief impulse, like the explosion that hurls the projectile from a gun. Some volcanic explosions are like that, but many are of longer duration—continuous blasts of outrushing gas that continue for several seconds or minutes, or even hours. The middle part of the great eruption of Vesuvius in 1906 was a tremendous outrushing of gas in a column a quarter of a mile in diameter and reaching 8 miles above the mountaintop that continued uninterrupted for some 12 hours. It was less like the explosion of a gun, or even a relatively slow quarry blast, than it was like the blowing off of steam from a boiler or the long-continued blast from a rocket. The

Vesuvius example is an extreme one, but most big volcanic explosions are continuing blasts of appreciable duration.

Instantaneous or long-continued, weak or violent, all volcanic explosions are the result of escape of gas that has been confined under pressure. The gas responsible for some explosions originates within the magma, separating from it as described in Chapter 4. This is *magmatic gas,* and the explosions caused by it are *magmatic explosions.* Other gas originates outside the magma, primarily by the transformation of water into steam. These *hydroexplosions* result from the sudden generation of steam where water comes in contact with hot rock or magma, as when molten lava rises through water-saturated rocks or is extruded into a lake or the ocean. The type of hydroexplosion resulting from transformation into steam of groundwater in near-surface rocks is known as a *phreatic explosion* (after the Greek word meaning a well). Explosions resulting from both magmatic gas and extraneous steam are called *hydromagmatic* or *phreatomagmatic.* Different sorts of explosions produce somewhat different types of ejecta.

Volcanic ejecta may be classified by general composition, by origin, by size, by condition at the time of ejection and at the time of striking the ground, and by the degree of consolidation of the deposit formed by accumulation of the ejecta. The different bases of classification are useful for different purposes.

Considering them first from the standpoint of origin, we find that ejecta may be derived from the molten magma itself (magmatic ejecta), or from rock that was already solid (nonmagmatic ejecta). The latter may have already solidified from magma of the same eruption, or they may be related rocks of the same volcano but formed in earlier eruptions, or still older rocks derived from the crust underlying the volcano and totally unrelated to it except by the accident of location. The names that are in most common use for these various classes of fragments were proposed by H. J. Johnston-Lavis in 1885. *Essential ejecta* are derived directly from the molten magma of the same eruption. Essential ejecta may be magmatic or they may be fragments of already solidified parts of the magma, such as a crust formed on a mass of lava in the crater of the volcano. Since magmatic ejecta are thrown out in a molten condition and cooled rapidly in the air or on the surface of the ground, they are partly or entirely glassy (*vitreous,* or *vitric*). The nonmagmatic essential ejecta also are usually at least partly glassy. *Accessory ejecta* are fragments of older rocks that were formed by the same volcano during previous eruptions. Most commonly they are bits of older lavas that are partly or wholly crystallized, but with fine grain. They have a stony appearance and are said to be *lithic* (Plate 7-1). Occasionally, accessory ejecta are coarse grained, resembling moderately deep-seated intrusive rocks except that they are often somewhat open textured with open spaces between the grains. These coarse fragments represent parts of the magma that crystallized at depth, in part as minor intrusions within the body of the volcano, and perhaps in part on the outer edge of the magma reservoir. They may be torn from

PLATE 7-1 Lithic explosion debris (top) resting on well bedded vitric magmatic ash, Kilauea Volcano. The lithic ejecta were thrown out by phreatic explosions; the vitric ash was formed by lava fountains of Hawaiian-type eruptions. Hawaii Institute of Geophysics photo by G. A. Macdonald.

the walls of the conduit by the outrushing gas, or they may be carried upward in the rising magma and blown free of it by the explosion. Fragments of nonvolcanic rocks or of volcanic rocks formed during periods of volcanic activity preceding the birth of the volcano from which they were ejected, torn from the basement beneath the volcano, are *accidental ejecta*.

The most important classification of tephra is that based on the size of the fragments. The fragments larger than $2\frac{1}{2}$ inches in average diameter are further subdivided on the basis of their shape, which reflects their physical condition at the time they were ejected. The general classification of tephra is given in Table 7-1. It should immediately be emphasized, however, that the size limits of the various types of ejecta are completely arbitrary. There is complete gradation from one size group to another, and there is no genetic significance to the boundary selected. Furthermore,

TABLE 7-1. Classification of tephra

SIZE OF FRAGMENTS (average diameter)	SHAPE OF FRAGMENTS	CONDITION ON EJECTION	NAMES	
			Individual fragments	*Accumulations of fragments*
Greater than about $2\frac{1}{2}$ inches	Round to subangular	Plastic	Bombs	Agglomerate
	Angular	Solid	Blocks	Breccia
About $2\frac{1}{2}$ inches to $\frac{1}{10}$ inch	Round to angular	Liquid or solid	Lapilli	Lapilli agglomerate or lapilli breccia
Less than about $\frac{1}{10}$ inch	Generally angular, but may be round	Liquid or solid	Ash	Ash when unconsolidated, tuff when consolidated

124

the usage in the past has been far from uniform. The sizes given in the table are the most recent ones suggested [R. V. Fisher (1961)].

Bombs (Plate 7-2) are defined as ejecta larger than 64 millimeters (approximately $2\frac{1}{2}$ inches) in average diameter that were thrown out in molten condition. Because of the fluidity of the fragments, their shapes were somewhat modified during their flight through the air. Highly to moderately fluid magma is ejected both as long irregular strings and as discrete blebs of liquid. The strings commonly break up into short segments during flight. Segments that fall to the ground intact are known as *cylindrical* or *ribbon bombs* (Plate 7-2 and 7-7). They are more or less circular or flattened in cross section and typically show pronounced longitudinal flutings (Fig. 7-1). Ribbon bombs may still be very plastic when they strike the ground, and often they are much twisted (Plate 7-2). The thicker portions of the ribbons often separate from the rest during flight, and both these and the masses that were ejected originally as separate blebs tend to be pulled into spheres by the surface tension of the liquid. As a result, there may be formed *spherical bombs* (Plate 7-3); but more

PLATE 7-2. Volcanic bombs and a block. In the left foreground is a cow-dung bomb, seen from above. Behind it is a fragment of a ribbon bomb, and in the rear is a bipolar fusiform ("spindle") bomb with its rough lee side up. In the center is a unipolar fusiform bomb, in front of it are three small fusiform bombs, and at the right is a block ejected during a phreatic explosion. The cow-dung bomb and the block are from Kilauea, the other bombs are from Mauna Kea, Hawaii. Hawaii Institute of Geophysics photo by G. A. Macdonald.

FIGURE 7-1. Sketches of volcanic bombs. (A) Bipolar fusiform bomb with stoss side down; (B) cross section of (A); (C) unipolar fusiform bomb; (D) almond-shaped bomb; (E) cross section of (D); (F) cross section of bomb with broad equatorial fin; (G) cylindrical ribbon bomb; (H) cross section of (G); (J) cross section of cow-dung bomb; (K) cow-dung bomb. (From Macdonald, 1967.)

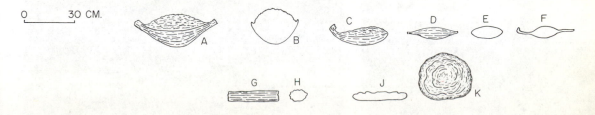

PLATE 7-3 Nearly spherical bomb at the foot of Cinder Cone, Lassen Volcanic National Park, California. U. S. Geological Survey photo by G. A. Macdonald.

commonly the attainment of spherical shape is only partial and the bomb is shaped like a sweet potato, or an almond, or the spindle of an old-fashioned spinning wheel. These are often referred to as *spindle bombs* or *rotational bombs*, and it was formerly believed that they owed their shape to spinning in the air. Actually, however, the amount of spinning is very small—generally only enough to give the bomb a slight twist. In an effort to escape the implication of spinning, C. K. Wentworth and I have suggested that they be called *fusiform bombs*. Typical shapes of fusiform bombs are shown in Figure 7-1 and Plate 7-2, 7-4, and 7-5. They generally show longitudinal fluting, and one side is smoother and slightly broader than the other. The smooth, or "stoss," side is the one that was on the front as the bomb fell through the air. Frictional resistance of the air commonly has dragged the still-plastic skin of the bomb toward the back, or "lee," side, and often has formed a thin projecting rim along the edge of the stoss side. Most fusiform bombs have prominent projections, generally twisted, at one or both ends. These "ears" are simply the remaining stumps of the broken-off ribbon.

Although fusiform bombs are generally regarded as the typical bombs, and illustrated in most textbooks, they actually constitute only a very small portion of the bombs formed during most eruptions. By far the greater number of bombs are simply irregular, and generally very vesicular, lumps known as *cinder* or *scoria*. Fusiform bombs may be entirely absent, and when they are present are commonly concentrated in the deposits formed at the very end of the eruption. They are denser

PLATE 7-4. Regular fusiform bomb, Haleakala Volcano, Hawaii. Hawaii Institute of Geophysics photo by G. A. Macdonald.

PLATE 7-5. Irregular fusiform bomb, Haleakala, Hawaii. Hawaii Institute of Geophysics photo by G. A. Macdonald.

than the cinder and form during a stage when the amount of gas in the magma has started to decrease.

Practically all bombs are at least somewhat vesicular, and in cross section they often show concentric layers of greater and lesser vesicularity (Plate 7-6). Bombs with a large hole in the center are rare; and still rarer are the "explosive bombs" that burst explosively, due to the pressure of contained gases, after they have struck the ground or, perhaps, sometimes in the air. Exceedingly vesicular cinder, so light that it will float on water, is *pumice*. In rhyolite, rhyodacite, and dacite pumice, the vesicles typically are much stretched out into long very thin tubes, giving the material a rather silky appearance; but in other pumices the vesicles are more equidimensional. Basaltic pumice is far less abundant than that of more siliceous composition, but it is formed in Hawaii both as pyroclastic fragments and as a thin layer of froth on the surface of some lava flows. It is often extremely vesicular, consisting only of thin glass threads that mark the intersections of the vesicles. This extremely vesicular pumice, also known as "thread-lace scoria" and "reticulite," is the lightest rock known on earth, with a specific gravity of as little as 0.3. Paradoxically, although rhyolitic pumice commonly will float for months and has been known to drift as much as 4,000 miles across the ocean, the still lighter basaltic pumice generally sinks almost immediately. The vesicles are so freely interconnected that the material quickly becomes waterlogged.

Some bombs have a more or less spherical center with a thin disk-like equatorial fin (Fig. 7-1F), and in others the central swelling is absent and only the disk is left, usually bent up at the edges and resembling a saucer or bowl. The variation in forms of bombs is enormous. H. Tsuya (1939) has described and named 14 different types from the slopes of Mt. Fuji alone, but there seems little point in carrying the classification to such great detail. Only a few special forms are mentioned here.

Many bombs are formed around a core of solid older rock. Some of the cores are accessory or accidental fragments, and some are bits of lava

PLATE 7-6. Cross sections of fusiform bombs, Mauna Kea, Hawaii. Hawaii Institute of Geophysics photo by G. A. Macdonald.

formed earlier during the same eruption. Very commonly, chunks of cinder fall back into the pool of molten lava in the erupting vent and become wrapped up in the liquid and reejected as the centers of these *cored bombs*. Sometimes the cores are coarse-grained fragments brought up from depth. During the 1801 eruption of Hualalai Volcano in Hawaii, thousands of fragments of bright green dunite were rafted up in the rising magma, and bombs with dunite cores are common around the vent. They resemble candies with green fondant centers wrapped in dark brown or black chocolate coatings.

Bombs that are still liquid when they strike the ground flatten out (Plate 7-7) or even splash, typically forming an irregular roundish disk (Plate 7-2). These have been called "pancake" bombs, but far more descriptive is the term *cow-dung bomb* used by A. Lacroix. The formation of cow-dung bombs requires very fluid lava and projection to only a moderate height so that the bomb has not cooled to solidity during its flight. They are typical of the gentle eruptions of fluid basalt magma. Showers of still-fluid blebs striking the ground around the vent flatten out and mold themselves to the underlying surface, and frequently their still-plastic edges stick together. This accumulation of flattened and welded fragments is known as *spatter* (Plate 7-8), or, using a term coined by G. W. Tyrrell (1931), as *agglutinate*.

In contrast to spatter, the fragments of *cinder* produced by more explosive eruptions, often of less fluid magma, fall to the ground in an essentially solid condition. The cinder remains mostly unwelded, though it may later be cemented together by deposition of mineral matter from circulating water. All types of bombs, including cinder, are magmatic ejecta and are generally largely glassy.

At the other extreme from cow-dung bombs are those which are so viscous when they are ejected that they acquire very little rounding during their flight through the air. Commonly, however, although the outside of the bomb is nearly solid, the inside is still sufficiently plastic to expand as the gases in it escape and form vesicles. The result is that the skin becomes too small to fit the expanded center and is torn open, forming deep cracks resembling those that form on thick-crusted bread (Plate 7-9). These fragments are known as *bread-crust bombs*.

Masses of tephra containing a large proportion of bombs are called *agglomerate*. They generally form either in the throat of the volcano itself or on the flanks close to the vent.

Most bombs are less than a foot across, but bombs several feet across are not uncommon. Rather irregular spheroidal bombs 1 to 3 feet in diameter are common on the cone of Paricutin in Mexico, though many of them broke into angular fragments on striking the ground or while rolling down the side of the cone. (Commonly, bombs are much cracked internally due to stresses set up in cooling.) During particularly violent projections, some bombs as much as 10 inches in diameter fell as much as a mile from the base of the cone, and a few irregular elongate bombs more than 20 feet long were reported near the base of the cone. Very regular fusiform bombs 2 to 4 feet long are found on some of the cinder cones of Mauna Kea. Cow-dung bombs up to 4 feet across were plastered on rocks near the southern active vent of Stromboli in early 1965. Gorshkov (1970) records a bread-crust bomb with a volume of more than 130 cubic yards on the cone of Kozyrevskii Volcano in the Kuril Islands.

Blocks (Plate 7-2 and 7-10) are angular fragments greater than 64 millimeters ($2\frac{1}{2}$ inches) in diameter ejected in a solid condition. Some are

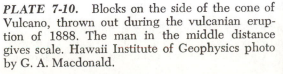

PLATE 7-9. Bread-crust bombs, formed during the eruption of 1888 at Vulcano, Italy. Hawaii Institute of Geophysics photo by G. A. Macdonald.

PLATE 7-10. Blocks on the side of the cone of Vulcano, thrown out during the vulcanian eruption of 1888. The man in the middle distance gives scale. Hawaii Institute of Geophysics photo by G. A. Macdonald.

PLATE 7-11. Block 40 feet across on the rim of the crater of Asama Volcano, Japan, thrown out by an explosive eruption in September 1950. Note the man sitting on the smaller fragment of the block. Photo by T. Minakami, Earthquake Research Institute, University of Tokyo.

many feet across (Plate 7-11). They may be bits of older rocks, either volcanic or nonvolcanic and either accessory or accidental, torn from the walls of the conduit or the roof of the magma chamber and carried up by the escaping gas. Accessory blocks often are fragments from the walls of the crater that have tumbled down into the vent either before or during the eruption. During the course of the eruption, individual explosions tend to core out the vent and steepen the lower walls of the crater, and between explosions the oversteepened crater walls collapse and fragments slide and roll into the vent to be hurled out by the next explosion.

Some blocks are essential, formed by disruption of the crust of a lava pool or dome that has formed in or over the vent during the eruption. Many of the blocks ejected by Vulcano (Plate 7-10) are of this sort. They may be entirely cold when they are thrown out, but commonly they are warm, and they may be incandescent. Generally, they are completely solid, but some are still slightly plastic, and all gradations are found into bombs that show appreciable rounding of the corners and pronounced bread-crust cracking.

Some blocks are fragments of older rocks that have been reheated by the proximity of magma or the passage of hot gases. These commonly show a cracking of the surface that somewhat resembles bread-crust cracking, but typically the cracks are narrower and more closely spaced. Gradations into typical bread-crust cracking do occur, however. Some bread-crusted blocks appear to have been formed in the same manner as bread-crust bombs, except that the vesiculation of the center has resulted from reheating.

Sometimes blocks are repeatedly tossed and rolled about in the vent, gradually having their corners knocked off and becoming more and more rounded. Some of these milled lava balls are nearly spherical and are easily mistaken for bombs, but careful examination usually shows that their surfaces have a hammered and pitted character that serves to distinguish them.

Accumulations of blocks are known as *breccia* (Plate 7-12). Because breccia is a general geological term for any rock composed of large angular

PLATE 7-12. Breccia filling a volcanic vent, Diamond Peak, Lassen Volcanic National Park, California. U. S. Geological Survey photo by G. A. Macdonald.

fragments, it is often desirable to specify those formed by volcanic explosion as *pyroclastic breccia* or *explosion breccia,* or by the type of eruption that produced it, as *vulcanian breccia* (Plate 7-13) or *phreatic breccia.* Pyroclastic breccias may be loose, or they may be made solid by later cementation.

Fragments between 64 and 2 millimeters (approximately $2\frac{1}{2}$ inches to $\frac{1}{10}$ inch) in average diameter are known as *lapilli.* (The singular form of lapilli is *lapillus,* derived from a Latin word meaning "little stone.") Lapilli may be essential, accessory, or accidental, ejected either in a liquid or a solid condition, and may show any of the forms shown by bombs or blocks. The most abundant fragments of cinder are usually of lapilli size. Very fluid lapilli may weld together to form spatter, or agglutinate. There is no consistency in the terminology applied to accumulations of lapilli. Fisher (1961) has suggested that consolidated masses of lapilli be called "lapillistone," but thus far the term has not been generally accepted. Perhaps it is best to call masses of rounded bomb-like lapilli, *lapilli agglomerate,* and those of angular lapilli, *lapilli breccia.*

A special form of lapilli consists of drops of lava that were ejected in very fluid condition and solidified in the air. These may be spherical or elongated rod-like bodies with rounded ends, but most typically they are drop-shaped (Plate 7-14). They are formed in large numbers during some Hawaiian eruptions, such as the Kilauea Iki eruption of 1959; and they have been named *Pele's tears,* after Pele, the legendary goddess of Hawaiian volcanoes. They are dark brown to black in color and are com-

PLATE 7-13. Breccia resulting from vulcanian explosions, exposed in a cut on highway 299 in northeastern California. U. S. Geological Survey photo by G. A. Macdonald.

PLATE 7-14. Pele's tears—more or less drop shaped basaltic lapilli, from Kilauea Volcano. The crescentic lapillus in the center is approximately one inch long. Photo by F. A. Perret. From Perret, 1950. Courtesy of Carnegie Institution.

PLATE 7-15. Pele's hair—natural spun glass, from Kilauea Volcano. Photo by F. A. Perret. (From Perret, 1950. Courtesy of Carnegie Institution.)

posed almost wholly of glass. Commonly, as each droplet is ejected by explosion through the surface of a pool of lava it trails behind it a thread of liquid. The thread is chilled in the air to a filament of golden brown to dark brown glass. These threads of natural spun glass (Plate 7-15), known as *Pele's hair,* may be drifted for many miles by the wind.

Tephra fragments less than 2 millimeters (about $\frac{1}{10}$th inch) in diameter are known as *ash.* This long-established term is somewhat misleading, and it should be emphasized that volcanic ash is in no sense a product of burning. It is simply pulverized rock material. Ash that is larger than $\frac{1}{16}$ millimeter (about $\frac{1}{400}$ inch) is coarse ash, and that smaller than $\frac{1}{16}$ millimeter is fine ash. The fragments may be essential, accessory, or accidental, and may be either solid or liquid when they are thrown out, though because of their small size the liquid ones cool and solidify very quickly. Accessory and accidental ash is stony in appearance and is said to be *lithic.* Essential ash formed by ejection of material in liquid condition is glassy, or *vitric.* Sometimes, when the magma contains numerous crystals, the solid bits may be blown free of the liquid to form *crystal ash,* each grain consisting of a single crystal or of groups of crystals with only traces of glass adhering to them. It is quite common to find nearly perfect crystals of olivine and augite blown out in this manner by basaltic volcanoes; and Mt. Erebus in Antarctica and some Japanese volcanoes are renowned for ejected crystals of the calcium feldspar, anorthite. Ash consisting of more than one type of material may be given a compound name: vitric–crystal ash, vitric–crystal–lithic ash, etc.

Accretionary lapilli are more or less spherical masses of cemented ash. The cementation is often weak. They are also known as volcanic *pisolites*. Most of them are slightly flattened spheroids, but some are quite roller-shaped. They are usually between $\frac{1}{16}$ and $\frac{1}{2}$ inch in diameter, but a few are as large as 2 inches. They are usually formed by accretion of particles around a wet nucleus, such as a raindrop, falling through a cloud of ash. The resulting mud balls may roll on the surface of loose ash and grow like snowballs rolling downhill. Others are formed by raindrops striking directly on an ash-covered ground surface and rolling downhill or being rolled across the surface by wind.

By far the commonest variety of ash is vitric ash formed by the disruption of liquid lava by expanding gas (Plates 7-16A and 7-16B). As the magma approaches the surface, gas comes out of solution to form a froth, and as the bubbles continue to grow, the froth is literally torn apart. Some of the larger masses of froth remain as lumps of pumice, but much of the froth is disintegrated to the point that all that remain are the septa that separated the bubbles, chilled to glass, and carried upward by the outrushing column of gas. The shapes of the ash fragments clearly reveal their origin in the concave surfaces that once were the surfaces of bubbles

PLATE 7-16A. Vulcanian explosion cloud from the eruption of Bezymianny Volcano, Kamchatka, in 1956, seen from a distance of 27 miles. The cloud rose to a height of more than 24 miles. Photo by V. A. Shamshin, Kamchatka Volcano Station.

PLATE 7-16B. Small explosion at the summit of Paricutin Volcano, Mexico. The dark, ash-laden, tightly convoluted explosion cloud is overhung by the lighter fume cloud. Photo by Tad Nichols, Tucson, Arizona.

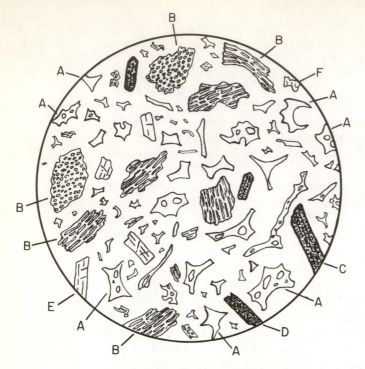

FIGURE 7-2. Typical vitric-crystal ash (dacitic), Cascade Range, northern California, under the microscope. The diameter of the field is about 2 mm. The ash consists of angular glass shards (A) showing typical arcuate and forked forms, bits of pumice (B) showing vesicles that are nearly round in cross section in one direction and much stretched in the direction at right angles to the first, and crystals of hornblende (C), biotite (D), and feldspar (E), and a little quartz (F). The fine powdery matrix has been omitted. (See also Fig. 5-6(A).)

and the Y-shaped bits that once separated adjacent bubbles (Fig. 7-2). The curved and forked fragments of vitric ash are often referred to as "shards."

Deposits of ash are known as ash layers, ash beds, or sometimes as ash blankets. Consolidated ash deposits (Plate 7-17) are called *tuff*. Ash and tuff often contain some fragments of larger size. Those in which moderately to very abundant lapilli are scattered through the finer matrix are called *lapilli-ash* or *lapilli tuff*. Those containing blocks are known as *tuff-breccia*, and those containing bombs may be called *tuff-agglomerate*.

Near the vent each individual explosion during an eruption results in a shower of fragments that fall as a layer over the adjacent country. Each layer is the result of a separate explosion. However, only the finest ash is carried by the wind to great distances, and at places remote from the vent it commonly is impossible to distinguish the deposits of individual explosions. Instead, the layer represents the accumulated ash of an entire eruption.

PLATE 7-17. Bomb sag in well-bedded tuff, Koko Crater, Oahu, Hawaii. The bomb is 8 inches across. U. S. Geological Survey photo by G. A. Macdonald.

Because they are formed by the fragments settling more or less vertically from the air above, ash beds tend to form a continuous mantle over whatever topography the ash falls on. The layer runs uninterrupted over hill and dale rather than being confined to valleys as are the volcanic deposits formed by various types of flows. Both ash and lapilli beds commonly are well sorted according to size of the fragments, and individual beds commonly show a size gradation both vertically and laterally. The fragments are usually larger near the base of the bed, because the larger fragments thrown out by any one explosion fall through the air faster than the small ones and strike the ground first. For the same reason, the larger fragments fall closer to the vent, while the smaller ones tend to be carried farther by the wind. Occasionally, ash beds are found in which the grain size increases upward. These may result from increasing strength of explosion, larger fragments being thrown higher and drifting farther from the vent so that at any one place the fragments falling to the ground are larger than those that preceded them. On the other hand, they may instead result from decreasing strength of explosion, the magma being less completely blown apart so that the fragments formed are somewhat larger in later stages than they were earlier.

Although subaerial ash beds are generally well sorted, the ash deposited close to the vent by very voluminous eruptions may show little or no sorting. The great abundance of material settling through the air prevents effective separation of fragments of different size and they are all deposited together.

Violent explosive eruptions may throw fine ash high into the upper levels of the atmosphere, where it may drift for great distances. Ash from the 1883 eruption of Krakatoa Volcano in the strait between Java and Sumatra is commonly believed to have drifted around the earth three times, refraction of the sunlight by the very fine dust in the upper atmosphere producing brilliantly colored sunsets as far away as England. Similar brilliant sunsets were observed in many parts of the United States during 1963, after the eruption of Agung Volcano in Bali. The atmospheric effects persisted, in the case of the Krakatoa eruption for more than 5 years, and following the Agung eruption for 3 years. There appears, however, to be considerable doubt whether these long-continued optical effects actually were caused by ash. Meinel and Meinel (1967) have pointed out that the settling rate of the particles is slower than it should be if the particles were ash, and also that the height of the refracting layer is constant and independent of the strength of the eruption. They suggest that, although there is indeed an initial widespread ash layer in the atmosphere, this largely settles out within a few weeks or months, and that the long-continued effects are due to an aerosol formed by precipitation of sulfates on condensation nuclei. The sulfates are believed to result from interaction of volcanic sulfur dioxide with atmospheric ozone. The layer coincides with a sulfate layer always present in the upper atmosphere but which becomes intensified following big volcanic eruptions.

The amount of ash that drifts to great distances in the atmosphere is so small that it is generally undetected when it finally falls to the ground; but, in combination with the intensified sulfate aerosol layer, it may be great enough to appreciably reduce the amount of heat from the sun that reaches the ground surface, and thereby affect the weather. Measurements suggested that the ash introduced into the air by the eruption near Mt. Katmai, Alaska, in 1912, reduced by about 20 per cent the amount of solar radiation reaching the earth's surface at Mt. Wilson, more than 2,000 miles away in southern California. Dust from the great Laki fissure eruption in Iceland in June, 1783, drifted over Europe and appears to have caused abnormally cold weather for several months. The actual lowering of average temperature was probably only 1 or 2 degrees, but the results were so noticeable that the winter of 1783–1784 was long known as "the cold winter." The famous American meterologist, W. J. Humphreys, was convinced that a lowering of the amount of solar heat reaching the earth's surface, and consequently of average surface temperatures, during the years 1884–1886 was brought about by the eruption of Krakatoa in 1883; that a similar decrease during the years 1888–1892 was caused by the eruptions of Bandai in 1888, Bogoslof in 1890, and Awoe in the Sangihe Archipelago in 1892; during 1903 by the outbreaks of Santa Maria, Mt. Pelée, Soufrière, and Colima in 1902 and 1903; and during 1912–1913 by the Katmai eruption. Wexler (1952) still supports the idea, though Gentilli (1948) found no evidence to confirm it in a study of worldwide temperature records.

An extensive study by Lamb (1970) appears to indicate that volcanic dust veils in the atmosphere are related in some way to some climatic changes, that they do tend to bring about lowering of the surface temperature and may prolong periods of cold climate caused primarily by other factors, but that they are not the only cause of exceptionally cold periods.

It has been suggested that large amounts of ash introduced into the atmosphere during periods of increased volcanic activity may have lowered the average temperature of the earth's surface enough to bring about the glacial climates of past geologic times. Budyko (1968) estimates that 50 to 100 great explosive eruptions during a single century would reduce the direct sun radiation by 10 to 20 per cent and lower the average air temperature 1 to 3°C. Budyko's basic assumption, that the frequency of great eruptions during the last century is close to the average frequency during the entire Quaternary period (about 2 million years), is questioned by Lamb (1970, p. 495); but the geologic evidence suggests that the assumption may be conservative. Volcanic activity during the Pleistocene epoch appears to have been appreciably more intense than during the last century. However, it appears very doubtful that activity during the Pleistocene was more intense than it was during several earlier periods in which glaciers were absent or very restricted. Volcanic ash veils may have contributed to the lowering of temperature that brought about the Pleistocene

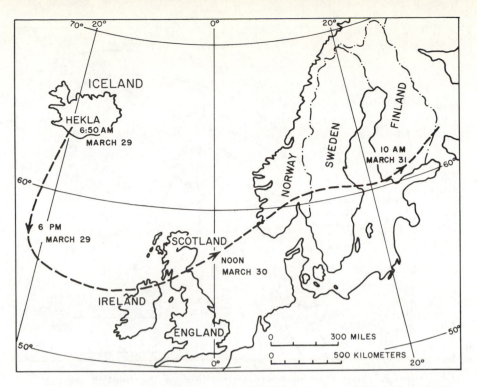

FIGURE 7-3. Map showing the path of ash movement from the eruption of Hekla Volcano in March, 1947. (After Thorarinsson, 1954.)

glaciation, but it seems unlikely that they were the sole, or even the principal, cause. At present the question remains open.

The speed of movement of ash in the atmosphere depends on high-level wind velocities. Ash from the 1947 eruption of Mt. Hekla drifted 3,000 miles by a circuitous route from Iceland, across Scotland and Norway to Finland in about 52 hours (Fig. 7-3). The rate of travel was nearly 60 miles an hour! In 1932 the volcano Quizapu in the Chilean Andes erupted explosively, throwing huge amounts of ash into the air, much of it reaching a height of 45,000 feet. The ash was carried northeastward across South America, reaching Buenos Aires, 700 miles to the east, in about 17 hours, and Rio de Janeiro, 1,850 miles away, in about 120 hours (Fig. 7-4). The rates of movement thus ranged from about 15 to more than 40 miles per hour. Ash darkened the sky in Buenos Aires and fell to a thickness of about a quarter of an inch in the streets. The total volume of ash erupted was more than 5 cubic miles. It fell over an area of about 1 million square miles on land and probably at least as great an area of ocean.

The Katmai eruption in Alaska in June, 1912, was one of the greatest in historic time. Nearly 6 cubic miles of ash and pumice were blown into the air (in addition to the ash flows down the valley mentioned on a later page). Ash fell over an area of 100,000 square miles, reaching a thickness of nearly a foot at the village of Kodiak, 100 miles from the site of the eruption (Fig. 7-5). In Kodiak, day was turned into night as the ash cloud eclipsed the sun, and even with lanterns men had to grope their way along the street from house to house. The 1883 eruption of

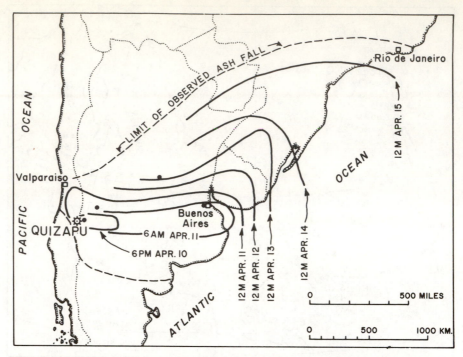

FIGURE 7-4. Map showing successive positions of the front of the ash cloud from the eruption of Quizapu Volcano, Chile, in April 1932. The solid dots indicate the location of the analyzed samples of ash in Fig. 7-6(A). (After Larsson, 1937.)

FIGURE 7-5. Map showing the thickness of ash deposited by the Katmai eruption of June, 1912. (Modified after Wilcox, 1959.)

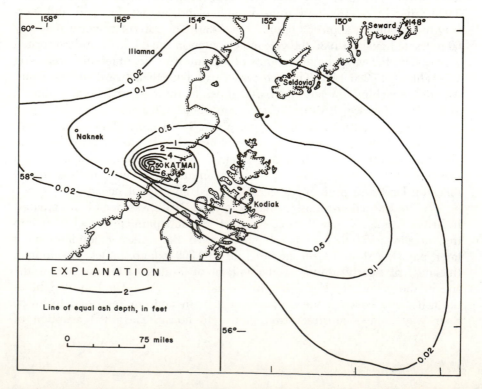

Krakatoa is said to have produced nearly 4 cubic miles of ash. That of Mt. Mazama, which resulted in the formation of Crater Lake, Oregon, about 4,000 B.C., threw 7 to 9 cubic miles of ash into the air and deposited a layer of ash over the surrounding country that reached a thickness of 5 inches as much as 100 miles away (Williams and Goles, 1968), in addition to several cubic miles of glowing avalanche deposits. The eruption of Coseguïna, Nicaragua, in 1835 formerly was said to have ejected 30 cubic miles of ash, but although ash from the eruption fell in Jamaica 800 miles to the east, studies by Williams (1952) indicate that the total volume of ash thrown out probably did not exceed 6 cubic miles. The tremendous explosion of Tambora in the eastern part of the East Indies in 1815, which was probably by far the greatest explosion of historic times, is estimated to have thrown up some 20 cubic miles of ash. Another very large eruption was that which, some 1,400 years ago, spread more than 10 cubic miles of ash over an area of more than 140,000 square miles in the upper Yukon basin of Alaska.

Ash layers interbedded with ancient rocks of other types often are of great importance geologically, because they supply a widespread time datum of unrivaled precision. A single ash bed covering tens of hundreds of thousands of square miles and often extending over several different geologic provinces was everywhere formed within a period of a few days— a mere instant in the eons of the earth's history. It furnishes a means of correlating the associated rocks in time—rocks that may have been forming under very different conditions and consequently be of very different character and contain very different types of fossils in different parts of the ash-covered region. As an example, we may cite the ash that was laid down over the Mississippi Valley region, from Alabama to southern Canada and from New York westward to Minnesota and Missouri, in the Ordovician period some 450 million years ago.

In general, however, ash layers have proved most useful in the correlation of very young rocks (late Tertiary to Recent). By the use of "tephra chronology," Thorarinsson (1951, 1967a) has been able to correlate late prehistoric and early historic volcanic and other historical events over large parts of Iceland. In the United States, also, "ash chronology" is becoming more and more useful (Wilcox, 1965). Ash from the great eruption of Mt. Mazama has been traced as far east as central Montana and northward into British Columbia and Alberta, establishing the synchronism of associated rocks in the Cascade Range, Columbia Plains, Rocky Mountains, and western Great Plains. Ash erupted at the time of formation of the Bishop Tuff, an ignimbrite formed about 700,000 years ago in the northern end of the Owens Valley, California, has been identified as far east as central Nebraska (Izett et al., 1970). Ash from the eruption of Glacier Peak, Washington, about 12,000 years ago, also has been traced eastward as far as Montana; and the Pearlette ash, erupted during the Pleistocene (late Kansan) Ice Age, is found from western Texas to southeastern South Dakota, and possibly westward into Nevada. It establishes

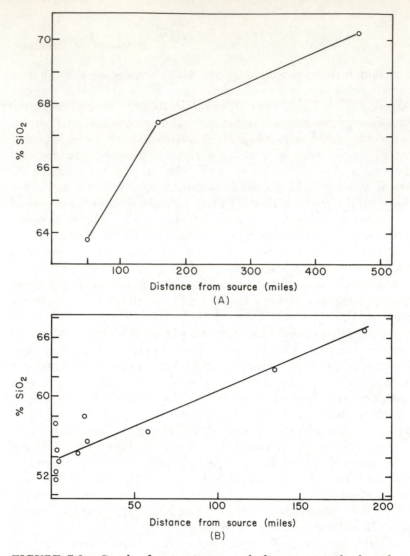

FIGURE 7-6. Graphs showing increase of silica content of ash with increasing distance from the volcano; (A) during the eruption of Quizapu Volcano in 1932 (after Larsson, 1937); and (B) during the eruption of Klut Volcano, Java, in 1919 (modified after van Bemmelen, 1949).

the synchronism of the enclosing alluvial deposits in south-central United States with deposits of glacial outwash hundreds of miles to the north.

Ash layers are often very much alike, and it may be difficult or impossible to be sure that exposures at different localities are of the same ash layer. A given ash is recognized at various places primarily by its constituents, though other features such as thickness, color, and stratigraphic position may be helpful. Most useful are the composition and refractive index of the glass fragments, and the nature and relative abundance of the crystals (phenocrysts). Thus, for instance, the Mazama ash can be told from the otherwise very similar Glacier Peak ash by the presence in it of crystals of augite, which are lacking in that from Glacier Peak (Powers and Wilcox, 1964). An ash layer erupted from Mt. Rainier about 2,000 years ago can be told from the Mazama ash by the higher refractive index of its glass (Wilcox, 1965).

Another interesting aspect of ash falls that can be of considerable importance to the geologist studying them is the change in composition of the ash at varying distances from the point of eruption. When it is ejected, most ash consists of a mixture of crystals and glass fragments. The crystals are denser than the glass, and both individual crystals and bits of glass containing crystals tend to fall faster than the crystal-free glass fragments. Thus, crystals are more abundant in the ash deposited close to the vent and become less and less numerous at increasing distances. In the acid magmas that cause most violently explosive eruptions, the crystals generally contain considerably less silica, and more iron, magnesium and calcium, than the liquid portion of the magma that forms the glass; consequently, the portions of the ash that fall at greater distances and contain less crystals are progressively richer in silica. The effect is illustrated in Fig. 7-6. This change of composition of ash by aerial sorting has been called "aeolian differentiation."

SUGGESTED ADDITIONAL READING

Capps, 1915; Fisher, 1961; Gentilli, 1948; Humphreys, 1942, p. 302–303; Lacroix, 1930; Lamb, 1970; Macdonald, 1967; Parsons, 1969; Pirsson, 1915; Reck, 1915; Verhoogen, 1951; Wentworth and Macdonald, 1953; Wentworth and Williams, 1932; Wexler, 1952; Wilcox, 1959; Williams, 1952.

8

Fragmental Flows

The phenomena to be discussed in the present chapter have the general behavior of lava flows, in that they act as heavy fluids controlled in their movement by gravity and the topography of the land surface along their courses, and they can be considered to be lava flows of special sorts; but they leave behind them deposits of material that resemble those formed by volcanic explosion, described in the last chapter. Many of the deposits have in the past been interpreted as explosion-generated rocks; and the same names, such as tuff and tuff-breccia, are still commonly used for them. Indeed, many of the flows are the direct result of volcanic explosion, and others involve gas expansion which, although perhaps not explosive in the strict sense, certainly approaches it. These flows of volcanic fragments often move at great speed and to great distances, and they include the most destructive phenomena of volcanism.

Glowing Avalanches

The dome and great spine that formed in the crater of Mt. Pelée, Martinique, during the eruption of 1902, have already been mentioned. The dome probably started to grow early in May. The volcano had al-

ready been erupting since April 23, or even before, throwing cinder and
ash into the air and building a small cone in the crater. The ash drifted
down over the city of St. Pierre situated at the coast 6 miles south-southwest
of the summit of the mountain (Fig. 8-1), and, coupled with the stench of
sulfur gases, it made life in the city decidedly unpleasant. Birds fell dead
in the streets, suffocated by the gases or by clogging of their respiratory
passages by the fine ash. Many people left the city, and undoubtedly many
more would have done so had they not been urged by the government to
stay. An important election was impending, and in order to vote the people
must be in their home districts! They were less alarmed than they might
have been had it not been for the fact that the last eruptions of the
volcano, in 1792 and 1851, had done no important damage. The persons
who did leave were replaced by others who came in from country districts
on the slopes of the mountain, where conditions were even less pleasant
than in St. Pierre, so the population of the city remained nearly the same
at about 30,000 persons. A government-appointed commission reported no
immediate risk to St. Pierre, and the governor himself came to the city
to reassure the people. He never left!

Stream valleys radiate outward in all directions from the summit
of Mt. Pelée. One of them, the valley of the Rivière Blanche, starts at a
V-shaped notch nearly 1,000 feet deep in the south wall of the crater,
trends southward almost directly toward St. Pierre for about 2 miles, then
bends southwestward to enter the sea 2 miles north of the city. The crater
itself, before the eruption, was a bowl-shaped hollow containing two
smaller depressions. The more northerly depression contained a small permanent lake. The more southerly, known as L'Etang Sec (Dry Lake), contained water only after torrential rains and normally was dry. On April
27 L'Etang Sec contained a pool of water more than 600 feet across.

On May 5 flows of mud swept down the canyons on the mountain
flanks, and at the mouth of the Rivière Blanche buried at sugar mill and
about 30 workmen. It is generally thought that explosion threw the water
of L'Etang Sec out into the head of the Rivière Blanche, thus generating
the mudflow, but there is also some suggestion that the amount of water
represented by the mudflows all around the mountain was too great to
be accounted for by the lake and the contemporaneous rainfall. Can it be
that there was actually an expulsion of water from the mountain by some
mechanism that we do not yet understand?

On May 6 and 7 more mudflows occurred and the strength of
the explosive activity at the summit of the mountain became even stronger.
Then at 7:50 A.M. on the morning of May 8 a series of violent explosions
took place. A great black cloud of ash was projected many miles upward
above the mountaintop, and simultaneously another cloud shot southward
through the notch in the crater wall into the headwaters of the Rivière
Blanche and on toward St. Pierre (Plate 8-1). In less than 2 minutes it
had engulfed the city, and within another very few minutes nearly every
one of the 30,000 inhabitants was dead!

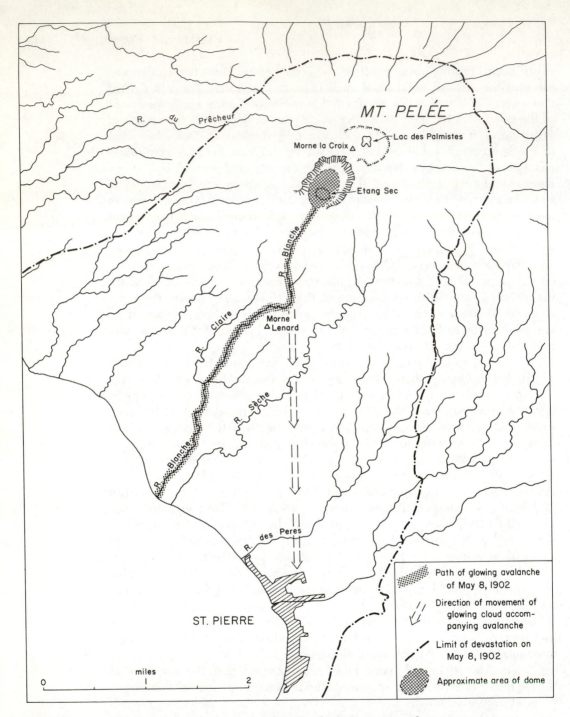

FIGURE 8-1. Map of the northern end of the Island of Martinique, showing the location of Mt. Pelée and the City of St. Pierre, the Riviere Blanche, and the course of the glowing avalanche and glowing cloud of May 8, 1902. (Modified after A. Lacroix.)

PLATE 8-1. Glowing avalanche ("nuée ardente") on the flank of Mont Pelée, Martinique, December 16, 1902. The main avalanche is hidden by the dust cloud. Photo by A. Lacroix, courtesy of Masson et Cie., Paris.

The velocity of the cloud in its descent on St. Pierre has been variously estimated, but it must have been in the vicinity of 100 miles an hour! The blast struck the city with tremendous force. Masonry walls 3 feet thick were knocked over and torn apart, big trees were uprooted, 6-inch cannon were torn from their mounts, and a 3-ton statue was carried 40 feet from its base. Trees that remained standing were stripped of leaves and branches, and on many the bark was stripped away on the side toward the volcano leaving bare wood that bore the marks of having been sandblasted. Most of the ships in the harbor were upset and sunk or destroyed by fire. Only two escaped. Most of the few survivors of the tragedy were on these two ships or had been thrown into the water from the ships that were sunk, and nearly all of them were horribly burned. It is often said that within the city itself there was only one survivor—a prisoner who was in a dungeon with only one tiny window opening on the side away from the volcano. Actually there appear to have been about four survivors, two of them on the very edge of the cloud, and another who by some strange accident escaped even though everyone around him was killed. The survivors had little to tell of the blast other than the sudden pitch darkness, clouds of hot dust that mixed with water to form scalding mud, a short period of intense heat, and a sense of overpowering suffocation. The initial great heat due to the blast itself seems to have been of very short duration—at most only a few minutes.

The injuries to the dead were grotesque. In many instances the actual cause of death probably was the inhaling of the very hot gas. The bodies were intensely burned, as also were those of the survivors. Many were stripped of clothing by the force of the blast; but others remained clothed and the clothing was not ignited, even though the body beneath it was severely burned. Body tissues were distended, and in many instances skull sutures had been opened up. The injuries were such as would result from sudden heat intense enough to turn water in human tissues into steam, but not high enough or of long enough duration to raise fabrics to kindling temperature.

The temperature of the blast itself is difficult to appraise. Much of the city burned, and the high temperatures must be attributed in part to the fires, fed by hundreds of thousands of gallons of rum stored in warehouses. But the temperature was high enough to ignite the wooden decks of ships in the harbor, where the hot dust accumulated on them, and in parts of the city where there were no extensive fires, the temperature was nevertheless high enough to soften glass objects. It is generally estimated that the temperature of the blast as it left the crater was about 1000°C, and that the temperature of the cloud that swept over the city was still between 700 and 1000°C. The thickness of the layer of dust left by the cloud in the city averaged only about a foot.

Destruction of the city was almost total. Little was left save the wrecked masonry walls, twisted sheets of iron roofing, and other metal debris.

Understanding of the nature of the cloud that destroyed St. Pierre emerged only gradually. Trained scientific observers soon were on the scene, and several more similar blasts were observed during the remainder of the eruption. They rushed down the river valleys at tremendous speed— by day, masses of black tightly convoluted cloud rising as they came and often leaning forward as though eager to accomplish their dread purpose; by night, glowing a dull red. The cloud was the conspicuous feature and led Lacroix to give them the name "nuée ardente" (glowing cloud); but studies of the deposits left by them soon made it apparent that the most important feature was not the cloud at all but an avalanche of incandescent rock fragments that flowed down the valley like a lava flow or a stream of water, but far more rapidly. The cloud was only the dust rising above the avalanche. The name "glowing cloud" seems, therefore, to give too much emphasis to a relatively minor feature, and many volcanologists today prefer to call the phenomenon a *glowing avalanche*.

At Mt. Pelée, as elsewhere, the avalanches were confined to the bottoms of valleys, while the dust clouds spread laterally, sometimes to considerable distances. At Hibokhibok in 1951 the fine dust from the cloud formed a thin deposit that extended half a mile or more beyond the margin of the avalanche deposit. In the case of the blast that destroyed St. Pierre, the avalanche started southward toward the city but followed the canyon of the Rivière Blanche around a sharp bend to the southwest and reached the ocean nearly 2 miles north of the city; but the dust cloud jumped the ridge on the south side of the valley and continued southward over the city (Fig. 8-1). The destruction of the city was wholly the work of the dust cloud and the fire that followed it.

The earliest good description of a glowing avalanche was by Tempest Anderson and J. S. Flett, who had been sent by the Royal Society of London primarily to study the nearly simultaneous eruption of Soufrière Volcano on the neighboring island of St. Vincent. They observed one of the blasts from a ship lying off the shore of Mt. Pelée on the evening of July 9. Like the one that destroyed St. Pierre, it issued through the notch in the crater rim and rushed down the valley of the Rivière Blanche. They write (1903, p. 442), "In an incredibly short span of time a red-hot avalanche swept down to the sea. . . . It was dull red, with a billowy surface, reminding one of a snow avalanche. In it there were large stones, which stood out as streaks of bright red, tumbling down and emitting showers of sparks. In a few minutes it was over."

The cloud from the avalanche continued across the water toward them. They write (p. 443),

It was globular, with a bulging surface, covered with rounded protuberant masses, which swelled and multiplied with a terrible energy . . . . In its face there sparkled innumerable lightnings . . . . The cloud itself was black as night, dense and solid, and the flickering lightnings gave it an indescribably venomous appearance. It moved with great velocity, and as it approached it got larger and larger, but it retained its rounded form. It did not spread out laterally, neither did it rise into the air, but swept on over the sea in surging globular masses.

They estimated that it was about 2 miles broad and a mile high. Fortunately, about a mile before it reached them, it suddenly began to lose energy and velocity and to disintegrate. Otherwise their account might never have been written!

They continue (p. 444),

There can be no doubt that the eruption we witnessed was a counterpart of that which destroyed St. Pierre . . . . The most peculiar feature of these eruptions is the avalanche of incandescent sand and the great black cloud which accompanies it . . . a mass of incandescent lava rises and rolls over the lip of the crater in the form of an avalanche of red hot dust . . . . It rushes down the slopes . . . carrying with it a terrific blast which mows down everything in its path. The mixture of dust and gases behaves in many ways like a fluid.

It should be emphasized that the great majority of the fragments in most glowing avalanches are of new rock consolidated from magma just reaching the surface. A few fragments of old rock from the crater walls or torn from the walls of the conduit are scattered through the mass, but they generally form less than 5 per cent of the total. Regarding the disruption of the new rock to form the fragments, Anderson and Flett (1903, p. 507) concluded that as the magma "rose in the throat of the volcano, the relief of pressure allowed the gases to expand, and to free themselves from the liquid in which they were held. Sooner or later the cohesion of the liquid was overcome, and from a spongy froth the mass changed to a cloud of particles, mostly solid, but perhaps in some part liquid, each surrounded on all sides by films of expanding gases."

Rarely, the amount of old rock material in a glowing avalanche may be large. Neumann van Padang (1933) has described such an avalanche with a volume of 7.5 million cubic meters that took place at Merapi in Java in 1930. Only about one tenth of the material was new lava. Nevertheless, the avalanche traveled 8 miles and was hot enough to cause many fatal burns. At Stromboli Volcano in 1930, glowing avalanches were formed wholly of old rock fragments, heated to incandescence, torn from the walls of the conduit, and ejected by steam explosions.

The day before the tragedy at St. Pierre a very similar event took place on the island of St. Vincent. (The two form one of the rather rare examples of the simultaneous eruption of neighboring volcanoes.) There, also, great clouds rolled down the mountainside like ominous black to reddish or purplish curtains, leaving deposits of fragmental debris several tens of feet thick in the valleys and taking about 2,000 lives. The loss of life would have been much greater had not the people living on the leeward side of the volcano seen the beginnings of the eruption on the day before and fled to safer places. On the windward side, the top of the mountain was hidden by the usual trade-wind clouds, and by the time the inhabitants realized the volcano was erupting it was too late; the roads to safety were already blocked by torrents of boiling mud rushing down the unbridged stream valleys.

The volcano responsible for the St. Vincent disaster is Soufrière, which forms the northern end of the island. (In French-speaking regions, "Soufrière" is a common name for volcanoes giving off sulfurous gases. There are several in the Lesser Antilles alone.) The Soufrière of St. Vincent is a composite volcano (see Chapter 11) with a newer cone occupying the large crater (caldera) of an older one much in the same way that the new cone of Vesuvius occupies the caldera formed by the eruption of 79 A.D. (see Chapter 10). Before the eruption the top of the new cone of Soufrière was occupied by a crater nearly a mile across and more than 1,600 feet deep below the lowest point on the irregular crater rim. The latter ranged from 3,000 to 3,600 feet above sea level. The bottom of the crater was occupied by an opalescent green lake more than 500 feet deep. A smaller crater, formed by an eruption in 1810, adjoined the main crater on the northeast, and to the north the rim of the older caldera stood more than 400 feet higher than the top of the new cone. The outer slopes of the volcano are quite gentle, averaging only about 15°.

The eruption of May 7, 1902, was somewhat different from that of May 8 at Mt. Pelée, despite the overall similarities. There were many more survivors from within the cloud-covered area, and these reported the same general sensations of intense heat and overpowering suffocation that lasted, fortunately, only a very few minutes. But the temperature of the cloud was lower than at St. Pierre and the force of the blast was much less. Relatively few fires were started and many buildings survived. Many of the fires, and much of the destruction, particularly that of chimneys, appears to have been by lightning (Anderson and Flett, 1903, p. 398–399), which as usual was very abundant in the clouds of ash. Furthermore, the clouds and the glowing avalanches that caused them descended all sides of the mountain instead of being confined to a single sector. They were even projected over the high outer rim of the caldera onto the northern slope. It is noteworthy also that the deposits of the avalanches were mostly sand-sized particles with a much smaller proportion of large fragments than those of Mt. Pelée. The form of the mountain with its deep crater completely eliminated the possibility of the hot avalanches having been caused by blasts directed at a low angle. The material must have been thrown up nearly vertically, and the avalanches resulted from the fall of great volumes of hot gas-charged fragments on the upper slope of the mountain. The movement of the material down slope was caused wholly by gravity, and the comparatively slow movement (only 20 to 30 miles per hour) resulted from the rather gentle slope.

A controversy soon developed between Lacroix and Anderson and Flett. At Soufrière it was clear that the explosive ejection of material that initiated the glowing avalanches was in a vertical direction. Part of the material continued to rise vertically, forming the towering ash cloud characteristic of many volcanic eruptions, but part of the heavily laden edges of the cloud fell back onto the slope of the volcano and rushed down it as glowing avalanches (Fig. 8-2B). The driving force that caused

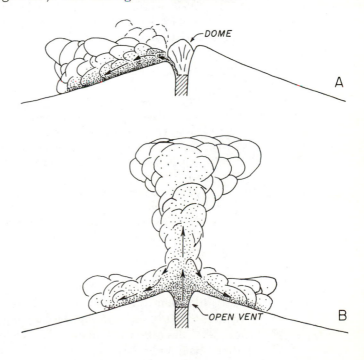

FIGURE 8-2. Diagram illustrating different types of glowing avalanches. (A) Pelée type; (B) Soufrière type; (C) Merapi type.

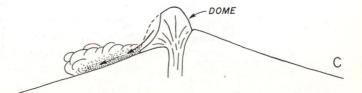

the movement of the avalanche down slope was wholly that of gravity; the movement was the flowing of a heavy but very mobile fluid. In contrast, at Mt. Pelée Lacroix saw evidence that the initial ejection of material was directed laterally and gave an added impulsion to the avalanche. There could be no doubt of the Soufrière mechanism, but evidence was insufficient to demonstrate whether or not Lacroix's concept of the Peléean explosions was correct. It was not until 1930, during a later eruption of Mt. Pelée, that F. A. Perret obtained further evidence on it. The avalanches were smaller than those of 1902, and Perret was able to observe some of them at close range—one actually from a distance of less than 100 feet! He was convinced that many of them had indeed been started by explosions that shot the material out at a low angle. The explosion he regarded as originating within the ejected material itself. He writes (1935, p. 86),

> In the type of explosion which I envisage as the cause of a *nuée ardente*, it is the projected lava itself which explodes. The gas-charged substance, when the critical point [of gas saturation] is reached, suffers a sudden vesicular expansion throughout its entire mass, an explosive process so distributed that it may merely lift the material soundlessly, without marked violence, from a pocket and down upon a slope, where it descends gravitationally as a hot avalanche.

On the other hand,

> Where the original lava is retained beneath the carapace of a dome, it may remain quietly until competent energy is stored up, when it bursts forth with cataclysmic violence from the weakest point of its prison [often the basal margin of the dome] as a horizontally projected blast, clearing valleys and hills, avalanching down slopes, spreading out fan-wise and annihilating towns many kilometers away . . . . At the moment of explosion liquid masses of lava, instead of being hurled high into the air to form bombs, are converted more or less completely into ash by the rapid discharge of gas and with the ash are carried along ejectamenta of all sizes; blocks, boulders, and the roots of spines, highly heated but not fused.

Perret's careful observation of several hundred glowing avalanches left little room for doubt, but confirmatory evidence has been found elsewhere. For instance, during the glowing avalanches at Hibokhibok volcano in 1951, described in Chapter 1, blocks were hurled out in a trajectory that could only have resulted from explosions directed at a low angle from near the base of the dome.

In the meantime, workers at other volcanoes, notably Merapi in Java, had demonstrated still another mechanism by which glowing avalanches are generated. The latest of a series of domes formed in a line across the crater of Merapi extended out beyond the crater rim onto the outer slope of the mountain. As the dome continued to grow in normal fashion, its flank repeatedly became unstable and collapsed, sending avalanches of incandescent rock fragments down the slope of the mountain. These had much the same character as the glowing avalanches of Mt. Pelée, including great speed. According to Neumann van Padang (1933), some of the avalanches at Merapi are set off by heavy rain chilling the outer part of the dome and causing it to crack and crumble. Essentially the same as the Merapi avalanches are those reported by H. Williams at Fuego Volcano in Guatemala and Izalco in El Salvador, where they have resulted from the collapse of the steep fronts of block lava flows on the slope of the mountain.

Glowing avalanches commonly deposit little or no material on the steep flanks of the volcano. They may, indeed, have an erosive effect, sometimes carving out gullies several feet deep in older deposits and producing scratches resembling crude glacial striae on the canyon sides. It is not until they lose velocity on the gentler slopes at the base of the volcano that they deposit their load. The deposits consist of an intimate mixture of finely pulverized rock material (ash) with angular blocks of rock ranging up to several yards in diameter and often many fragments of pumice (Plate 8-2). The great turbulence in the avalanche prevents any great degree of sorting of the material. Some deposits show a slight degree of layering, in some there is a slight tendency for the larger blocks to be segregated toward the bottom, and in some the fragments of very light pumice tend to be carried farther than the denser, heavier fragments and concentrated near the terminus of the flow. The dust that forms the cloud above the avalanche often settles to form a thin layer of fine material on the top of the avalanche deposit and extending sometimes as much as a mile, or even more, laterally beyond the edges of the main deposit. The proportion of large blocks to ash in the avalanche deposit varies greatly. Avalanches in which the blocks are very abundant are sometimes referred to as "block and ash flows."

Still another type of glowing avalanche takes place on the steep slopes of volcanoes heavily covered with hot ash and other ejecta during violent eruptions. Such avalanches were described by Perret (1924, p. 89) during

PLATE 8-2. The deposit left by the glowing avalanches of December, 1951, in a canyon on the flank of Hibokhibok Volcano, Philippines. Boulders on the surface of the deposit range from less than a foot to about 10 feet across. U. S. Geological Survey photo by G. A. Macdonald.

the 1906 eruption of Vesuvius. The accumulated material is unstable with much of the quality of a dry quicksand, and any disturbance—an earthquake, a falling bomb—may start it in motion. There results an avalanche that may travel with speeds of several tens of miles per hour for half a mile or more.

Thus we can recognize several types of glowing avalanches that may be classified, following Lacroix, A. G. MacGregor (1952), and others, as:

1. Explosively generated avalanches $\begin{cases} \text{Caused by vertical explosions} \\ \text{(Soufrière type)} \\ \text{Caused by low-angle explosions} \\ \text{(Pelée type)} \end{cases}$

2. Dome-collapse avalanches (Merapi type)

3. Hot-ash avalanches (Vesuvius type)

The first three types are illustrated in Figure 8-2.

All these share the characteristic of great mobility and resultant great speed of flow to great distances. The cause of the great mobility unquestionably is the buoying up and separation of the fragments by gases between them, so that the friction of movement is very greatly reduced. This was clearly recognized by Lacroix and by Anderson and Flett in 1902. An additional factor was suggested by C. N. Fenner as a result of his study of the "sand flow" in the Valley of Ten Thousand Smokes, described in the next section, and the idea was elaborated by Perret in his report on the glowing avalanches of Mt. Pelée in 1930. The idea was simply that the release of gas was not restricted to the initial explosion, but that the fragments continued to give off gas for some time as they were carried along in the avalanche. The avalanche and the dust cloud above it were in a state of "auto-explosivity." Each fragment was cushioned from the adjacent fragments by an envelope of expanding gas that was continually being added to by escape of more gas from the fragments themselves.

McTaggart (1960) has suggested that the mobility of glowing avalanches is the result of entrapment of air beneath and within the on-rushing avalanche, the heating of the cold air causing it to expand. There seems to be little question that this is an important factor; and, indeed, its importance in adding to the mobility of glowing avalanches has long been recognized by volcanologists working in Indonesia (Bemmelen, 1949, p. 193). In some instances, as for example in the hot-ash avalanches of the Vesuvius type, it is probably the dominant or even the sole factor. In most glowing avalanches, however, both mechanisms probably play important parts, with the effects of heating of entrapped air being especially important in the distal portion of the flow and perhaps largely restricted to it. At least two lines of evidence indicate that gas does continue to evolve from the fragments throughout the movement of the avalanche. Blocks in many glowing avalanche deposits, such as those of the 1968 eruption of Mayon Volcano in the Philippines and a prehistoric avalanche on the northwestern flank of Mt.

Lassen in California, have glassy surfaces that are deeply and intricately divided by bread-crust cracking that has resulted from expansion of gas in the interior of the block after the outer portion had become rigid. Moore and Melson (1969) have pointed out that these surfaces are so fragile that the blocks could not possibly have been transported any appreciable distance in the avalanche without the surfaces being destroyed. Therefore, gas must still have been coming out of solution and expanding in the interiors of the blocks during the very last stages of movement of the avalanche and after it came to rest. A still more dramatic demonstration of the continued evolution of gas is furnished by the explosion of blocks after the avalanche has stopped, like the big block of dacite on the top of the Hibokhibok avalanche described in Chapter 1.

Another interesting phenomenon observed during the 1968 eruption of Mayon, and in some other eruptions, is a blast of cool air that moves directly in front of the glowing avalanche (Moore and Melson, 1969). The avalanches of the 1968 eruption were of the St. Vincent type and advanced down the mountain slope at an average speed of about 65 miles an hour. The initial blast of cool air appears to result simply from pushing of ordinary air ahead of the descending avalanche.

In Indonesia glowing avalanches are known as *ladus*. The term has the merit of brevity, but it has not as yet been generally accepted in other parts of the world.

Ash Flows

For a century geologists were puzzled by a type of volcanic rock that shows some of the characteristics of lava flows and some of those of pyroclastic materials thrown into the air by explosions. In many instances it was clear that the material had flowed down valleys or spread out over plains, assuming an essentially level surface in the manner of a liquid instead of forming a layer mantling the hillsides and ridgetops as would a shower of fragments falling from the air. At the same time, however, much of the material was obviously of fragmental origin. Large pieces of pumice and bits of other types of rock scattered through it could be seen with the naked eye, and the microscope showed it to be made up of angular bits of glass and crystals identical with those of exploded ash. The obviously fragmental rock often grades downward, and sometimes laterally, into denser rock resembling lava flows. At lower levels in the mass, the pumice fragments commonly become flattened and the vesicles in them more and more closed up, until each fragment becomes a dense flat disk. In cross section the disks appear as conspicuous black lenses of obsidian, often with fuzzy ends, in a gray or brown matrix (Plate 8-3). They are perhaps the most conspicuous features of these rocks and have received the Italian name *fiamme*, or "flames" (singular: fiamma). Under the microscope the bits of glass are seen to be-

PLATE 8-3. Specimens of ignimbrite, showing dark fiamme in a lighter matrix. (A) Bear Creek member of the Nomlaki Tuff northwest of Mount Lassen, California. The specimen is 4 inches wide. (B) Tertiary ignimbrite capping the Providence Mountains, southeastern California. The scale is the same. Hawaii Institute of Geophysics photo by G. A. Macdonald.

come interlocked and molded around each other and around the crystal fragments, and increasingly flattened and drawn out in a direction essentially parallel to the surface of the mass. This parallel structure, resembling flow structure in lava flows, was early given the name *eutaxitic*. Megascopically, the rock often first assumes the appearance of a rather streaky lava flow, which in turn may grade into a layer of dense black obsidian. The obsidian layers may be very extensive and retain rather uniform thickness over broad areas; but in other instances they are markedly lenticular and may pinch out, for example from 30 feet to 1 foot or even to zero, within horizontal distances of a few hundred feet.

The clue to the origin of these rocks came from recognition of the mechanism of glowing avalanches. In 1912 there was a great eruption close to the base of the volcano Katmai in Alaska. West of the volcano lay a deep glaciated valley heading at Katmai Pass. The eruption laid a thick deposit of ash over the surrounding countryside and destroyed the vegetation. A few years later the botanist, R. F. Griggs, was studying the return of plant life to the devastated area. Crossing the Katmai Pass, he found the valley tremendously altered. It had been filled to a depth of many tens of feet by a deposit of new material, and from the surface of the fill rose hundreds of jets of steam (fumaroles). He named it the Valley of Ten Thousand Smokes. Soon afterward he headed an expedition sent by the National Geographic Society to study the valley, and among the geologists in the expedition were C. N. Fenner and E. G. Zies of the Geophysical Laboratory of the Carnegie Institution of Washington. Zies' principal studies were on the gases being given off and the materials deposited by them. His results will be mentioned in Chapter 13. Fenner studied the deposit itself and found that it was made up of sandy material consisting of bits of rhyolite glass and crystals. Scattered through it were many lumps of pumice. The material had flowed down the valley with great fluidity, burying the older topography and coming to rest with a surface that sloped very gently from the head of the valley

154

to the end of the deposit, about 14 miles downstream. Fenner called it a "sand flow" and concluded that it had formed in much the same way as the deposits of the glowing avalanches of Mt. Pelée. He suggested (1923) that its great mobility had resulted from cushioning of the individual fragments by expanding envelopes of gas given off from the particles themselves—the same idea of "autoexplosivity" later adopted by Perret to explain the movement of glowing avalanches. The "sand flow" has a volume of about 2.6 cubic miles, but all of it appears to have been emplaced in less than 20 hours (Curtis, 1968).

Shortly afterward, P. Marshall (1935) recognized the similarity of the "sand flow" material to the less consolidated portions of the great sheets that make up the "rhyolite plateau" in the center of the North Island of New Zealand. To indicate the similarity of their origin to that of the deposits of glowing avalanches ("nuées ardentes"), he named the deposits ignimbrites ("glowing-cloud rocks"). But in New Zealand the loose surficial parts of the deposits grade downward into well-consolidated rocks that contain the lumps of collapsed pumice, lenses of black obsidian, and softened and twisted glass shards described above, and these in turn grade into massive obsidian. Marshall pointed out that these rocks must have been formed by the welding, or sticking together, of still-plastic bits of glass and pumice in flows of fragmental material like the "sand flow," and that the plastic condition of the fragments must have resulted from the high temperature of the deposit when it came to rest. Not only had the fragments been welded, but the slow cooling of the deposit and the effects of gases had caused the glass to partly devitrify. Fine needle-like crystals had formed in it extending inward from the edges of individual fragments and in some instances crossing the boundaries from one fragment to another. Commonly, these microscopic crystals form radiating spherical masses known as *spherulites,* or more elongate masses called *axiolites.* The crystallization tends to obscure the fragmental character of the original material and adds to the consolidation of the deposit.

Currently, the flows that produce these deposits are more commonly called *ash flows.* The rocks produced by them, which were called ignimbrite by Marshall, have commonly been called by other writers "welded tuff." Correlatively, the flows that produced them have been called "tuff flows." The term is a poor one, because "tuff" denotes a consolidated rock, and obviously the material was far from consolidated at the time it was flowing. "Ignimbrite" likewise is out of favor with many writers, partly because of its implication of the origin of the material from a cloud—a very minor feature of the flow—and partly because of the vagueness of Marshall's original definition of the term, which did not make clear whether it was based on the mode of origin of the material or on its composition or physical nature. However, both the etymological structure of the word and Marshall's comparison of the deposits to that formed in the Valley of Ten Thousand Smokes seems to imply clearly that Marshall intended the term to designate rocks formed by flows of the "sand flow" type, regardless of composition or details of structure. I prefer to use the term *ash flow* for the eruptive mechanism,

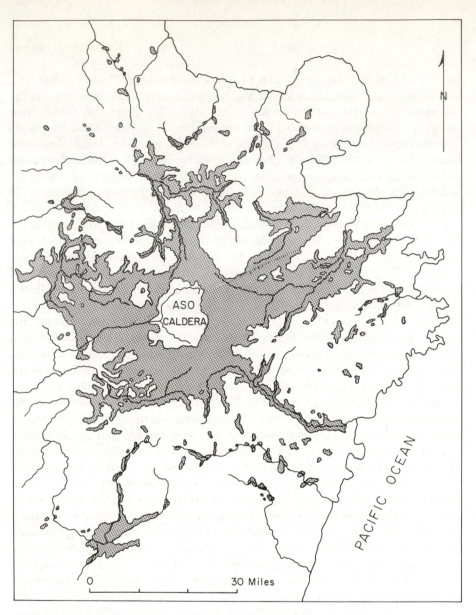

FIGURE 8-3. Map of part of Kyushu, Japan, showing the distribution of ignimbrite around Aso Caldera. To a large degree the flows followed valleys radiating outward from the caldera. The deposits have been considerably eroded, and were formerly more extensive and continuous. (Somewhat simplified after Matumoto, 1943.)

and to define *ignimbrite* as *the rock formed by an ash flow* (welded or not). The term ignimbrite thus is synonymous with the more cumbersome "ash-flow deposit."

In some areas ignimbrites have been referred to as "mud lavas," and in parts of Japan they have been called "Aso lavas" because of their widespread development around the caldera of Aso Volcano (Fig. 8-3). Much of the "piperno" of the Neapolitan region of Italy is the same sort of material

156

(but most of the "peperino" near Rome is of mudflow origin). Weakly consolidated porous varieties are sometimes called by the Peruvian name, sillar. In them the consolidation is largely the result of devitrification of the glass shards rather than welding.

In most ignimbrites the predominant material is of sand to dust size. Scattered through this there are usually lumps of pumice or the remnants of collapsed pumice up to a foot or more across. In some, however, fine material is relatively minor and the lumps of pumice predominate. These have been called *pumice flows*, or *lump-pumice flows*. The deposits may be termed lump-pumice ignimbrites. Aramaki (1956) has suggested the general name *pyroclastic flow* for all types of flows composed of incandescent fragments.

The material of ignimbrites generally shows little sorting or bedding. However, as in glowing-avalanche deposits, there may be some segregation of the larger lumps of pumice at the surface and along the edges and snout of the deposit. Slight traces of bedding can sometimes be seen (Plate 8-4), and it may result either from successive flow units or from laminar flowage within a single unit. Occasionally, as at Crater Lake in Oregon, the color may change from bottom to top of the deposit, or from the distal to the proximal part of the deposit, due to change in composition of the magma in the course of a single eruption. At Crater Lake the great eruption that brought about the collapse of the mountaintop some 6,000 years ago (p. 305) began with ejection of dacite that formed pale gray ash-flow deposits, then changed to darker gray deposits of andesite (Williams, 1942). The deposit of the ash flow in the Valley of Ten Thousand Smokes consists at its terminus largely of nearly pure rhyolite with few crystals of pyroxene; but in the parts near the vents pyroxene crystals become much more abundant, plagioclase

PLATE 8-4. Ignimbrite layer exposed in the wall of the crater of Broken Top, a composite volcano near South Sister in the Cascade Range of Oregon. The lower part of the bed is nearly white, but the upper part is pale brownish orange as a result of oxidation of iron by rising gases. The ash is very little welded. Photo by G. A. Macdonald.

crystals are richer in calcium, the refractive index of the glass increases indicating a more femic composition, and the pumice lumps are banded with darker streaks of andesite. The latter indicate the admixture of andesite magma with the rhyolite magma in the later stages of the eruption (Curtis, 1968).

Most ash flows are of rhyolite, dacite, or trachyte composition. Andesite ash flows are fairly common, but basaltic ones are much rarer. The erupted magma and the glass formed from it may be almost devoid of crystals brought up from depth (phenocrysts), but commonly such crystals are abundant. They tend to be very uniform in type and relative abundance throughout the flow and, consequently, provide a characteristic feature that can be useful in distinguishing the deposit formed by one flow from others that are otherwise similar. J. H. Mackin (1960) and P. L. Williams (1960) have been able to identify a sequence of ignimbrites over an area of several thousand square miles in Utah and Nevada largely on the basis of their phenocryst contents.

Many ignimbrites contain fragments of foreign rock picked up from the basement beneath the volcano by the rising magma, and sometimes these fragments are very abundant. Examples have been recorded in which the fragments make up nearly half of the ignimbrite, but more usually they constitute only a few per cent. Commonly, they increase somewhat in abundance downward in the deposit and decrease in number as the distance from the vent increases. The size of the fragments also commonly decreases with increasing distance from the vent. In contrast, lumps of pumice in the ignimbrite may show little variation in abundance and size either vertically through the deposit or longitudinally from the vent to the terminus of the flow. The foreign fragments are generally nonvesicular and considerably denser than the pumice lumps, and their change in abundance is clearly the result of settling out during the progress of the flow. Kuno and his associates (1964) have pointed out that since the pumice fragments do not settle out, the bulk density of the surrounding gas–particle cloud must have been approximately equal to the density of the pumice lumps (0.2–0.8) but decidedly less than that of the foreign fragments. They find that at Towada Volcano in Japan at distances greater than 12 miles from the vent, the pumice fragments also began to settle out, owing to a decrease in the turbulence within the moving flow or to decrease in the density of the cloud, or both.

Other flows show a tendency for the pumice lumps to settle even close to the vent, and still others show no signs of sorting even at great distances from the vent. There must be considerable differences between flows, both in the degree of turbulence and in the density of the cloud.

The lack of sorting in ignimbrites appears to result from the high degree of turbulence that commonly continues to exist within the flow right up to the point where it becomes immobile. Deposition by the flow is brought about by the entrance of fragments of all sizes, more or less at random, into a bottom zone of relatively low velocity that results from friction with the underlying ground (Fisher, 1966).

As in the case of glowing avalanches, ash flows erupted high on volcanic mountains may form deposits only on the lower slopes, where their velocity decreases. On the upper slopes they may even erode the underlying ground. An example is the great eruption of Bezymianny Volcano, Kamchatka, in 1956 (Gorshkov, 1959), where nothing was deposited on the upper slopes of the mountain, although thick deposits were formed in valleys as much as 15 miles from the vent.

The features of ash flows and ash-flow deposits have been thoroughly reviewed recently by Smith (1960, 1960a) and by Ross and Smith (1961). Ash-flow deposits range in thickness from a few feet to several hundred feet. Many ash flows travel more than 10 miles, and some more than 50 miles. The Nomlaki "tuff" in northeastern California probably traveled at least 65 miles from the vicinity of Lake Almanor to the western side of the Sacramento Valley. In southwestern Utah and adjacent Nevada, single beds of ignimbrite extend for more than 100 miles (Mackin, 1960, p. 95).

The fact that ash flows can extend over such broad areas, reaching distances of tens of miles from the vent with a temperature still high enough to bring about welding of the fragments after the flow comes to rest, implies very rapid extrusion of the fragmental material, very rapid spreading, little cooling due to adiabatic expansion or to admixture of air, and little dissipation of the cloud upward into the atmosphere. Tazieff (1969) suggests that the last three factors, together with the ground-hugging character of the cloud, may be partly the result of abundant carbon dioxide making the gas of the cloud denser than the atmosphere, and thus lessening its tendency to adiabatic expansion and mixture with the overlying air.

Volumes of the deposits formed by individual ash flows are difficult to estimate, but those of groups of deposits formed by series of flows are fairly well known. The ash-flow deposits of Crater Lake, formed during the catastrophic eruption that created the caldera, have a volume of about 8 cubic miles (Williams, 1942). The upper Bandelier tuff in the Jemez Mts. of New Mexico has a volume of about 50 cubic miles (Smith and Bailey, 1966). Ignimbrites in the San Juan Mountains of Colorado had an original volume, before erosion, of nearly 5,000 cubic miles (Lipman and Steven, 1969). Howel Williams (oral statement, 1965) believes some individual ignimbrites in Nevada cover areas as great as 7,000 square miles, and even assuming an average thickness as small as 200 feet, these individual sheets must originally have had volumes in excess of 250 cubic miles! According to Cook (1968), Williams estimates that ignimbrites once covered more than 80,000 square miles in the Basin and Range Province of Nevada and Utah with an average thickness of 1,000–1,500 feet and a total volume of 16,000–25,000 cubic miles.

One of the most conspicuous features of many ash-flow deposits is the development of columnar jointing (Plates 8-5 and 8-6), particularly in their lower and middle parts. The jointing tends to be coarser and less regular than in many lava flows, and the columns are more commonly four-sided. Especially in arid regions, the columnar jointing commonly can be seen from

PLATE 8-5. Weathered and eroded columnar jointing in the moderately welded zone of vapor-phase crystallization in the Bear Creek member of the Nomlaki Tuff (ignimbrite) northwest of Mt. Lassen, California. U. S. Geological Survey photo by G. A. Macdonald.

PLATE 8-6. Columnar jointing in the upper Bandelier Tuff, a series of ignimbrites in the Jemez Mountains of New Mexico. At this locality sub-units 1 and 2 are respectively nonwelded and partly welded parts of a zone of vapor-phase crystallization, sub-unit 3 is a densely welded devitrified zone, and sub-unit 4 is a partly welded vapor-phase zone. Talus at the bottom of the cliff obscures part of 1 and 2. U. S. Geological Survey photo by R. L. Smith.

a distance of several miles, and it is often the first feature that suggests the ash-flow origin of the bed to a geologist entering a new area.

The coherence of lithified ignimbrite is due in varying degree to two different processes: welding and crystallization. Welding is the sticking together of the molten edges of the glass grains. All degrees of welding are possible, from incipient welding, in which the grains barely adhere to each other, to intense welding in which the grains adhere strongly and tend to merge. Near the surface of the flow, welding may take place without deformation of the grains; but at greater depths welding of any degree greater than incipient is nearly always accompanied by compression and flattening of the grains, due to the weight of the overlying material, and soft glassy grains may wrap around each other and around solid crystals and rock fragments.

The compression is accompanied by closing of vesicles and squeezing out of much of the gas that they contained when the flow came to rest, so that fragments of pumice tend to be transformed into flattened disks of dense obsidian. The degree of welding and compression commonly increases downward from an unwelded surficial zone to a zone in which welding becomes incipient and then weak, but porosity is still high and the grains are essentially undeformed, through deeper zones of increasingly strong welding and deformation, to a zone in which the original grains have lost their identity and merged into a layer of dense obsidian. Even in the dense obsidian, however, the grain boundaries often are still clearly discernible under the microscope as intricately curving and convoluted lines marked by grains of iron oxide. The zone of most intense welding is usually somewhat below the middle of the deposit. At the base, rapid cooling against the underlying former ground surface results in a reversal of the zones of progressive welding, and in the very bottom of the deposit the fragments commonly are unwelded and the original porosity and form of the fragments are preserved.

Locally, the deposit may be welded right to its base and, more rarely, to its top, especially where the flow was buried while it was still hot by another flow. The zone of intense welding is missing in some flows, and in some thin flows there is not even partial welding. The succession of zones may be entirely within a single flow, but where several flows were emplaced in rapid succession, they may at first have about the same temperature throughout the entire mass and may cool as a single unit, constituting what Smith (1960) terms a *cooling unit*. In this case the succession of zones may be developed across the entire series of flows that constitute the cooling unit. In the San Juan Mountains of Colorado, the Bachelor Mountain Rhyolite is a series of ash flows that issued from vents associated with a caldera near the town of Creede. At a distance from the vents, the formation consists of three separate members, but close to the caldera it consists of a single cooling unit more than 3,000 feet thick. The accumulation of ash-flow deposits near the vents was so nearly continuous that one did not have time to cool appreciably before the next one was deposited, but only occasionally did exceptionally big surges reach the marginal areas (Ratté and Steven, 1967). According to Peter Lipman (oral statement, 1969), other groups of ignimbrites that accumulated within some of the calderas of the San Juan region formed single cooling units as much as 1,500 feet thick that are almost wholly densely welded.

The degree of welding in ignimbrites varies with several factors, the principal of which are the thickness of the flow, its temperature when it came to rest, and the amount of gas it contained. Laboratory experiments show that the minimum temperature of welding of "dry" glass shards is probably about 750°C, but slight welding may take place in the presence of gases at temperatures as low as 535°C (Smith, Friedman, and Long, 1958). The slow cooling and weight of overlying material favor welding in the middle and lower parts of a thick flow, and a flow burying hilly topography may be unwelded where it is thin over hills and densely welded where it is thick over valleys. That thickness alone is not the only factor is shown by the fact that thin flows may be thoroughly welded, whereas some thick flows show little or no welding. The Walcott Tuff in Idaho is only 25 feet thick but is densely welded, whereas the Battleship Rock ignimbrite in New Mexico shows no dense welding in a cooling unit 250 feet thick (Smith, 1960). The Súlur Tuff in eastern Iceland is strongly welded in places where it is only two feet thick (Walker, 1962). Such very thin flows showing more than incipient welding must have been emplaced at very high temperatures. In some deposits the degree of welding decreases with the increase of distance from the source, reflecting a cooling of the ash during flowage.

Smith (1960a) recognizes four different types of crystallization in ignimbrites: devitrification, vapor-phase crystallization, granophyric crystallization, and fumarolic alteration. A few geologically recent ignimbrites consist of particles of fresh glass, but all glass is unstable and, particularly when it is held at high temperature in the presence of volatiles, it tends to crystallize. This process of crystallization of the glass is devitrification. Most ignimbrites show some degree of devitrification, and in many it is intense. In many ignimbrites a large part of the devitrification takes place during the cooling of the deposit. Especially in very thick cooling units, devitrification may be almost complete throughout the majority of the mass by the end of the cooling period, and undevitrified glass may be present only in the chilled top, base, and thin margins. In rhyolitic ignimbrites, devitrification consists in the formation of tiny crystals of cristobalite and alkalic feldspar with minor amounts of other minerals, largely in the form of spherulites, which are sometimes so fine grained that the individual fibers cannot be made out clearly even under the highest magnification of the optical microscope. The crystals are largely confined within the boundaries of individual glass fragments and formed within the glass itself. The crystal fibers tend to develop at right angles to the boundary of the glass fragment. Where the shards have been elongated by stretching, the crystal fibers lie for the most part across the length of the shard, giving rise to *axiolites* (Zirkel, 1876).

The flattening out and squeezing together of glass shards and the collapse of pumice fragments during welding, as a result of the weight of the overlying material, results in compaction of the ignimbrite that may amount to a volume loss of more than 50 per cent. The gas squeezed out during compaction moves outward, and particularly upward, from the zone of intense welding. It carries some dissolved material and deposits some of this in the more porous zones as silica minerals (tridymite and cristobalite), alkalic feldspar, and minor amounts of other minerals, resulting in a zone of *vapor-phase crystallization* that is best developed just above the zone of intense welding. In contrast to devitrification, vapor-phase crystallization depends on the formation of new crystals in the open spaces between shards or in pores in incompletely collapsed pumice. It is, therefore, absent in densely welded portions of the deposit except where locally trapped gases have produced cavities. Where such cavities exist, they are commonly lined with crystals and may show the petal-like or shell-like growths of lithophysae. The vapor-phase minerals are generally coarser than those formed by devitrification. Devitrification and vapor-phase crystallization are in part coeval.

In the inner parts of some very thick cooling units, quartz is found instead of tridymite or cristobalite, combined with alkalic feldspar in a micrographic (granophyric) intergrowth similar to that found in slowly cooled rhyolite domes and thick lava flows. Smith (1960a) believes that in some instances this granophyric crystallization is an original result of very slow cooling, but that it may also result in older ignimbrites from conversion of original tridymite and cristobalite into quartz.

In the upper part of ash flows the loose material along the edges of channels through which gas is rising to escape from fumaroles at the surface may be altered and firmly cemented by deposition of new minerals. More resistant than the surrounding material, these cemented "fossil fumaroles" may stand up in relief when the deposit is partly eroded, forming conspicuous columns such as those to be seen along Annie and Sand Creeks at Crater Lake, Oregon, and mounds and ridges as much as 45 feet high on the Bishop Tuff in eastern California (Sheridan, 1970). At Crater Lake the cementing material is largely iron oxide, kaolin, and opal (Williams, 1942). Surprisingly, fossil fumaroles are very rare (Ross and Smith, 1961).

Not all of the crystallization in ignimbrites takes place as a result of the rising hot gases. Like other glass, that of ignimbrites is unstable and tends to crystallize with the passage of time, aided by groundwater and other fluids that may circulate through the rock. Most typically, the resulting minerals are zeolites, such as clinoptilolite.

Sperenskaia (1967) has related the variations in mobility, degree of welding, and crystal content of ash flows in the Okhotsk region of northeastern Siberia to eruption from different depths in underlying granitic magma chambers. The first eruptions liberated magma derived from the top of the chamber which was poor in suspended crystals, rich in volatiles, and relatively cool. They formed widespread sheets up to 650 feet thick which, because of temperatures that probably did not much exceed the minimum temperature of welding of rhyolitic glass (ca. 600°C), were little welded. On the other hand, because of the high gas content, such elements as potassium, beryllium, and rare earths are abundant, and vapor-phase recrystallization of the glass is extensive. They were, in general, followed by eruptions of magma from a lower level in the chamber that was poorer in gas, but hotter, and contained more suspended crystals. Again, the flows were very moible and formed widespread sheets that, however, were much welded. The temperatures are believed to have been above 800°C. Finally, there was erupted magma very rich (40 to more than 60 per cent) in broken crystals, presumably from deep in the magma chamber. The flows were not very mobile and piled up to form irregular mounds as much as 3,000 feet thick along the vent fissures. They contain many inclusions of medium-grained granite but few pumice fragments or fiamme formed by collapse of pumice, although both of the latter are common in flows of the first two types. That their temperature was high is shown by the high degree of welding of the glass matrix.

The mechanism of generation of ash flows appears to be an extreme frothing of gas-rich magma in the vent and upper part of the feeding conduit. The expansion of the gas first inflates the magma to froth (which may consolidate to pumice) and then literally tears the froth apart to form angular bits of ash. The process is essentially the same as that which produces ordinary explosive magmatic ash (Chapter 7), and in both cases the debris consists largely of the curved and Y-shaped fragments of the septa that once separated the bubbles in the froth. Some portions escape complete disruption and survive as lumps of pumice. The emulsion of gas and solid fragments rises to the lip of the vent and in large part simply overflows, though probably always with at least minor accompanying explosive activity (Fig. 8-4). Lubricated by the interstitial gas, the mixture flows with great rapidity to great distances and assumes a nearly level surface of equilibrium. The residual heat results in welding of the fragments and the still-soft lumps of pumice are flattened into fiamme.

The fiamme in ignimbrites generally are nearly equant in horizontal dimensions. Although they may be slightly stretched in the direction of movement of the flow, the distortion that has formed them is very largely vertical compression. An unusual instance of the stretching of both pumice fragments and fiamme in ignimbrites has been described by Schmincke and Swanson (1967) at Grand Canary Island. The ignimbrites consist of several cooling units of trachytic ash flows. In the uppermost, unwelded parts of the cooling units, the pumice fragments are equidimensional or only slightly elongate, but the elongation of the fragments increases downward, and in the zone of maximum welding the fragments are as much as 30 times as long as they are thick or wide. This deformation is accompanied by other unusual structures, all of which indicate unusually high viscosity of the flows during their last few meters of movement. Some stretched pumice blocks have been broken into fragments by fractures perpendicular to their length and the pieces slightly separated, some pieces being rotated in a downhill direction by movement of the overlying material. Similar tension cracks resulting from internal shearing are present in the welded-tuff matrix. Elongate foreign inclusions have been rotated out of parallelism with the flow planes and are partly surrounded by open spaces that the matrix was too viscous to fill. Both pumice fragments and matrix in the welded zones have locally been folded, sometimes into open folds a few millimeters to several meters across, sometimes into sharp chevron-like crinkles, and sometimes into tightly appressed isoclinal folds. Ramp structures, like those in some lava flows (Chapter 5), have developed in association with the folding, cutting sharply across flow-unit boundaries within the cooling unit and producing ridges 1 to 4 meters high on the surface of the deposit. Schmincke and Swanson believe that these flows probably never were greatly inflated, and that they gradually degassed and grew denser as they slowed and began to

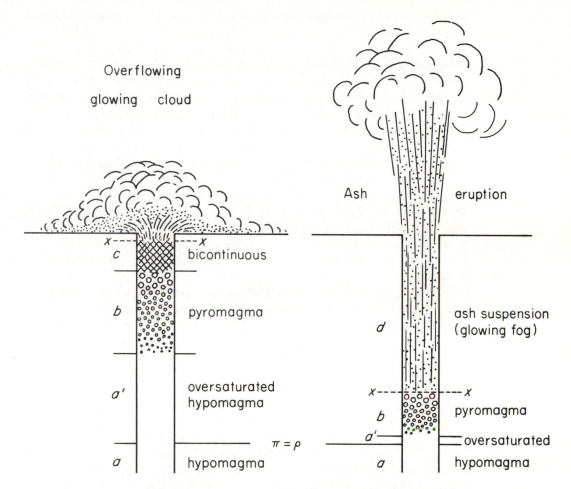

FIGURE 8-4. Diagram illustrating the difference between a normal ash eruption and an ash-flow eruption. (From Rittmann, 1962a.) The hypomagma at depth (zone a) is saturated or undersaturated with gas. As it rises into zones of lower pressure it becomes oversaturated (zone a′) and bubbles start to form in it (pyromagma, zone b) but the expansion of the liquid-and-gas mixture is restrained by the high viscosity of the liquid. In zone c the gas becomes so abundant that there are present two continuous phases, instead of a gas phase dispersed in a liquid. Eventually, with further rise, the explosion level (X - X) is reached, and the gas rushes out, bearing in it a cloud of liquid and solid particles. In the ash eruption (right) the explosion level is deep, and the expanding gas is directed upward as though by a gun barrel. In the ash-flow eruption (left) the shallow explosion level results in an overflow of the gas-and-ash mixture with ash flows and glowing clouds spreading out from the vent. The higher the viscosity of the magma, the lower the external pressure that is required to initiate explosion, hence the shallower the explosion level, so that the more viscous siliceous magmas (e.g. rhyolite) are more apt to produce ash flows than are the less viscous basic ones.

weld while some movement still continued. They may represent a gradation into the froth flows described in the next section.

Also probably related to froth flows are the ignimbrites described by Gibson and Tazieff (1967) at Fantale Volcano in Ethiopia. The flow is about 60 feet thick on the surrounding plain, but thins to as little as 1 foot on the flanks of the volcano. It is highly welded throughout and contains many very elongate fiamme of black glass in which are numerous unde-formed, nearly spherical vesicles. The fiamme are present throughout the deposit, including the upper part of the flow on the plain and the very thin portions on the slopes of the volcano, showing that their flattening cannot be the result of collapse of original pumice fragments under the weight of overlying material. The undeformed vesicles also indicate absence of stretching of the fiamme after the vesicles were formed. Gibson and Tazieff conclude that the gas–ash emulsion contained many nonvesiculated blebs of magma that on deposition became much flattened even when the weight of overlying material was very small. (They may also have been much drawn out by laminar flowage before the flow finally came to rest.) After movement ceased, gas separated in them to form the spherical vesicles. It is not clear, however, why the vesiculation was so long delayed.

McBirney (1968) has put forward still another hypothesis for the origin of fiamme. Certain ignimbrites in Central America contain many fiamme in restricted areas, but lumps of pumice in the higher parts of the bed are too small to produce the observed fiamme by compaction and flattening. The fiamme appear to be restricted to areas where the ignimbrites rest on river-laid sand and gravel that may have been saturated with water when it was buried by the ash flow. McBirney suggests that water vapor streaming upward through the hot ignimbrite was absorbed in the glassy shards, locally lowering their melting temperature sufficiently to allow the glass to remelt, forming the fiamme. Clearly, there is still not complete agreement among highly competent investigators as to the origin of some features of ignimbrites, and it appears probable that they are formed in more than one way.

In some instances welding and compaction of an ignimbrite has re-sulted in the development of sufficient mobility in the middle and lower por-tion of the mass to allow it to resume flowage under the influence of gravity. These are known as *rheo-ignimbrites* (Rittmann, 1958; 1962, p. 81). The amount of renewed flowage probably is generally small, though just how great it has been is difficult to ascertain. Its most characteristic expression is in the formation of dike-like masses of the lower more fluid portion that are intruded into the upper portion. On slightly eroded surfaces these auto-intrusions may be manifested as arcuate ridges of large blocks or more continuous wall-like masses of rock. These portions commonly show upward-curving joints formed by shearing of the very viscous reborn lava similar to those formed by the last movements in many block lava flows (Chapter 5).

Generally speaking, welding is an indication that a "tuff" was formed by an ash flow. There are, however, a few known examples of the welding of air-fall ash by overlying hot materials. In southcentral Washington, the Pomona basalt, an extensive lava flow of the Columbia River flood basalts, overlies an air-fall vitric tuff. In many places the tuff is welded at the contact with the basalt, the welded zone sometimes reaching a thickness of as much as 3 feet. The texture and minerals found in the tuff are identical to those of welded ash-flow tuffs (Schmincke, 1967). Similar welded air-fall tuffs are recorded beneath ash flows in Arizona (Enlows, 1955), in Yellowstone National Park (Boyd, 1961), and adjacent to a flow of rhyolite lava in Nevada (Christiansen and Lipman, 1966).

The nature of the vents from which ash flows have issued is discussed in Chapter 11.

Froth Flows and Tuff-Lavas

In ash flows the continuous fluid is gas with solid, or in some instances perhaps partly liquid, fragments dispersed through it. A lesser degree of gas expansion in the erupting magma may fail to disrupt the foaming liquid, resulting in a froth in which the continuum is a liquid and the dispersed phase consists of very numerous gas bubbles. Flows of this sort have been called *froth flows* (Boyd, 1961). The frothiness decreases downward, and the center and lower part of the flow may become only moderately vesicular or even dense. Upward, the degree of vesicularity may increase to extremely frothy pumice, and movement may break the pumice into blocks and finer debris that resembles the surficial parts of some ash–and–pumice flows.

The concept of froth flows has been elaborated by Locardi and Mittempergher (1965, 1967). In central Italy, near the calderas of Lago di Vico and Lago di Bolsena, certain lava flows issued as moderately to highly viscous magma that was transformed during flowage into pumice by expansion of its abundant contained gas. Flowage within the magma was laminar. Because of the high viscosity of the magma, vesiculation was in general retarded, but shearing between laminae locally induced more rapid release of gas from solution and the formation of highly vesicular bands. Movement was easier on these bands than elsewhere, and continued shearing along them resulted in collapse of the bubbles, thus transforming the originally highly vesicular bands into fiamme of dense glass. Meanwhile, vesiculation of the rest of the magma was progressing, forming a mass of pumice surrounding the fiamme. In the center of the flow the pumice remained continuous, but in the upper and lower parts of the flow it was broken into fragments by movement. The pumice fragments were crushed and abraded by mutual friction to form sandy and powdery "ash" that constitutes a fine matrix between the larger blocks. To some extent, fine material may also have been formed by autoexplosive disruption of the blocks. Thus, the upper portion of the flow was transformed into a mass of fragments and expanding gas that was more mobile than the continuous pumice phase beneath it and, in some instances, moved faster, leaving the pumice phase behind and forming an independent ash-flow phase. In these flows we have a continuous gradation from relatively little-vesiculated lava into frothy pumiceous lava, and thence into unwelded ignimbrite. Ash flows of this sort, generated on lava flows after extrusion, are probably never as extensive as some of the great ash flows mentioned in the previous section, which appear to have been generated during extrusion or in the upper part of the conduit before extrusion.

At the front of the Italian froth flows, the early-vesiculated blebs of magma richest in gas have survived as nearly spherical masses of pumice, although throughout most of the flow they were transformed into dense fiamme. It is worth noting that the fiamme are not disk shaped, as they are in typical ignimbrites, but are much elongated in the direction of flow.

In Armenia extensive deposits containing lenticular fiamme have been called *tuff-lavas*. Some workers have classed them as ash-flow deposits, but others insist that they are different and constitute a transition between lava flows and explosion-generated ash. Descriptions such as those by Shirinian (1963) and Petrov (1963) suggest that they may represent lavas of somewhat lesser gas content than those that form ash flows and in which the gas is not uniformly distributed. Inhomogeneity in gas content is a common condition in lava flows and frequently results in alternating bands of greater and lesser vesicularity, though, as pointed out above, shearing between flow laminae may also result in bands of greater vesicularity. In obsidian flows the alternating layers often consist, respectively, of light-colored pumice and dark-colored dense glass. In the Armenian flows the portion richer in gas commonly has frothed into pumice, whereas clots of gas-poor lava, drawn out into thin bands by flowage, have consolidated as dense black obsidian. These are in essence froth flows.

True ignimbrites, formed by ash flows, also are present in Armenia (Shirinian, 1963; Westerveld, 1952) and have been called tuff-lavas by some writers. However, Petrov (1963) considers that H. Abich (1899), in proposing the term tuff-lava, clearly referred to pumiceous lava resulting from the frothing of volatile-rich magma, which he regarded as intermediate between ordinary lavas and explosively generated tuffs.

At Suswa Volcano in Kenya, some phonolitic lava flows have surface portions 1 to 3 feet thick composed of masses of highly vesicular globules up to 2 inches long. The underlying parts of the flows, 10 to 75 feet thick, have the structures and textures of ordinary lava flows. The globules are somewhat flattened parallel to the flow surface and are molded around each other. Each has a glassy skin and a crystalline core. In some the septa between vesicles have partly ruptured, and some are hollow. Johnson (1968), who has described these flows, believes that the globules were formed by disruption of the top of the flow by vesiculation, forming molten globules each of which consisted of a thin plastic skin enclosing a fluid core. The globules settled on top of each other, becoming flattened and welded into a coherent rock. A few flows, 1 to 3 feet thick, consist wholly of globules. Johnson considers that they were probably emplaced as emulsions of hot globules and gas that flowed down the slopes of the volcano. He further suggests that the globule-surface portions of some flows higher upslope were more mobile than the normal lava beneath and slipped off the main mass of the flow to form a globule flow farther downslope. The mechanism has similarities to that suggested for froth flows in Italy.

Also in Kenya, lavas of a wholly different character have been called "froth flows" by McCall (1964). In them, clots of magma presumably once richer in gas than the surrounding magma have been drawn out into parallel bands and lenses by flowage and have developed coarser crystallinity than their surroundings. Although minor amounts of clastic structure may be present, the abundant relics of angular, Y-shaped, and irregular hooked and horned shards that are generally recognizable even in densely welded portions of ash flows are absent. The enclosing mass was a continuous dense or vesicular liquid, not a cloud of discrete solid or semisolid particles. Neither, however, was it a markedly pumiceous froth. The application of the term "froth flow" to these rocks appears undesirable.

Flows that have been designated as "tuff-lava" in Kamchatka appear to be of quite different origin than those of Armenia. They contain "fiamme" of porphyritic rhyodacite in a matrix of dacite that has the texture of an ordinary lava flow. V. I. Vlodavetz (1963) believes that a body of differentiated magma in a shallow chamber consisted of fluid dacite with a top of nearly solid but still plastic rhyodacite. Upward movement during eruption resulted in breaking the rhyodacite into fragments, which were carried out in the liquid dacite, being drawn out into thin streaks by flowage. "Tuff-lavas" in eastern Siberia, described by V. A. Keegai (1966), are rhyolitic lava flows crowded with inclusions of older rock, many of them lenticular. The older rocks were shattered by tectonic movements and the rhyolite magma rose into the resulting breccia, engulfing the fragments, many of which were carried in it as it poured out onto the earth's surface. The only close resemblance of "tuff-lavas" of this sort to the deposits of ash flows or froth flows is in the presence of "fiamme." It is apparent that highly lenticular inclusions in flows can originate in various ways. The presence of fiamme, although highly suggestive, cannot in itself be taken as a definite indication that the rock containing them originated as an ash or froth flow.

The three-dimensional forms of the fiamme seem usually to offer a clue to the mechanism of formation of the particular rock body that contains them. In the true ash-flow deposits, the fiamme are more or less equidimensional in horizontal section. They have been formed by vertical compression and flattening of more or less equidimensional lumps of pumice after the flow had nearly or completely come to rest, and consequently have suffered little or no stretching in the direction of flow. During movement of the flow, each lump of hot plastic pumice is discrete, and the viscosity of the surrounding material is too low to bring about deformation of the lumps by flowage. In contrast, the clots in froth flows that form the fiamme are not discrete and are drawn out by flowage of the enclosing relatively viscous mass. The resulting fiamme should be long and narrow in horizontal cross section as well as in vertical section. This is indeed the case in the Italian froth flows.

Volcanic Mudflows

The prosaic name, *mudflow*, designates one of the most destructive phenomena of volcanism. During the last few centuries volcanic mudflows have destroyed more property than any other type of volcanic action and have killed thousands of people.

Mudflows are just what the name implies—slurries of fine material mixed with water to form a mud that flows down the mountainside under the driving force of gravity. The fine material is generally of sand, silt, or clay size. It is most commonly volcanic ash, but it includes also soil and rock altered to clay by the action of acid in volcanic gases and hot-spring waters. Mixed with the fine material are varying amounts of coarse debris: bombs, blocks that may be several yards in diameter, tree trunks, and indeed any other movable objects that may be encountered by the moving mud. Some "mudflows" are water-saturated masses of gravel-size volcanic cinder. Whatever the material, the mélange moves down the mountainside, following stream courses where they are available, with a speed dependent on the steepness of the slope, the freedom from obstructions, and the viscosity of the mud. Speeds of 20 to 30 miles an hour are common, and some of more than 60 miles an hour have been recorded. The distance traveled also depends to a large extent on the nature of the terrain over which the flow moves, though loss of water plays a part in slowing and stopping the flow. Frequently, mudflows originating on the steep slopes of a volcanic cone continue only a short distance after they reach the gentler slopes at the base of the cone. Others, however, continue for great distances. Mudflows that travel 5 to 10 miles are common, and some have traveled more than 100 miles.

Individual mudflows may have huge volumes and may cover large areas. The Osceola mudflow from Mt. Rainier in Washington, about 5,000 years ago, had a volume of more than half a cubic mile and covered an area of 125 square miles along the White River Valley and in the now heavily populated Puget Sound lowland (Fig. 16-1).

Mudflows that follow valleys are long narrow tongues, but on surfaces of low relief mudflows spread out into broad sheets, often with lobed margins.

Not all mudflows are of volcanic origin. They may result from any sort of flood, and they are particularly common as a result of heavy rain on slopes that have been denuded of protecting vegetation by fire, overgrazing, or artificial clearing. For precision, therefore, it is best to specify those of volcanic origin as volcanic mudflows.

In Indonesia mudflows of all types are called *lahars*, and the term is beginning to be used in other parts of the world.

PLATE 8-7. Mudflow breccia, Tuscan Formation, in the Cascade Range near Whitmore, California. The fragments are of basalt and andesite lava flows. U. S. Geological Survey photo by G. A. Macdonald.

The deposits left by mudflows typically show an almost complete lack of sorting (Plate 8-7), though larger and heavier fragments may show some tendency to be concentrated toward the bottom, and water squeezed out of the top as the mass of the deposit settles after coming to rest may carry with it silt and clay and leave them as a layer a fraction of an inch thick on the surface of the deposit. The deposits of old mudflows often are very difficult to distinguish from those of glowing avalanches. Sometimes, however, they contain fragments of wood that are not charred, as they would be if they had been enclosed in very hot material. At the snout of a mudflow the water may drain away, carrying with it some of the material and depositing it as ordinary sediments. Thus, mudflow deposits often grade downstream into stream-laid sand and gravel. Successions of mudflow deposits also often contain interbeds of sandstone and conglomerate.

Mudflows may be either hot or cold, depending on their manner of origin. The upper limit of temperature is, of course, the boiling temperature of water.

The causes of volcanic mudflows include

1. Ejection of the water of a crater lake by eruption.

2. Release of the water in a crater lake by breaking down of the crater wall.

3. Rapid melting of ice or snow on the slope of the volcano.

4. Explosion-induced avalanches of old rock material into streams.

5. Descent of glowing avalanches or ash flows into streams.

6. Entrance of autobrecciated ("self-broken") lava flows into streams.

7. Brecciation of lava flowing over snow or ice or very wet ground on the slope of the volcano.

8. Extrusion of material already brecciated in the conduit before reaching the ground surface.

9. Heavy rains on loose material on the mountain slope.

10. Movement of water-saturated material down the slope of the mountain set off by an earthquake.

Types 2, 3, 9, and 10 may occur independently of any eruption.

Lakes often form as a result of the accumulation of rain and snow in volcanic craters, even while the volcano is still active. The lake may disappear during eruptions and form again during the time of quiescence between eruptions. The rocks in the crater walls commonly are partly altered to clay by gases that contain sulfuric, hydrochloric, and hydrofluoric acid that issue from gas vents (fumaroles) within the crater. Fine material is washed down into the crater, sealing the pores in the rocks of the crater bottom so that water will stand in it. Explosions through the crater lake, caused partly by gas rising from the conduit below the lake and partly by hot volcanic material coming in contact with the water in the lake or in the rocks below the lake and generating steam, may result in the water of the lake being thrown out and falling on the outer slope. The water may be already mixed with rock debris when it is thrown out, and it generally finds abundant loose material on the mountain slope. The resulting mud flows down the mountainside. As examples of this sort of mudflow may be mentioned those at the beginning of the devastating eruption of Soufrière Volcano on the island of St. Vincent in 1902. The early explosions of the eruption ejected a large part of the water of the big lake that occupied the crater, lowering the lake level several hundred feet, and the resulting mudflows rushed down the valleys on the south side of the mountain into the sea. They were followed by the death-dealing glowing avalanches of incandescent ash.

In Java in 1822, the volcano Galunggung exploded through its crater lake, ejecting the lake water and forming a great hot mudflow with a volume of 40 million cubic yards that traveled a distance of 40 miles.

Kelut Volcano, also on Java, periodically ejects its crater lake, causing mudflows that have taken thousands of lives. After a particularly disastrous eruption in 1919, during which about 130 square kilometers of farmland was destroyed and some 5,000 lives were lost as a result of mudflows, Dutch engineers constructed a series of tunnels through the flank of the mountain to drain away most of the water of the crater lake so that future eruptions would do less damage (Fig. 8-5). First a tunnel was driven through the crater wall at a level just above the lake surface. Water was then siphoned from the lake through the tunnel until the lake level was lowered enough to allow another tunnel to be driven about 30 feet lower, and this process was repeated until the water level in the lake had been lowered 185 feet. The siphoning was then discontinued and the water level rose again about 12 feet but was maintained at that level by drainage through the lower tunnel. The volume of water in the lake was reduced from about 85 million to 4 million cubic yards. The scheme was successful. Another violent eruption took place in 1951, but most of the water was evaporated in the crater and no large mudflows were formed. Only the uppermost part of the mountain was blanketed by tephra, and only seven persons were killed (two of them observers working for the Volcanological Survey).

The 1951 eruption of Kelut had two unfortunate results, however. The intakes of the tunnel system were destroyed, and the crater was

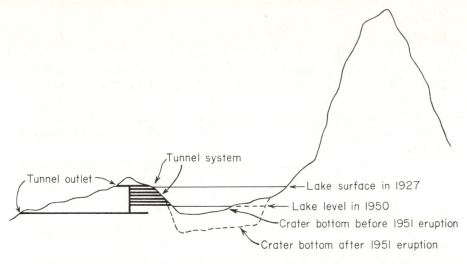

Tunnel system

Tunnel outlet

Lake surface in 1927

Lake level in 1950

Crater bottom before 1951 eruption

Crater bottom after 1951 eruption

FIGURE 8-5. Tunnel system constructed at Klut Volcano, Java, to lower the level of the crater lake and reduce the danger from future mudflows. (After Zen and Hadikusumo, 1965.)

deepened about 230 feet (Fig. 8-5). Only the main shaft and the lowest tunnel could be rehabilitated (Zen and Hadikusumo, 1965), and by the time the water level regained the level of the tunnel, the deepened basin contained about 50 million cubic yards of water. It was apparent that if this volume of water remained, the risk of devastating mudflows was again present. Another tunnel was driven 66 feet lower, but stopped short of the lake. It was hoped that seepage through permeable materials in the walls of the lake basin would drain the lake to the level of the tunnel, but the hope proved futile. In 1964 the lake contained about 52 million cubic yards of water, and Zen and Hadikusumo (1965) pointed out that if eruption came within the next few years, as appeared probable, it would again bring disaster. It did! The eruption came in 1966, and again mudflows killed hundreds of people! A new, lower-level tunnel was completed in 1967, and the lake is again drained to a low level.

The water of crater lakes may be highly acid, and mudflows containing such water may be even more destructive than those formed by ordinary water! A disastrous mudflow of this type took place at Kawah Idjen Volcano, Java, in 1817. Later, Dutch engineers constructed a sluice at the lowest point on the crater rim to attempt to keep the level of the crater lake low and thus reduce the risk of future acid mudflows.

The wall of a volcanic crater may be weakened by explosions, by gas alteration, by landsliding, or other causes, and as a result it may collapse, releasing the water of the crater lake. The violent local earthquakes that directly precede some eruptions are sometimes the immediate cause of the collapse. The resulting mudflows are composed of debris from the crater wall and material picked up by the water on the outer slope of the volcano. In 1875 a collapse of this sort took place at Kelut Volcano.

In 1914 a landslide from the crater wall of the White Island Volcano in New Zealand filled the shallow crater lake and blocked big steam vents that had been active within the lake basin. Steam pressure mounted beneath the new plug, and eventually the vents cleared themselves by blasting out the landslide debris mixed with mud from the lake floor. The mixture flowed seaward, destroying part of a sulfur-reclamation factory and taking the lives of 11 men. The deposit left by the mudflow has a very irregular, hummocky surface. Surfaces of this type, found on many mudflows, are discussed on a later page.

The collapse of part of the flank of an unstable young volcanic cone may produce a landslide that, if the rocks are saturated with water or, as often happens, if it occurs during or directly following a heavy rain, may become transformed into a mudflow. A collapse of this sort took place on the western flank of Raung Volcano in Java during prehistoric times, and produced a mudflow 35 miles long (Bemmelen, 1949, p. 194).

Melting of ice and snow and the resultant mudflows may be caused by volcanic eruption or simply by warm weather or warm rains. Mudflows of the latter sort were formed on the slopes of Mt. Shasta, California, in 1926 and 1931 by rapid melting of the Konwakiton and other glaciers due to warm weather. They had nothing to do with eruptions and are regarded as volcanic only because the mud was formed of volcanic debris. However, in 1915 a lava flow issuing from the crater at the summit of Mt. Lassen caused rapid melting of the snow on the upper east flank of the peak, and the resulting mudflows swept 30 miles down the valleys of Lost and Hat Creeks. Still more recently, in 1963, a lava flow from the crater of Villarica Volcano in Chile melted the ice and snow near the summit. Mudflows rushed down the mountainside and out onto the plains to the west doing great damage to fields and completely destroying a village on the lower flanks of the volcano. In 1877 a mudflow from near the summit of Cotopaxi Volcano in Ecuador reached a village 150 miles from its place of origin after following a circuitous course of more than 200 miles. Its average speed over the entire distance was about 17 miles an hour, and on the slopes of the mountain it was about 50 miles per hour.

Even more spectacular are the tremendous floods that result from eruptions beneath the glaciers in Iceland. Many of Iceland's active volcanoes are buried beneath glaciers, and eruptions of any of these may cause sudden melting of the ice. The two most frequent offenders are Katla Volcano, which lies beneath part of the Myrdals glacier, and Grimsvötn, beneath the Vatna glacier, both in south-central Iceland. Volcanic heat results in melting of the bottom of the glacier. At Katla the water accumulates in a chamber beneath the ice, but at Grimsvötn melting extends all the way through the ice, forming a lake visible at the surface. As the amount of water increases, it eventually becomes deep enough to float the edge of the glacial ice slightly upward, allowing the water to escape under it. In the case of Grimsvötn, it is possible, by keeping careful track of the amount of water in the lake, to predict when the escape of the water will occur. The water rushes out from beneath the ice as a tremendous flood, known as a "jökulhlaup" (glacier burst). Individual bursts may contain volumes of as much as $1\frac{1}{2}$ cubic miles of water, and the rate of discharge of some of the Katla bursts has reached more than

120,000 cubic yards per second—more than that of the Amazon River! The floods of water carry with them vast amounts of sand and coarser debris that have been spread out over the coastal lowlands to form the "sand plains" characteristic of that part of Iceland. They do great damage to farmsteads and have taken many lives.

Previous to 1934, the bursts from the Vatna glacier were frequently accompanied by visible eruptions in the Grimsvötn crater. The water level in the lake rises quite steadily between eruptions, however, and it appears that most of the melting must be caused by fumaroles or other more or less constant activity beneath the ice rather than by the visible eruptions. Indeed, though there have been no visible eruptions since 1934, the floods have continued. The release of the flood results in a rapid lowering of the level of the lake water by about 650 feet, and it is uncertain weather this abrupt reduction of pressure on the volcanic vent beneath may not have been the triggering force that set off the eruptions.

It has been suggested that mudflows at Mt. Lassen in 1915, and others at other volcanoes, may have resulted from sudden melting of snowfields by glowing avalanches rushing over them or by the fall of hot ash. R. H. Finch, who was a meterologist as well as a volcanologist, doubted this. He wrote (1930), "A few feet of snow can absorb several inches of rainfall so that the rain produces but little immediate runoff . . . . A hot blast unless long continued, or a slight deposit of volcanic ash, would produce the same effect as rain." It is commonly observed that lava flows produce relatively little melting of snow or ice with which they come in contact. Lava flows at a temperature of about 1000°C near the vents on the upper part of Mauna Loa in 1949 melted the 3 or 4 feet of snow directly below them, but caused the snow along their sides to melt back only a few feet. Lava flows on the upper slopes of Etna have buried masses of ice, but later act as insulators to preserve the buried ice from the summer heat. Since Roman days, this "fossil" ice has been mined during warm weather. On the other hand, the ash flows of Bezymianny Volcano appear to have lowered the level of the snow near the base of the mountain about 6 feet (Gorshkov, 1959).

Fiske, Hopson, and Waters (1963) consider that a very large proportion of the abundant breccias in Mt. Rainier have resulted from shattering of lava flows extruded onto ice, snow, or wet ground. They write, "Where thin lava flows slid downhill mixing with large amounts of slushy snow and melt water, the entire flow was disrupted by steam explosions, and the resulting mixture of sand and blocky debris continued down the slope in mudflows. In thicker flows irregular tongues and streaks of lava, still unshattered, have survived in the chaotic mixture. All gradations between autobrecciated lavas, breccias resulting from shattering of lava flows by steam explosions, and mudflow breccias are found on Mt. Rainier."

Explosions may cause avalanches on the flanks of volcanoes by ejecting large quantities of loose rock material onto a steep slope, the avalanche often picking up also unstable loose material that is already present; or they may undermine part of the slope, resulting in its collapse. The material involved may be largely or wholly old; it may be either warm or cold, depending on the proximity to the volcanic vent and to fumaroles; and it may be fresh rock, or part or all of it may be partly or wholly altered to clay minerals by weathering and/or decomposition by fumarole gases or hot acid water. The explosions commonly are low in temperature, caused largely or wholly by steam. In 1888 a low-temperature steam explosion (phreatic explosion) blasted away part of the flank of Bandai-san Volcano in Japan, causing the slope above the explosion craters to break free and slide, breaking up and gathering speed as it went. Most of the material had been much altered by acid fumarole gases. The avalanche rushed down into the stream valleys at the base of the mountain, mixed with water, and formed mudflows that traveled along the stream courses, destroying villages and farmlands and killing more than 400 persons.

Glowing avalanches and ash flows entering streams may be transformed into mudflows. At Merapi in central Java, glowing avalanches from the summit dome frequently form mudflows that have done as much, or more, damage as have the avalanches themselves. At Santa Maria Volcano in Guatemala in 1929, glowing avalanches entering rivers formed mudflows that traveled downstream more than 60 miles. In 1956 the tremendous eruption of Bezymianny Volcano (Gorshkov, 1959) produced huge ash and pumice flows that rushed down into the Hapitsa River valley, forming mudflows that went as much as 50 miles from the base of the volcano.

Tremendous amounts of mudflow deposits have been formed in many volcanic districts during past geologic ages. In northern California the Tuscan Formation (Anderson, 1933) once covered an area of almost 2,000 square miles and is as much as 1,700 feet thick. It is composed largely of mudflow breccias the total volume of which is approximately 300 cubic miles (Lydon, 1968). Individual breccia beds range from more than 100 feet thick near their sources to a few feet thick 30 miles away. In the Sierra Nevada of California, Curtis (1954) believes the Mehrten Formation, also composed largely of mudflow deposits, to have once covered an area of 12,000 square miles and to have had a volume of 2,000 cubic miles. The mudflow deposits of the Mehrten Formation can be found grading into brecciated andesite or basalt lava flows or the fillings of vents, and the brecciated lava in turn grades into massive lava. It appears that much of the fragmental material that formed the mudflows in these extensive formations must have resulted from autobrecciation of the lava during the process of extrusion—a fragmentation that resulted partly from continued movement, breaking the viscous lava into blocks, and partly from the expansion of gas in vesicles near the bounding surfaces of the blocks causing spalling of the block surfaces. It has been shown (Durrell, 1944) that some of the fragmentation took place in the conduit before the lava reached the surface. Lydon (1968) also has found breccia-filled dikes that appear to be sources of part of the mudflows of the Tuscan Formation,

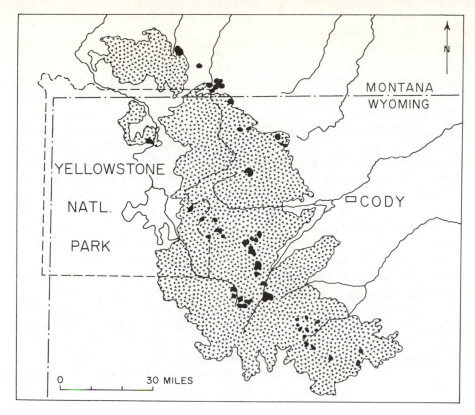

FIGURE 8-6. Map showing the extent of the Absaroka Volcanic Field, Montana and Wyoming. (After Parsons, 1967.)

but reports that gradation into brecciated lava flows is uncommon in that formation.

The breccias erupted from fragmented dikes are essentially mono-lithologic—that is, nearly all of the fragments composing them are of the same kind of rock. Other widespread bedded breccias are heterolithologic, consisting of a mixture of fragments of different types of volcanic rocks, and sometimes of nonvolcanic rocks derived from the walls of the conduits. In the Absaroka Volcanic Field in the Rocky Mountains along the eastern edge of Yellowstone National Park (Fig. 8-6), breccias and associated lava flows of middle Eocene to Oligocene (?) age extend over an area of about 4,000 square miles and in places reach thicknesses of as much as 6,500 feet. Close to the vents the rocks are poorly bedded, very poorly sorted, massive breccias and tuff-breccias associated with a minor amount of tuff and occasional lava flows. Individual layers of breccia range from about 10 feet to several hundred feet in thickness. About 80 per cent of the breccia is heterolithologic. In the northern part of the area the dark-colored fragments are andesite, but farther south light-colored fragments of dacite or latite are most abundant. In a few areas remnants of volcanic cones have been recognized (Parsons, 1967). Away from the vent areas the breccias become better bedded and grade into characteristic mudflow deposits that in turn grade into sedimentary conglomerates, sandstones, and siltstones composed of the same volcanic materials. W. H. Parsons reports about a dozen volcanic plugs and many other dikes and irregular intrusive bodies filled with breccias identical to those making up the bedded breccias. The brecciation in these intrusive masses clearly took place underground, probably in the ways mentioned in the discussion of the origin of breccias in volcanic necks and plugs in Chapter 15. Parsons (1967) suggests that the breccias formed in underground conduits were driven to the surface by the thrust of rising magma beneath, or carried upward in a fluidized state by rising gases, perhaps in part steam derived from groundwater in the adjacent rocks. Similar "fluidization" of tuff-breccias in and around volcanic necks is described in Chapter 15. Extruded onto the surface, the masses of fragments formed essentially cold block or block-and-ash flows. Condensation of water from the fluidizing gases would undoubtedly help lubricate the flows. Transformation downslope into typical mudflows was aided by the abundant rainfall in a normally humid region.

Although in some areas mudflows appear to have been formed in great abundance by the entrance into streams of autobrecciated lava or by extrusion of breccias formed in underground pipes, by far the commonest cause of subaerial mudflows during the last century of scientific observation has been simply heavy rain on the flank of the volcano. Particularly during and just after eruptions, the mountainsides often are covered with loose ash, which may reach a thickness of several feet and commonly is in a very unstable condition with a tendency to slide. Rain falling on the ash soaks it with water, and the sodden mass then starts to flow downhill, gathering both momentum and additional material as it goes. The movement of the flow may be started by one of the numerous earthquakes that accompany eruptions, but probably it more commonly results just from the increase of weight of the water-soaked material.

The rains that set off the mudflows may have various origins. Condensation of the steam in the cloud of gas given off during an eruption may produce heavy rainfall in small areas, provided the mixture of gas and air is saturated with water. Some evidence suggests that the saturation may in many instances be due more to ordinary meteorological processes than to the addition of steam to the air from the volcano. A very large steam cloud may actually contain relatively little water, due partly to the very large volume of steam as compared with that of water and partly to the great dilution of the cloud with air. At any rate, once saturation is reached the formation of rain may be aided by nuclei of finely divided sulfur or droplets of acid in the cloud. Also, the heat given off during eruption may cause a strong convective rise of the air over the volcano, and as the air rises to higher, cooler levels, it may become saturated and the water condense to form clouds and rain. Small cumulus cloudcaps often can be seen forming over volcanic vents that are not giving off any appreciable amount of gas. Unquestionably, most of the rain that causes mudflows is of ordinary storm origin. For instance, most of the mudflows that have buried the whole base of Mayon Volcano in the Philippines probably have resulted from torrential monsoon rains on the ash-covered

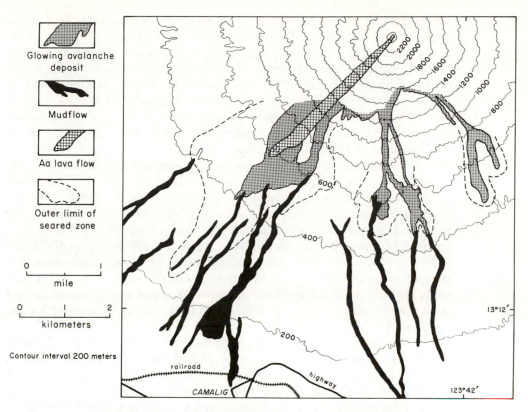

Glowing avalanche
deposit

Mudflow

Aa lava flow

Outer limit of
seared zone

0   1
mile

0   1   2
kilometers

Contour interval 200 meters

railroad

highway

CAMALIG

13°12'

123°42'

FIGURE 8-7. Map of Mayon Volcano, Philippines, showing deposits of glowing avalanches and mudflows formed during the eruption of 1968. (After Moore and Melson, 1969).

slopes of the mountain. During the 1968 eruption of Mayon, mudflows were generated by rapid erosion of the distal parts of glowing-avalanche deposits by torrential rains (Fig. 8-7), in part due to formation of rain-drops around nuclei of dust particles rising from the avalanches (Moore and Melson, 1969).

Some evidence suggests that the water of mudflows may originate within the volcano, or even within the magma. Lydon (1968) believes it is improbable that enough water to account for the mudflows of the Tuscan Formation could have been derived from rainfall and/or melting snow. He points out, however, that basaltic magma can contain up to about 3 per cent by weight of dissolved water at 1100°C and 1 kilobar pressure (corresponding to a depth of about 12,600 feet within the earth). A reduction of pressure to 0.1 kilobar (corresponding to a depth of 2,500 feet) reduces the solubility of water in the magma to 1 weight per cent. Thus, basalt magma saturated with water at a moderate depth should release water on approaching the surface. The solubility of water in andesitic magma under pressure is greater than in basalt magma, and saturated andesitic basalt magma such as that which formed the Tuscan rocks should release about

2.5 weight per cent of water, or about 7 per cent by volume. Such water might aid greatly in mobilizing the breccia forming in dikes and moving to the surface, particularly as large parts of it are transformed into steam at very shallow levels. However, the volume still appears wholly inadequate to account for mudflows with sufficient fluidity to travel tens of miles from their sources, in part over slopes of gentle gradient.

In some instances voluminous mudflows directly precede or accompany the beginning of volcanic eruptions. During the early stages of the 1902 eruption of Mont Pelée, mudflows descended all sides of the mountain, one of them destroying a sugar mill at the mouth of the Rivière Blanche along which the great glowing avalanches later descended. The volume of water in the mudflows appears to have been far too great to be accounted for by the ejection of the small crater lake that existed before the eruption. Furthermore, although the deep notch in the crater wall would have made it easy for the lake water to gain access to the headwaters of the Rivière Blanche, in the absence of violent explosions it is difficult to understand how it could have been ejected over the high crater walls onto the other slopes of the mountain. Rainfall on the mountain had not been unusually heavy and also appears inadequate to account for the mudflows (Jaggar, 1949).

During the beginning of the 1947 eruption of Mt. Hekla in Iceland, about 100 million cubic feet of water rushed down the mountainside in 6 hours—an amount which Kjartansson (1951) considers far too great to have been derived from rainfall or melting snow.

What mechanism could have caused a large and abrupt increase in spring discharge on the mountains? Is it possible that heating of the lower part of the groundwater body within the highly permeable and largely saturated volcanic cone may have produced steam, the expansion of which literally pushed the overlying water out onto the surface of the mountain? If so, the supply of groundwater accumulated within the volcano may be a major contributor to the water of mudflows.

One more interesting feature of mudflows should be mentioned. The surfaces of some mudflow deposits are dotted with innumerable small hills. At the foot of Galunggung Volcano, the "Ten Thousand Hills" on the plain of Tasikmalija (actually there are about 3,600 of them) are hillocks a few tens of feet high scattered over the surface of a huge mudflow that had a volume in the vicinity of 170 million cubic yards, formed in prehistoric times when an explosion destroyed a dam that confined a crater lake (Escher, 1925). A similar area of "many thousand hills" was formed at the base of Raung Volcano by the great landslide and mudflow mentioned on an earlier page. The hills were once thought to be cones formed by lateral eruptions, but Neumann van Padang (1939) has shown that they are protuberances on the surface of the mudflow.

At the foot of Yatsuga-dake Volcano in Japan, many isolated hills, 30 to 200 feet high and 250 to 2,000 feet across, rise above the surface of a prehistoric mudflow deposit. They are especially numerous on the end of the deposit farthest from the volcano. Where the deposit as a whole and one of the hills are both exposed in cross section, flow layers curve from horizontal in the main mass of the deposit to vertical where they extend upward into the overlying hill. Mason and Foster (1956) concluded that under hydrostatic pressure of that part of the mudflow still on the slope of the volcano, material of relatively low viscosity from the still-liquid interior part of the flow on lower ground was squeezed upward through fractures on the drying, hardened upper crust of the flow to form the hills.

Subaqueous Debris Flows

In some areas, particularly in sinking geosynclines, there have accumulated enormous volumes of layered rocks composed of volcanic fragments and obviously deposited beneath water. Perhaps most abundant are tuff-breccias consisting of angular to slightly rounded fragments from a fraction of an inch to several feet across in a fine ashy matrix. These grade into and are interbedded with sandstones and siltstones composed largely or wholly of volcanic fragments. The tuff-breccias occur in beds from a few feet to more than 100 feet thick that can be traced with certainty over distances of a mile or more and probably extend over many square miles. Within each bed the components show almost no sorting, though sometimes there is some concentration of the larger fragments toward the bottom. Fragments of uncharred wood often are present. The similarity to subaerial mudflow deposits should be apparent, and indeed these deposits are formed by mudflows beneath the water. Many of the associated sandstones also were deposited by "turbidity" currents—suspensions of solid fragments in water that move across the sea floor because they are denser than the surrounding clearer water. Beds of these sandstones commonly show an upward decrease in grain size due to faster settling of the larger grains as the current comes to a stop. Similar settling of the larger fragments in mudflows is largely prevented by the greater concentration of solid fragments in the suspension and, consequently, greater viscosity.

In the Cascade Range of Washington, the Ohanapekosh Formation consists of a thickness of 10,000 feet or more of mudflow deposits and associated sandstones and siltstones, lava flows, and ash flows. The vast majority of the mudflows appear to have formed subaqueously, some of them as a result of mudflows formed on land entering the water, but most of them by eruptions in or under the water (Fiske, 1963; Fiske, Hopson, and Waters, 1963). Similar huge deposits of subaqueous mudflows have been found in Japan (Fiske and Matsuda, 1964), in the Coast Ranges of Oregon and Washington (Snavely and Wagner, 1963), and in other parts of the world.

SUGGESTED ADDITIONAL READING

Glowing Avalanches
Anderson and Flett, 1903, p. 353–553; Hay, 1959; Lacroix, 1904, p. 196–368; Macdonald and Alcaraz, 1956; MacGregor, 1952; McTaggart, 1960; Perret, 1924, p. 89–92; Perret, 1935, p. 40–49, 84–100; Taylor, 1958.

Ash Flows
Cook, 1962, 1966; Curtis, 1968; Enlows, 1955; Fenner, 1923; Gilbert, 1938; Gorshkov, 1959; Mackin, 1960; Marshall, 1935; Martin, 1959; Peterson, 1970; Ross and Smith, 1961; Smith, 1960, 1960a; H. Williams, 1942, p. 68–98; 1957, p. 57–89; P. L. Williams, 1960.

Mudflows
Anderson, 1933; Crandall and Waldron, 1956; Curtis, 1954; Fisher, 1960; Fiske, Hopson, and Waters, 1963, p. 83–86; Lydon, 1968; Mullineaux and Crandall, 1962; Murai, 1960, 1960a; Parsons, 1967; 1969, p. 283–287; van Bemmelen, 1949, p. 191–195.

Subaqueous Debris Flows
Fiske, 1963, 1969; Fiske and Matsuda, 1964; Fiske, Hopson, and Waters, 1963, p. 9–10; Snavely and Wagner, 1963.

9

Minor Structures at Vents

The accumulation of erupted material around a vent forms a mound or hill, the form of which depends partly on the form of the vent and the violence of the eruption, and partly on the physical character of the material—on the angle of rest of loose fragments and the degree of welding of the fragments, or, in the case of lava flows, on the volume of the outpourings and the viscosity of the liquid. The hill may consist wholly of tephra, wholly of lava-flow material, or of a mixture of the two. Hills built by single eruptions vary from a few feet to several hundred feet in height and from a few feet to more than a mile across. Repeated eruptions build much larger structures, but these will be treated in Chapter 11. Only the smaller structures built by single eruptions will be dealt with in the present chapter.

Tephra Cones

One of the most familiar of all volcanic structures is the *cinder cone*—a cone-shaped hill or small mountain nearly always with a truncated top in which is a bowl-shaped crater (Plates 9-1 and 9-2). It results from

PLATE 9-1. Cinder cone near the base of Mauna Kea, Hawaii, showing the typical form of such cones and their craters. Photo by U. S. Air Force.

PLATE 9-2. Sunset Crater, a large cinder cone in Arizona formed by Strombolian eruption. Tree-ring studies show that the last activity occurred in 1064 A.D. Photo by Tad Nichols, Tucson, Arizona.

the heaping up around a more or less circular vent of cinder thrown into the air during moderately explosive eruptions. The conical form of the hill results from the fact that the largest fragments and the largest proportion of fragments of all sizes fall closest to the vent, so the hill is highest close to the vent and decreases in height away from it. The form can be shown mathematically to be related to the probability curve for the distribution of fragments of varying size falling around the vent (Becker, 1885). The angle of slope is close to the angle of rest for piled-up loose irregular fragments and is generally about 30°.

The crater at the top of the cone is most typically rather smoothly bowl shaped or funnel shaped (Plate 9-3). The sides are the result of

PLATE 9-3. Cinder cone near the summit of Mauna Kea, Hawaii, with a lava flow that issued from low on its side. Hawaii Institute of Geophysics photo by A. T. Abbott.

loose fragments rolling and sliding down toward the vent until they attain equilibrium. Sometimes the slopes meet in the center to form a pointed funnel, but at other times the center is a rather flat floor, generally the result of fine material being washed down the sides during rains and spread over the bottom. The crater may consist of a single depression, indicating a single vent active at the end of the eruption, or it may be multiple with several depressions, each surrounding a former vent. Most typically, multiple craters are aligned, as the result of the arrangement of the vents along a fissure. Where multiple craters are present during early stages of the eruption, they may be buried and replaced during later stages by a single crater as all but one of the vents becomes inactive. The crater is largely the result of building up of the surrounding walls, the area of the vent being kept relatively clear of falling ejecta by the force of the escaping gas. To some extent, however, it is often partly the result of collapse at the end of the eruption, the lowering of the magma level in the conduit removing some support and allowing the overlying material to sink in and the loose material of the crater walls to slide to a new position of rest. Sometimes the resulting collapse is very extensive and greatly alters the shape of the crater and even of the whole cone, but often it is comparatively minor and the original constructional form of the cone is little modified.

Rarely, a diminution in the strength of ejections toward the end of the eruption results in filling of the crater and formation of a round-topped craterless cone. Most commonly, however, craterless cones are the result of later erosion that has destroyed the crater rim.

Typically, young cinder cones consist almost wholly of loose material; but with the passage of time groundwater moving through them may deposit calcium carbonate, or some other type of cement, that sticks the fragments together. The cone is composed of superimposed layers formed by successive showers of fragments thrown up by successive explosions (Plates 9-4 and 9-5). The first layer forms a low mound on the ground around the vent, and each succeeding layer forms a mantle draped over the one before it, sloping from the crest of the growing ridge both

PLATE 9-4. Bedded cinder, in a cinder cone on the flank of Mauna Kea, Hawaii. Hawaii Institute of Geophysics photo by G. A. Macdonald.

PLATE 9-5. Close view of bedded cinder shown in Plate 9-4, showing typical irregular bombs. Hawaii Institute of Geophysics photo by G. A. Macdonald.

outward away from the vent and inward toward it. This arrangement of layers has been termed "mantle bedding" by C. K. Wentworth. On the outer slope of the cone the layers often are quite regular, and individual layers extend over large segments of the cone; but within the crater the layers commonly are very irregular, distorted and discontinuous, owing to truncation of their lower edges by succeeding explosions and resultant slumping of the material on the side of the crater downward toward the vent. On the outer slope, also, slumping and sliding are fairly common, causing some disturbance of the layering.

The cinder fragments range from a fraction of an inch to several feet in diameter, but most of them are between $\frac{1}{4}$ inch and a foot (Plate 9-5). Within individual layers the size of the fragments generally decreases upward, because in general in any one explosion the larger fragments are thrown less high, fall faster, and strike the ground sooner than the smaller ones. The size of the fragments depends in part on the strength of the explosion, more violent expansion of the gas tending to tear the magma into smaller shreds. Commonly, individual cinder cones are characterized throughout by a more or less uniform size of fragments (mostly fairly coarse, or mostly fairly fine) resulting from fairly uniform explosiveness of the entire eruption. However, it is also common to find a systematic increase in the size of fragments in the uppermost layers resulting from a decrease in gas content of the magma and explosiveness toward the end of the eruption. It is also common to find occasional large bombs imbedded in a haphazard manner in finer cinder.

Fusiform and spherical bombs often are associated with the cinder, though generally in very minor proportion, and in some cones they are lacking. Commonly, they are most abundant in the outer portion of the cone, and this also seems to result from a decrease in the gas content of the erupting magma and, consequently, in the explosiveness of the last stages of the eruption. Commonly, the impact of the larger bombs forms distinct pits, sometimes a foot or two deep, in the surface of the cone; and it may rupture the underlying layers or bend them downward in a "bomb sag." Sometimes, though comparatively rarely, the explosiveness decreases to such a degree that the ejecta change from cinder to spatter, and a layer of welded spatter may form over the crater rim or even over a large part of the outer slope of the cone. Spatter accumulating on the crater rim may build a nearly vertical wall crowning the cone. Such cones have been called "ruffed cones," because of the fancied resemblance to an old-fashioned ruff.

Rarely, also, a pool of molten lava in the crater may rise high enough to overflow and form a layer of lava over part or all of the outer slope of the cone. In receding again, it may veneer the crater wall also. These "armored cones," protected by outer shells of spatter or lava, are more resistant to erosion than are ordinary cinder cones, though it should be noted that even unarmored cones are remarkably resistant to erosion, because water from rain or melting snow tends to sink into them instead of running down over the surface.

Cinder cones range in height up to about 1,500 feet. Seldom do they get much higher, apparently because even if the eruption continues, the instability of the piled-up loose material causes it to slide and slump instead of building higher. Thus, the cone of Paricutin Volcano in Mexico reached a height of about 1,200 feet within the first year of the eruption (Plate 9-6), but changed little in height during the following 8 years of activity. Successive collapses reduced its height as rapidly as it was built up. Higher cones generally require the strengthening effect of lava flows interbedded with the cinder in the cone walls. These "composite cones" are discussed in Chapter 11.

Many cinder cones are nearly circular in ground plan. Where the vent is elongate, however, the cone also is elongate, and a fissure vent may be bordered either by a row of partly coalescing cinder cones or by a long ridge of cinder. Some cones are almost perfectly symmetrical, but most are lower on one side than on the other, and sometimes the notch in the low side extends all the way to the base of the cone so that the cone is horseshoe-shaped in ground plan. These unsymmetrical cones may result from nonuniform building because of inclined explosive jets that deposit more material on one side of the vent than on the other, or because of a strong wind in a constant direction during the eruption that blew the majority of the ejecta in one direction, thus building one side of the cone faster than the other. At other times a lava flow may burrow through the side of the cone and carry away part or all of the cone wall above it. Sometimes the burrowing seems to result simply from the greater density of the liquid lava as compared to the mass of cinder, the latter being lifted or thrust aside much as water would displace a mass of dry wood or sawdust. At other times the lava melts its way through the cone wall. First, wisps of fume start to rise from a small area on the side of the cone, then the area starts to glow and sometimes bulges slightly, and finally the molten lava stream emerges. Pouring out through the aperture in the cone, the lava may then lift and float away the portion of the cone above the aperture. Fragments of cinder cones as much as 100 feet across have been carried away on the backs of lava flows, some-

PLATE 9-6. The symmetrical cinder cone of Parícutin Volcano, Mexico, in mild eruption in October, 1944. The jagged surface of a new aa lava flow is visible in the left foreground, and the lateral cone of Zapicho, formed by an outbreak at the base of the main cone, lies at the extreme left. Photo by Tad Nichols, Tucson, Arizona.

times for distances of several miles. However, the commonest cause of "breached cones" in which the notch extends almost or entirely to the base of the cone is the pouring out of a stream of lava from one side of the vent throughout much or all of the period of cone building. Cinder falling on the surface of the lava stream is carried away, and the cone is prevented from building on that side. A breach due to this cause is generally on the downhill side of the cone, though not always, because the initial ejections may obstruct the passage on the downhill side and make it easier for the lava to escape elsewhere.

The initial building of cinder cones may be quite rapid. The cone of Paricutin was about 450 feet high at the end of the first week of eruption and 1,000 feet high within 2 months. Jorullo Volcano, some 100 miles farther southeast in Mexico, commenced its eruption in 1759 with phreatic or phreatomagmatic explosions that continued for about 10 days before the activity became more purely magmatic. In $1\frac{1}{2}$ months the cone had been built to a height of about 820 feet. The first recorded "birth of a new volcano," in contradistinction to the opening of another vent on the flank of an older major volcano, took place in the Phlegraean Fields, northwest of Vesuvius, in 1538. The cinder cone, known as Monte Nuovo (New Mountain), is only 440 feet high but was built wholly within 7 or 8 days.

With a decrease in the explosiveness of eruption, or an increase in the fluidity of the magma, or both, cinder cones grade into *spatter cones*. Spatter and cow-dung bombs become mixed with the cinder and commonly become partly welded to adjacent fragments. Sometimes layers that are almost wholly spatter alternate with others that are largely or wholly cinder.

Showers of spatter may be so voluminous that the individual fragments run together on the flank of the cone to form a "rootless" lava flow (one not directly connected with the source of lava at depth) that trickles on down the slope of the cone (Plate 9-7). These flows range from a few

PLATE 9-7. Spatter cone of the 1940 eruption, cut by the eruptive fissure of 1949, in Mokuaweoweo Caldera, Mauna Loa, Hawaii. The cone is approximately 100 feet high. Small rootless flows, formed by the coalescence of copious showers of spatter, can be seen on the lower right slope of the cone. Hawaii Institute of Geophysics photo by A. T. Abbott.

inches to a foot or two in thickness and from a few feet to several feet wide, and often are found interbedded with the layers of spatter or cinder. Other flows break through the cone wall from the central feeding conduit and partly veneer the cone side. Both cinder cones and cinder-and-spatter cones are commonly cut by dikes, often very irregular in form, representing intrusions into the cone walls or feeders of flows that broke through them.

A still further decrease in the proportion of cinder leads to the formation of purely spatter cones (Plate 9-8). Typically, they are smaller than cinder cones, rarely reaching a height as great as 100 feet, and most of them are less than 50 feet. Their slopes tend to be steeper than those of cinder cones, because the fragments stick together and the slopes are no longer dependent on the angle of rest of loose material. Welded spatter can stand in a bank that is essentially vertical. Also, within the crater less sliding occurs, and the crater wall may be very steep and irregular; and occasionally a pipe-like or fissure-like conduit may remain open to a depth of several tens of feet below the bottom of the crater. Like cinder cones, spatter cones are often breached, most commonly by the outflow of a stream of lava preventing the building of one side of the cone.

"Rootless" spatter cones (Plates 5-12 and 9-9) commonly form on the surface of lava flows, particularly pahoehoe flows, by the escape of

PLATE 9-8. Welded spatter, in a spatter cone formed in 1954 at Kilauea Volcano. Hawaii Institute of Geophysics photo by G. A. Macdonald.

PLATE 9-9. Rootless driblet cone on the surface of a late-prehistoric pahoehoe lava flow near the summit of Mauna Loa, Hawaii. The cone probably grew over a small tumulus. U. S. Geological Survey photo by G. A. Macdonald.

PLATE 9-10. Driblet spire—a small hornito—on the 1919 lava flow on the floor of Kilauea Caldera, Hawaii. U. S. Geological Survey photo by G. A. Macdonald.

PLATE 9-11. Row of tuff cones at the southeastern edge of the Island of Oahu, Hawaii. In the foreground is Koko Crater, a double cone breached on the near side. The far rim is higher because the wind was blowing most of the ash in that direction during the eruption. Behind it are Kahauloa Crater, Hanauma Bay (also the crater of a tuff cone), and the craters of Koko Head. Hawaii Institute of Geophysics photo by A. T. Abbott.

still-fluid gas-charged lava from the central part of the flow upward through breaks in the crust. They are generally small, from less than a foot to 10 or 15 feet high, and are sometimes referred to as "driblet cones." Very steep sided ones (Plates 5-11 and 9-10) have been called "driblet spires." They are types of hornitos (see p. 79).

Where the eruptive vent was a fissure, the spatter cone may be very elongate, or a series of partly coalescing spatter cones may be formed. Where lava fountaining is more or less continuous for short periods over considerable lengths of an eruptive fissure, long low walls of welded spatter are formed along one or both sides of the fissure and occasionally merge to form arches over it locally. It is sometimes possible to cross a still-active erupting fissure on one of these natural bridges. The wall built along the fissure is known as a *spatter rampart*. It is generally less than 10 feet high, but occasionally is as much as 20.

Cones built by the accumulation of ash around the vent are *ash cones,* and where moderately to very abundant blocks are imbedded in the ash, they are *block-and-ash cones.* The ash commonly alters readily to clay or to palagonite. Ash cones cemented together by deposition of secondary cement between the ash grains or by palagonitization are *tuff cones* (Plate 9-11). Ash cones and tuff cones may closely resemble cinder cones in form. Often, however, and particularly in the case of basaltic ash cones, the explosions are partly or wholly hydromagmatic (Chapter 10) and take place at very shallow levels. These explosions, essentially at the surface of the ground, throw the ejecta out at a low angle and the fragments accumulate at a considerable distance from the vent. In contrast, ordinary magmatic explosions typically take place at a moderate depth within a pipe-like conduit that acts like a gun barrel, directing the blasts more or less vertically upward; as a result, the falling ejecta accumulate quite close around the vent. Because of this difference in the mechanism of building, ash and tuff cones commonly have a much broader and lower profile than cinder cones, and their craters are more like saucers than bowls or funnels. Typical profiles are shown in Fig. 9-1. Very broad steep-sided tuff cones are sometimes referred to as "tuff rings."

Ash and tuff cones vary greatly in size. Diamond Head (Fig. 9-1) in Honolulu is a rather large one, nearly 1.5 miles across at the base, with a crater a little less than a mile across from rim to rim and averaging about 400 feet deep. The southwestern rim of the cone rises to 775 feet above sea level, whereas the northeastern rim rises only to 460 feet. The greater height of the southwestern rim was caused by the northeast trade wind during the eruption blowing the preponderance of ash southwestward from the vent.

Although they are not, strictly speaking, formed at vents, littoral cones are described here because of their resemblance to true vent structures. *Littoral cones* are formed by steam explosions where lava flows enter water. They are common along the shorelines of some young volcanic islands, and if a person is studying the internal structure of the volcano,

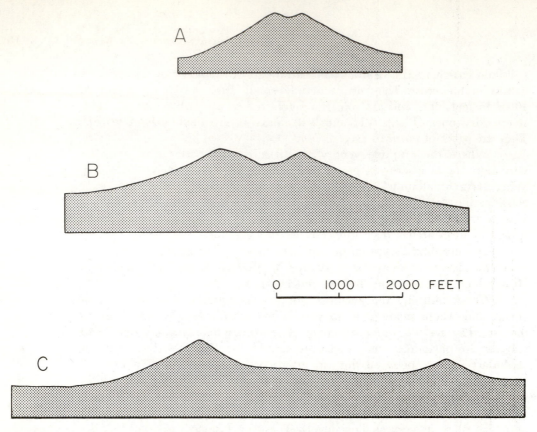

FIGURE 9-1. Typical profiles of tuff cones and cinder cones. (A) Cinder Cone, Lassen National Park, California; (B) Puu Makanaka, a cinder cone on Mauna Kea, Hawaii; (C) Diamond Head, a tuff cone in Honolulu, Hawaii.

it is important to recognize that these cones do not mark true vents where the lava rose from depth. Where a lava flow enters the ocean or a lake, the water may penetrate into the very hot central portion of the flow and be quickly transformed into steam, which rushes out again carrying with it a shower of solid and semisolid fragments derived from the outer part of the flow and liquid clots and droplets derived from the still-molten center. Most littoral explosions are caused by aa flows, because their fragmental surfaces allow the water easy access to the center of the flow. Block lava flows rarely cause large littoral explosions, because their advance usually is so slow that the amount of very hot lava newly exposed to the water within a small area at any one time is insufficient to generate a large, concentrated, and continuous volume of steam. Perhaps even more rarely are they caused by pahoehoe flows, which are encased within a fairly continuous skin that serves to insulate most of the very hot portion of the flow from the water. The brief exposure of red-hot surfaces of toes protruding from time to time along the front of the pahoehoe flow results in only minor steam generation. Where pahoehoe does produce littoral explosions, as did the 1868 lava flow of Mauna Loa (Fisher, 1968), the flow was probably unusually rapid, and perhaps also unusually hot.

The larger clots of molten material thrown out in littoral explosions solidify into bombs and lapilli. Generally, the bombs are irregular and rather dense, and characteristically their surfaces show a rather finely meshed shallow breadcrust-like cracking that is perhaps better described as a crackling. At the cone formed by the littoral explosions on the 1868 flow, some of the bombs were still sufficiently fluid to flatten out into cow-dung forms on impact, but this is unusual. The smaller drops of liquid spray freeze to little rounded pellets and irregular fragments of glass. Sand-size material of this sort may be washed along shore to accumulate as beaches of black sand formed predominantly of glass, with only minor amounts of stony debris.

Where littoral explosions are long continued, they build cones that may reach more than 200 feet in height and more than half a mile in breadth at the base. Puu Hou, the littoral cone formed by the lava flow of 1868 from Mauna Loa, reached a height of about 270 feet during the 5 days that the lava flowed into the ocean. The cone commonly is built on the surface of the lava flow itself at the edge of the main feeding river where the contact of hot lava with the water is most continuous. Commonly, also, a large percentage of the ejecta falls into the water and is washed away, so the cone is semicircular in plan with only the landward portion remaining. It may be quite regular in form with a single rim; or, as is the case at Puu Hou, explosions at a series of different centers may build a complex cone with several rims. Often, two separate cones are built at the two sides of the lava river; or if more than one lava river entered the water, three or more cones may be built. Mantle bedding arches over the rim of the cone, but bedding and sorting of the material often are poor. Some beds are nearly pure ash, but others contain numerous lapilli and bombs. Where the lava was very fluid, the ejecta may be partly agglutinated in portions of the cone close to the site of the explosions. Local unconformities and slump structures are common in the cones. In fact, the general structure of the cone often resembles quite closely those in cinder and ash cones built at true vents.

It may be difficult or impossible to be sure whether a given prehistoric cone at or near the shoreline was formed at a true vent or by a littoral explosion. Usually, however, the ash grains in a littoral cone are denser than ordinary vitric ash formed by true magmatic explosions and show fewer of the arcuate forms ("Bogenstruktur") resulting from the rupturing of vesicles. The difference results from the fact that the ordinary ash is formed by disruption of the magma from within by expansion of its own contained gas bubbles, whereas the littoral ash is formed by blasting apart of the magma by gas (steam) that originates outside it. The degree of contrast depends on the amount of gas that is still contained in the lava when it reaches the shore. Where the lava has flowed for a long way and lost most of its gas, the fragments produced by the littoral explosion are quite dense. On the other hand, where gas is still coming out of solution in the lava in fair abundance and forming still-expanding vesicles, as it generally is in pahoehoe flows, the fragments may be moderately vesicular. The rapid chilling of the liquid droplets thrown out by littoral explosions generally results in a large proportion of pale brown glass (sideromelane), though some black essentially opaque glass (tachylite) also is present. The same is true of the ash formed by hydroexplosions at true vents.

The ash of cones formed by hydromagmatic explosions, such as Capelinhos and Surtsey (Chapter 10), is intermediate in character but is generally far more vesicular than the littoral ash, because the gas in the magma was still actively expanding when the magma came in contact with water and the explosion occurred.

The pale brown or reddish-brown sideromelane glass formed by rapid chilling of liquid magma during hydroexplosions (either littoral or hydromagmatic), like that of the hyaloclastite formed by granulation of subaqueous lava flows (Chapter 5), is far more susceptible to alteration than is the common black tachylite. The blackness of the latter appears to be caused by dispersed very fine grains of magnetite, which are largely absent in the sideromelane, and the ease of alteration probably results from retention of the iron in solution in the glass. The sideromelane alters by hydration and oxidation, and dissolving out of some of its constituents, forming a yellowish- or reddish-brown waxy-appearing material known as palagonite. The material dissolved during the alteration commonly is redeposited between the palagonite grains as opal, calcite, and zeolite. The result is a consolidated rock called *palagonite tuff*. Basaltic ash cones more than a few hundred years old are nearly always altered to palagonite tuff. It was formerly believed that a large part of the alteration was caused by steam that permeated the cone during and just after its formation. However, the ash in the new cones of Capelinhos and Surtsey is unaltered or shows only the very beginnings of alteration even several years after the eruption, and the sideromelane of the 1868 cone (Puu Hou) is largely unaltered after a century. Moreover, the contact between palagonitized and unpalagonitized ash in the Koko Crater cone on Oahu quite closely parallels the gullied surface of the cone, showing that the alteration took place after the erosion of the cone. It is becoming clear that palagonitization is largely the result of ordinary weathering (Hay and Iijima, 1968).

Ash cones may form either on land or in water. In the latter case the cone commonly grows above water level, the base of the cone forming subaqueously and the upper part subaerially. The subaerial part of the cone consists partly or wholly of air-fall ash, with rather regular bedding on the flanks, mantle bedding arching over the rim, and both normal and reverse graded bedding. Sorting ranges from poor to good. The thin beds that result from the fall of ash from moderate to small explosions are generally moderately to well sorted, the degree of sorting increasing with distance from the vent. Thick massive beds formed close to the loci of strong explosions may have very poor sorting. Slumping commonly distorts the bedding on the crater side of the rim, and less commonly on the outer slope. Falling bombs and blocks cause compaction and distortion of the ash beds beneath them and form local basins in the underlying beds known as bomb-sags or block-sags. Heavy rains may accompany the eruptions, due in part to the condensation of steam from hydro-explosions, and rain drops falling through the ash cloud and striking on loose ash form accretionary lapilli, which commonly are abundant. The rains also may cause erosion of the flanks of the growing cone, resulting in local unconformities which may be erroneously interpreted as meaning that the cone was built during two or more separate eruptions. The eruptions are often accompanied by base surges (Moore, 1967), and the base-surge deposits show dune (strictly speaking, antidune) structures and often conspicuous low-angle cross bedding (Fisher and Waters, 1970, 1970a).

In the subaqueous portion of the cone the beds may show typical sedimentary features, and are apt to be better sorted than those of the subaerial part. Normal graded bedding, with the grains in each bed becoming finer upward, is often present, and may be conspicuous. Fisher and Waters (1970a) attribute these well-graded beds to underwater turbidity currents.

Lava Cones

Repeated overflows of fluid lava around a vent may build a cone consisting wholly or almost wholly of thin lava flows or flow units. The cone may take the form of a broad low dome—a small *shield volcano* (Plate 9-12) that is essentially a miniature of the large shield volcanoes built by repeated eruptions of fluid lava described in Chapter 11. Shields of this sort are known in Iceland, in Hawaii, and many other places. They may mark the vents of eruptions of flood basalt, as for example in the Snake River Plains of Idaho. Good examples are the small shields that have been built around vents on the rift zones of the major shield volcanoes, such as Kane Nui o Hamo, Heiheiahulu, and Mauna Iki on the flanks of Kilauea in Hawaii. Kaimuki in Honolulu is a small independent shield built on the same line of fracture as the tuff cone of Diamond Head. These small shields generally range in width from ½ to 1½ miles and in height from 100 to 350 feet, and their sides slope at an average angle of 2 to 5°. At the summit there is generally a small crater formed by

PLATE 9-12. Crater Lake Mountain, a small shield volcano on the Modoc Plateau northeast of Mt. Lassen, California. U. S. Geological Survey photo by G. A. Macdonald.

collapse when the magma was withdrawn from the upper part of the vent conduit at the end of the eruption. The crater of Kane Nui o Hamo, 1,000 feet wide and 200 feet deep, is an unusually large one. Small amounts of spatter often are associated with the lava flows near the summit of the shield; some, such as Kaimuki, are crowned by a small spatter cone.

Repeated overflows that spread less far from the vent, either because they are more viscous or because their volume is smaller, congeal one on top of another to build a steeper-sided cone. A good example is the lava cone built in the summit caldera of Mauna Loa, Hawaii, in 1949. After the initial phase of intense lava fountaining died down, a small lava lake, only 20 to 30 feet across, was formed. For a month the lava level in this lake fluctuated, dropping a few feet below the brim and then rising to overflow it. None of the lava overflows was voluminous, however, and most of them traveled less than 100 feet before they froze to immobility. This resulted in the building of a cone about 100 feet high and 300 feet across the base, sloping at an average angle of about 35°. At the top is a vertical-sided pit 20 feet across and 8 feet deep that was occupied by the lava lake.

The larger lava lake that existed in Halemaumau Crater at Kilauea for many years repeatedly built lava cones of a very special sort. At the edge of the lake, secondary fountains at sink holes (see p. 208) built a ridge of spatter, and repeated small overflows of the lake added to the ridge. There resulted a sort of natural levee around the edge of the lake that at times actually contained the lake at a level as much as 20 feet above the adjacent crater floor (Plate 10-4). This sort of structure has been called by R. A. Daly a "lava ring."

More or less intermediate between the steep-sided lava cones like that of the 1949 eruption and the miniature shield volcanoes are rounded lava hillocks that have sometimes been referred to as *lava cupolas*. Good examples are Colle Umberto and Colle Margherita at Vesuvius. These two "cupolas" were built over vents near the base of the main cone of Vesuvius, but fed from the main conduit of the volcano, by repeated overflows of moderately viscous lava. Colle Umberto, formed between 1895 and 1899, is 480 feet high and about half a mile across. Similar but smaller mounds, termed by Rittmann "rootless flow domes," form on the surface of lava flows around "rootless" vents where fluid lava from the interior of the flow escapes through a break in the crust. Some of these in the Valle dell'Inferno, between the central cone of Vesuvius and the encircling rampart of Monte Somma (Fig. 10-2), attain heights of as much as 200 feet and are formed largely of "entrail pahoehoe" (Plate 5-10). The extrusion of the lava resulted from the hydrostatic pressure of the fluid central part of the flow extending back up the steep slope of the central cone.

SUGGESTED ADDITIONAL READING

Bullard, 1947; Fisher, 1968; Fisher and Waters, 1970, 1970a; Macdonald, 1967, p. 52–57; Macdonald and Orr, 1950, p. 20–22; Palmer, 1930; Stearns, 1928, 1963; Stearns and Vaksvik, 1935, p. 13–17, 133–137; Stearns and Macdonald, 1942, p. 20–23; Wentworth, 1926; Wentworth and Macdonald, 1953, p. 22–26.

10

Kinds of Volcanic Eruptions

Volcanic eruptions have been classified on several different bases, but no classification so far devised is wholly satisfactory. The usual ones are based on the form of the vent from which the eruption is taking place, the location of the vent in relation to the volcanic mountain, or the general character of the eruption—that is, whether it is violent or gentle, explosive or nonexplosive, whether the lava is very fluid or viscous, and so forth. Each sort of classification is useful under its own special circumstances.

Classifications Based on Form and Location of Vent

The opening through which volcanic material issues onto the surface of the earth may be a crack or fissure, or it may be more or less cylindrical or pipe-shaped. Depending on the form of the vent, eruptions are commonly classified as *fissure eruptions* (Plates 10-1 and 10-2) or as *central-vent eruptions*. Although it is a fact that the central vents of most continental volcanoes are pipe-like, some of them are not, and the central

198

vents of most oceanic volcanoes are fissures. Therefore, it appears better to avoid the term "central vent" to imply the form of the vent and instead to refer to eruptions from cylindrical vents as *pipe eruptions*. By a *central-vent eruption* we then mean one from the vent at the apex, or center, of the volcanic mountain. A central vent eruption may be either a fissure eruption or a pipe eruption.

Eruptions at the top of a volcanic mountain thus are *central eruptions* or *summit eruptions*. They are the commonest sort of eruptions; but it is also very common for the mountain to be ruptured and for the volcanic material to issue from its side as a *flank, lateral,* or *adventive eruption*. Eruptions from vents near or beyond the base of the mountain are sometimes termed *excentric eruptions*. Eruptions in the summit crater are sometimes called *terminal eruptions,* and flank eruptions close to the summit are called *subterminal eruptions*. Both terminal and subterminal eruptions are best regarded as summit eruptions, the subterminal eruption representing simply a splitting of the crater wall. Commonly, terminal and subterminal eruptions produce no appreciable lowering of the top of the magma column in the conduit, whereas lateral and excentric eruptions result in a marked lowering and increase in gas activity at the summit.

PLATE 10-1. The eruptive fissure extending across Mokuaweoweo Caldera, at the summit of Mauna Loa, Hawaii, on January 7, 1949. In the right foreground a line of small lava fountains is playing along the fissure. In the middle distance the fissure has bisected the cone built by the eruption of 1940. Official photograph, U. S. Navy.

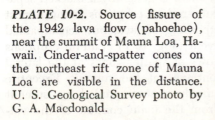

PLATE 10-2. Source fissure of the 1942 lava flow (pahoehoe), near the summit of Mauna Loa, Hawaii. Cinder-and-spatter cones on the northeast rift zone of Mauna Loa are visible in the distance. U. S. Geological Survey photo by G. A. Macdonald.

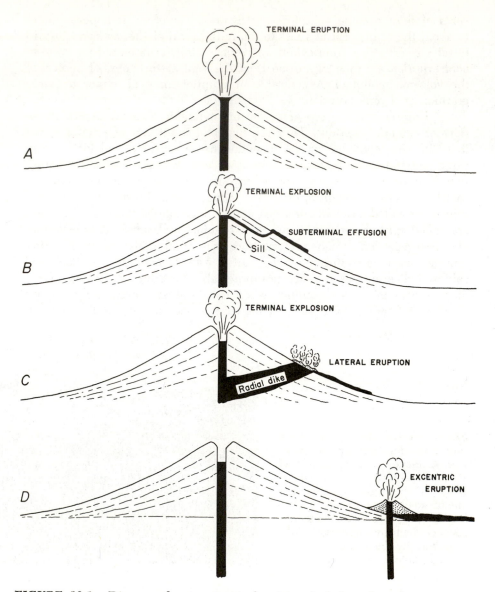

FIGURE 10-1. Diagram showing terminal, subterminal, lateral, and excentric eruptions. (After Rittmann, 1963.)

Thus, at Etna Volcano (Rittmann, 1963) there is generally a marked separation of gas and liquid phases, with subterminal eruptions being almost wholly effusive with relatively quiet outpouring of lava, but accompanied by explosive gas release at the terminal vent (Fig. 10-1). Lateral eruptions at Etna are mildly explosive, building rows of spatter cones at the lateral vents while explosive gas liberation continues at the summit. Excentric eruptions are independent of, and commonly unaccompanied by, summit activity. They apparently are not fed from the main conduit of the volcano, at least at shallow levels. Rittmann believes that their vents lie on fractures produced by regional tectonic movements rather than by any mechanism within the major volcano. They are more explosive than lateral eruptions and build large cinder and ash cones often with extensive lava flows.

At volcanoes in general, summit eruptions often take place without any associated flank activity. Flank eruptions also may occur entirely independently of any activity at the summit, but more commonly they are either accompanied, or immediately preceded, by summit eruption. The vent of a flank or lateral eruption commonly shifts progressively downslope as the flank of the mountain splits open farther and farther down. Small cones built on the flank of larger volcanoes (Plate 10-2) by lateral eruptions are sometimes called *parasitic* or *adventive* cones.

The outstanding examples of fissure eruption are the great masses of flood basalts (Chapter 11) and the almost equally voluminous eruptions of rhyolitic ash flows. Some eruptive fissures are very long. For example, the Eldgja ("Old Fissure") in Iceland erupted continuously over a length of 18 miles, and the Great Crack in the southwest rift zone of Kilauea Volcano in Hawaii is more than 8 miles long. The fissures generally appear to have been opened simply by the rocks on the two sides being pulled apart with little or no slipping parallel to the length of the fissure. Projections on one side of the fissure commonly fit into reentrants in the other side of the fissure directly opposite them. The width of the fissures ranges from a few inches to as much as 50 feet, and rarely even more. The walls of the fissure are generally veneered with lava. Locally, explosions may blast out funnel-like craters along the fissure; and cinder, spatter, and ash cones, and spatter ramparts may be built along them.

Most eruptions of oceanic shield volcanoes (see Chapter 11) are fissure eruptions. In contrast, most summit eruptions of volcanic mountains on the continents are pipe eruptions. Flank eruptions of continental volcanoes may be pipe eruptions, but are very commonly fissure eruptions. Often it appears that the magma first rises high in the cone, producing a summit eruption, but that the cone walls are unable to sustain the high pressure resulting from the weight of the column of heavy magma within it and rupture, allowing the magma to escape from the resulting fissure at a lower level. When this happens, it is common to observe a more or less complete "separation of phases," the gases escaping mostly from the summit vent, whereas the flank eruption produces a higher proportion of liquid lava with comparatively little gas and, consequently, a much lesser degree of explosion.

The eruption of Vesuvius in 1906 furnishes a good example both of separation of phases and of vents of different types. The eruption began with mildly explosive activity from the pipe vent at the summit with the magma standing at a high level within the mountain. Early in 1905 the level of the liquid had been nearly up to the lip of the crater. In late May, 1905, vents opened on the side of the cone at a 4,000-foot altitude,

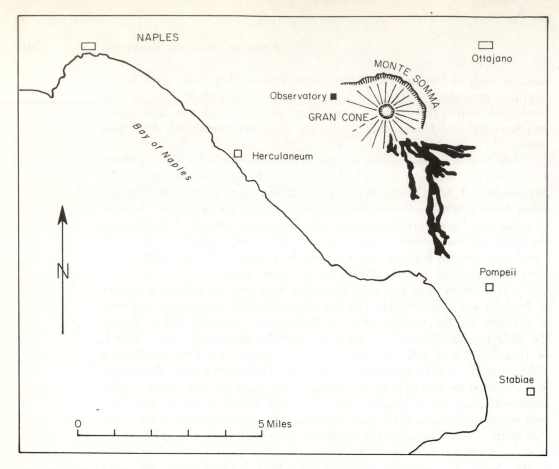

FIGURE 10-2. Map of Vesuvius, showing Monte Somma, the central cone, the lava flows of 1906, and the locations of Pompeii, Herculaneum, and Stabiae. (After Perret, 1924, Courtesy of Carnegie Institute of Washington.)

only about 400 feet below the summit (Fig. 10-2), and for 10 months fluid lava poured from them down the northwest side of the mountain. At the summit vent, mild to fairly strong explosion continued. On April 4, 1906, another vent opened on the south-southeast side of the cone at about the same altitude as the vents of 1905, and lava flowed down that side also. The cone continued to split downward, and at midnight another vent opened 1,750 feet below the summit and a copious outflow of lava began. The level of liquid in the central pipe was soon lowered below the older vents on the northwest side, and the northwestern lava streams ceased to flow. Explosive activity at the summit increased. As the now unsupported inner walls of the upper part of the conduit began to collapse, much of the material that fell into the vent was blown upward by the escaping gas and great volutes of black ash-laden cloud rolled forth. On the morning of April 6, a new vent opened on the flank of the cone at an altitude of 2,000 feet, about 650 feet vertically below the earlier vent, and still another rapid outflow of lava began. Lava poured downslope from the vent at a rate of 15 feet per second. Perret (1924, p. 39) writes: "At a

202

moment when we were observing and measuring the velocity of the outflow at the vent, this was suddenly extended upward [upslope] for some 20 meters or more with a sputtering roar and the ripping and tearing open of solid rock, and a sheet of the glowing lava shot, for an instant, vertically upward from the long rent to a height of 5 meters and then fell to the new level a redoubled river of fire." Thus, the flank vent was of the fissure type, and the outflow of lava there was accompanied by only mild spattering, though violent gas release continued at the summit vent.

During the afternoon of April 7, the violence of activity at the summit increased, and an increase in the quantity of glowing bombs and lapilli being ejected indicated that magma had again risen to a high level in the conduit. The upper part of the cone was covered with incandescent debris and great geyser-like jets of incandescent fragments rose above the crater rim. At 10:20 and 10:40 P.M., activity increased at the flank vents and torrents of liquid lava poured from them. At about the same time the cone was fissured high on the northeastern side and still another lava flow poured out.

By midnight the ground at the Observatory, a little more than a mile west-northwest of the summit, was in constant motion—"a continuous earthquake, and for some hours . . . it was impossible to stand quite still. Within the building it was difficult to cross a room without steadying oneself with a hand against the wall." The column of incandescent pasty fragments rising from the crater was 1,000 feet in diameter and 10,000 feet high. A strong updraft of cold air blew up the mountainside. Perret writes: "The most alarming feature at this time was the continuous increase—each earth shock felt above the regular pulsation was stronger than its predecessor; each wave crest on the sea of sound was louder than the one before; the jets of the great fiery geyser shot ever higher into the dark, overhanging pall of blackness that extended over our heads. . . ." The climax was approaching!

During the early hours of April 8, a branch of the incandescent jet from the top of the mountain gradually changed its direction, shooting more and more obliquely to the northeast over the crest of the arcuate ridge of Monte Somma, while the rest of the jet continued straight upward. The falling debris caused great destruction in the towns of Somma Vesuviana, Ottaiano, and San Giuseppe on the northeast slope of the mountain (Fig. 10-2). This oblique jet must have resulted from a change in form of the volcanic conduit at a level not far below the crater.

The simultaneous drainage from so many lateral vents, together with the voluminous ejections at the summit, brought about a lowering of the level of the magma in the conduit. Lava outflow from even the low-level vents stopped on April 8. As the level of magma in the conduit dropped, pressure on the magma at greater depths was reduced, allowing more and more gas to come out of solution and rush up the conduit. Fracturing of the mountain may also have allowed groundwater to enter the hot chamber and be rapidly transformed into steam, adding to the bulk of escaping gas. Beginning in the early morning of April 8, for a whole day a tremendous column of gas rushed forth with great velocity to a height of 8 miles above the mountaintop. The whole mountain trembled with the force of the blast; but despite the violence of the discharge, the gas carried up relatively little ash. Apparently, the great gas pressure tended to prevent the collapse of the sides of the vent. By April 9, however, gas pressure was diminishing and collapse resumed. As material from the sides slid into the conduit it was carried out with the gas, forming a billowing black "cauliflower" cloud such as is characteristic of many explosive eruptions. The blackness of the eruptive column was in strong contrast to the incandescent jets of the earlier part of the eruption. Activity of this sort continued with gradually abating strength until April 22. When it finally came to an end the mountain had been transformed from a high pointed cone with a small summit crater some 600 feet across to a truncated cone with a crater 2,200 feet wide and 1,600 feet deep, and the level of the summit had been lowered an average of about 550 feet (Fig. 10-3). The upper end of the pipe conduit at the bottom of the crater was about 1,500 feet in diameter.

As mentioned earlier, the opening of a flank fissure commonly begins high on the volcano and progresses downslope. Another good example is furnished by the eruption of Mt. Etna in 1928. The eruption began with ash ejection at the summit of the mountain, about 10,200 feet above sea level, on November 2. Less than 2 hours later a fissure opened at an 8,600-foot alti-

FIGURE 10-3. Cross section of Vesuvius, showing the change of form of the cone resulting from the eruption of 1906, and the refilling of the crater up until August 1920. (Modified after Perret, 1924.)

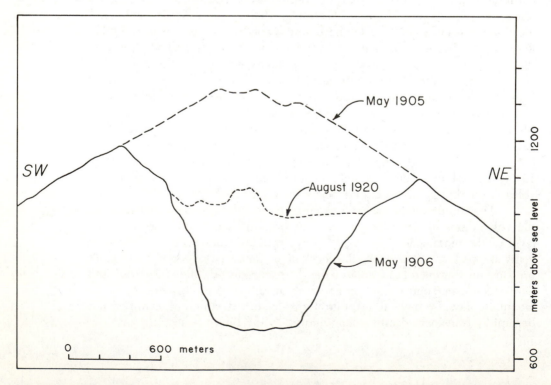

tude, and a small lava flow was poured out accompanied by ejection of cinder. This lasted only a couple of hours. At 3:30 A.M. the next morning another fissure appeared to the accompaniment of loud rumblings, rapidly extending downslope from an 8,250 to a 6,300-foot altitude. Cinder was ejected at 12 points along the fissure, and from the lowest a lava stream poured out. On November 4, still more fissures opened, extending downslope as far as an altitude of 4,000 feet, and a big lava flow commenced, which continued until November 20 and destroyed the town of Mascali.

The formation of a fissure vent by cracking or tearing open of the crustal rocks is easily understood, but the mode of formation of a pipe-like vent is less apparent. Pipe vents often are seen to be related to fissures, and even where no fissure is visible, the common alignment of several vents suggests that their position has been governed by a fissure in the underlying rocks (Fig. 10-4). At other times a pipe vent can be seen to be merely an enlarged portion of a fissure, or to have been formed at the intersection of two fissures. Pipe vents probably are formed by the coring action of gases

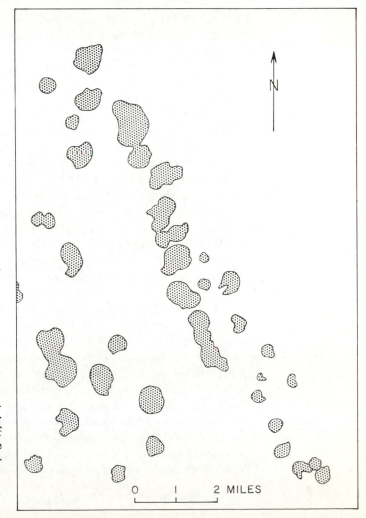

FIGURE 10-4. Map showing north-northwest alignment of cinder cones in the southwestern part of the Harvey Mountain Quadrangle northeast of Mount Lassen, California.

rushing out where they have found an escape to the surface along a fracture or the intersection of two fractures, the gas tearing fragments from the side of the channel and abrading the wall rocks; or they may be formed by fragmentation of the rocks due to stresses set up by heating or by melting of the rocks (the "blowpipe" action suggested by R. A. Daly) by the gas accumulated at the top of a mass of magma rising along a fissure. The rarity of pipe vents on oceanic shield volcanoes (Chapter 11) and in the great basaltic "plateau" areas probably results at least in part from the gas-poor character of the magma and the correlative lack of explosion.

Rittmann (1962, p. 30–46) distinguishes eruptions respectively from open and closed vents and "initial" eruptions that mark the beginning of new volcanoes. A completely open vent allows no possibility for the accumulation of gas under pressure beneath a tight "lid." Actually, however, it appears doubtful whether the closing of a vent can ever be sufficiently tight to permit the development of much pressure of confined gas. In general, the abundant joints in rocks would allow the gas to escape before the pressure became very high. Violent explosion appears to require the rapid generation of gas rather than storage of gas under high pressure. Some of the greatest explosions have taken place from open vents. The tremendous explosions of Krakatoa in 1883, described on a later page, took place from a volcano at which the vents had been open and erupting for several weeks; and as we have just seen, the great outrush of gas at Vesuvius in 1906 took place from a vent that had been freely open for more than a year. On the other hand, even mild explosions at the beginning of eruption from a vent that has been closed may throw out solid accessory fragments of the rocks that were blocking the vent.

An initial eruption from a pipe vent constitutes an extreme case of an eruption from a closed vent. The first breakthrough is often explosive and throws out a shower of fragments of older rock. In more detail, the first things to be seen are apt to be a cracking and slight sagging of the surface followed by a rather gentle oozing out of sulfurous gas that increases in strength until an explosion occurs. The first deposits around the new vent may consist largely or wholly of accessory or accidental debris. Except in the case of nonmagmatic explosions, these are succeeded by essential materials.

In contrast, the initial opening of a fissure vent may be no more explosive, and sometimes is less so, than the later activity. Eruptions in Hawaii commonly begin with the quiet opening of a fissure from which spurts a row of fountains of liquid lava only a few feet or tens of feet high, but sometimes several miles long. As the eruption progresses, the row of fountains becomes shorter and the remaining fountains become taller. To be sure, sometimes the outbreak is accompanied by a puff of gas, but the gas is not under high pressure. The rocks of the Hawaiian shield volcanoes (see Chapter 11) are so permeable that it probably is not possible under ordinary circumstances to accumulate within them gas under much pressure. On the other hand, the opening fissure vent of the 1947 eruption of Hekla

Volcano in Iceland released a great gas cloud that for a short time reached a height of 90,000 feet. Fissure vents are nearly always new vents. It is seldom that the same fissure produces more than one eruption.

Long-continued activity at an open vent takes different forms, depending on the viscosity and gas content of the lava. If the magma remains at a low level in the conduit, we may have nothing given off at the surface but a cloud of gas, rising quietly with rolling convolutions into the air. Where the gas issues at an essentially uniform rate, it probably indicates a quiet bubbling out of gas from a very fluid magma. More commonly, the gas issues in puffs, and at times the sound of muffled explosions deep in the conduit can be heard. Each puff represents the gas given off by a mild explosion, which does not throw the ejecta high enough to be visible at the surface. When the magma level is higher, the tops of showers of spatter, or cinder and bombs, become visible in the vent. On days when low-level winds are gentle, the gas cloud may rise as a narrow nearly straight-sided column until it encounters higher-level winds or the "inversion layer" at the top of the convection cells of the lower atmosphere, where it spreads out with a form like that of a mushroom or a wide-spreading flat-topped tree. Writing of the eruption of Vesuvius in 79 A.D., Pliny the Younger described the cloud as resembling the flat-topped Italian pine, and since then many other writers have commented on the "pine-tree cloud."

Lava lake activity (Plate 10-3) is a special variety of activity at an open vent. The classic locality for such activity is Kilauea volcano, where for a century a lava lake was nearly always present in the Halemaumau Crater. The lake disappeared in 1924, and since then lava lakes have been present only for a few short periods at Kilauea. Short-lived lava lakes are

PLATE 10-3. Lava fountain and beginning of a spatter cone in the lava lake in Halemaumau Crater, Kilauea, July 21, 1952. Many thin lava flows are visible in cross section in the crater wall. Photo by Fred Rackle, Carter's Camera and Gift Shop, Honolulu.

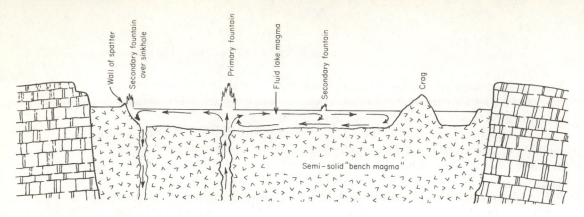

FIGURE 10-5. Cross section of Halemaumau lava lake at Kilauea Volcano, showing the circulation pattern, primary fountains, sinkholes, and secondary fountains.

occasionally formed at other volcanoes, as at Nyamlagira in the Congo in 1938, and Iwo Jima, Japan, in 1951; but the only long-lived lake presently active is in the crater of Nyamlagira's northerly neighbor, Nyiragongo.

Careful studies by T. A. Jaggar (1917a, 1917b, 1947) demonstrated the nature of the Kilauea lava lake. It consisted of a broad shallow pool, generally 1,000 to 1,500 feet across and averaging only about 50 feet deep (Fig. 10-5). Lava rose through vents near the center of the pool, marked by "primary" lava fountains a few tens of feet high, and flowed outward across the lake surface to descend again at "sinkholes" usually near the lake's margin. The surface of the lake cooled quickly to form a thin gray crust, but movement of the liquid beneath it broke the crust and revealed the red-hot liquid through the cracks between the fragments. Where the crust fragments were carried down in the sinkholes into the underlying hot liquid, they were partly remelted, and entrapped gases were released to bubble forth at the surface and form "secondary" fountains a few inches to a few feet high (Plate 10-4). The drifting of sunken crust fragments by subsurface currents often resulted in "traveling" secondary fountains that moved slowly across the surface of the lake. Thus, the lake displayed a convectional circulation, hot gas-charged lava rising at the central vents, moving outward, losing gas, and cooling to descend again in the sinkholes. In addition, from

PLATE 10-4. Lava lake in Halemaumau Crater, Kilauea, in 1910. Note the many small secondary fountains on the lake surface, and the levee built at the edge of the lake by the fountains where the convectional circulation carries the liquid lava and its crust downward. Photo by Ernest Moses, Hilo, Hawaii.

time to time cooling and degassing of the surficial part of the lake resulted in a destruction of the thermal equilibrium in the lake. At such times the crust would suddenly break up over the whole lake surface and sink, to expose for a few moments a complete surface of red liquid, which in turn quickly became chilled to a thin gray crust. Sudden convectional overturns of this sort have been seen more recently in the lava lakes that formed briefly in Kilauea Iki and other pit craters in the years since 1958.

The bottom of the Halemaumau lake consisted of partly degassed and cooled pasty aa-type lava, called by Jaggar *epimagma* or *bench magma,* that was far less mobile than the overlying *lake magma* or *pyromagma* (Plate 10-5). The Halemaumau lake appears to have been in essence the top of the column of liquid magma filling the conduit of the volcano. The upper part of the conduit was filled with a semisolid plug of epimagma that was transected by fissures through which the liquid pyromagma reached the surface. There, confined by the crater walls, the liquid spread out to form the lake. At times the pressure of magma beneath the plug was reduced, perhaps by drainage out into fractures in the flanks of the volcano or by flank eruption, and both the plug and the lava lake sank in the conduit. At such times the greater mobility of the pyromagma allowed it to drain away more rapidly than the underlying semisolid epimagma, revealing the lake bottom. At other times, as the pressure of magma beneath it increased, both the plug and the lake rose, the very fluid pyromagma of the lake rising faster than the plug. Sometimes the liquid rose high enough to pour over the crater rim or escape through fractures just below the rim and flood the adjacent floor of the larger Kilauea Crater (caldera) around it. In 1919 the lake overflowed onto the crater floor in this manner for more than 10 months.

PLATE 10-5.   Islands of "epimagma" projecting through "pyromagma" in Halemaumau lava lake at Kilauea Volcano in January 1918. Crags of this sort commonly shifted laterally in the lake with movements of the viscous epimagma that formed the lower portion of the lake. Hawaiian Volcano Observatory photo by T. A. Jaggar.

Where no lava lake is present, lava may overflow quietly from an open vent as terminal or subterminal lava flows, like those of Vesuvius in 1905 mentioned above; or more viscous lava may pile up over the vent for many months or years, forming a dome or a series of domes, like those built at Santa Maria, Guatemala, between 1922 and 1925.

Classifications Based on Character of the Eruption

Eruptions may be classified according to the proportion of explosion in them. *Explosive eruptions* may consist entirely of explosive ejection of tephra. On the other hand, *effusive eruptions* may involve very little explosion and consist almost wholly of a relatively quiet outpouring of lava. *Mixed eruptions* involve both lava outpouring and explosion. Most eruptions are actually either explosive or mixed. Eruptions wholly devoid of explosion are very rare, if indeed they ever occur at all; but if the explosive aspect is very gentle and minor it is commonly ignored, and the eruption is considered effusive.

Traditionally, different types of eruptions have been designated in part by the names of volcanoes at which they constitute the common or characteristic type of activity. Thus, we have Hawaiian-, Strombolian-, Vulcanian-, and Peléean-type eruptions. Objection has sometimes been raised to these names on the basis that no volcano always exhibits the same sort of activity. In fact, two or more different types of activity may go on simultaneously at different vents on the same volcano. It is quite possible to find three different vents, for instance in the crater of Stromboli, producing at the same time Strombolian, Hawaiian, and Vulcanian eruption. But it is also a fact that most volcanoes have a characteristic habit of eruption, and although they may depart from that habit in varying degree from time to time, so long as we remember that the name designates only a particular sort of activity there seems to be no real objection to using for it the name of a volcano. At any rate, the names are thoroughly entrenched in the literature and must be understood until they are replaced by some better nomenclature.

A classification of this sort is given in Table 10-1. It will be noted that some of the names of eruption types are those of volcanoes. Others ("flood eruptions" and "fumarolic activity") indicate the nature and scale of the activity; and one ("Plinian") is taken from the name of the famous Roman naturalist, Pliny the Elder, who lost his life in the earliest recorded eruption of that type. It should be emphasized that every gradation exists from one type to another. Thus, Mercalli (1907, p. 123) recognized a "mixed" type, which he placed between Strombolian and Vulcanian, in which a significant quantity of triturated older solid lava is mixed with the new magmatic tephra.

Mercalli grouped Strombolian and Hawaiian activity together in a single class, but they were separated by Lacroix (1908, p. 86), and the dis-

TABLE 10-1. Classification of volcanic eruptions

Eruption type	Physical nature of the magma	Character of explosive activity	Nature of effusive activity	Nature of dominant ejecta	Structures built around vent
Basaltic flood	Fluid	Very weak ejection of very fluid blebs; lava fountains	Voluminous wide-spreading flows of very fluid lava	Cow-dung bombs and spatter; very little ash	Spatter cones and ramparts; very broad flat lava cones; broad lava plain
Hawaiian	Fluid	Weak ejection of very fluid blebs; lava fountains	Thin, often extensive flows of fluid lava	Cow-dung bombs and spatter; very little ash	Spatter cones and ramparts; very broad flat lava cones
Strombolian	Moderately fluid	Weak to violent ejection of pasty fluid blebs	Thicker, less extensive flows of moderately fluid lava; flows may be absent	Spherical to fusiform bombs; cinder; small to large amounts of glassy ash	Cinder cones
Vulcanian	Viscous	Moderate to violent ejection of solid or very viscous hot fragments of new lava	Flows commonly absent; when present they are thick and stubby; ash flows rare	Essential, glassy to lithic, blocks and ash; pumice	Ash cones, block cones, block-and-ash cones
Peléean	Viscous	Like Vulcanian, commonly with glowing avalanches	Domes and/or short very thick flows; may be absent	Like Vulcanian	Ash and pumice cones; domes
Plinian (exceptionally strong Vulcanian)	Viscous	Paroxysmal ejection of large volumes of ash, with accompanying caldera collapse	Ash flows, small to very voluminous; may be absent	Glassy ash and pumice	Widespread pumice lapilli and ash beds; generally no cone building
Rhyolitic flood	Viscous	Relatively small amounts of ash projected upward into the atmosphere	Voluminous wide-spreading ash flows; single flows may have volume of tens of cubic miles	Glassy ash and pumice	Flat plain, or broad flat shield, often with caldera
Ultravulcanian	No magma	Weak to violent ejection of solid fragments of old rock	None	Accessory and accidental blocks and ash	Block cones; block-and-ash cones
Gas eruption	No magma	Continuous or rhythmic gas release at vent	None	None; or very minor amounts of ash	None
Fumarolic	No magma	Essentially nonexplosive weak to moderately strong long-continued gas discharge	None	None; or rarely very minor amounts of ash	Generally none; rarely very small ash cones

tinction is useful. Lacroix defined four main types of eruption—Hawaiian, Strombolian, Vulcanian, and Peléean—in terms of the freedom of release of the gas from the magma, which in turn is related to the viscosity of the magma. The more viscous is the magma, the less free the gas release, and in general the more explosive is the eruption. Lacroix's classification was accepted by Sapper (1927, p. 83, 159) and has been widely used since. The freedom of the gas release or the viscosity of the magma seldom can be measured directly, but they are indicated to a considerable extent by the nature of the ejecta, as is described in the following pages.

All the types of eruption vary considerably in the volume of material ejected and in the strength of the explosions. The Strombolian type, for example, ranges from rhythmic mild explosions that throw out sparse showers of scoria to heights of only a few tens of feet to violent blasts that project voluminous showers of scoria and bombs to heights of hundreds or thousands of feet, accompanied by a dense black ash cloud. The unifying feature in these widely differing Strombolian eruptions is that in each case the ejecta are new magmatic material, liquid when they are thrown out, but solid by the time they strike the ground. Mercalli (1907) called the mild activity "normal Strombolian," because it is the commonest type of activity at Stromboli, and the violent explosions "Strombolian paroxysms." However, since the latter are sometimes of quite long duration, instead of being truly paroxysmal, it seems best to call them violent Strombolian eruptions and to classify Strombolian activity as mild or gentle, moderate or violent, long-continued or brief, continuous or rhythmic. If this classification is accepted, such highly explosive eruptions as that of Cerro Negro, Nicaragua, in 1968, and the magmatic portion of the Tarawera eruption of 1886 (see p. 246), become violent Strombolian and are distinguished from similarly violent Vulcanian eruptions in which the ejected magma is more viscous. The fundamental factor in the classification is the fluidity of the ejected magma; the strength of the explosion is secondary. Vulcanian eruptions may be less violent than Strombolian eruptions. Nevertheless, there is a strong tendency for Strombolian explosions to be more violent than Hawaiian, and Vulcanian explosions more violent than Strombolian.

Peléean and Plinian eruptions can be regarded as special varieties of Vulcanian activity so far as the nature of the ejected magma is concerned, but it appears desirable to set them apart in the classification because of their special characteristics, described later.

The usages of Mercalli, Lacroix, and Sapper have been followed in Table 10-1, except that it has appeared desirable to add a few additional types. Basaltic flood eruptions are much like Hawaiian eruptions in general character, but not in the resulting structures, and rhyolitic flood eruptions bear close resemblance to the ash flows that occur during some Plinian eruptions; but because of the extreme volume of flood eruptions, it appears worthwhile to set them apart in the classification.

Hawaiian Eruptions

The great fluidity and small gas content of the magmas reaching the surface at the presently active Hawaiian volcanoes result in quietly effusive eruptions accompanied by relatively small amounts of weak explosion. The magma reaching the surface commonly is shot into the air as *lava fountains* by the hydrostatic pressure on the liquid and the expansion of the bubbles of gas forming in it (Plate 10-6). Usually the fountains are a few tens to a few hundreds of feet high, but occasionally they exceed 1,000 feet. The tremendous fountain of the 1959 eruption of Kilauea reached heights of 1,400 or 1,500 feet! Spectacular though they be, the fountains are not truly explosive. They are essentially just jets of incandescent liquid shot into the air like the water from a fire hose, or perhaps more like the stream of liquid from a soda-water siphon. A minor amount of weak explosion does indeed occur in them, in the sense that the escaping gas tends to disrupt the edges of the fountain and tear the liquid into shreds. Falling to the ground around the base of the fountain, the still-liquid shreds form spatter and cow-dung bombs and build spatter cones. Very light pumice is often formed, but generally in relatively minor amounts. Commonly, the eruptions take place from fissure vents, and particularly in early stages of the eruption, a line of closely spaced fountains

PLATE 10-6. Lava fountain about 40 feet high at one of the vents of the Mauna Loa eruption on October 25, 1919. In the foreground is the rim of the cone of welded spatter (agglutinate) that is being built by the fountain. Hawaiian Volcano Observatory photo by T. A. Jaggar.

PLATE 10-7. The "curtain of fire"—a row of coalescing lava fountains as much as 600 feet high playing along a fissure on the southwest rift zone of Mauna Loa, Hawaii, June 2, 1950. Official photograph, 199 Fighter Squadron, Hawaii Air National Guard.

PLATE 10-8. Lava fountain, and cascade pouring from a fissure in the northeast wall of Halemaumau 300 feet into a lava lake in the bottom of the crater, May 31, 1954. Photo by R. T. Kanemori, Modern Camera Center, Hilo, Hawaii.

may extend along the fissure for several miles (Plate 10-7) and build a spatter rampart. Drops of liquid escaping from the fountain may trail behind them threads of Pele's hair. Lava lake activity may occur (Plate 10-8), but it is present only rather rarely and is not an essential part of this type of eruption.

Hawaiian-type eruptions take place from open vents, generally of fissure type, in which the magma is at high level and generally overflowing.

The magma is usually basaltic or even more basic, but may be andesitic. The lava flows are thin (generally less than 50 feet), very fluid (Plate 10-9), and often very extensive (commonly with areas of 5 to 20 square miles and lengths up to 30 miles or more). They are of both pahoehoe and aa types. Quite rarely, an extended period of repeated small overflows around a short segment of the eruptive fissure may build a low gently rounded mound of lava (a small "shield volcano," see Chapter 9) or a steeper-sided lava cone such as the one built in the summit crater of Mauna Loa in 1949.

The 1955 eruption of Kilauea, described in Chapter 1, was a typical, though rather small, Hawaiian-type eruption. Perhaps even more typical was the eruption of Mauna Loa in 1942. Commonly, eruptions of the Hawaiian volcanoes come in pairs, a summit eruption being followed a few months later by a flank eruption. A summit eruption of Mauna Loa had taken place in 1940. In the early spring of 1942 earthquakes indicated that the zone of fissures extending down the northeast flank of Mauna Loa (the "northeast rift zone") was being torn open. Finally, after about 3 weeks of such quakes, on March 26 lava broke out again in the summit crater (called Mokuaweoweo), flooded part of the crater floor, and spread small flows over the upper northeast flank of the mountain. This summit activity lasted only a few hours. Eruption then stopped, but earthquakes indicated that the rift in the mountain flank was still being torn open, and on April 28 a new outbreak took place 8 miles northeast of the summit and 4,000 feet vertically below it. A series of fissures a mile long opened in the mountainside, and for a few hours a nearly continuous line of lava fountains, a few feet to 50 feet high, spurted from them. Falling ejecta built a spatter rampart up to about 10 feet high along the fissures. In places the rampart was a continuous double wall along both sides of the fissure, but elsewhere lava flowing out of the fissure carried away the falling ejecta and prevented the building of the wall. Soon, however, erup-

PLATE 10-9. Flood of lava on the west flank of Mauna Loa, June 2, 1950. Note the braided character of the flow, and the "kipukas" left between branches of the flow. Official photograph, U. S. Navy.

tion began to be restricted to a continually lessening length of the fissure, and at the same time the fountains near the mid-point of the fissure began to grow in height. There, for a length of about ¼ mile, activity continued for 13 days, the fountains reaching a height of 600 feet, and a row of coalescing cones of spatter and cinder 100 feet high was built. Lava pouring from the vent flowed for 16 miles. The flow is partly pahoehoe and partly aa, has an average thickness of about 15 feet, covers an area of approximately 7.3 square miles, and has a volume of about 90 million cubic yards. An additional 10 million cubic yards had been poured out in the summit region at the beginning of the eruption.

Basaltic Flood Eruptions

Basaltic flood eruptions are very much like Hawaiian-type eruptions in general character, differing from them only in the enormous amounts of lava poured out and the even smaller proportion of explosive activity. Single flows commonly cover areas of hundreds of square miles and have volumes of several tens of cubic miles. The structures formed at the vents are often so inconspicuous that the vents are difficult or impossible to locate. It appears, however, that the vents are nearly always, if not always, of fissure type. Some vents are marked at the surface by rows of low spatter cones and some by very broad low "shields" (see Chapter 11), sometimes with small spatter cones at their summits or along fissures on their flanks. In some instances small spatter cones or ramparts have been built along the fissure vents during early stages of the eruption, only to be buried by the thickening lava flow during later stages when the amount of gas in the erupting magma had become even smaller. It is quite possible that this situation is much commoner than has been recognized, and that the featureless character of the final lava plain is the result of burying of the early formed vent structures. The general features of lava plains and plateaus are further described in the next chapter.

Less commonly, the vents of basaltic flood eruptions are marked by sizable cinder or cinder–and–spatter cones. Several large cones dot the surface of the Snake River Plain in Idaho. In Craters of the Moon National Monument, which is probably the latest area of eruption of the Snake River basalts, a row of 55 cones 50 to 800 feet high marks the vent fissure. Explosive activity of this magnitude is decidedly exceptional in basaltic flood eruptions, however, and represents a departure from the usual conditions of eruption. In the case of the Craters of the Moon, the rise of magma to the surface may have been less rapid than usual, allowing some accumulation of gas in the upper part of the conduit. At other times, and possibly also at Craters of the Moon to some extent, shallow groundwater may become involved, adding to the explosiveness of the eruption (see p. 218).

The only basaltic flood eruption witnessed during historic times was an abnormal one, resembling in many respects the one that must have occurred at Craters of the Moon. The Laki eruption, which took place in southern Iceland in 1783, began with earthquakes accompanying the opening of a series of fissures 15 miles long and the sinking of a shallow trough (graben) between two faults. The fissures extended in a northeast–southwest direction through Laki Hill (Fig. 10-6). On June 8 eruption began along the part of the fissure zone southwest of the hill with strong explosions and the ejection of great black clouds of ash. After a day of purely explosive activity, lava reached the surface and poured out of the fissure forming a huge lava flow that advanced southwestward and, on

FIGURE 10-6. Map of part of south-central Iceland, showing the lava flows and the cones along the eruptive fissure of the Laki eruption of 1783. (Simplified after Thorarinsson, 1970.)

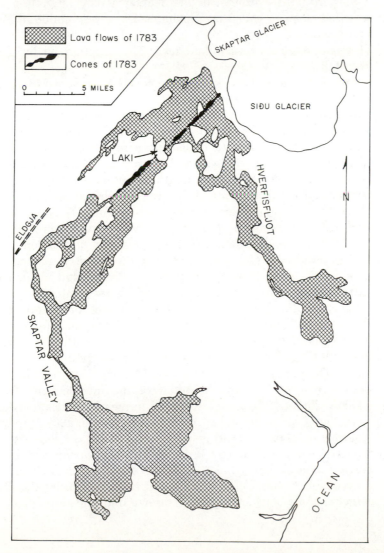

June 12, poured into the valley of the Skaptar River and down it toward the southern coast. In a single day the lava advanced 9 miles. The flow gradually filled the valley to the brim and spilled over the edges onto the surrounding hilly surface. On the coastal lowland it spread out like a great fan. At the vents the ash ejection was replaced by a row of lava fountains. On June 13 a second lava flow started to spread southward from the vents. About June 15 activity ceased, and the vents remained quiet except for fuming until June 26, when activity resumed and still another big lava flow was poured out. Activity came to an end along the southwestern part of the fissure zone about June 30, but on July 14 eruption began on the fissures northeast of the hill. Again the first activity was explosive, and it was not until July 30 that voluminous discharge of lava began. The lava effusion reached a climax on August 9, but continued into early September. Great volumes of lava poured down the Hverfisfljot Valley, 20 miles northeast of the Skaptar Valley (Fig. 10-6). Again came a period of quiet, ended on September 26 by resumption of lava discharge. On October 25 a very strong explosion took place, followed by the extrusion of huge volumes of very fluid lava. The eruption finally ended in early November.

The lava of the Laki eruption covers an area of 218 square miles and has a volume of about 2.9 cubic miles (Thorarinsson, 1970). Huge as it is, this is small as compared with that of some older flood basalt flows (Chapter 5). Along the Laki fissure there were built more than 100 small spatter and cinder cones, most of them only a few tens of feet high, but a few of them as much as 200 feet. At least two are tuff cones, and one of these is nearly 300 feet high. The total amount of tephra, including both the spatter and cinder cones and the ash, which fell all over Iceland and as far away as Scotland and Norway, was about 0.07 cubic mile. The eruption was a catastrophe for Iceland! Several farms were destroyed by the lava flows, but far more important was the destruction caused by the bluish sulfurous haze that hung over the country, damaging crops and stunting the growth of forage plants. It is said that about half of all the cattle and three fourths of the sheep and horses of Iceland died as a result of starvation; and to make matters even worse, the haze from the ash and gas reduced visibility to the point where fishermen feared to go to sea. The famine that resulted from loss of crops and cattle and lack of fish killed one fifth of the total human population of Iceland!

The pattern of the Laki eruption strongly suggests that its explosiveness was at least partly the result of the involvement of water—either shallow groundwater or the water of former lakes destroyed by the eruption. The descriptions are very reminiscent of the 1960 eruption of Kilauea Volcano in Hawaii. That eruption took place on the east flank of the volcano near the shoreline. It began with the opening of fissures and the sinking of a shallow graben in an area where brackish groundwater lay only about 80 feet below the ground surface. During the first few days, large amounts of black ash were thrown out, and throughout the eruption

PLATE 10-10. Stromboli Volcano, seen from the northwest. The long smooth slope of the Sciara del Fuoco is the result of cinder and lava flows tumbling down to the sea from the "crater terrace." Photo by Fred M. Bullard.

the activity was much more explosive than that of typical Hawaiian eruptions. The large amount of salt in the ash clearly indicated that the rising lava had generated steam from the salty groundwater.

Strombolian Eruptions

The most typical activity of Stromboli Volcano (Plate 10-10) off the west coast of Italy consists of rhythmic ejection of incandescent cinder, lapilli, and bombs to heights of a few tens or hundreds of feet. This may or may not be accompanied by discharge of a lava flow. Typically, the lava is somewhat more viscous than that of Hawaiian eruptions and the flows are somewhat shorter and thicker. Usually the ejecta are too nearly solid when they strike the ground to spatter or even to flatten appreciably, but rarely cow-dung bombs as much as 3 feet across are formed. The ejecta are mostly irregular chunks of cinder with a small proportion of well-formed fusiform or spheroidal bombs and lapilli. They accumulate around the vents to form typical cinder cones. Ash is relatively minor in amount, and the eruption cloud is generally yellowish to white in color beyond the limit of projection of the lapilli.

Mild Strombolian activity of this sort takes place at open vents where moderately fluid lava stands at a high level in the conduit, but generally a little way below the surface. Because of the greater viscosity of the magma, gas escapes from it less readily than from the very fluid magma of Hawaiian activity, and the bursting of bubbles at the surface of the magma constitutes a series of small explosions that throw up clots of molten lava. Some of the clots strike the walls of the conduit near the magma surface while they are still molten and form spatter; but those that reach the level of the lip of the vent have cooled somewhat during their flight up the conduit and cool still more during their flight through the air, so they strike the ground in an essentially solid condition. Commonly, they are still glowing red when they leave the vent, but have become black by the time they strike the ground. If the magma level rises closer to the surface, more of the ejecta may reach the surface in a partly fluid condition and strike the ground around the vent as spatter, and the eruption then grades into one of Hawaiian type. In typical Strombolian activity, however, the jets of incandescent material at the vents are occasional showers of discrete fragments thrown up every few seconds or few minutes, instead of the continuous (though often pulsating) fountains of liquid during Hawaiian eruptions.

Mild Strombolian activity may continue with little variation for periods of months or even years. The "semipermanent" nature of Strombolian activity is commonly cited as one of its chief characteristics, as indeed it is characteristic of Stromboli itself, but closely similar activity also takes place during brief eruptions.

The typical mild activity of Stromboli is punctuated at intervals of a few months to a few years by brief periods of more violent activity, in the stronger of which showers of incandescent cinder and bombs are thrown to heights of a few thousand feet and a great black ash cloud rises above the volcano. Bombs may fall at a distance of several kilometers from the vent. The general nature of the ejecta is the same as in the milder eruptions, except that glassy ash becomes much more abundant and occasional blocks of old rock are found. The violent activity usually lasts for only a few hours or days and is followed commonly by a short interval of quiet during which only fumarolic activity occurs.

At other times violent Strombolian activity may constitute a single relatively brief eruptive episode of a few hours or days, or it may be a phase of a much longer eruption in which most of the activity is mild to moderate. The activity of Paricutin Volcano in Mexico, which continued uninterrupted from 1943 to 1952, was mostly moderate Strombolian in type, at times becoming violent. The ejecta were glassy cinder, spheroidal bombs and lapilli, and glassy ash formed largely by disintegration of the cinder. The ash formed thick and fairly extensive deposits (Fig. 10-7).

The magma that produces Strombolian eruptions is generally basaltic or andesitic. The lava flows are most typically block lava, but may be aa or even pahoehoe.

A good example of long-continued Strombolian eruption is furnished by Izalco Volcano in El Salvador. From the time of its birth, about 1770 A.D., the volcano was continually active until 1958, building a composite cone of alternating beds of lava and tephra (bombs, lapilli, and ash) to an average height of about 2,700 feet above its base. The activity consisted primarily of ejection of showers of cinder and bombs with occasional lava flows, generally from lateral vents. The ever-present mild activity became a tourist attraction, and the government of El Salvador built a road to the summit of the neighboring older cone, Cerro Verde, and a handsome hotel from which visitors could view the active volcano. Almost immediately, the volcano ceased erupting!

Shorter Strombolian eruptions build cinder cones, generally with associated lava flows. Such eruptions may last for only a few weeks, or they may continue several years, as did that of Paricutin in Mexico (Fig. 10-7). Once these eruptions have ended, it is rare that a second one occurs at the same place. Cinder cones are commonly one-eruption features.

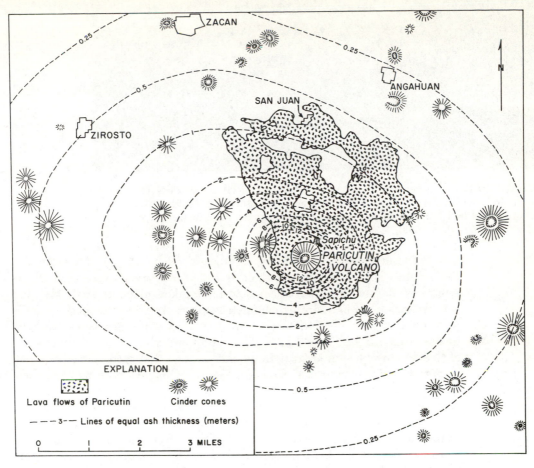

FIGURE 10-7. Map showing thickness (in meters) of ash deposits around Paricutin Volcano, Mexico, in October 1946, and the extent of the lava flows in August 1947. (After Williams, 1950.) Many older cinder cones are scattered around the new cone of Paricutin.

Often, however, many eruptions occur in the same general area, each forming its own cinder cone and lava flows. This is the case with Paricutin, which is only the last in a series of several dozen similar cones (Fig. 10-7).

Vulcanian Eruptions

As early as 1888, the pioneer Italian volcanologist, O. Silvestri, recognized that the eruptions that took place at Vulcano during that year were quite different in character from those usually observed at Stromboli, and he suggested that they be designated as a "vulcanian phase" of eruption. Although agreeing in a general way with Silvestri's suggestion, G. Mercalli thought it better to consider these particular sorts of eruptions as types rather than phases of volcanic activity, since they can occur simultaneously or alternately at the same volcano.

PLATE 10-11. The main cone of Vulcano, from the northwest. The lateral lapilli-and-block cone of Forgia Vecchia, and its associated obsidian lava flow, formed in 1739, lies on the near slope. Hawaii Institute of Geophysics photo by G. A. Macdonald.

The first records of activity at Vulcano (Plate 10-11) date from the fifth century B.C., and between then and 1800 A.D. there were at least 10 eruptions. A small eruption appears to have taken place in 1831, but this was followed by 40 years of complete repose. Activity resumed in 1873 with weak explosions, and these were repeated with increasing strength in the years 1876–1879 and 1886. The explosions threw out an abundance of fine ash mixed with angular fragments of rock that were sometimes hot enough to glow at night but showed no signs of having been molten when they were ejected. On August 3–5, 1888, there occurred violent explosions that threw out rocks weighing several tons. Some of the rock fragments were thrown nearly a mile and were still hot enough to set fire to boats in the harbor at Porto di Levante (Fig. 10-8). However, all the fragments were of preexisting rocks; none were of newly consolidated lava. After two weeks of inactivity, explosions began again on August 18 and continued at brief intervals for 19 months. During the times of most violent activity, explosions occurred every few minutes, but in less active periods they were separated by times of quiet reaching an hour or more.

The resumption of activity on August 18 brought a change in the sort of material ejected. Some blocks of older rock were still being thrown out, but fragments of new lava were greatly predominant. Most abundant were ash and lapilli, but the stronger explosions threw out also many angular fragments of rock, some of them glassy, and bombs with centers of very light pumice enclosed in thin crusts of dense obsidian, commonly with prominent bread-crust cracking. The ejected material appeared dark in daylight but was incandescent at night. The bread-crust bombs must have been sufficiently plastic when they were ejected to allow their centers to puff up into pumice as gas separated from the magma; and rarely the bombs were still sufficiently plastic to flatten out very slightly, without breaking, when they struck the ground. Other than that, however, there were no evidences that the material was ejected in a molten condition. The blocks were sharply angular, and round or spindle-shaped bombs such as characterize Strombolian eruptions were completely absent.

In the most violent explosions, bombs were absent and the larger ejecta consisted wholly of massive irregular fragments of new, but already solid, lava. One of these that fell near the rim of the crater had a volume of more than 50 cubic yards and weighed more than 100 tons!

Mercalli (1907, p. 132–133) points out that the general aspect of the explosions was very different from those characteristic of Strombolian eruptions. His description, freely translated, follows:

> In the less violent explosions large ejecta were lacking and the jet consisted of a dense gray mass of lapilli, sand, and ash that rose slowly, taking the form of a great cauliflower or giant mushroom. . . . The strongest commenced with a pine-tree cloud that was absolutely black in daylight, culminating in arrow-like projections which rose very rapidly, within a few seconds reaching heights of many hundreds of meters, while from the flanks and summit of the cloud separated black streaks of stones and fine detritus. Large black rocks shot higher than the cloud, and within the cloud darted lightning flashes, followed by short sharp claps of thunder, quite different from the rumbling that accompanied the beginning of the explosion. Then the cloud expanded in dense globes and volutes, finally building up to a height of 3 or 4 km, and becoming gray and then whitish as it gradually freed itself of the heavier solid materials.

The bright lightning flashes within the ash cloud or between the cloud and the ground are characteristic features of Vulcanian eruptions. They result from differences in electrical potential due at least in part to generation of static electricity by friction between the particles in the cloud.

Thus, Vulcanian activity consists in the explosive ejection of frag-

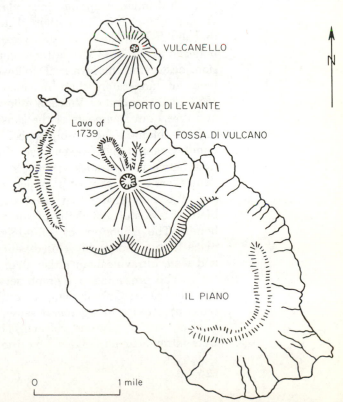

FIGURE 10-8. Map of the Island of Vulcano, showing the main cone and crater (Fossa di Vulcano), and the young cone of Vulcanello, formed about A.D. 183. The southern end of the island and the Lentia Ridge on the west are older than the main cone.

PLATE 10-12. Okmok Volcano, Umnak Island, Aleutians, in eruption in 1947. The black vulcanian eruption cloud is heavily laden with ash. U.S. Army Signal Corps photo by R. E. Wilcox.

ments of new lava, commonly incandescent when they leave the vent but either solid or too viscous to assume any appreciable degree of rounding during their flight through the air—in other words, essential blocks. With these there are often bread-crust bombs or blocks and, generally, large proportions of ash (Plate 10–12). The material may form deposits of blocks and ash on the flanks of an older cone, or, in the case of eruptions from a new vent, it may form a block-and-ash cone around the vent. Lava flows may be absent, as they were during the 1888 eruption of Vulcano; and when they form, they are generally very short and thick because of the high viscosity of the magma. The latter is usually andesitic, dacitic, or trachytic, but may be basaltic or rhyolitic.

Vulcanian eruptions take place from open vents in which highly viscous molten lava lies a short distance below the surface, or from vents that are lightly closed by the freezing of the top of the magma column between explosions. The latter situation may result in a Vulcanian explosion, destroying the lava seal, followed by Strombolian explosions ejecting blebs of moderately fluid magma. The strongest explosions during the 1888–1890 eruption of Vulcano followed the longest intervals of quiescence and threw out fragments of the consolidated crust that had formed on the magma column. The closely spaced explosions at intervals of only a few minutes cannot have taken place from a truly closed vent, because the time between explosions was not sufficient to allow the formation of more than a very thin skin of solidified rock on the top of the magma body; and it is noteworthy that these explosions threw out large numbers of blebs of lava still sufficiently plastic to form the pumice-cored bread-crusted bombs. The explosions of 1873–1886 and August 3–5, 1888, which took place from a thoroughly closed vent, threw out only old, accessory debris and were ultravulcanian rather than truly Vulcanian in character.

The preceding paragraph serves to emphasize once again the fact that the names Strombolian, Vulcanian, etc., serve to designate different types of activity in a general sense, rather than types that represent the total activity of any one volcano. The first explosions of Vulcano in 1888 were ultravulcanian, followed by true Vulcanian activity. Many other initial explosions are ultravulcanian, no matter what the nature of the later part of the eruption. Strombolian-type bombs are found, albeit rarely, in the products of the predominantly Hawaiian-type eruptions of Kilauea Volcano. The 1906 eruption of Vesuvius, described above, commenced with Strombolian-type activity at the summit followed shortly by Hawaiian-type activity at some of the lateral vents, and still later by ultravulcanian ejections of the debris from the collapsing walls of the conduit, and so forth. Each type of activity indicates the physical nature of the magma, the copiousness of gas discharge, the level of the magma in the conduit, and the condition and form of the vent at the particular moment of the discharge, rather than any permanent character of the volcano.

G. Imbo has suggested that long-continued powerful gas streamings, such as that of April 8, 1906, at Vesuvius (see above), be termed "Vesuvian activity." Similar long periods of gas outflow have been observed in other eruptions, as for example that of Vesuvius in 1944, when falling ejecta did great damage to Allied airfields. Several such periods, lasting as long as 3 hours, occurred during the 1957 eruption of Capelinhos Volcano (p. 247).

Peléean Eruptions

Activity of the sort first witnessed and described at Mt. Pelée in 1902–1903 is known as Peléean eruption. Actually, it is a special type of Vulcanian eruption, since the ejecta are either solid or extremely viscous when they are discharged and remain angular. The two characteristic features are the formation of domes and glowing avalanches (Plate 10-13).

PLATE 10-13. Mayon Volcano, Philippines, in eruption, April 30, 1968. A glowing avalanche is rushing down the slope of the composite cone at the same time that a typical vulcanian eruption cloud is rising vertically from the summit vent. Photo by Dainty Studio, Daraga, Albay, Philippines.

PLATE 10-14. Bezymianny Volcano, Kamchatka, before (left photo) and after (right photo) the eruption of March 30, 1956. The eruption destroyed a large portion of the cone. In the right photo a dome can be seen growing in the crater. In the foreground is the surface of the ash-flow deposit formed during the eruption. Photos by G. S. Gorshkov and others, Kamchatka Volcano Station, Academy of Sciences, U. S. S. R.

Both may occur, as in the eruptions of Pelée in 1902 and 1929, or either one may take place without the other. The eruption of Soufrière on the island of St. Vincent in 1902, with its devastating glowing avalanches, took place from an open crater without any dome formation, but is nevertheless classified as a Peléean-type eruption.

Two of the greatest Peléean eruptions of recent years are those of Bezymianny, Kamchatka, in 1956, and Mt. Lamington, New Guinea, in 1951. The Peléean eruption of Hibokhibok Volcano in 1948–1951 has been described in Chapter 1.

The great eruption of Bezymianny was studied soon afterward by the Russian volcanologist, G. S. Gorshkov (1959). Before the eruption, Bezymianny rose as a snow-covered cone to a height of 10,180 feet above sea level (Plate 10-14, left). It had no record of activity during historic times and was generally regarded as extinct. Associated as it is with other, spectacularly active volcanoes such as Klyuchevskaya, it had in fact attracted almost no attention, and the very designation "Bezymianny" means "no name." The mountain consisted of a large dome to the west of which was a younger cone consisting of alternating beds of lava and tephra with a crater at its summit containing a small terminal conelet. From the rim of the crater a deep gorge descended southeastward into the head of one of the branches of the Dry Hapitsa River.

About September 29, 1955, earthquakes from the area of Bezymianny began to be recorded at the town of Kliuchi, 25 miles to the north. Their frequency gradually increased until by October 12 they numbered 100 to 200 a day, and by October 21 the total number recorded was 1,285. At 6:30 A.M. on October 22 the volcano began to erupt. From then until the end of November a series of strong explosions of Vulcanian type threw ash 3 to 5 miles into the air. This was followed by weaker activity of the same general sort until late March, 1956. The old dome was slowly upheaved more than 300 feet by magmatic pressure from below.

On March 30 a tremendous explosion destroyed the whole top of the mountain (Plate 10-14, right), lowering the height of the summit some 600 feet and forming a crater roughly a mile across. A great Vulcanian cloud was projected obliquely upward toward the east at an angle of 30–40° to the horizon, reaching a height of more than 24 miles. At a distance of 15 miles, trees a foot in diameter were felled by the force of the blast. Eighteen miles away the bark of living trees was scorched and dry dead wood was set afire. Snow 3 to 6 feet deep was melted by the hot ash along the center line of the blast. Simultaneously, great glowing avalanches swept down the mountain slopes, particularly into the Dry Hapitsa Valley. Six to eight miles east of the crater the ground was covered with sandy ash 1½ feet thick, and 11 miles away the valley of the river was completely filled with the deposit of the glowing avalanche. The avalanche gave rise to mudflows that continued on down the valley.

Following the paroxysmal explosion, a dome appeared in the crater and continued to grow, accompanied by occasional weak to moderate explosions and small glowing avalanches, through the spring and early summer. In August it was more than 1,000 feet high. In September and October a second dome grew against the southwestern flank of the first one. By late autumn the eruption was over. The total volume of material erupted was about half a cubic mile.

Previous to 1951, Mt. Lamington also was regarded as extinct. The mountain is situated in a region of sugar plantations at the southern edge of the coastal plain that lies along the northern edge of Papua. Rising nearly 6,000 feet above sea level, it is dwarfed by the towering Owen Stanley Range behind it. It consisted of a deeply eroded volcanic mountain, formed partly by coalescing volcanic domes, with a deep horseshoe-shaped crater opening northward onto the plain and drained by the Ambogo River. Within the crater rose a remnant of an old dome, and ravines cut into the sides of the mountain revealed the deposits of ancient glowing avalanches, as well as beds of ash and air-laid pyroclastic breccia, and lava flows. The mountain was covered by heavy forest and small scattered patches of cultivation. There was no record of past eruption either in history or in the legends of the native people.

The 1951 eruption of Mt. Lamington was thoroughly studied and described by the Australian volcanologist, G. A. M. Taylor (1958), who arrived on the scene only 2 days after the climactic explosion. The eruption was not unheralded, but unfortunately the dire nature of the warning symptoms was not recognized. On Monday, January 15, 1951, a thin column of "smoke" was seen rising from the crater, and new landslides scarred the steep slopes. For several days occasional small earthquakes had been felt. On Tuesday and Wednesday the "smoke" became stronger and earthquakes increased in number and intensity. Many more landslides occurred and rumbling noises came from the ground. On Thursday the increase in activity became more rapid, the gas column became dark with ash, and the emission of gas became pulsatory. During Friday and Saturday the pulses became stronger and more frequent, and the ash cloud rose 15,000 to 30,000 feet with nearly constant lightning in the cloud. Within the crater activity spread as new vents opened. The mountain slopes became white with ash. At Higaturu, 6 miles north of the crater, earthquakes became almost incessant. Thus far it was a typical Vulcanian eruption.

At 8 P.M. on Saturday the very frequent earthquakes stopped, and only occasional quakes were felt through the night. At 10 A.M. on Sunday, January 21, something that may have been a small glowing avalanche was observed on the west flank of the mountain.

At 10:40 A.M. came catastrophe! A huge black ash-laden Vulcanian cloud rose rapidly upward, within 2 minutes reaching a height of 40,000 feet and spreading out like a great billowing flat-topped mushroom. Within 20 minutes the edge of the cloud in the stratosphere had spread more than 60 miles north of the volcano. Heard from 6 miles away, irregular rumblings gave place to a continuous roar of escaping gas that continued for 3 or 4 minutes. Around the base of the rising ash column, dark gray clouds of ash spread rapidly outward marking the rush of glowing avalanches down the mountainside and out onto the plain. From Sangara Plantation, 9 miles north of the crater (Fig. 10-9), the cloud advancing over the ground surface appeared incredibly solid, "whirling and billowing like an oil fire." Its summit leaned forward like the curling top of a breaking wave, and it seemed certain that the plantation would be overwhelmed; but when the front was less than a mile away a strong breeze suddenly sprang up and rolled it back again. High above, the ash cloud continued to expand and within a few minutes ash began to fall over the area, soon changing to a rain of mud, and then again to dry ash mixed with accretionary lapilli.

At Issivita, 6 miles northwest of the crater, the cloud rolled halfway across the mission station before it was suddenly stopped and swept back by a strong wind. Its farthest advance was marked by the sharp edge of a layer of ash 2 inches thick. Similar strong winds blowing toward the volcano have been noted during other eruptions. For instance, during the eruption of Vesuvius in 1906, at the town of Ottaiano an inward-directed gale resulted in the breaking of windows by falling ejecta on the sides of the buildings away from the volcano. These winds are air rushing in from the sides to replace that moving upward over the volcano. To their seemingly miraculous intervention we probably owe the survival of the witnesses to the eruption at Sangara and Issivita.

The glowing avalanches were of the St. Vincent type resulting from the overflowing of a gas–ash emulsion on all sides of the crater; but the principal outflow took place to the north, guided by the low notch in the crater rim and the valley that led out of it (Fig. 10-9). The area covered by the avalanches was more than 90 square miles. The average velocity of the avalanches was probably about 60 miles per hour. Over most of the area destruction was almost total, but around the edge was a narrow zone in which the devastation was less complete. Everywhere the movement of the avalanches was closely governed by topography. The dense rain forest was leveled, big trees were broken off or uprooted, and in some

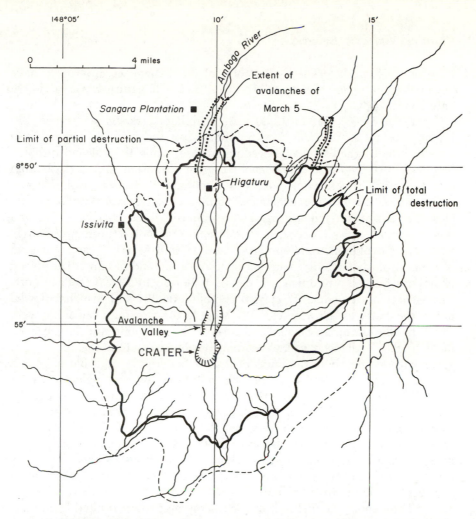

FIGURE 10-9. Map of the region around Mt. Lamington, New Guinea, showing the limits of total and partial destruction during the eruption of January 1951, and the extent of the glowing avalanches of March 5, 1951. (After Taylor, 1958.)

places the ground was swept bare, not even stumps remaining. Trees were overturned and aligned parallel to the movement of the blast, and those that remained standing were strongly sand-blasted on the side toward the crater. At Higaturu one large house was pushed 15 feet northwards and severely damaged on the south side by flying debris, and most of the other houses were carried away completely. Nearly 3,000 persons lost their lives. No one within the central area survived.

Within 2 miles of the crater the avalanches caused considerable erosion. The effects were particularly great at the foot of the mountain, where the steep slopes merged into the plain. It was there that the avalanches attained their greatest velocity. The ground surface was sand-blasted and grooved, and "in many places the only evidence of the forest cover was charred root ends carved off level with the grooved soil surfaces"

(Taylor, 1958, p. 42). The temperature of the avalanches appears to have been considerably lower than at Mt. Pelée, and at Higaturu it was probably only about 200°C.

From 11:00 A.M. to 12:30 P.M. complete darkness enveloped Mt. Lamington and its environs, and for the rest of the day the region lay in a reddish half-light like that preceding sunrise, while the volcano rumbled ominously. At 8:45 P.M. came another great explosion, hurling ash high into the air. This one, however, was a normal Vulcanian explosion un-accompanied by glowing avalanches. Still another, smaller explosion occurred at 2 A.M. on January 22. There followed three days of quiet, and then a period of frequent strong explosions that lasted until mid-March, with major explosions on February 6 and 18 and March 5, and a period of lesser explosive activity that continued until the end of June. The strong explosions formed Vulcanian ash clouds that rose to 30,000 feet or more. The weaker ones frequently ejected copious quantities of ash that flowed out of the crater as "glowing clouds." Most of the glowing avalanches were small, hardly extending beyond the base of the mountain and largely confined to the "avalanche valley" leading northward out of the crater; but some extended nearly to the limits of that of January 21, and that of March 5 actually surpassed it. The latter was witnessed by volcanologist Taylor at close range. It swept down the channel of the Ambogo River, passing less than half a mile from his observation post at Sangara Plantation. Taylor comments, "The realization that the main body of the nuée ardente was being strictly controlled by topography was the only reassuring point in an alarming situation." Several separate flows rushed down the valley during a period of a little more than an hour, the passage of each being marked by a loud "rustling" noise.

Throughout the first half of 1951 many mudflows resulted from rains on the ash-covered surface.

Within a few days of the eruption of January 21, a dome started to grow in the crater. The growth began with a bodily elevation of the whole crater floor several hundred feet above its previous level, changing its shape from that of a steep-sided funnel to a nearly level platform. The center then bulged upward and a typical spine-covered dome emerged, partly mantled with explosive debris from the crater floor. Within 6 weeks it was more than 1,500 feet high. Between February 3 and 9 the summit of the dome rose at a rate of about 100 feet a day.

The strong explosions of March 5 shattered the dome, and about two thirds of it was removed as part of the glowing avalanches that descended the avalanche valley. The dome was quickly rebuilt, and growth continued until mid-August, followed by two months of quiet and crumbling of the flanks of the mass. A new phase of growth started in late October and continued spasmodically through 1952 with minor movements continuing until 1955, when the dome was 1,850 feet high with basal diameters of 3,000 and 4,500 feet, and a volume of about ¼ cubic mile.

Peléean eruptions, particularly the dome-building phase, demand lava of at least moderate viscosity. For that reason it might be expected that most Peléean eruptions will liberate lavas of moderate to high silica content, and this is actually the case. Most of them produce andesite, dacite, or rhyolite, or more rarely trachyte. However, Peléean eruptions of basaltic composition, such as those of Manam Volcano, north of New Guinea, in 1957 and 1960 (Taylor, 1963) also are known.

It has sometimes been stated that Peléean activity is a sign of volcanic decadence, indicating the approach of extinction of the volcano. This probably is true in some instances, but it is patently far from true in others. It was pointed out on a preceding page that Mt. Lamington is largely built of the products of long-past Peléean eruptions. Hibokhibok Volcano, and its southerly neighbor, Mt. Mambajao, also are built largely of accumulations of Peléean domes. The same is true of several of the volcanoes of the Lesser Antilles and other volcanoes elsewhere. Far from marking their end, Peléean activity seems to have characterized a large part of the life span of these volcanoes.

Plinian Eruptions

Only one type of volcanic eruption bears the name of a man. The catastrophic outburst of Vesuvius in 79 A.D. took the life of the famous Roman naturalist, Pliny the Elder, and eruptions of that type nowadays are generally known as Plinian eruptions. In a sense, however, it is his nephew, Pliny the Younger, who is immortalized in the name of the eruption type. Although his account lacks some details we would like to have had, the younger Pliny has given us a description of the eruption that was so discerning and accurate, and so filled with human warmth, that it has come down to us through the centuries as fresh and full of interest as the day it was written; and it enables us to recognize with considerable certainty the nature of the events that transpired. It can rightfully be regarded as the first scientific description of a volcanic eruption.

It is a great temptation to quote Pliny's glowing account of the eruption, but it has been repeated so often that the urge to do so again must be rejected! His description has been quoted in full by several writers in slightly differing translations (see, for example, Phillips, 1869, pp. 13–25; and Bullard, 1962, pp. 138–144), and only a brief synopsis will be given here. Pliny's account can, of course, give only part of the picture, since the observations he records are limited and were made wholly from the region to the west of the volcano; but careful geological studies of the mountain and the products of the eruption, especially those by A. Rittmann, have filled in details and resulted in a reasonably complete picture. This evidence also will be summarized, since it furnishes a good example of the use of geology and petrology in deciphering the history of a volcano. This particular piece of scientific detective work has been greatly aided, if not actually made possible, by Rittmann's demonstration of the changes in the erupting magmas, which started with a trachytic composition and became progressively less rich in silica and richer in magnesium, iron, and alkalies—a change that Rittmann attributes to assimilation of magnesium-rich limestone (dolomite) by the magma in the chamber beneath the volcano. The present-day lavas of Vesuvius are predominantly leucitites—basic rocks resembling nephelinites (Table A2-2) but richer in potassium. In addition to the overall change, Rittmann recognizes other changes brought about by differentiation of the magma during periods of volcanic quiescence. During each such period, the upper part of the magma body became richer in silica and the lower part richer in iron and magnesia than the average of the magma body as a whole. Thus, the first lava erupted in 79 A.D., derived from the top of the magma body, was leucite phonolite; whereas the magma erupted from lower in the chamber later in the same eruption was leucite tephrite (a rock intermediate in composition between leucitite and basalt).

Like many volcanoes, Vesuvius has had a complicated history. It began some 10,000 years ago with the eruption of trachyte ash and pumice, forming a cone that later was partly eroded and covered with soil during a long period of volcanic quiet (Rittmann, 1933). When the volcano returned to activity, the materials produced were rather acid tephrite close to phonolite in composition, and a series of eruptions built a cone (known as the Older Somma) that almost completely buried the original trachyte cone. Still another period of inactivity ensued, but again activity returned and another cone (the Younger Somma) of leucite tephrite largely buried the earlier one. This cone, roughly 6,000 feet high, was the mountain known to the early Romans, but it had even then been long inactive and was somewhat eroded and heavily covered with vegetation. At its summit was a broad bowl-shaped crater with precipitous walls (Fig. 10-10) that in 72 B.C. served as the refuge of Spartacus and his rebellious gladiators. The volcano was regarded by Strabo (ca. 20 A.D.) as extinct.

The beginning of the most recent reactivation of Vesuvius was marked by a violent earthquake, which in 63 A.D. did great damage to the cities near the base of the mountain. Suetonius tells us that the earthquake occurred at the moment when the Emperor Nero was making his concert debut at Naples and that he did not stop singing until he had finished the number! Many more earthquakes came during the following years, and with our present knowledge of volcanoes it would almost surely have been recognized that Vesuvius was approaching another eruptive cycle. But the probability was not recognized by the Romans, and when about noon on August 24, 79 A.D., a great cloud suddenly appeared over the mountain, it came as a surprise. The cloud rose quickly from the mountain-top as a slender column, spreading out in the upper atmosphere to resemble the flat-topped Italian pine tree. The whole coastline to the west along

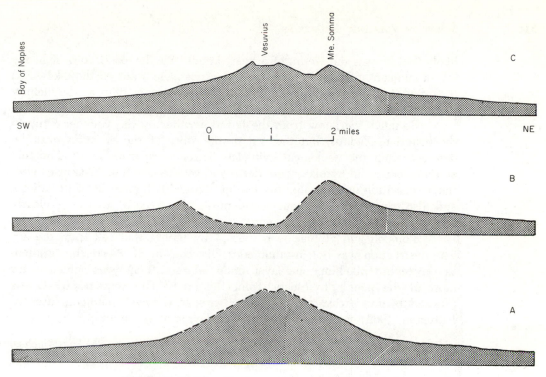

FIGURE 10-10. Cross sections of Vesuvius, showing the approximate profiles of the cone before (A) and after (B) the eruption of 79 A.D., and the profile in 1927 (C).

the shore of the Bay of Naples appears to have been heaved up temporarily several feet. Light-colored ash and pumice of leucite phonolite composition started to rain down over the region, falling on the Elder Pliny as he took his galleys (he was serving as admiral in command of a fleet) from Micenum across the Bay of Naples toward the foot of the mountain (Fig. 10-2) on his double mission of observing the eruption at closer range and rescuing friends in distress. Unable to land where he had intended, near the present site of Torre del Greco, because of the upheaval of the shore, he turned southward to Stabiae near the present Castellammare. There things were not yet as bad as they were farther north, but adverse winds prevented the ships from putting back to sea, and he decided to spend the night there with his friend, Pomponianus.

During the night the fall of ash and pumice in the courtyard of the house where he was sleeping was so heavy that it threatened to block the doorway, and the group took to the open fields, with pillows tied on their heads to protect them from the falling stones. Even with the advent of day, it was so dark that even with torches they could see only a few feet. Pliny, who was a very corpulent man, laid down for a few minutes rest, but when he tried to rise, he fell back again, dead. His companions believed he had been poisoned by noxious gases, but at that distance from the volcano, well away from any likely vents, and particularly considering the absence of serious effects on others in the group, it appears more likely that he was the victim of a heart attack. Similar conditions of heavy fall of pumice and ash, impenetrable darkness, incessant earthquakes, and disturbance of the shore were described by the younger Pliny in the vicinity of Micenum.

So much we know from the letters written by the younger Pliny to the historian, Tacitus, but the rest of the story of the eruption must be deduced from the geological evidence. Three prosperous cities, Pompeii, Herculaneum, and Stabiae, were destroyed by the eruption. Centuries later their excavation has revealed fascinating details of Roman life and culture, and also exposed the sequence of deposits that record, almost as clearly as the letters of Pliny and far more completely, the events of the eruption.

Pompeii and Stabiae were buried by tephra that fell from the air. The destruction was not instantaneous, like that of St. Pierre, but gradual as the tephra piled up one layer upon another. Time was sufficient for most of the people to escape from the cities. The sequence of layers exposed by the excavators at Pompeii are as follows (modified after A. Rittmann, 1962) with the first-deposited layers at the bottom:

	Thickness (inches)
10. Ash (glassy) with accretionary lapilli	12.
9. Lapilli (accessory)	1.2
8. Ash (glassy)	0.8
7. Lapilli (accessory)	1.2
6. Ash (glassy tephrite) with accretionary lapilli	25.
5. Lapilli (accessory)	1.2
4. Sandy ash	2.
3. Pumice, greenish gray (phonolitic tephrite) with some fragments of limestone and deep-seated intrusive rocks	
2. Pumice, light gray (tephritic phonolite) with some fragments of limestone	100.
1. Pumice, white (phonolite) with small fragments of lavas from the Young Somma cone	

Layers 1, 2, and 3 consist very largely of essential pumice, representing the frothed-up magma that caused the eruption. Fragments of limestone in layer 2 came from a formation (of Eocene age) that lies about half a mile below sea level beneath the volcano, and those in layer 3 came from an older limestone formation (dolomitic marble of Triassic age) that lies at a depth of about 3 miles. The source of the explosions was becoming deeper as the upper part of the magma column was thrown out. The lapilli of layers 5, 7, and 9 are predominantly fragments of rocks from the two Somma cones, and the ash of layers 6, 8, and 10 represents bits of the erupting magma torn apart by expanding gas.

At the northern foot of the mountain, Rittmann found a lava flow that closely resembles in chemical and mineral composition the magmatic ash of layers 6–10. The city of Herculaneum on the western slope was buried not by the fall of pumice or by lava flow, but by a succession of three mudflows containing fragments of pumice like those at Pompeii.

From the foregoing, plus evidence from other localities, Rittmann has deduced the following story. The eruption began with clearing of the vent, followed by rapid frothing of the phonolitic magma at the top of the magma body. Violent explosions threw pumice and ash high into the air. Pumice fell in great volume near the volcano, burying Pompeii, but most of the ash drifted to greater distances. As deeper and deeper levels in the magma body were ejected, the magma changed composition (layers 1–3). Following this, a great gas blast, probably resembling that of the intermediate phase of the eruption of 1906, blew out sandy pulverized material from the upper walls of the conduit (layer 4) but little magma. Then a decrease in the strength of eruption allowed the crater walls to slide in, blocking the vent, but the shattered material was blown out by another explosion (layer 5). This was followed by another ejection of magma spray (layer 6). Twice more the vent walls collapsed into the conduit and the debris was blown out (layers 7 and 9), and each time there followed a spray of liquid magma from the reopened vent (layers 8 and 10). Simultaneously with the latter activity, a flow of lava escaped from a lateral vent low on the north flank of the cone. Rain falling through the ash clouds from time to time formed accretionary lapilli, and, saturating the thick ash and pumice deposits on the western flank of the cone, it produced the mudflows that swept down and buried Herculaneum.

As the underlying magma reservoir was drained by the eruption of magma, the upper part of the mountain lost its support and caved in. When the eruption came to an end, the clearing ash clouds revealed only the stump of the mountain. The whole top was gone, and in its place was a broad crater, known to volcanologists as a *caldera* (Chapter 12).

After this paroxysmal effort, Vesuvius rested for nearly a century; but starting with an eruption in the year 172 A.D. a new cone has been built in the caldera formed in 79 A.D. This new cone is the present Mt. Vesuvius (Plate 10-15). The remains of the old cone, forming the northern and eastern rims of the caldera, are now known as Monte Somma (Figs. 10-2 and 10-10).

In view of the foregoing, we can summarize the essential charac-

PLATE 10-15. The cone of Mount Vesuvius, with part of Resina in the foreground. On the left is Monte Somma, part of the rim of the caldera formed during the eruption of 79 A.D. On the right the caldera rim has been buried by later lava flows. The main cone of Vesuvius has been built in the caldera. Between Monte Somma and the main cone can be seen the rounded profile of the Colle Umberto, a "lava cupola" (small shield volcano) formed by outwelling of lava from a lateral fissure. Hawaii Institute of Geophysics photo by G. A. Macdonald.

teristics of a Plinian eruption. It consists in the explosive disgorgement of a large volume of magma (commonly several cubic miles), resulting in the collapse of the mountaintop to form a collapse crater or caldera. Simultaneous lava flows may or may not occur. The expansion of magmatic gas transforms most of the magma into pumice or tears it completely apart to form ash. The ash and pumice are thrown high in the air and fall as a wide spread blanket over the surrounding area. Glowing avalanches and/or ash flows often occur and may be more voluminous than the high-flung air-fall debris, but their presence is not essential. It is apparent from this that the Plinian eruption is in fact a very violent Vulcanian-type eruption, and there is no set dividing line between them, or between Plinian and Peléean eruptions. An eruption of which dome formation is a part is by definition a Peléean eruption, but if it is of extreme violence and accompanied by large-scale collapse of the upper part of the cone, it is also a Plinian eruption. The eruption of Bezymianny, described on an earlier page as a Peléean eruption, could equally well be called Plinian.

The other characteristic feature of Peléean eruptions—glowing avalanches—may also occur in Plinian eruptions. None seems to have taken place during the 79 A.D. eruption of Vesuvius, but they have been prominent features of several otherwise very similar eruptions. They were present, for instance, in the eruption of Bezymianny. The tremendous eruption that destroyed the top of Mt. Mazama and formed the caldera now occupied by Crater Lake in Oregon about 6,000 years ago ejected some 13 to 17 cubic miles of magma in the form of pumice and ash showers and glowing avalanches (Williams and Goles, 1968). An area of 5,000 square miles was covered to a depth of 6 inches or more, and pumice fragments from the eruption have been found as far away as Montana and southern Canada. Simultaneously, great glowing avalanches rushed down the mountainsides; and interestingly, as at Vesuvius, the composition of the magma changed during the eruption from dacite to basaltic andesite as the reservoir was drained to lower levels.

Still another example of a Plinian eruption is that of Krakatoa Volcano in 1883, one of the greatest volcanic eruptions of recent times. Krakatoa is situated in the Sunda Strait between Java and Sumatra. Before the eruption the visible part of the volcano consisted of a group of three small islands and a tiny rock (Fig. 10-11A). Lang and Verlaten Islands and the rock called Polish Hat were projecting portions of the rim of a caldera formed by destruction of the top of a big volcanic cone in prehistoric time. Krakatoa, the main island, consisted of three overlapping volcanic cones. The oldest of the three, Rakata, was a basaltic cone built over another projecting portion of the caldera rim. To the north of it lay the successively younger andesitic cones of Danan and Perbuwatan. Several eruptions of the Krakatoa vents were recorded in Indonesian history, the last one in 1680, when a flow of andesitic pitchstone (water-rich obsidian with a pitch-like luster) issued from Perbuwatan; but for 200 years the volcano had lain quiet.

On May 20, 1883, the volcano returned to activity with moderately

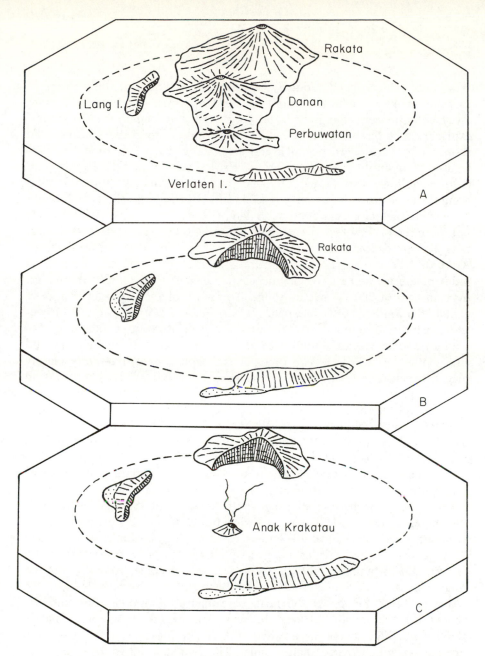

FIGURE 10-11. Diagrams showing the islands of the Krakatoa group (A) before the eruption of 1883, (B) after the eruption, and (C) in 1960. In (B) the submarine contours show the form of the hollow (caldera) in the sea floor formed during the 1883 eruption. (Modified after Escher, 1919.)

strong explosions that ejected pumice and ash together with fragments of older lava from Perbuwatan. The activity continued with gradually declining strength for a little more than a week. The volcano then was quiet again until June 19, when new explosions occurred at Perbuwatan, and a few days later another vent opened at the foot of Danan. Weak to moderate eruption continued, at least intermittently, through July; and by August 11 Rakata also had joined in the activity.

The climax came suddenly. At approximately 1 P.M. on August 26 there occurred a violent explosion, the noise of which was heard 100 miles away at Buitenzorg and Batavia on Java. At 2 P.M. came an even greater explosion that threw ash to a height of 17 miles above the volcano, and shortly afterward there began a series of short sharp explosions that increased in intensity until about 5 P.M. Explosions continued all night, and their rumblings were heard all over Java and Sumatra. For 100 miles around the volcano the country was shrouded in falling ash. Day brought no end to the darkness. Even with lamps and torches the visibility was not more than a few feet. More than 100 miles away this stygian blackness persisted for 22 hours, and on the near end of Sumatra it lasted for $2\frac{1}{2}$ days! At 10:02 A.M. on August 27 came the strongest blast of all. Ash rose 50 miles in the air and rained down heavily, mixed with chunks of pumice, over an area of 300,000 square miles. The noise of the explosion has been called "the loudest noise on earth." It was heard 2,200 miles away in central Australia, and nearly 3,000 miles away at Rodriguez Island in the western Indian Ocean. Another great explosion came at 10:52 A.M., and still another at 4:35 P.M. The times of the explosions can be very closely placed because of their effect on the pressure gages at the gas works in Batavia. Through the night of August 27 explosions continued with gradually diminishing intensity. By midmorning of August 28 the eruption was essentially over, although sporadic weak activity continued for several months and explosions loud enough to be heard at Batavia occurred on September 17 and 26, October 10, and February 20, 1884.

Accompanying the explosions were a series of giant "tidal waves." These waves actually were unrelated to the tides and were caused by the volcano. They are better called *tsunamis*. The first of them swept up onto the shores of Java and Sumatra shortly after a series of strong explosions at about 5 P.M. on August 26. Others came during the night, doing much damage to low-lying villages along the western end of Java and the southeastern end of Sumatra, but the worst was yet to come. About 7 A.M. on August 27 a great wave lifted the gunboat *Berouw* completely over the beach at Telok Betong at the head of Sumatra's Lampong Bay and deposited it in the town—but even this was soon exceeded! At approximately 10:30 A.M. there swept in a wave that again picked up the ship and carried her inland more than a mile! The height reached by the water at Telok Betong was about 87 feet above normal sea level. Along all the shores of the Sunda Strait the water reached heights of 65 to 100 feet, and at Merak, near the northwest tip of Java, it must have reached more than 130 feet! Farther south, at the head of Pepper Bay, it swept as much as 10 miles inland. The great wave completed the destruction of the dozens of coastal villages that had already been heavily damaged by the earlier waves; the additional great wave that came in about 11:20 A.M. could do little more. Destruction of the lowland areas by the waves was almost absolute, and more than 36,000 persons were killed.

When visibility finally returned, it was found that nearly two thirds of Krakatoa Island had disappeared (Fig. 10-11B). The cones of Perbuwatan and Danan were completely gone, and Rakata had been chopped in two. Its southern half was still there, truncated on the north by a cliff half a mile high. All that remained in the area farther north was a single small spire of rock, later named Bootmansrots, where the east flank of Danan had been. Beneath the site of the former west flank of Danan the water was nearly 900 feet deep, and this basin extended westward toward the south end of Verlaten Island.

The immediate puzzle was, of course, what had happened to the missing part of the island? The answer was found by R. D. M. Verbeek in a study of the materials ejected during the eruption. They were overwhelmingly new material—mostly pumice and crystal–vitric essential ash with only scattered bits of older rock. The lowermost, earliest deposits on Verlaten and Lang Islands are well bedded and mostly moderately to well sorted, indicating that they settled from the air. A thickness of 50 feet of deposits contains more than 30 separate layers representing that many separate explosions. Above these lie 200 feet of unstratified debris consisting of a chaotic mixture of fragments of pumice up to 3 feet or more across with lapilli and ash, again with only a small proportion of accessory fragments. Clearly, these deposits were the products of glowing avalanches. Finer ash and pumice were carried to great distances. On the slopes of Rajah Bassa Volcano at the southeastern tip of Sumatra the falling ash was so hot that it burned persons' faces and hands and any other skin surfaces that were directly exposed to it (although it was not hot enough to set fires), and some deaths resulted. In the eastern part of the Sunda Strait, rafts of floating pumice accumulated on the water to thicknesses of more than 10 feet, and ships experienced great difficulty in forcing their way through. Ash fell to an appreciable thickness over an area of more than $1\frac{1}{2}$ million square miles, and as was stated in Chapter 7, some fine ash drifted around the world. Verbeek calculated that the total volume of ejecta was at least 3.8 cubic miles—but he also demonstrated that only about 5 per cent of this material was old rock derived from Perbuwatan, Danan, and Rakata cones or the underlying basement.

If the volume of dilated pumice and ash is recalculated to what it would be if the material were dense magma, its volume is roughly the same as that of the hollow that occupied the site of the missing part of the island. But the total volume of fragments of old rocks is far less than that of the missing part of the island. Obviously, therefore, the island cannot have been simply blown into the air. The only reasonable alternative explanation is that the missing portion sank, dropped down into the void left by the eruption of stupendous quantities of magma. This is the conclusion reached by Verbeek shortly after the eruption and the one we accept today. It is strengthened by the fact, demonstrated by M. Neumann van Padang, that the sinking did not cease with the eruption but continued for several decades after it. Careful study of the deposits of the eruption by Charles Stehn (1929) has demonstrated that they can be closely related to various phases of the eruption recognized by observers at a distance. Thus, the great glowing avalanche deposits were formed at the time of the great explosions at 10:02 and 10:52 A.M. The collapse occurred piece-meal. Perbuwatan disappeared at 4:40 A.M., and Danan at 10:52 A.M.

The tsunamis occurred repeatedly through the night and morning, and although only a few of them can be correlated with times of apparent collapse of the volcano, many can be correlated with known explosions, and the greatest waves correspond in time with the greatest explosions. It seems clear that the tsunamis were largely the result of the explosions, caused either directly by the violent outward thrust on the water or indirectly by the impact of the huge volumes of ejecta falling into the sea around the vent, or perhaps jointly by both mechanisms.

Brief notice of the later history of Krakatoa will be taken later.

Rhyolitic Flood Eruptions

"Rhyolitic" is here used in a broad sense. The magma of these eruptions is most commonly rhyolite, but may be rhyodacite or quartz latite (similar to rhyodacite but somewhat more alkaline), or rarely dacite, quartz trachyte, or trachyte. Like the basaltic flood eruptions, the rhyolitic flood eruptions produce great volumes of magma and spread to great distances from their vents as very fluid flows that build broad nearly level plains, in part consisting of broad very flat coalescing shields (Chapter 11). The two types of flood eruption are similar in two other respects: both appear generally, if not always, to be fed from fissure vents; and we have no really typical example of either in historic times. The great fluidity is the result of movement of the viscous magma in the form of ash flows (Chapter 8).

The closest approach to a typical rhyolitic flood eruption that we have had in recent centuries was that in the Valley of Ten Thousand Smokes, just northwest of Mt. Katmai, Alaska, in 1912. Indians living in the vicinity had moved away, alarmed by earthquakes that preceded the outbreak, and there are no known close-range witnesses of the eruption. Its events must be deduced from studies of the deposits left by them.

The eruption began with explosions heard 600 miles away and the ejection of huge amounts of pumice and ash, which fell to a thickness of 10 inches at Kodiak, 100 miles from the volcano. Early studies led to the conclusion that the ash had been erupted from Mt. Katmai itself, but later work (Curtis, 1955, 1968) has shown that it came from vents situated in the head of the valley that leads northwestward from near the west base of Katmai (Fig. 10-12). The actual nature of the vents cannot be seen, because they have been buried by later deposits, but fissures in the adjacent mountain slopes trend across the valley head, and it is presumed that the ash issued from fissure vents, concentrating in one place to build a pumice cone within which later was built the dome of Novarupta. Following the initial ash ejection, there issued from the same vents an ash flow that traveled down the valley for a distance of 14 miles (Chapter 8). Recent seismic and gravity studies (Gedney, Matteson, and Forbes, 1970) indicate, however, that the average thickness of the flow is less than 100 feet—far smaller than some earlier estimates. The valley floor was transformed into a flat plain as much as 2½ miles wide from which, for many years, there rose an untold multitude of fumaroles. Thence came the name given to the valley by its discoverer, R. F. Griggs—the Valley of Ten Thousand Smokes. The rise of the gas-rich magma that formed the ash flow was followed by that of viscous magma poorer in gas that built the Novarupta dome in the crater of the small pumice cone. The last major event of the eruption was the collapse of the summit of the volcanic cone of Mt. Katmai, presumably because of drainage of magma from beneath it. The height of the mountain was reduced by about 1,150 feet, leaving a caldera 2.7 miles long, 1.9 miles wide, and 1,600 to 2,000 feet deep. The collapse was followed by the building of a small dacite cinder cone on the floor of the caldera and deposition of a small amount of dark ash over the surrounding country.

FIGURE 10-12. Map showing the relationship of the ash flow of the Valley of Ten Thousand Smokes to Katmai and other neighboring volcanoes. (Modified after Curtis, 1968.)

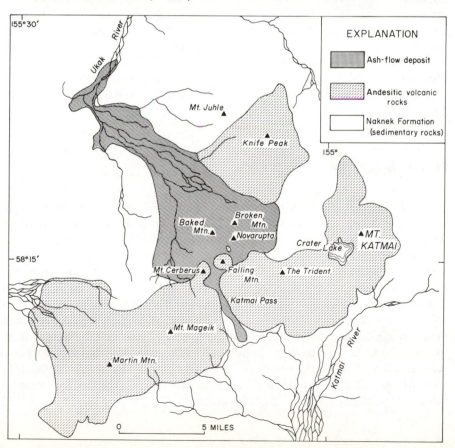

The most important thing in the present connection is the nature of the ash flow itself. In the ensuing years streams have cut deep gorges into it, revealing its internal structure. The deposit has been briefly studied by Bordet, Marinelli, Mittempergher, and Tazieff (1963), who have reached the following conclusions: (1) the ash flow is weakly welded in its lower part, (2) it was extruded as an aerosol of solid fragments in gas at a high temperature, (3) the flow down the valley was laminar, and in the lower end of the valley it became separated into a series of sheets that advanced one over another, (4) the flow was fed from a series of fissures in the upper end of the valley, and (5) the advance of the flow at its terminal end was slow and gentle enough so that trees were simply enclosed in it without being knocked over. The characteristics are in accord with a rather gentle overflow of an incandescent ash–gas mixture spreading down the valley at a speed of only a few miles an hour, governed by gravity, the gentle slope of the valley floor, and its own rather low density. Far from being a violent blast, it appears to have been a rather gentle flooding.

The great volume of some of these eruptions has been mentioned in Chapter 8 and should again be emphasized here. Single flows commonly have volumes of several tens of cubic miles, and some appear to have volumes of several hundred cubic miles. These volumes are equaled only by some of the flows of basaltic flood eruptions (Chapter 5). Furthermore, successive flows commonly are erupted one over another at such short intervals that earlier flows are still hot when later ones are emplaced, and an entire succession of flows cools as a single unit.

Ash-flow deposits are commonly underlain by air-fall ash and pumice showing that the eruptions start with moderate to strong explosive activity, but the volume of air-fall tephra usually is small compared to that of the ignimbrite.

Ultravulcanian Eruptions

Eruptions in which only solid fragments of older rocks are ejected are known as ultravulcanian, or sometimes as semivolcanic. The fragments may be cold, or they may be hot and even incandescent, but they are not derived from newly risen magma. The heat of some fragments may be residual, the rock not having cooled completely since it was emplaced during some former eruption, or the heating may have been brought about by rising hot gases or, perhaps rarely, by the combustion of gas. The ejecta may be either accessory or accidental and often consist of both. They range in size from blocks weighing many tons to very fine ash resulting from the attrition of solid rocks. The ash is generally lithic or crystal–lithic. Vitric ash, which is rarely present, is the result of the ejection of ash from an earlier magmatic eruption or of the pulverization of older volcanic glass during the explosions.

Initial explosions at new vents throw out showers of accidental debris, which commonly accumulates around the vent to form a low block or block–and–ash cone. Some explosion craters have only one brief period of eruption, and the cone consists wholly of accidental fragments—chunks of whatever rocks the crater has been blasted through. Commonly, however, the initial explosions are followed by others in which the magma rises nearer the surface and more and more magmatic ejecta are formed, so that the initial ultravulcanian block–and–ash cone becomes buried beneath a normal cinder or ash cone, formed by Strombolian or Vulcanian eruption, in which lava flows may be interbedded.

The first phase of eruptions of long-established volcanoes also may be ultravulcanian. The explosions that clear the way for the rising magma may throw out the material that has clogged the conduit and vent as showers of accessory fragments, sometimes wholly cold and sometimes partly glowing. The first explosions of the 1888 eruption of Vulcano, mentioned above, were of that sort. They were followed by ordinary Vulcanian or Strombolian activity.

The gas that causes ultravulcanian explosions may be magmatic in origin, or it may be the result of heating of groundwater (phreatic explosions). Where no magmatic ejecta are thrown out, it may be difficult to be certain whether or not magmatic gas was involved in the explosion. Thus, for instance, some of the explosion craters (maars) in the Rhine region of Germany are surrounded by low block–and–ash cones composed wholly of fragments of the surrounding sedimentary rocks. The explosions that formed them may have been wholly phreatic; but the presence of magmatic ejecta in some otherwise similar cones nearby suggests that magmatic gases played a part in the explosions that formed the latter cones, and they may well have done so at the first-mentioned craters also, even though no molten material reached the surface. The cones surrounding the Ubehebe Craters at the north end of Death Valley, California, consist largely of accidental ejecta but contain some magmatic bombs, showing that although the explosions that formed them may have been very largely phreatic, magma and magmatic gases also were involved.

One of the best examples of a phreatic ultravulcanian eruption is that of Kilauea Volcano in 1924 (Plate 10-16). For several years a lake of molten lava had been present in Halemaumau Crater, at times rising to the crater brim and overflowing. Early in 1924 the level of the lake started to drop, and on February 21 the liquid magma disappeared from view leaving a fuming pit 380 feet deep. Through March and April the crater remained empty, while numerous earthquakes along the zone of fractures extending eastward from the summit suggested that this "east rift zone" was opening and the magma draining from beneath the summit of the mountain out into the fissures in the eastern flank. The floor of Halemaumau Crater continued to sink. On April 30 the crater was 500 feet deep, and by May 7 it was 700 feet deep. On the night of May 10 a small explosion in Halemaumau threw out accessory blocks and dust. More explosions

PLATE 10-16. Ash-laden steam cloud from a phreatic explosion in Halemaumau Crater, Kilauea Volcano, in May 1924. The base of the column is about 2,000 feet across. Photo by Tai Sing Loo.

followed, increasing in violence until the morning of May 18, when one block weighing about 8 tons was thrown more than half a mile from the crater rim and dense clouds of ash were projected to a height of 4 miles. After that, explosions continued with decreasing strength until May 27.

The explosions threw out approximately 1 million cubic yards of debris (Plate 10-17). All of it was old rock. Some of the fragments were red hot, but these could be recognized as pieces of still-uncooled intrusive bodies exposed in the walls of the crater. No fresh magmatic material was ejected, and the gas was wholly steam with no detectable trace of magmatic constituents. With the exception of the few glowing fragments, both the rock debris and the steam were quite cool, only a little above the boiling temperature of water.

The end of the eruption left Halemaumau a steaming chasm 1,300 feet deep. Its diameter had more than doubled, from $\frac{1}{4}$ to more than $\frac{1}{2}$ mile. The volume of the crater was approximately 264 million cubic yards—roughly ten times as great as the volume of rock fragments thrown out of it. As was pointed out by R. H. Finch, obviously the enlargement of the

PLATE 10-17. Blocks thrown out by phreatic explosions at Kilauea Volcano, Hawaii, in 1924. The hat gives scale. Hawaii Institute of Geophysics photo by G. A. Macdonald.

crater was brought about more by sinking and collapse than by blasting out by explosion.

Measurements indicated that the collapse at Halemaumau had been accompanied by a general sinking of the whole mountaintop. A benchmark at the outer rim of Kilauea caldera went down $3\frac{1}{2}$ feet, and another on the caldera floor near the edge of the inner crater of Halemaumau went down 13 feet. The sinking was accompanied by hundreds of earthquakes. There can be little doubt that the explosions were the result of groundwater that drained from the surrounding rocks into the hot conduit of the volcano through the fractures formed by the sinking. It has been suggested that the repeated explosions at fairly regular intervals resulted from clogging of the vent by rock fragments falling and sliding into it after each explosion, forming a plug beneath which steam accumulated until the pressure became great enough to blast out the plug in another explosion. However, Finch (1943) doubts that the plug could have been tight enough to retain the steam at the pressure necessary to bring about the explosion (more than 1,000 pounds per square inch) and suggests that instead the explosions were due to repeated surges of water into the conduit, the rate of inflow being more or less constant, as in geysers that have regular intervals of eruption.

The explosions of Kilauea in 1790 were much like those of 1924, except that some magmatic bombs and lapilli were thrown out with the accessory debris. Spherical cored bombs are moderately abundant in some areas but absent in others. It is noteworthy that the shell of congealed magma on the bombs commonly is quite dense, as though most of the gas had been lost from it before it was ejected and solidified. Some magmatic gas may have been involved in the explosions, but more likely the explosions were wholly phreatic like those of 1924, and the magmatic ejecta represent merely remnants of the incompletely drained lava lake, or magma that drained back into the growing crater from still-liquid intrusive bodies in its walls.

Another well-known ultravulcanian eruption was that of Bandai-san, Japan, in 1888. It is not certain when the last previous eruption of Bandai-san took place. Mudflows formed on the slopes of the mountain in 1783 and 1808, and small explosive eruptions may have occurred at those times. At any rate, the volcano had been quiet for at least 80 years except for rather gentle gas release at fumaroles. On July 15, 1888, rumblings from the mountain were heard soon after 7 A.M., and at 7:30 A.M. there was a moderately strong explosion followed by a continuous trembling of the ground. At 7:45 A.M., while the ground was still trembling, came a moderately strong explosion, followed during the next few hours by 15 to 20 more. Blocks and lapilli were thrown to a height of 4,000 feet, and the black dust-laden cloud of steam drifted on up to 20,000 feet or more. At the foot of the mountain rain falling from the cloud produced a shower of scalding-hot mud.

The explosions took place on the northern flank of the mountain near a point where steam had been issuing for many years. They produced an amphitheater-shaped crater 7,460 feet long and 8,080 feet across at the mouth with precipitous sides. The volume of material blown out was approximately ¼ cubic mile. All of it consisted of old rock, some of it partly decomposed to clay (kaolinized) by the action of acid from volcanic gases escaping through it. On the north side of the mountain the debris formed an avalanche that rushed down into stream valleys and was transformed into mudflows, which in turn swept on down the valleys for several miles and took the lives of about 460 persons.

Another phreatic ultravulcanian eruption of somewhat different character took place in the Suoh Basin, a swampy depression in southcentral Sumatra, in 1933. The region had been one of hot springs, small geysers, and a few solfataras (fumaroles from which sulfur-bearing gas was escaping). On June 25 it was shaken by a violent earthquake, and 13 hours later the gas pressure in the geysers and solfataras began gradually to increase until, on July 10, violent steam explosions occurred heard 350 miles away. The explosions burst out at more than 100 places along cracks in the marshy floor of the basin, but primarily at two places, where moderate-sized craters were blasted out. The material ejected was almost wholly mud and covered an area of about 12.6 square miles with a layer of mud 65 feet thick at the center and a total volume of about 250 million cubic yards. No new magmatic material was erupted. Dutch volcanologists who studied the eruption concluded that the earthquake of June 25 had opened cracks that allowed water to descend to the proximity of a body of magma or still-hot intrusive rock at depth, where it was converted into steam.

The outbreak of Tarawera Volcano on the North Island of New Zealand in 1886 is an example of an eruption that varied greatly in character from one area to another owing to the local reaction of rising magma with water. The eruption was a tragedy, not only because of the loss of life occasioned by it, but also because of the destruction of the famous pink and white terraces of Lake Rotomahana. These magnificent stepped structures built by the deposition of calcium carbonate by hot springs were considered one of the natural wonders of the world. Mt. Tarawera is one of a row of prehistoric rhyolite domes northeast of Lake Rotomahana. On July 10, 1886, a series of fissures opened in a northeast–southwest direction across the top of the mountain, and there followed an eruption that ejected nearly a cubic mile of magmatic basaltic cinder and ash, forming a deposit as much as 250 feet thick along the fissure. Southwestward the fissures extended beneath Lake Rotomahana, and the rising magma encountered groundwater in the rocks beneath the lake, transforming it into steam. The resulting low-temperature hydroexplosions completely destroyed the pink and white terraces and threw out large amounts of lake-bottom mud and fragments of partly kaolinized rock, but no new magmatic material. Although the eruption at Mt. Tarawera itself was of violent Strombolian character, the low-temperature nonmagmatic explosions at Lake Rotomahana were ultravulcanian.

Shallow Submarine Eruptions

Probably, the explosiveness of all sorts of eruptions is increased where the rising magma comes in contact with water at shallow depths with resultant generation of steam. However, the effect is most conspicuous in the case of Hawaiian- or Strombolian-type eruptions that otherwise would be gentle. The eruption of Kilauea Volcano in 1960 has already been mentioned (p. 218) as a case in point, and the explosiveness of the Laki eruption in Iceland was probably also in part due to the same cause.

An even more conspicuous example is furnished by the change in type of activity during the Capelinhos eruption at the western end of Fayal Island in the Azores in 1957–1958. From September 16 to 26 the western end of Fayal was shaken by frequent small earthquakes. On September 27 the ocean surface was seen to be discolored, brownish to yellowish, over an area some half-mile across centering about 3,000 feet west of the western tip of the island. Occasional wisps of steam rose from the discolored water, and soon the ocean began to boil and a dense turbulent column of steam arose. About 2 A.M. on September 29 showers of incandescent fragments began to shoot up out of the water to a height of 300 feet, and by that afternoon the top of a cinder cone appeared. The cone had been built from the ocean floor, 250 to 300 feet below sea level, in 48 hours.

The strength of the explosions rapidly increased. By October 1 bombs and blocks were being thrown to a height of 1,500 feet and a dense black ash cloud was rising to 20,000 feet. By late October the new island stood 260 feet above sea level and was shaped like a horseshoe half a mile across, open to the sea on the northwest side. On October 30 eruption suddenly stopped, and within a few hours a large part of the island had disappeared. As Tazieff (1958) has pointed out, the destruction was far too rapid to have been the result of wave erosion and must have been brought about by collapse of the vent area as the magma withdrew from an underlying shallow chamber. Two days later eruption recommenced and the cone was rebuilt, eventually being joined to the main island as a peninsula and adding about half a square mile to the area of Fayal.

Throughout the early part of the eruption, the crater of the cone remained open to the sea on the northwest side and the vent was submerged beneath the water. Contact of the rising magma with the seawater resulted in violent steam explosions. Clusters of dark gray to black jets shot upward to heights of 500 to 1,500 feet at angles ranging from about 60° to vertical, giving the general impression of a dense clump of fir trees or cypress trees with their projecting pointed tops (Plate 10-18). Similar explosion clouds during the 1944 eruption of Vesuvius have been called *cypressoid* by G. Imbo. Streamers and curtains of lapilli and ash fell around the edges of the eruption column; around its base rose clouds of gray ash kicked up by bombs and blocks falling on the flanks of the cone, and billowing puffs of white steam rose from the water where it was heated by falling ejecta. Above the pointed jets a tightly convoluted ash-laden "cauliflower" cloud rose another several thousand feet. In general appearance the explosion clouds of many submarine eruptions closely resemble those of true Vulcanian eruptions.

By December the cone had built to such an extent that the breach in the ring was closed, and the vent became isolated from the ocean. The eruption changed in character to Strombolian, and at times even Hawaiian, with showers of incandescent bombs and lapilli accompanied by only a small amount of ash. Later during the eruption occasional collapses of the cone again allowed water to enter the crater, and each time the erup-tion column again temporarily assumed the explosive cypressoid character. Further confirmation that the explosive character was due to contact of the magma with water is furnished by Tazieff's observation on June 14, 1958, of two vents simultaneously active, one above water producing mild Strombolian eruption and one below water producing violent cypres-soid blasts.

The parts of the cone built by the Strombolian portions of the eruption consist of typical Strombolian cinder, bombs, and lapilli. In con-trast, the parts built by the steam explosions consist of bombs and blocks mixed with ash. Many of the latter bombs have a dense chilled skin a fraction of an inch to an inch in thickness, often with rather fine-meshed irregular surficial cracking resembling incipient bread-crust cracking. The cone shows the same broad low profile with broad saucer-shaped crater that typifies older tuff cones (such as Diamond Head and Punchbowl in Hawaii) formed by hydromagmatic explosive eruptions.

The best studied of all submarine eruptions began on November 14, 1963, in the ocean just south of Iceland (Thorarinsson, 1964). The island built by it has been named Surtsey, after the giant Surtur who, in Nordic mythology, will set fire to the earth at the Last Judgment (Sigvalda-son, 1965). At 8 A.M. on November 14 black bursts of tephra were seen rising from the water to a height of 200 feet at three separate places along a northeast-trending line 6 miles southwest of the southernmost of the tiny Westman Islands. By 11 A.M. these cypressoid jets were shooting to heights of 400 to 500 feet at intervals of about 30 seconds, and a cloud of steam and fume rose 2 miles above them. The length of the line of vents was about a quarter of a mile. Ejecta piled up around the vents, and by November 16 an island had appeared. On November 19 the island consisted of a ridge of ash and bombs 200 feet high and 2,000 feet long split from end to end by the eruptive fissure, which was flooded by the sea. By the end of November the island had become horseshoe shaped, with the crater open to the sea toward the southwest.

Hydroexplosions continued for the next several months (Plate 10-18). At times when the sea had easy access to the vent, the explosions were intermittent at intervals of a few seconds to a few minutes, producing

PLATE 10-18. Surtsey Volcano, south of Iceland, in eruption in November, 1963, showing the black "cypressoid" or "cock's-tail" jets, the white steam cloud, and the cone being built in the ocean. Photo by Sigurdur Thorarinsson.

typical cypressoid jets. When the explosions took place at a moderate depth in the vent, the jets rose more or less vertically, reaching heights of as much as 1,600 feet, with some bombs thrown as high as 3,000 feet. When the explosions occurred close to the surface, the jets spread out into a fan of gracefully curving plumes likened by Thorarinsson (1964) to cocks' tails. Bombs fell into the water three quarters of a mile from the island. In contrast, when access of water to the vent was partly or wholly cut off by building of the cone, there was instead a continuous but pulsating outrush of gas and tephra reaching heights of 3,000 to 6,000 feet and continuing often for several hours.

By early April, 1964, the cone had grown to a point where the ocean was effectively excluded from the vent, and the type of activity changed. Lava fountains of Hawaiian type played in the crater building spatter conelets around themselves, and lava flows poured from the crater into the sea armoring the southern portion of the cone (Fig. 10-13). As in the Capelinhos eruption, the character of the explosions clearly was governed by the ease of access of external water into the vent.

Without the lava cover the island would have been short lived. Thorarinsson records that during a single violent storm in February, 1964, waves cut a bench 300 feet wide across the edges of the tephra cone. The lava is much more resistant to the waves than is the loose ash, and the cover of lava will make it possible for the island to survive.

The activity at the main Surtsey vent ended on May 7, 1965. Two weeks later submarine eruptions began again about 2,000 feet to the east-northeast, and another island ash cone was built. The character of the activity was much like that of the early phase of Surtsey. By mid-September Syrtlingur (Little Surtsey) was about 1,000 feet across and rose 230 feet above sea level. However, activity came to an end in early October, and by October 24 the island was completely washed away.

Shortly afterward, submarine eruption began again half a mile southwest of Surtsey. The activity first became visible at the sea surface on December 26, and the new ash island was named Jólnir—Christmas Island. Again the activity resembled the submarine phase of Surtsey. During the ensuing few months the island was washed away 5 times. When activity

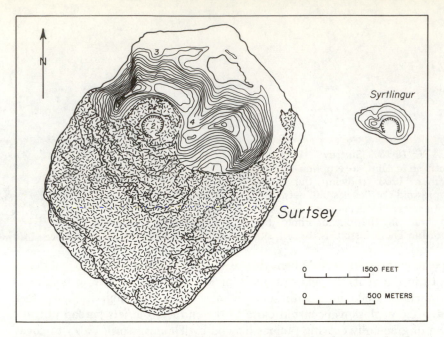

FIGURE 10-13. Map of Surtsey Volcano, Iceland, showing the lava veneer on the southern side. (After Thorarinsson, 1967.) The patterned area is lava covered, the unshaded area is tephra; the numbers represent vents that were successively active. The contour interval is 10 meters.

ended, on August 10, 1966, it was more than 200 feet high, but again it was soon washed away.

On August 19 lava broke out again on the main island. The activity was of Hawaiian type, and the lava flowed mostly toward the south-southeast building the island outward at a rate of more than 2,000 square yards a day (Thorarinsson, 1967). At the end of March, 1967, the eruption was still continuing, and the total volume of lava and tephra produced since the beginning of the eruption was about 0.7 cubic mile.

One of the features commonly shown by hydroexplosions of all types is a cloud that spreads out from the base of the vertical eruption column, often with great velocity. This ring-shaped expanding cloud appears to be the same as the *base surge* observed in nuclear explosions (Moore, 1967). It is closely related, if not identical, in origin to the glowing avalanches of St. Vincent type (Chapter 8). Commonly, the cloud is heavily laden with ash or with mud formed by mixing of water with the ash, and sometimes with lapilli and bombs, or even large blocks. It sandblasts, or even knocks down, trees and other objects in its path, and it may plaster the side of the object toward the eruption center with mud. Close to the center it may erode radial channels in the tephra cone around the vent, and it may form deposits of ash that show both the external forms and the internal bedding structures that are typical of sand dunes. Farther from the center more or less horizontal layers of ash represent the deposits of successive base surges. Bombs or blocks up to several feet in diameter may be present in the poorly sorted matrix of ash and lapilli. Base surges have been recognized in the Capelinhos and Myojin eruptions and at Anak

Krakatoa, and at Surtsey the bigger explosions were followed by "tephra-vapor avalanches" that swept down the slopes of the cone and traveled out as much as a quarter of a mile over the surrounding water (Moore, 1967). Base surges are clearly recognizable in photographs of the 1924 eruption of Kilauea.

One of the most spectacular developments of base surges occurred in the eruption of Taal Volcano in the Philippines in 1965. The volcano is located in Lake Taal, which occupies the floor of a volcano-tectonic depression (see Chapter 12) in southwestern Luzon about 35 miles south of Manila. Near the center of the lake, Volcano Island consists of a series of overlapping cones built by previous eruptions. Shortly after 2 A.M. on September 28 eruption commenced from a new vent on the southwestern side of the island. At first the eruption was of the Strombolian type, throwing incandescent bombs and cinder high in the air and building a cinder cone around the vent. About 3:25 A.M. the character of the eruption changed, and enormous ash-laden clouds rose 10 to 12 miles into the air. The change appears to have been caused by the lake water gaining access to the vent (Moore, Nakamura, and Alcaraz, 1966). Violent explosions continued until about 9:20 A.M. Fine ash fell as much as 50 miles to the leeward. In the area nearer the volcano, much of the ash was in the form of accretionary lapilli, owing to the abundant water in the eruption cloud. Base surges swept out across the lake and onto the outer shores (Fig. 10-14), transporting material horizontally with hurricane velocity. Half a mile south of the vent cross-bedded sand-dune deposits of the base surges are 8 feet thick and contain blocks as much as 18 inches in diameter. Dunes several feet high were formed. Three miles to the southwest the deposits still were more than a foot thick. The material thrown out was mostly old rock blasted out of the side of Volcano Island. The effects of the horizontal blasts extended to a distance of about 3.5 miles from the vent. Within half a mile of the vent all the trees were broken off or uprooted; and in the next zone, about 800 feet wide, the trees were strongly sandblasted on the side toward the volcano and as much as 6 inches of wood was scoured away, although the bark still remained on the side away from the volcano. Nowhere in the entire area of the blasts was there any evidence of charring or burning, and in the outer part of the area thick deposits of mud formed on trees and other objects, showing that the temperature could not have been as high as the boiling point of water.

After 9:20 A.M. the explosions became less intense, and about 11 A.M. it could be seen that a crater 0.2 mile across and 0.9 mile long had been blasted out of the side of the island along a southwest-trending fissure. The crater was connected with the lake forming a long, narrow bay. Explosions of decreasing violence continued until 6 A.M. on September 30 when another change in the character of the activity occurred. From then until 4 P.M. that afternoon, weak explosions hurled up black magmatic ejecta mixed with steam and built a small cinder cone in the crater. It is interesting to note that bombs in the cone show weakly bread-crusted

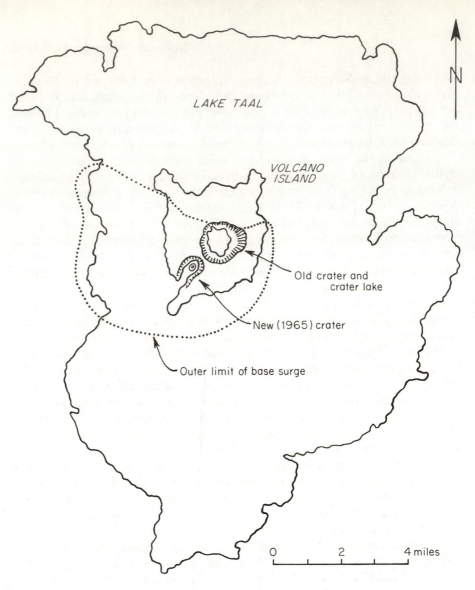

FIGURE 10-14. Map of Lake Taal and Volcano Island, showing the location of the vent of 1965 and the extent of blast effects from base surges. (After Moore, 1967.)

surfaces resembling those found at Capelinhos and in littoral cones formed where lava flows enter water.

The 1965 eruption killed about 190 persons. A much more violent eruption of Taal in 1911, which killed more than 1,300 persons, appears to have been much the same in character.

It will be noted that the effects of the Taal eruption were much like some of those of the Tarawera eruption of 1886. Descriptions of that eruption are not adequate to indicate for certain whether or not base surges were formed, but it appears very probable that they were and that they caused much of the destruction around Lake Rotomahana.

Cypressoid eruption clouds of the sort described on the preceding pages are very characteristic of shallow submarine eruptions, though they are observed in other types of eruption also. That their general character is the result of violent steam generation external to the magma is shown by the fact that they are much the same even though the character of the magma may be quite different. The steam explosions that attended the growth of the dacitic submarine dome at Myojin Reef, south of Japan, in 1952–1953, and those that resulted from the basaltic Strombolian eruptions at Fayal and at Krakatoa, and the Hawaiian eruption at Surtsey, were essentially identical. The Krakatoa activity differs in one respect from that of Capelinhos. After the great eruption and collapse of Krakatoa in 1883, the volcano was quiet until 1927. In that year activity resumed with eruption of basaltic ejecta from a vent nearly midway between the former vents of Danan and Perbuwatan and close to the foot of the submarine escarpment formed by the 1883 collapse. The character of the explosions was precisely like that of the cypressoid explosions of Capelinhos. Repeatedly, as activity started and stopped during the ensuing years, the cone (known as Anak Krakatoa—the "child of Krakatoa") was built above water and destroyed again, largely by wave erosion. In 1960 (Fig. 10-11C) the rim of the cone was 350 feet above sea level and the crater was isolated from the sea. In spite of this, however, the explosions continued to be cypressoid (Decker and Hadikusumo, 1961). Apparently the base of the cone was not sufficiently impermeable to exclude the seawater, which still found access to the vent. Shortly afterward, however, the vent became sealed off from the water, and between 1960 and 1963 lava flows flooded the crater (Zen and Hadikusumo, 1964).

Brief mention should be made of the "disappearing islands" that are reported from time to time. These are the tops of either tephra cones or domes built by eruptions in fairly shallow water. Their disappearance may be caused either by destruction of the top of the mass by explosion and collapse or by wave erosion, which may work with great rapidity on loose ash and cinder. Sometimes both explosion and erosion are involved. Explosions are common on subaerial domes (Chapter 6), and on those formed in water they are even commoner. The island formed by the rise of a dome at Myojin Reef, mentioned above, was soon destroyed by explosions that blew away the sides of the dome and allowed the upper part to collapse. Similar destruction by explosion, aided by wave erosion, was the fate of the McCulloch Dome at Bogoslof Island, Alaska, in 1907, only 10 months after it was built (Jaggar, 1908). Falcon Island, at the north end of the Tonga Archipelago is a tephra cone that periodically builds above sea level during eruptions, but is generally eroded away within the following few months by the ocean waves. The same fate met Graham Island in the Mediterranean Sea in 1831. Mention has already been made of the repeated washing away of the tephra cones of Surtsey and Anak Krakatoa, and several other examples could be cited.

Eruptions very similar in character to shallow submarine eruptions may occur on land, where rising magma encounters abundant water in rocks close to the surface. Such eruptions have been called *phreatomagmatic,* because the gas that causes the explosions is partly steam derived from the groundwater and partly of magmatic origin. The ash cones formed by these eruptions resemble closely the cones formed by shallow submarine eruptions. They have been described in Chapter 9. Examples include many of the tuff cones of the island of Oahu, Hawaii, such as Diamond Head and Punchbowl. The *littoral explosions* that occur where some lava flows enter water also are very similar in character to the hydromagmatic explosions of submarine eruptions, though commonly on a smaller scale. They also have been described in Chapter 9.

SUGGESTED ADDITIONAL READING

Hawaiian Eruptions
Jaggar, 1917; Macdonald, 1943, 1954, 1959.

Lava-lake Activity
Jaggar 1917a, 1917b; Tazieff, 1966.

Basaltic Flood Eruptions
Thorarinsson, 1970; Tyrrell, 1937.

Rhyolitic Flood Eruptions
Bordet, Marinelli, Mittempergher, and Tazieff, 1963; Curtis, 1968.

Strombolian Eruptions
Bullard, 1947; Foshag and Gonzalez, 1955; Gonzalez and Foshag, 1946; Perret, 1916.

Vulcanian Eruptions
Day and Allen, 1925; Fisher, 1939.

Peléean Eruptions
Anderson and Flett, 1903; Gorshkov, 1959; Lacroix, 1904; MacGregor, 1952; Perret, 1935; Taylor, 1958.

Plinian Eruptions
Bullard, 1962, p. 133–156; Furneaux, 1964; Judd, 1888; Rittmann, 1933; Stehn, 1929; Verbeek, 1886; Williams, 1941b, p. 28–35; 1942, p. 68–98.

Ultravulcanian Eruptions
Corwin and Foster, 1959; Jaggar and Finch, 1924; Sekiya and Kikuchi, 1889; Smith, 1887; Stearns, 1925.

Shallow Submarine Eruptions
Decker and Hadikusumo, 1961; Machado, Parsons, Richards and Mulford, 1962; Stehn, 1929; Tazieff, 1958; Thorarinsson, 1967.

Deep-ocean Volcanism
McBirney, 1963a.

11

Major Volcanic Edifices

The smaller structures such as cinder, spatter, and lava cones, built directly around vents by single eruptions, have already been treated in Chapter 9. The present chapter briefly describes the larger land forms that are built generally by repeated eruptions either at the same vent or in the same general area.

Lava Plains and Plateaus

Throughout most if not all of the geological history of the earth, repeated flood eruptions of basalt have taken place within certain areas, burying the land surface or sea bottom and spreading out to form nearly level plains. Some of the plains are at high altitude and, consequently, can be classed as plateaus; and the basaltic lava flows that build the plains have commonly been called *plateau basalts*.

Some of the plains are small: a single eruption or a sequence of a few eruptions may partly fill a valley transforming its formerly V-shaped bottom to a nearly level surface (Fig. 11-1A); but where many successive flood eruptions have taken place, the plain may attain huge size. The Deccan

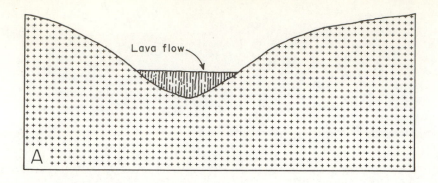

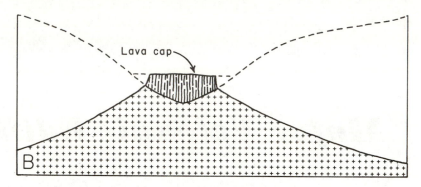

FIGURE 11-1. Diagram showing (A) a lava flow partly filling a valley, transforming it from V-shaped to flat bottomed; and (B) erosion of the adjoining rocks leaving the former valley floor standing as a flat-topped ridge above its surroundings.

plain in northwestern India now covers 100,000 square miles (Fig. 11-2) and probably was originally at least twice that big, as it extends beneath the Arabian Sea, and lavas that were probably once continuous with the main mass are found far to the northwest of it. The Columbia River plain in Washington and Oregon covers an area of some 50,000 square miles; and farther southeast, in eastern Oregon and Idaho, the Snake River plain has an area of about 20,000 square miles (Fig. 11-2B). The youngest eruptions of the Snake River lavas, in and near Craters of the Moon National Monument, are less than 2,100 years old (Prinz, 1970). Extending southward from the Columbia River plain is a series of plains with intervening mountain ridges known in northeastern California as the Modoc Plateau. This region, covering about 30,000 square miles, and also the Snake River plain have sometimes been included as part of the Columbia River plain, but their lavas are younger and of somewhat different composition.

Smaller basalt plains of rather recent geologic age are known in Manchuria, southern Vietnam, northern and central British Columbia, and Patagonia.

Many other similar basaltic plains, or remnants of former plains, are known. One of the oldest is the Keweenawan basalt, which contains the rich copper deposits of Michigan. It is some 700 million years old. The copper forms amygdules and fills other spaces in the lavas. Somewhat younger are flood-basalt masses in South Africa, central Siberia, Abyssinia, the islands such as Kerguelen off the east coast of Africa, the Paraná and Patagonian regions of South America, and the Newark Series of the eastern United States. Perhaps the most extensive of all was a great basaltic plain that, 40 to 30 million years ago, may have extended over 700,000 square miles of the northeastern Atlantic Ocean region. This vast "Thulean plateau" has been generally believed to have been broken up by foundering of the earth's crust to form the present ocean basin; but modern evidence suggests that instead it was pulled apart as North America drifted westward in relation to Europe. In the latter case, it may originally have been much less extensive. At any rate, it is now visible only in small remnants in northern Ireland, western Scotland, the Faroe Islands, Jay Mayen, Iceland, and Greenland.

The volume of lava that entered into the building of some of the lava plains is enormous. The Columbia and Snake River lavas buried mountainous landscapes with a relief of several thousand feet. Near the edges of the plain, mountain ridges of older rock extend into it like peninsulas, and peaks project from it like islands in a sea of lava. (These "islands" have been called *steptoes, dagalas,* and *kipukas.*) Farther from the edge of the plain the old surface has been completely submerged. A well drilled in the south-central part of the Columbia plain passed through 6,000 feet of lavas, and farther north the lava mass is probably even thicker. The volume of the Columbia basalts is probably close to 100,000 cubic miles. In the Paraná basalts of southern Brazil and Uruguay, a well 10,000 feet deep failed to reach the bottom of the lavas, and their volume may be as much as 200,000 cubic miles! The thickness of the plateau-forming lavas in Iceland reaches

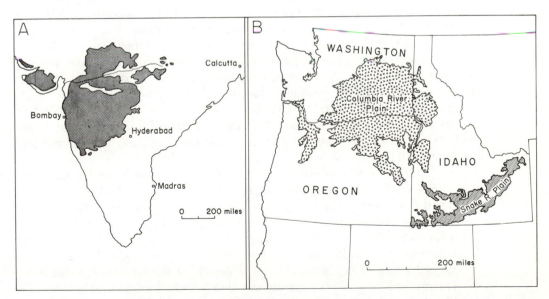

FIGURE 11-2. Maps showing (A) the Deccan basalts of India; and (B) the Columbia, Snake River, and Modoc basalts of northwestern United States. (A) after H. S. Washington, 1922; (B) after Waters, 1955.)

PLATE 11-1. A very low broad shield volcano on the Snake River Plain in southern Idaho. The surface in the foreground is on flood basalt flows of the Snake River lavas. U. S. Geological Survey photo by G. A. Macdonald.

at least 15,000 feet and may be twice that much. The great depth to the base of the lavas in the central parts of these plains probably indicates that the underlying former land surface sank, forming a great basin, during the time the lavas were being erupted. The sinking may have been entirely an adjustment to the great weight of the accumulating lavas, but more likely it resulted in part from a transformation of the outer part of the earth's mantle, which became denser as the relatively lighter basaltic material was removed from it (Chapter 15).

Individual flood-basalt flows have vast areas and volumes (Chapter 5) and must have been erupted rapidly. Locally, large masses of flows accumulated in a short time, as in the Steens Mountain area of southeastern Oregon, where it appears that a thickness of about 5,000 feet of basalt was extruded within 50,000 years (Watkins and Gunn, 1969). However, the formation of the total masses of the lava plains required millions of years. Many thousands of separate flows were involved, and in any one small area there were often lengthy periods between successive flows. Deposits of sand and gravel, and soil beds formed by weathering of the lava surface, were buried by later flows. Other deposits interbedded with the lavas show that the flows interfered with the surface drainage and caused the formation of lakes and swamps that were later filled or drained by erosion. The accumulation of the Columbia River basalts may have taken as much as 10 million years, and the average rate of extrusion of lava was probably not much if any greater than that of the Hawaiian volcanoes during recent times. (At the rate of eruption during historic times the entire 10,000-cubic-mile bulk of Mauna Loa could have been built in less than a million years, and Kilauea may have been built in half that time.)

Most basaltic plains and plateaus have been partly eroded and somewhat folded and/or faulted, and it is no longer possible to determine in detail the nature of the original surfaces. However, the Snake River plain is so young that its surface is nearly intact, and very probably it is typical of such plains. The surface is amazingly flat. I. C. Russell (1902, p. 102–103) writes of it: "On the plain the lava spread out and formed what may be termed a lake of liquid rock . . . the margin of the lake is approximately a contour line . . . No eye can observe that it is not a perfect plain." Actually, the surface is not quite as horizontal as it seems. It was not formed by a single great sheet of molten lava that covered all of it at the same time and was able to assume a surface of hydrostatic equilibrium. Rather, it was formed by many flows from many widely separated vents overlapping one another, and even very fluid basalt flows must have a surface slope in order to spread. It is not surprising, therefore, to find that the surface actually consists of a series of very broad flat cones with slopes for the most part less than 1°. Near the vents some of these cones steepen to form obvious but very broad rounded mounds (shields) 100 to 200 feet high and several miles across (Plate 11-1). At the actual vent there is sometimes preserved a little spatter in the form of a cone, a row of cones, or a spatter rampart. The shield constitutes only a relatively small central portion of the area covered by the eruption and merges imperceptibly into the surrounding broad plain made up of interfingering flows from various vents. Individual flows may extend more than 100 miles from the vent.

The slopes of these very broad shields are too gentle to be readily recognized on the surfaces of the older, eroded plains. In Iceland, however, they have been recognized in cross section in the walls of some of the valleys (Rutten, 1964), where lava beds of one shield may rest with a small angular discordance on those of another shield or on essentially horizontal beds formed by fissure eruptions (Fig. 11-3). In the Faroe Islands detailed studies of the thickness of the lavas above a recognizable widespread nearly

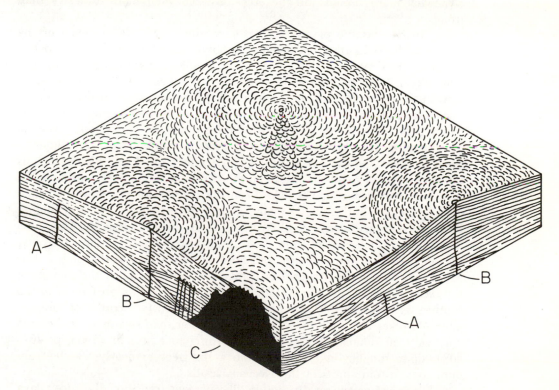

FIGURE 11-3.   Diagram illustrating the structure of a typical lava plain or plateau. (A) dike; (B) pipe conduit merging into a dike at depth; (C) dike feeding fissure eruption. (Modified after Rutten, 1964.)

horizontal surface have demonstrated the presence of three separate shields with slopes of only about 0.5° (Noe-Nygaard, 1968). Two of these shields have central thicknesses of 130 and 180 feet, respectively, areas of approximately 30 and 50 square miles, and volumes of about 1.7 and 0.8 cubic miles. Only a fraction of the third shield is preserved.

In most areas of flood basalts the flows are mainly pahoehoe, though both aa and the aa-like lava described in Chapter 5 may also be present. Individual beds range from a few feet to more than 100 feet thick, but most of them are between 15 and 30 feet. Most flows lack columnar jointing, but in some it is well developed and conspicuous.

In northern Ireland the period of basalt effusions began with associated explosions, the products of which are now seen in tuff beds underlying and intercalated with the lava flows (Patterson, 1955). In general, however, ash and tuff are nearly absent in flood-basalt accumulations; though in some of them tuff, and even lava flows, from adjacent areas are interbedded with the basalts near the edge of the plain. The Bardarströnd area in northwestern Iceland is exceptional both in the presence of abundant tuff (some beds containing fossil leaves) and in the prevalence of aa-type flows (Rutten, 1964). The magma reaching the surface there must have been somewhat more viscous and the eruptions somewhat more explosive than usual.

In the basaltic plains there is generally very little evidence of the nature of the vents from which the lava flows issued. A few lines of spatter cones (as at Craters of the Moon, Idaho) indicate fissure vents, and it is generally believed that the vents were largely if not entirely fissures, probably distributed over rather wide areas. Even where vents are nearly circular, like those preserved at the summits of some of the Icelandic shields, the conduits probably merge downward into fissures at shallow depths. Magma consolidating in a fissure forms a *dike* (Chapter 15). Dikes, sometimes in great numbers, cut the lava beds in some deeply eroded lava plains, such as those of western Scotland. Most of the dikes cut completely through the lava beds and hence cannot have been the feeders for the flows in which they are found, but probably many of them were feeders for later, higher flows since eroded away. A. C. Waters (1955) believes that the Columbia River lavas issued largely from three groups of dikes (*dike swarms*) near the southwestern, southeastern, and northwestern edges of the plain. Near Monument in central Oregon basalt dikes cut older rocks at the margin of the basalt plain. Along the Grande Ronde River and Joseph Creek, in the southeastern corner of Washington and the northeastern corner of Oregon, about 40 dikes cut the basalt flows; and another dike swarm is in the area northwest of Yakima, Washington. According to Krishnan (1968, p. 407–408), dikes ranging in thickness from a few feet to nearly 200 feet are numerous in some parts of the Deccan basalts.

It is extremely rare to find a dike passing transitionally into a lava flow and thereby giving clear evidence that it was the feeder of the flow. One such was recorded in the Columbia River lavas by Fuller (1927). Two dikes passing into lava flows have been found in the Grande Ronde dike swarm (Gibson, 1969); and along the "Great Rift" in Idaho, 25 miles south of the Craters of the Moon, a dike belonging to the Snake River basalts can be seen passing into the flow it fed. The rareness of this observation is probably due to two factors: by chance, the comparatively limited actual vent area must be visible; and furthermore, the actual connection between the feeder and the flow probably is commonly broken by recession of the magma in the dike at the end of the eruption. This draining back of the magma has been observed repeatedly along the feeding fissures at the end of eruptions in Hawaii.

Erosional dissection of the basaltic plains commonly results in formation of a step-like topography on the sides of the valleys caused by the alternation of more and less resistant parts of the lava beds. These steps gave rise to an old name for these basalts, which were once widely known as "traps" or "trap rocks." In America the term is now almost obsolete. Where the beds have been tilted the treads of the steps may be inclined, or a series of hogbacks or cuestas may be formed.

It is rare that lava flows more silicic than basalt are sufficiently fluid to spread out to form a nearly flat surface; and lavas less silicic than basalt are usually erupted in too small volume, at least on the land surface, to form very extensive plains. Flood eruptions of trachyte and related rocks built an extensive plateau in Kenya (Johnson, 1969). Generally, however, extensive plains formed by silicic volcanics are not the result of true lava flows, but of ash flows (see next section). In some volcanic regions, such as the Cascade Range in northwestern United States and the volcanic chains of Central America, the formation of the big central-vent volcanoes was preceded by the eruption of large volumes of thin flows of pyroxene andesite, perhaps in sinking geosynclinal basins (Chapter 14), and these accumulations may have had extensive nearly plain surfaces or may have formed broad very gently sloping ridges. There are few relics of pipe vents in them, and the flows appear to have been erupted mostly from fissure vents forming a complex of broad low overlapping shields.

In northern Nevada, the Circle Creek Rhyolite is a mass with an area of 36 square miles and unknown thickness. Its original surface appears to have been essentially horizontal. It is believed (Coats, 1968) to have resulted from upwelling of magma through numerous fissures to form a pool in a basin that resulted from sagging of the upper part of the earth's crust. Coats (1968, p. 71) suggests the name *lekolith* for a lens-shaped basin-filling extrusive mass of this sort. The name seems undesirable, however, because of the verbal confusion that inevitably will result with the much older and well-established term, laccolith (Chapter 15).

Deep-ocean volcanism probably has built broad basaltic lava plains similar to those found on land and even more extensive, though they are not yet known in any detail. Certainly, the evidence indicates that most of the floor of the deep ocean basins is composed of basalt beneath a thin and discontinuous cover of sediment.

Ash-Flow Volcanoes and Ignimbrite Plains

The only flows other than basalt that are sufficiently fluid and voluminous to form very extensive plains are ash flows. The central part of North Island of New Zealand is a broad, slightly eroded ignimbrite plateau covering an area of about 9,000 square miles. It is formed of a series of partly welded ash flows. The total volume of the ignimbrite is about 1,800 cubic miles. Slight weathering of the surfaces of some of the buried flows indicates that there was at least a moderate interval of time between successive eruptions. The same is suggested by the reversal of the direction of remnant magnetism in some successive flows, the north pole of the magnetization in one flow corresponding in direction to the south pole in the next. The orientation of the magnetization in the flow is believed to represent that of the earth at the time the flow was extruded and cooled, and investigations of rocks that have been dated by means of radioactive-isotope studies suggest that in recent geologic time such reversals of the earth's field have taken place at intervals ranging from about 70,000 to 800,000 years. Several reversals indicate, therefore, a period of several million years for the accumulation of the New Zealand ignimbrites. The plateau has been broadly arched, possibly by the distension of magma forming beneath it, and somewhat broken into fault blocks.

Other big ignimbrite masses are found in Armenia, west-central Sumatra, the Chiricahua region in Arizona, the Jemez Mts. of New Mexico, the San Juan Mts. of Colorado, southern Nevada, Yellowstone National Park, eastern Siberia, and several other areas. At the north end of the Owens Valley, in eastern California, the Bishop Tuff (Gilbert, 1938) is a great sheet of ignimbrite averaging more than 200 feet thick (400 feet thick before compaction) that buried the earlier hilly topography and formed a plain with an area of about 400 square miles (Fig. 11-4). It formed approximately 700,000 years ago as the result of a series of ash-flow eruptions so closely spaced in time that they cooled as a single, or in some places as two, cooling units. Ignimbrites associated with the Lake Toba graben in Sumatra cover an area of more than 9,000 square miles. In the San Juan Mts. the volume of the ignimbrites is estimated to be about 2,000 cubic miles. In British Columbia, early Tertiary time was marked by the eruption of extensive sheets of rhyolitic to andesitic ignimbrites associated with large calderas (Souther, 1970).

Perhaps the most extensive known ignimbrite plain is that which occupied much of central and southern Nevada and adjacent Utah during Miocene time, 20 to 30 million years ago. It has since been broken up and tilted during the formation of the fault-block mountain ranges of that part of the Great Basin, but in its original development it must have been a vast nearly level plain with an area of some 50,000 square miles (Mackin, 1960).

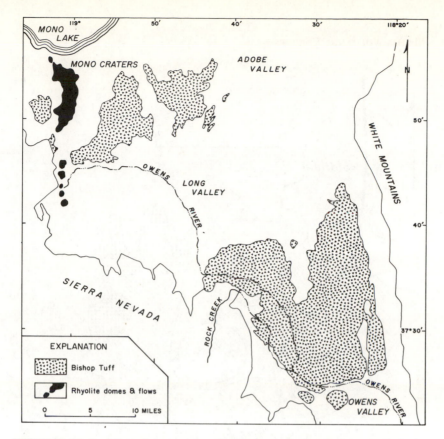

FIGURE 11-4. Map showing the distribution of the Bishop Tuff (ash-flow deposit) in eastern California. (After Gilbert, 1938.)

The most recently recognized type of major volcanic structure consists of a cone built up wholly, or almost wholly, by repeated ash flows from vents concentrated in the central area. The cones are very broad flat shields of ignimbrite, usually with a caldera at the apex (Fig. 11-5). Eruption of the ash flows is commonly preceded by regional or local doming. The most recent and one of the best studied of these ash-flow centers is in the Jemez Mts. of New Mexico (Fig. 11-6). The geology of the area has been worked out in great detail, but only preliminary reports have as yet been published (Smith, Bailey, and Ross, 1961; Smith and Bailey, 1966, 1968).

The volcanic history of the Jemez Mts. area started in late Miocene or early Pliocene time, about 11 million years ago, with the building of a broad volcanic highland by the eruption first of a series of basalt and rhyolite lava flows and tephra beds, followed by a more varied series of basalt, andesite, dacite, and rhyolite flows and tephra. This was followed by a period of volcanic quiet during which the highland was eroded into a mountainous terrain. Then, in mid-Pleistocene time about a million years ago, a series of rhyolite ash flows was erupted, burying the older topography and forming a broad gently sloping cap over the central part of the highland and extending out over the adjacent lowland. These flows comprise the lower Bandelier Tuff and had an original volume of about 50 cubic miles. Their eruption

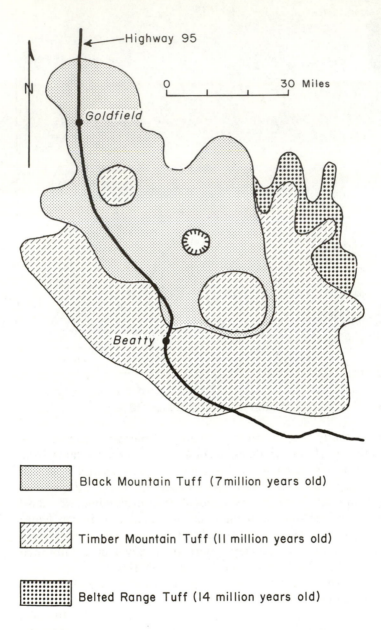

Black Mountain Tuff (7 million years old)

Timber Mountain Tuff (II million years old)

Belted Range Tuff (14 million years old)

Black Mountain Caldera

FIGURE 11-5. Map of part of southwestern Nevada showing the distribution of ignimbrite sheets around the Black Mountain Caldera. The two round structures filled with Timber Mountain volcanics are respectively the former Stonewall Mountain and Timber Mountain Calderas. (Modified after Ekren, 1968.)

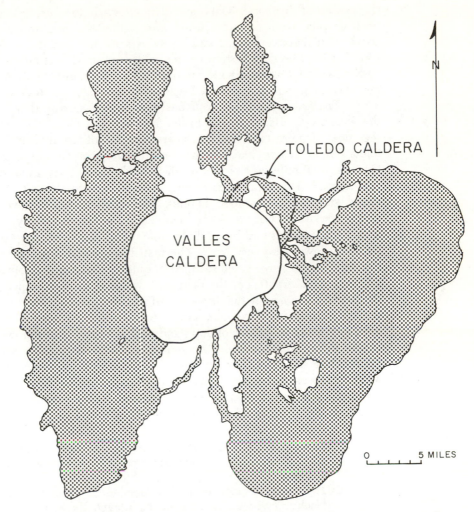

FIGURE 11-6.   Map of part of the Jemez Mountains, New Mexico, showing the distribution of the Bandelier Tuff (ignimbrites) around the Valles
Caldera. (After Smith and Bailey, 1966.)

was followed by collapse of the summit of the pile to form the Toledo
Caldera. This caldera has been largely obliterated by later events. There
followed another period of erosion, lasting about 300,000 years, during which
deep canyons were cut into the lower Bandelier Tuff. Then came another
series of ash flows, again with a volume of about 50 cubic miles, filling the
Toledo Caldera and burying the canyons and ridges cut in the lower tuff.
This later series of ash-flow deposits is known as the upper Bandelier Tuff.
The eruption of the upper Bandelier Tuff was preceded by a regional up-
doming of the Jemez highland, presumably above an underlying magma
body, the distension of the area resulting in a series of arcuate fractures near

the summit of the dome. The upper Bandelier ash flows are believed to have been erupted from those fractures, and within the fractures a subcircular block with diameters of 12 and 15 miles sank to form the Valles Caldera (Fig. 11-6). The later history of the caldera is described on page 314. The upper Bandelier ignimbrites are underlain by a layer of air-fall pumice, showing that the period of eruption began with magmatic explosions.

The lower Bandelier Tuff has been partly destroyed by erosion and the remaining parts are largely buried by the upper tuff. The latter reaches a thickness of more than 800 feet near the crest of the highland and in the filled Toledo Caldera and becomes progressively thinner outward, forming a lens about 60 miles across in a north-to-south direction, and 40 miles across east-to-west. The total mass forms a broad gently sloping shield-shaped dome with the caldera at its summit. The total number of flows within the unit is not known, but there were many; and the volume of any one flow was only a small fraction of the total 50 cubic miles. However, the time intervals between flows were very brief. The first flows, which filled the canyons in the older rocks, were cooled sufficiently quickly that they seldom show welding or crystallization; but the degree of welding increases upward through the lower six tenths of the deposit, and in the upper portion of this part of the tuff, groups of flows combine to form single cooling units, indicating both increasing frequency of flows and higher temperatures of emplacement. In the upper four tenths of the sequence, the recognizable ash flows are thinner, the divisions between flows are more distinct, and zones of dense welding separated by much less welded zones indicate that flows were becoming less frequent than earlier. Smith and Bailey (1966) summarize the events during the formation of the upper Bandelier Tuff as follows:

1. Rapid eruption of some 20 cubic miles of magma [expanded to 30 cubic miles of tuff] with concomitant lowering of total pressure in the magma chamber.
2. Preliminary sagging or partial foundering of the cauldron [caldera] block and wedging of the conduits, bringing the eruption to a temporary halt. . . .
3. Disturbance of equilibrium due to lowered pressure causing resorption of quartz and feldspar in the magma chamber. [The abundance of phenocrysts of quartz and feldspar, particularly of quartz, in the tuff decreases greatly at a level about six-tenths of the way from the bottom to the top.]
4. Continued sporadic eruptions with short time breaks, allowing development of local disconformities, sandy partings, and fumaroles.
5. Reopening of conduits and eruption of remaining 10+ cubic miles of magma. . . .
6. Final collapse of the cauldron block into the magma chamber, thus forming the Valles Caldera.

In the Tibesti region of north Africa, Vincent (1960, p. 141; 1963) has shown that some of the ignimbrite sheets are lenticular disks tapering outward in all directions from the central source area. In surface form they are very flat domes resembling the basaltic shield volcanoes described in the next section, but the shield-like form is partly the result of doming of the surface by intrusive masses beneath. At the summit the shields are indented by collapse calderas. The Yirrigue shield, which is the youngest and best preserved, is approximately 40 miles across. Outside the caldera its summit is nearly flat, and the side slopes of the shield average only 2 to 3°, merging gradually into the surrounding plains. In the walls of the caldera the ignimbrite is only about 300 feet thick and is underlain by older rocks. At the outer edges of the shield the ignimbrite thins to less than 50 feet. The total volume of the ignimbrite lens is about 25 cubic miles. The ignimbrite shields of Tibesti are "central" volcanoes fed from relatively small central vent areas within the present calderas, though Vincent believes the actual feeding conduits to have been fissures. In the oldest and most deeply dissected of the shields, he has described (1960, p. 143) about a hundred rhyolite and trachyte dikes ranging in thickness from about 15 to 50 feet. The dikes form two groups, trending respectively nearly north to south and west-northwest to east-northeast. Arcuate dikes have not been found.

Detailed study of the geology in and around the U.S. Atomic Energy Commission's Nevada Test Site has led to the discovery of a whole series of ash-flow eruption centers in southern Nevada (Figs. 11-5 and 12-6). One of the oldest of the units, the 26.5-million-year-old Monotony Valley tuff, has a volume of more than 1,000 cubic miles, but its total extent and characteristics are still largely unknown (Ekren, 1968). Later units are known in considerable detail.

Each is a roughly lenticular mass with an irregular base owing to its having buried a preexisting hilly topography; and each was formed by a large number of ash flows erupted at intervals so short (probably not more than a few tens of years) that they have merged into a small number of cooling units. Most are distributed more or less symmetrically around collapse calderas. As an example, the Rainier Mesa Member of the Timber Mountain Tuff has an original volume of more than 285 cubic miles, a radius of 35 to 50 miles, and a thickness near the center of more than 800 feet (Byers et al., 1968). An elliptical caldera with diameters of 18 and 20 miles formed during or after the eruption of the ash flows. A later ignimbrite sheet, the Ammonia Tanks Member, has about the same distribution and a volume of about 180 cubic miles. There appears to be no question that the ash was erupted from the general area of the caldera, presumably from arcuate fractures related to the caldera collapse, but there is no direct evidence of the nature of the conduits. Just north of the Timber Mountain caldera, the older Silent Canyon caldera is surrounded by the ignimbrite sheets of the Belted Range Tuff (Figs. 11-5 and 12-6). The hypothesis that the ash flows were erupted from arcuate fissures related to the formation of the caldera is there supported by the presence of four minor vents lying along a curved line just northeast of the caldera boundary (Noble et al., 1968).

The rocks of most of the ash-flow centers in southwestern Nevada are normal calc-alkaline rhyolites and rhyodacites ("quartz latites"), but two of them, the Black Mountain and Silent Canyon centers, are characterized by peralkaline (alkali-rich) rhyolites (comendites) and quartz trachytes.

Ninety miles east of the Silent Canyon center, the Kane Springs Wash center also erupted peralkaline ash flows that covered an area of 3,000 to 4,000 square miles and had an original volume of more than 200 cubic miles (Noble, 1968). Activity at the center commenced with the eruption of lava flows, followed by voluminous ash flows that formed the Kane Springs Wash Tuff. The latter consists of at least six and possibly more than twelve separate cooling units, at least three of which were formed by several separate ash flows. The major sheets thicken and show an increase in welding and crystallization, and several thinner and less extensive sheets appear toward the center of the area, where collapse formed a caldera 12 miles long and 8 miles wide. The caldera later was filled to overflowing by a series of silicic to basic lava flows, domes, air-fall tuffs, and ignimbrites.

The recognition of these ignimbrite shields in a few well-studied areas suggests that the broad ignimbrite plains may consist in large part of coalescing shields with very low angles of slope, just as do the basaltic plains. Noble (1968) writes: "The Kane Springs Wash center . . . is of the arcuate fissure-central vent type, in which pyroclastic eruption culminates in the formation of large, roughly equidimensional collapse calderas, that appears to be typical of large-scale ash-flow volcanism throughout the world."

As with the basaltic flood eruptions, there is comparatively little evidence of the nature of the conduits that fed most of the ash-flow floods. In general, the flows have buried and hidden their vents. The evidence for fissure eruptions in the Tibesti and Silent Canyon shields has been stated above. On the basis of logic, it seems impossible that the great ash flows could have been erupted from pipe vents. In some instances the huge volume of gas–ash emulsion flowed for a hundred or more miles, reaching its final resting place still so hot that the settling ash particles were plastic enough to flatten out and weld themselves together. The emulsion must have been poured out with extreme rapidity. Even the comparatively small flow of the Valley of Ten Thousand Smokes issued at an average rate of more than 700 million cubic yards an hour! Some relatively small ash flows have been erupted from pipe vents; but as Rittmann (1962a) has pointed out, only extensive fissures with their large surface areas making possible simultaneous frothing and blowing apart of large volumes of magma can account for the very large flows. Nevertheless, actual examples of dikes that fed ash flows are rare.

Marshall (1935) described one dike of ignimbrite believed by him to be a feeder for an ignimbrite sheet in New Zealand. The ash flow of the Valley of Ten Thousand Smokes was believed by Fenner to have issued from fissures in the valley floor, but the evidence was largely presumptive. The similar flow from Bezymianny in 1956 is known to have issued from the summit crater, and Gorshkov (1959) suggested that the flow in the Valley of Ten Thousand Smokes issued from the caldera of Katmai rather than from vents on the valley floor. However, work by Williams, Juhle, and Curtis

(1956), by Bordet and others (1963), and by Curtis (1968) has supported Fenner's earlier belief, at least in a general way. Curtis's detailed studies show that the flow issued on the valley floor, not from the summit of Katmai, and that both the ash flow and the associated air-fall deposits of tephra came from the pipe vent later occupied by the dome of Novarupta or from vents along fissures in a circular zone of collapse surrounding Novarupta.

Luedke and Burbank (1961) have described a small welded ash flow that issued from a collapsed crater about a mile in diameter in the San Juan Mts. of Colorado. Such craters could, of course, easily be buried by additional flows during the building of an ignimbrite plateau, but there is no evidence that this has commonly been the case.

In the Hot Creek Range of western Nevada, Cook (1968) has described both dikes and "plugs" of ignimbrite that presumably represent the feeders of adjacent ash flows. The plugs are fillings of large crateriform depressions, one of them 3 miles long and half a mile wide, the other 1.5 miles long and 500 to 2,500 feet wide. One of the dikes is 100 to 300 feet wide and the other ranges from 50 to 400 feet. Each has been traced for about 1.5 miles. The depth of exposure is as much as 1,300 feet. In the dikes the flow structure, defined by the orientation of elongate glass shards and lumps of pumice, dips inward toward the center at angles of 75 to 90°. In the larger of the two plugs, the flow planes dip inward 65 to 90° in the lower part, but fan outward toward the top, where they dip only 3 to 10°. In the dikes and plugs, the pumice fragments and glass shards show no flattening or distortion, although in the adjacent ash flows both flattening and distortion are moderate to extreme. The reason why the shards and pumice lumps in the dikes and plugs were not flattened by the weight of as much as 1,300 feet of overlying material, whereas those in the ash flows were flattened under a much smaller load, is obscure.

In the Elbrus region between the Black and Caspian Seas, Milanovsky and Koronovsky (1966) describe volcanic pipes, dikes, small sills, and even laccoliths of ignimbrite. One dike, filled with a breccia of older rock fragments in a matrix of glassy tuff, "forms a branching columnar body with blind upper ends." The descriptions are reminiscent of the small dikes of tuff associated with diatremes in the Swabian Alb and elsewhere (Chapter 15), and while the masses may not be actual feeders of ignimbrites, they do confirm the disruption of magma into ash in channelways beneath the earth's surface. The disruption is the result of low confining pressure rather than necessarily of eruption onto the surface.

Although it seems very probable that the vents for most if not all large ash flows are fissures, the form and distribution of the fissures is less certain. Mackin (1960) and others have suggested that the feeding fissures for the ash flows of the Great Basin area were linear groups related to the basin–range faulting. On the other hand, Noble (1968) considers that the fissures were probably arcuate, associated with caldera collapse.

Rittmann (1962a) believes that ash flows near San Vincenzo in Tuscany issued from linear fissures along the crest of an uplifted block (horst). The resulting ignimbrites have been removed from the uplifted

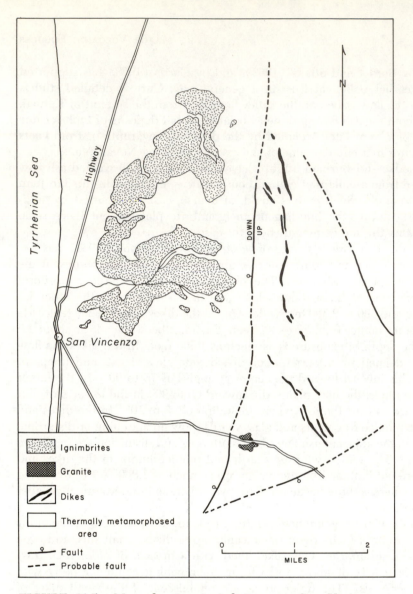

FIGURE 11-7. Map showing ignimbrite near San Vincenzo in Tuscany, and dikes that are believed to have been the conduits that brought the ignimbrite-forming magma to the surface. (After Rittmann, 1962a.)

region by erosion, remaining only in the lower region to the west, but the source fissures are marked by dikes of rock of closely similar chemical composition (Fig. 11-7). At nearby Mt. Amiata, ash flows have issued from fissures on the borders of a central horst, the uplift of which probably was caused by a mass of light magma beneath (Marinelli, 1961).

Westerveld (1952) considered that the ash flows of central Sumatra probably issued from fissures related to the formation of the Lake Toba graben.

270

Ash flows commonly are associated with the formation of calderas (Chapter 14). Indeed, the caldera collapse often is attributed to the removal of support from beneath the top of the volcanic mountain by partial emptying of the underlying magma reservoir as a result of the eruption of great volumes of airborne ash and ash flows. The latter may issue at the summit vent, as they did at Bezymianny, but commonly they come from arcuate fissures part way up the flank of the mountain. The same fissures, or closely related ones, may later become the faults bounding the sinking caldera. As an example, Matumoto (1965) has shown that the extensive ash flows around the caldera of Aso in Japan (Fig. 8-3) issued mostly from fissures near the present caldera boundary.

Branch (1967) describes, in Queensland, Australia, curving dikes of vertically flow-banded ignimbrite that fed ignimbrite sheets that have been preserved within ancient sunken calderas of which the curved dike-filled fissures are the boundaries. The cauldrons have individual areas ranging from 25 to 2,250 square miles, and the ignimbrites probably once covered an area much more extensive than the cauldrons.

It thus appears that ash flows have issued, in different regions, from both linear and arcuate fissures, but it does not yet appear possible to say whether one or the other was the prevalent type of vent for the great ignimbrite accumulations.

Many of the greatest ash-flow accumulations are associated with broad uparchings of the earth's crust that have later collapsed to form grabens and volcano-tectonic depressions (Chapter 12). It is tempting to think of the arches as resulting from the generation of light magma beneath (as appears to be the case at the Mt. Amiata horst) and the collapse to be at least partly the result of the extrusion onto the surface of the huge volumes of magma that formed the ignimbrites (see Chapter 15).

Shield Volcanoes

Predominantly effusive eruptions of Hawaiian or Strombolian type build around their vents broad flat cones composed very largely of lava flows (Plate 11-2). Typically, these have a broadly rounded profile, resembling the upper one eighth or less of a sphere cut off and laid flat side down on a flat surface. Because of a fancied resemblance in profile to the round shields of early germanic warriors, these have been named *shield volcanoes*. The resemblance often is heightened by the presence of a spatter or cinder cone at the apex of the volcano, corresponding to the central protuberance of a shield, and sometimes by lateral cones corresponding to the bosses of a shield. Shield volcanoes have also been referred to as "domes" or "exogenous lava domes," but that usage is confusing because of the many other uses of the term "dome" in geological literature. The sides of shield

PLATE 11-2. The shield volcano of Mauna Loa, Hawaii, with the step-faulted western wall of Kilauea Caldera in the foreground. The caldera wall is 400 feet high, and the summit of Mauna Loa is 20 miles beyond it. The dark streaks on the side of Mauna Loa are aa lava flows. The many thin flows that built the Kilauea shield are visible in the caldera wall, as also are several sills, and a short distance to the right of the step-fault blocks is a double laccolith. Hawaii Institute of Geophysics photo by A. T. Abbott.

volcanoes generally slope at an angle between 2 and 10°, rarely as much as 15°, and at the base the slope merges imperceptibly with the surroundings (Fig. 11-8).

Shield volcanoes were originally named in Iceland. The Icelandic shield volcanoes are all rather small, ranging in basal diameter up to about 9 miles and in height up to about 3,000 feet above their surroundings. They were built by eruptions from a pipe vent or a very short segment of a fissure, and consequently they are nearly circular in ground plan (Fig. 11-9). It is probable, however, that at the beginning many of the eruptions were along considerably more extensive fissures and that only later did the activity become concentrated into a small area. Single eruptions may produce a small shield volcano, commonly with a steep wall a few feet to a few tens of feet high surrounding a small summit crater. A shield of this type is known in Iceland as an *eldborg* ("fort mountain"), because of the resemblance of the summit wall to a fortification (Thorarinsson, 1960). The wall is formed of spatter from lava fountains in the crater, sometimes with a thin veneer of lava formed by overflow of a lava lake. Perhaps the best known of Icelandic shields is the Skjaldbreidur Volcano, 6 miles across at the base, that rises 1,700 feet from the northern edge of the plains of Thingvellir, near Reykjavík, with a very regular profile and slopes averaging 7 to 8°. At its summit is a slightly elliptical crater 1,000 feet across. The nearby shield volcano, Lyngdalsheidi, has slopes of only 2 to 3° and approaches in form the very low shields, already mentioned, around the vents of some flood eruptions on the basaltic plains. Kjartansson (1967) gives the volumes of several of the Icelandic shields, as follows:

Skjaldbreidur	4.08 cubic miles
Kjalhraun	0.96 cubic miles

Leggjabrjótur	0.96 cubic miles
Baldheidi	0.48 cubic miles
Selvogsheidi	0.24 cubic miles

    Many small shield volcanoes of Icelandic type, often crowned with a cinder or spatter cone, are scattered over the Modoc Plateau region and the adjacent Cascade Range in northeastern California. Good examples are Table and Badger Mountains on the northern boundary of Lassen Volcanic National Park, Black and Crater Lake Mountains farther northeast, and the

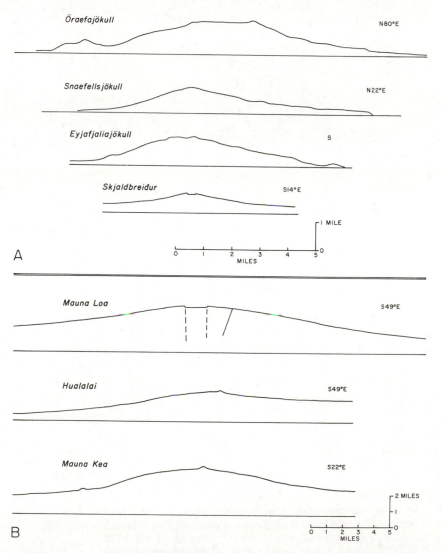

FIGURE 11-8. Profiles of (A) Icelandic and (B) the upper part of Hawaiian shield volcanoes. Note that the scale of (A) is nearly twice that of (B). (After Thorarinsson, 1960, and Stearns and Macdonald, 1946.)

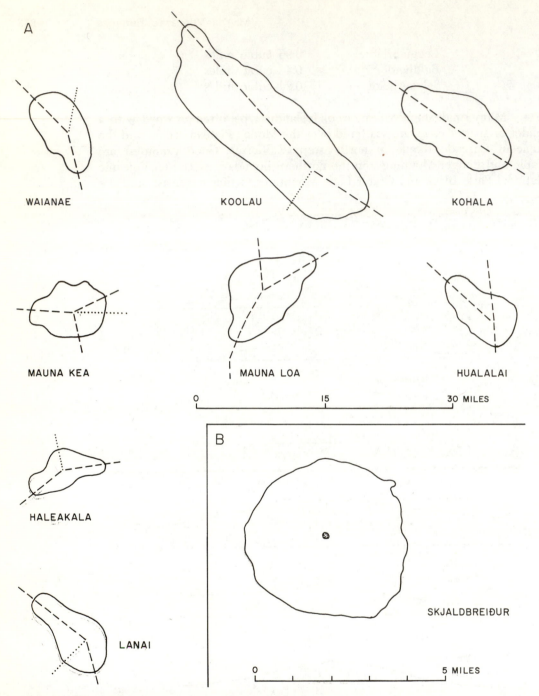

FIGURE 11-9. (A) Ground plan of Hawaiian shield volcanoes at a level about 3,000 feet below their summits. The dashed lines represent the rift zones. In comparison, (B) is a plan of Skjaldbreidur, Iceland, about 1,500 feet below its summit. The more nearly circular form of Skjaldbreidur is the result of predominant central eruptions rather than eruptions on the lateral rift zones. Note the difference in scale between (A) and (B). ((A) after Wentworth and Macdonald, 1953; (B) after Tryggvason, 1943.)

Whaleback near Mount Shasta. There are many other examples in other parts of the world, including the Rangitoto and Whatitiri cones of New Zealand, and Kaimuki in Honolulu. Although most of the small shield volcanoes are basaltic, some are andesitic.

Although the cinder cones that often cap small shield volcanoes may be the result of an increase in explosivity of the eruption toward its end, more commonly the cinder cone starts to build at the beginning of the eruption and is partly buried by the accumulation of lava around it until finally only its upper part protrudes.

Small shields are generally the result of single eruptions, and even shields as big as Skjaldbreidur may be built by a single prolonged eruption (Walker, 1965) lasting perhaps sometimes for several years. However, most of the larger shields probably result from repeated eruptions from the same summit vent, sometimes with lateral outbreaks as well. All consist of many overlapping thin flows or flow units.

Quite different in scale and structure from the small shields just described are the giant shield volcanoes of the Hawaiian and other midocean islands. The islands are the tops of huge mountains rising from the deep-sea floor. The lowest of the Hawaiian Islands rise nearly 3 miles above their bases; and Mauna Loa and Mauna Kea on the island of Hawaii have absolute heights of about 30,000 feet. In terms of elevation above their surroundings, they are the highest mountains on earth! Unlike the Icelandic shields, those of Hawaii are built by eruptions from fissure vents (Plate 11-3), and many of the eruptions take place on their flanks rather than at the summit. Like the Icelandic shields, they have been built almost wholly by thin fluid basalt lava flows. Tephra comprises less than 1 per cent of their visible masses above sea level. Cones and ramparts at the vents are small (Plate 11-4) and consist very largely of spatter. The unmodified slopes of the Hawaiian shield volcanoes range from about 2 to 12°, though in late stages of activity, a steeper cap of andesitic and related lavas may be built on top of the shield.

The form of Hawaiian shields is controlled largely by the presence of

PLATE 11-3. Vertical air view of cinder-and-spatter cones along eruptive fissures in the southwest rift zone of Mauna Loa. An elongate pit crater is visible near the center of the picture. Lava channels lead past it toward the top. Photo by U. S. Air Force.

PLATE 11-4. Fissures, spatter cones, and lava flows along the southwest rift zone of Mauna Loa, looking toward the summit. The broadly rounded profile of the shield volcano is seen on the skyline. Hawaii Institute of Geophysics photo by A. T. Abbott.

zones of fissures (Plates 11-3 and 11-4), known as *rift zones*, that have served as the channelways to bring the lava to the surface. Typically, there are three rift zones radiating from the summit of the mountain with angles of about 120° between them. Usually, however, two of the rift zones are much more prominent than the third (Fig. 11-9). The major rift zones range from less than a mile to about 2 miles in width and contain hundreds of fissures that have served as eruptive vents. These are marked at the surface by open cracks, spatter ramparts, rows of spatter cones, a few spatter–cinder cones, collapse craters, and even some minature Icelandic-type shields (e.g., Mauna Iki and Kane Nui o Hamo on Kilauea). At depth, where they have been exposed by cutting of canyons into the older shields, the rift zones are seen to consist of innumerable thin dikes (Chapter 15).

The ground plan of the Hawaiian shields is the direct result of the position and strength of development of the rift zones. Where the latter are poorly developed, and eruption has taken place from fissures radiating more or less uniformly in all directions from the summit, as in West Maui Volcano (Fig. 11-9), the ground plan is more or less circular. But where the rift zones are well developed, the eruptions and the consequent growth of the shield are concentrated in the sectors occupied by the rift zones and the ground plan is lobate, often approaching the form of a three-pointed star (Fig. 11-9).

The shield consists of innumerable long narrow lava flows extending radially down the mountain slopes from their vents either at the summit or along the rift zones (Plate 11-2) and overlapping at their edges. In traveling around Mauna Loa on the highway, one crosses something on the order of 400 separate flows.

At the summit of the Hawaiian shields, the rift zones converge in a sunken crater, or *caldera* (Chapter 12, Plate 11-5). Eruptions occur, on the average, somewhat more frequently in the calderas than on the flanks of the shield, but they are generally smaller. Although it is more or less circular, the caldera does not mark a pipe vent. Eruptions within the caldera take place from fissures that cross the caldera floor and often extend up the caldera wall and beyond onto the upper slopes of the volcano. Such pits as Halemaumau Crater, long the site of the lava lake at Kilauea, may be exceptions, representing pipe-like perforations of the roof above a shallow

276

magma chamber; but even within Halemaumau, eruptions generally take place from fissures that cut through the plug of solid and semisolid material in the bottom of the crater.

Unfortunately, we have very little information on the constitution and mode of building of the great oceanic shield volcanoes from the ocean floor to sea level. We believe that in deep water the weight of the overlying ocean restrains the escape of gas and prevents explosion. Lavas dredged from depths of more than 6,000 feet on the slopes of the Hawaiian shields (Moore, 1965) lack the vesicularity of subaerial lavas or those dredged from shallow water, and photographs of the bottom show no trace of tephra. In shallow water, however, eruptions tend to be explosive (Chapter 10), and the part of the mountain formed within a few hundred feet below sea level may contain a considerably larger proportion of tephra than the portions formed in deep water or above sea level. Gravity studies indicating rather low gross densities of the mountains also suggest that this may be the case. If so, however, the portion of the mountain containing more abundant tephra has been entirely hidden by later lava flows. At the most, the total proportion of tephra is probably not more than 2 or 3 per cent because it would be limited to the conelets immediately surrounding the vents, and even much of this may have been removed by quasi-contemporaneous submarine erosion and scattered over the adjoining deeps. No signs of abundant tephra have been found by dredging and submarine photography along the rift zones of the shields. A long narrow mass of palagonitized "ash" on the southern flank of Kilauea (J. G. Moore, personal communication, 1966) is probably hyaloclastite formed by lava flows entering the sea and drifted to its present location by currents.

The flattening of the profile of the upper part of the shield is due to a combination of collapse of the summit in the formation of the caldera and the fact that the most copious discharges of lava are from flank vents rather than at the summit. If it were otherwise, the slope would remain the same to the edge of the caldera, or even become steeper, because the same number of flows of the same width and thickness would cover a greater proportion of the circumference of the shield near the summit than farther downslope, and, consequently, would build up the summit region faster than the middle

PLATE 11-5. The summit of the shield volcano of Mauna Loa, Hawaii, with Mauna Kea in the background. In the foreground are three pit craters along the upper end of the southwest rift zone of the volcano, and behind them is Mokuaweoweo Caldera. The mountain is covered with a light fall of snow. Photo by U. S. Air Force.

flanks. Similarly, the common flattening of shields near the base is due to the increase in circumference downslope and the smaller number of flows that reach that extreme distance, so that building of the lower slope is slower than that of the middle slope.

However, some other cause must be sought for the common flattening of Hawaiian shields in some places just above sea level. Gently sloping shore terraces, as much as two miles wide, are seen for instance on the west slope of Hualalai Volcano and the northeast slope of Haleakala Volcano. To some extent these may be the result of the burial of coral reefs or wave-cut platforms, or a combination of the flattening of the shield with increasing distance from the summit and steepening again below sea level due to eruption beneath water. But there may be yet another cause. Where subaerial lava flows enter the water, they sometimes tend to dam themselves back and build a sort of natural levee, piling up behind it and sometimes spreading laterally parallel to the shoreline. (This behavior was observed, for example, during the 1911 eruption of Matavanu Volcano in Samoa, and at Kilauea Volcano in 1960.) There is as yet no certain explanation for the near-shore flattening.

The flanks of several Hawaiian shields are broken by series of scarps formed along faults that are approximately tangential to the slope of the shield. Along these faults the downslope portion of the shield has moved relatively downward (or the upslope portion has moved relatively upward), in some instances more than 1,000 feet. The faults are usually considered to be the result of instability of the shield, with the unsupported flank sliding off toward the ocean. However, to me it appears more probable that they result from the central part of the shield being thrust up by magma beneath it, the margins of the shield lagging behind. It is well known that the summits of Hawaiian shields are pushed up several feet during intervals between eruptions (Chapter 15); and although they sink again after eruptions, the sinking in the long run may be less than the uplift, and the marginal faults may be the net result of uplift exceeding sinking. In other parts of the world it is not uncommon for basement rocks to be pushed to high levels in the central parts of volcanoes, and on Etna, Pleistocene marls have been elevated more than 1,200 feet above sea level.

The forms of some Hawaiian shield volcanoes have been modified during late stages of their activity by a change in the character of the eruptions and the erupted products. The main mass of the shield above sea level is composed of thin wide-spreading flows of tholeiitic basalt (see Appendix 2) extruded in eruptions of Hawaiian type. During this stage, eruptions are so frequent that there is very little weathering or erosion of the surface between one flow and the next. But toward the end of the life of the volcano, eruptions become less frequent and commonly more explosive, and the lavas change in composition to alkalic basalts and rocks more like andesite (mugearite and hawaiite) with minor amounts of trachyte. Many of the eruptions are Strombolian in character and build large cinder cones. Flows tend to be shorter and thicker than in the earlier stage, and some trachyte domes are formed. Furthermore, the activity is commonly more restricted to the summit part of the mountain. As a result, the caldera becomes buried, and a steeper cap is built on the top of the shield with a much bumpier pro-file than that of the original shield. This is well exemplified by Mauna Kea (Fig. 11-8), where the broadly rounded profile of the shield is still visible on the lower slopes surmounted by a steep humpy cap of later rocks.

The big shield volcanoes of the Galapagos Islands differ in both general form and structure from those of the Hawaiian Islands (McBirney and Williams, 1969a). Eruptive fissures and dikes are much less commonly radial than in Hawaii; most of them are concentric. The slopes of the shields are much steeper, averaging about 25° and reaching as much as 35°. The cause of such steep slopes is intriguing! They resemble much more the slopes of composite volcanoes (see p. 284) than they do those of typical shield volcanoes. Can the steep Galapagos shields, like some steep-sided lava cones described in the next section, be the result of lava flows mantling pyroclastic cones formed in an earlier stage of activity?

Lava Cones

Some mountains built largely of thin lava flows cannot appropriately be called shield volcanoes, because they lack the characteristic broadly rounded form of the shield. Instead they are truncated cones, commonly with a slightly concave profile becoming steeper toward the top, like many cinder cones or the composite volcanoes discussed in the next section. There is in fact a complete gradation from the Icelandic type of shield volcano to these *lava cones*. Such shields as Skjaldbreidur, with relatively steep sides and little rounding at the top, are essentially very flat lava cones. Nearly all lava cones terminate with a summit crater, sometimes small and sometimes large, formed by the collapse of the top of the cone as a result of with-drawal of magma in the underlying conduit at the end of the eruption. Small lava cones formed during a single eruption have been described in Chapter 9, but larger ones result from repeated eruptions of either Hawaiian or Strombolian type.

The resemblance in form of many cones that appear to be built wholly of lava to cinder or composite cones has led to the suggestion that they may have been formed by lava flows burying an earlier cone of one of the other types. This in fact does occur. For instance, Magee Mt. (Crater Peak), just north of Lassen National Park, California, consisted of a largely pyroclastic cone completely veneered with lava flows. At the end of its eruptive history, the Magee cone would have appeared to consist entirely of lava flows; but glacial erosion cut through the lava shell and revealed its pyroclastic core. Similarly, Nyiragongo in Belgian Congo consists of a lava-flow veneer over a pyroclastic core. However, some large rather steep-sided cones consist almost wholly of lava flows throughout. The conical shape may have resulted wholly from rather short flows poured out of the summit vent, their shortness being due either to their viscosity or their smallness of volume. In some the flows are basalt, but in others they are andesite and, more rarely,

PLATE 11-6. Mayon Volcano, Philippines. This composite cone, nearly 8,000 feet high, is reputed to be the most symmetrical in the world. The city of Legaspi lies in the foreground. U. S. Geological Survey photo by G. A. Macdonald.

PLATE 11-7. Layers of ash and cinder interbedded with lava flows, exposed in a glacial cirque cut into North Sister, a composite volcano in the Cascade Range of Oregon. Photo by G. A. Macdonald.

dacite (e.g., Crescent Crater in Lassen National Park) or trachyte. Examples of such lava cones include Batur Volcano on the island of Bali, and Sugarloaf in Hat Creek Valley just north of Lassen National Park. Some, like Sugarloaf, have small cinder or spatter cones at their summits or at vents on their flanks.

Composite Cones

Except for the midocean shield volcanoes, most of the great volcanic mountains of the earth, and especially those famed for their beauty (Plate 11-6), are made up of interbedded lava flows and layers of ash and cinder (Plate 11-7). Often these are referred to as "strato-volcanoes," but shield volcanoes also consist of strata (beds) of lava, and it appears preferable to call those consisting of both lava and tephra *composite volcanoes*. Close groups of overlapping cones that are difficult to separate from each other also have been called "composite volcanoes," but it seems better to use for them the equivalent term, *multiple volcanoes*. The relative proportions of tephra and lava flows in composite cones vary greatly, and every gradation can be found from purely ash or cinder cones to lava cones.

The eruptions that build composite volcanoes may be Strombolian, Vulcanian, or Peléean, and two or all three types of eruption may take place in the history of the same volcano. Plinian eruptions also may occur, as rare events (Chapters 10, 12). The lava flows are most commonly block lava, but they may be aa and rarely pahoehoe. The tephra is usually cinder or ash, but small amounts of spatter may be present. Depending on the viscosity of the magma, the lava flows may be thin and extensive or thick and short, and domes also are common. Indeed, some composite volcanoes, such as Hibok-hibok in the Philippines and some of the mountains of the Lesser Antilles, consist to a large degree of an aggregation of domes, glowing-avalanche deposits, ash, and cinder. Glowing-avalanche deposits are common on composite volcanoes, but even more abundant are the deposits of mudflows. Dome growth and glowing avalanches characterize the late stages of many composite volcanoes; but at others, such as Mt. Lamington in New Guinea (Chapter 10), Peléean eruptions have taken place through a large part of the history of the volcano. The growth of a dome is not sufficient justification to regard the volcano as approaching extinction.

Composite cones range in height from a few hundred to several thousand feet and in basal diameter up to about 20 miles. Mt. Fuji in Japan rises some 12,000 feet above the surrounding lowlands, Mt. Shasta in California rises about 10,000 feet, and Mt. Rainer in Washington about 8,000 feet above the nearby peaks of the Cascade Range. (Although both Mt. Shasta and Mt. Rainier reach heights of more than 14,000 feet above sea level, their cones are built on masses of older rocks the surface of which is several thousand feet above sea level.) Most composite volcanoes are built by eruptions that come principally from a single central pipe vent, and consequently their ground plan is roughly circular. This may be greatly modified, however, where considerable proportions of their eruptions have been from lateral vents. Where the main vent has shifted its position, there may result double volcanoes, such as Mts. Shasta and Shastina, or even a line of several quasi-independent cones. The departure from circularity of ground plan is even greater in the rare cases where composite volcanoes are built around lengthy fissure vents. One of the outstanding examples of the latter is Mt. Hekla in Iceland. Hekla is a composite volcano built around a fissure 3 or 4 miles long, and the basal plan of the mountain is an oval about 6½ miles long and only 3 miles wide. Viewed in a direction parallel to the fissure, Mt. Hekla has the general form of a typical composite volcano, but viewed at right angles to the fissure it appears as a broadly rounded dome resembling a shield volcano.

The structure and profile of a typical composite volcano are shown diagrammatically in Fig. 2-1. On some composite cones the principal part of the slope is nearly straight (Plate 11-8) with an angle ranging from about

PLATE 11-8. South Sister, a composite volcano in the Cascade Range, Oregon. The irregular surface of a block lava flow lies in the foreground. Photo by G. A. Macdonald.

10 to 35°; on others the slope steepens progressively upward to a rather narrow crater rim. At the base, the slope generally flattens gradually to near horizontality. The flattening appears to be due principally to two factors: the more abundant eruption of lava near the base of the cone from lateral vents produced by rupturing of the cone walls, as in the 1906 eruption of Vesuvius (Chapter 10); and the movement of loose debris down the slopes of the cone and deposition at its base by rainwash, streams, and mudflows. Not uncommonly, the base of the cone consists largely of lava flows and the upper part largely of tephra (Plates 11-9 and 12-8A). In humid regions, particularly in the tropics, the amount of loose material (largely tephra, but including also blocky debris from lava flows) brought to the base of the mountain by mudflows may be tremendous. At Mayon Volcano in the Philippines, for instance, nearly the entire broad gently sloping skirt of the cone (Plate 11-6) seems to be composed of mudflow deposits with only minor amounts of air-laid tephra. The upward steepening of the cone is simply the result of deposition of a larger amount of material in any given surface area in the same length of time on the part of the cone nearest the vent. In the case of explosive eruptions, most of the coarsest debris falls at or near the crater rim; and the thickness of even the fine deposits decreases more or less logarithmically with increasing distance, both because of the tendency for more material to fall near the vent and the increasing surface area to be covered with increasing radial distance. Lava flows escaping over the crater rim or from subterminal vents may also be largely restricted to the upper part of the cone, as in the case of lava cones.

The crater may be simply a funnel-shaped hole at the top of the cone kept open by blasting out of the fallen material by successive explosions. Commonly, however, it is much enlarged by collapse of its walls, as a result of withdrawal of magma from the upper part of the conduit at the end of the eruption, removing the support from the still-loose masses of tephra and allowing them to slide toward and into the conduit, or as a result of the coring out of the cone by explosions, as in the 1906 eruption of Vesuvius. The steep walls resulting from collapse usually are soon made gentler by slumping of loose materials, which accumulate as taluses against the foot of the crater walls to form a series of banks sloping into the central conical or bowl-shaped depression. On ash cones, water running down the slopes dur-

PLATE 11-9. Farallon de Pajaros, a composite volcano in the northern Mariannas Islands, in mild eruption in March 1953. The upper part of the cone consists largely of cinder, but the lower slopes are predominantly of lava flows. The bulge on the left slope a short distance below the summit was formed by a lava flow breaking out on the flank of the cone. At the extreme left are remnants of an older cone. Official photograph, U. S. Navy.

ing heavy rains may wash fine material out onto the bottom of the crater and deposit it, sometimes in temporary lakes, to form a flat central floor. Sometimes lava wells up into the crater to form a flat floor, or a dome may rise to form a rounded hump within the crater. The pyroclastic beds are originally deposited as mantle beds wrapping over the rim and sloping both away from and into the crater. The portions of the beds sloping into the crater are commonly destroyed by collapse, however, so that the edges of the beds exposed in the crater walls slope outward.

Rarely, composite cones are devoid of a crater. In a few instances this may be due to filling of the crater by tephra during very weak eruptions. It may also be due to lava rising in and filling the crater. Perhaps most commonly, however, it is the result of a crater having been filled by a dome, which may overlap the crater rim (Fig. 11-10) and give rise to Merapi-type glowing avalanches.

Most, if not all, of the big and beautifully symmetrical cones of the world are composite. Purely pyroclastic cones appear to become unstable when they reach a certain height, generally between 1,000 and 1,500 feet, and their symmetry is destroyed by slumping. To attain large size and

FIGURE 11-10. Sketch of Merapi Volcano, Java, showing the crater filled by a series of domes. The ridge on the right is an old crater rim. (After a photograph by George de Neve, 1952.)

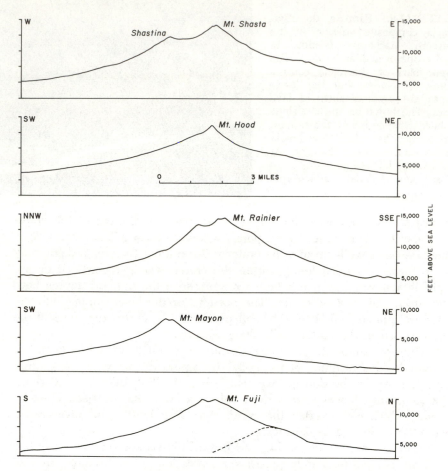

FIGURE 11-11. Profiles of large symmetrical composite volcanoes. Shastina is a younger cone on the flank of Mount Shasta. The hump on the northwest side of Mount Rainier is part of the rim of an old crater largely buried by the younger summit cone. The bulge on the north side of Mount Fuji is caused by an older volcano now largely buried by Fuji.

still retain symmetry, the cone requires the strengthening effect of ribs of lava interbedded with the tephra. Such big symmetrical cones as Mt. Shasta (Fig. 11-11), Mt. Fuji, Mayon in the Philippines, Mt. Hood in Oregon, El Misti in Peru, and Klyuchevskaya in Kamchatka (Plate 11-10) all are composite volcanoes.

A high degree of symmetry also requires that the eruptions take place exclusively from a single summit vent and that the vent remain in the same position. If, as quite commonly happens, the summit vent shifts somewhat in position from time to time, the building of the cone is not related to a single central point and the top of the mountain becomes irregular. An excellent example of constancy of position of the vent is furnished by

PLATE 11-10. Kliuchevsky Volcano, an active composite cone reaching an altitude of 16,000 feet in Kamchatka. Photo by G. S. Gorshkov, Kamchatka Volcano Station.

PLATE 11-11. Crater Peak (Magee Mtn.), in the Cascade Range northwest of Mount Lassen, California. Originally composed very largely of cinder, its outer slopes are now completely covered with lava flows. U. S. Geological Survey photo by G. A. Macdonald.

Mayon, where the upper part of the cone has been destroyed several times by explosive eruptions, but rebuilt in so nearly the same position and form that the traces of the crater rims formed by the explosions are barely detectable (Plates 11-6 and 11-10). Large lateral eruptions may result in double or multiple cones, as at Mt. Egmont, New Zealand, and Mt. Shasta, California.

Some fairly large cones have a core composed largely of tephra enclosed in a shell consisting almost entirely of lava flows. They are sometimes called armored cones. Crater Peak (Magee Mt.) in the Cascade Range of northern California has this structure, revealed by deep erosion in glacial cirques (Plate 11-11). The lava armor of Crater Peak extends all the way to the foot of the cone. Fuss Peak on Paramushiro Island in the Kurils is an armored cone on which the lava shell is restricted to the upper part of the cone (Gorshkov, 1970).

Radial segments of the cones may be dropped down between faults as *sector grabens*. Segments may also be displaced by landslides, which may produce troughs in the crater rim and slopes of the cone that resemble grabens (Fig. 11-12) or may form spoon-shaped depressions similar to those characteristic of many landslides in other types of rocks. The slides result from the instability of the poorly cemented pyroclastic material in the steep flanks of the cone increased by loading of the upper slopes by debris from later eruptions and often by saturation with water from heavy rainfalls, either accompanying eruptions or at other times. In some instances, erosion by glowing avalanches may have gouged valleys into the sides of the cones. Minor erosion of this sort is well established.

285

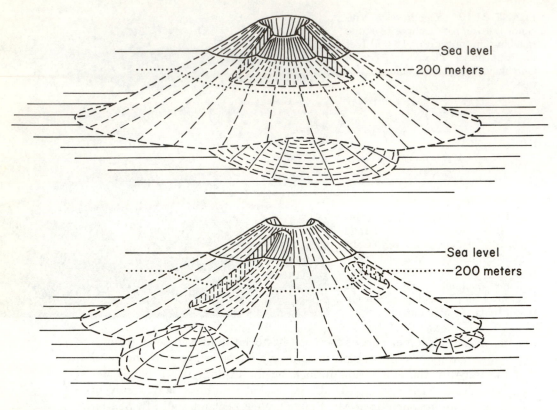

FIGURE 11-12. Diagrams showing landslides on the slopes of Api Volcano, an island in the Banda arc of Indonesia. The one in the upper diagram resembles a sector graben. (From Kuenen, 1935.)

Williams (1934) has suggested this origin for Diller Canyon, a cleft a quarter of a mile wide and 400 feet deep on the flank of Shastina in California, but although glowing-avalanche deposits are associated with the canyon, it remains in doubt whether the canyon was largely cut by the avalanches or merely guided them.

The Valle del Bove, a great depression on the eastern side of Mt. Etna in Sicily, is the caldera (Chapter 12) of an older volcano (Trifoglietto) now largely buried by the younger Etna cone.

Much of the irregularity of the sides of composite cones appears to be the result of stream erosion. In late stages of growth of the cone, the eruptions may become widely spaced in time, separated by quiet intervals of tens or hundreds of years, and during these intervals streams may cut sizable valleys into the poorly consolidated tephra. Later eruptions may partly or wholly fill the valleys and mask their origin.

SUGGESTED ADDITIONAL READING

Basalt Plains and Plateaus
> Geikie, 1882, p. 237–238, 242–245; Russell, 1902, p. 59–66; Rutten, 1964; Stearns, Crandall, and Steward, 1938, p. 5–7, 56–84.

Ignimbrite Plains and Plateaus
> Boyd, 1961; Grange, 1937, p. 16–19, 58–64; Mackin, 1960; Marshall, 1935; Westerveld, 1952, 1957.

Shield Volcanoes
> Macdonald, 1956, 1967; Stearns and Macdonald, 1946, p. 24–42; Thorarinsson, 1960; Trygvasson, 1943.

Composite Volcanoes
> Cotton, 1952, p. 226–236; Perret, 1950, p. 3–24; Rittmann, 1962, p. 122–138, 148–151; Russell, 1897, p. 80–90; Tyrrell, 1931, p. 128–153.

12

Craters, Calderas, and Grabens

Negative land forms, or depressions, of volcanic origin are of several different kinds and are formed in different ways. Those of small to moderate size, when they are more or less circular in plan, are referred to as *craters*, but even these have varying origins. The larger quasi-circular depressions also are craters in a general sense, but are more specifically called *calderas*. Rather arbitrarily, the lower size limit for the diameter of calderas is placed at 1 mile, but it turns out that this actually is a good choice because most, if not all, volcanic depressions larger than that are of different origin from most of the smaller craters. Elongate depressions include open fissures, *grabens* formed by dropping of long narrow blocks between faults, and larger down faulted basins or troughs known as *volcano-tectonic depressions*. Volcanic depressions can be conveniently divided into those

PLATE 12-1. The crater of Tjerimai Volcano, a composite cone, in Japan. Photographer unknown.

formed by explosion and those formed by collapse or down faulting. In addition, there must be recognized depressions that are formed by erosion of volcanic mountains rather than directly by volcanic action.

Explosion Craters

The craters formed normally at the summits of lava, spatter (Plate 9-7), cinder, ash cones, and composite volcanoes (Plates 12-1, 12-2A, and 12-2B) have already been mentioned and require no further lengthy discussion here. They result partly from the inability of the cone to build up directly over the vent because explosions continually blow out the material that accumulates there, and partly from collapse of the summit of the

PLATE 12-2A. The summit of Farallon de Pajaros, a composite volcano in the Volcano (northern Mariannas) Islands. A lava flow has spilled out of the crater in the foreground. A small explosion is taking place in another crater, beyond. Official photograph, U. S. Navy.

PLATE 12-2B. The crater of Prevost Peak, Simushir Island, Kuriles. Note the smaller cone nested within the older, larger crater. Photo by G. S. Gorshkov, Kamchatka Volcano Station.

PLATE 12-3. Craters in an old air field on the volcanic island of Iwo Jima. The left-hand crater was blasted out by a series of explosions in 1957. The crater to the right was formed by collapse about 50 minutes later. The dark area around the crater is covered with a thin layer of ash. U. S. Geological Survey photo by Helen L. Foster.

cone due either to coring out of the cone by explosions (as in the 1906 eruption of Vesuvius) or to removal of support by withdrawal of the liquid magma from the upper part of the conduit at the end of the eruption. These craters may be considered a normal part of the construction of the cone. Other craters may form on the flanks of cones as holes blasted out by lateral explosions. Still other craters form by explosive destruction of a large part of the summit of a composite volcano, leaving a funnel-shaped depression resembling that formed by more ordinary activity, but commonly larger. Explosion craters of this sort may be as much as a mile, or a little more, in diameter, but it is doubtful if they are ever much larger. Many calderas have been attributed in the older literature to decapitation of the volcano by explosion, but more recent investigations have shown many of these instead to be the result of collapse, and the existence of true explosion calderas must be regarded as doubtful.

In some volcanic regions there are found craters that are not directly related to any large volcanic cones and that perforate more or less flat-lying bedded rocks that sometimes are not even volcanic in origin. Some of these craters may be formed partly by collapse, but careful study of others has shown that they are surrounded by very low, inconspicuous cones of fragmental debris. Some of the latter craters may have been formed by the impact of meteors on the earth's surface, but around many of them the debris includes lapilli and bombs that are clearly of magmatic origin, and these craters without question were formed by volcanic explosion. Probably many of the explosions were dominantly phreatic, since the ejecta that make up the surrounding ring are very largely accidental; but even where magmatic ejecta are absent, the close association of the craters with others of demonstrated volcanic origin implies that they also were formed by ultravulcanian explosions. Other similar craters probably result from the explosive release of gas from underlying magma. In the Eifel region of Germany, where craters of this sort have formed in nonvolcanic rocks, many of them extend down to the groundwater table and are occupied by lakes. From this is derived the name *maar* ("lake"), which is generally applied not only to the craters of the Eifel but to similar craters everywhere, whether or not they contain lakes. Maars are found, for instance, in New Zealand, on the Philippine island of Luzon north of Manila, in the Alban Hills near Rome, Italy, and on the plateau surface southeast of Bend, Oregon (Hole-in-the-Ground and Deep Hole Craters). A crater formed by low-temperature explosions in the runway of the old airfield on Iwo Jima in 1957 is a maar (Plate 12-3).

Most maars are less than half a mile across, less than 500 feet deep, and roughly circular. They grade into explosion craters surrounded by low, but obvious, ash or tuff cones, such as the Ubehebe Craters in Death Valley. As an example, Hole-in-the-Ground Crater in central Oregon (Peterson and Groh, 1961) is 5,000 feet across and 425 feet deep below the rim of a very gently sloping debris ring about 100 to 150 feet high and half a mile in radius (Fig. 12-1). The ejecta are largely fragments of underlying older lavas, some of which, according to G.W. Walker of the U.S. Geological Survey, come from depths of 1,000 to 1,500 feet below the surface, but rare magmatic lapilli also are present. The explosion that formed the crater resulted from the contact of rising magma with ground-water in sedimentary rocks beneath the lavas. The floor of the crater is nearly flat, and although it sometimes contains a pond following heavy rains, it is usually dry. Hole-in-the-Ground is associated with a series of other maars and palagonitized tuff cones. Many maars probably are the surface expressions of diatremes (Chapter 15).

Large tuff cones such as Diamond Head in Hawaii and the Fort Rock cone in central Oregon have been referred to by a few writers as maars (Ollier, 1967; Fisher and Waters, 1970a), but the term is better reserved for the explosion craters surrounded by low inconspicuous cones like those described above.

Collapse Craters

Along the rift zones of the shield volcanoes Kilauea and Mauna Loa in Hawaii are found nearly circular craters that perforate the surface of the volcano without any surrounding debris cone (Plate 11-5). Indeed, in the dense rain forest it is possible to come right to the edge of these craters without any forewarning. A very small amount of phreatic ex-

FIGURE 12-1. Cross section of Hole in the Ground Crater, central Oregon, showing the low encircling debris cone.

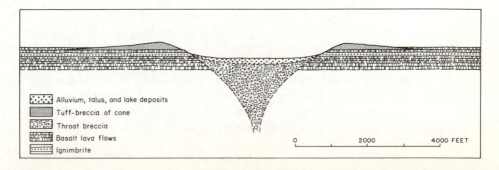

Alluvium, talus, and lake deposits
Tuff-breccia of cone
Throat breccia
Basalt lava flows
Ignimbrite

0   2000   4000 FEET

plosion debris is scattered near the edges of a few of these craters, but most have none whatever; and even where it is present, it equals only an infinitesimal part of the volume of the crater. Obviously, these craters could not have been formed by explosion and must have resulted from the sinking in of segments of the surface of the volcano. To distinguish them from explosion craters, these sunken-in craters were named *pit craters* by Charles Wilkes, commander of the U.S. Exploring Expedition that visited the islands in 1840. A line of 12 pit craters is followed by the Chain of Craters Road in Hawaii Volcanoes National Park. Similar pit craters have since been found in other volcanic regions. As an example may be mentioned Deep Hole Crater on the slope of Brokeoff Volcano northwest of Mt. Lassen, California.

Pit craters range in diameter from a few tens of feet to about a mile and in depth from a few tens of feet to more than 1,000 feet. In ground plan they are generally roughly circular, or broad ovals, except that where two adjacent ones overlap, the form resembles a figure eight. In early stages, their walls are nearly vertical, but their rims soon begin to fray and the fallen rock fragments accumulate as great sloping banks (taluses) against the foot of the walls.

Several pit craters in Hawaii are known to have formed during historic times, but only two have been seen immediately after they first formed. One of these is the Devil's Throat, near the Chain of Craters Road in Hawaii Volcanoes National Park; the other is Lua Nii, formed during the 1955 eruption on the east rift zone of Kilauea 20 miles east of the summit of the mountain. Both initially had openings only about 25 or 30 feet across, and in both the crater became larger downward, so that the walls were overhanging. Collapse of the upper part soon transformed the walls to vertical.

Some pit craters are located at or near the summit of major shield volcanoes (Plate 12-4A), and others indent small shields within calderas (Plate 12-4B) or on the flanks of larger volcanic structures. These shields have been built by local lava effusion before the formation of the crater, and the crater may fill up and overflow from time to time. However, many pit craters seem to have no direct association with preexisting vents, nor have they been the source of lava flows. Occasionally, later eruptions take place in or adjacent to a pit crater and pour lava into it, but the association of the eruption with the crater appears to be a matter of chance, the eruptive fissure just happening to open across or near the crater.

The initial breakthrough of Lua Nii was witnessed by J. P. Eaton and me from a distance of about half a mile. It was marked by a dull explosion and projection of a small dark cloud of ash a few hundred feet into the air. The amount of ash thrown out was, however, less than 1 per cent of the volume of the hole, which clearly was the result of the sinking in of the older rocks rather than explosion. The explosion can have represented only the final disruption of the roof over a hole already formed or forming by sinking of the underlying rocks. The puff of gas and ash was the result of a small excess of gas pressure in the hole.

PLATE 12-4A. Craters of Erta Alè Volcano, Ethiopia. Both craters contained active lava lakes at the time the photograph was taken, in March 1971. The crater in the foreground is about 750 feet across. Both are surrounded by flows of pahoehoe. Photo by Giorgio Marinelli, University of Pisa.

PLATE 12-4B. Halemaumau Crater, in Kilauea Caldera, Hawaii, during the eruption of 1952. The crater, approximately 3,000 feet in diameter, occupies the summit of a very flat shield built on the caldera floor. A lava lake lies in the bottom of the crater. Photo by U. S. Department of the Interior, National Park Service.

The collapse that forms a pit crater probably is the result of withdrawal of magma from the upper part of an underlying plug-like intrusive body that ate its way upward to a level fairly close to the surface. When the magma was withdrawn, possibly by moving laterally into rift-zone fractures or by some other mechanism, the overlying roof was too weak to support itself and sank along more or less cylindrical or conical fractures, the position of which was governed by the form and location of the intrusive body. The mechanism resembles that of cauldron subsidence described in Chapter 15. In some instances the roof may be broken into fragments as it sinks, but in others it may sink largely *en masse*, as a single block, perhaps tilting somewhat as it does so. The latter was the case at the pit crater Lua Poholu at the summit of Mauna Loa, where a lava floor that was formed in the crater by an eruption after the initial formation of the crater was tilted sharply upward on one side during a later resumption of subsidence (Stearns and Macdonald, 1946, Fig. 10).

Some small pit craters appear to form by collapse of the roof of unusually large lava tubes (Plate 12-5).

Calderas

The big sunken-in craters, or *calderas*, that form at the summit of Hawaiian-type shield volcanoes have been mentioned in Chapter 11. In both form and origin they resemble large pit craters (Plate 12-4A) from which they appear to differ only in their larger size.

Calderas are still present as great open depressions on the active volcanoes Kilauea (Plate 12-6) and Mauna Loa (Plate 11-5). The caldera of Kilauea is approximately $2\frac{1}{2}$ miles long and 2 miles wide. On its western side it is 400 feet deep, but at the southern edge it is so shallow that in 1921 a small lava flow escaped over the edge of the caldera. The difference in height of the walls is caused by the fact that the sunken block was not centered exactly on the summit of the shield. Mokuaweoweo Caldera, at the summit of Mauna Loa, is about 3 miles long, $1\frac{1}{2}$ miles wide, and 600 feet deep at its western edge (Plate 12-7). At the northeast

PLATE 12-5. Pit craters formed by collapse of the surface above an unusually large lava tube, on the southwest rift zone of Kilauea Volcano. The nearer crater is approximately 150 feet across. U. S. Geological Survey photo by G. A. Macdonald.

PLATE 12-6. Kilauea Caldera, with Mauna Kea in the background. Halemaumau Crater, within the caldera, is approximately 3,000 feet across. To the right of it, the black patch on the caldera floor is the lava flow of 1954. Note the step faulting at the distant (northeastern) edge of the caldera. Official photograph, U. S. Air Force.

PLATE 12-7. The 1940 spatter cone on the floor of Mokuaweoweo Caldera, Mauna Loa, with the 600-foot cliff at the western side of the caldera behind it. Note the step faults in the background. Hawaii Institute of Geophysics photo by A. T. Abbott.

and southwest, the main caldera merges with adjacent pit craters (Plate 11-5). Both on Kilauea and Mauna Loa, curved faults lie outside the main calderas and more or less parallel with the caldera walls, and have allowed the surface of the shield between them and the caldera to sink a few feet or tens of feet (Fig. 12-2). Some of the other Hawaiian calderas are much larger. That of Kauai Volcano, for instance, is about 11 miles across. The walls of the calderas are steep cliffs, formed by faulting, with banks of talus at their base formed by falling of fragments from the cliffs above.

As with the pit craters, there can be no question that the Hawaiian calderas were formed by collapse. The small amounts of exploded fragments on the surfaces of the shields around the calderas are vastly less than the volumes of the calderas. That the caldera was not always present,

at least as a depression even approaching its present size, is shown by
the fact that outward-sloping lava flows in the walls are abruptly cut off
(Plate 12-8) and project upward into space toward vents that must formerly have existed where there is now only air (Fig. 12-3).

The floor of Kilauea Caldera is now a very broad flat shield rising
to an apex in its southwestern part, where it is perforated by the collapse
crater of Halemaumau (Plate 12-4B). All of it is composed of lava flows
less than 100 years old. The history of Kilauea Caldera has consisted of a

FIGURE 12-2.   Map of Mokuaweoweo Caldera, at the summit of Mauna
Loa, Hawaii. The late pre-caldera flows shown on the map are only the
most readily identifiable of many. They can be traced to the caldera rim;
but their sources, which lay within the area of the present caldera, have
been dropped down and buried by later caldera-filling flows. The faults
east and southeast of the caldera proper mark the outer limit of subsidence
of the mountain top. Line A–A is the line of the cross section in Figure 12-3.
(After Macdonald, 1970.)

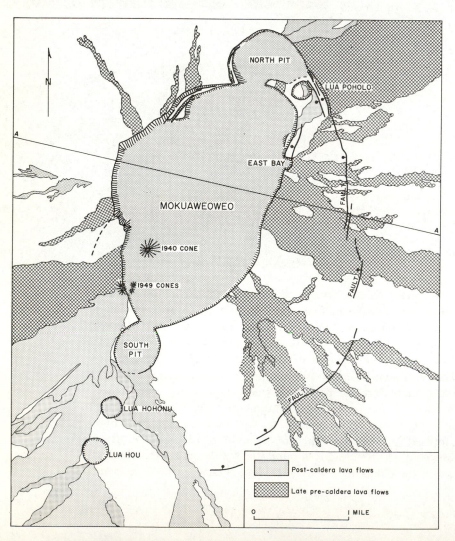

PLATE 12-8. Eastern edge of Mokuaweoweo Caldera, Mauna Loa. The cliff is approximately 200 feet high. The darker lava near the foot of the cliff is aa, overriden by the lighter pahoehoe at the left. The apparent lighter color is due to the greater reflection of light from the surface of the pahoehoe. Note how the cliff truncates the lava flows, which were erupted from vents within the area of the present caldera, at its summit. Hawaii Institute of Geophysics photo by A. T. Abbott.

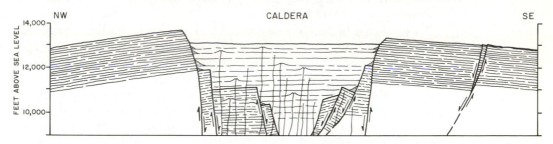

FIGURE 12-3. Cross section of Mokuaweoweo Caldera, showing lava flows in the cliffs projecting into space. They were erupted from vents nearer the summit of the mountain before the collapse of the caldera.

series of collapses and refillings. In 1825 the caldera consisted of a central pit 900 feet deep and nearly 1½ miles across. Around this was a narrow "black ledge" covered with very recent lava flows at a level about 100 feet below that of the present floor. Obviously, the caldera had been filled with lava to the level of the ledge not long before, and the central pit was the result of a recent sinking, quite likely at the time of the lateral eruption of 1823. Lava flows poured onto the floor of the central pit and rapidly filled it, until by 1832 lava was again overflowing the black ledge; but in that year, at the time of minor eruptions on the east rift zone, the central part of the caldera again collapsed, reestablishing the pit much as it had been in 1825. Once again the pit was refilled, and by 1840 it was again overflowing onto the ledge; but again collapse accompanied flank eruptions and the pit was reformed, though a little smaller than previously (Fig. 12-4A). Through the next 25 years it was again refilled, but this time only in part by lava flows. The entire central floor rose as a unit, pushed up like the floor of an elevator, carrying with it the talus banks that had formed at the foot of its boundary cliffs until finally they stood as a curved

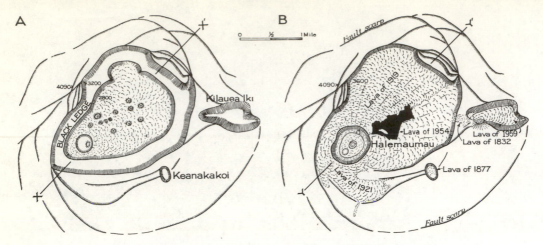

FIGURE 12-4. (A) Map of Kilauea Caldera in 1825 (after Malden); and (B) in 1965 (from Macdonald and Hubbard, 1970).

ridge of broken rock fragments above the level of both the central floor and the black ledge! A series of other important collapses took place in 1868, 1886, and 1891, each a little smaller than the previous one, and each time the basin was refilled by lava flows until finally the present condition was attained (Fig. 12-4B).

The history of Mokuaweoweo Caldera has been similar, though less complicated. In 1840 a deep central pit lay between crescentic black ledges at the northeast and southwest ends, but the pit has been gradually refilled until the ledges have been buried and lava has spilled out of the caldera into both of the adjoining pit craters (South Pit and North Bay, Fig. 12-2).

The Hawaiian calderas appear to have grown by gradual coalescence of a number of pit craters that formed, one after another, on the summits of the shields (Stearns and Clark, 1930, p. 49). The Karthala Caldera, on Grande-Comore Island, appears to be forming in a similar manner. It consists (Strong and Jacquot, 1971) of several neighboring and overlapping pit craters, some with smaller pit craters within them, forming a depressed area 2.4 miles long and 1.8 miles wide at the summit of the volcano. Fault scarps more or less tangent to the group of pit craters indicate sinking of the summit area as a whole, in addition to the localized subsidences at the pit craters.

During late stages of their activity, the Hawaiian volcanoes tend to fill their calderas and build a cap of lava flows and pyroclastic cones over the top of the shield (Chapter 11). Activity may stop at any stage; and at some volcanoes, such as that of Lanai, the caldera is not quite filled. Even in the old, deeply eroded volcanoes, the caldera can easily be recognized by the difference in character of the lavas that filled it as compared with those that built the outer, main part of the shield. The latter are thin bedded and slope outward approximately parallel to the shield surface at angles averaging about 6°. In contrast, the lavas erupted in the caldera are unable to spread freely, because they are confined by the caldera walls, and form thick beds that are essentially horizontal. Because they remain liquid much longer, the thick, caldera-filling flows lose more of their gas before they solidify than do the thin flows on the flanks of the shield; con-

PLATE 12-9. Island of Molokai, Hawaii, looking westward. In the middle distance is the erosional caldera of Molokai, formed of the coalescing heads of Wailau and Pelekunu Valleys, cut by streams. The precipice along the north side of the island is a sea cliff. Official photograph, U. S. Air Force.

sequently, the caldera-filling lavas are commonly less vesicular than the flank flows. In the walls of canyons cut into the old volcanoes, the thick, dense, horizontal caldera-filling flows can be seen abutting against the edges of the thin, vesicular, outward-sloping flows along a surface that marks the former boundary cliff of the caldera. In places, also, the caldera-filling flows are separated from the others by masses of breccia that represent the taluses formed against the base of the old caldera wall and buried by the accumulating caldera-filling lavas (Fig. 12-3).

Erosion tends to progress less rapidly in the thick, dense caldera-filling flows than in the outer part of the shield; as a result, in deeply eroded Hawaiian-type shields the central filled caldera may stand up in high relief above its surroundings. This is the case, for instance, at the main caldera of the Kauai Volcano and also at the smaller filled lateral caldera known as Haupu or Hoary Head on the southeast side of Kauai. Although they have as yet been little studied, it is probably also the cause of the high, massive central parts of the Marquesas Islands. Directly the opposite effect is found, however, in some other ancient calderas, such as those of the Koolau Volcano on Oahu and the East Molokai Volcano (Plate 12-9), both also in Hawaii. There gases moving upwards for thousands of years through the caldera-filling rocks have so altered and softened them that they became easy prey to erosion and the caldera fill has been deeply eroded, leaving the outer part of the shield standing high above it. The great cliff of the Nuuanu Pali on Oahu was formed in the same way.

The total amount of sinking that has taken place in the Hawaiian calderas cannot be determined, because the present-day calderas have been partly filled, and the base of the caldera-filling lavas in the older ones has nowhere been reached by erosion. However, in several of the older calderas the sinking exceeded 2,000 feet, and in that of the Kauai Volcano it was more than 4,000 feet.

Rarely, calderas may also form on the flanks of Hawaiian-type shield volcanoes. A circular depression averaging nearly 8 miles across on the east flank of the Kauai shield appears to be of this type (Macdonald, Davis, and Cox, 1960).

Collapses in the caldera of Kilauea in 1823, 1840, and probably in 1790, closely followed voluminous flank eruptions, suggesting that the collapse was related to the removal of underlying magma. A smaller collapse in 1868 was accompanied only by small lava eruptions, but magma moved into both rift zones of the volcano and a fairly large volume of magma may have been injected as dikes.

On Hawaiian volcanoes caldera collapse has stopped before the formation of the late caps of alkalic lavas, but on some other volcanoes that appear otherwise to be similar in structure, such as those of Samoa, calderas have formed in the late-stage alkalic caps. The visible portion of the mid-Atlantic Azores Islands is very largely, if not wholly, formed of alkalic rocks, including large amounts of trachyte, though the basal parts of the volcanoes are believed to consist of tholeiitic basalt, as in Hawaii. Calderas have formed in the tops of the trachyte volcanoes. On São Miguel Island there are three such calderas, one of them occupied by the famous hot-spring resort of Furnas. Although large amounts of trachyte ash are present, the calderas seem to have formed by collapse, not by explosion. At the caldera of Sete Cidades on the western end of São Miguel, the air-deposited ash beds mantle the rim of the caldera, showing that they were laid down after the sinking in of the caldera.

Calderas are formed also at the summit of many composite volcanoes. The great caldera formed in Mt. Somma during the Vesuvius eruption of 79 A.D. (Plate 10-15) and that of the Krakatoa Volcano have been mentioned in Chapter 10, and many others are known. Typically, they are nearly circular in plan and range in depth from a few hundred to several thousand feet. New ones are bounded by precipitous walls that cut sharply across the beds of lava and tephra, though in older, somewhat eroded ones the boundary slopes may be quite gentle. One of the best known and best studied is that of Crater Lake, Oregon (Williams, 1942). It is 5 to 6 miles across and about 3,700 feet deep from the rim to the bottom of the lake (Fig. 12-5).

Some calderas form in volcanic complexes built of several overlapping volcanoes and/or fissure-fed lava flows, but are not obviously related to any single volcanic mountain. In some instances, and perhaps in most, the area was domed up, presumably by a relatively shallow intrusive body beneath, before the formation of the caldera.

The largest calderas are those associated with ash-flow volcanoes. The Timber Mountain Caldera in southwestern Nevada (Figs. 12-6, 12-11) is elliptical with diameters of 18 by 20 miles; the nearby Silent Canyon Caldera has diameters of 12 and 15 miles, the Kane Springs Wash Caldera

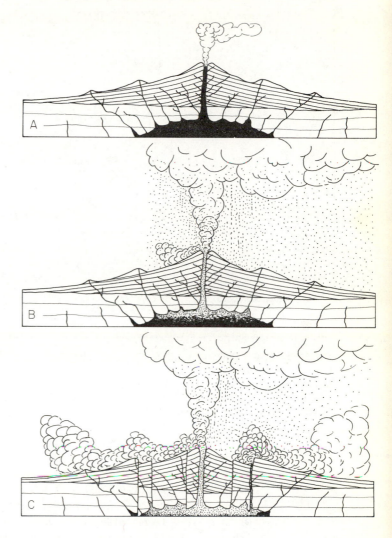

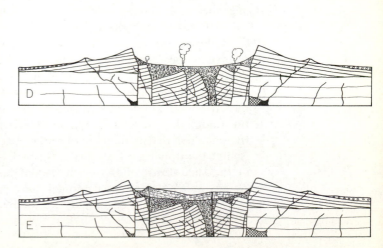

FIGURE 12-5. Diagrams illustrating the formation of the Crater Lake caldera, Oregon. (A) before the eruption; (B) during an early stage of the caldera-forming eruption, showing a vulcanian ash cloud and a small ash flow from the central vent; (C) during the climax of the eruption, with big ash flows issuing from the central vent and from ring fractures part way down the slope while the summit starts to sink as a series of big blocks; (D) after the eruption; (E) in its present state, with new eruptions on the floor and the caldera partly filled with water. (Modified after Williams, 1942.)

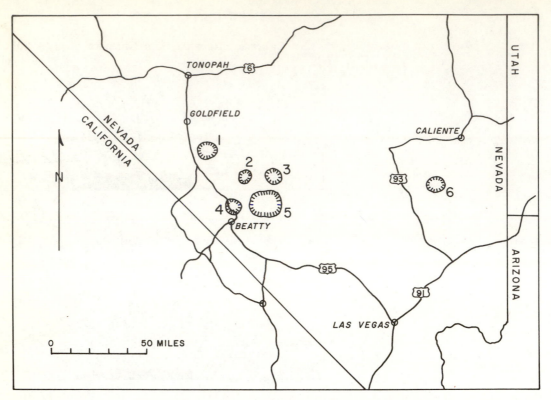

FIGURE 12-6. Map of southern Nevada, showing the location of several large calderas associated with voluminous ash-flow deposits. (1) Stonewall Mountain Caldera, (2) Black Mountain Caldera, (3) Silent Canyon Caldera, (4) Paintbrush Caldera, (5) Timber Mountain Caldera, (6) Kane Springs Wash Caldera. (After Ekren, 1968, and Noble and others, 1968.)

in southeastern Nevada has diameters of 8 and 12 miles. The La Garita Caldera in the San Juan Mountains of Colorado has a north to south diameter of about 30 miles, an east to west diameter of 25 to 30 miles, and its original depth was 6,000 to 7,000 feet (P. E. Lipman, oral statement, 1969). The diameters of some other calderas are listed in Table 12-1. Some of these very large calderas are resurgent (p. 313), but not all of them. For instance, the Kane Springs Wash Caldera (Fig. 12-6) shows no signs of resurgence (Noble, 1968).

Formation of the caldera usually takes place late in the history of the volcano and often follows a long pause in activity during which the cone may become fairly deeply eroded. The magmatic material ejected during the caldera-forming eruption is usually dacitic or rhyodacitic in composition, less commonly andesitic or trachytic. It is generally believed that the long quiescence preceding the eruption allows differentiation of the underlying magma body, producing a mass of magma at the top of the chamber that is more acidic than that lower down. Another possibility is that the upper acid magma is formed by *local anatexis*—melting of part of the sialic crust of the earth by hot basic magma from greater depths. At any rate, if eruption continues long enough it may exhaust the upper magma, and dacitic ejecta may be followed by andesitic or basaltic ejecta

TABLE 12-1. Diameters of some calderas

CALDERA		AVERAGE DIAMETER (miles)
Name	*Location*	
Aso	Kyushu Island, Japan	12.5
Kikai	Kyushu Island, Japan	12
Towada	Honshu Island, Japan	7
Batur	Bali	7
Kawah Idjen	Java	11
Krakatoa	Between Java and Sumatra	5
Santorin	Aegean Sea	8.5
Monte Albano	Italy	6
Conca di Bolsena	Italy	10
Somma (Vesuvius)	Italy	2
Emi Koussi	Tibesti (N. Africa)	8.5
Tarso Yega	Tibesti (N. Africa)	11
Tarso Voon	Tibesti (N. Africa)	9.5
Trou de Natron	Tibesti (N. Africa)	4
Suswa	Kenya	6.5
Sete Cidades	Azores	1.5
Aniakchak	Alaska	5.5
Katmai	Alaska	3
Okmok	Aleutian Islands	7
Tanaga	Aleutian Islands	6.6
Buldir	Aleutian Islands	19
La Garita	San Juan Mts., Colorado	28
Valles	Jemez Mts., New Mexico	13
Crater Lake	Oregon	6
Kilauea	Hawaii	2.5
Mauna Loa	Hawaii	2.2
Koolau	Hawaii	6
Kauai	Hawaii	11

derived from deeper in the magma body, as was the case at Crater Lake (Chapter 8).

Many calderas, and probably all of the very large ones, are associated with voluminous ash-flow deposits. Sometimes several layers of ignimbrite separated by zones of weathering and soil formation are associated with one caldera, indicating a succession of ash-flow eruptions at considerable intervals of time and probably a series of caldera collapses. Thus, at Towada Caldera in Japan (Fig. 12-7) two major collapses were

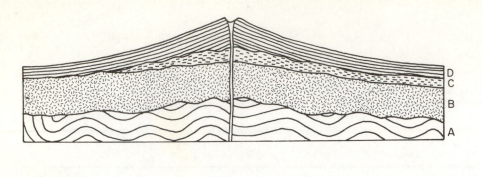

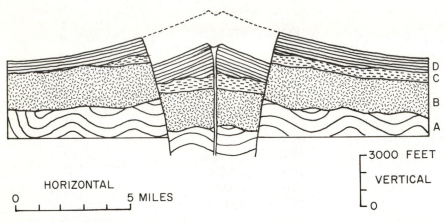

FIGURE 12-7. The earlier of two calderas at Towada Volcano, northern Honshu, Japan. (A) folded Paleozoic sedimentary rocks of the pre-volcanic basement, (B) Tertiary volcanic rocks, (C) Pleistocene welded tuff, (D) composite volcano. (Simplified after Kuno, and others, 1964.) Inward dipping caldera-boundary faults, such as are hypothesized here, imply an extension of the whole area, as by updoming. It is likely, however, that the faults are more nearly vertical than they are shown.

accompanied respectively by the formation of voluminous ignimbrite and pumice-and-ash-fall deposits (Kuno et al., 1964). Other calderas are surrounded, and sometimes partly or wholly filled, by a single great ignimbrite mass that cooled in the vicinity of the caldera as a single cooling unit, and must have originated in a single great eruption or eruptions so closely spaced in time that they may be regarded as a single eruptive episode, probably with a single essentially continuous caldera collapse. A remarkable example of this association of a single big ignimbrite mass with each caldera is found in the San Juan Mountains of Colorado (P. E. Lipman, oral statement, 1969). Careful mapping in that region has demonstrated the presence of 11 major ignimbrite masses, plus some minor ones, and probably 11 calderas, situated in each case near the center of one of the major ignimbrite sheets. (Nine of the calderas are certain. The San Juan volcanoes are old enough—about 20 million years—so that their original forms have been greatly modified by erosion and much geological investigation is required to elucidate their details.)

Commonly, the ash flows appear to have been erupted from the same series of arcuate fissures on which the circular block subsided to form the caldera, probably in most instances combined with at least some eruption from the summit vent. Where the caldera formed on a composite cone, the eruptive fissures in some instances, as apparently at Crater Lake in Oregon, were part way down the slope of the cone. In other instances, however, as at some of the Japanese calderas (S. Aramaki, oral statement, 1969), the distribution of the associated air-laid ash and pumice deposits indicates that the ejections came from a restricted vent at the summit of the volcano rather than from arcuate fissures part way down the slope.

The great volumes of fragmental debris found on the slopes of the composite volcanoes surrounding the calderas suggested to early workers that violent explosions had blown the top off the volcano to form the caldera. Great explosions there were indeed! But careful study of the tephra deposited by the explosions has shown that only a very small proportion of it consists of fragments of the old mountaintop. Generally, 95 per cent or more is new magmatic material brought up from depth during the caldera-forming eruption and spread over the slopes of the volcano and the nearby region as showers of pumice and ash, and usually very voluminous glowing avalanches and ash flows. The volume of old material thrown out by the explosions equals only a few per cent of the volume of the caldera. It is clear, therefore, that the caldera has resulted not from explosive decapitation of the mountain, but from subsidence of the summit along ring-shaped fractures; and the huge volume of new magma erupted points to partial drainage of an underlying magma chamber and suggests removal of support from beneath the top of the mountain as the cause of the collapse. An alternative hypothesis suggested by the Dutch volcanologist, Wing Easton, invokes a caving in of the top of the mountain as a result of coring out of a central pipe by violent discharges of gas like that during the 1906 eruption of Vesuvius (Chapter 10). Wing Easton's (1916) mechanism probably accounts for some craters formed by collapse of the summit of composite cones, as it undoubtedly did for the enlargement of the crater of Vesuvius in 1906, but it is not adequate to explain the larger calderas such as Crater Lake, if for no other reason than that the volume of ejected old cone material is not great enough to account for the requisite cored-out cylinder. To allow the mountaintop to slump into it, such a cylinder would have to have a volume at least equal to that of the resulting caldera, and thus the mechanism is ruled out by the same objection that has been raised to the hypothesis of the destruction of the mountaintop by explosion. The quantity of ejected old material is far too small.

The history of the formation of Crater Lake, as deduced by Williams (1942), may be taken as an example of the formation of a caldera on a composite cone (Fig. 12-5). Briefly, it is as follows. The mountain in which the caldera is located was formerly an andesitic volcano some 12,000 feet high. It has been named Mt. Mazama. Late in its history concentric fissures opened on its middle slope and dacitic magma was erupted to form a series of cones, domes, and short thick lava flows. These now are Mt. Hillman, Llao Rock, Grouse Hill, Rugged Crest, and other prominences on the north side of the mountain. A period of volcanic quiet then allowed streams to cut canyons into the cone, and these were enlarged and changed from V to U shape by glaciers. Debris deposited by the glaciers formed moraines on the mountainside. Then, about 6,000 years ago, while glaciers still occupied the upper ends of the valleys, came the climactic eruption. Explosions threw out showers of dacite ash and pumice mixed with relatively few fragments of older andesite from the cone. The explosions rapidly increased in violence, a great vulcanian eruption cloud rose miles above the mountaintop, and ash and pumice rained down over the surrounding country. Some ash fell as far away as Alberta in Canada. Then came great glowing avalanches of ash and pumice rushing down the canyons, burying the glacial moraines, and extending as much as 35 miles from their source. As the avalanches continued, the composition of the magma changed from dacite to basaltic andesite, and the color of the pumice changed from pale to dark gray. The deposits are well exposed along Sand and Annie Creeks, where the dark gray material can be readily seen resting on the pale gray material of earlier stages in the eruption. At about the time of the culmination of the ash and pumice avalanches, the top of the mountain collapsed, probably by degrees, to form the caldera (Fig. 12-5). Along its northern edge the collapse was localized by the same concentric fracture that had earlier determined the position of the row of dacitic eruptions.

Since its formation, the caldera has been partly filled with water from rain and melting snow to form the lake, and also partly with lava from basaltic eruptions within the caldera, one of which built the cinder cone and lava flows of Wizard Island. Another large cone is wholly submerged in the lake. The later eruption of basic lavas within the caldera is a common occurrence (Plate 12-10), as we have seen also at Krakatoa (Chapter 10).

The sinking-in of the top of a volcanic cone implies the presence of a fairly sizeable magma reservoir fairly close to the surface. The actual presence of such a magma body in Kilauea Volcano has been demonstrated by geophysical evidence (Chapter 15). Two principal mechanisms that may bring about the collapse have been suggested: (1) removal of support by draining away of the underlying magma, and (2) upward displacement of the underlying magma by the heavier overlying block sinking into it.

PLATE 12-10. The composite cone of Karymsky Volcano, rising within an older caldera, in Kamchatka. Photo by G. S. Gorshkov, Kamchatka Volcano Station.

The latter mechanism was suggested as early as 1909, by Clough, Maufe, and Bailey, to explain the cauldron subsidence at Glencoe in Scotland. (See Chapter 15.) Although it may be effective at some places, it is improbable at the Hawaiian volcanoes and many others because of the almost complete absence of any indication of magma rising along the fractures that bound the sinking block (Macdonald, 1965). Even at the Galapagos volcanoes, where eruptions on concentric fissures are common, the volume of lava thus erupted appears to be very much smaller than the volume of the caldera.

The favored hypothesis today is that of the removal of support by some sort of drainage of the underlying magma—a mechanism suggested, as we have seen, both by the association of Hawaiian caldera collapse with flank eruptions of lava, and by the huge volumes of tephra associated with the calderas of composite volcanoes (Williams, 1941a). But the evidence is not as clear cut as it appears on casual inspection. In 1840 the estimated volume of lava erupted by Kilauea Volcano (281 million cubic yards) was nearly the same as the volume of collapse in the caldera (287 million cubic yards)—apparently an excellent corroboration of the hypothesis; but in other eruptions the volume of caldera collapse was very much greater than that of the extruded lava. In 1823, for example, the collapse was about 705 million cubic yards, whereas the volume of lava extruded was only 15 million. Even allowing for considerable error in the estimates, it is necessary to hypothesize a large amount of dike or sill intrusion to account for the smaller volume of extruded lava. Similarly, the volume of ash and pumice erupted during the collapse of calderas in composite vocanoes, reduced to the unexpanded state of the nonvesicular magma in the reservoir, nearly always appears to be considerably smaller than that of the associated caldera. For instance, Katsui (1963) has found a volume of about 14.4 cubic miles of ejecta associated with the Shikotsu Caldera in Hokkaido, Japan, which has a volume of 19 cubic miles; and Williams and Goles (1968) find the volume of material ejected from Mt. Mazama to be approximately 10 cubic miles, as compared to 14.9 cubic miles for the Crater Lake Caldera. Some of the discrepancies may be accounted for by ash that has drifted to very great distances and formed deposits that are so thin they have escaped detection and by underestimates of the volume of material removed from the easily eroded tops of ignimbrites, but it is unlikely that amounts of several cubic miles, as in the examples above, can be thus explained.

Thus, although it seems quite clear that caldera collapse must be related to the loss of support of the mountaintop caused by removal of magma beneath, at least in many cases the removal is only partly by eruption of the magma at the surface. Some of it must be due to movement of magma within the earth. If so, this suggests the possibility that the extreme vesiculation of the magma that brings about the ash eruptions may also be due to the internal withdrawal of magma, resulting in a decrease of pressure in the upper part of the magma chamber. In this way, an internal withdrawal of magma may lead to vesiculation and expansion of the remaining magma with resulting eruption and removal of a still larger volume of magma, and this in turn leads to collapse. But more specifically, just what becomes of the magma removed internally? The caldera problem is still far from solved!

Recently, McBirney and Williams (1969) have suggested the following revision of Williams earlier (1941a) classification of calderas:

> **Group I.** Calderas associated with voluminous explosive eruptions of siliceous magma.
>
> A. *Krakatoa type.* Collapse results from copious eruptions of magma as pumice falls and pumice flows. In part at least, the eruptions issued from the summit vents of mature composite volcanoes.
>
> B. *The Katmai type.* Collapse results from drainage of the central conduit of a volcano and perhaps also of some of the underlying reservoir by discharge of magma through adjacent conduits not in the volcano itself.
>
> C. *The Valles type.* Collapse follows discharge of colossal volumes of ash and pumice as pyroclastic flows from arcuate fissures unrelated to pre-existing volcanoes.
>
> **Group II.** Calderas associated with effusive eruptions of basaltic magma.
>
> A. *The Masaya type.* Formed by piece-meal collapse over areas much broader than any pre-existing volcano. Eruptions from rifts outside the caldera play no part in its formation.
>
> B. *The Hawaiian type.* Formed by collapse during late stages of growth of large basaltic shield volcanoes. The summit block subsides along steeply inclined ring fractures following tumescence of the shield and drainage of magma into rift zones, with or without flank eruptions of lava.
>
> C. *The Galapagos type.* Also formed by collapse during late stages of growth of large basaltic shield volcanoes. But engulfment results chiefly from injection of sills and from eruption of lavas from circumferential fractures near the summit.

The Glencoe, cryptovolcanic, and miscellaneous types of the earlier classification have been abandoned, the name Kilauea type has been changed to Hawaiian type, and the Katmai type has been redefined. The Valles type, Masaya type, and Galapagos type, have been added.

The Katmai type of caldera was formerly conceived to have been formed by collapse resulting from a combination of internal solution of the volcanic cone by magma standing at a high level, pumice explosions, and caving in of the crater walls. Few, if any, volcanologists today accept the idea of solution of the upper part of the Katmai cone by a lava lake in the crater, as proposed by Fenner (1920), and it is now known that the eruption of magma that accompanied the collapse took place from vents beyond the edge of the Katmai cone. There is no evidence that remelting played any part in the formation of the Katmai Caldera. On the other hand, partial remelting of the deeper central parts of some volcanic cones probably does take place. It probably is responsible for the formation of the shallow magma reservoir that appears to lie above the level of the original base of the cone in the Hawaiian shield volcanoes (see Chapter 15) and is probably an essential part of the mechanism of formation of calderas of the Hawaiian type.

Cryptovolcanic depressions are now believed by many geologists not to be of volcanic origin, but instead to have been formed by the impact of meteorites on the surface of the earth. Others, however, still believe in the origin of at least some of them through "muffled" subterranean explosions, and these persons probably would retain a class of cryptovolcanic calderas.

Vincent (1960) believes that the calderas of the Tibesti region, North Africa, have resulted from tumescence of the ignimbrite shields (Chapter 11) and the underlying nonvolcanic terrane, with resultant sinking of a "keystone" block at the summit, not from eruption of underlying magma. In the Jemez Mts. also, updoming preceded the formation of the Valles Caldera, and the Tibesti calderas can probably be included in the Valles type. Tumescence may also have been a factor in the formation of calderas in some basaltic shield volcanoes. The distension of the shield by inflation of an internal magma chamber may have sufficiently stretched the carapace of the shield to allow the summit portion to sink a short distance into the less dense magma in the reservoir beneath it.

There is very little difference in the mechanisms of formation of the Hawaiian and the (now abandoned) Glencoe types of calderas, except that in the former the drainage of magma that brings about caldera sinking takes place by eruptions on the flanks of the shield volcano, whereas in the latter the magma moves up through ring fractures that bound the sinking block, giving rise to eruptions around the edges of the caldera. Such eruptions from circumferential fissures are one of the marks used to distinguish calderas of the Galapagos type from Hawaiian calderas. The distinction between the latter two types of calderas does not seem to be altogether clean cut. Both mechanisms may be involved in the formation of the same caldera. Though eruptions on circumferential fissures are rare in Hawaii (only two such cases are known at Kilauea), they are common, along with flank eruptions, on some of the shield volcanoes of Samoa. Likewise, although they are less abundant, radial eruption fissures do exist, along with the circumferential ones, on the Galapagos volcanoes. In both Hawaiian and Galapagos volcanoes some of the drainage of magma from beneath the caldera clearly takes place by intrusion, but the distinction between sill and dike intrusion is in large part hypothetical. Many sills can be seen in the walls of the Hawaiian calderas.

Smith and Bailey (1968) suggested that another difference between calderas of the Glencoe and Krakatoa types is that collapse of the former involves a fairly regular sinking of the floor block along ring fractures, whereas the Krakatoa-type calderas result from chaotic collapse of many blocks in which ring fractures do not play an essential part except to bound the general collapsing mass. Actually, the importance of piecemeal collapse in the formation of calderas may have been considerably overemphasized.

It appears that in many calderas, if not in most, the underlying block may have sunk pretty much as a unit. A recent example is the collapse in the Fernandina Caldera, Galapagos Islands, in 1968, in which an old tuff cone and the surrounding part of the caldera floor went down as much as 900 feet with slight basining but only minor breaking up (Simkin and Howard, 1970). The volume of magma extruded during this eruption was only a small fraction of the volume of the caldera collapse, thus illustrating the importance of intrusion into the flanks of the cone in the formation of the Galapagos calderas.

The calderas of McBirney and Williams' groups I and II are distinct not only in the type of magma with which they are associated, but also in their geophysical properties. Calderas of group I have moderate to strong negative gravity anomalies (deficiencies of gravitative attraction), whereas those of group II have moderate to strong positive anomalies (Yokoyama, 1963). The negative anomalies in group I appear to be the result of deep fills of light fragmental material. In group II the sunken caldera block is denser, but the positive anomaly may be largely the result of a mass of very dense rock only a mile or two beneath the surface (Strange, Machesky, and Woollard, 1965; Macdonald and Abbott, 1970, p. 283). It is noteworthy that while the heavy masses lie nearly below the centers of some of the calderas, they are distinctly offset with respect to some of the other calderas (Kinoshita, 1965; Macdonald, 1965). The nature of the very dense rock is still uncertain. The masses may consist of upward protrusions of the dense peridotite of the earth's mantle, or they may be accumulations of heavy crystals (predominantly olivine) that lagged behind in the rising magma in the conduits of the volcano.

Volcanic Grabens

The stretching of the surface of Hawaiian-type shield volcanoes that forms the rift zones may also allow long narrow blocks of the surficial rocks to sink between faults parallel to the rift zones, like the keystone block of a slightly stretched arch. These *grabens* are well developed on both the east and southwest rift zones of Kilauea, but not on Mauna Loa. They range in width up to about a mile and in length to several miles. Their present depth varies from a few feet to about 50 feet, but the total amount of sinking is unknown because they have been partly filled with more recent lava flows. Grabens also may form on shield volcanoes away from the rift zones. On the southwest side of the Kauai Volcano, the sinking of a triangular block 4 miles across left a graben valley that has since been partly filled with lava flows that poured into it from the caldera.

In Hawaii, graben collapse does not appear to have taken place after the beginning of formation of the late cap of alkalic lavas; but in the Azores, grabens, as well as calderas, have formed in the alkalic cap.

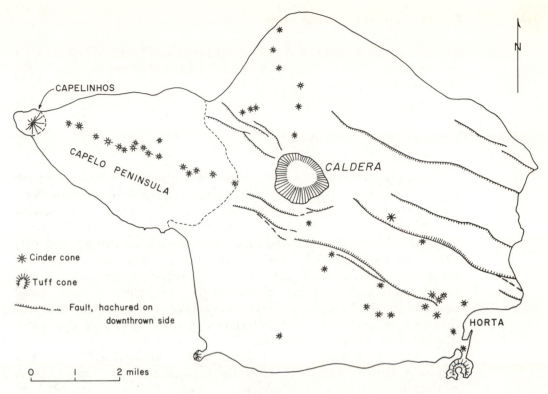

Cinder cone

Tuff cone

Fault, hachured on downthrown side

CAPELINHOS

CAPELO PENINSULA

CALDERA

HORTA

0   1   2 miles

FIGURE 12-8. Map of Fayal Island, in the Azores, showing the caldera and the graben extending across the summit of the volcano.

On both Fayal and Pico Islands big grabens trend west-northwestward across the top of the volcanoes (Fig. 12-8). That on Fayal is 10 miles long, 4 to 6 miles wide, and about 500 feet deep, the sides descending in a series of giant steps, each of which is the surface of a down-dropped fault block. Whether these are the result of the removal of magma from an underlying chamber, or of stretching of the surface of the volcano or even of the entire underlying crust of the earth due to a spreading of the Atlantic Ocean basin, is not known.

Radial grabens may also form on composite volcanoes. They have been called by some writers *sector grabens*. Unusually big valleys that extend down the flanks of some cones may be sector grabens. For example, this is thought by R. W. van Bemmelen to be the origin of certain big gorges on Indonesian volcanoes. However, some such big canyons, like the Koolau, Kaupo, and Kipahulu Valleys on Haleakala Volcano in Hawaii, have been shown to be wholly the result of stream erosion, and caution must be used in attributing the big valleys on other volcanoes to graben collapse. Diller Canyon, on the side of Shastina in California, may be a sector graben, though it is thought by Williams (1934, p. 236) to be more probably the result of erosion of the flank of the cone by glowing avalanches. The Valle del Bove on the flank of Mt. Etna in Sicily has been said by some to be a sector graben and by others to be the result of stream erosion; but, as was recognized by Sartorius von Waltershausen in 1880, it is clearly the caldera of an older volcano (Trifoglietto), breached on the northeastern side, and now being buried on the western side by the growing cone of Etna.

Volcano-Tectonic Depressions

Similar genetically to the calderas of Krakatoa and Valles type are great downfaulted troughs (grabens) called *volcano-tectonic depressions*. These are often, though apparently not always, formed on the crests of broad arches created by the upbending of the rocks of the earth's crust. These arches have generally been attributed to mountain-building (tectonic) forces, but the associated volcanic events suggest that they may be the result of the expansion of large volumes of relatively light magma generated in the underlying part of the earth's crust, rather than of lateral compression. The troughs are many miles long, several miles wide, and thousands of feet deep. They are known in several parts of the world. The following are a few examples.

The Taupo basin on North Island of New Zealand is 60 miles long and 15 to 20 miles wide (Fig. 12-9) and contains the big composite cones of Tongariro and Ngauruhoe Volcanoes, as well as Tarawera Volcano, Lake

FIGURE 12-9.   Map of the Taupo region, North Island of New Zealand, showing the alignment of volcanic vents along graben formed by volcano-tectonic collapse. (After Gregg, 1961.)

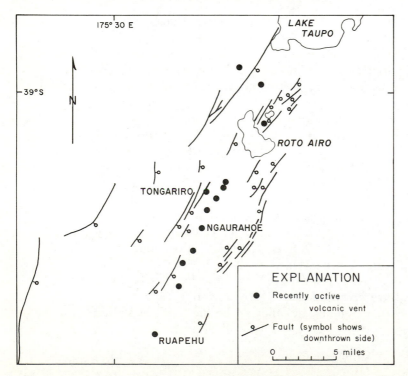

Taupo, and the once-renowned pink and white terraces destroyed by the eruption of Tarawera in 1886. The basin was formed by the collapse of the crest of a broad arch, forming a series of grabens, and at about the same time great masses of rhyolite ash flows were erupted from fissures in the crest of the arch or from the fault fractures that bounded the grabens. The present big cones have grown in the basin following its collapse.

In west-central Sumatra the basin occupied by Lake Toba is 60 miles long, 18.5 miles wide, and 1,400 feet deep (Fig. 12-11C). Like the Taupo basin, it was formed by the sinking of a series of grabens along the crest of a broad arch (Bemmelen, 1929). The great volume of ignimbrites associated with the Toba depression has been mentioned in Chapter 10, and it was presumably the eruption of this huge volume of magma from beneath that allowed the top of the arch to collapse.

The Ata depression, which lies largely beneath the ocean at the southern end of Kagoshima Bay on Kyushu Island, Japan, is a complex area of foundered blocks about 12 miles across. The sinking was associated with the formation of three big ignimbrite sheets separated by soil layers, indicating that the collapse probably took place in a series of widely separated events (Aramaki, 1969).

In central America, the basin of Lake Ilopango in El Salvador and the elongate depression in Nicaragua that contains Lakes Managua and Nicaragua are broad shallow grabens that developed on the crests of broad arches after the eruption of large volumes of ignimbrites (Williams and Meyer-Abich, 1955; McBirney and Williams, 1965). Indeed, most if not all of these great depressions are associated with huge volumes of rhyolitic to dacitic ash-flow deposits, and presumably in each case room for the sunken blocks was furnished at least in part by removal of the magma represented in these deposits.

Resurgent Calderas

It has already been pointed out that volcanic activity commonly continues after caldera collapse. The caldera may eventually be completely filled and obliterated by later volcanic rocks—lava flows in Hawaiian-type calderas, a combination of lava flows and tephra in Krakatoa-type calderas, and ash-flow deposits with or without other volcanics in Valles-type calderas. The renewal of activity in Valles-type calderas appears commonly to be accompanied by up-bowing of the caldera floor, sometimes by an amount of several thousand feet, and calderas in which this has taken place are called by Smith and Bailey (1962) *resurgent calderas*. The up-domed floor is stretched and cracked, and grabens commonly form across the dome (Figs. 12-10, 12-11 and 12-12). Later eruptions are largely localized along the grabens and along the ring fractures that bound the caldera floor. It should be noted that not all Valles-type calderas are resurgent.

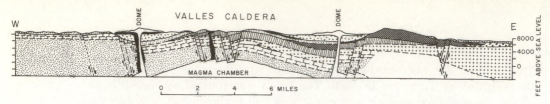

FIGURE 12-10. Cross section through part of the Jemez Mountains, New Mexico, showing the structure of the Valles Caldera. Note the updoming of the sunken central block of the resurgent caldera. The Bandelier Tuff is the stippled layer near or at the top of the section. Rhyolite domes have been built over the ring fractures. (After Smith, Bailey, and Ross, 1970.)

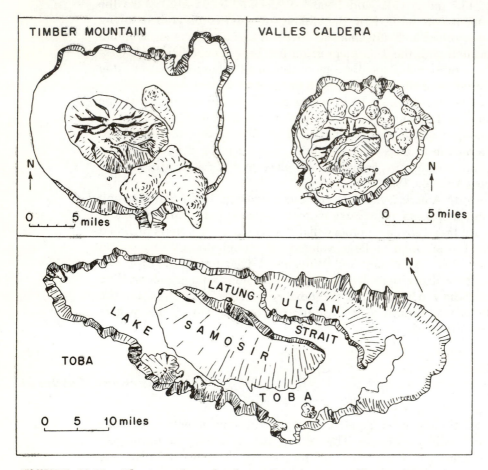

FIGURE 12-11. Physiographic sketches of resurgent calderas. (From Smith and Bailey, 1968.) (A) Valles Caldera, New Mexico; (B) Timber Mountain Caldera, Nevada; (C) Lake Toba volcano-tectonic depression, Sumatra.

The concept of resurgent calderas was first developed during studies of the Jemez Mts. in New Mexico, and the history of that region may be taken as typical of resurgent calderas in general (Smith and Bailey, 1968). The general character and history of the Jemez Volcano has already been described (p. 263). During and after the formation of the upper Bandelier ignimbrites, the summit of the highland collapsed to form the Valles Caldera (Figs. 12-10 and 12-11A)—a subcircular depression 12 to 15 miles in diameter and with a visible depth of more than 2,000 feet in spite of partial refilling by later volcanics. Approximately in the center of the caldera lies a mountain mass 8 to 10 miles across and 3,000 feet high composed of up-domed beds of ignimbrite and lake deposits, and crossed by a large graben and many lesser faults. The history of the caldera is outlined by Smith and Bailey as follows:

1. Regional doming of the Jemez highland and formation of a series of ring fractures above an underlying magma body.

2. Eruption of the upper Bandelier Tuff from vents along the ring fractures.

3. Sinking of the block inside the ring fractures to form the Valles Caldera. The caldera was bounded by arcuate step faults and floored mainly by Bandelier Tuff.

FIGURE 12-12. Diagrammatic cross sections showing the difference between a simple caldera of the Glen Coe or Hawaiian type and a resurgent caldera. (After Smith, Bailey, and Ross, 1961.)

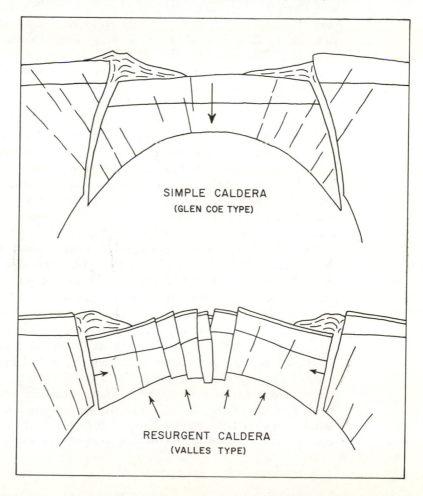

SIMPLE CALDERA
(GLEN COE TYPE)

RESURGENT CALDERA
(VALLES TYPE)

4. Formation of a lake within the caldera, and eruption of rhyolite lava flows and tephra. The caldera floor was completely buried by talus and landslides from the walls, lake deposits, and tephra.

5. Up-bowing of the center of the caldera floor, and eruption of rhyolite lavas from the ring fractures at the northwest edge of the caldera and within the graben that formed across the central uplift (Fig. 12-11A). Lake deposits and lava flows continued to accumulate in the moat between the central uplift and the caldera walls.

6. Eruption of rhyolite, forming a discontinuous circle of tephra cones, domes, and lava flows in the moat.

7. Hot-spring and solfataric activity continuing to the present day.

Smith and Bailey recognize many other resurgent calderas and volcano-tectonic depressions. Among them are the Creede, Silverton, and Lake City Calderas in Colorado, the Timber Mountain Caldera in Nevada (Fig. 12-11B), and the Lake Toba depression in Sumatra (Fig. 12-11C). The Timber Mountain Caldera, described by Christiansen, Lipman, Orkild, and Byers (1965), and Carr and Quinlivan (1968), is 18 by 20 miles in diameter, and within it the central uplift rises 2,000 to 3,000 feet above the caldera floor. The collapse of the caldera followed the eruption of more than 250 cubic miles of rhyolitic ash flows, and the resurgence was accompanied and followed by eruptions from fractures in the central uplift and from the ring fractures.

The San Juan Mountains of Colorado contain the eroded remains of a mass of volcanic rocks about 7,000 feet thick and covering an area of 6,000 square miles. The rocks were erupted from several centers. The Silverton and Lake City resurgent calderas lie within the rocks of the western center. There, during Oligocene time (about 30 million years ago), lava flows, tuffs, tuff-breccias, mudflow deposits, and ignimbrites of andesitic to rhyodacitic composition erupted from a series of volcanoes, and sedimentary rocks derived from them built a more or less shield-shaped mass about 60 miles across and a mile or more thick (Luedke and Burbank, 1968). Within this, collapse formed a huge caldera or volcano-tectonic depression 30 miles long and 15 miles wide. This was the San Juan Caldera. The collapse followed eruption of several hundred cubic miles of quartz latite to rhyolite ash flows (the Eureka Tuff), much of which is preserved within the caldera. An unknown additional amount was erupted outside the caldera area and has since been largely eroded away. Later, up-arching of the caldera floor caused outward tilting of these once-horizontal beds of ignimbrite. The elongate central uplift was broken by a longitudinal graben, known as the Eureka graben (Fig. 12-13B). Continued eruptions, principally from vents along the ring fractures at its borders, nearly filled the caldera. Further eruption of 200 to 300 cubic miles of quartz latite to rhyolite ash flows resulted in the collapse of the smaller Silverton and Lake City Calderas within the former San Juan Cal-

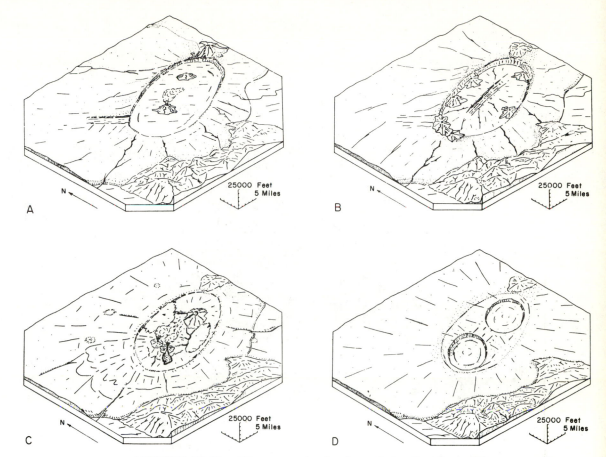

FIGURE 12-13. Diagrammatic sketches of the San Juan, Silverton, and Lake City Calderas. (After Luedke and Burbank, 1968.) (A) San Juan Caldera, with volcanic cones on the caldera floor and a graben extending outward northwestward from it; (B) San Juan resurgent caldera, with central uplift and graben, and volcanic cones formed along the boundary fracture; (C) Resurgent caldera nearly filled by later volcanics; (D) Silverton and Lake City Calderas formed by collapse within the area of the former San Juan Caldera.

dera (Fig. 12-13D). In turn, resurgence caused the up-bowing of the floors of both of these calderas, and the Eureka graben was reactivated. Further eruptions took place along the ring fractures around the calderas and along radial fractures outside the calderas that appear to be related genetically to a broad up-doming of the whole volcanic district. Luedke and Burbank suggest that this broad uplift is in turn related to an underlying rather shallow-seated batholith. As in several other of the resurgent calderas of the southwestern United States, the volcanic activity was followed by extensive mineralization and the formation of shallow-seated (epithermal) ore deposits.

In eastern Idaho, 40 miles west of Yellowstone Lake, the Island Park Caldera has diameters of 18 by 23 miles. It lies at the summit of a broad rhyolite ignimbrite shield with rhyolite domes along the caldera boundary (Hamilton, 1965). The eastern edge of the Island Park Caldera has been

317

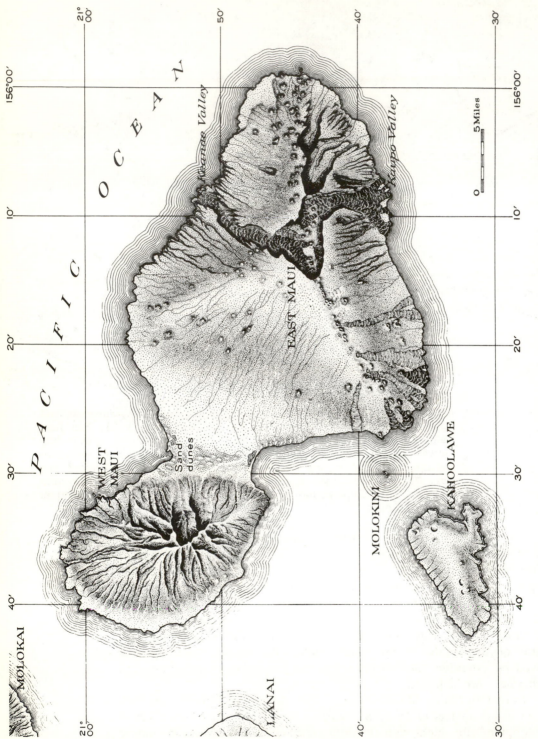

FIGURE 12-14. Relief map of the Island of Maui, Hawaii, showing Haleakala Crater, and big stream-cut valleys on the slopes of the volcano. (After Stearns and Macdonald, 1942.)

buried by huge rhyolite flows that form the western edge of the Yellow-stone Plateau. Work just being completed by Robert L. Christiansen and H. Richard Blank, Jr., of the U.S. Geological Survey, has shown that the Yellowstone Plateau was built during three separate volcanic cycles, each of which culminated in the eruption of a huge composite rhyolitic ash-flow sheet and the collapse of an enormous caldera (Christiansen and Blank, 1969, and letter of March 12, 1971). The formation of the Island Park Caldera was related to the middle volcanic cycle about 1.2 million years ago. The oldest caldera, related to rocks erupted about 2 million years ago, was at least 50 miles long and covered parts of both the Yellowstone and Island Park areas. It appears to be the largest caldera yet recognized on earth. Nearly as large, however, is the youngest caldera, formed about 600,000 years ago. The collapse occurred on two intersecting sets of ring fractures and resulted in a caldera nearly 50 miles long in a northeast-southwest direction and more than 30 miles wide. Later, two resurgent domes formed in the caldera, one in its southwestern part in the vicinity of the Upper Geyser Basin, the other at its northeastern end just north of Yellowstone Lake. Volcanic structures of this enormous size, even such very young ones as those of the Yellowstone region, can be demonstrated only by such careful detailed mapping and stratigraphic studies as those done by Christiansen and Blank. Similar work elsewhere no doubt will reveal more of them.

Erosional Calderas

Haleakala Crater on the island of Maui, Hawaii, is 7 miles long, 2 miles wide, and 2,000 feet deep at its western end (Fig. 12-14). In terms of size, it is a caldera. However, careful geologic studies indicate that it has been formed by erosion rather than by direct volcanic processes (Stearns, 1942). Leading out of the crater are two deep valleys closely similar in form to amphitheater-headed stream-cut valleys on the eastern flank of the mountain. The head of one of the latter valleys is separated from the crater only by a narrow knife ridge. A comparatively small amount of additional erosion will extend it headward to merge with the crater. During a long pause in volcanic activity, a series of stream valleys started to develop around the mountain. The two largest of these appear to have excavated a great cavity in the heart of the mountain, the heads of the valleys eventually coalescing to the point where they were separated only by a narrow and relatively low divide. Later, renewed volcanic activity flooded the valleys with lava flows and built cinder cones on the resulting flat floor of the depression (Plate 12-11). Similar caldera-size topographic depressions formed by erosion are fairly common on other volcanoes (Plate 12-9) and are probably best called *erosional calderas*.

In some instances, and perhaps in most, the erosional calderas coin-

PLATE 12-11. Cinder cones in Haleakala Crater, Maui Island, Hawaii. In the background the wall of the crater is partly mantled with long banks of wind-blown ash. Lava flows, also mantled with ash, surround the cones. The crater was formed by stream erosion, then later partly refilled by renewed volcanic eruptions. Hawaii Institute of Geophysics photo by A. T. Abbott.

cide quite closely with former calderas of strictly volcanic origin. On West Maui Volcano, Hawaii, the Iao Valley has cut deeply into the center of the shield volcano. Its walls approximate the boundaries of a former caldera 2 miles across, which later was completely filled by lavas. The present depression is wholly the result of erosion. On the neighboring island of Molokai, also, a filled caldera 4 miles long and 1½ miles across has been reexcavated by stream erosion (Plate 12-9). On nearby Oahu the filled calderas of both the major shield volcanoes that built the island have been deeply eroded. The spectacular cliff of the Nuuanu Pali on the northeastern side of Oahu in its central part follows closely the former caldera boundary (Fig. 12-15). The lava flows that filled the West Maui, East Molokai, and Koolau (Oahu) calderas were extensively altered by gases and hot hydrous solutions, and the resultant softening of the rocks has greatly speeded their erosion. The alteration is nearly restricted to the area of the caldera, however, and the more resistant unaltered rocks outside the caldera stand up in high relief. Similar alteration may have aided the scooping out of the center of Haleakala Volcano.

In contrast, the lavas that filled the caldera of Kauai Volcano, also in Hawaii, have suffered little or no alteration. The thick, massive beds that formed as a result of pooling of lava flows within the caldera are more resistant to weathering and erosion than are the thinner and more vesicular beds that formed the flanks of the volcano outside the caldera; consequently, the caldera fill stands up as a great central mass capped by a poorly drained plateau. Similar erosion-resistant caldera fills appear to account for the steep-sided central massifs of eroded volcanoes in the Marquesas Islands and elsewhere.

Erosional calderas have been described in other parts of the world as well as in Hawaii. Williams (1941, p. 308) considers that the central depression of the main cone of Tahiti, 4 miles in diameter with precipitous walls as much as 5,000 feet high, was formed by stream erosion. The Lyttelton and Akaroa Volcanoes, which make up the Banks Peninsula in New Zealand, have central depressions 6 to 7 miles across, 11 miles long, and as much as 2,000 feet deep, which Speight (1917) believes were formed

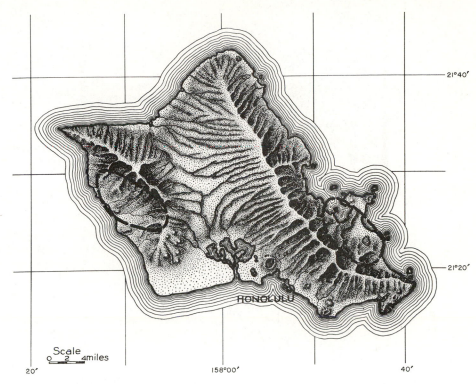

FIGURE 12-15. Relief map of the Island of Oahu, Hawaii. The heavy dashed lines show the approximate boundaries of the filled calderas of the Waianae (western) and Koolau (eastern) Volcanoes. (Modified after Stearns, 1939.)

by stream erosion. The caldera of Hakone Volcano in Japan originated by collapse, but has been considerably enlarged by stream erosion (Kuno et al., 1969).

Surprisingly, there is still great disagreement on the origin of the depression for which the term *caldera* was first introduced into geologic literature. The word "caldera" is used by natives of the Canary Islands for any large bowl-shaped or cauldron-shaped topographic depression, and is applied by them in that sense to the amphitheater-shaped heads of many large valleys. One of them, the Taburiente Caldera on La Palma Island, is about 3 miles across and is drained southwestward by a deep valley (Fig. 12-16). A similar but less conspicuous amphitheater lies just to the south. In his pioneer study of the island, von Buch (1818) believed the Taburiente Caldera to be a rent in the summit of a "crater of elevation" torn open by the distension of the up-bowed volcanic beds. Later it was attributed by Lyell (1855, p. 498–508) and Scrope (1862, p. 201, 421) to explosion, though they recognized that erosion also had played a part in its formation. Friedlaender (1915) considered the Caldera to have been formed by collapse, though he too recognized that it had been much

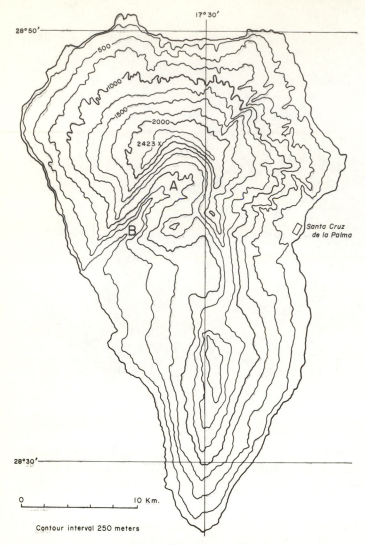

FIGURE 12-16. Topographic map of the Island of La Palma, Canary Islands, showing (A) the Taburiente Caldera, and (B) the baranco (valley) leading out of it. (After Bravo, in Neuman van Padang, and others, 1967.)

modified by erosion. The great importance of erosion in sculpturing the depression is now generally accepted, but there is still no agreement on the part played by other processes. Only von Buch's rent hypothesis seems to have been wholly abandoned! Bravo (in Neumann van Padang, et al., 1967, p. 57) considers it to be an eroded explosion crater, whereas Machado (1965, p. 61) believes it to be an eroded depression formed originally by collapse. Krejci-Graf (1964, p. 424) mentions neither explosion nor collapse but points to the decomposed character of the underlying rocks as contributing to the formation of an "erosion cirque." Obviously, the type Caldera still needs further study.

SUGGESTED ADDITIONAL READING

Anderson, 1941; Bemmelen, 1929, 1949, p. 210–212; Kingsley, 1931; McCall, 1963; Noll, 1967; Oftedahl, 1953, 1960; Reynolds, 1956; Smith and Bailey, 1968; Wentworth and Macdonald, 1953; Westerveld, 1952; Williams, 1941, 1942, 1960; Williams and Meyer-Abich, 1955; Yokoyama, 1963, 1969.

13

Fumaroles, Hot Springs, Geysers and Geothermal Power

Vents from which volcanic gases (fumes) issue at the surface, exclusive of true eruptive vents, are *fumaroles*. Such gas vents are associated with most active and dormant volcanoes and commonly persist for thousands of years after the volcano has become extinct. The major exception is at highly permeable volcanic structures, the bases of which are saturated with water. Thus, on the Hawaiian shield volcanoes, fumarole activity is sparse even when the volcano is active; and during dormancy, as well as after extinction, it is wholly absent. Probably the gases rising from the magma body at depth are cooled and condensed, or dissolved, in the thick water-saturated zone they must traverse to reach the surface. Lack of fumarolic activity is no guarantee that the volcano will not again become active. On the other hand, eruptions of volcanoes are sometimes heralded by the appearance of new fumaroles, increase in strength or temperature of existing ones, or change in the composition of the gases being given off.

Fumaroles may be situated within the crater of the volcano, on the outer flanks of the cone, or in the region surrounding the base of the cone. Thus, like eruptive vents, they may be terminal, lateral, or excentric. Commonly, groups of fumaroles are aligned along either concentric or radial fissures.

There is no essential difference between the long-continued quiet emission of gas that takes place at some vents of active volcanoes and high-temperature fumarolic activity. Conventionally, however, the former is not referred to as fumarolic.

Fumarole gases are nearly always predominantly water. The second most common constituent is carbon dioxide (CO_2) followed by sulfur gases and hydrochloric acid (HCl). Carbon monoxide (CO), hydrofluoric acid (HF), boric acid (H_3BO_3), carbonyl sulfide (COS), ammonia (NH_3), sulfocyanic acid (HCNS), free hydrogen, and nonreactive gases, such as argon, are often present in smaller amounts. The compositions of some typical fumarole gases are given in Table 13-1.

Where halogen gases (Cl and F) are present, we often find the

TABLE 13-1.   Compositions of some fumarole gases.[a]

Active gases	1	2	3	4	5	6	7	8	9	10
CO_2	65.0	91.7	59.9	—	—	59.6	96.	73.	100.	96.2
CO	—	—	3.0	28.	—	0.3	—	—	—	1.7
CH_4	0.08	0.15	—	—	—	0.2	0.1	—	—	0.4
NH_3	0.06	0.003	—	—	—	—	—	—	—	—
H_2	25.0	4.45	5.3	26.	—	(?)	0.3	—	—	—
HCl	5.39	1.76	1.1	46.	68.	—	—	25.	—	—
HF	2.76	0.53	—	—	23.	—	—	—	—	—
H_2S	0.10	1.02	—	—	9.	40.0	3.	—	—	—
S	—	—	—	—	—	—	—	—	—	—
SO_2	1.66	0.42	31.5	—	—	—	—	2.	—	1.6
SO_3	—	—	—	—	—	—	—	—	—	—
Temp., °C	750°	300°	280°	148°	350°	255°	89°	129°	75°	97°
% H_2O in sample	99.25	99.07	—	—	99.87	99.96	98.7	95.±	—	—

[a] The sum of the "active" gases is recalculated to 100 per cent by volume. Data from White and Waring, 1963, p. 14–19.

1. Fumarole A-1, Showa-shinzan, Usu Volcano, Japan.
2. Fumarole B-46, Showa-shinzan, Usu Volcano, Japan.
3. Central 1 fumarole, Sheveluch Volcano, Kamchatka.
4. Fumarole B-2, Biliukai Crater, Klyuchevskaya Volcano, Kamchatka.
5. Fumarole S-20, Valley of Ten Thousand Smokes, Alaska.
6. Fumarole 29-G, Valley of Ten Thousand Smokes, Alaska.
7. Fumarole D, Mount Hood, Oregon.
8. Fumarole near Lot's Wife, White Island, New Zealand.
9. Fumarole Prêcheur, Mont Pelée, Martinique.
10. Well at Sulphur Bank solfatara, Kilauea Volcano, Hawaii.

deposition around the fumaroles of chlorides of various constituents brought up by the gases or derived from the alteration of the surrounding rocks. The commonest are ammonium, aluminum, and ferric chloride, the first two forming bright white, and the last brilliant orange, incrustations. Sulfates also are common and include anhydrite ($CaSO_4$), gypsum ($CaSO_4 \cdot H_2O$), alunite ($K_2SO_4 \cdot Al_2(SO_4)_3$), alum ($KAl(SO_4)_2 \cdot 12H_2O$), and epsom salt ($MgSO_4 \cdot 7H_2O$). Hydrogen sulfide ($H_2S$) rising from depth is oxidized at the surface to sulfur dioxide (SO_2) or to native sulfur that often forms masses of beautiful delicate needle-like crystals ("flowers of sulfur"). Minor amounts of metallic minerals may also be formed, including chlorides, sulfates, or oxides of iron, copper, lead, zinc, arsenic, antimony, and mercury (Zies, 1929). Gold-bearing veins near Rodalquilar in southeastern Spain are thought by DeRoever and Lodder (1967) to be fumarolic deposits in ignimbrites. Water may combine with ferric chloride to give soluble hydrochloric acid and insoluble ferric oxide (Fe_2O_3) that is deposited on the walls of the vent as a lining of tiny brilliant steel-gray to black plates of specular hematite.

Around fumaroles the rocks are attacked by the acid gases and condensates. In addition to the acids already mentioned, SO_2 and SO_3 combine with water to give sulfurous and sulfuric acids (H_2SO_3 and H_2SO_4). The silicate minerals in the rocks are broken down, and the metallic elements and alkalies are partly or wholly removed in solution. The common products left behind are opal (silica plus water), clay minerals, and hydrated iron oxides, sometimes with lesser amounts of alum, alunite, and sulfur. At Kilauea Volcano it has been found that the products of rock decomposition vary with rather small changes in the acidity of the altering solutions. When the acidity is marked though still low (pH 3±), the iron is removed with the other bases and the residue is a white to cream-colored rock composed almost wholly of opal and clay (kaolinite). The structures of the rock and its component minerals are almost perfectly preserved during the alteration. The rock has the same vesicular appearance as the fresh lava, and under the microscope not only the outlines but also the cleavages and fractures of the original minerals are perfectly preserved. In fact, in casual microscopic observation with ordinary light the altered material can easily be taken for the fresh rock, though when the polarizing prisms of the petrographic microscope are crossed, the total darkness of the field emphasizes the fact that all that is left is a pseudomorph of opal replacing the original rock minerals. With slightly less acidity of the altering solutions (pH 5–6), the silica is removed and the residue is a red to brown mixture of limonite ($Fe_2O_3 \cdot nH_2O$) and clay minerals that closely resembles the lateritic soils produced by ordinary tropical weathering. Alterations similar to those at Kilauea are common in other fumarole areas, as for example in Lassen National Park (Plates 13-1, and 13-2) and at Sulphur Bank in California. At some places the removal of other things has been so complete that there is left only a spongy mass of opal.

Around some fumaroles, deposition of secondary minerals in the rocks

PLATE 13-1. Bumpass Hell, a solfatara in Lassen Volcanic National Park, California. The white color of the rocks is the result of alteration by rising volcanic gases and hot water. U. S. Geological Survey photo by G. A. Macdonald.

PLATE 13-2. Steaming pools in Bumpass Hell, Lassen Volcanic National Park, California. U. S. Geological Survey photo by G. A. Macdonald.

(often tuff) has made them more resistant to erosion than the surrounding less cemented rocks. Where erosion has worn away part of the rocks, the cemented cylinders around the fumarole channels may stand up in relief as irregular columns. Such columns are conspicuous along the sides of Annie and Sand Canyons at Crater Lake in Oregon.

On Mt. Erebus and other less well known volcanoes in Antarctica water-rich fumarole gases have been frozen around the vents to form towers of ice as much as 60 feet high (LeMasurier and Wade, 1968).

Fumarolic deposits have sometimes been mined, particularly for sulfur and alum. Sulfur formerly was mined in the craters of Vulcano in Italy and Popocatepetl in Mexico, among other places. At both, the mining was brought to an end by volcanic eruptions that destroyed the mine workings but, fortunately, took no lives. Miners in the crater of White Island Volcano, New Zealand, were less fortunate. In 1914 a landslide from the crater wall blocked the vents of large fumaroles. Steam explosions cleared the vents and caused a hot mudflow which moved across the crater floor, destroying the processing plant and killing 11 men (Hamilton and Baumgart, 1959). Mining of volcanic sulfur has now largely been brought to an end by the much cheaper production of sulfur from nonvolcanic sources, as in the Gulf Coast region of the United States.

Fumarole gases come from two different sources: (1) magmas that are giving off gases at depth and igneous rocks that, although largely or entirely solidified, are still losing gas; and (2) from the heating of groundwater, either by direct contact with hot igneous rocks or by mixing with rising superheated gases. As they issue from the vent, they generally also contain a considerable proportion of admixed air. Probably some steam from heated groundwater is nearly always present, and sometimes the gases may be largely or even wholly of groundwater origin. The proportions from the two sources are very difficult to determine. Where sulfur and halogen gases are present, they are probably magmatic, though even sulfur may be derived from nonvolcanic sources such as sulfate minerals. Most problematical of all is the predominant water. It is generally believed that the heavy isotope of hydrogen (deuterium) is more abundant in surface water than in magmatic gases, and if further research confirms this, we may eventually have a means of ascertaining the proportion of magmatic water in fumarole gases. Heavy sulfur (^{34}S) seems to be more abundant in magmatic sulfur than in that from other sources. Heavy argon (^{40}Ar) has been found to be more abundant in some fumarole gases, such as those at Larderello in Tuscany, than it is in the atmosphere.

Some fumaroles have no connection with deep sources and derive their gases wholly from the lava flow or ash flow on which they occur. Again, the gases of these "rootless" fumaroles are of two origins. Some of the gas comes from the cooling rock itself, but some of it is from rain or stream water that finds entrance into the hot center of the flow. Thus, it has been shown that the gas of the fumaroles in the Valley of Ten Thousand Smokes, Alaska, was more than 90 per cent water from surface streams that seeped into the ash flow (Allen and Zies, 1923). Rootless fumaroles are always short lived. Some last only a few hours or days, and none last more than a few decades. Those of the Valley of Ten Thousand Smokes have now mostly disappeared. The ones that remain are restricted to the area of the vents from which the ash flow issued and are probably fed from deep sources.

In contrast to the short life of rootless fumaroles, deep-seated ones may continue active for thousands of years. There appears to have been little change in the fumaroles of the Solfatara Crater (the ancient "Forum Vulcani") in the Phlegraean Fields north of Naples since Roman times.

Fumaroles are classified on the basis of both temperature and composition of the escaping gases. In a general way, those at a greater distance from the eruptive center have a lower temperature than those close to it (though many exceptions can be found), and the temperature decreases with the passage of time. Fumarole temperatures range from close to 1000°C to less than 100°C. High-temperature fumaroles contain relatively larger proportions of HCl, HF, CO, COS, and free hydrogen; those of lower temperature (less than about 650°C) contain less of these gases and a relatively greater proportion of sulfur gases. However, in all of them by far the most abundant constituent is superheated water (steam). Fumaroles in which sulfur gases are the dominant constituent after water are known as *solfataras*.

In areas where there is a superabundance of water, fumarole temperatures are generally only a degree or so above the boiling temperature of water at the altitude of the fumarole vent, and they may be a little below it. C. Sommaruga (quoted by Rittmann, 1962, p. 9) has demonstrated this relationship of temperature to the altitude of the fumarole vent in Table 13-2.

TABLE 13-2

Place	Altitude of vent (feet above sea level)	Boiling temp. at vent (°C)	Temperature of gases (°C)
Phlegraean Fields, Italy	0	100	101
Ischia, Italy	0	100	101
Forgia Vecchia, Vulcano, Italy	925	99	99.5
Izalco, El Salvador	3,630	96.3	97
Soufrière, Guadeloupe, Antilles	4,850	95	96
Vulcarolo, Etna, Italy	9,900	89.8	91

Fumaroles with temperatures much below the boiling point of water, and sometimes nearly as low as that of the surrounding air, are generally rich in CO_2 and have received the special name of *mofettes*. When topographic and wind conditions are right, the CO_2 may accumulate in hollows (because it is denser than air) or even in small valleys. Animals and birds wandering into such pools of CO_2 may die from lack of air. A "death gulch" of this sort was found by early geological explorers in the Absaroka Range near Yellowstone National Park. Although the wind was in such a direction as to clear out the CO_2 when the men entered the gulch, the bodies of several grizzly bears indicated the deadly potential of the place. Similarly, during the 1947–1948 eruption of Hekla in Iceland, CO_2 accumulated in hollows near the base of the volcano. Sheep pastured in the hollows drowned, but the heads of men accompanying them were above the level of the rim of the basin and the men suffered no ill effects. Some investigation was necessary to detect the reason for the death of the sheep. Flows of CO_2 gas have been described in gulches on the flanks of Tankuban Prahu in Java.

Another interesting phenomenon should be mentioned. It is common knowledge in fumarole areas that bringing a flame, or even a glowing cigar or cigarette, close to the windward side of a fumarole vent often causes a spectacular increase in the amount of visible vapor. The famous American volcanologist, Henry S. Washington, once commented, "No volcanologist should ever be without a cigar!" It was a precept he did his best to follow! Drivers of tour cars at Kilauea produce the same result by stopping the car just to windward of the vent and racing the engine, allowing the exhaust to drift over the fumarole. The increase of vapor is, of course, only apparent. Invisible steam becomes condensed into tiny droplets around nuclei and then becomes visible. The nuclei are partly tiny smoke particles, but they are also ions produced by ionization of the air by the heat of the flame or glowing ash. Electrical sparks will also cause ionization of the air with the same increase in visibility of the vapor.

Hot Springs

Space permits here only a very brief treatment of the big subject of hot, or thermal, springs. They may be defined as springs that issue at temperatures appreciably above the average temperature of the air in the particular region. Not all hot springs are volcanic. Some are far removed from any visible or likely occurrences of volcanic rocks and appear to owe their temperature to deep circulation of the water that brings it into the lower parts of the earth's crust, where the temperature of the rocks is high because of the normal temperature gradient of the earth. However, hot springs are very common in volcanic regions.

Volcanic hot springs owe their temperature to the same causes as do fumaroles. Indeed, the two phenomena are often closely associated. Just as with fumaroles, it is as yet generally impossible to say with certainty how much of the water is ordinary groundwater and how much is of magmatic origin. Undoubtedly, in most instances groundwater greatly predominates. In Iceland, for instance, there appears to be no addition of volcanic volatiles to most of the hot water (Bodvarsson, 1960), and the heating must be almost wholly the result of contact of the circulating water with hot rocks. The dependence on groundwater is shown by the fact that volcanic hot springs are almost absent in desert regions. It is shown also by the fact that in Hawaii, where groundwater is very abundant, in spite of the presence of volcanic heat hot springs are few and of low temperature. Instead of a small amount of water being heated to high temperature, a larger amount is heated to a lesser degree.

There is a considerable variation in the composition of the waters of volcanic hot springs, depending partly on the nature and abundance of volcanic emanations mixed with the groundwater, and partly on the composition and solubility of the rocks the water has passed through. Some hot springs are acid because of admixed acid volcanic gases. Some are slightly alkaline, presumably because of neutralization of the acid by reaction with the rocks and dissolving of some of the alteration products.

In Yellowstone National Park the smaller and hotter springs tend to be acid, and the larger and cooler ones alkaline, apparently because of a larger proportion of volcanic emanations in the springs with smaller ground-water supplies. Many volcanic hot springs give off hydrogen sulfide. The methane sometimes found is probably of organic, not volcanic, origin. Table 13-3 gives some typical compositions of volcanic hot-spring waters.

TABLE 13-3. **Analyses of hot spring waters, in parts per million** (*From White, 1957*)

	1	2	3	4	5	6
Type of water	Sodium chloride	Sodium chloride	Acid sulfate chloride	Acid sulfate	Sodium bicarbonate	Calcium bicarbonate
Temperature of water °C	89.2	84	59	70	100	70.5
pH	7.9	7.45	3.0	2.2	6.7	6.9
SiO_2	293	529	428	364	191	56
Fe	—	—	3	2.9	—	—
Al	—	—	4	1.6	—	—
Ca	5.0	5.8	17	2.6	12	209
Mg	0.8	0.2	4	1.0	1.7	78
Sr	0.1	—	—	—	—	—
Na	653	439	607	27	230	129
K	71	74	70	24	17	56
Li	7.6	8.4	—	0.1	1.2	1.4
NH_4	1	0.1	—	10	0.24	—
As	2.7	3.1	—	—	—	—
Sb	0.4	0.1	—	—	—	—
CO_3	0	0	—	—	—	—
HCO_3	305	27	0	0	670	526
SO_4	100	38	262	482	11	529
Cl	865	744	953	6.0	2.7	169
F	1.8	4.9	—	—	3.7	—
Br	0.2	0.1	—	—	—	—
I	0.1	0.1	—	—	—	—
B	49	11.5	14	1.5	0.5	4.4
H_2S	4.7	0	0	—	0	2.4
CO_2	—	—	—	—	0	—
Total	2359	1885	2362	922.7	1141.04	1760.2

1. Spring 8, Steamboat Springs, Nevada.
2. Spring 200 feet southwest of Pearl Geyser, Norris Basin, Yellowstone.
3. Frying Pan Lake, New Zealand.
4. Acid pool, Norris Basin, Yellowstone.
5. Well 5, Wairakei, New Zealand.
6. Blue Spring, Mammoth Hot Springs, Yellowstone.

PLATE 13-3. Boiling mudpot in Bumpass Hell, Lassen Volcanic National Park, California. The bursting bubble is approximately 14 inches across. Photo by G. A. Macdonald.

Some hot springs contain appreciable quantities of radioactive substances, such as radon, probably derived from volcanic emanations. Such radioactive springs are among the most popular health resorts in some parts of the world. An outstanding example is the island of Ischia near Naples, Italy. It seems a paradox that in this age when so many people fear an increase of radioactivity in the atmosphere as a result of atomic explosions, people still flock to these springs to expose themselves to the presumed beneficial effects of radiation!

Rock alteration around hot springs resembles that around fumaroles. The rocks are commonly altered to clay, with deposition of such things as alunite, iron oxide, and iron sulfide (pyrite or marcasite), the latter often as a fine black powder. The spring often consists of a pool of moderately viscous mud formed of fine clay with various mixtures of iron oxide, iron sulfides, and other substances, giving it colors ranging from white and cream colored to gray, yellow, brown, red, or green. These "paint pots" commonly are boiling (Plate 13-3), and even when their temperature is lower than the boiling point, their surfaces may be constantly disturbed by bursting bubbles of gas. Such boiling mud pools are well seen, for instance, in Yellowstone and Lassen National Parks (e.g., Bumpass' Hell). The "Frog Pond" in the Rotorua region of New Zealand is so called because the repeated small jets of mud thrown up from the surface of the pool are reminiscent of jumping frogs. Spattering of the mud often builds around the pool a low conical rim known as a "mud crater," or "mud volcano" (Plates 13-4 and 13-5), though these also are formed by springs that have no relationship to volcanoes or volcanic heat.

Hot springs containing considerable dissolved silica may deposit it to form *siliceous sinter*. The deposition may occur within the spring itself or around the spring where the water overflows. The latter deposits may build a mound, sometimes several feet high, with the spring at its top. Springs containing dissolved calcium carbonate commonly deposit it to form *calcareous tufa*. In this case, the deposition is greatly aided by escape of dissolved CO_2 reducing the concentration of carbonic acid in the water. Deposition within the spring often coats various objects, such as twigs, with calcium carbonate. In central France it is a common practice to place

PLATE 13-4. Mud volcano, 5 feet high, in the crater of Solfatara, Phlegrean Fields, Italy, formed by spattering of boiling mud in a hot spring. Hawaii Institute of Geophysics photo by G. A. Macdonald.

PLATE 13-5. Mud volcano, about 3 feet high, in Bumpass Hell, Lassen Volcanic National Park, in 1926. Photo by R. H. Finch.

religious medals and other objects in the springs to be encrusted with calcium carbonate. (These objects are then said to be "petrified," although the result is quite different from the replacement of material that takes place in true petrifaction.) Overflow of the springs may build mounds, spires, or stepped terraces of calcareous tufa. Excellent examples of this are to be seen at Mammoth Hot Springs in Yellowstone National Park. The finest of all were the gorgeous pink and white terraces of the Rotorua region, New Zealand, destroyed by the eruption of Tarawera in 1886.

Geysers

Great Geyser in Iceland is a hot spring that, in the 1770s, every half hour threw a jet of hot water and steam as much as 200 feet into the air. There are many other similar spouting hot springs, or geysers, in the same region, and the name *geyser* has been extended to periodically spouting hot springs all over the world. Geysers are essentially ground-water phenomena that derive their heat in the same way as other hot springs. Many of them are closely associated with volcanoes or young volcanic rocks. The principal geyser areas of the world are central Iceland (30 geysers), the central part of North Island of New Zealand (22 geysers), and Yellowstone National Park (200 geysers). The numbers are approximate and constantly changing as some geysers become inactive and new ones appear. Individual geysers or small groups of geysers are known at many other places. The Beowawe Geyser in western Nevada is an example. In the Steamboat Springs area of Nevada, 21 different geysers were observed in eruption during the years 1945–1952 (White, 1967). Many of them were short lived, and most eruptions were only a few feet in height; but in 1924 and 1925 one geyser erupted to 25 feet, and in the 1860s eruptions of more than 50 feet were reported (by Dan DeQuille). Other examples are in Indonesia and nearby islands, Japan, Kamchatka, and the Aleutian Islands. Rittmann (1962, p. 4) reports one in the crater of the extinct volcano Socompa in Chile at a height of more than 18,000 feet above sea level.

Artificial geysers have been created by drilling wells, generally in attempts to obtain natural steam. Left open, these may spout rhythmically just as do natural geysers. The "Old Faithful" geyser at Calistoga, California, is an artificial geyser (spouting boiling well) of this sort, commonly kept shut in, and nearby wells once behaved in a similar manner (Allen and Day, 1927, p. 98). Farther north, the region known as The Geysers now contains only hot springs and artificial steam wells, though small geysers may have been present when the area was first explored.

Some geysers throw water only a few inches into the air; others throw it tens or hundreds of feet. The greatest geyser on record was Waimangu ("Bird Water") in New Zealand, which during its short life from 1899 to 1904 periodically threw a great column of steam, muddy water, and rock fragments to a height of 1,500 feet. The interval between eruptions of a single geyser ranges from a few minutes to many months. Some geysers are quite regular in their period, others very irregular. Probably the best known example of a regular geyser is Old Faithful in Yellowstone National Park. For many years Old Faithful has erupted on an average of about once in 65 minutes, but the actual intervals between eruptions range from about 35 to 90 minutes. Generally, the time between successive eruptions of a geyser gradually increases. The period of Great Geyser in Iceland increased from about 30 minutes in 1772 to 20 days in 1883.

Geysers are short-lived phenomena. Many have become inactive in the short span of historic time. In some cases the cause of death is external. Waimangu became inactive as a result of the lowering of the groundwater level when destruction of a natural dam caused the lowering of the surface of the neighboring Lake Rotomahana. The great Montana earthquake of 1959 caused the death of several Yellowstone geysers by disrupting their feeding channels; but it also caused the appearance of new ones. Many geysers cease to exist because of internal changes in their feeding channels, as a result of clogging by collapses of their walls, or by deposition of opal.

Some geyser waters contain volcanic gases, though apparently never in an amount more than 5 per cent by weight, and others appear to contain none. Most geyser waters are alkaline, but some are acid. Most are clear, but some are muddy.

Geysers commonly deposit siliceous sinter, forming sometimes broad gently sloping mounds around the vent and sometimes steep-sided cones that may have a rounded shape resembling that of an old-fashioned beehive. Beehive Geyser in Yellowstone National Park is an example of the latter. The sinter is sometimes called geyserite. Some geyser cones reach heights as great as 10 feet.

Geysers vary a great deal in the details of their behavior. One of the common patterns consists in a slow rise of the water surface in the vent until the water finally overflows. This is soon followed by the beginning of an explosive ejection of water and steam that increases to a climax within a few seconds or minutes and then quickly declines. The upper part of the conduit is left empty, but gradually refills. Old Faithful in Yellowstone Park shows this general pattern.

Many hypotheses have been proposed to explain geyser action. Probably the best known is that put forward by Bunsen, about 1880, to explain the general pattern of behavior described above. According to him, a tube-like opening is filled with water nearly to the level of the ground surface. The lower part of the column is heated by rising volcanic gases or by contact with hot rocks. The temperature of the water at the bottom of the column rises above the boiling point appropriate to the altitude of the vent, but the water is prevented from boiling by the additional pressure resulting from the weight of the overlying column of water. Eventually the temperature of the water in the bottom of the tube reaches the boiling point even under the high pressure, and a few bubbles of gas form in the water causing a slight expansion of the heated water column, which in turn lifts its top sufficiently for it to overflow. The reduction in pressure at the bottom of the column due to the loss of some water from the top allows the water at low levels to boil, and the expansion of the steam pushes still more water out at the top with still greater reduction of pressure at low levels. The whole heated lower part of the column then quickly transforms into steam in a sort of chain reaction, and the mixture of steam and hot water is ejected in the climactic eruption. The ejection of water is followed by a period of steam emission. The hole then refills with water, and the cycle is repeated. The length of time between eruptions is governed by the rapidity with which the hole is refilled with water and the lower part again heated to the requisite temperature.

The eruption of a geyser can sometimes be hastened by putting soap or detergent into the pool of water in the vent, inducing frothing and lowering the surface tension of the water. However, "soaping" of the geysers is strictly forbidden in Yellowstone National Park and some other geyser areas.

Th. Thorkelsson, in studying the geysers of Iceland, found that Bunsen's explanation could not be entirely correct for all geysers, because the temperature of the water at the depth where the eruption begins does not reach the boiling point at the pressure corresponding to the weight of the overlying column of water. He attributed the reduction in pressure that brings about the boiling at depth to the introduction of volcanic gases into the water column, the expansion of the water-saturated gas bubbles near the surface producing a frothing, which in turn results in overflow with reduction of pressure at depth. The rest of the mechanism is much like that suggested by Bunsen. The importance of gas bubbles in bringing about geyser eruption is supported by Barth (1950). His graphic description of the action of Uxahver Geyser in northern Iceland is worth reading. "In the lulls between eruptions the water is clear and one can see far down into the spring. Just before a new eruption one will see something like a whitish cloud from great depths (about 5 meters) rapidly ascending. This is a swarm of tiny gas bubbles. As they rise they rapidly expand and, near the surface, become 2 to 5 cm in diameter. One must be careful not to become too absorbed in watching, though, for at this moment a new eruption starts, and the observer has to make a rapid retreat." However, although gases may be important in some geyser eruptions, they cannot be the general cause of them, because in most geyser waters they are present in far too small a proportion.

Exploratory drilling in geyser areas has shown that the geysers are part of a groundwater system with a convectional circulation that extends to great depths—at least a mile and probably more than two miles (White, 1967). In most instances the heating of the water cannot be caused by rising volcanic gases, since the amount of the latter in the water is far too small; furthermore, the temperature of the water does not continue to increase downward indefinitely, as it should if the heat were being brought up by gases rising from below. The maximum temperatures are reached at an intermediate depth and remain fairly constant below that. The ultimate source of heat is probably igneous intrusive masses at greater depth, but the immediate heating of the water appears to be by contact with hot wall rocks along the fissures through which the water is circulating. In the areas investigated by White, the temperature of the near-surface water is always at least as high as 150°C, and probably above 170°C (338°F). White's careful studies lead him to the conclusion that deep-circulating water is heated at depth to temperatures well above the boiling point at the surface, but because of the high pressure, does not boil. It rises beneath the geyser area because the density of the heated water is less than that of cold water. (Water at 250°C is 20 per cent lighter than water at 4°C.) As the water rises, the weight of overlying water decreases until finally boiling begins. (If dissolved gases are present, the level of boiling is somewhat deeper than with pure water.) Expansion of the boiling water causes

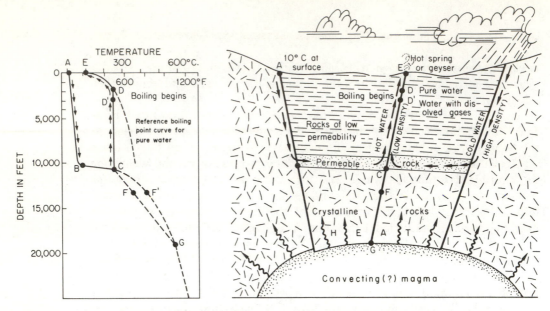

FIGURE 13-1. Diagrammatic representation of a hot spring and geyser system with deep convectional circulation of meteoric water. (From White, 1967.)

overflow at the surface, and this in turn further reduces the pressure at depth allowing a further increase in boiling, and so on until eruption results. The general structure of the system is shown in Fig. 13-1.

In recent years the period between eruptions of Old Faithful has varied from about 40 to 80 minutes, and the duration of the fountaining has ranged from 1.5 to 5 minutes. The eruption is not a single continuous jetting of water, but consists of a series of pulses or bursts. Longer eruptions are followed by longer intervals before the next eruption. Close observation has shown that during the longer intervals the previous eruption is followed by 20 to 30 minutes of complete quiet terminated by ground vibrations that continue until the next eruption. The vibrations are sometimes accompanied by audible booming noises. During the shorter intervals, the quiet period is lacking (Rinehart, 1965). Probing of the geyser tube with weighted thermistors (electrical thermometers) indicates that the tube is probably more than 575 feet deep and also has yielded information on temperature changes in the water at various depths (Rinehart, 1969). Following eruption, the geyser tube rapidly refills with water that quickly becomes superheated, but in the upper part of the tube the water again becomes cooler as the level of boiling gradually extends downward. Below about 200 feet, however, heating continues, and at the 300-foot depth the water reaches about 120°C just before the next eruption. Finally, the hot water from depth rises rapidly upward, bringing the upper part of the water column above boiling point and causing the eruption to begin. However, the temperature of the water in the deeper parts of the tube is still far below the boiling point, because of the pressure of the overlying water. (At a depth of 200 feet the boiling temperature is about 204°C, whereas the water temperature is only 120°C.) Ejection of the water in the uppermost part of the tube reduces the pressure on the water below it, resulting in ejection of that water, and so on, the stepwise lowering of the boiling level producing the series of pulses in the eruption (Rinehart, 1969).

Some geysers may consist of a single tube, as pictured by Bunsen, but the complications of geyser activity have led most investigators to visualize one or more subterranean chambers connected to the tube. Local enlargements of the tube itself by the tearing loose of wall-rock fragments by the outrushing steam must be present in many geysers. At least one ancient, now-dry geyser that has been explored consists of a series of opal-lined chambers interconnected by fissures. The structure suggested by Barth (1950) for Great Geyser is shown in Fig. 13-2.

It was earlier pointed out that the general behavior shown by such geysers as Old Faithful and Great Geyser is only one of various patterns. In some geysers the shallow part of the tube and even the surficial basin are not emptied during the eruption. Benseman (1965) has suggested a mechanism to explain the action of these *flooded geysers*. Essentially, it consists of two or more water-filled subterranean chambers connected in series to each other and to the geyser tube with overflow channels to regulate the water level (Fig. 13-3). When the water in the chamber nearest the vent (X, Fig. 13-3) becomes hot enough to generate steam, the fluid expands pushing some water out through the overflow system and reduc-

FIGURE 13-2. Diagram illustrating the hypothetical structure of Great Geyser, Iceland. (After Barth, 1950.)

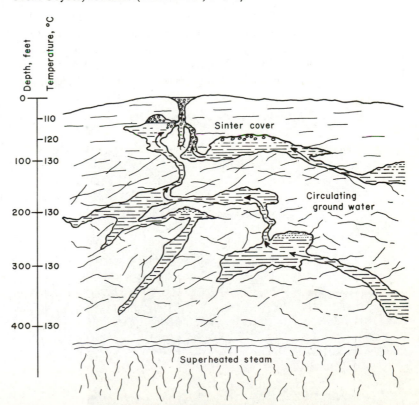

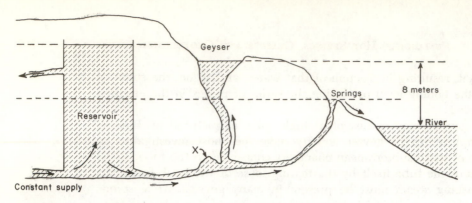

FIGURE 13-3. Diagram illustrating the hypothetical eruptive apparatus of Wainui Geyser, New Zealand. (After Benseman, 1965.)

ing the water pressure on the rest of the system. As a result, hot water flows rapidly from the second chamber into the first and on into the geyser tube, producing the eruption. Once the water level in the second chamber drops to a level where the flow through the geyser vent cannot be maintained, the eruption stops and the system gradually refills. The combination of circumstances required to produce the operating system are so special that it appears unlikely it can have any very general application.

Geothermal Power

Since time immemorial, hot-spring waters have been used for bathing, laundry, and cooking, but it is only in the last few decades that natural steam and hot water have been put to more sophisticated uses. During the nineteenth century, chemicals, particularly boric acid, were extracted from the gases (largely steam) in the Larderello area in Tuscany, northern Italy (Plate 13-6), and in 1904, M. Ginori Conti made the first

PLATE 13-6. Steam well in the Larderello area, Italy. Photo by Giorgio Marinelli, University of Pisa.

attempt to use the steam for the generation of electric power. At first the enterprise was fraught with great difficulties, the most serious being that the acid gases attacked and destroyed the metal parts of steam engines, and therefore the natural steam could not be used directly in the engines. Instead, it had to be used to heat pure water to steam, which was in turn used to run the generators. This, of course, entailed the loss of a great deal of heat. During the last 20 years, new alloys have been developed that withstand the acid gases, which can now be used directly in the turbines. The present generator installations at Larderello are capable of furnishing about 3 billion kilowatt hours of electricity per year, and at the same time the gases support an important chemical industry for the extraction of boric acid, carbon dioxide, ammonia, and helium. (Though helium was first identified in the lines of spectra from the sun, it was first found on earth at Larderello.) A new but thus far much smaller natural-steam development is now under way at Monte Amiata, also in Tuscany.

In Iceland, natural hot water was first used to heat dwellings and greenhouses near Reykjavík in 1925, and in 1928 the drilling of wells for hot water commenced. At present about one fourth of the total population of Iceland lives in houses heated by natural hot water. Heating of Reykjavík with natural steam results in the city being wholly free of the smoke that once plagued it, as it does many other cities. Use of the steam from high-pressure wells to generate electricity is just beginning, with the completion in 1964 at Hveragerdi, near Reykjavík, of a power plant with a capacity of 15,000 kilowatts.

In California, at The Geysers, 75 miles north of San Francisco, wells were drilled to obtain steam for the generation of electricity as early as 1921, but the project was temporarily abandoned. It was revived in 1955 (Plate 13-7) and in June, 1960, a 12,500 kilowatt generating plant was in

PLATE 13-7. Blowing steam well at The Geysers, California, during an early stage of the development of the thermal area. Photo by G. A. Macdonald.

operation, with additional units planned for early construction. Some difficulty is being encountered, however, with rapid corrosion of the pipes that lead the steam from the wells to the generators. The Geysers is the only thermal area except Larderello that produces dry steam. In all the others the steam reaching the surface is accompanied by varying amounts of hot water. Other thermal areas being developed in California include Casa Diablo, just east of the Sierra Nevada about 40 miles northwest of Bishop, and the Salton Sea area, 3 miles southeast of Niland. Wells in the latter area also produce carbon dioxide and brine from which potash and other chemicals may be commercially recoverable.

At Wairakei on North Island of New Zealand natural steam from drilled wells during 1963 was producing about 200,000 kilowatts of electricity (Evrard, 1964), and the operation was still being expanded. In all these areas, electricity is produced by natural steam power at much less cost than it could be by the use of fuels to heat water to steam to drive generators. Consequently, there is great interest in finding natural steam in other areas, particularly those lacking in hydroelectric potentials and cheap natural fuels. Development of natural steam is in various preliminary stages in Mexico, El Salvador, Japan, Indonesia, Chile, and other areas.

Individual steam wells probably will usually be relatively short lived. The rising steam and hot water deposit silica and calcium carbonate, and sometimes other things, in the well and gradually clog it. Many wells will probably become unusable within 15 to 25 years, and new wells will have to be drilled to replace them. In contrast to individual wells, most projections indicate that the thermal areas will continue to yield large amounts of steam for several centuries.

Despite the wide extent of volcanic districts on earth (Chapter 15), the possibility of finding many regions where large amounts of electricity can be generated with natural steam is far less than might be supposed. Certain special conditions are necessary that are seldom encountered in volcanoes. The steam must have high pressure or must be heated appreciably above the boiling point, or both. The supply of water to be heated must be adequate to furnish large amounts of steam, but must not be excessive. Too great a supply of water results in heating of more water to a lower temperature, just as in Hawaii the very abundant groundwater results in a dearth of hot springs. Where heating depends on contact of water with hot rocks at depth, as is nearly always the case, if the circulation of water is too rapid, the transfer of heat to the water is faster than the flow of heat through the rock to the water-contact surface, and the contact surface is cooled down so much that the water-heating system soon ceases to function. (It is important in this connection to remember that rocks are very poor conductors of heat.) Accumulation of large amounts of steam under high pressure demands favorable geologic structure, just as does the economic accumulation of petroleum or natural hydrocarbon gas. A permeable, cavernous, or fissure-riven reservoir rock must exist in a suitable relationship to the water-circulation and heating systems. A tight cap rock also is advantageous, though it may not be absolutely necessary. In volcanoes sufficiently impermeable confining rocks and appropriate confining structures are seldom found; lacking them, any development of natural steam must depend on other, very special features. Appropriate structures are commoner in other types of rocks.

Thus far, none of the big natural-steam power developments are on volcanoes, and two of the three are in regions where recent volcanic rocks are absent at the surface. At Larderello the steam is accumulated in solution cavities in limestone, underlain by metamorphic schists cut by many fissures that serve as passageways for the steam, and overlain by tight impermeable clays (Fig. 13-4). The pressure of the steam reaches as much as 25 atmopheres, and the temperature reaches 230°C. On the island of Elba about 35 miles west of Larderello, and at other places near the west coast of Italy, there are exposed bodies of late Tertiary granitic rock (some 7 million or so years old), and presumably similar bodies underlie the Larderello region and are still yielding heat and gases to the circulating groundwater (Marinelli, 1963); but there are no volcanic rocks exposed within the region itself. At The Geysers, California, the steam rises along fault zones cutting sedimentary rocks and serpentine some 100 million years old. However, Tertiary volcanic rocks lie only a short distance to the southeast, and Pleistocene volcanoes probably less than 1

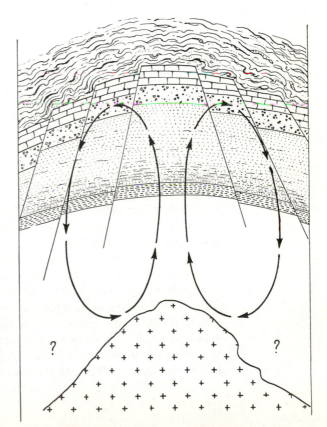

FIGURE 13-4. Diagram illustrating general conditions in a geothermal area such as Larderello. (From Marinelli, 1963.) A hot mass of igneous rock at depth heats deep-circulating ground water, setting up a convectional circulation. The rocks above the igneous body have been pushed up between faults forming a horst. Nearer the surface less brittle sedimentary rocks have suffered intense small-scale crumpling without faulting, and constitute a poorly permeable cap rock for the system.

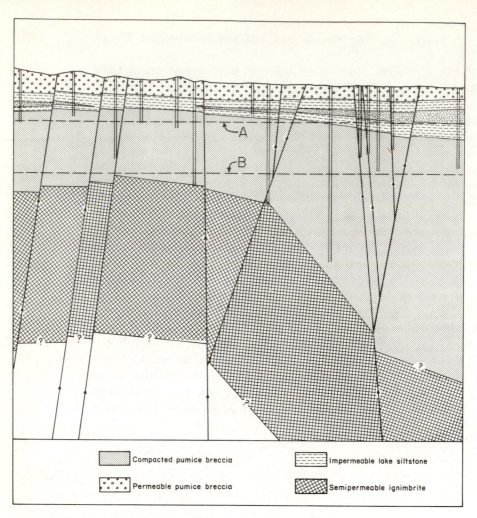

FIGURE 13-5. Simplified diagram showing the structure of the hydro-thermal field at Wairakei, New Zealand. (After Studt, 1958.)

million years old are found on the west side of Clear Lake, 10 miles to the north. No definite cap rock has been recognized at The Geysers, and Facca and Tonani (1967) have suggested that in such areas, where there is no apparent rock, the permeability of the rocks above the steam-producing zone may have been greatly reduced by deposition of silica and calcium carbonate and formation of clay by the rising steam and hot water. The latter thus produce their own seal.

At Wairakei water with temperature up to 265°C is encountered in an aquifer consisting of pumice breccia, with interbedded tuff and lacustrine sediments. The breccia is probably of glowing-avalance origin, the material having been reworked by wind and water and deposited at least partly in a lake. The aquifer is overlain by a series of lacustrine shales, mudstones, sandstones, and tuffs. The water is fed into the aquifer by faults cutting poorly permeable ignimbrites (Fig. 13-5). Another, similar aquifer occurs at greater depth. The bedded rocks, of Pleistocene age, are arched over a horst in the basement rocks. The source of the heat is believed to be a hypothetical underlying Pleistocene batholith (Grindley, 1965).

Thus, the best prospects of finding large amounts of high-pressure high-temperature steam appear to be in areas of deformed sedimentary rocks close to late Tertiary or younger volcanic rocks or intrusive bodies. Beyond that, no useful generalizations can be made. Each prospective region must be carefully investigated by geological and geophysical methods as well as by exploratory drilling.

The amount of energy available from natural steam is tiny as compared to the tremendous stores of heat energy in volcanoes. These latter stores of energy are as yet wholly unusable, but it is certainly not impossible that we will find a way to use them, by new types of heat exchangers, or by some other technique. Very large artificial blasts, possibly utilizing atomic explosives, may be used to shatter spherical or chimney-like bodies of hot rock into which water can then be introduced to generate steam. Removing the heat directly from the rocks, by means of heat exchangers or heat pumps without the intermediary water or other fluid, will encounter the disadvantage that the rocks in contact with the exchanger will cool down, and, because of the low thermal conductivity of rock, heat will not flow rapidly into them from the hotter rocks farther away. If an exchanger can be introduced directly into a reasonably large body of magma, this difficulty will be at least partly removed, because convection in the magma will constantly bring new hot material into contact with the exchanger. I fully expect that within the next century, and probably within the lifetime of many of my readers, we will have found the way!

SUGGESTED ADDITIONAL READING

Fumaroles

Allen and Zies, 1923; Deville, 1857; Naboko, 1959; White and Waring, 1963; Zies, 1924, 1929. See also extensive bibliography in White and Waring, 1963, p. 11–13.

Hot Springs and Geysers

Allen and Day, 1935; Barth, 1950; Benseman, 1965; Day, 1939; Day and Allen, 1925, p. 86–175; Grange, 1937, p. 86–128; Rinehart, 1969; White, 1955, 1957, 1967.

Volcanic Steam Power

Allen and Day, 1927; Benseman, 1959; Bodvarsson, 1960; Grindley, 1965; Keller and Valduga, 1946; Marinelli, 1963; McNitt, 1963; Studt, 1958.

14

Distribution and Geological Relationships of Volcanoes

Probably there is no part of the earth that has not been the scene of volcanic activity at some time in the past. Lava flows appear among the oldest known rocks and among rocks of all later ages. Today, however, volcanism is restricted to certain geographic areas and certain geologic environments; and there is no doubt that in the past also it was restricted to similar environments, the geographical location of which shifted with the gradual evolution of the earth's crust. The structural conditions that bring about the generation and rise of magma are determined by the geological processes that are continually modifying the earth's surface, heaving up folded or faulted mountain ranges, elevating the crust in broad arches where former folded mountains have been eroded away, or tearing open the crust in great rifts that may extend for hundreds or thousands of miles. Indeed, volcanism is an integral part of these events; and an understanding of volcanism, when we finally achieve it, will aid greatly in understanding the fundamental forces that bring them about.

GEOGRAPHICAL DISTRIBUTION

Today, a vast majority of active and recently extinct volcanoes are concentrated in a belt that encircles the Pacific Ocean and coincides in a general way with regions of recent mountain building. This "girdle of fire" extends from New Zealand northward through Melanesia into eastern Indonesia, the Philippines, Japan, and Kamchatka, eastward through the Aleutian Islands and southern Alaska, and southward along the western coast of the Americas to southern Chile (Fig. 14-1). Outliers in Antarctica complete the circle. To be sure, there are gaps in the line, such as that from Alaska to southern British Columbia, and northern California to Mexico, but these gaps are to a considerable extent more apparent than real and due largely to the short span of history in those areas. Volcanoes have been active in them in the not-distant past.

About 150 volcanoes have been active in British Columbia and Yukon during Pleistocene and Holocene (Recent) time. Most are cinder cones and associated basaltic lava flows resembling those of Paricutin and probably formed by single eruptions, but at least 20 are composite volcanoes formed by repeated eruptions ranging in composition from basalt through andesite and dacite to rhyolite. One of the latter, Mt. Edziza, consists of a basaltic shield formed during Pliocene time, overlain by a complex of andesite, dacite, and rhyolite domes formed during the Pleistocene, surrounded by about 30 very young basaltic cinder cones and associated lava fields. At least three eruptions of the latter have taken place during the last 1800 years (Souther, 1970). Farther south, the Aiyansh Volcano produced a cinder cone and a lava flow of alkalic basalt with an area of about 15 square miles and a volume of about 0.1 cubic mile only about 220 years ago (Sutherland Brown, 1969).

In the Mohave Desert of southeastern California several cinder cones and associated lava flows of alkalic basalt, including Mt. Pisgah and Amboy Crater, were formed during Pleistocene and Holocene time. Farther north, in Death Valley, the Ubehebe Craters also are very recent. In the northern end of the Owens Valley the Bishop ignimbrite was erupted only about 700,-000 years ago. Still later are the Mono Craters to the north and basaltic cinder cones and lava flows along the foot of the Sierra Nevada to the south. The basalt flow of Devil's Postpile, within the Sierra Nevada, is of Pleistocene age.

A very important spur of the circum-Pacific belt extends eastward through Indonesia in the region where the folded mountain ranges of southern Asia join the structures of the Pacific rim. The loop of volcanoes that extends through the Lesser Antilles, east of the Caribbean Sea, probably should be regarded as an eastern outlier of the circum-Pacific belt. The Scotia arc also is a loop of folded mountains swinging eastward into the Atlantic from Cape Horn and connecting with the Palmer Peninsula of Antarctica, with active volcanoes in the South Sandwich Islands at the eastern end of the arc and at least two active volcanoes close to the Palmer Peninsula. About three quarters of the earth's active volcanoes lie in the Pacific girdle as thus defined, and 14 per cent are in Indonesia alone.

Still other groups of active volcanoes lie in the Mediterranean region, northern Asia Minor, the vicinity of the Red Sea, and central Africa. Most of the latter are associated with the great Rift Valleys within which lie Lakes Victoria, Tanganyika, Albert, Edward, and Kivu. At the head of the Gulf of Guinea on Africa's west coast, Cameroon Mt. is one of a line of volcanoes that is continued offshore by Fernando Poo, Principe, São Tomé, and Annobón Islands. Beyond Lake Chad, 1300 miles inland but on the same alignment, is the Tibesti region with its recently extinct volcanoes. The classical volcanoes of the Mediterranean are mostly in Italy, west of the Apennine Mts.; but in the Cyclades Islands southeast of the peninsula of Greece lies Santorin (Thera) Volcano, a great eruption of which may have been largely responsible for the destruction of the Minoan civilization. Mt. Ararat, of Biblical fame, is one of the volcanoes of northern Asia Minor, but it does not appear to have erupted in historical times.

Only about 17 per cent of the known active volcanoes of the world lie within the true ocean basins; 83 per cent are continental. The locations of known submarine eruptions are shown in Fig. 14-1, as well as those of active island volcanoes. However, the proportion of known eruptions in the oceans to those on the continents is certainly misleadingly small. Many historic submarine eruptions, and even some eruptions above sea level on remote islands, must have escaped observation, and still more have gone unrecorded. Not only is the area of the ocean very large and the chance of a literate observer being in the right place at the right time very small, but eruptions at deep-ocean depths probably seldom produce recognizable disturbances at the surface. A great deal of volcanic activity has taken place in the ocean basins in the past. There is little question that the floors of the deep-ocean basins consist very largely of basaltic lava flows, and although some of them are probably moderately old, many are geologically young. Rittmann (1962) hazards the opinion that submarine volcanism has been at least equal to, and probably greater than, that of the continents, and I would suggest that it has probably been much greater.

About 1,000 islands are scattered within the Pacific Ocean basin, excluding the numerous islands around the edges that actually belong to the margins of the continents. Some of the islands consist of volcanic rock and are obviously volcanoes; some are still active, and others are in various stages of erosional dissection. Other islands consist of reef limestone and limy sand. It has long been believed that the latter islands are simply caps of limestone on volcanic pedestals, and this has now been confirmed by both seismic surveys and drilling. The limestone ranges from a few hundred to nearly 5,000 feet in thickness, but below it the mountain consists of basalt lava. All of the mid-ocean islands are primarily volcanic. However, only a small proportion of the volcanic mountains are high enough to emerge as islands. Menard (1964) estimates that the Pacific Basin contains about 10,000 seamounts more than 1,000 meters (3,300 feet) high but not high enough to reach the sea surface. In addition, there may be as many as 100,-000 *abyssal hills* less than 1,000 meters high. In form, the seamounts closely resemble subaerial shield volcanoes. They are broadly rounded with slopes ranging from about 25 to 5° merging into the surrounding ocean floor (Fig. 14-2). In plan, they range from nearly circular to ovoid or lobate (Fig. 14-3), again resembling the outlines of the island shield volcanoes. The summits of many, if not most, are indented by steep-walled craters 1,000 to

3,000 feet across and up to 600 feet deep. Some craters have flat floors probably formed by flooding with lava. There is little possible question that most, if not all, of them are in fact shield volcanoes. The abyssal hills are closely similar in form, and most of them also are almost certainly small shield volcanoes, though some may be up-domings of the ocean floor above shallow intrusive bodies (laccoliths). Indeed, relief maps of many parts of the ocean floor look amazingly like some land areas, such as parts of the

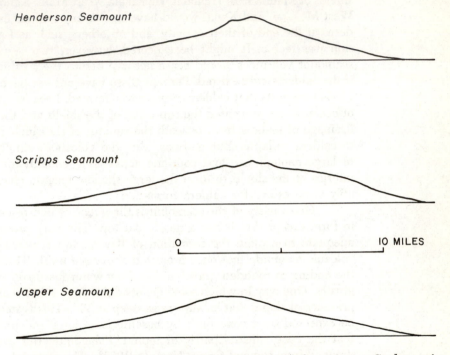

FIGURE 14-2. Profiles of typical seamounts. (After *Marine Geology of the Pacific,* by H. W. Menard. Copyright 1964 by McGraw-Hill, Inc. Used with permission of McGraw-Hill Book Company.)

FIGURE 14-3. Plans of three typical seamounts: (A) Gilbert Seamount; (B) seamount GA-5; (C) Henderson Seamount. (After *Marine Geology of the Pacific,* by H. W. Menard. Copyright 1964 by McGraw-Hill, Inc. Used with permission of McGraw-Hill Book Company.)

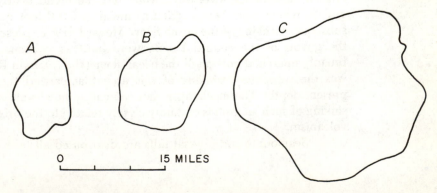

Modoc Plateau in northeastern California, that are made up of closely spaced small shield volcanoes.

One feature that has bothered some investigators is the apparent lack of calderas on the seamounts, like those found on the big island shield volcanoes such as Mauna Loa and Kilauea. Actually, most of the big sub-aerial shields of central Pacific islands had partly or entirely filled their calderas by the time they became inactive. In Hawaii, none of the great shields of Mauna Kea, Hualalai, Haleakala, West Maui, Kahoolawe, East and West Molokai, and Kauai would have shown any surface expression of calderas at the end of their activity, and on others, such as Lanai, the expression was feeble. It might be expected, however, that some of the 10,000 seamount volcanoes would cease activity before their calderas were filled, if the calderas ever existed. Perhaps these have not yet been found. Menard (1964) suggests that calderas were never formed, because the high pressure of ocean water prevented the rupturing of the shield and the resulting rapid drainage of magma from beneath the summit of the shield that would lead to caldera collapse. But perhaps, also, the volcanoes simply did not grow to large enough size and continue active long enough for melting of the interior of the shield to form the large shallow magma chamber that probably is necessary for caldera formation.

One variety of the seamount is the *guyot,* which resembles the others in form except that it has a nearly flat top. The only process that appears adequate to explain the formation of the flat top is wave truncation of a volcanic mountain that once projected above sea level. This is supported by the finding of rounded gravel and shallow-water fossils on the tops of some guyots. One way in which some guyots differ from other seamounts is in the presence of slopes that locally are as steep as 40°. This is steeper than would be expected on a cone built by basaltic lava flows and probably indicates that the cone consists partly of tephra. Palagonitic tuff actually has been dredged from some of them (Nayudu, 1962). The material may be partly or wholly hyaloclastite. If it is actually tephra of explosive origin, this would constitute further evidence that the volcano built into shallow water, since large-scale explosive activity would not be expected in deep-water eruptions. The occasional over-steep slopes might be accounted for also by up-doming of cones either of lava flows or of hyaloclastite by magma intruded into the interior of the cone, as suggested by Nayudu. But nothing except wave erosion close to sea level can account for the broad nearly flat tops of the guyots, which have been carried as much as 6,000 feet below sea level by subsequent sinking of the ocean floor. Menard (1964) presents evidence that the guyots of the central Pacific were built as volcanic mountains on a broadly uparched portion of the ocean floor (the "Darwin Rise"), and that it was the subsequent sinking of this arch that carried the guyots to their present depth. The mechanism that can cause the elevation and subsequent sinking of such an arch is certainly closely related to the origin of mid-Pacific volcanism.

Seamounts and abyssal hills are distributed all over the Pacific Basin

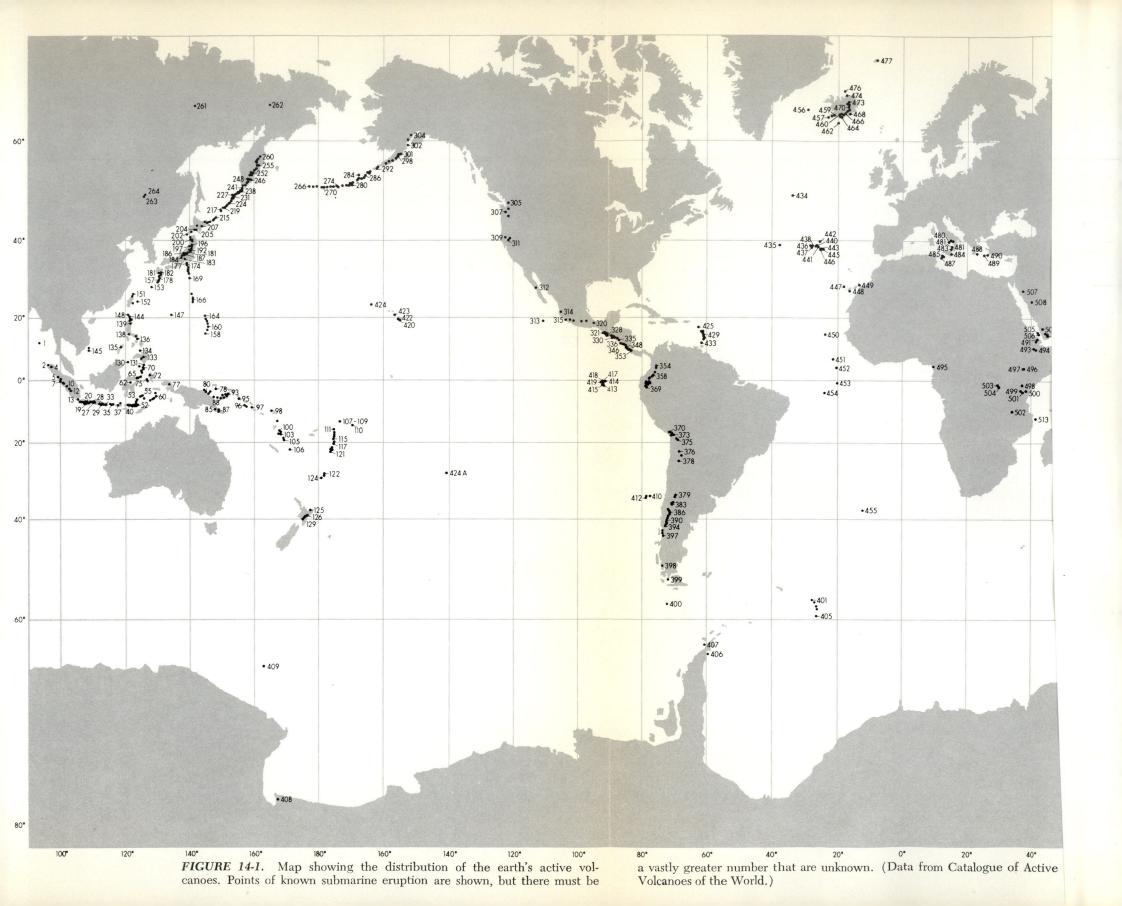

FIGURE 14-1. Map showing the distribution of the earth's active volcanoes. Points of known submarine eruption are shown, but there must be a vastly greater number that are unknown. (Data from Catalogue of Active Volcanoes of the World.)

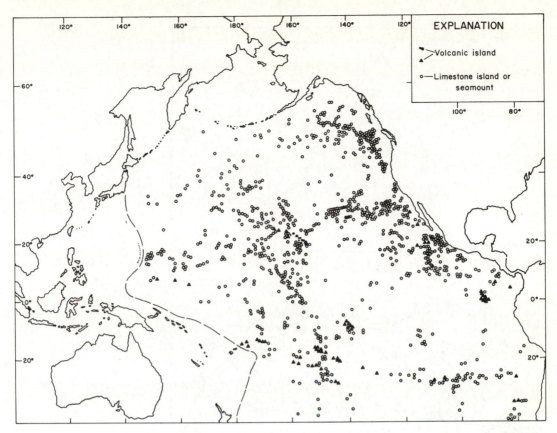

FIGURE 14-4. Young volcanoes more than 3,000 feet high in the Pacific Basin. Undoubtedly, many more remain undiscovered. Older seamounts, such as the guyots of the Darwin Rise, are not included. The dashed line marks the edge of the true ocean basin in the western and southwestern Pacific. (Modified after *Marine Geology of the Pacific,* by H. W. Menard. Copyright 1964 by McGraw-Hill, Inc. Used with permission of McGraw-Hill Book Co.)

(Fig. 14-4), but not in uniform abundance. The larger volcanoes—islands and large seamounts—are more numerous in the southwestern part of the basin. On the other hand, smaller seamounts are more abundant in the northeastern part. In the part of the basin west of North America, where we have more detailed information than elsewhere, the abundance of volcanoes varies from one more or less east-west segment of the ocean floor to another. These segments are separated by great east-west-trending faults, or *fracture zones.* Thus, in the segment between the Mendocino and Murray fracture zones (Fig. 14-5) volcanoes are relatively few as compared to the number in the segments to the north and south.

Table 14-1 gives the volumes estimated by Menard (1964, p. 95) for the volcanic features of the Pacific Basin. It will be noted that by far the largest volume is in the *archipelagic aprons*—broad gently sloping plains that border many of the archipelagos and groups of guyots (former islands). Based largely on seismic evidence, Menard believed the aprons to consist of lava flows erupted in deep water, but more recent work has demonstrated

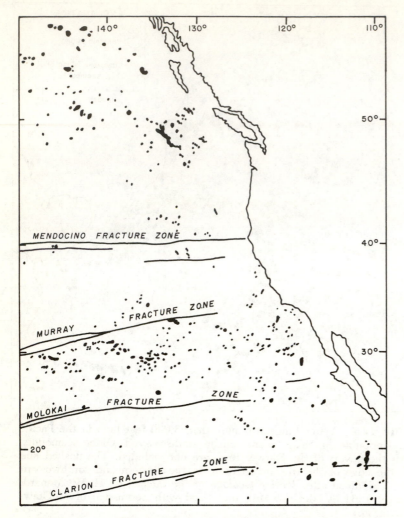

FIGURE 14-5. Map showing great faults (fracture zones) and the distribution of volcanoes in the northeastern Pacific Ocean basin. (After *Marine Geology of the Pacific,* by H. W. Menard. Copyright 1964 by McGraw-Hill, Inc. Used with permission of McGraw-Hill Book Co.)

that at least the Hawaiian apron is a great bank of sediment. Perhaps both types are present. Actually, for the present purpose it does not make a great deal of difference. The sedimentary aprons must be composed very largely of volcanic material eroded from the volcanic islands, so in either case the aprons are ultimately the product of volcanic eruption.

Fossils dredged from the seamounts and potassium–argon dates from volcanic rocks suggest that all of the features are geologically young, formed within the last 100 million years. Menard estimates that in most of geologic time—4 billion years—the total volume of volcanic rocks erupted on the continents was only about 2,400,000 cubic miles, whereas the volume erupted in the Pacific in only 100 million years was about 5,700,000 cubic miles. If the Pacific is representative of all the ocean basins, and if the rate of oceanic volcanism was about the same during the last 100 million years as it was

TABLE 14-1. Volumes of volcanic rocks in the Pacific Basin [1]

Types of Structure	Approximate Volume	
	Cubic kilometers	Cubic miles
Archipelagic aprons (assuming an average thickness of 2 kilometers)	20,000,000	5,000,000
Major volcanic ridges (measured above regional depth)	2,300,000	550,000
Large island groups (measured above regional depth)	1,000,000	250,000
100 relatively isolated islands (measured above regional depth	300,000	70,000
10,000 smaller volcanoes (measured above regional depth)	300,000	70,000
	23,900,000	5,940,000

[1] The volume of the suboceanic crust apart from these structures is not included. After Menard, 1964.

during earlier geologic time, this would mean that the rate of oceanic volcanism over all of geologic time averaged more than 100 times as great as that of continental volcanism. Menard's estimate of the volume of continental volcanic rocks is probably a good deal too small, considering the large amounts that must have been removed by erosion (it seems probable that the volume of ignimbrites, for instance, may have been reduced by as much as 50 per cent by erosion); but even allowing for this it is obvious that the ocean basins must have witnessed a much greater amount of volcanic activity than the continents. The 3 per cent of the world's active volcanoes that are located in the Pacific are a very feeble and inadequate indicator of the total volcanic activity of the area!

The same general facts are true for the other ocean basins. The Indian Ocean Basin contains only 1 per cent of the world's active volcanoes, but seamounts are scattered abundantly over the floor of the basin. About 13 per cent of the earth's active volcanoes lie within the Atlantic Ocean Basin, but again seamounts and extinct volcanic islands are vastly more numerous. A very prominent line of volcanic seamounts lies along the Mid-Atlantic Ridge—the great submarine range that roughly bisects the Atlantic Ocean in a north-south direction. It is generally believed today that the Ridge has grown over a zone of fissuring where the earth's crust is being torn apart as the parts of the Atlantic Ocean floor on the two sides of it are borne respectively eastward and westward by diverging convection currents in the underlying mantle. The Ridge extends through Iceland and into the Arctic Ocean north of Norway and Novaya Zemlya. Iceland, which appears to be an emergent part of the Ridge, contains about 3 per cent of the earth's active volcanoes; but in the period since 1500 A.D. it has produced about 24 per cent of the volume of erupted lava flows, thanks largely to the huge volume of the

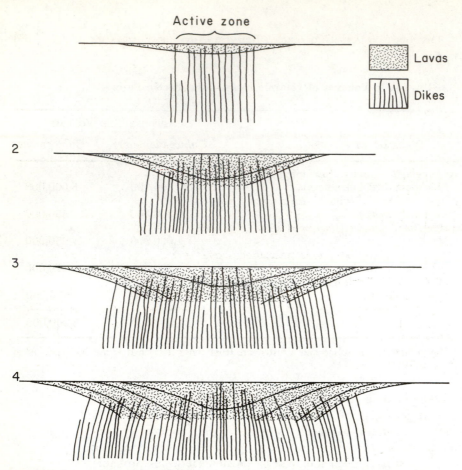

Active zone

Lavas

Dikes

2

3

4

FIGURE 14-6. Diagram illustrating the spreading of the earth's crust beneath Iceland, with the intrusion of vast numbers of dikes and gradual accumulation of volcanic rocks in the sinking graben at the surface. (After Bodvarsson and Walker, 1964.)

Laki eruption of 1783. The center of Iceland is a northeast-trending graben, and evidence suggests that the eastern and western parts of Iceland are being pulled apart (Fig. 14-6) at a rate of nearly 2 feet a century (Bodvarsson and Walker, 1964). The fractures left in the spreading crust are occupied by innumerable dikes. Farther south on the Ridge, the Azores are the summits of great volcanic mountains, some extinct and some still active; Ascension, Gough, and Bouvet Islands are extinct volcanoes, and Tristan da Cunha is an active one. St. Paul's Rocks is a mass of peridotite and serpentine that may have been squeezed up from the earth's mantle. Away from the Ridge, the Canary and Cape Verde Islands, Madeira, St. Helena, and the Fernando Noronha and Martin Vaz Islands, all are volcanic. The total number of volcanoes in the ocean basins is certainly several hundred thousand!

It is far more difficult to estimate the number of volcanoes that have been active on the continents during the last 100 million years. The sea-mounts are largely immune to erosional destruction and retain their external form indefinitely, but subaerial volcanoes are rapidly cut away by erosion. The oldest subaerial volcanoes that retain in any large degree their original constructional form are of Pliocene age—probably none of them more than 10 million years old. Many older volcanic centers can be recognized from their feeding channels that have been exposed by erosion or from the structural relationships of their lavas and tuffs to the surrounding rocks, but others are lost in the complexities of volcanic fields or buried by younger rocks. Thus, about 42 vents of the pre-Pliocene lavas of the Western Cascade Range have been recognized in central and northern Oregon, but the total number of vents certainly was several times that many (Peck et al., 1964). If we take the approximate volume of the pre-Pliocene lavas of the entire Cascade Range and divide by the approximate average volume of the later individual cones of the range, we come out with a figure of 1,500 to 2,000 separate volcanoes required to build the older part of the range. Some separate cones can be recognized in the younger part of the range, but these rest on a mass of basaltic lavas erupted from dozens of small cones. The total number of volcanoes probably was of the same general order as that required to build the earlier Western Cascades. Thus, there have probably been several thousand volcanos active within the area of the Cascade Range alone during the last 60 million years. Certainly the total number of volcanoes active on all of the continents during the last 100 million years (the same span of time as that covered by the estimate for the ocean basins) must also have been well over 100,000.

Appendix 1 lists the known active and recently extinct volcanoes of the world, but it must be apparent that this is only a small sampling of the total volcanic activity of the earth during recent geologic time.

GEOLOGICAL RELATIONSHIPS

Continental versus Oceanic Volcanism

Important overall differences exist between the volcanic activity on the continents and in the oceans. They stem largely from the fact that, while highly fluid basaltic magmas are erupted in both types of region, the more viscous andesites, dacites, and rhyolites are restricted to the continents or to certain island arcs near the continents that are generally considered to have continental affinities. A few possible exceptions exist. Thus, rhyolites have been described from Easter Island, and rhyodacite from Oahu in Hawaii, but in both instances the rocks are richer in sodium than the corresponding rocks characteristic of continental regions, and the erupting magma was less viscous. The magmas probably had a different origin from the typical rhyolites of the continents. Associated with the oceanic basalts are comparatively small quantities of trachyte and intermediate rocks (hawaiite, mugearite), and sometimes phonolites and nephelinites.

The entire oceanic association occurs also on the continents. It is thus only parts of the continents that can be considered volcanologically distinct from the oceans—but these parts include the borderlands of the Pacific and other folded-mountain regions in which more than three quarters of the world's active volcanoes are located. Within these belts the erupting magmas characteristically are not only more viscous but seem generally to contain more gas than do the oceanic magmas, and the result of greater viscosity and greater gas content is a greater degree of explosiveness of the eruptions. The really violent explosive eruptions take place at continental volcanoes. (It should be emphasized here that volcanoes within the ocean but on the submerged edges of the continents are continental.) Except for hydromagmatic explosions caused by contact of rising magma with water, explosion is minimal at oceanic volcanoes. Even the more explosive eruptions of their later stages are gentle as compared with many continental eruptions. Oceanic eruptions are essentially effusive; eruptions in the mountain-building belts of the continents are predominantly explosive.

Rittmann (1936, p. 162) designates as the *explosion index* the percentage of tephra in the total volcanic products of a region or of an eruption. Using data compiled by Sapper (1927) on the volumes of lava flows and of tephra erupted between the years 1500 and 1914 he finds, for instance, that in Kamchatka, tephra constitutes approximately 60 per cent and lava flows 40 per cent, of the material erupted. Thus, the explosion index for Kamchatka is 60. This index is low compared to indices for other parts of the Pacific borderland in which the general average exceeds 90. Among the most explosive areas are Indonesia and Central America for both of which the index is approximately 99. The Italian volcanoes and those of central Africa with indices of about 40 are less explosive than those of the Pacific rim. Historic eruptions of mid-Pacific volcanoes have indices of less than 1, and estimates for the prehistoric late-stage eruptions of Hawaiian volcanoes (which are more explosive than early-stage eruptions such as those of the presently active volcanoes) range from about 1 to 3. Indices for the volcanoes of the Atlantic and Indian Oceans are higher (Canary Islands 20, Azores 65). Inclusion of the rather explosive eruptions of Hekla and Katla brings the index for Iceland up to about 39 (Rittmann, 1962, p. 156), but the general index for Iceland excluding those volcanoes is much lower. Rittmann points out that although Sapper's data are certainly very incomplete, nevertheless the indices derived from them give a useful general comparison of the degree of explosiveness of the various areas. They serve to underline heavily the fact that oceanic volcanism is far less explosive than that of the continents, and that the degree of explosivity is much greater in the Pacific borderland (including Indonesia and nearby islands) than in any other part of the world.

Volcanic Rocks of the Ocean Basins

The major part of the Hawaiian shield volcanoes consists of basalt that is fairly rich in silicon in relation to alkalies (sodium and potassium). It is known as *tholeiitic basalt*. The eruptions are of Hawaiian type, and in

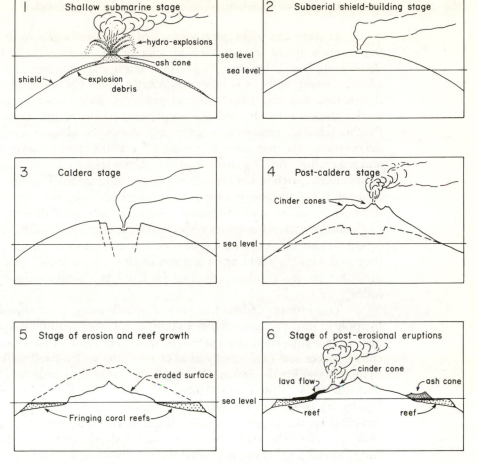

FIGURE 14-7. Diagrams illustrating the stages of development of Hawaiian volcanic mountains. (From Macdonald and Abbott, 1970; modified after Stearns, 1946.)

the part of the volcanoes visible above sea level, tephra makes up less than 1 per cent. Many of the lavas contain phenocrysts of olivine, and where these make up more than 5 per cent of the rock, it is called tholeiitic olivine basalt. Rocks containing more than 35 per cent olivine are called oceanite. It is believed that the entire shield from the sea floor up consists of these types of rock. To start with, at great depths in the ocean the eruptions must have been very effusive, without explosion, because of the restraining effect of the great weight of water on the expansion of gas. The lava flows are dense, as is confirmed by samples dredged from the lower slopes of the volcanoes. As the shield built close to sea level, however, water pressure decreased and hydromagmatic explosions became common. Part of the tephra and hyaloclastite no doubt was washed away into deep water, but part should have remained, and the portion of the shield built just below sea level should contain more fragmental material than the part formed above sea level. Eventually the summits of most of the shields collapsed to form calderas (Fig. 14-7), which were gradually filled by continuing eruptions.

At about this stage the frequency of eruptions begins to diminish, and the composition of the erupting magma begins to change. It is still predominantly basalt, but it is richer in sodium and potassium in relation to silicon; consequently, it is known as *alkalic basalt* (Macdonald, 1968; Macdonald and Katsura, 1965). The magma is a little richer in gas than the earlier tholeiitic basalt, and the eruptions become a little more explosive. Further change produces magma still richer in alkalies and poorer in magnesium, iron, and calcium, yielding "andesitic" rocks known as hawaiite and mugearite, and ultimately trachyte. Along with these are minor amounts of ankaramite, rich in big crystals of olivine and augite. This basalt–trachyte association has become known as the typical oceanic association. The eruptions of hawaiite and mugearite typically are Strombolian and build moderately large cinder cones associated with extensive lava flows. Trachyte eruptions may be moderately explosive, forming cones of pumice. Typically, they end with the building of a dome of trachyte over the vent, but sometimes the magma is sufficiently fluid for flows to extend outward for several miles.

This history, deduced at Hawaiian volcanoes, is commonly believed to apply at least in a general way to most or all other oceanic volcanoes. This has not actually been demonstrated, however. Most other oceanic islands consist above sea level wholly of alkalic basalts and related rock types. On Réunion Island in the Indian Ocean, alkalic basalts are underlain by rocks of tholeiitic type (Upton and Wadsworth, 1965). Both alkalic and tholeiitic basalts are present in the Galápagos Islands, but only on James Island do tholeiitic basalts clearly underlie alkalic basalts (McBirney and Williams, 1969, p. 126). The rocks of the volcanic islands along the Mid-Atlantic Ridge are all alkalic, but nearly all the basalts dredged from the Ridge itself are tholeiitic (Melson and Thompson, 1968). At least in places, rocks dredged from the walls of the median valley in the Ridge show a correlation of composition with depth, those from the upper part of the walls being alkalic basalt, and those from the lower part being tholeiitic (Aumento, 1968).

In Hawaii, after a period of volcanic quiet and erosion that may last as long as 2 million years, volcanism may resume (Fig. 14-7). The rocks formed in this late, post-erosional period are nephelinites, or basalts very poor in silica. It is still uncertain to what extent the same relationship holds in other mid-ocean islands.

To date, nearly all of the samples of lava that have been dredged from the deep-ocean floor away from ridges are tholeiitic basalt, and most are very poor in potassium oxide (less than 0.2 per cent). Some, but by no means all, are richer in alumina than the typical tholeiitic basalts of Hawaii. It is currently believed by many workers that this "low-potassium basalt" is characteristic of the deep-ocean floor, and it has been suggested (Engel, Engel, and Havens, 1965) that it is the most "primitive" type of basalt from which all others have been derived. It should be emphasized, however, that the total number of samples from the deep-ocean floor is still comparatively small, and many large areas are still unsampled. In contrast to the deeper areas, basalts dredged from rises not uncommonly are alkalic, though tholeiitic basalts may be found on others parts of the same rise.

Orogenic versus Nonorogenic Continental Regions

The process of formation of mountains is known as *orogenesis*. Mountains are of various types, but the typical mountains of continental regions are the ranges that are formed by folding and uplift of long narrow belts of the earth's crust, and it is to these that the term orogenesis is usually applied. The belts in which the mountains are formed are *orogens*, or *orogenic regions*. Other parts of the continents may have undergone great uplift, but without folding. They are *nonorogenic* or *kratogenic* regions. Volcanic activity typically is different in the two sorts of regions.

The volcanism of the nonorogenic regions is commonly much like that of the ocean basins, though somewhat more explosive. The rocks are often alkalic. The basalt–trachyte association is common, and silica-deficient nephelinites or leucitites (potassium-rich) may appear. Tholeiitic basalts also occur, however, and the great flood eruptions are usually tholeiitic. An exception is the Thulean region of the northeast Atlantic. In the southeastern part of this region, in Scotland and Ireland, the earliest lavas of the Thulean cycle were flood eruptions of alkalic basalt followed by tholeiitic central volcanoes. In Iceland, however, the flood eruptions were tholeiitic, followed by dominantly alkalic basalt eruptions. The latter are associated with the central graben—a trench formed by downfaulting presumably as a result of the stretching of the mid-Atlantic crust as the continents of Europe and North America drift farther apart.

Other volcanoes associated with tension in the earth's crust are those of central Africa (Fig. 14-8). The Rift Valleys are generally believed to be the result of the pulling apart of the crust with sinking of a long narrow block (a graben) between two fault scarps. The sides of the graben have been slightly elevated. The volcanic rocks are moderately to very deficient in silica and rich in sodium or potassium, or both. Some of them are among the poorest in silicon and richest in alkalies of any volcanic rocks on earth. Another example is the Rhine Graben—a Y-shaped split in the crust resulting from, or accompanying, a gentle broad up-arching, possibly due to intrusion of magma beneath. Several volcanic fields are associated with it (Fig. 14-9). The Vogelsberg field lies directly astride the eastern arm of the Y, and the Kaiserstuhl lies within its leg. To the east of the arms lie the volcanoes of the Hesse and Rhön districts, between the arms lie those of the Westerwald, and to the west those of the Eifel (Cloos, 1939). The Hegau volcanoes lie on

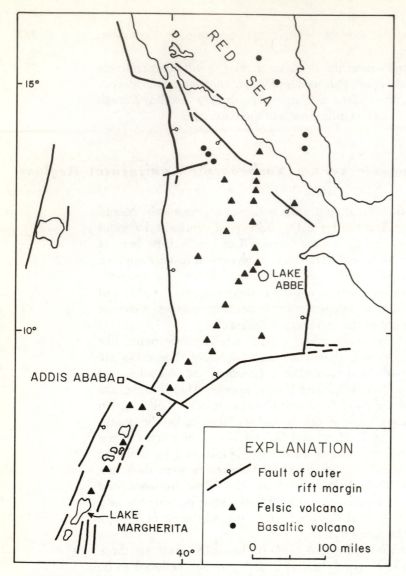

FIGURE 14-8. Map of the Ethiopian rift valley (graben) and associated volcanoes, northeastern Africa. (After Mohr, 1967.)

a lateral graben southeast of the leg, and farther east and north lie the diatremes of the Swabian Alb (Chapter 15). Again, the volcanic rocks are alkalic and deficient in silica.

Orogenic Volcanism

Space cannot be devoted here to all the complexities and variations in the history of orogenic regions. The following comments are only a gross generalization.

358

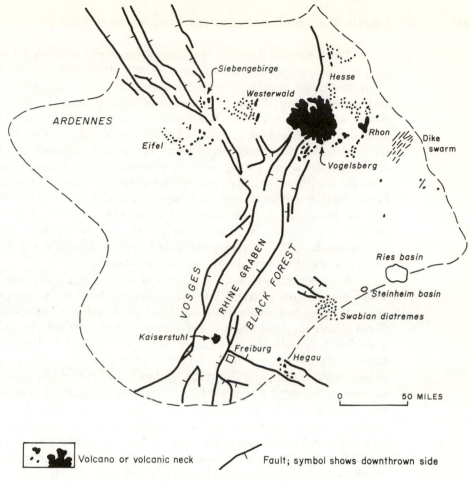

Volcano or volcanic neck   Fault; symbol shows downthrown side

FIGURE 14-9. Map of the Rhine graben, Germany, showing the associated volcanic fields. The dashed line indicates the edge of the Rhine upwarp, as defined by the shoreline of the Upper Cretaceous sea. (After Cloos, 1939. From Arthur Holmes, *Principles of Physical Geology,* second edition, The Ronald Press Co., New York. Copyright 1965.)

In a general way, the history of most folded mountain ranges can be divided into several stages, as follows:

1. Geosynclinal period

2. Period of folding, thrust faulting, and elevation

3. Period of batholithic formation, with continued elevation

4. Period of erosion

5. Rejuvenation, by up-arching or faulting

6. Erosion

Most of the great mountain ranges of the world have passed through stage 5, and the present relief of the mountains is the result of differential erosion.

359

The history of a typical orogenic region starts with the formation of a long narrow trough flooded with ocean water, often at or near the margin of a continent, but sometimes with extensive continental areas on both sides. Sedimentary material eroded from adjacent land areas is washed into the trough and deposited there. Commonly, the rate of deposition keeps pace with the rate of sinking of the bottom of the trough, so that the depth of water is never great, and occasionally the trough becomes overfilled and nonmarine delta and swamp deposits may form in it. At other times, however, the supply of sediment may be insufficient to keep the sinking trough filled nearly to sea level, and the water may become very deep. The trough may be hundreds of miles long and many tens of miles wide. The total amount of sinking of the floor of the trough, and the thickness of sediment accumulated in it, often exceeds 30,000 feet and may reach 60,000 feet. These great sinking troughs are known as *geosynclines*.

Commonly, a geosyncline consists of a series of aligned basins, each of which may behave a little differently from the others; the entire geosyncline generally does not sink or become filled with sediment at the same rate. Geosynclines may become divided into two parallel troughs by the rising of a medial longitudinal ridge known as a *geanticline*. A geanticline often forms along the edge of the geosyncline also. The formation of the geanticline usually is primarily due to an up-bowing of the earth's crust, but very commonly the ridge is capped by a row of volcanoes. The resulting row of central islands and the marginal ridge, volcanic or otherwise, contribute eroded debris to the trough, and the volcanoes contribute ash, mudflows, and lava flows, and sometimes ignimbrites, which are interlayered or mixed with the sediments. Other lava flows are erupted within the geosyncline itself, sometimes forming recognizable volcanic cones, but often forming extensive sheets, probably erupted from fissures, that do not seem to be related to distinct cones.

Not all geosynclines contain volcanic material mixed with the sediments. Following Stille (1940), those containing volcanic rocks are commonly called *eugeosynclines*, and those devoid of volcanics, *miogeosynclines*. In general, eugeosynclines seem to have sunk more and accumulated a greater thickness of rocks than have miogeosynclines. However, great variation is found within a single geosyncline. Parts of it may have accumulated great thicknesses of volcanic rock, whereas other parts have little or none. One example of a geosyncline that received a large volume of volcanic rock is the one that later evolved into the Olympic Mts. and Coast Range of Washington and Oregon. There, during Eocene time (about 60 to 35 million years ago), basalt lava flows were poured out over a series of sandstones and shales thousands of feet thick. The flows are mostly pillow lavas and hyaloclastites, the latter often partly reworked by water currents and containing many marine fossils. Many submarine mudflow deposits also are present (Snavely and Wagner, 1963). Sedimentary rocks are interbedded with the lavas, showing that much of the deposition was submarine; but also in places old soil zones on the lavas show that the surface of the growing pile was at times above sea level. The total thickness of the lavas eventually reached more than 15,000 feet in places, and the total volume reached about 40,000 cubic miles (Waters, 1955). Lenticular masses of lava and hyaloclastite up to 5,000 feet thick probably represent individual shield volcanoes. Most of the lavas are typical tholeiitic basalt, but sodium-enriched spilites (discussed later) are present in places.

To the north, during the Mesozoic era, the Coast Range eugeosyncline of western Canada was divided into two northwest-trending troughs. In the Insular trough, including the area of the present Vancouver and Queen Charlotte Islands and other islands farther north, rapid sinking during late Triassic time was accompanied by the eruption of at least 14,000 feet of sodic basalt, mostly as pillow lavas. Simultaneously, in the Whitehorse-Nechako trough of central British Columbia, submarine eruptions and eruptions of volcanic islands produced a thick accumulation of predominantly andesite and basaltic andesite lava flows, pyroclastic rocks, and sediments derived from them. Following a brief interval of quiet, widespread andesitic explosive volcanism took place in both troughs in Jurassic time (Souther, 1970).

Not many examples of typical geosynclines appear to exist today. A commonly cited example is the northern Gulf of Mexico and adjacent southern United States, which is slowly sinking and has accumulated a great thickness of sediments. Volcanic rocks are absent in it except for very minor amounts of ash. The very deep troughs that border the island arcs of the western Pacific Ocean may be examples. They form the deepest parts of the ocean, and very little sediment appears to have accumulated in them; but that may be because the supply of sediment from the adjacent small land areas is very small and the troughs themselves are young. The sediment may be carried downward beneath the edge of the island arc about as rapidly as it accumulates, by the downward-plunging edge of the spreading crust of the sea floor (see page 368). The island arcs themselves are rows of largely andesitic volcanoes capping geanticlines, and considerable amounts of volcanic material, particularly tephra, undoubtedly are being contributed to the troughs. However, since the most characteristic feature of a typical geosyncline is the accumulation of great thicknesses of sedimentary rocks, these troughs can hardly be considered typical geosynclines.

The volcanic rocks of the geosynclines are predominantly basalt. Tholeiitic basalt appears to be most abundant, but very widespread is a peculiar variety of basalt known as spilite. It contains abundant sodium, and the characteristic light-colored mineral is the sodium feldspar, albite, or a feldspar close to it in composition, in place of the calcium-rich labradorite or bytownite feldspar of ordinary basalts. The place of pyroxene in the ordinary basalts is largely taken by chlorite. Much more rarely, similar rocks rich in potassium may occur. The origin of the spilites is uncertain. Some of them seem clearly to be the result of alterations by sodium-rich hydrous solutions after the lava solidified. Ragged remnants of original labradorite are found in the albite, and remnants of pyroxene in the chlorite. In some areas, such as the Olympic Mts. of Washington (mentioned above), sedimentary rocks above or below the spilites have also been albitized by migrating sodium-rich solutions. Some geologists believe these sodic solutions to have resulted from migrating heated seawater squeezed or boiled out of the sediments in the lower part of the geosyncline. Others, working in regions where only the lavas were affected, believe that the alterations are the result of late-stage sodium-rich solutions concentrated within the lava while it crystallized. In still other cases, there is no sign of alteration of earlier feldspar and pyroxene, and both the albite and the chlorite appear to be original products of crystallization from the basalt magma. If so, the crystallizing magma must have been unusually rich in sodium and water. It has been suggested that this richness is the result of absorption of seawater by lavas erupted at great depths in the ocean, or that it is due to the retention in the crystallizing magma, owing to the high confining pressure of overlying seawater, of water and other volatiles that normally escape. Against this, on the other hand, we have the facts that many basalts erupted in deep water are not spilitic, and that many spilites appear to have been erupted in shallow water. There is as yet no general solution of the spilite problem. However, spilites are decidedly characteristic of the geosynclinal environment, and although a few examples of replacement spilite are found in other types of regions, the great majority of spilites are found in geosynclinal associations. It seems certain that there must be a genetic relationship between them.

Many of the lava flows in geosynclinal associations are pillow lavas. Probably most spilites are pillow lavas, but on the other hand most pillow lavas are not spilites. Hyaloclastites are commonly present, associated with the pillow lavas.

In some areas small amounts of more silicic soda-rich rocks (keratophyres and quartz keratophyres), both lava flows and tuffs, are associated with the spilites.

Sheets of serpentine often are interbedded with the geosynclinal sediments. Some of these probably were intruded as sills before the folding of the geosynclinal rocks, but others have recently been shown to have been extruded as lava flows (probably as peridotites, later altered to serpentines). The first to recognize these serpentine lavas were Bailey and McCallien (1954), working in Turkey. Rittmann (1958a) has described what appear to be serpentine pillow lavas in Egypt, and serpentine lavas have since been recognized in other regions. Flows of serpentine or other ultrabasic rocks have never been found except in geosynclinal environments and under circumstances that suggest eruption in very deep water. The erupting magma that formed them must have been very rich in olivine (picrite or peridotite). Rittmann (1962) has suggested that it is so heavy that it cannot be lifted to high levels and, therefore, can only be erupted at great oceanic depths. It is generally believed that under surface conditions these ultrabasic magmas would require impossibly high temperatures to keep them molten, but Clark and Fyfe (1961) have shown that under the high confining pressure of water at great depths the temperature required is within a reasonable range. In the Alps, sheets of serpentine several thousand feet thick have been reported to pass upward into thick accumulations of basaltic pillow lavas, and it has been suggested that the basalts were derived from the peridotite magma.

The chloritized basalts of orogenic regions often are referred to as *greenstones*, and the combination of these with serpentines is known as the *ophiolite suite*. (Ophiolites are spilitic rocks consisting of roundish masses of albite in a matrix of chlorite probably formed by the alteration of original glass.) It was long ago pointed out by G. Steinmann that these two rock types very generally are associated with chert (SiO_2 rock), and "Steinmann's trinity" has come to be recognized as characteristic of geosynclinal associations world over. Bailey, Irwin, and Jones (1964) suggest that the chert is formed by precipitation of silica dissolved in seawater as a result of reaction between the water and hot lava. Under high pressure at great depths in the ocean, large amounts of silica can be dissolved in the hot water directly overlying a lava flow, but as the hot water rises and cools it becomes greatly oversaturated with silica and precipitates silica gel, which settles back to the ocean floor to form a layer of chert above the lava.

Other types of volcanic rocks also are found in geosynclinal assemblages. Andesite flows, tuffs, and mudflow deposits, and tuffs of dacite and rhyolite composition are common in some geosynclines, such as the Coast Range geosyncline of British Columbia (Dickinson, 1962), but in general they are far less abundant and characteristic than are the basalts, spilites, and serpentines. In many instances they probably are the products of the volcanoes on the adjacent geanticlines.

The life of a typical geosyncline is measured in hundreds of millions of years, though it may be punctuated by relatively brief and often local periods of folding, faulting, and uplift. Eventually, however, the existence of the whole geosyncline is terminated by folding, thrust faulting, and uplift.

The early stages of folding of the geosynclinal rocks are accompanied by intrusion of small masses of peridotite and gabbro, but surficial volcanic activity generally is absent. As folding progresses, high temperature and probably the action of volatiles in the lower part of the mass brings about metamorphism of the rocks and ultimately alteration of part of them into granite. (Granite in the broad sense. In a restricted sense it is generally quartz diorite to quartz monzonite.) This *granitization* takes place essentially in the solid state, but ultimately it may reach a stage in which part of the rock becomes mobile and moves upward as magma, intruding the overlying rocks to form higher-level batholiths and stocks. In some cases the magma breaks through to the surface to produce synorogenic volcanism, usually predominantly andesitic to dacitic. In other cases, there is no indication of this. Indeed, in some folded belts even granitic intrusions are small and few, or totally absent at levels now visible, though it is possible that they exist at greater depth. Such variations may occur even within the same orogenic belt.

The andesitic eruptions form belts of composite volcanoes. The duration of activity of each belt is generally comparatively brief—a few million years, but the end of activity in one belt may be followed by the beginning of activity in another roughly parallel belt, coinciding with a new zone of folding of geosynclinal rocks. The successive development of belts of folding and volcanism has commonly been from the continent side toward the ocean, resulting in a seaward growth of the continent. Elsewhere, however, the later volcanic belt lies on the inland side of the earlier one (McBirney, 1970). This was the case, for instance, in the Cascade Range, where the belt of Pleistocene and Holocene volcanoes (the High Cascade) lies to the east of the Miocene Western Cascade belt (Peck, Griggs, Schlicker, Wells, and Dole, 1964).

Volcanic activity also takes place in many (but not all) folded belts after the end of folding. This post-orogenic volcanism sometimes follows closely after the period of maximum deformation, but more commonly there is a considerable interval of time between them. A general uplift of the region takes place, partly as a result of the folding and thickening of the upper, lighter part of the earth's crust, but probably partly because of the large masses of relatively light granite in the roots of the folded belt. The uplift results in erosion, which carves the area into high mountain ridges, and then lowers the ridges to a region of low relief. The advent of volcanism may not take place until after a long period of erosion, sometimes lasting tens of millions of years. Thus, in the Sierra Nevada of California most of the folding had been completed by the end of the Jurassic period, about 135 million years ago, and the youngest of the granitic intrusions had consolidated by about 80 million years ago, but post-orogenic volcanism appears not to have started until about 50 million years ago.

In contrast, in the Rocky Mountains, although only small granitic masses were emplaced following the folding, volcanism began in some areas almost immediately. The folding and thrust faulting of the Rocky Mountain geosyncline is generally believed to have culminated in early Eocene time, about 55 million years ago; but in some parts of the region, such as the Absaroka Range near Yellowstone National Park, volcanism had already started by middle Eocene time, possibly while folding was still going on in other parts of the geosyncline. As in the geosynclinal stage, variations in synorogenic and post-orogenic volcanism are great even within a single orogenic belt, and those between belts are even greater.

In regions such as the Sierra Nevada in which there was a long interval between the folding and the beginning of post-orogenic volcanism, erosion commonly had exposed the upper parts of the granitic intrusives, and the volcanic rocks in places rest directly on the eroded surface of the granites. It is difficult to believe that the volcanics could have been derived from the still-unconsolidated lower parts of the granitic intrusives. More probably, there had been a new generation of magma beneath the region.

The volcanic rocks erupted during and after the folding of orogenic belts range from basalt to rhyolite and most characteristically are andesite and dacite. These rocks are rich in silicon and calcium, as compared to alkalies, and are said to be *calc-alkaline*. The assemblage of calc-alkaline volcanic rocks is typical of orogenic regions and may be called the *orogenic*

PLATE 14-1. Composite volcanoes in the central Cascade Range, Oregon. In the distance are Mt. Washington and Mt. Jefferson. The closer peaks are, from left to right, Middle Sister, North Sister, South Sister, and Broken Top. Oregon State Highway Department Photograph.

suite. By far the most abundant are rather basic andesites (basaltic andesites and pyroxene andesites) and basalts. Not uncommonly, the early eruptions build a broad welt of basalt, basaltic andesite, and andesite, erupted as fissure flows and broad, flat, often coalescing, shield volcanoes. This is followed by eruptions of more silicic andesite, dacite, and less commonly rhyolite, that form composite volcanoes (Plate 14-1). This, for instance, is the case in the Cascade Range, where the composite volcanoes form the well-known conspicuous peaks along the crest of the range. Another characteristic feature is the eruption, generally later than most of the activity of the composite volcanoes, of isolated flows of basalt with associated cinder cones that often fill valleys eroded into the earlier rocks. The early basalts are generally tholeiitic—relatively low in alkalies and alumina and grading into the basaltic andesites; the late-stage basalts are often high in alumina, and may be somewhat alkalic.

Although the foregoing is the most characteristic sequence of rock types, other sequences also occur. Thus, in the Sierra Nevada the earliest post-orogenic lavas are rhyolitic, followed by predominant andesites and eventually by basalts.

The tremendous volumes of rhyolitic to dacitic ash flows (ignimbrites) that are found in some regions, such as North Island of New Zealand, Sumatra, Kamchatka, and Nevada, are post-orogenic. They have been erupted in regions of mountain building that have undergone considerable amounts of erosion and commonly have been reduced to rather low relief. Several of the regions had been broadly uparched following the long erosion, with fracturing of the crust allowing the arch to collapse, resulting in the formation of grabens (New Zealand and Sumatra) or of block-faulted mountains with intervening valleys (Basin and Range Province of the western United States). It is possible that the original arching was due to the presence of large volumes of light granitic magma in the earth's crust, and that the fracturing allowed part of the magma to escape at the surface, forming the ash flows.

Very commonly, the eruption of calc-alkalic rocks of the orogenic suite within the main orogenic region is accompanied or followed by eruption of alkalic rocks in adjacent regions outside the folded belt. Most commonly, these alkalic rocks range from alkalic basalt to trachyte and closely resemble the typical assemblages of mid-ocean islands. Others, however, are leucite-bearing rocks rich in potassium. These eruptions usually take place in the region behind or on the concave side of arcuate belts of folding, but sometimes they are in front. A typical example is furnished by Japan and the nearby margin of the Asiatic continent. In that region a series of geosynclines, successively closer to the Pacific basin, were folded during Triassic, Cretaceous, and early Tertiary times (respectively about 190 million, 80 million, and 50 million years ago), after which the present volcanic arcs of Japan were formed. In the latter, predominantly tholeiitic basalts in the area closest to the Pacific are succeeded inland by predominant andesites and associated rocks of the typical orogenic suite. Still farther west, along the coast of the Japan Sea, the rocks are alkalic, and alkalic volcanics are found also in Manchuria.

In contrast, the volcanic rocks of central and southern Italy, in front of the fold belt of the Apennine Mts., are strongly potassic, as is well exemplified by the leucite-bearing rocks of Vesuvius. It is noteworthy that farther north, in Tuscany, the volcanic rocks and associated shallow granitic intrusives west of the Apennines are typical calc-alkaline types (Marinelli and Mittempergher, 1966). East of the fold belt of the Rocky Mts., also, highly potassic alkalic rocks occur in the Little Belt Mts. and Leucite Hills of Wyoming.

Episodes of intense compression that result in folded and thrust-faulted mountain belts are sometimes followed, usually after a considerable interval, by crustal tension that may be associated with volcanism. Thus, in British Columbia, the northeast–southwest compression that formed the Coast Range structures in late Mesozoic time was followed by east-west crustal tension in late Tertiary and Quaternary time with the formation of two north-south belts of alkalic basalt volcanoes related to normal faults. A contemporary east-west belt of Quaternary volcanoes is parallel to fracture zones in the floor of the Pacific Ocean to the west and may be related to them genetically (Souther, 1970).

The association of volcanoes with grabens and crustal tension in non-orogenic regions has already been mentioned. In orogenic regions, also, the post-orogenic volcanoes often lie along and in a large graben. Appearances suggest that the crust of the region has been elevated into a broad arch elongated approximately parallel to the folded belt, possibly by the buoyancy of large granitic masses beneath the surface or by general heating and expansion of subsurface rocks, and that resulting tension in the outer part of the arch has allowed a graben to sink in along the crest. Excellent examples are to be found in Central America. Thus, in El Salvador the great Quaternary and Holocene volcanoes lie along a nearly east-west graben formed by foundering of the crest of a broad arch (Williams and Meyer-Abich, 1955); and in Nicaragua (Fig. 14-10) the volcanoes lie within and along the boundary faults of a similar northwest-southeast graben (McBirney and Williams, 1965). A similar relationship is shown by the row of volcanic vents that lie along the Taupo graben in North Island of New Zealand (Fig. 12-7).

Currently, the hypotheses of sea-floor spreading and "plate tectonics" are gaining wide acceptance, although they certainly cannot as yet be considered proven, and important objections to them have been raised (Beloussov, 1970). Briefly, the concept is as follows. Large rigid plates of lithosphere (the crust and uppermost part of the earth's mantle) are considered to move laterally over an asthenosphere (zone of lower rigidity) beneath. The lithosphere plates move outward from broad ridges, or "rises," most of which are beneath the oceans. The outward flow of heat on the ridge is generally several times as great as it is in adjacent areas, and it appears probable that the ridge is the result of local heating and expansion of the underlying mantle. Outward movement of the plates at approximately right angles to the ridge tears the lithosphere apart along the crest of the ridge, and magma rises into the tensional rift creating new lithosphere, partly by volcanic eruptions and partly by very numerous shallow intrusions. Such a zone is the Mid-Atlantic Ridge, and other mid-ocean ridges such as the East Pacific Rise are thought to be similar. The rate of broadening of the lithosphere over the ridge ranges from less than an inch per year on parts of the Mid-Atlantic Ridge to more than 3 inches per year on parts of the East Pacific Rise. Since other evidence demonstrates that the earth's circumference cannot be increasing at a rate equalling more than a small portion of this, if it is increasing at all, it follows that lithosphere must be destroyed elsewhere at a rate approximately equal to that of creation of new lithosphere on the ridges. This destruction occurs at the distal edges of the plates, where

FIGURE 14-10. Map of Nicaragua, showing the alignment of the volcanoes along the major graben. (Simplified after McBirney and Williams, 1965. Originally published by the University of California Press; reprinted by permission of The Regents of the University of California.)

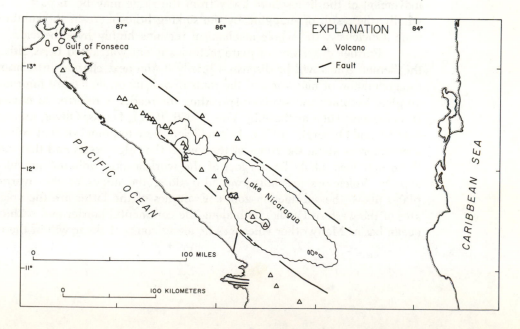

the lithosphere plunges downward beneath the edges of the bordering plates along underthrust fault zones, commonly called "Benioff zones" after the seismologist, Hugo Benioff, who first demonstrated their existence (Benioff, 1954). This "subduction" of the lithosphere commonly occurs at the boundary between ocean and continent. The downward-moving oceanic plate may scrape off an accumulation of sedimentary and associated volcanic rocks against the edge of the overriding continental plate, and this scraped-off mass, together with sedimentary material on the edge of the continental plate, may be crushed and thickened into belts of folded mountains. The entire edge of the Pacific Ocean, with its festoons of folded mountain ranges, is of this nature, and it is worthwhile noting the common association of volcanic activity with the folded belts. The subduction zones may, however, be located within the continents or within the oceans, instead of at their border, and such volcanic island arcs as the Mariana and Tonga Islands, with oceanic crust on both sides of them, are thought to mark intra-oceanic subduction zones.

The cause of the movement of the lithosphere plates away from the ridge crests and of their sinking in the subduction zones is still very uncertain. Most commonly the outward movement is attributed to convection currents, rising beneath the ridge and moving outward in the top of the asthenosphere and rafting along the overlying lithosphere, but there is also a possibility that the motion is caused partly, or even entirely, by gravitative sliding of the plate down the slope of the ridge. In the subduction zone the lithosphere may be dragged down by a descending convection current or pushed down by the sliding crust behind it; or it may sink, because of its greater specific gravity, into less dense heated asthenosphere beneath; or all three mechanisms may contribute. As the lithosphere plate descends, it is presumably transformed into asthenosphere, but partial melting may release magma which moves upward through the edge of the overlying plate. The movement of the lithosphere away from the ridge may be in part, or even wholly, the result of dragging by the sinking lithosphere in the subduction zone. Obviously, the whole mechanism remains highly hypothetical.

Further discussion of plate tectonics is not warranted here, although the Benioff zones will be discussed briefly in the next chapter in relation to the generation of magmas and the roots of volcanoes. For more information on plate tectonics and sea-floor spreading the reader is referred to numerous recent papers such as those by Vine (1966, 1971), Isacks, Oliver, and Sykes (1968), and Oxburgh (1971). It is sufficient here to point out that volcanoes are numerous along the zones of tension on the ridge crests and that indeed these may very likely be the loci of the world's most voluminous volcanic activity. Volcanoes are numerous also along the edges of the overriding plates above the subduction zones. Examples of the latter are the volcanic arcs of the western Pacific, both along the continental border and within the ocean basin. Many other volcanoes lie along zones of shear within the moving plates, such as the great fracture zones of the eastern Pacific (Fig. 14-5). Still others, however, cannot as yet be related in any specific way to plate tectonics.

SUGGESTED ADDITIONAL READING

Aubouin, 1965; Bailey, Irwin, and Jones, 1964; Battey, 1956; Buddington, 1959; Erlich, 1968; Gorshkov, 1962; Hentschel, 1961; Holmes, 1965, p. 1109–1192; Kay, 1951, pp. 1–6, 69–77; Knopf, 1960; Lehmann, 1952; Menard, 1964, p. 55–95; Turner and Verhoogen, 1960, p. 164–321; Tyrrell, 1955; Verhoogen, et al., 1970, p. 287–316; Waters, 1955; Williams, 1953.

15

The Internal Structure and Mechanism of Volcanoes

Evidence on the internal constitution and workings of volcanoes is of two sorts: direct geological observation of the interior of old cones and the underlying rocks exposed by erosion or by mining operations, and geophysical observations that indicate something about the properties of the rock materials below the levels that are accessible to direct observation. Geophysical observations are, of course, often subject to more than one interpretation and, hence, are less certain indicators of structure than are direct geological observations; but, except for the occasional fragments of underlying rocks brought to the surface by rising magma or explosions, they are our only means of studying the substructure of active volcanoes. In this chapter we will consider first the volcanic "plumbing" that is actually visible and its implications as to the mechanism of volcanoes, then the geophysical evidence and its interpretation in view of the visible structures.

Dikes, Sills, and Laccoliths

The walls of collapsed craters and cross sections of eroded cones commonly reveal intrusive bodies. In some cases they are very numerous, but in others they are few. Most abundant are *dikes* (Fig. 2-1) formed by magma

PLATE 15-1. Dike merging upward into a small sill, intruded into thin-bedded lava flows in the wall of Mokuaweoweo Caldera, Mauna Loa. The sill is 26 feet thick at its thickest point. U. S. Geological Survey photo by G. A. Macdonald.

filling fissures that cut across the tephra beds and/or lava flows in the cone; but *sills* intruded parallel to the beds also are common (Plate 15-1), and irregular or roughly cylindrical intrusive masses are sometimes found. The latter are known as *stocks* or *bosses*.

Less common are sill-like bodies known as *laccoliths*, roughly planoconvex in cross section and bending the overlying beds into a conspicuous arch (Plate 11-2). Every gradation exists between laccoliths and sills. The mechanics of intrusion are essentially the same. Both lift the overlying beds to make room for themselves, and both pinch out laterally. In general, sills are formed by less viscous magma that spreads out to form a thin sheet with nearly parallel top and bottom, whereas more viscous magma spreads less freely and forms a thick mass close to the feeder. Thus, sills can be considered the intrusive equivalents of lava flows, and laccoliths the intrusive equivalents of domes. Both sills and laccoliths can be fed either by dikes (Plate 15-1) or directly from a central pipe conduit or a stock (Fig. 15-1).

FIGURE 15-1. Diagram showing: (A) and (B) laccoliths fed from central feeding pipes (after Gilbert, 1877); (C) laccolith fed from a stock, Henry Mts., Utah (after Hunt, Averill, and Miller, 1953); (D) cross section at a right angle to (C).

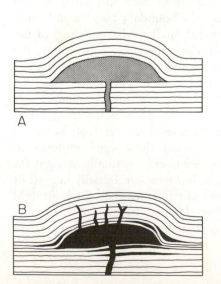

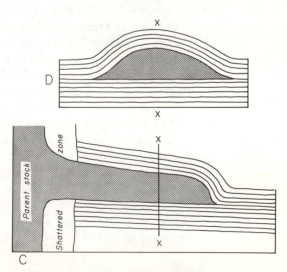

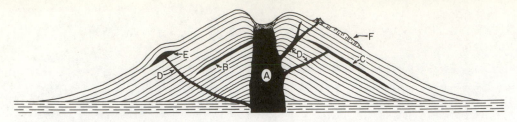

FIGURE 15-2. Diagrammatic cross section of a composite volcano, showing a plug (A), a mantle sill (B), a sill (C), dikes (D), a laccolith (E), and a lava flow (F).

    A. Rittmann believes that some of the layers of dense lava parallel to the other beds in the cone of Vesuvius are "mantle sills" (Fig. 15-2) formed by lava being forced part way through the cone wall as a dike and then spreading downslope between older beds, or entering directly between the other beds where they abut against the upper part of the central pipe conduit. These mantle sills may extend around large segments of the cone.

    Although dikes and sills are common in volcanic cones, they are also common in other environments, both the folded rocks of orogenic regions and the relatively flat-lying rocks of nonorogenic regions. Laccoliths are relatively rare in volcanic cones, and most big laccoliths are found in "plateau" regions of nonfolded rocks. The rocks overlying big laccoliths are most commonly sedimentary, probably because the relative lightness of the sedimentary rocks makes it easier for the magma to lift the overlying beds than to break through them to the surface.

    It has already been pointed out (Chapter 10) that although a single pipe vent commonly produces many eruptions, most fissure vents erupt only once. Occasionally, however, fissures may be reopened, most commonly along the edge of the dike formed by solidification of the earlier magma in the fissure, but sometimes through the center of the dike. At the end of the second eruption, consolidation of the magma within the fissure forms a second dike directly against the first, and, rarely, the same thing may happen several times. Usually the boundaries between successive dikes are sharp and distinct, and commonly the edge of the second dike shows evidence of having been chilled against the earlier dike with the formation of a thin glassy selvedge; but if the first dike was still hot or even still partly molten at the time of formation of the second one, the boundary may be indistinct or even gradational. Dikes made up of several smaller adjacent dikes of the same composition are known as *multiple dikes,* and those in which the several adjoining dikes are of different composition are known as *composite dikes.* Single dikes are far commoner than multiple or composite ones.

    Deep erosion of a composite cone commonly reveals many dikes cutting the beds of lava and tephra. In width the dikes range from a few inches, and rarely even less than an inch, to several tens of feet; but most commonly they are between 2 and 20 feet. They show some tendency to cut the beds at approximately right angles. Some are essentially straight for long distances, rarely even for several miles, but most are broadly curved or bent in plan; in detail they commonly consist of numerous short fairly straight segments separated by abrupt bends. The detailed courses of many are obviously governed by preexisting joints, particularly in the lava flows. Dikes cutting tephra tend to be quite regular and sharply bounded at deep levels in the cone, but may become very irregular or even feather out into the tephra at high levels, where confining pressure was low. Many dikes were once feeders of lateral eruptions, though in other cases the magma rising in the fissure did not reach the surface.

Dikes commonly are bounded by selvedges of glass, generally only a fraction of an inch thick, resulting from chilling of the liquid magma against the cooler wall rocks. Some dikes are highly vesicular, but most are denser than the enclosing lava flows. The denseness may in part be due to escape of the gas bubbles before consolidation of slowly cooled intrusive magma, but even the quickly chilled glassy selvedges commonly are dense, and thin dikes must have cooled faster than thicker lava flows unless the surrounding rocks were hot; if the latter were the case, a chilled glass selvedge should not form. The common denseness of dikes exposed by erosion probably results from repression of bubble formation by the weight of the overlying column of magma, in the same way that bubbles are prevented from forming in lava flows in deep water (Chapter 5). Under lesser pressure the escaping gas expands to form bubbles in the liquid, and a highly gas-charged magma at high levels in the dike may completely blow itself apart, forming fragmental dikes such as appear to have fed some fragmental flows (Chapter 8). Some dikes show a microstructure resembling that of ignimbrites or the fluidized tuffs of the tuff necks mentioned later, and probably result from welding of the glassy fragments of gas–ash emulsions that were injected into fractures. Some of them probably were the feeders of fragmental flows on the surface.

Cooling of dikes by radiation and conduction of heat from their two approximately parallel boundary surfaces commonly results in well-developed columnar jointing approximately at right angles to the dike walls (Plate 15-2), and in the case of nearly vertical dikes, the exposed masses of columns may look surprisingly like great stacks of cordwood (Plate 15-3).

PLATE 15-2. Dike, with columnar jointing normal to its walls, Island of Kauai, Hawaii. U. S. Geological Survey photo by G. A. Macdonald.

PLATE 15-3. Columnar-jointed dike, exposed by erosion of the surrounding rocks, 17 miles south of Adin, northeastern California. U. S. Geological Survey photo by G. A. Macdonald.

Usually, both in composite cones and in the large shield volcanoes, most of the dikes radiate outward from near the apex of the cone. On active and recent cones these are attested to by the radial lines of minor vent structures described in earlier chapters. Thus, Klyuchevskaya Volcano in Kamchatka bears on its flanks about 80 minor cones arranged along 12 lines radiating from the summit. In addition, 3 arcuate lines are concentric to the summit and probably are the surficial expression of cone sheets, described on a later page. In older, dissected volcanoes the dikes themselves are exposed. In some cones the distribution of radial dikes is more or less regular, like the spokes in a wheel; but in many of the Hawaiian volcanoes the dikes are largely concentrated into certain relatively restricted radial segments of the shield that represent the subsurface portions of the rift zones (Chapter 11). Typical examples of radial patterns are shown in Figs. 11-9A and 15-3.

The regions of very abundant dikes in Hawaiian-type shield volcanoes are known as *dike complexes*. Most of the dikes in them are between 1 and 5 feet thick and stand at angles between 70° and vertical, though occasional ones with flatter attitudes are found. The dikes sometimes are in direct contact with each other and sometimes are separated by thin septa composed of the lava flows that built the shield. They commonly cross each other, often with the formation of a glassy selvedge, showing that the earlier dike was already relatively cool when the second dike was intruded. Frequently, in crossing the dike complex one can count as many as 300 to 600 dikes per mile. The dike complexes, like the surface rift zones, generally are from about 1 to 2 miles in width.

FIGURE 15-3. Maps showing radial dike patterns at (A) the Sunlight District, Wyoming (after Parsons, 1939); (B) Spanish Peaks, Colorado (after Hills, 1901).

Although there can be no question that many or most of these dikes are the fillings of conduits that once fed surface eruptions, it is rare that one of them can be seen to pass into the lava flow it produced. This is at least partly because of a tendency for the lava to sink back a little way into the conduit at the end of the eruption, breaking the direct connection with the flow.

In some regions, vast numbers of subparallel dikes form *dike swarms* (Fig. 15-4). Swarms of this sort are generally believed to have fed the flood

FIGURE 15-4. Map showing regional dike swarm of western Scotland. (After Richie, 1961.)

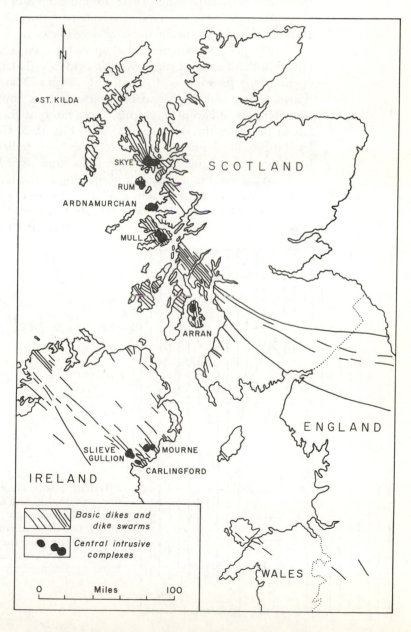

eruptions that built lava plains and plateaus like those of the Deccan region in India and the Columbia Plain of northwestern United States (Chapter 11). However, as in the Hawaiian shield volcanoes, it is very rare that a dike can actually be traced directly into a lava flow.

Most volcanic dikes appear to be *dilatational*—that is, the magma appears to have occupied a fissure formed by the bodily moving apart of the walls. Projections on one wall commonly match reentrants on the other. At deeper levels in the earth's crust some dikes are nondilatational: room for them has not been made by moving apart of the walls; instead, there has been a transformation of the rock by volatile materials moving along some fracture or permeable zone. There are indications of this same process in the deep root regions of some eroded volcanoes, but it does not appear to happen at the shallow depths ordinarily considered volcanic.

The precise mechanism that opens the dike fissures is generally uncertain. For the most part, there is little evidence that the fissure was wedged open by the pressure of the entering magma. Many dikes cross beds of coarse tephra and the fragmental parts of lava flows without appreciably disturbing the adjacent fragments. Only rarely is there definite evidence of strong thrust by the dike magma, as in Fig. 15-5. Generally, the rocks cut by the dike-filled fissures appear to have been pulled apart by underlying forces and the magma to have risen in them more or less passively.

Whatever the mechanism of opening of the fissures, there is no question that the opening indicates a dilation, or stretching, of the rocks cut by the dikes, and in some instances this stretching can be shown to be great. Whether uniformly distributed or concentrated in dike complexes, the radial

FIGURE 15-5. Diagram of a basalt dike cutting gneissoid biotite quartz diorite in the Repetto Hills, near Los Angeles, California. For nearly two feet directly in line with the terminus of the dike the normally straight plates of biotite mica are crumpled into accordion-like forms by the pressure of the dike magma.

dikes represent an appreciable stretching of the outer part of a volcanic cone. In some composite volcanoes, the lengthening of the circumference of the midpart of the cone amounts to several per cent. The swarm of hundreds of northwest-trending dikes associated with the ancient (Tertiary) volcanic center of the Island of Mull in western Scotland (Fig. 15-4) represents a distension of the earth's crust in a northeast-southwest direction of nearly half a mile. A little farther south, near the Island of Arran, the distension is even greater—probably more than 6,000 feet (Richey, 1961, p. 111). Similarly great distension results from the thousands of dikes that cut the Hawaiian shield volcanoes. The roughly parallel dike complexes of the Waianae and Koolau volcanoes of the Island of Oahu (Fig. 15-6) each represent a northeast-southwest stretching of the bases of the volcanic structures of nearly half a mile. Even this amount of stretching of the crust is small compared to the distension of possibly as much as 240 miles in central Iceland (Bodvarsson and Walker, 1964) and probably at least that much in other parts of the Mid-Atlantic Ridge (Chapter 14), or to that in the Island of Cyprus, where dikes cutting pillow lavas and an underlying serpentinized peridotite and gabbro complex make up more than 90 per cent of the rock and represent a stretching of at least 45 miles (Gass and Masson-Smith, 1963).

In some instances, the radial fissuring of volcanic cones may be the result of lateral thrust due to the weight of a column of liquid magma occupying a central pipe conduit. This was strongly suggested by the splitting of

FIGURE 15-6. Map of the Island of Oahu, Hawaii, showing the dike complexes and calderas of the Koolau and Waianae Volcanoes.

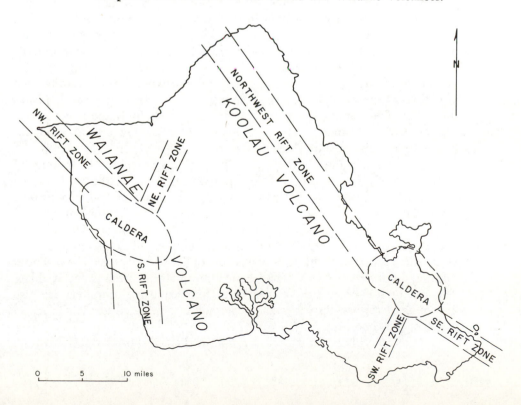

the Vesuvius cone, with resultant lateral eruptions and lowering of the magma level that led to the great explosive eruption of 1906 (Chapter 10), and by similar phenomena accompanying many other eruptions. It is probably the commonest cause of radial dike intrusion in small composite cones; but it appears to be wholly inadequate to explain the stretching of big Hawaiian-type shields, where some other mechanism must be involved. This will be discussed further later.

Volcanic Plugs and Necks

Pipe conduits of inactive volcanoes are filled with more or less cylindrical masses of congealed magma or tephra, commonly referred to as *plugs*. The development of a plug of solidified magma is, of course, a gradual process, and in dormant volcanoes the solid plug may overlie a still-fluid column of magma. The explosions that mark the resumption of activity at such volcanoes commonly throw out numerous fragments of the solid plug, and the initial explosion breccias may consist wholly of such debris. Sometimes the plug is pushed upward by more gradual pressure from beneath, forming a *plug dome* (Chapter 6). The plug is commonly more resistant to erosion than the enclosing rocks, and in deeply eroded volcanoes it may stand up in bold relief as a tower or irregular column commonly known as a volcanic *neck*. The term "neck" is, however, often used synonymously with "plug," regardless of whether or not the mass stands up in relief.

At shallow levels the plug formed by solidification of the magma is fine grained and is commonly referred to as a lava plug. At greater depths, however, the rock is coarse grained, granitic or gabbroic, and often porphyritic. The composition of the rocks covers the entire range of erupted lavas and includes some types, such as dunite or other varieties of peridotite, that are nearly or quite unknown as lava flows, except perhaps at great depths in the ocean. These rocks, which may never exist as wholly liquid magmas, are *cumulate rocks* formed by the accumulation of sinking crystals that are denser than the magma in which they form.

Many plugs and necks are largely or wholly composed of fragmental material, partly of volcanic rock and partly fragments of the walls of the pipe, which may be of any type of rock. The fragments of both types range from dust size to blocks several tens of feet across. The fragmental material of magmatic origin is generally glassy ash and bits of pumice. The material may be all fine, constituting a tuff neck or plug, or all coarse in a breccia neck; but most commonly it is a mixture of large blocks in a fine matrix forming a tuff–breccia neck. The fragmentary material often is cut by dikes. The tuff or tuff–breccia necks resulting from explosive eruptions are also known as *diatremes*. Probably, they commonly terminated at the surface in maars or tuff cones.

Volcanic plugs (and necks) range in diameter from a few yards to

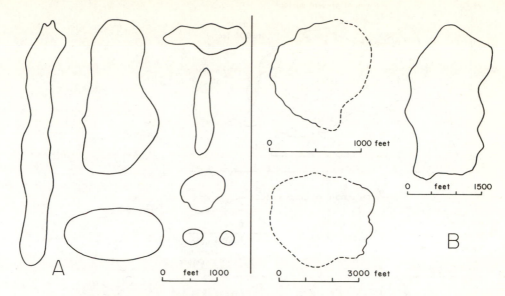

FIGURE 15-7. Outlines of volcanic necks and plugs (A) in central Scotland (after Geikie, 1897a), and (B) in Arizona (after Hack, 1942; McBirney, 1959; and Shoemaker, Roach, and Byers, 1962).

about a mile. Some are nearly circular in ground plan, but others are oval, and in extreme cases they are gradational into fissure fillings. Other examples, such as some of the necks described by Geikie (1897) in Scotland, are very irregular in plan (Fig. 15-7). In some instances, as in some of the pipes of South Africa that have been mined for diamonds, a plug that has a subcircular cross section at the ground surface is found to become more and more elongate at depth (Fig. 15-8). Some plugs have nearly vertical walls and a few appear to enlarge downward, but most converge downward like very steep walled funnels opening upward. In a few instances, where the presently exposed level was close to the surface at the time of eruption, the uppermost part of the funnel is seen to flare out very abruptly. Remnants of tuff cones can sometimes be found around the mouths of these flaring pipes. In natural exposures the plug walls can seldom be seen through vertical ranges of more than a few hundreds of feet; hence, the downward convergence of the walls to any great depth can only be inferred. However, at the Kimberley Mine in South Africa, the convergence was found to continue to the limit of mining operations at a depth of 3,500 feet below the present surface and about twice that below the surface at the time of the formation of the pipe (Fig. 15-8). Where a plug cuts nearly horizontal sedimentary or volcanic rocks, the beds of the latter adjacent to it can sometimes be seen to be bent upward by upthrusting of the central area. More commonly, however, they have sagged inward in a conical or bowl-like structure owing to subsidence of the area because of removal of support from beneath. Around some of the necks near Dunbar, Scotland, the beds in a zone a few tens of feet thick immediately adjacent to the walls have been dragged downward into nearly vertical attitudes (Francis, 1962). In some of the necks, nearly horizontal layers of tuff, which must have been formed at the surface, have subsided several hundred feet into the pipe, presumably due to removal of

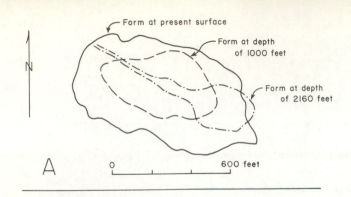

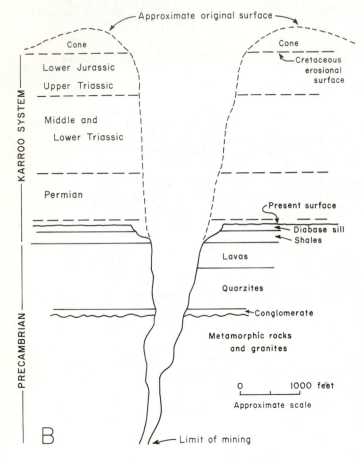

FIGURE 15-8. Kimberly diamond pipe, South Africa, showing form and dimensions at various levels. (A) plan (after Wagner, 1914); (B) diagrammatic cross section showing probable original form above present land surface (after Arthur Holmes, *Principles of Physical Geology*, second edition, The Ronald Press Co., New York. Copyright 1965).

support at the end of the eruption. Tuff consisting partly of sedimentary debris, presumably mobilized by gas, has been injected into fractures forming dikes and sills in the neck and along its boundaries.

The quasi-cylindrical form of volcanic pipes and plugs is sometimes the result of subsidence of cylindrical blocks along ring fractures, as described in the later section on cauldron subsidences, but in many instances it must result from enlargement of an original fissure. Not only do some pass downward into fissure-like forms, but commonly the alignment of several plugs suggests very strongly their localization along regional fissures (Fig. 15-9), and sometimes the position of a particular plug appears to be governed by the intersection of two such fissures. The enlargement of the original fissure to a pipe-like form appears to be the result of abrasion and/or stoping. The latter is a process of separation of blocks of rock from the walls of the vent, either by forceful dislodgement by magma or gas or by simple dropping off of an unsupported block through the influence of gravity as material is removed from around it. Abrasion of the walls results from the rubbing and collision of fragments carried past them by outrushing gas. The possibility of enlargement of the conduit by melting of the wall rocks must also be kept in mind, though there is seldom any evidence of it.

Very instructive as to the ways of development of the pipes are the tuff necks of Swabia, described in detail by the German geologist, Hans Cloos (1941). These necks cut sedimentary rocks of Jurassic age and are filled with a mixture of tuff and sedimentary blocks. The tuff consists partly of comminuted sedimentary rock and partly of bits of glassy ash and lapilli solidified from molten magma. The blocks are of the same sedimentary rocks that make up the walls of the neck. The original suggestion that the mixture resulted simply from ejected material falling back into the open explosion funnel has been shown by Cloos to be unacceptable. The sedimentary blocks are not arranged helter-skelter, as they would be if they had fallen

FIGURE 15-9. Map of three volcanic necks (diatremes) in the Hopi Buttes region of Arizona, showing their relation to basalt dikes (black). (After Hack, 1942.)

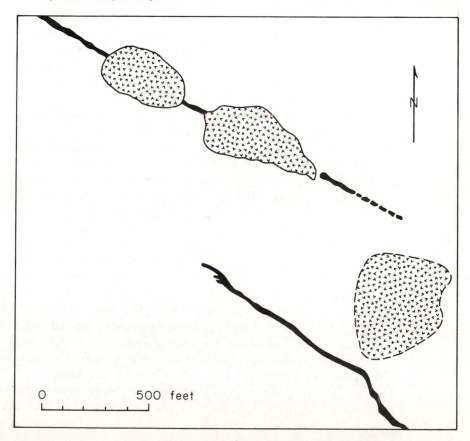

0   500 feet

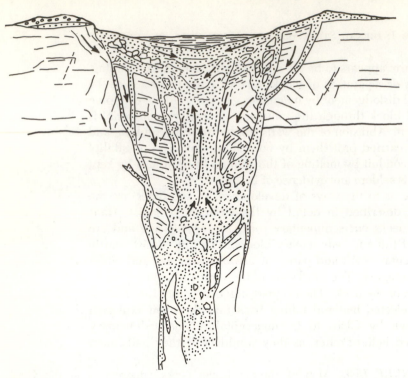

FIGURE 15-10. Vertical cross section of a tuff neck in Swabia (after Cloos, 1941). Intrusive tuff (stippled) contains large and small fragments of massive limestone (white).

back into the funnel after being thrown into the air. Instead, many of them, particularly the larger ones, are derived from the immediately adjacent wall rocks, which may be different from those a short distance above or below, and have simply moved outward and a little downward into the neck (Fig. 15-10). Commonly, flow structure is conspicuously developed in the tuff. Both in the wall rocks and in the sedimentary blocks thin and often wedge-shaped fissures have been filled by the tuff.

There appears to be little question that the mechanism of formation of these necks deduced by Cloos is correct. Highly gas-charged magma at relatively shallow depth encountered fissures (possibly formed by slight upheaval and distension of the overlying rocks), which locally relieved the confining pressure on the magma and allowed it to vesiculate explosively. Gas laden with bits of magmatic ash rose through the fissures, more freely at some places than others, abrading the walls and tearing loose small fragments of the wall rocks and carrying the fine debris upward to the surface, where it was ejected to build ash cones around the vents. As the conduit was gradually widened in this way, larger blocks of the wall rocks became loosened and slid outward into the conduit, their great mass causing them to move downward through the rising current of ash-laden gas. Some of the blocks moved downward several hundred feet below the level of their parent beds at the same time that the rising gas was carrying upward smaller fragments of rock from levels well below any now visible.

The suspension of ash particles in gas represents the same sort of "fluidization" that takes place in glowing avalanches and ash flows. The resulting emulsion is exceedingly mobile and enters and fills very small cracks. In some places the solid particles are largely or wholly magmatic ash, but at other places, as in the Carboniferous necks of Scotland, they consist mainly of tiny bits of sedimentary rock from the walls of the conduit. Cloos has suggested the name *tuffisite* for these intrusive tuffs to distinguish them from extrusive tuffs.

Numerous volcanic plugs and necks are found in parts of western United States, as for example in the Cascade Range, the Rocky Mountain region, and the Great Basin. A group of them has been described in southeastern Missouri (Rust, 1937) and another in north-central Montana (Hearn, 1968); but perhaps the best known are those in Arizona, Utah, and New Mexico (Williams, 1936; Hunt, 1937; Hack, 1942; McBirney, 1959, 1963; Barrington and Kerr, 1961; Shoemaker, Roach, and Byers, 1962). About 200 necks and plugs are known in the Hopi Buttes volcanic field alone.

Williams (1936), in discussing the plugs of the Navajo-Hopi country, recognized two types, referred to by McBirney (1959) as the Hopi type and the Navajo type. The latter (Fig. 15-11), which is found in Monument Valley and nearby fields, is a roughly cylindrical pipe filled with fragmental material and closely resembles the diatremes of Swabia, described above. Some of the pipes flare out, funnel-like, near the original surface. The tuff that fills the pipes consists of a chaotic mixture of bits of minette (alkali-rich basic subvolcanic rock), pulverized sedimentary material from the walls, and pieces of granitic rock from the deep underlying basement. It is well cemented with calcite. Many of the granitic fragments are well rounded as a result of attrition in the pipe. At the top of the neck the tuff may be bedded and may show a basin structure, indicating that it accumulated in a surficial crater, and it is sometimes

FIGURE 15-11. Idealized vertical cross sections of volcanic necks: (A) Navajo type (tuff-breccia cut by dikes); (B) Hopi type (filled with columnar lava). (Modified after Williams, 1936.) The heavy line represents the present surface; the dashed lines represent the former surface and structures now eroded away.

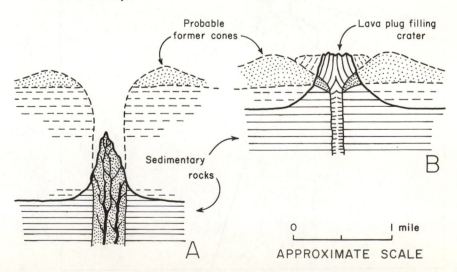

interbedded with lake-deposited sediments. The tuff is cut by dikes of minette. The Hopi type, well-developed in the Hopi Buttes volcanic field of Arizona and the Mount Taylor region of New Mexico, consists of a pipe filled with lava (an alkali-rich basic volcanic rock known as monchiquite), in some cases expanding at the top into a mass that represents the filling of a surficial maar or crater of a tuff cone. Some of the expanded heads show downward-diverging columnar joints (Fig. 15-11). In some, the crater-filling lava head is underlain by inward-dipping beds of tuff that contain abundant pulverized debris of sandstone and other underlying rocks. Both types of pipe filling are usually more resistant to erosion than the surrounding rocks and stand up as steep-sided castle-like or chimney-like buttes or mesas. Both also are sometimes associated with radial dikes (Fig. 15-12), which also often stand up as walls running across the countryside. Typical examples of the Navajo type are Agathla (Fig. 15-11) and Shiprock (Fig. 15-12), and of the Hopi type, Smith Butte (Fig. 15-11) and Haystack Butte. The Agathla neck is 1,000 feet high and 3,000 feet across at the base.

Sedimentary fragments in the tuffs of the necks are derived mainly

FIGURE 15-12.   Map of Shiprock, Arizona, a tuff-breccia neck, showing associated dikes and smaller necks. (After Williams, 1936.)

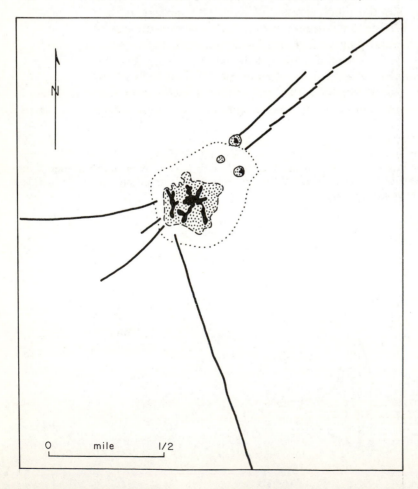

0   mile   1/2

from sandstones and shales of the walls immediately adjacent. Fragments from deeper origins are fairly common, but fragments from overlying levels are commoner. The latter frequently have been displaced downward several hundred feet, and fragments of granitic and metamorphic rocks in the Navajo necks have been brought up from the basement more than 3,000 feet below. Shoemaker and Moore (1956) have shown that in some necks an outer zone contains fragments from beds nearer the surface, whereas an inner zone contains fragments brought up from below. In some instances the tuff surrounds a core of massive igneous rock. The flaring upper portions of the pipes were no doubt caused by surficial hydroexplosions, and the rounding of fragments in the tuff was the result of repeated tossing and churning in the pipes; but McBirney (1959) attributes the removal of sedimentary material in the enlargement of the pipe to a sort of convectional movement in which a cooler mixture of gas and solid fragments moves downward near the edge of the pipe, while a hot column of gas and fragments moves upward in the center.

In the Shoshone Range of Nevada, three plugs cut sedimentary rocks of Paleozoic age (Gates, 1959). The Horse Canyon plug is elliptical with diameters of 1×0.75 mile. It is exposed by erosion through a depth of 1,600 feet. The walls of the pipe flare upward, and the contacts with the wall rocks are sharp but irregular. Along one side, the wall rocks are shattered through a thickness of 1 to 20 feet, but the blocks have not been much displaced. The outer portion of the plug consists, however, of a coarse breccia made up of angular fragments of the sedimentary wall rocks, ranging in size from microscopic to 100 feet long. At any given level the fragments are very largely of the same type as the immediately adjacent wall rock, showing that vertical movement of the breccia has been slight; but some blocks are found as much as 300 feet below the level at which they originated. A fine breccia consisting of angular to rounded fragments, mostly less than an inch across, of many different varieties of rock occupies the center of the plug and intrudes the coarser breccia in a series of dikes ranging from minute to several feet across. Some of the dikes lie between the coarse breccia and the walls. The matrix is finely comminuted rock flour now much altered by hot solutions. A small mass of subvolcanic rock (quartz monzonite porphyry) intrudes the fine breccia.

Gates suggests that the separation of fragments from the walls of the pipe to form the coarse breccia may have been partly the result of relief of pressure due to opening of the pipe, allowing the wall rocks to expand explosively, as they do in the drifts of deep mines. This tendency may even have been increased by the "Venturi effect" of rapidly outrushing gas streaming upward through the pipe, further reducing the pressure on the walls. It may also have been aided, as previously suggested by Rust (1937), by the expansion of water or other fluids that had been held under pressure in pores in the wall rocks.

The Montana diatremes typically consist of a discontinuous outer ring of downfaulted arcuate slices of the sedimentary wall rocks, some of

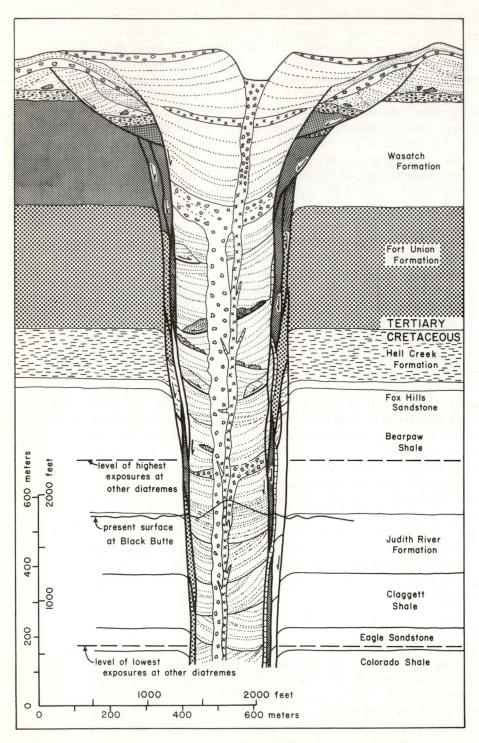

FIGURE 15-13. Hypothetical vertical cross section of diatremes in Montana. (After Hearn. Copyright 1968 by the American Association for the Advancement of Science.)

which have moved downward more than 4,000 feet (Fig. 15-13), within which a series of inward-dipping bedded tuffs is cut by a core of unbedded breccia and by dikes and irregular intrusive bodies of igneous rock. The intrusive igneous bodies and fragments of igneous rock in the tuff and breccia are kimberlite, an alkali-rich ultrabasic rock rich in altered olivine, resembling the commonest rock of the South African diamond pipes. The bedded tuffs are believed by Hearn (1968) to have been originally laid down from the air at higher levels and to have sunk thousands of feet in the pipes, dragging down with them the thin marginal slices of wall rocks. Each diatreme was filled by the debris of its own eruptions, and repeated eruptions alternated with subsidence to keep the pipe filled to a level near the surface.

Also, in some tuff necks in Fifeshire, Scotland, there is evidence of a considerable amount of subsidence (Francis, 1969). The necks are filled with basaltic tuffs and agglomerates, generally well bedded. The bedding is mainly the result of subaerial deposition of the ash, but in places the material was reworked by streams. The beds have been dropped at least 900 feet by subsidence on ring fractures at the boundary of the neck. The mechanism resembles that of formation of calderas and pit craters (Chapter 12).

In general, however, the enlargement near the surface of the pipes now occupied by necks or plugs seems probably to have resulted from pulsating explosions or series of explosions producing brecciation of the rocks along the walls of the original channelway and allowing the fragments to move into the resulting opening, where they tend to move downward under the influence of gravity but may be transported upward by the streams of gas and entrained debris. The churning action in the pipe may round some fragments and produce considerable admixture of fragments of different types of rock from various levels in the walls with variable amounts of essential volcanic material from depth. The separation of fragments from the walls is probably aided at moderate depths by the processes suggested by Gates and Rust. In many instances, the emulsion of gas and solid particles is exceedingly fluid and penetrates fractures in the wall rocks, aiding or bringing about their detachment. At the end of the explosive activity, depletion of magma and gas in the underlying reservoir and conduit may result in loss of support, which allows the pipe filling to sink by various amounts, sometimes hundreds or even thousands of feet.

Ring Complexes

In mapping the geology of the volcanic districts of western Scotland, it was found that many dikes are arcuate in ground plan, some of the arcs extending around almost a full circle (Richey, 1961; Stewart, 1965). Similar structures have been found in other denuded volcanic districts all over the world. Because of their form, these dikes are often referred to as *ring intrusions* and groups of them as *ring complexes*. Two

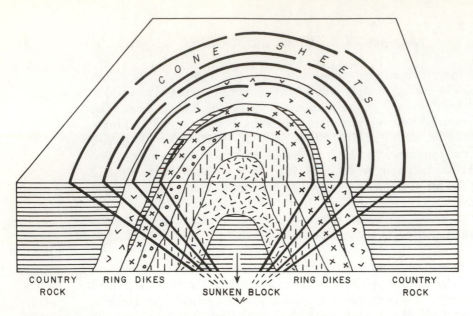

FIGURE 15-14. Idealized block diagram showing ring dikes and cone sheets. (After Richey, 1961. Acknowledgments are due to the Director, Institute of Geological Sciences, London, for permission to reproduce Figures 15-14, 15-15, and 15-17.)

types of ring intrusions have been recognized: *cone sheets* dip inward toward the volcanic center, and *ring dikes* are nearly vertical or dip outward, usually at angles greater than 70° (Fig. 15-14). Cone sheets are thin, seldom exceeding 15 feet in thickness and commonly less than 6 feet. In the Scottish centers they are usually fine grained and basaltic. Ring dikes are generally much thicker—from a few hundred feet to more than a mile in width. They are usually coarse grained and range from very mafic gabbros and peridotites to granite. The centers of the complexes are commonly occupied by stocks of similar coarse-grained rocks. Radial dikes are associated with some of the ring structures. The ring complexes underlay big volcanic cones, at least some of which contained big calderas, and in part the ring structures intrude the base of the caldera-filling lavas. Several of the Scottish districts show clear evidence of migration of volcanic activity from one to another of as many as three successive nearby centers.

The Loch Bà ring dike on the Island of Mull, which has been called the most perfect known example of a ring dike (Bailey et al., 1924), is a nearly continuous oval 3.6 × 5.3 miles in diameter. The maximum width of the dike is about 1,000 feet. The rocks within the ring fault along which the dike was intruded have subsided about 500 feet (Lewis, 1968). However, the cylinder enclosed by the ring fault and dike is not vertical, but is inclined northwestward at an angle of about 75° (Skelhorn, MacDougall, and Longland, 1969).

Around some of the Scottish centers cone sheets were formed in enormous numbers. Several hundred of them surround the centers in the Island of Mull and on the peninsula of Ardnamurchan (Fig. 15-15). The outermost sheets dip at angles of only 35 to 45°, but they steepen toward the center of the complex and the inner sheets dip at steeply as 75°. They also tend to steepen downwards. Projections of the dips of the cone sheets converge toward a focus at a depth of about 3 miles beneath the center of the complex (Fig. 15–16). They have been explained (Anderson, 1937) as the result of an upward thrust by a magma body at that depth, lifting the roof above it and producing upward-diverging fractures that were injected with magma. Radial dikes also may result from the up-doming and stretching of the roof above a magma body.

If the above interpretation is correct, the cone sheets indicate an uplift of the volcanic center that, in the case of the Ardnamurchan and Mull centers, must have amounted to considerably more than 1,000 feet. This is supported at Ardnamurchan by other evidence that indicates up-arching of the overlying rocks. Around the northern center in the Island of Arran, also, the neighboring rocks are dragged sharply upward around the cental stock; and in the Island of Rum the igneous rocks of the main intrusive mass have been uplifted several thousand feet on a great ring fault.

The ring dikes were interpreted by Anderson as the result of the decrease of pressure or removal of support from below. Withdrawal of

FIGURE 15-15. Simplified geologic map of Ardnamurchan, showing ring dikes and cone sheets surrounding three successive centers of volcanic activity. (After Richey, 1961.)

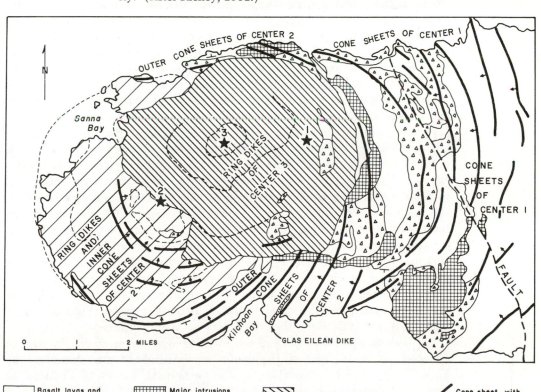

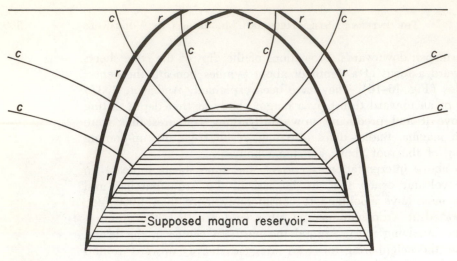

FIGURE 15-16. Diagram illustrating the formation of (c) cone sheets, and (r) ring dikes. (After Anderson, 1937.)

magma results in the formation of vertical or steep upward-converging fractures in the roof and sinking of the block bounded by the fractures, with magma invading the resulting space (Fig. 15-16). At times the fractures may break across before reaching the surface, and magma fills the space left between the sinking block and the roof. Probably some of the stocks at the center of ring complexes were formed in that way. At other times, the fractures reach the surface and the entire cylinder of rock above the magma body may sink, forming a more or less circular basin at the surface. Such a basin is, of course, a caldera. Where only the roots of the volcanic structure remain, however, it is often impossible to tell whether or not the subsidence extended all the way to the surface. In these cases the term caldera is avoided, and the subsurface structure is referred to as a *cauldron subsidence*. Unfortunately, the use of the term is not always consistent, and some sunken basins that existed on the surface and in which surficial lava flows accumulated have been referred to as cauldrons.

The sinking of the block is not necessarily the result of prior withdrawal of magma. If the gross density of the block is greater than that of the magma, once the fractures are established the block may sink into the magma of its own weight, the magma moving up the boundary fractures to make room for it. The ring-dike opening may be further enlarged by stoping (physical removal) of fragments from its walls, the fragments sinking in the magma and perhaps being assimilated into it, or, in the case of rapidly rising magma, being carried upward and perhaps out at the surface. Indeed, enlargement of the fracture by some such method is necessary to account for the great width of many ring dikes. Volcanic cones commonly are built along the ring fractures at the surface.

The first cauldron subsidence to be recognized as such was that of Glencoe, in the Grampian Highlands of Scotland. It was described by E. B. Bailey and his coworkers of the Geological Survey of Scotland in 1909. The cauldron, formed in Devonian time (about 360 million years ago), measures 5 by 9 miles and is occupied by lava flows that were later partly eaten away by granitic intrusives. The block within the cauldron sank several thousand feet (Fig. 15-17).

Cauldron subsidences have been recognized in many parts of the world in addition to Scotland. A series of well-studied ones, formed during the Permian period (about 240 million years ago), lies in the Oslo graben near Oslo, Norway (Fig. 15-18). Their size is shown in Table 15-1. The cauldrons were formed by the sinking of nearly circular blocks accom-

FIGURE 15-17. Diagram of cauldron subsidences. (After Bailey and Maufe, 1960.)

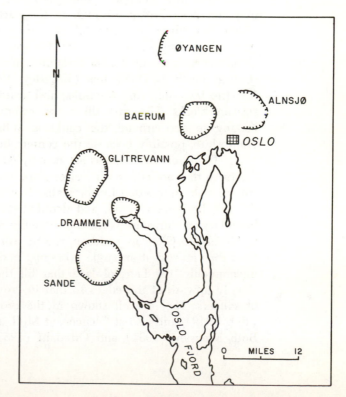

FIGURE 15-18. Map of cauldron subsidences in the Oslo graben, Norway. (After Oftedahl, 1960.)

TABLE 15-1. Dimensions of cauldron subsidences in Norway [1]

Name of cauldron	Diameter (miles)	Mean vertical subsidence (feet)	Volume of subsidence (cubic miles)
Baerum	7 × 5	3,000–4,500	17–26
Drammen	4	ca. 1,500	ca. 3.7
Glitrevann	10 × 6	4,500	ca. 40
Sande	7	1,500–2,500	12–17
Alnsjø [2]	9 (?)	4,500–6,000	—
Oyangen [2]	5 (?)	9,000–12,000	—

[1] After Oftedahl, 1960.
[2] Only a portion remains.

panied by surficial volcanic activity that poured lava flows into the resulting basins. Later stocks and irregular intrusive bodies ate their way upward into the lava flows within the cauldrons, in some cases destroying large parts of them. About 80 per cent of the lava that filled the Alnsjø cauldron has been replaced by intrusive bodies at the level now visible (Oftedahl, 1960).

Another well-known series of cauldron subsidences lies in New Hampshire and Vermont (Billings, 1945). Some of the subsiding blocks may not have broken through to the surface (Chapman and Chapman, 1940), but others certainly did so, since surficial lavas were carried down in the subsiding cylinder. In the Ossipee Mts. the volcanic rocks in the cauldron sank about 12,500 feet, and in other cauldrons they may have sunk as much as 17,000 feet (Kingsley, 1931). Ring dikes were intruded into the bounding ring fractures, and granitic intrusions have invaded the sunken blocks. The ring dikes are essentially vertical. Cone sheets are lacking in and around the cauldron subsidences of Norway and New Hampshire, possibly because the centers have been eroded too deeply.

Cauldron subsidences are usually considered to be bounded by ring fractures that are either vertical or slope outward leaving the central block free to sink unimpeded by the walls. It is rare, however, that the outward dip can be demonstrated, and detailed study has usually shown that the boundary fractures are vertical or actually dip inward at high angles. Even at the classic Glencoe cauldron, recent work has shown that the boundary fault dips inward at an angle averaging about 80° (Taubeneck, 1967). Not uncommonly, the beds of lava that fill the cauldron have been dragged steeply upward at the edges so that in cross section they resemble a stack of saucers. This is well shown in the cross section of the Ossipee Mts. (Fig. 15-19), and also at Glencoe, at Mull, and in the Norwegian cauldrons. Both Kingsley (1931) and Oftedahl (1953) point out that this suggests

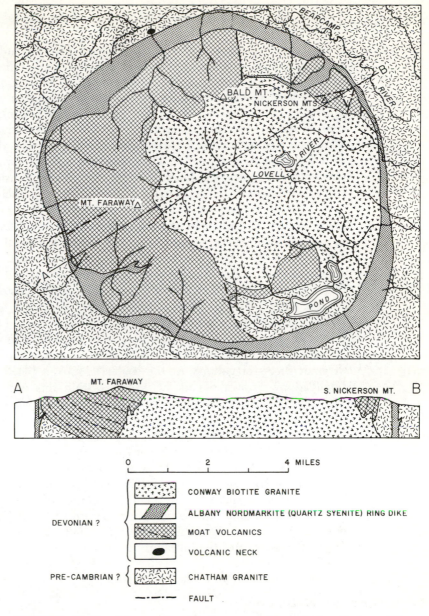

FIGURE 15-19. Map and vertical cross section of the Ossipee Mountains cauldron subsidence, New Hampshire. (After Kingsley, 1931.)

that the boundary fault dips inward, not outward, so that the sinking block has been squeezed at the edges by a wedging effect. At Skaergaard in Greenland, Wager and Deer (1939) have shown that the mass of intrusive gabbro underlying the cauldron is funnel-like in form, and there also the lavas that have sunk into it are strongly upturned at the edges. The evidence has been reviewed by Reynolds (1956), who points out the close link in genetic mechanism between ancient cauldron subsidences and modern calderas. She concludes that from a study of cauldron subsidences

393

it can be inferred that the boundary fractures of both cauldron subsidences and calderas commonly dip inward. This in turn, following Anderson's (1936, 1937) mechanical analysis, suggests that the original fractures were the result of pressure from below, and that only later did relaxation of pressure and/or removal of support, or some other mechanism, allow the central block to sink. Distension of the whole volcanic structure may allow the portion within a central ring fracture to subside in the manner of a keystone in a spreading arch, and the lack of support beneath the sinking portion may result simply from the greater density of the sinking block as compared to the magma in the underlying chamber.

Before leaving the subject of ring complexes, mention should be made of the Messum complex in southwest Africa. The complex is one of several that lie in a zone trending inland northeastward from Cape Cross, about 860 miles north-northwest of Cape Town. A large volcanic cone was built in the Messum area, projecting above, but apparently interfingering with, the Karroo flood basalt flows of Triassic age (Korn and Martin, 1954). The area has since been deeply eroded, exposing the core of the volcano. A central sunken area 15 miles across is bordered by once-horizontal Karroo lavas that have been bent sharply downward at angles of 30 to 75°. Within the sunken area there are exposed the edges of a series of great sheets of gabbro. At the center, a sunken block 4 miles across is bounded by ring dikes, and it is only within this innermost subsidence that remnants of the volcanic cone are preserved. Some of the rocks of the inner mass appear to have been much altered by gases with the introduction of sodium. The gabbro sheets have a total thickness of several thousand feet. They now tilt inward at angles of 5 to 60° and have been referred to as a "lopolith." The inward tilting is certainly at least partly the result of later sinking. The sheets were probably originally nearly horizontal, and their intrusion resulted in doming of the overlying volcanic structure. Restoration of the original structure (Fig. 15-20B) indicates that the central part of the gabbro sheets originally lay 10,000 to 15,000 feet below the summit of the volcano.

Structure of Kilauea

When seismographs were first installed at Kilauea Volcano, Hawaii, in 1911, it was soon found that the ground surface at the edge of the caldera was constantly tilting in one direction or another. The seismographs were of the type known as horizontal pendulums, in which a heavy mass is supported by a thin wire from the top of an upright post and hinged against the base of the post. Any tilting of the post from side to side causes a shift in the position of the pendulum (in the same way that an inclined gatepost causes the gate to swing in the direction of lean of the post), and this in turn results in a shift in the position of the line drawn

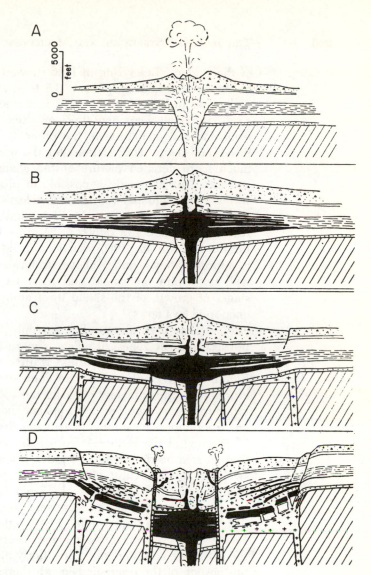

FIGURE 15-20. Vertical cross sections illustrating the evolution of the Messum complex, southwest Africa. (After Korn and Martin, 1954.) (A) The original volcanic structure; (B) Intrusion of gabbro sheets (black) and doming of the structure; (C) Subsidence of the structure and basining of the gabbro sheets; (D) Subsidence of the central cauldron and formation of ring dikes.

on the seismogram when the pendulum is at rest. Study of these records over many years, correlating them with the behavior of the volcano, showed that some of the tilting of the ground was due to seasonal temperature changes in the rocks of the caldera wall and some probably due to heavy rainfall; but some tilting was the result of the rise or fall of the top of the volcano with changes in magmatic pressure beneath. The volcano behaves almost like a great balloon, swelling up due to inflation before eruptions and deflating during eruptions. The indications from tilt measurements have been confirmed and made quantitative by differential leveling. Thus it was shown that between 1912 and 1921 the benchmark at the northeastern rim of the caldera rose 3 feet. In 1924 cracking along the east rift zone resulted in the magma draining out of the Halemaumau lava lake and from beneath the top of the volcano, allowing the top of the mountain to sink and causing a tilting of the ground toward the center of the caldera. Releveling in 1926 showed that the benchmark at the edge of the caldera had gone down 3.5 feet, and a benchmark at the edge of Halemaumau had gone down 13 feet since 1921.

In recent years new types of tiltmeters, relying on the flow of liquid from one end of a tube to the other as the surface beneath the tube is tilted, and many more stations for the measurement of tilt have yielded a much more detailed picture of the changes of shape of the top of the volcano. This has made it possible to project the pattern of tilting of the surface back into the core of the volcano, and to show that the changes are such as would be produced by inflation and deflation of a magma reservoir at a depth of only 2 to $2\frac{1}{2}$ miles below the summit of the volcano (Eaton and Murata, 1960; Macdonald, 1961). Since the top of the volcano is approximately 4 miles above its base at the sea floor, the reservoir is well up within the shield and must have been formed during the late stages of growth of the shield by heating, softening, and remelting of the once-solid lava flows.

It has been shown that not only the summit area of the volcano, but also the rift zones 20 miles or more away from the summit, swell up preceding eruptions and shrink again during eruptions (Macdonald and Eaton, 1964). Furthermore, the volume of lava extruded during a flank eruption is approximately equal to the volume of sinking of the mountaintop during the eruption. (It appears that a little of the magma moving out from under the summit remains as dike fillings in the rift zone instead of erupting at the surface.) During the years 1964–1967 it has been found that an area on the rift zone 6 miles east-southeast of the caldera has been swelling independently of the summit region, leaving an area between them lagging behind. It has also been found that the center of swelling beneath the summit does not remain constant, but shifts laterally through distances of more than a mile (Fiske and Kinoshita, 1969; Kinoshita, et al., 1969). Thus, the inflatable magma reservoir must extend outward along the rift zones, and there must be a fairly direct and easy connection between the portion of the reservoir beneath the summit and that in the rift zones.

The precise nature of the reservoir is still conjectural. It seems quite unlikely that it is a continuous large body of highly fluid magma, but it seems equally unlikely that it is merely a series of narrow dikes separated by rigid wall rocks. More probably it is a spongy mass of plastic or viscous very hot rock shot through with masses and channelways of more fluid eruptible magma. For weeks, months, or years magma slowly rises from a deeper source region into this plastic core of the volcano, and the settling of olivine crystals in the rising magma may produce a great mass of peridotite in its lower part. The more mobile pockets of magma increase in size and the whole volcano swells up, distending the surface more and more, until finally it ruptures and magma breaks through to the surface. The weight of the overlying mass of the volcano, aided near the surface by the expansion of bubbles of gas forming in the magma, causes the liquid magma to move upward and erupt. This in turn partly drains the mobile pockets of the reservoir and allows the volcano to shrink again.

There is a temptation to think of the Kilauea magma body as resembling the great sheets of gabbro exposed in the eroded core of the Messum volcano, described above. Indeed, in 1911 the great American geologist, R. A. Daly, suggested that Kilauea overlies a laccolith fed from Mauna Loa and, in turn, serving as the shallow magma chamber that feeds Kilauea. Thus far, however, the pattern of tilting does not appear to support such a simple concept. Furthermore, if a very widespread sheet-like or lens-like magma body existed at shallow level, it should be detectable by the delay of shear waves of earthquakes passing through it or following circuitous paths around it. Such is not the case, though there is some suggestion of delay of waves traveling through a small region below the caldera.

Other Shallow Reservoirs

Mauna Loa in Hawaii also swells before eruptions and shrinks during them. It is presumed that it also has a shallow magma reservoir, but the measurements are as yet inadequate to indicate its position or depth. At very few other volcanoes do we yet have any good indication of the depth of the magma chamber.

The magma erupted at Vesuvius brings up many fragments of limestone or of calcium silicate rocks derived by the alteration of limestone in contact with the magma. The less altered fragments are recognizable as being from a certain geologic formation, and since both the stratigraphy and the structure of the region are well known, the depth at which the limestone underlies Vesuvius also is known quite closely. Thus, if the fragments have been "stoped" from the wall and roof of the magma chamber, the latter lies at a depth of approximately 3 miles below sea level, or $3\frac{1}{2}$ miles below the mountaintop (Rittmann, 1933). This suggests that the shallow magma chamber of Vesuvius lies at a depth comparable with that of the shallow chamber of Kilauea.

The chamber beneath Klyuchevskaya Volcano in Kamchatka appears to lie somewhat deeper. Earthquakes arriving at a nearby seismograph station from origins in part of Japan pass directly beneath the volcano. From the delay in arrivals of shear waves, Russian volcanologists have been able to determine the approximate depth and size of the chamber. It lies between 30 and 40 miles beneath the surface, approximately at the top of the earth's mantle in that region, and appears to be a lenticular mass elongated in a north-south direction approximately parallel to the chain of volcanoes (Gorshkov, 1958). In Alaska, also, there has been observed a disappearance of the shear waves of earthquakes traveling along paths beneath the volcanic range in the vicinity of Katmai, and this has been attributed to the presence of magma bodies beneath the range (Kubota and Berg, 1967). The magma bodies range in depth from about 6 to 24 miles and appear to have the form of vertically flattened spheroids. Those at depths less than 12 miles are directly related to overlying volcanoes. The deeper ones cannot be closely correlated with individual volcanoes, but probably feed the shallower chambers.

From studies of earthquakes and volcanic tremor associated with Sakurajima, Sugimoto and Namba (1958) concluded that the volcano is underlain by a magma chamber at a depth of about 2 miles, which appears to be fed from another chamber about 6 miles deep which lies beneath Kagoshima Bay a little over a mile northeast of the volcano. The northern part of Kagoshima Bay occupies the Aira Caldera, and Sakurajima lies near the southern edge of the caldera, probably localized by one of the caldera-boundary faults. After the great eruption in 1914, subsidence in the area centered not at Sakurajima but at a point beneath Kagoshima Bay northeast of the volcano (Omori, 1916); and although the area near the volcano has since risen again, the center of the caldera has continued to sink, suggesting that magma has been shifting from that area to the reservoir beneath the volcano. From a consideration of the upward migration of the eruptive vents on the flanks of the volcano during the last 500 years, Taneda (1961) suggests that the magma chamber beneath the volcano has been working its way closer to the surface. This leads one to speculate whether the upward migration of the magma chamber may eventually lead to voluminous release of magma and collapse of the summit of the cone with formation of a summit caldera.

Gravity and magnetic studies have led to the conclusion that Avachinsky Volcano in Kamchatka is underlain by an ellipsoidal magma chamber with diameters of approximately 1 by 3 miles, 1.5 to 2 miles below the base of the volcano (Steinberg and Rivosh, 1965). It is interesting to note, however, that similar indications of shallow magma reservoirs beneath neighboring volcanoes have not been found. Also using gravity methods, Le Pichon and Talwani (1964) found an apparent magma chamber 6 miles beneath a submarine volcano in the Atlantic Ocean.

Abnormally dense masses of rock lie at depths of a few miles within the Hawaiian volcanoes (Kinoshita, 1965; Kinoshita and Okamura, 1965; Furumoto, Thompson, and Woollard, 1965; Malahoff and Woollard, 1966). The presence and approximate dimensions of one such mass beneath the Koolau Volcano on Oahu has been confirmed by seismic methods (Adams and Furumoto, 1965). Some of the masses, such as that in the Koolau Volcano, lie directly beneath the caldera; but others, such as those of Kilauea and Mauna Loa, are offset from the calderas by as much as several miles. The nature of the dense masses is still conjectural, but they are most probably accumulations of heavy crystals in the magma chambers and conduits of the volcanoes (Macdonald, 1965).

The magma chamber beneath Klyuchevskaya may lie in the zone where the magma is formed, but the shallow magma reservoirs of Kilauea and Vesuvius cannot mark the region of magma generation. They must be only storage chambers fed by magma from a considerably greater depth, through probably from zones that are shallow in terms of the earth as a whole. In general, the most likely zone for magma generation is the outer part of the earth's mantle, though locally magma may perhaps be formed in the base of the crust, particularly where the crust has been thickened and depressed during folding of a geosyncline (Chapter 14). Even there, however, there may be an admixture of magma from the outer mantle. Once again Kilauea provides us with some of the best evidence of depth of origin of the magma. This will be discussed briefly in the next section.

Source of Magma

The question of where the magma comes from and how it is generated are the most speculative in all of volcanology. We cannot see to any appreciable depth below the surface of the earth and have few direct measurements of the nature of the materials in the earth's interior. Deep mines and the deepest oil wells penetrate barely the outermost part of the earth's crust, and even where rocks have been tilted on edge and planed off by erosion in great folded mountain ranges, we see only the outer part of the crust. None of the earth below the crust or any material from there has ever been seen for certain, although in a few areas, such as St. Paul's Rocks on the Mid-Atlantic Ridge and the Island of Cyprus, masses of peridotite may be portions of the earth's mantle raised up through the crust. Possibly, also, some of the masses of serpentinized peridotite and eclogite in the California Coast Range, the Sierra Nevada, and elsewhere in the world are fragments of the mantle squeezed up by mountain-building forces. In addition, some lavas bring up from depth fragments of peridotite and eclogite, the minerals of which indicate that they were formed under such high pressure that they almost surely came from depths beneath the crust.

Space here does not permit a discussion of the evidence for the internal constitution of the earth, but this can be found in many standard textbooks (see references at the end of the chapter). Suffice it to say that the earth is generally believed to consist of three main parts—a core of nickel–iron with a radius of approximately 2,200 miles; a mantle 1,800 miles thick composed of peridotite and its high-pressure equivalents, with perhaps an increasing abundance of metallic sulfides in its inner part; and a crust of ordinary silicate rocks (Fig. 15-21). Beneath the continents the crust generally consists of an upper "granitic" portion composed of igneous rocks, such as granite, granodiorite, and quartz monzonite, with lesser volumes of gabbro and relatively small volumes of various lavas, sedimentary rocks, and metamorphic rocks formed by alteration of the lavas and sediments. Beneath the granitic crust there is generally a lower portion with the general properties, and presumably the composition, of basaltic rocks, though probably with the coarse granularity of gabbro. In places the granitic and basaltic portions of the crust are fairly sharply separated,

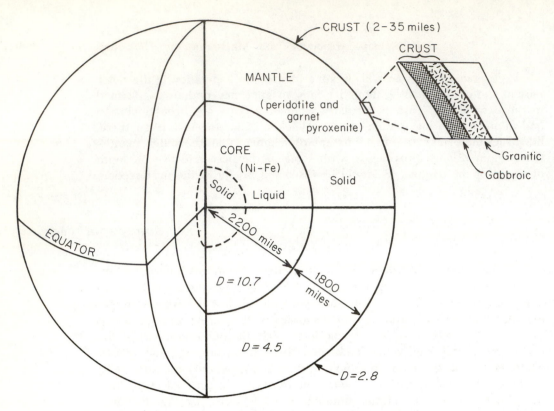

FIGURE 15-21. Diagrammatic cross section of the earth, showing the core, mantle, and the "granitic" and "gabbroic" portions of the crust.

but in other areas there is a gradual downward gradation from one to the other. The total thickness of the crust beneath the continents ranges from about 20 to 35 miles. Beneath the ocean basins the granitic portion is absent, and the crust consists wholly of more mafic materials. The suboceanic crust is very thin. Although it thickens to as much as 15 miles in places, as beneath the Hawaiian Islands, in other places it is as thin as 2 miles, and it averages only about 5 miles. The crust and mantle are believed to be essentially solid with only relatively small and local bodies of molten material. If any large masses of molten rock were present, they should be revealed by the cutting out of shear-type earthquake waves, which will not travel through ordinary liquids. Shear waves are, in fact, cut out at the boundary of the core, the outer part of which is believed to be liquid (although the inner part may again be solid).

Samples dredged from many places on the ocean floor are basalt (nearly all of tholeiitic type, rather poor in alkalies, particularly potassium), and it is generally agreed that the upper part of the crust beneath the oceans is basalt with a thin and discontinuous cover of sediment. But what lies below the upper layer? Hess (1962) suggested that the suboceanic crust consists mainly of serpentine formed by hydration of the outermost part of the earth's peridotite mantle, but this does not appear to be supported by seismic studies. On the other hand, the suggestion made by Hess (1962) and Dietz (1961) that the ocean floor is spreading outward from mid-ocean ridges (Chapter 14), appears to be somewhat better supported (Gilluly, 1969). One of the possible consequences of this seafloor-spreading mechanism is that the lower part of the crust may contain a very large number of dikes of basalt and perhaps also of peridotite (Vogt, Schneider, and Johnson, 1969). At any rate, most geologists today believe that the suboceanic crust is very largely basalt.

The outer portion of the mantle is believed to consist of peridotite made up largely of olivine and pyroxene with minor amounts of feldspar and other minerals. If water is present, the place of pyroxene is partly or wholly taken by amphibole. With increasing pressure, however, these mineral assemblages become unstable, the feldspar disappears, garnet appears, and the pyroxene becomes more sodic. This high-pressure assemblage is known as the *eclogite facies* (after the rock eclogite, which is the high-pressure equivalent of gabbro). The change in mineral composition of the mantle with depth appears to have important consequences on the composition of the magma derived from it.

We need not here be concerned with the composition of the deeper parts of the mantle or the core, since it appears fairly certain that magmas are generated at rather shallow levels. It should be noted, however, that the continued slow escape of hydrogen and other volatiles from the inner parts of the earth may well be of great importance in volcanic activity. Evidence at Kilauea Volcano, and less direct evidence elsewhere, suggests very strongly that basaltic magmas are formed within the outermost few tens of miles of the mantle. The level of origin of andesitic magmas is probably about the same, and that of rhyolitic ones even shallower.

The evidence at Kilauea is seismological. The numerous earthquakes recorded at the active volcanoes of the Hawaiian Islands are found to originate very largely in two different depth zones, one within about 5 miles of the surface and the other at a depth of 30 to 40 miles. Almost no earthquakes come from deeper than 40 miles in the Hawaiian area. The shallow quakes are mostly related to the change in shape of the volcanoes as they inflate and deflate before and during eruptions, but the deep quakes have long been thought to mark the region of magma generation. This belief has recently been strengthened by the discovery in close association with the quakes of a peculiar slight rhythmic trembling of the ground known as volcanic tremor. As early as 1914 less sensitive seismographs had recorded very similar but stronger tremor that we have since learned is closely associated with (and probably due to) the movement of magma through shallow feeding channels during eruptions. Consequently, there is a strong presumption that the tremor associated with the deeper earthquakes also results from movement of magma at or near the level of origin of the earthquakes. It is noteworthy that this level of apparent generation of magma coincides with a zone of low seismic velocities in the mantle. Such a decrease in the speed of earthquake waves could result from a softening and decrease in rigidity of the rocks as they approach the melting temperature. Perhaps the most easily melted constitu-

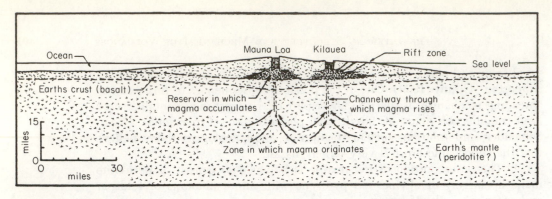

FIGURE 15-22. Diagram showing the probable substructure of Kilauea and Mauna Loa Volcanoes, Hawaii. (After Macdonald and Hubbard, 1970.)

ents of the mantle rocks are already liquid, occupying interstices between the still-solid more refractory portions. The earthquakes may result from the gradual yielding and readjustment of the solid material as the liquid portion moves out of it into the channelways that carry it eventually to the shallow magma reservoir. The general concept is illustrated by Fig. 15-22.

Since the magma appears at the surface, there can be no question that the melting does in fact occur, but the conditions that bring it about remain conjectural. Measurements in deep mines and wells show that everywhere the temperature increases downward within the earth. The rate of increase varies from one place to another, but averages about 1° per 100 feet. If this rate of increase were to continue, temperatures would be reached in the lower part of the mantle that for various reasons are regarded as impossible. Again, space does not permit here a discussion of the reasons or of the bases for the various estimates of the rate of temperature increase. Nearly all the estimates agree that at relatively shallow depths temperatures are reached at which rocks would be molten under the low pressures of the earth's surface. If the mantle is not as a whole molten, this must be the result of the known rise of melting temperature of rock with increase of pressure. Within the earth, pressure increases downward as a result of the increasingly great load of overlying rock. If we assume any specific distribution of particular types of rock, it is possible to calculate the pressure at any depth. In Fig. 15-23 the straight line shows the approximate melting temperature of basalt at increasing pressures downward within the earth. The figure also shows some recent estimates of the distribution of temperature within the earth. It will be noted that, in general, the melting-point curve lies above the temperature curves so that the rocks should remain solid. However, it will also be seen that the temperature curves, especially that of Verhoogen (1960), approach very close to the melting-point curve in the depth zone of 60 to 120 miles. The depth is about the same as that of the low-velocity zone in the mantle beneath the continents, but it is about twice as great as that of the low-velocity zone and the region of apparent magma generation beneath the Hawaiian Islands and other parts of the ocean basins. The increase of

402

temperature with depth beneath the oceans appears probably to be more rapid than beneath the continents. At any rate, if world over the temperature approaches close to the melting point at some level in the outer part of the mantle, any further local increase of temperature would bring about local melting and, if passageways to the surface are available, volcanism.

Increase of temperature is not the only possible cause of melting. Reduction of pressure by lowering the melting point would also bring about melting. The mechanism that might cause such reduction in pressure is obscure. It is doubtful that the crust has sufficient strength to allow reduction of pressure on the mantle by compressional up-arching of the crust. However, if open fissures can in any way be propagated downward into the appropriate zone, even briefly, melting should take place along the fissure. Gorshkov (1958) and others have pointed out the common occurrence of volcanoes in lines that may reflect underlying deep-seated fractures. The melting point may also be lowered by the introduction of volatile fluxes—gases migrating outward from the earth's deep interior.

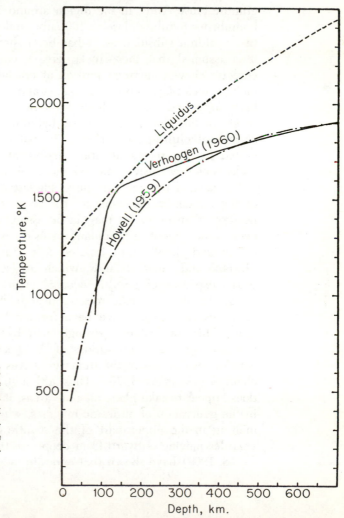

FIGURE 15-23. Graph showing probable temperature and pressure at various depths in the earth, and the melting temperature of basalt at various pressures. (After Macdonald. Copyright 1961 by the American Association for the Advancement of Science.)

Although it appears quite certain that basaltic magma comes from the outer part of the mantle, we have already seen that the outer mantle is believed to consist not of basalt but of peridotite. However, theoretically it is not difficult to obtain basalt magma from peridotite, since most peridotites contain several per cent of material of basaltic composition, and this material would be the first portion of the peridotite to melt. To obtain basalt magma, it is then only necessary to separate the liquid portion from the remaining solid, though just how this separation is accomplished we still do not know.

All the common volcanic rocks with compositions more siliceous than basalt *can* be derived from basalt magma by differentiation (see Appendix 2), and it appears certain that *some are* derived in this manner. But the volumes of these more siliceous rocks in many orogenic belts, and particularly the huge volumes of rhyolitic ignimbrite in some parts of the world, are too large to have been derived from the volume of associated basalt, and it is clear they must have been formed in some other way. Some, at least, probably have arisen from melting of lower parts of the continental granitic crust. Thus, in the region around Beatty, Nevada, where rhyolitic ignimbrites totalling close to 100 cubic miles in volume are associated with two cauldron subsidences, it has been shown by Cornwall (1962) that if it is assumed that these rocks have a composition corresponding to the eutectic (lowest-melting) portion of crustal rocks, the depth at which the melting took place should have been about 7 to 9 miles. Many investigators have suggested that the huge ignimbritic eruptions result from the fracturing of the roof above granitic batholiths and the escape of the magma of the batholith at the surface. The batholiths, in turn, appear to be generated by the recrystallization, mobilization, and melting of the crustal rocks that previously occupied the same region in the crust.

Several investigators have suggested that the voluminous andesites of the circum-Pacific belts are the result of the modification of the composition of rising basalt magma by assimilation of continental crust. However, some regions of abundant andesites with lesser amounts of associated dacite and rhyolite are isolated from the continents. Examples are the Mariana and Tonga Islands, which are separated from the continent by broad expanses of basaltic oceanic crust. Since, except for the volcanic masses themselves, sialic rocks appear to be absent in these regions, their andesites can hardly have been formed by remelting of continental-type crust. This conclusion is strengthened by the fact that within individual volcanic belts the compositions of the volcanic rocks remain the same, regardless of changes in the underlying crust, or vary independently of such changes (Gorshkov, 1970). Thus, although assimilation of continental crust does appear to take place in some areas, it cannot be a fundamental factor in the generation of andesitic magmas, which must instead arise by partial melting in the upper part of the mantle (possibly aided by addition of volatiles moving outward from deeper in the earth). Green and Ringwood (1968, 1969) have shown that andesite magma can be produced by partial melting of hydrous basalt or peridotite at pressures equivalent to depths of 9 to 48 miles or of quartz eclogite in the presence of water at depths of 48 to 90 miles. Variations in the composition of the parent material, the degree of partial melting, and the pressure under which melting occurs can result in differences in the composition of the resulting magma.

Over the ages, the generation of andesites and related calc-alkaline rocks in marginal belts, and the subsequent welding of these belts to the continents may have been largely responsible for the creation of the continental sialic plates, rather than assimilation of sial being responsible for the generation of andesites. Weathering, erosion, sedimentation, metamorphism, granitization, melting, and intrusion of the resulting magmas have reorganized the once-volcanic crust to the sialic plate as we now see it.

It has been stated on a previous page that current evidence suggests that the ocean floors are spreading. However, since the earth is not expanding, at least at anywhere nearly the same rate, the edges of the expanding areas must in some way be being destroyed. Arcuate belts of mountain building around the Pacific Ocean and in some other areas are associated with numerous earthquakes, many of which originate in zones that slope downward toward or beneath the edges of the continents. These *Benioff zones* have been interpreted as zones of shear along which the edge of the continent is moving relatively outward toward the ocean (Benioff, 1954) or along which the subocean crust and upper mantle are moving toward the continent and downward. As pointed out above, some of the arcs lie well within the area of oceanic crust rather than at the true edge of the continental platform. In 1959, Hisashi Kuno pointed out a change in the composition of the basalt magmas reaching the surface at increasing distance from the outer margins of the arcs and suggested that the magmas were generated along the Benioff zone, tholeiitic basalt magma being formed at relatively shallow levels and alkalic basalt magmas at greater depth on the side of the arc away from the ocean (Fig. 15-24). Recent laboratory experiments have shown that tholeiitic basalt magma can be obtained from partial melting of peridotite at low pressures, whereas at higher pressures

FIGURE 15-24. Diagrammatic vertical cross section across the edge of the Asiatic continent in the region of Japan, showing the generation of different types of basalt magma at different depths. The dashed lines indicate the zone of frequent earthquake foci. (Modified after Kuno, 1959.)

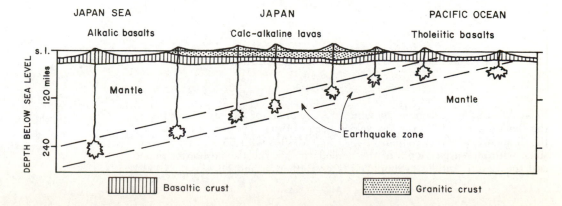

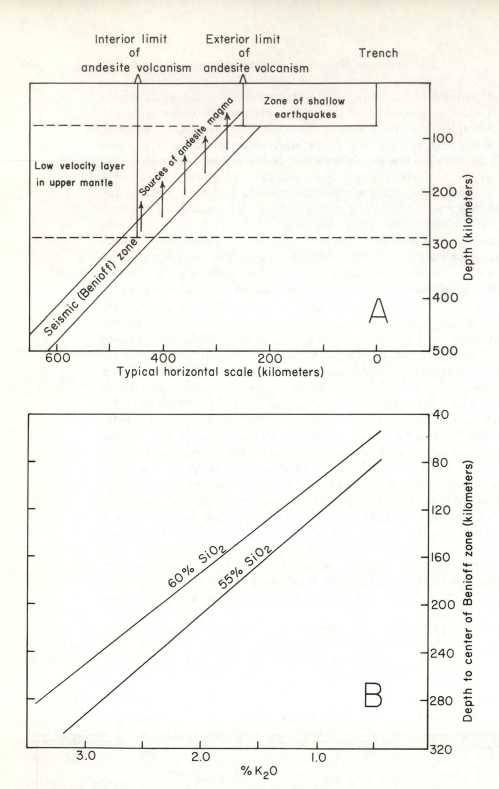

FIGURE 15-25. Diagram showing: (A) sources of andesitic magma in the Benioff zone within the low velocity layer of the upper mantle; and (B) the change in average content of K₂O in andesites with 55 and 60 percent silica with increasing depth of the Benioff zone in the Pacific border region and the Lesser Antilles. (Simplified after Hatherton and Dickinson, 1969.)

partial melting of eclogitic peridotite yields alkalic magma (Green and Ringwood, 1967). This evidence is in good agreement with Kuno's suggestion of the generation of the different basalt magma types at different depths along the Benioff zones.

Other evidence indicates that the formation of andesite magmas also is related to the Benioff zones. Hatherton and Dickinson (1969) have shown that the andesites in orogenic belts around the Pacific vary in composition across the belts, the proportion of potassium to silica increasing in direct relation to the depth of the underlying Benioff zone (Fig. 15-25)—a fact that suggests that the melting to form the magma takes place in, or close to, the Benioff zone.

One problem in deriving andesite magma by partial melting of peridotite in the presence of water is that rising temperature tends to drive off the water before the temperature of melting is reached. (The rate of diffusion of water in rock is greater than that of heat.) McBirney (1969) has suggested that this difficulty is eliminated if hydrous rocks of the suboceanic crust are carried down into the mantle along the Benioff zones and liberate water, which then rises into the already-hot mantle rocks above the zone. There the addition of water lowers the melting temperature to a level at or below the temperature that already exists in the rocks, and melting occurs. The evidence presented by Kuno and by Hatherton and Dickinson, cited above, suggests that if this mechanism is effective, the melting takes place not far above the Benioff zone.

The generation of andesite magma is, of course, not restricted to the margins of the Pacific Ocean or to regions in which there is indication of thrusting of crustal materials down into the mantle. In these other regions, also, it appears to have taken place by partial melting in the upper mantle. Minor chemical constituents of the andesites in the San Juan volcanic field of Colorado indicate that the andesite magma could not have been formed by melting of rocks such as those in adjacent parts of the crust (Doe, Lipman, and Hedge, 1969). They do, however, suggest that at least some of the andesite may have resulted from assimilation of crustal rocks by basalt magma rising from the mantle. Present indications seem to be that most andesites originate by partial melting in or at the top of the upper mantle; but the considerable variation in their chemical composition and the presence of many mineral grains that have been partly dissolved away and, hence, were obviously not in equilibrium with the surrounding liquid suggest frequent assimilation of crustal material and probably other disturbances of chemical and thermal equilibrium in the magma. Mixing of magmas of different composition has resulted in some places in formation of obviously banded rocks (Macdonald and Katsura, 1965; Wilcox, 1944; Williams, Curtis, and Juhle, 1956), and it is very likely that elsewhere the mixing has been so complete that the traces are no longer apparent.

Speculation on the origin of volcanic magmas could occupy another huge volume, but it should not be carried further here. It must by now be obvious to the reader that the nature of the interior of the earth and the causes and processes of magma generation are still very imperfectly known.

So also are many of the processes that go on within magmas and that bring about many of the structures in volcanoes and volcanic rocks that have been described in the foregoing chapters. We know vastly more today than we did only half a century ago, but we still have a tremendous amount to learn. Not all the remaining frontiers of exploration lie in outer space! Equally fascinating and challenging ones still exist within our own earth and are intimately related to such practical things as the origin and finding of ore deposits and the utilization of the enormous stores of energy within the earth. The exploration of inner space certainly rivals that of outer space in promise of returns of both cultural and material value. To the coming generation of earth scientists will go the thrill of at least some of these discoveries!

SUGGESTED ADDITIONAL READING

Interior of the Earth
  Hodgson, 1964; Howell, 1959.

Mechanism of Volcanoes
  Eaton and Murata, 1960.

Diatremes and Volcanic Necks
  Cloos, 1941; Francis, 1962; Geikie, 1897a, v. 2, p. 67–93; Hearn, 1968; McBirney, 1959; Shoemaker, Roach, and Byers, 1962; Williams, 1936.

Ring Intrusions
  Billings, 1945; Jacobson, MacLeod, and Black, 1958; Reynolds, 1956; Richey, 1961; Stewart, 1965.

Cauldron Subsidences
  Bailey and Maufe, 1960, p. 128–184; Chapman and Chapman, 1940; Clough, Maufe, and Bailey, 1909; Kingsley, 1931; Oftedahl, 1953, 1960; Taubeneck, 1967.

16

Volcanoes and Man

It was pointed out in the preface that volcanoes are both creators and destroyers, and that, as population pressure and the need for arable land increases, we must learn to live in close proximity to them while at the same time minimizing the inevitable dangers. Let us consider first the beneficent aspects of volcanoes, since it is due largely to these that people are encroaching more and more on the areas of danger. We will then turn to the destructive aspects, and some of the ways we may be able to deal with them.

VOLCANOES AS BENEFACTORS

Perhaps the most obviously beneficial aspect of volcanoes is that they build land for us to live on. It should be apparent from the discussion in Chapter 14 that volcanoes have been major contributors to the building of the continents, and all of the oceanic islands owe their existence either directly or indirectly to volcanoes. The high islands are volcanoes, in various stages of erosional dissection, and the low islands are the tops of thin limestone caps built on volcanic mountains beneath. None of the volcanic islands are very old; probably all of them that still exist as islands have been built within the last 25 million years, and most are much younger than that. And the process of building is still going on. In 1957–1958 the eruption of Capelinhos added a peninsula with an area of nearly a square mile to the Island of Fayal in the Azores; and in 1960 an eruption of Kilauea added half a square mile to the Island of Hawaii. This new land is not immediately useable to man for all types of agriculture, but it is useable for house and industrial sites, releasing other land for agriculture, and in suitable climates it becomes useable for certain types of agriculture surprisingly quickly. In the warm humid climate of eastern Hawaii the lava flow of 1840 is already heavily covered with forest.

Once they start to weather, lava flow surfaces may be very fertile, but the most fertile volcanic lands are those that have been covered by ash. The "fertilization" effect of a light to moderate ash fall during the 1955 eruption of Kilauea has been mentioned in Chapter 1. Even where vegetation is completely destroyed by an ash fall, it commonly becomes reestablished as luxuriantly, or more so, than before. Not only does the fine material of the ash retain water within reach of shallow plant roots, but the ash consists largely of readily weathered glass, which releases such plant foods as potassium comparatively rapidly. The effects of ash falls are especially important in subtropical and tropical regions, where leaching rapidly removes plant nutrients from the soil and reduces its fertility. The fertility is restored by new ash falls. One of the foremost students of tropical soils, E. C. J. Mohr, has pointed out the importance of this in Indonesia. He finds (Mohr, 1945) that there is a close correlation between population density and soil type, with by far the densest agricultural populations in areas where presently or very recently active volcanoes have been adding ash to the soil. Elsewhere also, many of the most fertile lands on earth owe their richness to volcanic ash.

The present and possible future benefits of geothermal power have been reviewed in Chapter 13. Not only is natural steam power cheap, but it does not present such grave environmental pollution hazards as do atomic power plants or generating plants burning coal or oil. Enormous amounts of heat energy are available in volcanoes, if we can find a way to harness it.

Not all the benefits from volcanoes are economic. Volcanoes have given us some of our most magnificent scenery. The recreational values of our volcanic national parks—Rainier, Crater Lake, Lassen, Lava Beds, Craters of the Moon, Yellowstone, Haleakala, Hawaii Volcanoes—and such other areas as Fuji and the volcanic national parks of New Zealand are incalculable, as is attested by the millions of persons that visit them each year. They can only be regarded as priceless.

Another gift of volcanic action is commonly overlooked, although it is as fundamentally important as that of the land we live on. Over the hundreds of millions of years of geologic time, all the waters on the face of the earth and all the atmosphere have been liberated from the body of the earth by volcanoes and by hot springs that derive their volatiles from cooling igneous intrusions (Rubey, 1951). Since organisms need water and air to live, it is not too much of an exaggeration to say that life on earth depends on past volcanic and other igneous action.

VOLCANOES AS DESTROYERS

The very fertility of volcanic lands, while overwhelmingly beneficial in the long run, leads to short-term trouble. Despite the risks, the richness of the land attracts people. For example, millions of persons live in the rich rice-growing districts of central Java, densely clustered around the bases of such active and potentially murderous volcanoes as Merapi and Kelut (Chapter 8), and plantations of other crops extend well up the flanks of the volcanoes themselves. Many other examples could be given, and we must not overlook the northwestern United States, where there are large and growing populations close to such volcanoes as Mts. Hood and St. Helens, and where the recreational attractions of Lassen, Shasta, Crater Lake, Rainier, and other volcanoes draw millions of visitors a year. The Cascade volcanoes cannot be considered extinct. A dozen or more eruptions have taken place from them in the last century and a half, and with little question there will be more eruptions in the future. Industrial developments also will lead men more and more onto volcanoes. Thus far, most of the important natural-steam areas are away from active volcanoes; but almost surely geothermal areas on and close to active volcanoes will be developed in the not-distant future.

Given the presence of man, his habitations, and his industrial installations on and close to active and potentially active volcanoes, the risk of volcanic catastrophe is obvious. Loss of life from lava flows has been rare and probably will remain rare in the future. Most lava flows advance very slowly, and even the fastest of them move slowly enough so that it is usually possible to warn people in their paths in time for them to get out of the way. In 1950, however, when the first flow came down the side of Mauna Loa at a speed of nearly 6 miles an hour, there was barely time for people to move out; and it is reported that the 1823 lava flow of Kilauea advanced so rapidly on a coastal village that some old people and small children were caught and killed. It must be expected, however, that lava flows will bury agricultural land and towns, as they did, for instance, in Hawaii in 1926 (Plate 16-1), 1955 (Chapter 1), and 1960; as flows from Etna buried Mascalli in 1928 and part of Catania in 1669; and as flows from Paricutin buried Paricutin village and most of San Juan Parangaricutiro. Lava flows onto snow or ice will generate floods and mudflows, as they did at Mt. Lassen in 1915 and at Villarica, Chile, in 1963. They will also start forest and grass fires.

Heavy ash falls will destroy vegetation, including crops, within a radius of many miles from the volcano. Ash from the 1912 eruption destroyed all the low vegetation at Kodiak, 100 miles from Katmai Volcano, although the bigger trees survived. At Paricutin even the big trees were

PLATE 16-1. Aa lava flow from Mauna Loa about to destroy the village of Hoopoloa, Hawaii, on April 18, 1926. Photo by Tai Sing Loo.

killed when the ash fell more than 3 feet deep within 2 to 4 miles of the vent. Even a few inches of ash is enough to smother grass and other low plants with temporarily disastrous effects to agriculture. Not only plants, but also animals, are affected. Grazing animals die, partly of starvation and partly because of clogging of their digestive systems from eating ash-laden vegetation. Several thousand cattle and horses died of this cause during the Paricutin eruption, and many more would have done so had they not been moved to other areas. Relatively small amounts of ash on the grass may cause severe grinding down of the teeth of grazing animals. During the 1947 eruption of Hekla Volcano in Iceland, and in some earlier eruptions, many animals in ash-covered areas died of fluorine poisoning, but such poisoning appears to be rare. More remote effects may also be expected. Sugarcane in the region west of Paricutin was badly affected, not directly by the ash fall, but by an infestation of cane borers that developed as a result of destruction by the ash of another insect that normally preyed on the borers and kept them under control. (Any disturbance in ecology may have unexpected and far-reaching results!) The great Icelandic famine that resulted from the Laki eruption of 1783 has been mentioned in Chapter 10. Because of modern communications and transportation it is unlikely that eruptions will cause such a famine again, but they may well cause great distress.

In areas of moderately heavy ash fall much damage is done by the accumulating ash (Plate 16-2) breaking branches from trees and causing roofs to collapse. A large proportion of the deaths in Pompeii during the eruption of Vesuvius in 79 A.D. was the result of persons in houses being

PLATE 16-2. Volcanic ash burying houses during the 1914 eruption of Sakurajima Volcano, Japan. Photographer unknown.

buried by ash when the roofs collapsed. Ash in the air may clog and abrade aircraft and other engines (Wilcox, 1959) and cause serious irritation to the respiratory systems of men and animals. Falling ash may temporarily contaminate water supplies and may cause local floods by clogging drains. Over a longer period, a poorly permeable ash cover may induce deep gullying of a volcanic terrane due to surface runoff on rocks that without the ash cover would be sufficiently permeable to allow most of the water to sink into the ground (Segerstrom, 1950; Williams, 1950). Ash falls may also add minor chemical elements to the soil that may affect grazing animals or people eating food grown in the area even long after the eruption that produced the ash. Some years ago it was found that sheep grazing in certain parts of New Zealand were suffering severely from a sickness that was eventually shown to be poisoning from excessive amounts of cobalt absorbed by plants from a particular prehistoric ash cover.

Mudflows will bury fields and towns, as they did Herculaneum in 79 A.D., Cagsaua at the foot of Mayon Volcano in 1814 (Plate 16-3), and broad areas at the foot of Kelut Volcano in 1919 (Chapter 8). A mudflow entering an artificial reservoir, such as those created along many streams for hydroelectric purposes or flood control, may cause the water in the reservoir to overflow the dam and bring about a catastrophic flood downstream. Crandell and Waldron (1969) have pointed out this hazard in the case of two reservoirs at the base of Mt. Baker in Washington and have suggested that similar mudflow-induced overflow of three reservoirs along the Lewis River, a tributary of the Columbia River south of Mt. St. Helens, might cause disastrous flooding along the heavily populated flood plain of the Columbia and in the city of Portland.

413

PLATE 16-3. Church in the village of Cagsaua, at the foot of Mayon Volcano, in the Philippines, buried to the top of the nave by a mudflow from Mayon in 1814. U. S. Geological Survey photo by G. A. Macdonald.

Glowing avalanches will wipe out villages, as they did at Lamington Volcano, New Guinea, in 1951 (Chapter 10), and even whole cities, as they did St. Pierre on Martinique in 1902 (Chapter 8). They may also, like mudflows, cause floods where they enter reservoirs, and they may generate mudflows by entering lakes or large streams. Ash flows wipe out everything in their paths, and flows as great or greater than that in the Valley of Ten Thousand Smokes may result in almost unthinkable calamities.

Volcanic gases may kill or adversely affect vegetation. Even at distances of several tens of miles, drifting acid gases wither leaves and cause fruit to drop. The damage to leaves closely resembles the smog damage that occurs in some urban areas. Gas drifting westward from Masaya Volcano in Nicaragua has done extensive damage to coffee plantations, and gas from Kilauea eruptions has damaged plum and other fruit trees at distances of as much as 30 miles. Heavy gases may accumulate in hollows, killing birds and animals. The "death gulches" in volcanic areas in which the corpses of birds and animals are occasionally found are well known. During the 1947–1948 eruption of Hekla Volcano bands of sheep were drowned by carbon dioxide gas that accumulated in shallow hollows, although men, with their greater height, walked through the hollows with immunity.

Eruptions in shallow water may cause tsunamis on adjacent shores, though the energy in these explosion-induced waves is not usually great enough for them to travel to great distances, as do tectonically generated

414

tsunamis. The steam cloud from shallow submarine eruptions may contain large amounts of salt, which, if the cloud drifts over agricultural areas on adjacent land, may be carried down with rain and do considerable damage to crops. Similar salt-laden steam clouds may result where lava flows from land enter the ocean.

This long list of destructive effects of volcanism is not given from the standpoint of sensationalism. These are simply some of the problems that we will have to face in volcanic districts. Some types of volcanic destruction seem unavoidable, and the risks must simply be balanced against the benefits of occupation of the area. Others can be avoided, or at least mitigated, by knowledge of how volcanoes behave, when and where eruptions are likely to occur, and by protective and corrective methods that already exist or will be developed in the future.

PREDICTION OF VOLCANIC ERUPTIONS

Obviously, if volcanic eruptions can be predicted, there are several ways in which loss of life and property can be eliminated or reduced. People can be evacuated from the threatened area. Moveable property can be moved. In some instances even such relatively immobile things as houses have been moved out of danger.

The effectiveness of predictions depends on their specificness and their accuracy. Too many false or inaccurate predictions will soon make all predictions ineffective; therefore, we must be conservative in predicting. The ultimate aim is to be able to state that an eruption will occur on approximately such a date, that it will be of a certain specified type, and will affect certain specified areas in specified ways. We are as yet far from being able to do this, but it has become urgent that we make every reasonable effort to learn to do it if we are to avoid volcanic catastrophes that will make those of the past appear small indeed.

Predictions of the time of eruption are of two sorts—general and specific. A general prediction consists of a statement that a volcano is likely to erupt in the near future. Since the "near future" can be anything from a few hours to several years, the usefulness of such a prediction is limited to alerting the population for other possible more specific indications. General predictions can be based on several different lines of evidence. Where a long enough record of past activity exists, a volcano may be found to have a more or less regular periodicity of eruption. In that case, once a period of quiescence approaches in length the average quiet period of the past, another eruption can be expected in the near future. Since the lengths of the individual quiet periods within one record usually vary greatly, this sort of prediction is usually very vague. On a short-term basis, however, it may be quite accurate. During the 1924 phreatic eruption of Kilauea, it was observed that the individual steam explosions came at quite regular intervals of 6 to 8 hours (Jaggar and Finch, 1924).

The only death resulting from an eruption of a Hawaiian volcano during recent years came as a result of ignoring a warning based on this periodicity. R. H. Finch, who at the time was in charge of the Hawaiian Volcano Observatory, warned a photographer not to go near the crater because an explosion was due. The photographer went to the crater rim regardless and was killed by falling blocks ejected by the explosion.

Another basis for general prediction is the behavior of fumaroles (Williams, 1954). At some volcanoes the temperature of fumarole gases is found to increase, the volume of the gas to increase, or the composition of the gas to change preceding eruptions. At other volcanoes there seems to be no change in the fumaroles. A long history of fumarole behavior at the specific volcano is necessary before any accurate forecasts can be made, and even then about the most that can be said usually is that the volcano will probably erupt "in the near future." Great care must be taken in interpreting fumarole changes. The actual and apparent volume of fumarole discharge may be greatly affected by the weather. Cold damp weather greatly increases condensation and, consequently, the visibility of steam. Recent rains may supply additional water to hot subsurface areas and increase the actual volume of steam discharge. The proportion or total amount of water in fumarole discharge is probably meaningless for prediction of eruptions, and attention must be given to the nature and proportions of the other gases. Very little specific can yet be said regarding their use in prediction, but future work may give valuable results, at least at some volcanoes.

As magma accumulates beneath a volcano and perhaps begins to rise toward the surface preceding an eruption, the heating of the surrounding rocks reduces their magnetic attraction, and it may be possible to measure this reduction by means of magnetometers at the surface or by aerial magnetometry. Periodic measurements of magnetic attraction and of variations in the direction of the magnetic field have been made at a few volcanoes. At Mihara Volcano on Oshima Island, Japan, Rikitake and his coworkers (1963) found marked shifts in the orientation of the magnetic field a few months before eruptions. Before two eruptions of Mauna Loa, Hawaii, peculiar disturbances were observed in the vertical component of the magnetic field 200 miles away in Honolulu (Macdonald, 1951), but the cause of these disturbances, or even whether they were actually related to the Mauna Loa eruptions, is not known. More recent eruptions of Kilauea have not been accompanied by similar disturbances. The magnetic measurements may prove to be valuable tools for prediction, but these studies are still in their infancy. Another possible method of detecting the increase of temperature at a volcano is by aerial infrared photography, repeated at regular intervals. This method is also as yet untested, but preliminary experiments suggest that it may be of value, particularly in areas that do not have too heavy a forest cover. Whether surface heating will be great enough to be recognized at a period sufficiently long before the eruption to make warnings possible remains to be seen.

Still another possibility is the use of variations in electrical currents in the volcano. Minakami (1935) noted marked rapid changes in earth currents several hours before individual strong explosions of Asama Volcano, but little in the way of similar studies has been reported since.

The tumescence of Kilauea Volcano preceding eruptions has been mentioned in Chapters 1 and 15. Apparently resulting from the inflation of a magma chamber at a depth of only 2 or 3 miles below the surface, it is detected by measurements of the tilting of the ground surface with instruments called tiltmeters. Formerly the horizontal-pendulum seismographs were used as tiltmeters, but these were exceedingly sensitive to temperature change. A horizontal-pendulum tiltmeter constructed of glass by A. Imamura is largely free from temperature effects but is very fragile. Most tiltmeters in use today consist of two vessels connected by a tube and partly filled with liquid. When the underlying ground surface tilts, some of the liquid runs from one vessel to the other, and the change in the liquid level in the two vessels can be measured very accurately by micrometers or in some other appropriate way. Analysis of the records from two such instruments placed at right angles to each other gives the true direction and amount of tilting at that particular place. The instruments and methods in use currently at the Hawaiian Volcano Observatory have been described by J. P. Eaton (1959). The earlier tilt measurements at Kilauea showed strong seasonal effects resulting from heating and cooling of an adjacent cliff, and it was necessary to eliminate these effects in order to use the records as a measure of tumescence (Finch and Macdonald, 1953); but present-day methods have gotten away from this difficulty, and it is now possible not only to measure the swelling very accurately, but to trace the migration of the center of swelling from place to place. However, eruptions have taken place at various degrees of inflation, and as yet tumescence can be used only to indicate that the volcano is in, or is approaching, a condition where eruption is possible.

Records are inadequate to be certain, but it appears probable that Mauna Loa, like Kilauea, tumefies before eruptions and detumefies during eruptions. Thus far, tilt measurements have been made at only a few other volcanoes. Whereas preeruption tumescence appears to occur at some of them, at others it appears to be absent. Whether or not it is detectable may depend on the shallowness of the magma chamber. At any rate, long records of tilting must be accumulated at each individual volcano before it can be used as more than a general indicator of coming eruption. Even at Kilauea, long periods of tumescence have not always led to eruption. Sometimes they are terminated by detumescence without eruption, indicating recession of the magma or intrusion into the flanks of the volcano.

Volcanic eruptions commonly are preceded by earthquakes. The Neapolitan earthquake of 63 A.D. was the beginning of a period of seismic activity that culminated 16 years later in the Plinian eruption of Vesuvius (Chapter 10). Since then earthquakes have been noted preceding many eruptions. At Kilauea shallow-seated earthquakes often numbering in the thousands precede most, if not all, flank eruptions, though some summit eruptions seem to have little or no seismic prelude. These earthquakes occur during times of tumescence and continue for periods of several hours to several days, commonly ceasing with the beginning of the eruption. However, similar swarms of shallow earthquakes occur during times of magma recession, when the top of the volcano is sinking, so a shallow earthquake swarm cannot be used as an indicator of impending eruption unless the character of the tilting also is known. In some instances earthquakes preceding Kilauea and Mauna Loa eruptions have come from progressively shallower sources, but in other instances no such pattern has been discernible. The seismic prelude to the 1955 eruption has been described in Chapter 1.

In 1942, R. H. Finch studied a series of earthquakes that started at a depth of 25 to 30 miles beneath the northeastern flank of Mauna Loa, followed by numerous quakes beneath the northeast rift zone of the volcano. On February 21 and 22 a swarm of quakes originated at shallow foci in the area between 9,000 and 10,000 feet altitude on the rift zone, followed by a series of others from foci that gradually migrated up the rift zone, reached the summit area on March 7, and then moved on down the southwest rift zone to a point about 5 miles from the summit on March 21. On March 28 another quake centered beneath the northeast rift (Finch, 1943). These earthquakes were contemporaneous with less-than-normal seasonal westward tilting at Kilauea, suggesting tumescence of Mauna Loa, 20 miles to the west; and these occurrences, combined with Finch's knowledge that a flank eruption of Mauna Loa was likely to follow the summit eruption of 1940 within about 3 years (based on the history of the volcano), formed the basis for one of the most successful predictions of an eruption that has yet been made. Because of wartime security restrictions, the prediction could not be published, but it is recorded in reports to the National Park Service. Finch predicted that Mauna Loa would erupt within the next few months at a point on the northeast rift zone, probably between 9,000 and 10,000 feet altitude. The eruption commenced on April 28 at 9,200 feet altitude.

It is noteworthy that this prediction was based not on one but on several lines of evidence. Thus far, no single tool is adequate to predict an eruption except in the most general way.

Minakami (1960) has classified earthquakes related to Japanese volcanoes into A-type quakes, originating at depths from about 0.5 to 6 miles; B-type quakes, originating from an area with a radius of about 0.6 mile beneath and around the crater; and explosion quakes, originating from explosions within the crater. He finds that at Asama Volcano about 2 months before an eruption the number of B-type earthquakes increases to a level several times that of the normal number during quiet periods, and several days before an eruption it increases to as much as 20 times the normal. The eruptions of Asama are generally of Vulcanian type. On the other hand, at Mihara and Aso Volcanoes, the eruptions of which are characteristically Strombolian, B-type earthquakes are absent; and although A-type earthquakes sometimes occur before and during eruptions, they also sometimes take place without any apparent relation to eruptions. Much more knowledge of earthquakes, particularly at volcanoes of types other than Hawaiian, is needed.

PROTECTIVE AND ALLEVIATIVE METHODS

Lava Flows

At least in some cases, lava flows can be dealt with in two very different ways. Under suitable conditions it may be possible to divert flows from particular areas into others in which they will do less damage. And once a lava flow has occupied an area, it may be possible to treat its surface in such a way as to make it useable either immediately or in a shorter time than it otherwise would be. Two methods of diverting flows have been suggested: bombing, and building of artificial channelways. In any case of diversion, it must be recognized that legal problems may arise from the directing of the lava into land that it would not have invaded without interference. The role of the volcanologist should be only to advise on whether or not diversion is possible and how best to accomplish it, not on whether the diversion should be attempted.

The use of explosives to change the course of lava flows was first suggested, so far as I know, by L. A. Thurston of Honolulu in the early 1920s. His original idea was to emplace dynamite or black powder by means of long poles, but at the time of the 1935 eruption of Mauna Loa, when a lava flow was threatening the city of Hilo, it was suggested that the explosives could be dropped as bombs from airplanes. The idea was elaborated by T. A. Jaggar (1931) and later by Finch and Macdonald (1951). Three general ways in which bombing can divert lava flows have been recognized, though possibly others exist. They are (1) by breaching a lava tube in a pahoehoe flow, (2) by breaching an open channel in an aa flow, and (3) by breaking down the wall of the cone built around the vent.

It is interesting to note that the idea of breaching the channel wall of an aa flow had already occurred to a resident of Catania, Sicily, in 1669. A lava flow from Etna was advancing toward the city. Under leadership of a man named Diego Pappalardo, 50 or so men from Catania covered themselves with wet cowhides for protection against the heat and dug a channel through the wall of hot lava at one edge of the flow. At first the operation was successful. Molten lava escaped through the gap thus created and flowed away at an angle to the path of the original flow, reducing the amount of lava moving toward Catania. However, the new stream was headed toward the town of Paterno, and 500 indignant citizens of that town armed themselves and drove the Catania men away. The channelway in the main flow wall soon clogged up and the flow continued toward Catania, where it came against the feudal city wall. For several days the wall withstood the flow and diverted it around the city toward the sea (Waltershausen, 1880, v. 1, p. 252), but eventually the lava broke through a weak place in the wall and flooded part of the city. Thus, the 1669 eruption provides examples of diversion both by destroying the flow wall and by turning the flow with an artificial barrier. The fact that neither was completely successful should not be taken to mean that the methods, used in a more adequate manner, will not succeed.

The bombing method will be only briefly summarized here. Fuller discussions can be found in the sources mentioned above. It has been pointed out in Chapter 5 that the feeding rivers of pahoehoe are open channels at first, but after the first few hours or days of the eruption they become roofed over by a crust of frozen lava creating a lava tube. If the tube can be broken open high on the mountainside, and particularly if the tube can also be partly clogged with debris, lava may spill out through the break and flood an area of relatively little importance, diverting some or all of the liquid that was feeding the main flow front. Clogging of the tube is partly with debris from the disrupted roof, but partly as a result of the violent stirring caused by the bomb explosion changing the liquid pahoehoe in the tube into more viscous aa. Reduction in the amount of liquid reaching the original flow front may cause the front to stagnate, and even though topography may guide the new flow along the same path as the old, days or weeks may pass before the new front reaches the position reached by the old one. At that stage, it may be possible to repeat the bombing. Such efforts to prevent inundation of particular areas by lava are in large part battles against time. If the inundation can be delayed long enough, the eruption will end.

Most aa feeding rivers remain open, and repeated overflows build up natural levees that may hold the stream at a level several feet above the surroundings. If the levee can be broken down, liquid lava spills out and the supply of liquid to the former flow front is reduced, with results as described above. Similarly, the cone at the vent often contains a pool of liquid lava at a level well above the adjacent land surface, and if the cone wall can be broken down, lava will flood around it, again reducing the supply to the former flow front.

The first method was tried by T. A. Jaggar during the 1935 eruption of Mauna Loa with at least partial success. The main pahoehoe tube was broken open high on the mountainside, partly clogged with aa and roof debris, and lava flooded around the break. The former flow front did not stop immediately, because liquid lava continued draining from the several miles of feeding tube and channel below the break, but it did slow almost immediately and stopped completely 6 days after the bombing. The second method was tried by R. H. Finch in 1942, when again a lava flow was advancing toward Hilo, and again it was partly successful. The levee was broken down and the liquid lava spilled out. A new flow front was formed, advancing alongside the earlier flow, but the new stream rejoined the older one a few miles beyond the bombing site. The advance of the main flow front was slowed but not stopped. The third method has not yet been tried, but a natural demonstration of it occurred during the same 1942 eruption. The cone wall broke down, releasing a flood of lava and depleting the supply to the flow, which slowed almost immediately and stopped a few days afterward.

Thus, all three bombing methods appear potentially useable, but they have serious shortcomings. They cannot be used successfully until the flow or the cone is in the right condition, and they cannot succeed unless the topography is favorable. A flow confined in a deep valley probably cannot be diverted. Furthermore, there is serious doubt as to whether the methods can succeed at all on any but very fluid, Hawaiian- or flood-type basaltic lavas. Fortunately, it is these that flow to the greatest distances and bury the greatest areas and, consequently, constitute the most serious threats.

The idea of building artificial barriers to divert lava flows also is not new. When the 1881 lava flow was approaching Hilo, W. R. Lawrence, an engineer for the Kingdom of Hawaii, suggested building an embankment to prevent the flow from spreading northward from the shallow gulch along which it was advancing and invading the main part of Hilo. The flow stopped before the project could be carried out, but not before the manager of a sugar mill had had a stone dam built across the gulch in front of the flow. It is quite possible that Lawrence's embankment would have been successful, but the dam could not possibly have succeeded. By chance, the flow stopped just after the lava reached the dam, and only a few tens of cubic yards of lava spilled over it; but if the flow had continued, it would have quickly filled the small reservoir behind the dam and continued on down the gulch essentially unimpeded. There is a good chance, however, that it would have simply buried the dam without pushing it over. Lava flow fronts commonly exert surprisingly little thrust. I know of several places where Hawaiian flows came against loose stone walls that lay roughly at right angles to their direction of advance and simply piled up behind the wall until they became deep enough to overflow it. Lava flows that entered the town of Bosco Trecase on the lower slope of Vesuvius in 1906 filled the streets to a depth of 15 to 20 feet and poured in through windows without crushing the weak masonry walls of the houses (Jaggar, 1945). The basalt lava flow from Matavanu, Samoa, in 1905 surrounded buildings without crushing the stone walls (Jensen, 1907), and the basaltic andesite flow from Paricutin surrounded the church at San Juan, with its surface at the level of the roof of the nave, without crushing the masonry walls. Other flows exert more thrust, however. For instance, several examples of flows pushing over walls are known on Mt. Etna.

The possibility of building barriers to deflect lava flows from the city of Hilo and its harbor has been discussed by Jaggar (1945) and by Macdonald (1958). The walls can be constructed by bulldozers, using whatever heavy rock material is available. Following Jaggar's suggestion, in 1940 barriers were designed by the U.S. Engineer Department. They averaged about 40 feet in height and created an available channel width for the possible flow of approximately 3,000 feet. Because lava does not behave quite like water, but actually piles up to a depth of several feet above any such diverting ridge, the height of the barriers probably could be somewhat lower, perhaps averaging 25 to 30 feet. It should be emphasized that the barriers are not intended to act as dams but are constructed at a low angle to the course of the flow and are intended simply to turn it into a new course where it will do less damage.

It has been objected (Wentworth, Powers, and Eaton, 1961) that the channels provided by the barriers might not be adequate to handle the volume of the flow. However, the possible volumes cited are those of the very rapid discharges close around the vents during early hours of some Mauna Loa eruptions. By the time the flow reaches the location of the proposed barriers, many miles from the vents, it is very unlikely that its volume of flow during any unit time will be more than a small fraction of the extreme figures cited. The probability is very great that the channels would be adequate. A more serious objection is the possibility that an early flow unit might congeal against the barrier, forming a dam that would cause a later flow unit, reaching the barrier on the up-hill side of the first, to overflow the barrier. Again, the likelihood of two large flow units reaching the barrier at such great distance from the vent is very small. The method does not guarantee success, but it appears to have considerable promise.

As yet we have had very little experience with lava-diversion barriers. Small, poorly designed and hurriedly constructed barriers had limited success during the 1955 eruption of Kilauea (Macdonald, 1958). Barriers built during the 1960 eruption of Kilauea were primarily dams, designed partly to give time for other construction and partly to prevent lateral spreading of the flows. Nevertheless, they did operate successfully for a time as diversion barriers (Macdonald, 1962). That they eventually were overflowed is an event that must be expected at any dam if the liquid behind it gets too deep. In spite of the overflow, I believe they were sufficiently successful to have greatly reduced the amount of destruction. The experience in 1960 clearly demonstrated the necessity of using heavy materials in the construction and of giving the walls a broad base and gentle slopes.

I know of few efforts elsewhere than Hawaii to control the spread of lava flows by means of artificial walls. Mason and Foster (1953) describe a wall built across a low gap in the rim of Oshima Caldera, Japan, to try to prevent lava that was spreading across the caldera floor from overflowing through the gap. However, the flow stopped before it reached the wall.

Like bombing, diversion barriers must have favorable topography to be successful, and it is doubtful if they can be used with success against any but rather thin fluid flows.

Similarly, little experience appears to exist in the treatment of lava-flow surfaces to make them useable. The surfaces of most aa flows and many block lava flows are quite easily leveled with bulldozers, making them suitable for construction sites and to a lesser extent for agriculture. The addition of small amounts of soil, as a continuous cover or in pockets, makes such leveled flow surfaces useable for certain types of crops.

In early 1841, J. D. Dana, the geologist of the U.S. Exploring Expedition, found crops of sweet potato thriving on the bare lava surface of the flow that had been formed less than a year before. The plants were rooted in handfuls of soil that had been carried in by the farmers. Within two years of the end of the 1955 eruption of Kilauea, several hundred acres of acerola for the production of vitamin C concentrate had already been planted on the lava flows. Again, the plants were rooted in small pockets of imported soil. The manager of the project reported that although preparations for planting were more costly than on older forested land nearby, lower costs for weed control on the otherwise bare new lava more than compensated for the higher costs of land preparation. The plantations have gone out of business, not because of agricultural conditions, but because of the development of cheaper synthetic vitamin C. Other crops that require only thin soil can be grown with equal success. The most essential factor in the treating of the surface of new flows for plantings of this sort consists in crushing the surface to produce abundant fine material that will hold moisture. Grass commonly starts almost immediately along the shoulders of roads bulldozed across the lava. The crushing also increases the surface area of the fragments exposed to weathering and thereby speeds up the release of plant nutrients. Pahoehoe is generally more difficult to treat than aa, because it is less easily leveled and crushed.

Mudflows

Volcanic mudflows are difficult to predict in any but a rather general way. They may occur at the beginning of an eruption (as at Mt. Pelée in 1902), at any time during an eruption, or for some time after the eruption has ended. Once they have started, they move so rapidly that it is very difficult to give adequate warning to people in their paths. The best approach seems to be to try to recognize in advance the conditions that may give rise to mudflows (Chapter 8) and take whatever steps are possible. Crater lakes with the water level close to the level of the crater rim or those with especially fragile rims should be partly drained, as was the Kelut lake (Chapter 8), if the ejection of their water would threaten important areas or large numbers of people. The growth of a dome or lava flow in the crater of a snow-covered volcano should be watched carefully for the possibility of meltwater-induced floods and mudflows if the lava, or a glowing avalanche, should go out onto the flank of the volcano. The heads of valleys on active volcanoes should be kept under careful observation during eruptions for signs of an impending or actual mudflow. At one time thermoelectric sensors were installed in the valley heads on Merapi, Java, to warn of the passage of hot mudflows or glowing avalanches, but they do not seem to have been particularly successful. Obviously, since the flow would be already in motion, the warning time would be very short—probably a very few minutes. The slopes of volcanoes and nearby hillsides should be watched during eruption for the accumulation of a cover of loose ash that might be transformed into mudflows by heavy rains, and the same possibility should be kept in mind after the eruption is over until the ash has become stabilized by compaction or plant cover. Since mudflows follow the valleys, the paths of possible mudflows on different sides of the volcano can be predicted with fair certainty, but the volume and extent of the flow may be much more difficult to foresee.

Possible alleviative measures against mudflow include the construction of diversion barriers, reservoirs to contain flows of relatively small volume, and artificial structures to serve as refuges. Mounds were built near some Javanese villages as places to which the villagers could flee to get above the level of possible mudflows. Small dams were placed across streams at the foot of Kelut Volcano to impound mudflows, but when the flows occurred, the reservoirs were quickly filled and the mudflows continued on downstream, wreaking havoc in the villages. On the other hand, larger reservoirs might contain mudflows of moderate volume very successfully. Crandell and Waldron (1969) point out that existing reservoirs near the base of Mt. Rainier could contain most or all of a mudflow such as the Electron

FIGURE 16-1.   Map of the region near Mt. Rainier, Washington, showing the areas of the Electron mudflow (about 500 years old), and the Osceola mudflow (5,000 years old). (After Crandell and Waldron, 1969.)

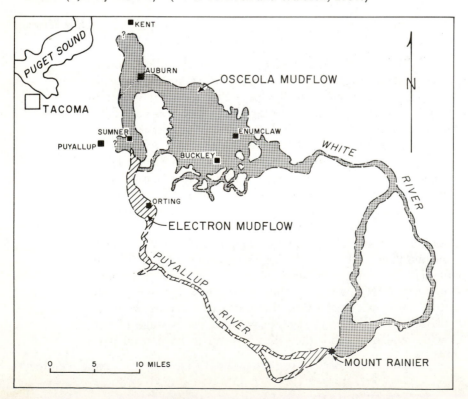

flow, with a volume of about 200 million cubic yards, which took place about 500 years ago (Fig. 16-1), though they would not begin to contain the Osceola mudflow, with its volume of 2.5 billion cubic yards. If any appreciable likelihood of mudflows into them exists, the water level in reservoirs near the volcano should be lowered to prevent floods in the valley below the dam.

I have been told (F. M. Bullard, personal communication, 1956) that for many years farmers on the slopes of Vesuvius have built low stone walls in an effort to prevent mudflows from entering their vineyards. There appears to be no reason why such methods, properly executed, might not be effective against small mudflows. Larger barriers, properly placed and constructed, might be used to divert mudflows of small to moderate volume in the same way as fluid lava flows, provided the surrounding topography is favorable to diversion and the velocity of the flow on reaching the barrier is not so great as to cause it to jump the barrier.

Most mudflows consist of material that is potentially fertile. Treatment of the surface to prepare it for agriculture may be difficult, because of the bouldery nature of many mudflow deposits; but suitable methods can be devised, particularly for small-scale family-type farming. Many mudflow areas, such as those around the base of Mayon Volcano, are intensely cultivated.

Glowing Avalanches

Domes enlarging beyond the wall of the summit crater or growing on the flank of the volcano are likely sources of dome-type glowing avalanches, and steps for warning and evacuation of persons in the threatened areas should be taken. The paths of the possible avalanches can generally be foreseen quite accurately from a study of the topography, but again it is difficult to forecast the volume or extent of the avalanche. The locations of explosively generated glowing avalanches of the Soufrière type are much more difficult to forecast, since they may occur on any flank of the mountain or on several flanks simultaneously. If an eruption of this type is feared, perhaps the best that can be done is to evacuate the entire circumferential area. The greatest difficulty is, of course, to foresee the eruption.

Careful watch should be kept on the upper slopes of erupting volcanoes for excessive accumulations of hot ash that might give rise to hot ash flows like those on Vesuvius in 1906 (Chapter 10).

Small glowing avalanches can, like mudflows, be contained in reservoirs, provided the velocity of the flow on reaching the dam is not too great. The water level in the reservoir should, of course, be lowered if an avalanche is thought likely. Larger glowing avalanches probably can neither be contained nor diverted. The depth of the flow is too great for any appreciable proportion to be turned by any artificial barrier of reasonable height, and the velocity is so great that even the lowest portion of the flowing mass would have a strong tendency to jump the barrier.

Ash Falls

The collapse of roofs from excessive loads of accumulated volcanic ash can be prevented simply by shoveling the ash off the roof at intervals. A simple dust mask, even just a damp piece of cloth over one's nose and mouth, prevents inhalation of the ash. Breaking of the branches of fruit trees by ash loading can be prevented by shaking off the ash before the load becomes too great. Even with a deep ash cover, the death of some large trees can be prevented by digging the ash away from their boles. Where aircraft or other engines must operate in ash-laden air, some sort of dust filter is desirable. If possible, grazing animals should be removed from ash-covered areas to prevent ingestion of excessive ash and damage to their teeth. Steps to reopen and keep open drains may be necessary. Surface water supplies may be physically contaminated with suspended solid particles, and it may be desirable to remove these with filters. Even a cloth bag tied over the faucet may be adequate. Temporarily, the water may become excessively acid. If an ash fall is anticipated, people remaining in the area should be advised to store enough drinking water for a few days.

Heavy ash falls greatly reduce visibility. It is commonly reported that "day becomes as dark as night," and even with lights it is impossible to see out of doors more than a few feet. Under these conditions, evacuation of an area becomes exceedingly difficult or impossible. In general it is probably best to advise people in such areas not to try to leave until visibility is restored, and to remain indoors except for brief excursions outside to clear off the roof if that becomes necessary.

Poisonous Gases

Very little work has yet been done on the prevention of damage to crops by drifting volcanic gases. As a preventive measure, it was once proposed to erect a giant funnel and flue in the crater of Masaya Volcano to collect the gases and lead them high enough into the atmosphere to cause their dispersal and dilution to a degree that they would no longer be damaging. Valuable chemicals would be removed from them in the process. Construction was started, but the installation was destroyed by the collapse of the crater bottom. Suggestions for local treatment of the affected plants have included spraying or sprinkling the plants with chemicals to neutralize the acid gases. Much more work is necessary, and consideration must, of course, be given to the cost of the treatment relative to the value of the plants that would be saved.

For persons caught temporarily in volcanic fume, general-purpose industrial gas masks are quite effective. There is ample air in the atmosphere inhaled, so if the harmful gases can be removed or neutralized, breathing is possible. If a gas mask is not available, as must often be the case, a wet cloth over the nose and mouth is quite effective, and if the cloth is wet with a dilute solution of vinegar or with urine, the effectiveness is increased. In the case of heavy gases that accumulate in hollows, the mask or wet cloth is ineffective because there is insufficient air in the mixture.

CONCLUSIONS

Additional surveillance of volcanic districts and additional study of means of prediction of times and types of eruptions and of ways to avert or minimize damage from eruptions are very much needed. It is time for volcanologists to put less emphasis on purely scientific aspects of their science, such as the generation and modification of magmas, and to give more attention to humanistic aspects—prediction and control of volcanic eruptions and the utilization of volcanic energy.

We should be watching not only such obviously dangerous volcanic districts as Indonesia and Japan, but others in which the lack of disastrous eruptions within the brief span of history has given a false impression of an absence of danger. In one of these, the Cascade Range, work has finally started to identify the types of volcanoes and the types of eruptions that are likely to occur at them, the probability of such eruptions, and to delineate the zones of different degrees and types of danger (Crandell and Waldron, 1969). The work is long overdue, and although both the U.S. Geological Survey and the Center for Volcanology at the University of Oregon are giving some attention to the problem, the work is still on a very inadequate scale. We need more geophysical surveillance—permanent installations of seismographs and tiltmeters to monitor the region and point out danger zones, and portable instruments to study the active areas in more detail; and we need a team of experienced volcanologists permanently assigned to the problem, working out the history of the individual volcanoes and the areas of danger from specific types of eruptions, and ready to concentrate on more specific predictions when signs indicate something may be brewing in a particular area.

As Crandell and Waldron remark (1969, p. 7), "We don't know which of the Cascade volcanoes will be the next to erupt . . . ." There seems to be no question that eruption *will* occur. Will it lead to catastrophe that could have been avoided?

APPENDIX 1

Active Volcanoes of the World

Volcanoes with certain or very probable records of eruptions during historic times are listed as active. Others, with solfataric activity or very well preserved forms, suggesting that they have been active during the last few tens of thousands of years are considered recent but are not listed individually. Their approximate number in each area is given in parentheses after the name of the area, together with the total number of active volcanoes in that area. Latitudes and longitudes are given to the nearest minute; altitudes converted from meters are given generally to the closest 5 feet. More approximate figures are marked c. (circa). Data are largely from the *Catalogue of Active Volcanoes of the World*, published by the International Association of Volcanology; those for the Aleutian Islands and Alaska from Coats, 1950; some for the Kurile Islands from Gorshkov, 1970; others are compiled from various sources.

Number (see map, Fig. 14-1)	Name	Location Latitude	Longitude	Height of summit (feet above sea level)	Number of eruptions recorded since 1700 A.D.	Arable land and/or property destroyed	Casualties	Types of activity (c, central crater; l, lateral crater; e, normal explosion; p, phreatic explosion; d, dome; f, lava flow; m, mudflow; g, glowing avalanche; s, submarine eruption)	Date of last reported eruption	Comments
					ANDAMAN ISLANDS (1 recent volcano, 1 active)					
1	Barren I.	12°15'N	93°50'E	1,005	4			c,e,f	1852	Central cone in caldera
					SUMATRA (29 recent volcanoes, 11 active)					
2	Silawaih Agam	5°25'N	95°36'E	5,695	1			l,e	1839	
3	Peuetsagoë	4°55'N	96°20'E	9,175	1			c,e,d,f	1918–1921	
4	Bur ni Telong	4°46'N	96°48'E	8,660	5			c,e,m	1924	
5	Sorikmarapi	0°41'N	99°32'E	7,080	5			c,l,e,p,m	1917	
6	Marapi	0°23'N	100°28'E	9,541	36			c,e	1967	Eruptions generally short
7	Tindikat	0°26'S	100°19'E	8,045	2			c,l,e,p	1914	
8	Talang	0°59'S	100°41'E	8,570	5			l,e	1968	
9	Kerintji	1°41'S	101°16'E	12,540	12			c,e,p	1968	Crater lake
10	Sumbing	2°25'S	101°44'E	8,275	2			c,l,e	1921	Crater lake
11	Kaba	3°31'S	102°37'E	6,440	7	X	X	c,l,e,m	1941	Crater lake
12	Dempo	4°02'S	103°08'E	10,470	18			c,e,p	1940	Crater lake
					SUNDA STRAIT (1 recent volcano)					
13	Krakatoa	6°06'S	105°25'E	2,685	2	X	X	c,s,e,p,g	1883–1884	Plinian eruption accompanied by caldera collapse
	Anak Krakatoa	"	"					c,e,s,p,f	1972	Cinder cone built in caldera since 1927
					JAVA (35 recent volcanoes, 20 active)					
14	Salak	6°43'S	106°44'E	7,295	5	X		l,e,p	1938	
15	Gedeh	6°47'S	106°59'E	9,760	19			c,e,p,f	1949	
16	Tankuban Prahu	6°46'S	107°36'E	6,875	7	X	X	c,e,p,m	1967	
17	Papandayan	7°19'S	107°44'E	8,795	2	X	X	c,p,m	1925	NE slope of mountain collapsed in 1772, destroying 40 villages

No.	Name	Lat	Long	Elevation (ft)	n				Last eruption	Products	Remarks
18	Guntur	7°08'S	107°20'E	7,420	21	X	X		1847	c,e,f	
19	Galunggung	7°15'S	108°03'E	7,155	3	X	X		1918	c,d,e,m	In 1822 a mudflow on the SE side killed 4,000 people
20	Tjerimai	6°53'S	108°24'E	10,155	4	X		X	1938	c,e,p,m	
21	Slamet	7°14'S	109°12'E	11,325	19		X		1967	c,e	
22	Butak Petarangan	7°10'S	109°49'E	7,335	3	X	X		1939	c,l,e,p,m	Crater lake
23	Dieng	7°12'S	109°54'E	8,465	3	X	X		1944	c,l,e,p	
24	Sundoro	7°18'S	109°59'E	10,397	6	X	X		1906	c,l,e,p	
25	Sumbing	7°23'S	110°03'E	11,125	1				1730?	c,f	
26	Merbabu	7°27'S	110°26'E	10,380	1				1797	c,e	
27	Merapi	7°32'S	110°26'E	9,605	40	X		X	1972	c,e,d,g,f,m	Very destructive glowing avalanches and mudflows
28	Kelut	7°56'S	112°18'E	5,710	18	X		X	1967	c,e,g,m,d	Mudflows formed by eruptions thru crater lake
29	Semeru	8°06'S	112°55'E	12,130	53	X		X	1972	c,e,l,f,m,d	Cinder cone in caldera
30	Bromo	7°56'S	112°57'E	7,685	44	X	X		1950	c,e	
31	Lamongan	7°59'S	113°20'E	5,506	37	X	X		1898	c,e,l,f,d,m	
32	Raung	8°07'S	114°02'E	10,995	35	X	X		1945	c,e,f,m	
33	Kawah Idjen	8°03'S	114°14'E	7,875	4	X	X		1936	c,e,p,m	Mudflows formed by eruption through a very acid crater lake
	SUNDA ISLANDS (29 recent volcanoes, 20 active)										
34	Batur	8°14'S	115°22'E	5,665	15	X		X	1968	c,e,l,f	Bali I. Composite cone in a caldera
35	Agung	8°20'S	115°30'E	10,370	4	X		X	1964	c,e,f,g,m	Bali I.
36	Rindjani	8°25'S	116°28'E	12,295	10				1966	c,e,d,l,f	Lombok I.
37	Tambora	8°15'S	118°00'E	9,410	3	X		X	1850?	c,e	Sumbawa I. A Plinian eruption in 1815 destroyed the top of the cone and threw out 100 km³ of tephra
38	Sangeang Api	8°11'S	119°03'E	6,430	7				1966	c,e,f	Sangeang I.
39	Iniё Lika	8°44'S	120°59'E	5,145	1				1905	c,p	Flores I.
40	Amburombu	8°48'S	121°11'E	7,008	5				1969	c,e,f,g	Flores I.

Number (see map, Fig. 14-1)	Name	Latitude	Longitude	Height of summit (feet above sea level)	Number of eruptions recorded since 1700 A.D.	Arable land and/or property destroyed	Casualties	Types of activity (c, central crater; l, lateral crater; e, normal explosion; p, phreatic explosion; d, dome; f, lava flow; g, glowing avalanche; m, mudflow; s, submarine eruption)	Date of last reported eruption	Comments
41	Ija	8°53'S	121°38'E	2,110	6			c,e	1969	Flores I.
42	Keli Mutu	8°45'S	121°50'E	5,410	2			c,p	1968	Flores I.
43	Puluweh	8°19'S	121°42'E	2,890	3	X		c,e,d,g	1966	Flores I.
44	Egon	8°40'S	122°27'E	5,620	2		X	c,e	1907	Flores I.
45	Lewotobi Lakilaki	8°32'S	122°46'E	5,225	11	X	X	c,e,d,f,m	1968	Flores I.
46	Lewotobi									
47	Perampuan	8°34'S	122°47'E	5,620	2			c,e,d	1935	Flores I.
	Leroboleng	8°21'S	122°50'E	3,685	3			c,e	1881	Flores I.
48	Ili Boleng	8°20'S	123°15'E	5,475	10			c,e,f	1950	Lomblen I.
49	Lewotolo	8°16'S	123°30'E	4,355	7	X		c,e	1920	Lomblen I.
50	Ili Werung	8°32'S	123°35'E	3,360	4	X	X	c,e,d,l,m	1948	Strombolian eruption
51	Batu Tara	7°47'S	123°35'E	2,470	1			c,e,f	1852	
52	Sirung	8°30'S	124°09'E	2,845	5			c,p	1947	Crater lake
53	Yersey	7°32'S	123°57'E	–	1			s	?	
	BANDA SEA				**(9 recent volcanoes, 8 active)**					
54	Emperor of China	6°37'S	124°13'E	–	2			s	1927?	
55	Nieuwerkerk	6°36'S	124°43'E	–	3			s	1927?	
56	Api	6°38'S	126°39'E	930	0			c,e	1699	
57	Damar	7°07'S	128°40'E	2,865	1			c,e	1892	
58	Teon	6°55'S	129°07'E	2,160	1	X	X	c,e	1904	
59	Nila	6°44'S	129°30'E	2,580	4			c,p	1968	
60	Serua	6°18'S	130°00'E	2,115	7	X	X	c,e,f	1921	
61	Banda Api	4°31'S	129°52'E	2,170	13	X	X	c,e,f	1901	
	CELEBES				**(13 recent volcanoes, 5 active)**					
62	Una Una	0°10'S	121°36'E	1,675	1	X		c,e,m	1898	
63	Soputan	1°06'N	124°43'E	5,886	18	X		c,e,l,d,f,g	1968	
64	Lokon-Empung	1°22'N	124°47'E	5,212	7	X	X	c,e	1970	
65	Mahuwu	1°21'N	124°51'E	4,390	4	X?		c,e,l,p	1904	
66	Tongkoko	1°31'N	125°11'E	3,790	4	X		c,e,d,l,f	1880	

No.	Name	Lat.	Long.	Elev. (ft)	No.	X	X	Composition	Date	Remarks
	SANGIHE ISLANDS							(5 recent volcanoes, 5 active)		
67	Ruang	2°17'N	125°25'E	2,355	15	X	X	c,e,d,f,m	1949	
68	Api Siau	2°47'N	125°29'E	5,885	22	X	X	c,e,m	1967	
69	Banua Wuhu	3°08'N	125°29'E	40	6	X		s,c,e,d,f	1968	Ephemeral island
70	Awu	3°40'N	125°30'E	4,355	14	X	X	c,e,p,d,f,m	1968	Crater lake
71	(Unnamed)	3°58'N	128°10'E	—	1			s	1922	
	HALMAHERA							(8 recent volcanoes, 5 active)		
72	Dukono	1°42'N	127°52'E	3,585	3	X	X	c,e,f	1951?	Continuous activity 1933–1951
73	Ibu	1°29'N	127°38'E	4,420	1			c,e	1911	
74	Gamkonora	1°22'N	127°31'E	5,395	3	X		c,e,f	1949	
75	Peak of Ternate	0°48'N	127°19'E	5,660	50	X	X	c,e,l,f,m	1963	
76	Makian	0°19'N	127°24'E	4,480	5	X		c,e,f	1890	
	MELANESIA							(58 recent volcanoes, 30 active)		
77	Umsini	1°11'S	134°00'E	8,795	1			c,e?	1864	Vogelkop, New Guinea
78	Tuluman	2°27'S	147°19'E	130	2			s,c,e,f	1955'	Built above s.l. in 1955
79	Bam	3°36'S	144°51'E	1,969	10	X		c,e	1956	New Guinea
80	Manam	4°06'S	145°03'E	4,265	15	X		c,e,f	1960	
81	Karkar	4°39'S	145°58'E	4,920	1			c,e,f	1895	
82	(Unnamed)	4°18'S	146°15'E	–	2			s	1951	
83	Long Island	5°21'S	147°07'E	4,278	2			c,e	1955	Caldera lake
84	Ritter Island	5°31'S	148°07'E	350	3		X	c,e	1888	Catastrophic eruption in 1888 destroyed top of cone 2,600 feet high
85	Lamington	8°56'S	148°10'E	5,840	1		X	c,e,d,g,m	1951–1956	Great Peléean eruption in 1951 killed nearly 3,000 people
86	Victory	9°11'S	149°04'E	6,090	2			c,e	1880	
87	Goropu	9°34'S	149°04'E	1,800	3		X	c,e,g,l,p	1944	
88	Langila	5°31'S	148°25'E	3,900	2			c,e	1954	
89	Benda	5°03'S	150°06'E	1,050	1	X	X	c,e,f	1920?	Cone in caldera lake
90	Pago	5°35'S	150°31'E	2,375	1	X		c,e,f	1900?	
91	Uluwan	5°02'S	151°20'E	7,546	?			c,e	1970	
92	Lolobau	4°55'S	151°10'E	3,058	1			c,e,l,f	1905?	
93	Vulcan	4°16'S	152°10'E	740	2			c,e	1937	Cone in Rabaul caldera
94	Matupi	4°14'S	152°13'E	750	5			c,e	1969	Cone in Rabaul caldera
95	Bagana	6°08'S	155°11'E	5,730	7			c,e,d,f,g	1953	
96	Cook	8°25'S	157°06'E	–	1			s	1964	

Number (see map, Fig. 14-1)	Name	Location Latitude	Location Longitude	Height of summit (feet above sea level)	Number of eruptions recorded since 1700 A.D.	Arable land and/or property destroyed	Casualties	Types of activity c, central crater; l, lateral crater; e, normal explosion; p, phreatic explosion; d, dome; f, lava flow; g, glowing avalanche; m, mudflow; s, submarine eruption	Date of last reported eruption	Comments
96A	Kovachi	9°01′S	157°57′E	–	9			s	1970	Ephemeral island
97	Savo	9°08′S	159°49′E	1,673	2?		X	c,e,g	1847	
98	Tinakula	10°28′S	165°45′E	3,000	?			c,e,f	1971	Active intermittently most of the time since 1595
99	Gaua	14°15′S	167°30′E	2,245	2			c,e	1967	Crater lake
100	Ambrym	16°15′S	168°05′E	4,377	15?	X		c,e,l,f,m	1967	Lava lake sometimes present
101	Lopevi	16°30′S	168°21′E	4,755	9			c,e,l,f	1967	
102	(Unnamed)	16°41′S	168°22′E	–	2			s	1953	
103	Karua	16°50′S	168°32′E	–	4			s	1971	Ephemeral island
104	(Unnamed)	18°45′S	169°11′E	–	1			s	1881	
105	Yasour	19°31′S	169°25′E	1,148	2			c,e	1969	Continuously active since 1774, with lava lake
106	Matthew Island	22°20′S	171°19′E	660	1			c,e	1953	
	SAMOAN ISLANDS				(about 20 recent volcanoes, 4 active)					
107	Mauga Afi	13°30′S	172°30′W	5,249	0	X		c,e,f	1690?	Savaii I.
108	Mauga Mu	13°36′S	172°31′W	5,490	1	X		c,e,l,f	1902	Savaii I.
109	Matavanu	13°31′S	172°22′W	2,335	1	X		c,e,l,f	1905–1911	Savaii I. A lava lake existed in the crater during part of the eruption
110	(Unnamed)	14°12′S	169°36′W	–	1			s,e	1866	Between Olosega and Tau Is.
	TONGA–KERMADEC REGION				(15 recent volcanoes, 14 active)					
111	Niuafo'ou	15°36′S	175°38′W	853	11	X		c,e,l,f	1959	Crater lake
112	Fonualei	18°09′S	174°19′W	600	4	X		c,e,l,f	1939	
113	Late	18°48′S	174°39′W	1,700	2			l,e,f	1854	
114	Home Reef	18°59′S	174°46′W	–	1			s	1852	

No.	Name	Latitude	Longitude	Elevation	No.			Type	Date	Remarks
115	Metis Shoal	19°11'S	174°52'W	—	7			s,p,d	1967–1968	Dome built above sea, eroded away again
116	Tofua Island	19°48'S	175°04'W	1,660	6			c,e,l,f	1958	
117	Falcon Island	20°19'S	175°25'W	475	9			s,c,e	1941	Frequent activity since 1894
118	(Unnamed)	20°34'S	175°23'W	—	3?			s	1959	Position doubtful
118A	(Unnamed)	20°40'S	175°50'W	—	1			s	1970	
119	(Unnamed)	20°51'S	175°32'W	—	2?			s	1923	
120	(Unnamed)	21°01'S	175°20'W	—	1?			s	1943	
121	(Unnamed)	21°27'S	175°46'W	—	2?			s	1932	
122	(Unnamed)	29°11'S	177°52'W	—	1?			s	1886	
123	Raoul Island	29°16'S	177°55'W	1,694	3			l,s,c,e	1872	
124	Brimstone Island	30°14'S	178°55'W	—	1			s	1825	Ephemeral island
NEW ZEALAND (about 6 recent volcanoes, 5 active)										
125	White Island	37°30'S	177°14'E	1,053	1?		X	c,p,m	1971	
126	Tarawera	38°16'S	176°34'E	3,770	1	X		c,e,p	1886	Catastrophic hydro-magmatic eruption
127	Tongariro	39°08'S	175°41'E	6,495	7			l,e	1927	Nearly continuous intermittent ash eruption since 1839
128	Ngauruhoe	39°10'S	175°42'E	7,515	59			c,e,f,g	1959	
129	Ruapehu	39°16'S	175°35'E	9,175	13		X	c,e,d,f,m	1971	
PHILIPPINES (31 recent volcanoes, 15 active)										
130	Jolo	5°55'N	121°10'E	?	2?		X	c,e,l?	1897	
131	Balut	5°23'N	125°22'E	2,915	1?	X	X?	c,e	1640–1641	
132	Ragang	7°40'N	124°31'E	9,290	9	X	X?	c,e	1915–1916	Mindanao I.
133	Calayo	7°50'N	124°41'E	995	1			c,e	1887	Mindanao I.
134	Hibokhibok	9°12'N	124°40'E	4,395	4?	X	X	c,e,d,f,g,m	1948–1952	Camiguin I.
135	Canlaon	10°24'N	123°08'E	8,135	8			c,e,f	1969	Negros I.
136	Bulusan	12°46'N	124°03'E	5,145	10?	X		c,e,l,f(d,g?)	1967	Luzon I.
137	Mayon	13°15'N	123°41'E	7,990	41?	X		c,e,f,m	1969	Luzon I.
138	Taal	14°01'N	121°00'E	990	19	X		c,e,l,p	1969	Luzon I.
139	Cagua	18°12'N	122°07'E	3,820	1			c,e	1860	Luzon I.
140	Camiguin de Babuyanes	18°51'N	121°51'E	2,380	1?			l,p,s?	1857?	
141	Didicas	19°04'N	122°11'E	150	4			s,e,d	1969	
142	Babuyan Claro	19°30'N	121°57'E	3,590	1			c,e	1919	
143	Smith	19°32'N	121°56'E	2,210	8	X		c,e	1924	
144	(Unnamed)?	20°20'N	121°45'E	—	3?			s	1854?	

Number (see map, Fig. 14-1)	Name	Location Latitude	Location Longitude	Height of summit (feet above sea level)	Number of eruptions recorded since 1700 A.D.	Arable land and/or property destroyed	Casualties	Types of activity c, central crater; l, lateral crater; e, normal explosion; p, phreatic explosion; d, dome; f, lava flow; g, glowing avalanche; m, mudflow; s, submarine eruption	Date of last reported eruption	Comments
				CHINA SEA	(7 known volcanoes, all active)					
145	Veteran	9°50'N	109°03'E	–	1?			s	1880?	
146	Ile des Cendres	10°09'N	109°00'E	80	1			s	1923	
147	(Unnamed)	20°56'N	134°45'E	–	1			s	1850	
148	(Unnamed)	21°50'N	121°11'E	–	1			s	1854	
149	(Unnamed)	24°00'N	121°50'E	–	1			s	1853–1954	
150	(Unnamed)	25°25'N	122°20'E	–	1			s	1867	
151	(Unnamed)	26°11'N	122°27'E	–	1			s	1916	
				RYUKYU ISLANDS	(13 recent volcanoes, 6 active)					
152	(Unnamed)	24°34'N	123°56'E	–	1			s	1925	
153	Okinawa-Tori-Shima	27°53'N	128°15'E	515	7?			c,e,p	1968	
154	Suwanose-Zima	29°32'N	129°43'E	2,635	15			c,e,f	1970	
155	Nakano Shima	29°50'N	129°55'E	3,235	2			c,e	1949	
156	Kutinoerabu-zima	30°26'N	130°13'E	2,140	7	X	X	c,e,l,p	1969	
157	Tokara-Iwo-zima	30°47'N	130°17'E	2,365	2			s,e	1935	
				MARIANA AND IZU ISLANDS	(23 recent volcanoes, 20 active)					
158	(Unnamed)	15°00'N	145°20'E	–	2			s	1964	
159	Guguan	17°19'N	145°51'E	1,025	2			c,e	1901	
160	South Pagan	18°06'N	145°47'E	1,880	1			c,e	1929–1930	Cone in caldera
161	North Pagan	18°07'N	145°48'E	1,810	5			c,e,f	1966	
162	Uracas	20°38'N	144°54'E	1,055	10			c,e,l,f,s	1969	
162A	Agrigan	18°45'N	145°40'E	3,185	1	X		c,e	1917	
163	Asongsong	19°40'N	145°24'E	2,940	5			c,e,l,f,m?	1924	
164	Uracas	20°38'N	144°54'E	1,055	10			c,e,l,f,s	1969	Also called Farallon de Pajaros
165	Sin-Iwo-sima	24°17'N	141°31'E	–	3			s,e	1968	Cinder cone 400 feet high, since eroded away
166	Iwo-sima	24°45'N	141°20'E	545	2?			l,p	1957	

No.	Name	Latitude	Longitude	Elevation	No.			Character	Last eruption	Remarks
167	Kita-Iwo-sima	25°26'N	141°14'E	—	2?			s	1889	
168	(Unnamed)	26°00'N	140°46'E	—	0			s	1543	
169	Tori-sima	30°28'N	140°14'E	1,330	3		X	c,e,p,f,s	1939	
170	Smith Rock	c.31°15'N	c.140°00'E	—	6			s	1916	Several eruption points
171	Myojin-sho	31°55'N	139°55'E	30	14			s,e,d	1970	A dome built in 1946 and 1952 with strong submarine explosions is 4 km north of Bayonnaise Rocks and part of the same structure; erupted again in 1960 and 1970
172	Aoga-sima	32°27'N	139°46'E	1,396	2	X	X	c,e,f	1785	
173	Hatizyo-sima	33°08'N	139°46'E	2,819	1?		X	c,e,l,s	1707?	
174	Miyake-zima	34°03'N	139°30'E	2,690	7	X	X	c,e,l,f	1962	
175	Kozu-sima	34°13'N	139°09'E	1,895	0			?	838	
176	Nii-zima	34°22'N	139°16'E	1,414	0			?	886	
177	O-sima	34°44'N	139°23'E	2,500	18			c,l,e,f	1969	Cone (Mihara-yama) in caldera
	JAPAN			(45 recent volcanoes, 31 active)						
178	Kaimon	31°11'N	130°32'E	3,050	0			e	882?	Southern end of Kyushu I.
179	Sakurajima	31°35'N	130°39'E	3,690	37	X	X	c,l,e,f	1972	
180	Kirishima	31°53'N	130°55'E	5,610	19		X	c,e,l,p	1959	
181	Unzen	32°45'N	130°18'E	4,487	1	X	X	c,e,l,f,m	1792	
182	Aso	32°54'N	131°06'E	5,255	54	X	X	c,e,p	1970	Group of cones in caldera
183	Fuji (Huzi)	35°21'N	138°44'E	12,460	2	X	X	c,l,e,f	1707	Honshu I.
184	Hakusan	36°09'N	136°47'E	8,917	0			c,e,m	1579	Shield volcano
185	Yake-dake	36°13'N	137°35'E	8,110	10	X	X	c,e,l,p,m	1963	Dome
186	Niigata-yake-yama	36°55'N	138°02'E	7,921	4			c,l,p	1963	Nearly continuous intermittent activity since 1900, with as many as 390 individual explosions a year
187	Asama	36°24'N	138°32'E	8,415	?	X	X	c,e,f,m	1965	
188	Kusatu-sirane	36°37'N	138°33'E	7,180	10		X	c,p,m	1939	
189	Akagi	36°32'N	139°11'E	6,034	0			?	1251	
190	Nikko-sirane	36°48'N	139°23'E	8,056	4			c,p	1889	
191	Nasu	37°07'N	139°58'E	6,325	3	X	X	c,e,p	1963	
192	Bandai	37°36'N	140°05'E	6,001	4?	X	X	c,p,m	1954	Devastating phreatic explosion and mudflow in 1888

Number (see map, Fig. 14-1)	Name	Location Latitude	Location Longitude	Height of summit (feet above sea level)	Number of eruptions recorded since 1700 A.D.	Arable land and/or property destroyed	Casualties	Types of activity c, central crater; l, lateral crater; e, normal explosion; p, phreatic explosion; d, dome; f, lava flow; g, glowing avalanche; m, mudflow; s, submarine eruption	Date of last reported eruption	Comments
193	Adatara	37°37′N	140°17′E	5,671	2			c,e	1900	
194	Azuma	37°44′N	140°15′E	6,516	5		X	c,e or p?	1950	
195	Zao	38°09′N	140°25′E	6,475	5	X	X	c,e,m	1939	Eruptions through crater lake
196	Kurikoma	38°57′N	140°47′E	5,371	3			c,e,p,m	1950	
197	Tyokai	39°05′N	140°02′E	7,359	2	X		c,e,d	1801	
198	Akita-Komaga-take	39°45′N	140°40′E	5,403	3			c,e,l,p	1971	
199	Iwate	39°51′N	141°00′E	6,734	3?	X		c,e,l,f,p?	1934	
200	Akita-Yake-yama	39°50′N	140°46′E	4,508	3?			c,p,e?	1951	
201	Iwaki	40°39′N	140°18′E	5,363	8?			c,p?, m	1863	Northern end of Honshu I.
202	Osima-O-sima	41°30′N	139°22′E	2,355	4?	X	X	c,e	1790?	Southern end of Hokkaido I.
203	Komagatake	42°04′N	140°41′E	3,760	14?	X	X	c,e,g	1942	
204	Usu	42°32′N	140°50′E	2,390	5	X	X	c,e,d,l,g,m	1943–1945	Composite volcano with domes
205	Tarumai	42°41′N	141°23′E	3,378	11?	X		c,e,d	1917	
206	Tokati	43°25′N	142°41′E	6,855	7?	X	X	c,e,g,m	1962	
207	Me-Akan	43°23′N	144°01′E	4,960	10?			c,p	1966	
208	Siretoko-Iwo-zan	44°08′N	145°10′E	5,160	4			l,p	1936	

KURIL ISLANDS (39 recent volcanoes, 33 active)

Number	Name	Latitude	Longitude	Height	Eruptions since 1700	Arable/property	Casualties	Types of activity	Date	Comments
209	Golovnin	43°53′N	145°32′E	1,805	1			e	c.1850	Domes in caldera
210	Mendeleev	43°59′N	145°42′E	2,935	2?			l,e	1900?	
211	Tiatia	44°21′N	146°15′E	6,015	1			c,e	1812	
212	Atsonupuri	44°49′N	147°07′E	3,975	2?			e,g	1932?	
213	Baransky	45°06′N	148°02′E	3,715	1?			e?	1951	
214	Chirip	45°23′N	147°55′E	5,160	2			e	1860?	
215	Kudriavy	45°23′N	148°48′E	3,270	3?			e,p?	1946?	Cone in caldera
216	Trezubets	46°03′N	150°03′E	4,390	1?			e	1924	
217	Berg	46°04′N	150°05′E	c.3,100	3			e	1952	Dome in crater

438

No.	Name	Lat.	Long.	Elev.	n	X		Year	Remarks
218	Snow	46°31′N	150°52′E	c.1,300	4		e,l,f	1879	Lava flows predominant
219	Cherny	46°31′N	150°52′E	2,060	2		e	1857	
220	Goriachaia sopka	46°50′N	151°45′E	2,940	6?		e,f,d	1944?	
221	Zavaritzky	46°55′N	151°57′E	2,060	2		e,f,d	1944?	
222	Prevo	47°01′N	152°07′E	4,490	2	X	e	c.1800	
223	Pallas	47°21′N	152°28′E	3,305	2		e	1924	Crater lake
224	Ushishir	47°31′N	152°49′E	1,325	2?		e,p?	1884	Cones in caldera
225	Rasshua	47°46′N	153°01′E	3,155	1		e	1846	
226	(Unnamed)	48°05′N	153°20′E	—	1		s	1924	
227	Sarychev	48°05′N	153°12′E	4,940	8		c,e,d,g	1965	
228	Raikoke	48°15′N	153°15′E	1,820	3	X	e	1924	
229	Chirinkotan	48°59′N	153°29′E	2,390	2?		e,f	c.1885	
230	Ekarma	48°57′N	153°56′E	3,865	1		e	1769	
231	Kuntomintar	48°45′N	154°01′E	2,730	3?	X	l,e	1927?	
232	Sinarka	48°52′N	154°10′E	3,080	3	X	e,d,g	1878	
233	Severgin	49°07′N	154°31′E	c.4,600	6		e	1933	Tsunamis accompanied the 1933 eruption
234	Krenitzyn	49°21′N	154°42′E	4,370	1		l,e,d	1952	Cone in caldera lake
235	Nemo	49°34′N	154°48′E	c.3,960	2		e	1906	Cone in caldera
236	Asyrmintar	49°36′N	154°54′E	1,880	1		e	1938	
237	Fuss	50°16′N	155°15′E	5,850	1		e,g	1854	
238	Karpinsky	50°09′N	155°22′E	4,440	1		c,e,f,g	1952	Caldera with edge cones
239	Chikurachki	50°19′N	155°27′E	5,995	5		c,e	1961	
240	Ebeko	50°41′N	156°01′E	3,755	4		c,e	1967	
241	Alaid	50°51′N	155°34′E	7,720	5		c,e,l,f,s	1972	

KAMCHATKA (28 recent volcanoes, 19 active)

No.	Name	Lat.	Long.	Elev.	n	X		Year	Remarks
242	Koshelev	51°21′N	156°45′E	5,980	1		e	c.1800	
243	Iliinsky	51°29′N	157°12′E	5,205	1		l,p	1901	
244	Zheltovsky	51°34′N	157°19′E	6,445	1		e	1923	
245	Ksudach	51°49′N	157°32′E	3,560	1		c,e	1907	Cones in caldera
246	Mutnovsky	52°27′N	158°12′E	7,670	14		c,e,f	1945	
247	Gorely Khrebet	52°33′N	158°02′E	6,035	5		c,e	1931	Cone in caldera
248	Opala	52°33′N	157°20′E	8,170	1		e	1776	Cone at caldera edge
249	Koriaksky	53°19′N	158°41′E	11,405	2		c,l,e,f	1957	
250	Avachinsky	53°15′N	158°50′E	9,080	13		c,e,f,g,m	1945	
251	Dzenzursky	53°38′N	158°25′E	7,540	1		e	1923	
252	Zhupanovsky	53°35′N	159°09′E	9,760	7		c,e	1957	
253	Karymsky	54°03′N	159°28′E	4,905	34		c,e,f,p	1970	Cone in caldera
254	Maly Semiachik	54°07′N	159°39′E	5,150	5		c,e	1952	Compound cone in caldera

Number (see map, Fig. 14-1)	Name	Location Latitude	Location Longitude	Height of summit (feet above sea level)	Number of eruptions recorded since 1700 A.D.	Arable land and/or property destroyed	Casualties	Types of activity c, central crater; l, lateral crater; e, normal explosion; p, phreatic explosion; d, dome; f, lava flow; g, glowing avalanche; m, mudflow; s, submarine eruption	Date of last reported eruption	Comments
255	Kronotsky	54°54′N	160°32′E	11,640	2			c,l,e	1923	Dome with crater
256	Kizimen	55°08′N	160°19′E	8,200	1			e	1927–1928	
257	Plosky Tolbachik	55°49′N	160°22′E	10,180	18?			c,e,f,l	1964	Lava lake in March, 1964
258	Bezymianny	55°58′N	160°35′E	10,180	15?			c,e,d,g,m	1970	Plinian eruption in 1956 destroyed top of cone, reduced height to 9,240 ft
259	Klyuchevskaya	56°03′N	160°38′E	16,000	72		X	c,e,l,f	1966	
260	Sheveluch	56°38′N	161°19′E	11,005	7			c,d,e,g,m	1964	

CONTINENTAL ASIA (number of recent volcanoes unknown, 5 reported active)

Number (see map, Fig. 14-1)	Name	Location Latitude	Location Longitude	Height of summit (feet above sea level)	Number of eruptions recorded since 1700 A.D.	Arable land and/or property destroyed	Casualties	Types of activity	Date of last reported eruption	Comments
261	Indigirsky	c.67°N	c.142°E	?	1?			e?	c.1770	
262	Anjuisky	67°10′N	165°23′E	3,465	0			e?	?	Eruptions between 1300 and 1700 A.D.
263	Laoheishan	48°41′N	126°20′E	c.1,730	1			e,f	1720–1722	
264	Huoshaoshan	48°43′N	126°21′E	c.1,500	1			e,f	1720–1722	
265	?	c.36°N	c.81°E	c.19,800	1?			e?	1951	Tibet ("Smoke was rising and stones were thrown out")

ALEUTIAN ISLANDS AND ALASKA (about 60 recent volcanoes, 39 active)

Number (see map, Fig. 14-1)	Name	Location Latitude	Location Longitude	Height of summit (feet above sea level)	Number of eruptions recorded since 1700 A.D.	Arable land and/or property destroyed	Casualties	Types of activity	Date of last reported eruption	Comments
266	Kiska	52°06′N	177°36′E	4,025	5			l,e,f	1969	
267	Little Sitkin	51°57′N	178°32′E	3,945	2			e	1828	
268	Cerberus	51°56′N	179°35′E	2,560	5			e?	1873	Semisopochnoi I.
269	Gareloi	51°48′N	178°48′W	5,370	8			e,f	1930	
270	Tanaga	51°53′N	178°07′W	7,015	4			e,f	1914	
271	Kanaga	51°55′N	177°10′W	4,450	6			e,f	1933	
272	Great Sitkin	52°04′N	176°07′W	5,775	5			e,f	1945	
273	Keniuji	52°13′N	175°08′W	885	3			e,f?	1828	
274	Korovin	52°23′N	174°10′W	4,885	3			e	1844	Atka I.
275	Sarichef	52°19′N	174°03′W	2,015	1			e?	1812	Atka I.

No.	Name	Latitude	Longitude	Elevation		Activity	Year	Notes
276	Seguam	52°19′N	172°23′W	3,465	5	e	1927	
277	Amukta	52°30′N	171°16′W	3,490	3	c,e,l,f	1963	
278	Yunaska	52°39′N	170°39′W	1,980	4	e	1937	
279	Carlisle	52°54′N	170°04′W	5,315	3	e	1838	
280	Cleveland	52°49′N	169°58′W	5,710	6	e,f	1944	Chuginadak I.
281	Kagamil	52°58′N	169°44′W	2,945	1	e?	1929	
282	Vsevidof	53°08′N	168°42′W	6,965	5	e	1880	Umnak I.
283	Okmok	53°25′N	168°03′W	3,540	10	e,f	1945	Caldera, Umnak I.
284	Bogoslof	53°56′N	168°02′W	c.150	11	e,d	1931	
285	Makushin	53°52′N	168°56′W	6,720	14	e	1938	Unalaska I.
286	Akutan	54°08′N	166°00′W	4,265	22	e,f	1948	Unalaska I.
287	Pogromni	54°34′N	164°42′W	7,545	4	e,f	1830	Unimak I.
288	Westdahl	54°31′N	164°39′W	5,055	1	l,e,f	1964	Unimak I.
289	Fisher	54°38′N	164°25′W	3,545	1	e?	1826	Unimak I.
290	Shishaldin	54°45′N	163°58′W	9,430	23	c,e,f	1963	Unimak I.
291	Isanotski	54°45′N	163°44′W	8,185	4	e	1845	Unimak I.
292	Pavlof	55°25′N	161°54′W	8,960	24	c,e,f	1963	Alaska Peninsula
293	Pavlof Sister	55°27′N	161°51′W	c.7,050	1	e?	1786	Alaska Peninsula
294	Veniaminof	56°10′N	159°23′W	c.8,450	8	e	1944	Alaska Peninsula
295	Aniakchak	56°53′N	158°10′W	4,450	1	e,f	1931	
296	Chiginagak	57°08′N	157°00′W	7,985	2	e	1929	
297	Peulik	57°45′N	156°21′W	5,030	2	e	1852	
298	Mageik	58°12′N	155°15′W	7,295	4	e	1946	
299	Trident	58°14′N	155°07′W	6,830	3	l,d,e,m	1968	
300	Novarupta	58°17′N	155°13′W		1	d,e,g	1912	Dome, with associated ash flow, Valley of 10,000 Smokes
301	Katmai	58°16′N	154°59′W	7,540	7	c,e,f	1931	
302	Augustine	59°22′N	153°25′W	3,995	5	e,f,d	1963	Augustine I.
303	Iliamna	60°02′N	153°06′W	10,140	6	e	1947	Alaska Range
304	Redoubt	60°28′N	152°45′W	10,265	7	c,e	1966	Alaska Range
304a	Spurr	61°17′N	152°17′W	11,070	1	l,c,m	1953	Alaska Range

CENTRAL BRITISH COLUMBIA, CANADA

No historic eruptions; but at least three eruptions of Mt. Edziza, at 57°41′N, 130°36′W, have occurred within the last 1,800 years, and the Aiyansh Volcano, at 55°07′N, 128°54′W, erupted about 220 years ago.

CASCADE RANGE, UNITED STATES (about 15 recent volcanoes, 7 active)

No.	Name	Latitude	Longitude	Elevation		Activity	Year
305	Mt. Baker	48°47′N	121°49′W	10,778	5	c,l,e	1870
306	Mt. Rainier	46°52′N	121°45′W	14,410	6	c,e	1882
307	Mt. St. Helens	46°12′N	122°11′W	9,671	6	c,e,f	1854
308	Mt. Hood	45°22′N	121°42′W	11,245	1	c,e	c.1801

441

Number (see map, Fig. 14-1)	Name	Location Latitude	Longitude	Height of summit (feet above sea level)	Number of eruptions recorded since 1700 A.D.	Arable land and/or property destroyed	Casualties	Types of activity c, central crater; l, lateral crater; e, normal explosion; p, phreatic explosion; d, dome; f, lava flow; g, glowing avalanche; m, mudflow; s, submarine eruption	Date of last reported eruption	Comments
309	Mt. Shasta	41°24'N	122°11'W	14,161	2?			e?	1855?	
310	Cinder Cone	40°32'N	121°20'W	6,907	1			c,e,f?	1851	Cinder cone and associated lava flows
311	Lassen Peak	40°29'N	121°30'W	10,453	4	X		c,e,f,g,m	1914–1921	Large dome with crater, in older caldera
			MEXICO AND CENTRAL AMERICA		(about 60 recent volcanoes, 42 active)					
312	Tres Vírgenes	27°28'N	112°35'W	6,585	2?			c,e,f?	1857?	Lower California
313	Bárcena	19°16'N	110°48'W	c.1,235	1			c,e,f,g?	1952	San Benedicto I., W of Mexico
314	Ceboruco	21°09'N	104°30'W	7,140	1			c,e,f,g	1870–1876	Mexico
315	Colima	19°25'N	103°43'W	13,070	13	X		c,e,f,g,d	1965	Dome growing in crater
316	Parícutin	19°29'N	102°15'W	10,460	1	X	X	c,l,e,f	1943–1952	Cinder cone and associated lava flows; started in 1943
317	Jorullo	19°02'N	101°40'W	4,390	1	X		c,l,e,f,m,g?	1759–1774	Cinder cone and associated lava flows; started in 1759
318	Popocatepetl	19°01'N	98°37'W	17,990	3			c,e	1920	
319	Orizaba	19°02'N	97°17'W	18,725	0			c,e,f	1687	
320	San Martín	18°35'N	95°10'W	5,115	1			c,e,f	1793	
321	Tacaná	15°08'N	92°06'W	13,300	2			l,e?	1855	On boundary between Mexico and Guatemala
322	Tajumulco	15°03'N	91°54'W	13,895	2?			c,e	1863?	Guatemala
323	Santa Maria	14°45'N	91°33'W	12,435	13	X	X	l,e,d,f,g	1969	Lateral domes
324	Cerro Quemado	14°48'N	91°31'W	10,490	1			l,f	1785	
325	Atitlán	14°35'N	91°11'W	11,630	10?	X		c,e	1856?	
326	Acatenango	14°30'N	90°52'W	13,070	2			c,l,e	1926–1927	
327	Fuego	14°29'N	90°53'W	12,655	31?	X	X	c,e,d,f,m	1971	

No.	Name	Lat.	Long.	Elev.	Eruptions			Rock types	Last activity	Remarks
328	Pacaya	14°23′N	90°36′W	8,400	6	X		c,e,l,f	1972	
329	Santa Ana	13°51′N	89°38′W	7,180	5	X		c,e	1920?	El Salvador
330	Izalco	13°49′N	89°39′W	6,485	53?	X	X	c,e,l,f,g	1966	First formed in 1770
331	San Marcelino	13°48′N	89°35′W	4,370	1?	X		l?,f	1722?	
332	San Salvador	13°44′N	89°17′W	6,490	2?	X		c,e,l,f	1917	
333	Islas Quemadas	13°40′N	89°03′W	c.1,485	1			s,d,e	1879–1880	Domes in Lake Ilopango
334	San Miguel	13°26′N	88°16′W	7,035	24?	X		c,e,l,f	1970	
335	Conchaguita	13°31′N	87°46′W	c.1,815	1			c,e	1892	
336	Coseguïna	12°58′N	87°35′W	2,879	1			c,e,g	1835	Great Plinian eruption, Nicaragua
337	El Viejo	12°42′N	87°01′W	5,875	0			c,e	1971	Active in 16th century
338	Chichigalpa	12°41′N	86°59′W	5,255	0			c,e?	?	
339	Telica	12°36′N	86°52′W	3,430	2			c,e	1971	Active in 16th century
340	Santa Clara	12°34′N	86°49′W	3,420	0			c,e?	?	First formed in 1850
341	Cerro Negro	12°31′N	86°44′W	1,615	12		X	c,e,l,f,m	1971	
342	Las Pilas	12°29′N	86°41′W	3,535	2			c,l,e	1954	
343	Momotombo	12°25′N	86°33′W	4,153	6			c,e,f	1905	
344	Masaya	11°57′N	86°09′W	2,121	14		X	c,e,f	1970	Nearly continuous activity from 1529 to 1946; fumes do great damage to plantations
345	Mombacho	11°50′N	89°59′W	4,620	2?			c,l,e	1850?	
346	Concepción	11°32′N	85°39′W	5,139	10?			c,e,f	1963	
347	Orosí	10°59′N	85°29′W	4,985	2?			c,e?	1849?	
348	Rincón de la Vieja	10°50′N	85°21′W	6,255	7	X		c,e,p	1970	
349	Arenal	10°29′N	84°43′W	5,390	2	X	X	c,l,e,f,g	1970	
350	Poas	10°11′N	84°13′W	8,985	13			c,e,p	1972	
351	Barba	10°08′N	84°05′W	9,625	1			c,e	1867	
352	Irazú	9°59′N	83°51′W	11,325	13?	X	X	c,e,p,m	1967	
353	Turrialba	10°02′N	83°45′W	10,980	?		X	c,e	1866	Quite active during the 18th and 19th centuries
SOUTH AMERICA					(60 recent volcanoes, 47 active)					
354	Ruiz	4°53′N	75°22′W	17,820	5	X		l,e,f?,m	1845	Subglacial eruptions produce mudflows
355	Tolima	4°39′N	75°22′W	17,210	4			c,e	1943	Volcanoes 354–360 are in Columbia
356	Puracé	2°22′N	76°23′W	15,145	21	X		c,e,f,m	1955?	
357	Doña Juana	1°31′N	76°56′W	14,025	1	X	X	c,e,d,g,m	1906	Continuously active 1897 to 1906

Number (see map, Fig. 14-1)	Name	Location Latitude	Location Longitude	Height of summit (feet above sea level)	Number of eruptions recorded since 1700 A.D.	Arable land and/or property destroyed	Casualties	Types of activity c, central crater; l, lateral crater; e, normal explosion; p, phreatic explosion; d, dome; f, lava flow; g, glowing avalanche; m, mudflow; s, submarine eruption	Date of last reported eruption	Comments
358	El Galeras	1°13'N	77°18'W	14,080	11?			c,e,d,f	1947	
359	Cumbal	0°59'N	77°53'W	15,720	2			c,e	1926	
360	Cerro Negro de Mayasquer	0°48'N	77°57'W	14,750	1?			c,e	1936	Possibly from Reventador
361	Reventador	0°05'S	77°40'W	11,500	16?			c,e	1972	Volcanoes 361–369 are in Ecuador
362	Guagua Pichincha	0°15'S	78°36'W	16,000	5			c,e,g	1881	
363	Antisana	0°30'S	78°08'W	18,995	4			c,l,e,f,d?	1801	Subglacial eruptions
364	Sumaco	0°34'S	77°38'W	12,770	?			c,e	1933	Several eruptions between 1700 and 1925
365	Cotopaxi	0°50'S	78°26'W	19,815	50	X		c,e,f,m	1942	Eruptions through crater lake
366	Quilotoa	0°52'S	78°55'W	13,135	3			c,e	1759	
367	Llanganate	1°13'S	78°15'W	?	?			e	?	Eruptions in early 20th century
368	Tungurahua	1°27'S	78°26'W	16,550	20?	X		c,e,f,g,m	1944	
369	Sangay	2°00'S	78°20'W	17,260	47			c,e,f,g?	1972	
370	El Misti	16°18'S	71°25'W	19,220	6			c,e	1878?	Dome growing in crater Volcanoes 370–373 are in Peru
371	Ubinas	16°21'S	70°54'W	18,720	11	X		c,e	1969	
372	Huaina-Putina	16°35'S	70°52'W	15,840	0	X	X	c,e	1600	
373	Tutupaca	17°01'S	70°22'W	19,160	4			c,e	1902	
374	Guallatiri	18°25'S	69°06'W	20,000	?			c,e	1960	Subglacial eruptions
375	Isluga	19°09'S	68°50'W	18,250	5	X		c,e,f	1960	Volcanoes 374–399 are in Chile
376	San Pedro	21°53'S	68°24'W	20,325	5?	X		c,e	1960	
377	Lascar	23°22'S	76°44'W	18,615	16?			c,e	1968	
378	Llullaillaco	24°43'S	68°33'W	22,185	3			c,e,l,f?	1877	
379	Tupungatito	33°24'S	69°48'W	18,610	16?			c,e,f	1964	
380	San José	33°48'S	69°55'W	19,405	7?			c,e	1931	

No.	Name	Latitude	Longitude	Elevation (ft)			Number	Type	Date	Remarks
381	Peteroa	35°15'S	70°34'W	13,500			7	c,e,f,m	1894	
382	Descabezado Grande	35°35'S	70°45'W	12,640			1	l,e	1932	
383	Cerro Azul	35°40'S	70°46'W	12,575			5	l,e,f	1932	The lateral crater, Quizapu, is the site of the recent eruptions
384	Nevados de Chillán	36°52'S	71°23'W	10,195			5	l,e	1906	
385	Antuco	37°24'S	71°22'W	9,850			9	c,e,l,f	1869	Active in 17th and 18th centuries
386	Los Copahues	37°51'S	71°10'W	9,935			?	e?	?	
387	Lonquimay	38°22'S	71°35'W	9,310			3	c,e,f	1889	
388	Llaima	38°42'S	71°42'W	10,310			20	c,e,l,f	1955–1957	Lava flows into snow cause mudflows
389	Villarica	39°25'S	71°57'W	9,370	X	X	13	c,e,f,m	1972	
390	Rinihue	39°56'S	72°02'W	8,020			1	e?	1864	Cone in caldera
391	Nilahue	40°22'S	72°06'W	c.900		X	2	c,e,m	1955	Maar
392	Puyahue	40°35'S	72°08'W	7,390			2	l,e,f	1972	
393	Osorno	41°06'S	72°30'W	8,780			8	c,e,l,f	1869	Subglacial eruptions cause mudflows
394	Calbuco	41°20'S	72°37'W	6,650		X	7	c,e,f,m	1961	
395	Huequi	42°20'S	72°40'W	3,465			5	c,e,f?	1920	
396	Minchinmávida	42°48'S	72°27'W	8,150			?	e,f	1835?	
397	Corcovado	43°11'S	72°48'W	8,150			?	e,f	1835?	
397A	Cerro Ventisquero	c.46°04'S	c.72°W	c.8,600		X	1	e,f	1971	Cone in caldera
398	Lautaro	49°01'S	73°33'W	11,155			?	e	1945?	
399	Mt. Burney	52°20'S	73°24'W	5,800			1?	?	1910?	

SCOTIA ARC AND ANTARCTICA (16 recent volcanoes, 10 active)

No.	Name	Latitude	Longitude	Elevation (ft)			Number	Type	Date	Remarks
400	(Unnamed)	56°15'S	72°10'W	—			1	s	1876	Built a few feet above sea level
401	(Unnamed)	55°54'S	27°54'W	—			1	s	1962	
402	Zavodovski I.	56°20'S	27°34'W	1,600			4?	e	1908?	
403	Candlemas I.	57°03'S	26°40'W	c.2,150			2?	e	1911?	
404	Mt. Michael	57°47'S	26°27'W	2,640			1	c,e	1819	Saunders I.
405	Mt. Darnley	59°03'S	26°30'W	c.3,600			5	e,f	1956	Bristol I.
406	Lindenberg I.	64°55'S	59°42'W	?			1	c,l,e	1893	
407	Deception I.	62°56'S	60°34'W	1,890			3	e	1970	Cinder cone built in bay
408	Erebus	77°35'S	167°10'E	13,200			7	c,e,f?	1947	Subglacial eruptions, Ross I.
409	Buckle I.	66°48'S	163°15'E	4,063			2	e	1899	

Number (see map, Fig. 14-1)	Name	Location Latitude	Location Longitude	Height of summit (feet above sea level)	Number of eruptions recorded since 1700 A.D.	Arable land and/or property destroyed	Casualties	Types of activity c, central crater; l, lateral crater; e, normal explosion; p, phreatic explosion; d, dome; f, lava flow; g, glowing avalanche; m, mudflow; s, submarine eruption	Date of last reported eruption	Comments
		PACIFIC OCEAN		(number of recent volcanoes unknown, 15 reported active)						
410	(Unnamed)	33°35'?S	76°50'W	–	1			s	1839	Ephemeral island
411	(Unnamed)	33°37'S	78°47'W	–	1			s,e	1835	Accompanied by a tsunami
412	El Yunque(?)	33°39'S	78°51'W	3,020	1?				1743	Mas a Tierra, Juan Fernández Is.
413	Santa Maria I.	1°18'S	90°27'W	2,100	1			e?	1813	Galápagos Is.
414	San Salvador I.	0°13'S	90°46'W	2,974	1			l,f	1897	Galápagos Is.
415	Cerro Azul	0°54'S	91°25'W	5,540	5?			c,e,f	1959	Shield volcano with caldera; Isabela I., Galápagos
416	Sierra Negra	0°50'S	91°10'W	4,890	3?			c,e,f	1953–1954	Shield volcano with caldera; Isabela I., Galápagos
417	Alcedo	0°26'S	91°07'W	c.3,700	2			c,e,f	1970	Shield volcano with caldera; Isabela I., Galápagos
418	Wolf	0°01'S	91°21'W	5,600	7			c,e,l,f	1948	Shield volcano with caldera; Isabela I., Galápagos
419	Fernandina	0°22'S	91°33'W	c.4,900	15?			l,e,f	1968	Great collapse of summit caldera in 1968
420	Kilauea	19°25'N	155°17'W	4,090	47	X	X	c,l,f,p	1971	Hawaii I. A lava lake was active in the caldera most of the time from 1823 to 1924
421	Mauna Loa	19°28'N	155°36'W	13,680	37	X		c,l,f	1950	Shield volcano with caldera; Hawaii I.
422	Hualalai	19°41'N	155°52'W	8,251	1	X		l,f	1800–1801	Shield volcano with caldera; Hawaii I.

No.	Name	Lat.	Long.	Elevation	No. recent volcanoes			Code	Date	Remarks
423	Haleakala	20°42′N	156°15′W	10,025	1			l,f	c.1790	
424	(Unnamed)	23°35′N	163°50′W	—	1			s	1955	
424A	Macdonald	29°01′S	140°17′W	—	1			s	1967	Submarine cone in Austral Is.

WEST INDIES (17 recent volcanoes, 9 active)

No.	Name	Lat.	Long.	Elevation	No. recent volcanoes			Code	Date	Remarks
425	Mt. Misery	17°22′N	62°48′W	3,792	2?			p?	1843	St. Kitts I.
426	La Soufrière de la Guadeloupe	16°03′N	61°40′W	4,813	6?			c,e,p,m	1956	Guadeloupe I.
427	(Unnamed)	16°08′N	61°17′W	—	1			s	1843	Between Guadeloupe and Marie Galante I.
428	Valley of Desolation	15°18′N	61°18′W	2,600	1			p	1880	Dominica I.
429	Mt. Pelée	14°49′N	61°10′W	4,584	4	X	X	c,e,d,g,m	1929–1932	Martinique I.
430	Hodder's Volcano	c.14°02′N	c.61°04′W	—	1			s	1902	
431	Qualibu	13°50′N	61°03′W	6,700	1			p	1766	St. Lucia I.
432	Soufrière of St. Vincent	13°20′N	61°11′W	3,864	6	X	X	c,l,e,p,g,m	1972	Many separate explosions in 1902–1903
433	Kick-em-Jenny	12°18′N	61°38′W	—	6			s	1966	

ATLANTIC OCEAN (number of recent volcanoes unknown, 22 reported active)

No.	Name	Lat.	Long.	Elevation	No. recent volcanoes			Code	Date	Remarks
434	(Unnamed)	49°00′N	34°30′W	—	1			s	1884	
435	(Unnamed)	38°45′N	38°05′W	—	1			s	1865	
436	Fayal I.	38°35′N	28°43′W	3,440	2	X	X	l,e,f,s	1957–1958	Azores. Capelinhos eruption was a lateral eruption on the western flank
437	Pico I.	38°28′N	28°24′W	7,760	3	X	X	c,l,e,f,s	1963	Azores
438	San Jorge I.	38°39′N	28°05′W	3,475	2	X	X	l,e,f,s	1964?	Azores
439	(Unnamed)	38°30′N	27°25′W	—	2			s	1902	
440	Santa Barbara	38°44′N	27°19′W	3,375	2	X		l,e,f,s	1867	Terceira I., Azores
441	Don João de Castro Bank	38°14′N	26°38′W	—	1			s,e	1720	Ephemeral island
442	(Unnamed)	39°57′N	25°50′W	—	1			s	1856	
443	Sete Cidades	37°52′N	25°47′W	2,825	4			c,l,e,f?,s	1811	San Miguel I., Azores
444	Agua de Pau	37°46′N	25°28′W	3,130	0	X	X	c,l,e,f	1652	San Miguel I., Azores
445	Furnas	37°46′N	25°19′W	2,655	0	X	X	c,e	1630	San Miguel I., Azores
446	Monaco Bank	37°36′N	25°53′W	—	2			s	1911	
447	La Palma I.	28°33′N	17°50′W	6,100	2	X	X	l,e,f,g	1971	Canary Is. Several lateral vents on southern half of island

Number (see map, Fig. 14-1)	Name	Location Latitude	Longitude	Height of summit (feet above sea level)	Number of eruptions recorded since 1700 A.D.	Arable land and/or property destroyed	Casualties	Types of activity c, central crater; l, lateral crater; e, normal explosion; p, phreatic explosion; d, dome; f, lava flow; g, glowing avalanche; m, mudflow; s, submarine eruption	Date of last reported eruption	Comments
448	Tenerife I.	28°18'N	16°38'W	12,250	5	X		l,e,f	1909	Canary Is.
449	Lanzarote I.	29°02'N	13°37'W	1,855	2			l,e,f	1824	Canary Is.
450	Fogo I.	14°57'N	24°21'W	9,335	6	X		c,l,e,f	1951	Cape Verde Is.
451	(Unnamed)	7°00'N	21°50'W	—	1			s	1824	
452	(Unnamed)	4°12'N	21°27'W	—	1			s	1878	
453	(Unnamed)	0°43'S	20°32'W	—	3			s	1836	
454	(Unnamed)	3°30'S	24°30'W	—	1			s	1852	
455	Tristan da Cunha	37°05'S	12°17'W	6,760	1	X		l,e,d,f	1961	
ICELAND AND JAN MAYEN					(number of recent volcanoes unknown, 22 reported active)					
456	(Unnamed)	c.66°N	c.29°34'W	—	0			s	1456	Ephemeral island
457	Eldeyjar	63°29'N	23°47'W	?	4			s	1926	Fissure eruption
458	Trölladyngja	63°56'N	22°11'W	1,250	0			f	1389–1390	
459	Meitill	64°00'N	21°24'W	?	0				c.1000	
460	Hekla	64°00'N	19°40'W	4,920	6	X	X	c,l,e,f,m	1970	
461	Krakatindur	64°01'N	19°29'W	?	2		X	f	1913	
462	Surtsey	63°18'N	20°37'W	570	1			s,c,e,f	1963–1967	New island built in sea
463	Eyjafjallajökull	63°38'N	19°38'W	5,500	1				1821	Subglacial eruption
464	Katla	63°36'N	19°00'W	c.4,750	6				1955	Subglacial eruption
465	Eldgja	63°58'N	18°36'W	?	0			f	c.950	Great flood eruption
466	Laki	64°05'N	18°14'W	2,700	1	X		f	1783	Great flood eruption
467	Grimsvötn	64°55'N	17°20'W	?	33				1954	Subglacial eruptions
468	Öraefajökull	64°00'N	16°38'W	c.6,900	1				1727	Subglacial eruptions
469	Kverkfjöll	64°39'N	16°42'W	c.6,100	3				1729	Subglacial eruptions
470	Askja	65°02'N	16°45'W	4,983	2			c,e,f,p	1961	Caldera
471	Sveinagja	65°23'N	16°30'W	c.3,100	1			f	1875	Fissure eruption
472	Myvatn fissure	c.65°40'N	c.16°50'W	?	1			f	1728–1729	Big lava flow
473	Krafla	65°42'N	16°44'W	2,700	1			e	1724	
474	Leirhafnarskörd	66°22'N	16°28'W	c.800	1			e	1823	
475	Mánáreyar	66°17'N	17°06'W	—	1			s	1867	

No.	Name	Lat.	Long.	Height	Eruptions			Code	Date	Remarks
476	(Unnamed)	c.66°40′N	c.18°05′W	—	0			s	1372	
477	Beerenberg	71°05′N	7°50′W	8,347	2			l,e	1970	Jan Mayen I.

MEDITERRANEAN REGION (about 25 recent volcanoes, 13 active)

No.	Name	Lat.	Long.	Height	Eruptions			Code	Date	Remarks
478	Monte Nuovo	40°50′N	14°06′E	460	1	X		c,e	1538	Cinder cone in Phlegraean Fields
479	Vesuvius	40°49′N	14°26′E	4,230	Many	X	X	c,e,l,f	1944	Nearly continuous activity from 1911 to 1944
480	Ischia	40°44′N	13°54′E	2,600	0	X	X	e,f	1301	Flow from Arso crater
481	Stromboli	38°47′N	15°13′E	3,055	Many	X	X	c,e,f,g	1971	Essentially continuous activity
482	Vulcanello	38°26′N	14°58′E	405	0			c,e,f	183 B.C.	
483	Vulcano	38°24′N	14°58′E	1,650	6?			c,e,f	1964	
484	Etna	37°44′N	15°00′E	10,855	75?	X	X	c,l,e,f	1972	
485	Giulia-Ferdinandeo	37°02′N	12°07′E	—	3			s	1863	Ephemeral island on Graham Bank
486	Pinne	36°09′N	13°00′E	—	2			s	1911	
487	Foerstner	36°08′N	11°09′E	—	1			s	1891	Just NNW of Pantelleria
488	Kameno Vouno	37°37′N	23°20′E	1,400	0			c,e,d,f	c.250 B.C.	Methana Peninsula, Peloponnesus
489	Santorin (Thera)	36°24′N	25°24′E	4,316	6	X	X	s,c,e,d,f	1950	Domes in caldera formed during a great prehistoric Plinian eruption
490	Nisyros	36°35′N	27°11′E	2,305	3?	X	X	c,e,p	1888	

AFRICA (43 recent volcanoes, 14 active)

No.	Name	Lat.	Long.	Height	Eruptions			Code	Date	Remarks
491	Dubbi	13°42′N	41°35′E	5,215	2	X	X	c,e,f	1863?	
492	Erta Alè	13°37′N	40°35′E	1,660	6?	X		c,l,e,f	1971	Shield volcano with lava lake in summit crater
493	Afderà	13°24′N	41°05′E	3,940	2	X	X	l,e,f	1915	
494	Abidà	10°04′N	40°50′E	4,290	2			e	1928	
495	Mt. Cameroon	4°12′N	9°10′E	13,430	9?	X	X	l,e,f	1922	
496	Teleki	2°22′N	36°37′E	2,120	5			l,e,f	1922	
497	Likaiyu	2°22′N	36°33′E	3,000	3?			c,e,f	1920?	
498	Longonot	0°55′S	36°27′E	9,111	1?			f?	c.1860	
499	Ol Doinyo Lengai	2°45′S	35°54′E	9,442	9?			c,e,f,p,m	1955	
500	Shaitani	2°52′S	37°58′E	c.5,500	1			c,e,f	c.1855	

Number (see map, Fig. 14-1)	Name	Location Latitude	Location Longitude	Height of summit (feet above sea level)	Number of eruptions recorded since 1700 A.D.	Arable land and/or property destroyed	Casualties	Types of activity (c, central crater; l, lateral crater; e, normal explosion; p, phreatic explosion; d, dome; f, lava flow; g, glowing avalanche; m, mudflow; s, submarine eruption)	Date of last reported eruption	Comments
501	Meru	3°15′S	36°45′E	14,978	3?			c,e,f	1910	
502	Kieyo	9°14′S	33°45′E	7,135	1			c,e,f	c.1800	
503	Nyamlagira	1°25′S	29°12′E	10,080	17	X		c,l,e,f	1971	Lava lake in summit caldera 1921–1938
504	Nyiragongo	1°29′S	29°14′E	11,380	13?			c,e	1972	Lava lake in crater most of the time since 1935
	ASIA MINOR (27 recent volcanoes, 8 active)									
505	Djebel Teyr	15°42′N	41°44′E	805	4?			e	1883?	Island in Red Sea
506	Saddle Island	15°07′N	42°06′E	585	2			e	1846?	Island in Red Sea
507	Halá-'l-Ishqa	c.27°35′N	36°48′E	c.5,600	0			f	640	Or at nearby Halá-'l-Bedr
508	(Unnamed)	24°20′N	39°36′E	c.3,000	0			c,f,d?	1256	12 miles SE of Medina
509	Djebel Yar	c.16°40′N	c.42°56′E	c.1,000	1?			e,f	1820?	
510	Kaulet Háttab	15°38′N	44°05′E	c.9,600	0	X		f	Between 400 and 600 A.D.	
511	Djebel Zebíb	15°36′N	44°07′E	c.9,700	0	X		l,f	Sometime after 200 A.D.	
512	Harras	c.14°30′N	c.44°30′E	c.8,500	1?			e	1937?	
	INDIAN OCEAN (number of recent volcanoes unknown, 4 reported active)									
513	Karthala	11°45′S	41°03′E	7,790	21	X	X	c,e,l,f	1972	Great Comoro I.
514	Piton de la Fournaise	21°14′S	55°43′E	8,680	Many			c,e,l,f	1972	Réunion I. Activity essentially continuous
515	Heard Island	53°06′S	73°31′E	9,005	15?			c,l,e,f	1960	Subglacial eruptions
516	St. Paul Island	38°43′S	77°31′E	820	1?			e?	1793	

Classification of Igneous Rocks

Igneous rocks are the result of solidification of magma (Chapter 2). They may consist wholly of minerals, or partly of minerals and partly of glass, or more rarely of glass alone. The nature and proportion of the minerals vary considerably, depending upon both the chemical composition of the magma and the physical conditions under which its consolidation takes place. The physical conditions are reflected also in the texture and structures of the rock. Except for rocks containing a large proportion of glass, the principal bases for the classification of igneous rocks are texture and mineral composition.

Textures of Igneous Rocks

Decrease of temperature and loss of dissolved volatiles result in solidification of magma. The liquid portion of a magma is a complex molten mutual solution of silicates and oxides (combinations of other chemical elements with silicon and oxygen), generally with only very minor amounts of other components. The magmatic solution follows the same general laws as other solutions. Just as in making rock candy, when a concentrated solution of sugar in hot water is cooled, sugar eventually reaches its saturation point and crystals of sugar start to form in the liquid, so also as the magma cools some of the constituents of the solution reach saturation and start to crystallize. Generally, one constituent reaches saturation first and crystallizes out for some time before one or more of the other constituents also reaches saturation and starts to crystallize. Thus, in the magmas of the Hawaiian volcanoes, the mineral olivine [$(Mg,Fe)_2SiO_4$—a compound of magnesium, iron, silicon, and oxygen] starts to crystallize first, and not until the magma has cooled down another 100° or so is it joined by the mineral pyroxene [$(Mg,Fe)Si_2O_6$]. Usually only a little more cooling is needed to start the crystallization of plagioclase feldspar ($NaAlSi_3O_8 \cdot CaAl_2Si_2O_8$). Thence onward, pyroxene and feldspar crystallize side by side until all the liquid is used up, or until there is some interruption due to external causes. In some magmas, olivine may continue to crystallize along with the pyroxene and feldspar to the very end; but in magmas of slightly different composition, when pyroxene starts to crystallize, the olivine crystals that have already formed become unstable and start to redissolve in the magma. Their constituents combine with additional silicon and oxygen and minor amounts of other things to form pyroxene.

The textures of igneous rocks depend on the size and shape of the crystals that form in the magma and on the mutual relationships of the crystals. The size of the crystals in turn depends on the rapidity of cooling and the viscosity of the magma.

The growth of crystals in the magma (or in any solution) depends on migration of the atoms of the chemical elements to the edges of the growing crystals. Under some circumstances, centers of crystallization start at only a few widely separated points; but under other circumstances there may be many closely spaced centers. With slow cooling we commonly find that crystallization begins at widely separated points, and if cooling continues to be slow, atoms have time to move through comparatively great distances (probably in most instances not more than a few centimeters) and accumulate to form large crystals, resulting in a coarse-grained rock. The distance through which atoms can migrate in any given length of time depends to a large degree on the viscosity of the magma. The less viscous the magma, the farther atoms can migrate, and consequently the larger the crystals. Viscosity, in turn, depends largely on three factors: the bulk chemical composition of the magma, the amount of dissolved gas it contains, and its temperature. Viscosity of magmas has been discussed on an earlier page, and here we need only say that in general the more silicon a magma contains, the more viscous it is. Thus, other things being equal, the more siliceous igneous rocks tend to be the finest grained. We have already seen that magmas tend to lose their dissolved gas as they approach the surface; consequently, intrusive magmas commonly contain more dissolved gas than extrusive ones, and for that reason tend to be coarser grained.

However, probably of considerably more importance in determining the grain size of an igneous rock is the rate of cooling of the magma. Slow cooling results in longer distances of migration of atoms and the formation of larger crystals. Even in the cases where large numbers of close-spaced centers of crystallization are formed (due to "labile" conditions, where the initiation of crystallization is delayed to a temperature somewhat below the saturation temperature for some or all of the minerals), if the continued cooling is slow, the large number of small crystals may be transformed into a smaller number of larger ones. At the boundary of each crystal, atoms are continually flying off into the surrounding magma and others are hooking on to take their places. The number that fly off are proportional to the surface area of the crystal, and since the surface of a large crystal has a smaller area in proportion to the total mass of the crystal than does that of a small one, the smaller crystals tend to lose more atoms back into the magma than the large ones. In other words, the small crystals tend to be redissolved in the magma and the large ones grow at their expense. Thus, due both to original crystallization and piracy of atoms by the larger crystals, slow cooling results in a coarser grain size in the crystallizing rock.

The rate of cooling depends, of course, on the rate of heat loss from the magma to its surroundings. The loss is due partly to radiation and partly to conduction of heat outward away from the magma. The rapidity of heat flow away from the magma due to conduction depends on the steepness of the temperature gradient—that is, how rapidly the temperature decreases outward away from the magma—much as the speed of flow of water down-hill depends on the steepness of the hillside. Magma poured out onto the earth's surface cools quickly, because the ground beneath it and the air above are cool, and heat transferred to the air is quickly carried away by air movements, so the air adjacent to the magma tends to stay cool. This is even more effective in the case of magma in contact with water. Magma intruded to levels near the surface, but still within the earth, comes in contact with relatively cool rocks, and at first the temperature gradient is high and cooling of the magma is rapid. But transfer of heat outward from the magma heats the surrounding rocks and the temperature gradient becomes less, resulting in slower and slower cooling. The parts of the solidified intrusive body that are in contact with the wall rocks may show evidence of very rapid cooling, whereas the central part of the body may be coarse grained as a result of much slower cooling. In general, however, intrusive igneous rocks formed near the earth's surface are finer grained than those formed at greater depth, where the original temperature of the surrounding rocks was higher and the cooling of the intrusive was therefore less rapid.

Slow or moderate rates of cooling result in igneous rocks that are coarse grained enough so that the individual mineral grains can easily be seen with the unaided eye. Rapid cooling, on the other hand, produces rocks in which the grains are so small that they can be seen only with difficulty, or not at all, with the naked eye, although the microscope may reveal them to be made up wholly of tiny crystals. With still more rapid cooling, some or all of the magma may not crystallize at all but may simply freeze into non-crystalline material known as *glass*. Ordinary window glass is simply a quickly frozen silicate melt, which, if it is allowed to cool more slowly, develops into a mass of tiny crystals. In a sense, glass is simply a very viscous undercooled liquid, and indeed if sufficient time is available, glass will crystallize even at quite low temperatures. Natural glasses more than

100 million years old are very rare. Most geologically old glasses have de-vitrified—that is, they have lost their glassy character and become masses of tiny crystals. Under high temperature, and especially in the presence of water, glass may crystallize rather quickly. The glassy glaze on tiles in the Roman baths at Bath, England, are very largely devitrified. Shallow intrusive bodies, especially small ones such as many dikes (see Chapter 15), often have thin glassy selvedges due to quick chilling of their edges against cold wall rocks. Most lava flows are partly glass. In silica-poor lavas, the glass commonly is restricted to small patches between crystal grains. Only the very last of the liquid lacked time to crystallize. But silica-rich lavas often are largely or entirely glass—a reflection of their slower rate of crystallization. Rocks that are made up of crystals too small to be seen without a microscope often can be discriminated from glass by the fact that they have a stony rather than a glassy appearance to the unaided eye.

When we speak of coarse, medium, and fine grain size we must realize, of course, that there are no sharp boundaries between them and that the categories are entirely arbitrary. Most geologists consider rocks consisting of grains larger than 5 millimeters (0.2 inch) in average diameter to be coarse grained, and those consisting of grains less than 1 millimeter (0.04 inch) across to be fine grained.

Some volcanic rocks are *equigranular,* consisting wholly of grains that are all of about the same size. Most, however, contain two distinct sizes of grains: some large grains are scattered through a matrix that consists of fine grains and/or glass, often with little sign of gradation from one to the other. This texture is referred to as *porphyritic,* and the rocks having it are called *porphyries.* The large crystals are called *phenocrysts,* and the finer grained or glassy matrix is called the *groundmass* (Fig. A2-1). Porphyritic texture

FIGURE A2-1. Microscopic drawings illustrating porphyritic texture in volcanic rocks, with large phenocrysts in a fine-grained groundmass; (a) and (b), basalts from the Island of Hawaii with olivine phenocrysts in a microcrystalline groundmass; (c) dacite from Mt. Lassen, California, with embayed phenocrysts of quartz, zoned and clouded phenocrysts of feldspar, and phenocrysts of hornblende and biotite in a cryptocrystalline, probably devitrified, groundmass.

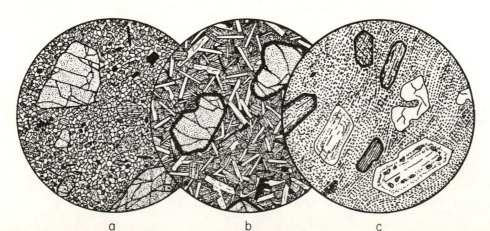

a   b   c

may originate in other ways, but in volcanic rocks the important cause is a sudden change in the physical environment in which the magma is crystallizing. Crystals start to form in an intrusive body of magma deep in the earth, where cooling is slow, and may grow to large size. Then the magma is abruptly moved upward to shallow levels or out onto the earth's surface, the large crystals being carried along with the enclosing liquid, and rapid cooling in the new, colder environment causes quick crystallization of the remaining liquid portion of the magma with development of a finely crystalline groundmass, or even chilling to a glass.

The change in environment may affect not only the coarseness of crystallization but also the composition of the minerals crystallizing from the magma. In particular, minerals that crystallize at depth do so in the presence of volatile substances such as water that are still held in solution in the magma under the prevailing high-pressure conditions. But as we have already seen, movement of the magma to a shallow level or the surface results in the volatile substances coming out of solution and being released as bubbles of gas. With the volatiles gone, minerals that depend on them for their formation can no longer form; and those already formed may react with the volatile-impoverished magma or with the freed gases and be partly redissolved and partly changed to new minerals. Water is the most abundant volatile and produces the most conspicuous results. Thus, the mineral hornblende, which contains water, commonly forms at depth and is brought up as phenocrysts in the rising magma, but because the dissolved water is largely lost from the magma during its rise, hornblende can no longer form among the fine-grained minerals of the groundmass. Furthermore, the hornblende phenocrysts commonly are reddened and otherwise changed, probably by the free gases and high temperatures associated with eruption, and partly redissolved in the magma, leaving in their place only ghost-like black outlines of fine grains of magnetite (iron oxide). Olivine phenocrysts also are commonly altered around the edges by the free gases to a reddish-brown mineral called iddingsite. Once the gases have bubbled out at the surface, however, olivine may again be stable in the magma and may again form during the crystallization of the groundmass. As a result, in some rocks we find phenocrysts consisting of a core of olivine surrounded by a shell of iddingsite and this, in turn, surrounded by an outer shell of olivine. Two changes in equilibrium conditions in the magma are clearly represented.

An exception to the above is the crystallization of hornblende and other hydrous minerals in the groundmass of volcanic rocks formed from magmas that were too viscous to allow the ready escape of volatiles.

The foregoing is the usual explanation for porphyritic texture, and no doubt most phenocrysts in volcanic rocks are formed in that way. But an important possible exception should be mentioned. Magmas commonly originate by melting of the upper part of the earth's mantle or the lower part of the granitic portion of the continental crust. This melting is not always complete, and some solid grains of the most refractory minerals may be left unmelted and carried up to the surface in the rising liquid magma. Some olivine "phenocrysts" in basalt, some quartz "phenocrysts" in rhyolite, and some feldspar grains in andesites, dacites and rhyolites, may be of this origin. (For definitions of the rock names, see the following section.)

Thus, the coarseness of grain of igneous rocks is indicative to a considerable degree of the depth of origin of the rock. Plutonic rocks are usually coarse to medium grained; and although they are sometimes fine grained, the granularity is always coarse enough so that individual grains are clearly visible to the naked eye. Rocks in which the grains are recognizable without the aid of a microscope are said to be *phaneritic*. (The study of even coarse-grained rocks is greatly aided by the use of a pocket magnifier.) Subvolcanic rocks vary greatly in grain size. Some are as coarse as plutonic rocks, but many are fine grained and some are partly glassy. Volcanic rocks generally are so fine grained that individual crystals can be made out with the unaided eye only with difficulty or not at all, and they are commonly partly glassy. These very fine-grained rocks are said to be *microcrystalline* or *aphanitic*. In dealing with porphyritic rocks it is the grain size of the groundmass that is significant. The phenocrysts are formed at depth, but the groundmass reflects the environment in which the magma solidified. It may be coarse in plutonic or subvolcanic rocks, but in volcanic rocks it is fine. Most volcanic rocks are porphyritic, though some are equigranular.

Classification of Igneous Rocks

The purpose of classification is to group together things with similar properties or characteristics. This at the same time serves to emphasize their differences from things placed in other categories. Classification is a constant and necessary, though often unconscious, part of man's mental processes. Science depends heavily on accurate classification of objects and phenomena, and the establishment of a useful classification commonly is the first step in the development of any particular scientific discipline. Classification can be on various bases. In biology the current highly successful classification of plants and animals is on a genetic basis. In geology also, genetic classification is employed to some extent, but to a large degree we avoid it, because we are not yet sufficiently sure of the precise origin of many types of rocks and other geological features to place them with confidence in a genetic classification. A wrong classification can be a great hindrance, because classifications serve as guides to thought, and erroneous classifications can lead to erroneous conclusions. As an example, we may take certain granites. Long classified as igneous rocks because of their resemblance to others that can definitely be shown to have solidified from a molten state, it was very difficult to think of their having any other origin. Yet now we are practically certain that they are in fact not igneous but have been formed by transformations brought about wholly in a solid state.

To try to avoid this sort of thing, we generally base our classifications as much as possible on things we know, or at least think we know—things based on actual observation rather than on deduction. The classification of igneous rocks that is in almost universal use today is based on texture and composition of the rock. Composition, in turn, can be either chemical or mineralogical, based either on chemical analyses of the rock as a whole or on a determination of the kinds and proportions of different minerals present in the rock. Chemical analysis is the more precise of the two, but it is expensive and until recently has been relatively slow, and it has not been possible to chemically analyze more than a small proportion of the rocks we have studied. Modern techniques of analysis may change this; but in the past, and still today, the only practical general classification of rocks has been based on their mineral content. The latter is, of course, governed by the chemical composition, but it is also affected by the physical conditions under which the minerals were formed. Some minerals or assemblages of minerals will form only under high pressure or only in the presence of dissolved volatile materials, whereas others form only under surficial conditions where pressures are low and dissolved volatiles nearly absent. Thus, the minerals that make up the rock tell us not only the approximate chemical composition of the rock but also the physical conditions under which the rock was formed, and as we learn more about the minerals themselves, they are becoming ever more useful in this regard. Chemical analysis will never wholly replace mineral analysis in the study of rocks.

Table A2-1 gives a simplified classification of igneous rocks based on composition and texture. Several things should be pointed out about it. In the first place, it is very much simplified in its number of subdivisions. It is possible to break down igneous rocks into very numerous categories. In fact, several thousand names have been given to different varieties. Most of these, however, are of very minor importance, and many of them differ so little from each other than only an expert can tell them apart (and not all experts agree on the divisions). To most professional geologists, let alone persons with a more casual interest in rocks, such a detailed classification is pointless. The classification given in Table A2-1 is adequate for most purposes. The rock names given in it can be augmented, where it is desirable, by preceding the rock name with the name of some characteristic mineral in the rock. Thus, some andesite lavas contain phenocrysts of pyroxene, and these rocks can be called pyroxene andesite to distinguish them from hornblende andesite that contains phenocrysts of hornblende, or from biotite andesite that contains grains of biotite mica, and so on.

Certain minerals are *essential* to a certain kind of rock; if they are not present, the rock is not of that kind. Thus, rhyolite must contain both alkali feldspar and quartz, if it has crystallized enough for minerals to form in it. In the case of glass, in which the minerals have not had a chance to form, we must use the chemical composition in classifying the rock, but even then

TABLE A2-1. Classification of common igneous rocks (*Names of aphanitic rocks are given in capitals, those of phaneritic rocks in lower-case letters*)

	FELSIC ROCKS — Light-colored minerals more than 60% of rock			MAFIC ROCKS — Dark-colored minerals 40% or more of rock		
				Soda-lime feldspar more than 90% of the total feldspar		Feldspar less than 10% of the rock
	Alkali feldspar[1] predominant	Alkali and soda-lime feldspar approximately equal	Soda-lime feldspar predominant (Alkali feldspar 10% or more of the total feldspar)	Feldspar more than 30% of the rock	Feldspar 30–10% of the rock	
More than 10% quartz	RHYOLITE granite	RHYODACITE quartz monzonite[4]	DACITE[3] quartz diorite[5] granodiorite[6]	QUARTZ BASALT quartz gabbro granogabbro		
Less than 10% quartz or feldspathoid[2]	TRACHYTE syenite	TRACHYANDESITE[7] monzonite	ANDESITE[7] diorite anorthosite[10]	BASALT[9] gabbro diabase[11]	PICRITE– BASALT picrite	dunite peridotite[12] perknite[12] carbonatite[13]
				TRACHYBASALT SPILITE[8] shonkinite		
More than 10% feldspathoid[2]	PHONOLITE[14] nepheline syenite[16]	TEPHRITIC PHONOLITE nepheline monzonite	PHONOLITIC TEPHRITE	TEPHRITE[15] BASANITE[15] essexite theralite[17]		NEPHELI-NITE LEUCITITE ijolite

458

1 Generally orthoclase, microcline, or albite in coarse-grained rocks; sanidine or anorthoclase in fine-grained rocks.

2 Silica-deficient equivalents of the feldspars, including nepheline, leucite, sodalite, kalsilite, analcite, melilite, etc.

3 Most dacites correspond in chemical composition to granodiorites rather than to quartz diorites.

4 Adamellite is approximately equivalent.

5 Tonalite is approximately equivalent.

6 In granodiorite alkali feldspar is approximately half as abundant as soda-lime feldspar.

7 Latite is approximately equivalent.

8 In spilite the feldspar is predominantly alkalic, usually albite. (See Chapter 14.)

9 When the rock contains more than 5% olivine it is called olivine basalt. Tholeiitic basalts are relatively low in alkalies and high in silica, whereas alkalic basalts are relatively high in alkalies and low in silica. Tholeiitic basalts usually lack alkali feldspar; alkalic basalts contain alkali feldspar, but in smaller amounts than the trachybasalts.

10 In anorthosite soda-lime feldspar makes up more than 90% of the rock.

11 Diabase tends to be coarser grained than basalt and is characterized by diabasic texture, in which well-formed (euhedral) lath-shaped grains of feldspar penetrate grains of augite.

12 Dunite contains more than 90% olivine, peridotite 90 to 10% olivine, and perknite less than 10% olivine. These ultramafic rocks, particularly peridotite and dunite, are very commonly altered to serpentine.

13 Carbonatites consist primarily of carbonates of calcium, magnesium, and iron, with variable amounts of other minerals such as nepheline, melilite, apatite, and magnetite.

14 Phonolites containing many large phenocrysts of leucite are leucitophyres.

15 Tephrite contains 10% or less olivine, basanite more than 10% olivine.

16 When alkali feldspar and feldspathoid are about equally abundant the rock may be called foyaite.

17 Theralite contains more feldspathoid and less soda-lime feldspar than essexite.

calculations show that the essential minerals would have formed if the glass had crystallized. Similarly, phonolite must contain both alkali feldspar and nepheline. (Quartz and nepheline cannot both be present, because nepheline represents a deficiency of silica and it would react with any free silica that might otherwise form quartz and be transformed into feldspar.)

The absence of certain minerals also is essential in certain rocks. For instance, trachyte must contain alkali feldspar, but it must not contain any large amount of either quartz or nepheline. Actually, a small amount of either may be present and the rock still be called a trachyte. Arbitrarily, the limiting amount is usually placed at 10 per cent. If a rock contains more than 10 per cent of quartz it is not a trachyte but a rhyolite; and if it contains more than 10 per cent nepheline, it is a phonolite.

Composition-wise, the primary division in the classification is on the relative abundance of light-colored and dark-colored minerals (top horizontal row in Table A2-1). Rocks composed predominantly of light-colored minerals are *felsic* (rich in feldspar); rocks containing more than 40 per cent dark minerals are *mafic* (rich in magnesium and iron). Felsic rocks are sometimes referred to as *salic* or *acid;* mafic rocks are sometimes called *femic* or *basic*. Rocks containing less than 10 per cent feldspar are called *ultramafic* or *ultrabasic*.

The principal light-colored minerals are feldspar, quartz, and feldspathoids. (The latter is a group of minerals having the same general chemical composition as feldspars, but containing less silica.) The principal dark-colored ones are pyroxene, hornblende, biotite, olivine, magnetite, and ilmenite. In coarse-grained rocks the relative abundance of light and dark minerals can be determined by estimating the number of individual grains of each. A word of caution is necessary: both feldspar and quartz rarely may be quite dark in color, but for the sake of classification they are nevertheless regarded as light-colored minerals. In very fine-grained (microcrystalline) rocks the individual grains are difficult or impossible to make out and, in this case, in the absence of a microscope we must rely on the general color of the whole rock to indicate the relative abundance of light and dark grains. A light-colored rock is presumed to have a predominance of light-colored minerals, a dark-colored rock to have a predominance of dark minerals, and rocks of transitional shade about equal amounts of light and dark minerals. In classifying lavas it is generally necessary to rely on the overall color of the rock, because they are very fine grained. Once again a word of caution is necessary. Volcanic glass is apt to be dark colored no matter what its chemical composition, and a silica-rich rhyolite or trachyte that contains a large proportion of glass may be as black as a basalt. The presence of much glass is usually indicated by a shiny glassy appearance. Such a rock can be named with confidence only if a chemical analysis of it is available, although an approximation can be made from the refractive index of the glass. In general, lacking a chemical analysis of a glassy rock, it is perhaps best simply to apply to it the general name for all volcanic glasses —*obsidian*. If the rock appears stony rather than glassy, however, it may be presumed that it contains a large proportion of crystalline material, and its general color may be used in assigning it a name.

The nature of the feldspar in the rock is important to the petrologist. It is given in the second horizontal row in the table. However, it is difficult or impossible to determine with certainty without the use of the microscope, particularly in microcrystalline volcanic rocks. In phaneritic rocks it is generally possible to distinguish alkali feldspar from soda-lime feldspar by the presence of fine parallel striations (albite twinning) on the latter. However, in very fine grained rocks it is generally necessary to neglect the nature of the feldspar and name the rock on its shade of color and the presence or absence of whatever other essential minerals can be identified.

The left vertical column of the table indicates the degree of "saturation" of the rock in silica. If more than enough silica is present to form feldspar of the alkalies and pyroxene or equivalent minerals of the iron and magnesia, some silica is left over in the form of quartz. Quartz-bearing rocks are shown in the third horizontal row of the table. Rocks in which there is neither a marked excess nor deficiency of silica are shown in the fourth row. In the fifth (bottom) row are rocks in which silica is insufficient to make feldspar of all the alkalies, and some or all of the feldspar is replaced by silica-poor feldspathoids.

The names of aphanitic rocks and porphyritic rocks with aphanitic groundmasses are given in capital letters. These are volcanic and shallow-seated subvolcanic rocks. The names of phaneritic rocks are in lowercase letters. They include both plutonic and some subvolcanic rocks.

The name granite requires special comment. It is used in two ways: a specific sense, as in the table; and a generalized sense in which it refers to all phaneritic quartz-bearing rocks from true granite to quartz diorite.

Average chemical compositions of the various types of volcanic rocks are given in Table A2-2. In the case of basalt two compositions are given: one for "tholeiitic" basalt, which is a variety comparatively rich in silica and poor in the alkalies (sodium and potassium); and one for "alkalic" olivine basalt, which in addition to containing the mineral olivine is also comparatively rich in the alkalies. (Tholeiitic basalts also may contain olivine, but are poorer in alkalies.) The average chemical compositions of the phaneritic rocks are much the same as those of their aphanitic equivalents. Thus, for example, the composition of diorite is much like that of andesite, that of syenite is much like that of trachyte, etc.

An additional comment should be made on rock classification in general: the sharp divisions between rock types in the table for the most part do not exist in nature. There is generally complete gradation in composition between adjacent rock types. Rhyolites grade into trachytes and trachytes into phonolites, rhyodacites grade into dacites, dacites into andesites, andesites into basalts, and so forth. Frequently, it is quite arbitrary whether a rock is placed in one group or another. Sometimes it is desirable to indicate the borderline character of a rock by means of a compound name, such as basaltic andesite.

TABLE A2-2. **Average chemical compositions of volcanic rocks** (*weight percent*) [1]

	Rhyolite	Trachyte	Phonolite	Rhyodacite	Dacite	Andesite	Tholeiitic basalt	Alkalic basalt	Nephelinite	Pyroxenite	Peridotite	Dunite	Serpentine
SiO_2	73.6	58.3	56.9	66.3	63.6	54.2	50.8	45.8	40.3	50.5	43.5	40.2	40.4
TiO_2	0.2	0.7	0.6	0.7	0.6	1.3	2.0	2.6	2.9	0.5	0.8	0.2	tr.
Al_2O_3	13.4	18.0	20.2	15.4	16.7	17.2	14.1	14.6	11.3	4.1	4.0	0.8	1.9
Fe_2O_3	1.2	2.5	2.3	2.1	2.2	3.5	2.9	3.2	4.9	2.4	2.5	1.9	2.8
FeO	0.8	2.0	1.8	2.2	3.0	5.5	9.1	8.7	7.7	7.4	9.8	11.9	4.3
MgO	0.3	2.1	0.6	1.6	2.1	4.4	6.3	9.4	13.3	21.7	34.0	43.2	36.0
MnO	0.3	0.1	0.2	0.1	0.1	0.1	0.2	0.2	0.2	0.1	0.2	0.2	—
CaO	1.1	4.2	1.9	3.7	5.5	7.9	10.4	10.7	13.0	12.0	3.5	0.3 }	0.7
Na_2O	3.0	3.8	8.7	4.1	4.0	3.7	2.2	2.6	3.1	0.4	0.6	0.1	
K_2O	5.4	7.4	5.4	3.0	1.4	1.1	0.8	1.0	1.4	0.2	0.2	0.1	0.2
H_2O+	0.8	0.5	1.0	0.7	0.6	0.9	0.9	0.8	1.1	0.5	0.8	0.4	10.5
P_2O_5	0.1	0.2	0.2	0.2	0.2	0.3	0.2	0.4	0.8	0.1	0.1	0.1	tr.

[1] After Nockolds, 1954.

The ultramafic rocks, especially peridotite and dunite, often are altered by the solutions left over at the end of their crystallization, or by other solutions at a later time, to form a rock made up largely of the serpentine group of minerals and called serpentine or serpentinite. Until recently, extrusive equivalents of the coarse-grained peridotites were unknown, but it now appears that some serpentine layers are lava flows of peridotite or very olivine-rich basalt composition poured out on the deep-ocean floor, the original olivine and other minerals having combined with ocean water to form serpentine.

Finally, bare mention may be made of three types of lava that are so unusual that they have not been shown in the classification table. Both lava flows and fragmental exploded debris of sodium carbonate (Na_2CO_3) are reported from Oldoinyo Lengai Volcano in central Africa (Dawson, 1964). Flows of native sulfur have formed at Siretoko-Iosan Volcano and Tokachi Volcano on the northern island of Japan (Watanabe, 1940), at Ebeko Volcano in the Kuril Islands (Gorshkov, 1970), and on the southwest rift zone of Mauna Loa in Hawaii (Skinner, 1970). The sulfur flows result from melting of sulfur previously deposited along fissures by rising fumarolic gases. Hamilton and Baumgart (1959) report that a bore hole in the crater of the White Island Volcano, New Zealand, penetrated a shallow chamber filled with molten sulfur. High in the Chilean Andes, Park (1961) has reported a flow, with a pahoehoe-type surface, of magnetite and hematite.

References

Abich, H., 1899, *Geology of the Armenian highlands, western part, western Caucasas Dept.*, All-Russian Geography, Book 21, Piatigorsk

Adams, W. M., and Furumoto, A. S., 1965, A seismic refraction study of the Koolau volcanic plug: *Pacific Sci.*, v. 19, p. 296–305

Alcaraz, A., Abad, L. F., and Quema, J. C., 1952, Hibok-Hibok Volcano, Philippine Islands, and its activity since 1948: *Volcano Letter*, no. 516, p. 1–6, no. 517, p. 1–4

Allen, E. T., and Day, A. L., 1927, Steam wells and other thermal activity at "The Geysers," California: *Carnegie Inst. Washington Pub. 378*, 106 p.

Allen, E. T., and Day, A. L., 1935, Hot springs of the Yellowstone National Park: *Carnegie Inst. Washington Pub. 466*, 525 p.

Allen, E. T., and Zies, E. G., 1923, A chemical study of the fumaroles of the Katmai region: *Natl. Geogr. Soc. Contrib. Tech. Papers, Katmai Ser.*, no. 2, p. 75–155

Anderson, C. A., 1933, The Tuscan Formation of northern California, with a discussion concerning the origin of volcanic breccias: *Univ. Calif. Berkeley Pub. Geol. Sci.*, v. 23, p. 215–276

————, 1941, Volcanoes of the Medicine Lake Highland, California: *Univ. Calif. Pub., Bull. Dept. Geol. Sci.*, v. 25, p. 347–422

Anderson, E. M., 1936, The dynamics of the formation of cone sheets, ring dikes, and cauldron subsidences: *Roy. Soc. Edinburg Proc.*, v. 56, pt. 2, p. 128–157

————, 1937, Cone-sheets and ring-dykes: the dynamical explanation: *Bull. Volcanol.*, ser. 2, v. 1, p. 35–40

Anderson, T., and Flett, J. S., 1903, Report on the eruptions of the Soufrière in St. Vincent, and on a visit to Montagne Pelée in Martinique, Pt. I: *Roy. Soc. London Phil. Trans.*, ser. A, v. 200, p. 353–553

Aramaki, S., 1956, The 1783 activity of Asama Volcano: Japan. J. Geol. Geograph., v. 27, p. 189–229, v. 28, p. 11–33

————, 1969, Pyroclastic flows, calderas, and other depressions in southern Kyushu, Japan: *Intern. Assn. Volcanology and Chem. Earth's Interior, Symposium on Volcanoes and their roots*, Oxford Univ., Abstracts vol., p. 77–78

Arsandaux, H., 1934, L'éruption de la Montagne Pelée en 1929: *Rev. Sci.*, année 72, no. 8, p. 248–251

Aubouin, J., 1965, *Geosynclines*, Elsevier Publishing Co., New York, 335 p.

Aumento, F., 1968, The Mid-Atlantic Ridge near 45° N. II. Basalts from the area of Confederation Peak: *Can. J. Earth Sci.*, v. 5, p. 1–21

Bailey, E. B., and McCallien, W. J., 1954, Serpentine lavas, the Ankara mélange and the Anatolian thrust: *Roy. Soc. Edinburg Trans.*, v. 62, pt. 2, p. 403–441

Bailey, E. B., and Maufe, H. B., 1960, The geology of Ben Nevis and Glen Coe and the surrounding country, 2nd ed., *Geol. Surv. Scotland Mem.*, 307 p.

Bailey, E. B., Thomas, H. H., and others, 1924, Tertiary and post-Tertiary geology of Mull, Loch Aline, and Oban, *Geol. Surv. Scotland, Mem.*, 445 p.

Bailey, E. H., Irwin, W. P., and Jones, D. L., 1964, Franciscan and related rocks, and their significance in the geology of western California: *Calif. Div. Mines Geol. Bull. 183*, 177 p.

Baker, P. E., and Harris, P. G., 1963, Lava channels on Tristan da Cunha: *Geol. Mag.*, v. 100, p. 345–350

Barrington, J., and Kerr, P. F., 1961, Breccia pipe near Cameron, Arizona: *Geol. Soc. Amer. Bull.*, v. 72, p. 1661–1674

Barth, T. F. W., 1950, Volcanic geology, hot springs, and geysers of Iceland: *Carnegie Inst. Washington Pub. 587*, 174 p.

————, 1962, *Theoretical petrology*, 2nd ed., John Wiley & Sons, Inc., New York, 416 p.

Basharina, L. A., 1965, Gases of Kamchatka volcanoes: *Bull. Volcanol.*, ser. 2, v. 28, p. 95–105

Battey, M. H., 1956, The petrogenesis of a spilitic rock series from New Zealand: *Geol. Mag.*, v. 93, p. 89–110

Becker, G. F., 1885, The geometrical form of volcanic cones and the elastic limit of lava: *Amer. J. Sci.*, 3rd ser., v. 30, p. 283–293

Beloussov, V. V., 1970, Against the hypothesis of ocean-floor spreading: Tectono-physics, v. 9, p. 489–511

Bemmelen, R. W. van, 1929, The origin of Lake Toba (North Sumatra): *Fourth Pacific Sci. Congr. Proc.*, v. 2A, p. 115–124

———, 1949, *The geology of Indonesia, v. 1A, General geology of Indonesia and adjacent archipelagos*, Govt. Printing Office, The Hague, 732 p.

Benioff, H., 1954, Orogenesis and deep crustal structure—additional evidence from seismology: *Geol. Soc. Amer. Bull.*, v. 65, p. 385–400

Benseman, R. F., 1959, Estimating the total heat output of natural thermal regions: *J. Geophys. Res.*, v. 64, p. 1057–1062

———, 1965, The components of a geyser: *New Zealand J. Sci.*, v. 8, p. 24–44

Billings, M. P., 1945, Mechanics of igneous intrusion in New Hampshire: *Amer. J. Sci.*, v. 243-A (Daly Volume), p. 40–68

Björnsson, S., 1968, Radon and water in volcanic gas at Surtsey, Iceland: *Geochim. Cosmochim. Acta*, v. 32, p. 815–821

Bodvarsson, G., 1960, Hot springs [of Iceland] and the exploitation of natural heat resources: *Intern. Geol. Congr., 21st Session, Norway, Guidebook to Excursion A-2, On the geology and geophysics of Iceland*, Reykjavik, p. 46–54

Bodvarsson, G., and Walker, G. P. L., 1964, Crustal drift in Iceland: *Roy. Astron. Soc. Geophys. J.*, v. 8, p. 285–300

Bonnet, G., 1960, Le rayonnement thermique du lac de lave du volcan Nyiragongo: *Acad. Roy. Sci. Outre-Mer Brussels*, n.s., v. 6, p. 709–714

Bordet, P., Marinelli, G., Mittempergher, M., and Tazieff, H., 1963, Contribution à l'étude volcanologique du Katmai et de la Vallée des Dix Mille Fumées: *Soc. Belg Geol. Mem.*, ser. in octavo, no. 7, p. 1–114

Boyd, F. R., 1961, Welded tuffs and flows in the rhyolite plateau of Yellowstone Park, Wyoming: *Geol. Soc. Amer. Bull.*, v. 72, p. 387–426

Branch, C. D., 1967, The source of eruption for pyroclastic flows: cauldrons or calderas: *Bull. Volcanol.*, ser. 2, v. 30, p. 41–50

Buch, Leopold von, 1818, Über die Zusammensetzung der basaltischen Inseln und über Erhebungskrater: *Abhandl. Akad. Wiss. Berlin*, 1818–1819

Buddington, A. F., 1959, Granite emplacement with special reference to North America: *Geol. Soc. Amer. Bull.*, v. 70, p. 671–747

Budyko, M. I., 1968, On the causes of climatic variations: *Sveriges Met. Hydrog. Inst. Medd.*, ser. B, no. 28, p. 6–13

Bullard, F. M., 1947, Studies on Parícutin Volcano, Mexico: *Geol. Soc. Amer. Bull.*, v. 58, p. 433–450

———, 1962, *Volcanoes: in history, in theory, in eruption*, University of Texas Press, Austin, 441 p.

Byers, F. M., Jr., Orkild, P. P., Carr, W. J., and Quinlivan, W. D., 1968, Timber

Mountain Tuff, southern Nevada, and its relation to cauldron subsidence: *Geol. Soc. Amer. Mem. 110*, p. 87–97

Capps, S. R., 1915, An ancient volcanic eruption in the upper Yukon basin: *U.S. Geol. Surv. Prof. Paper 95*, p. 59–64

Carr, W. J., and Quinlivan, W. D., 1968, Structure of Timber Mountain resurgent dome: *Geol. Soc. Amer. Mem. 110*, p. 99–108

Chamberlin, R. T., 1908, The gases in rocks, *Carnegie Inst. Washington Pub. 106*, 80 p.

Chaigneau, M., Tazieff, H., and Fabre, R., 1960, Composition des gaz volcaniques du lac de lave permanent du Nyiragongo (Congo belge): *Compt. Rend. Acad. Sci. Paris*, v. 250, p. 2482–2485

Chapman, R. W., and Chapman, C. A., 1940, Cauldron subsidence at Ascutney Mountain, Vermont: *Geol. Soc. Amer. Bull.*, v. 51, p. 191–211

Christiansen, R. L., and Blank, H. R., Jr., 1969, Volcanic evolution of the Yellowstone rhyolite plateau and eastern Snake River Plain, U.S.A.: *Intern. Assn. Volcanology and Chem. Earth's Interior, Symposium on Volcanoes and Their Roots*, Oxford Univ., Abstracts vol., p. 220–221

Christiansen, R. L., and Lipman, P. W., 1966, Emplacement and thermal history of a rhyolite lava flow near Fortymile Canyon, southern Nevada: *Geol. Soc. Amer. Bull.*, v. 77, p. 671–684

Christiansen, R. L., Lipman, P. W., Orkild, P. P., and Byers, F. M., Jr., 1965, Structure of the Timber Mountain caldera, southern Nevada, and its relation to Basin-Range structure: *U.S. Geol. Surv. Prof. Paper 525–B*, p. 43–48

Clark, R. H., and Fyfe, W. S., 1961, Ultrabasic liquids: *Nature*, v. 191, no. 4784, p. 158–159

Cloos, H., 1939, Hebung-Spaltung-Vulkanismus: *Geol. Rundschau*, v. 30, p. 405–527

———, 1941, Bau und Tätigkeit von Tuffschloten: *Geol. Rundschau*, v. 32, p. 709–800

Clough, C. T., Maufe, H. B., and Bailey, E. B., 1909, The cauldron subsidence of Glen Coe and the associated igneous phenomena: *Geol. Soc. London Quart. J.*, v. 65, p. 611–676

Coats, R. R., 1950, Volcanic activity in the Aleutian arc: *U.S. Geol. Surv. Bull. 974–B*, p. 35–49

———, 1968, The Circle Creek Rhyolite, a volcanic complex in northern Elko County, Nevada: *Geol. Soc. Amer. Mem. 116*, p. 69–106

Cook, E. F., 1962, Ignimbrite bibliography and review: *Idaho Bur. Mines Geol. Inform. Circ. 13*, 64 p.

———, 1966, editor, *Tufflavas and ignimbrites*, American Elsevier Publishing Co., Inc., New York, 212 p.

Cook, H. E., 1968, Ignimbrite flows, plugs, and dikes in the southern part of the Hot Creek Range, Nye County, Nevada: *Geol. Soc. Amer. Mem. 116,* p. 107–152

Cornwall, H. R., 1962, Calderas and associated volcanic rocks near Beatty, Nye County, Nevada: *Petrol. Studies Volume, Honor A. F. Buddington,* Geol. Soc. Amer., *1962,* p. 357–371

Corwin, G., and Foster, H. L., 1959, The 1957 explosive eruption of Iwo Jima, Volcano Islands: *Amer. J. Sci.,* v. 257, p. 161–171

Cotton, C. A., 1952, *Volcanoes as landscape forms,* 2nd ed., John Wiley & Sons, Inc., New York, 416 p.

Crandell, D. R., and Waldron, H. H., 1956, A recent volcanic mudflow of exceptional dimensions from Mt. Rainier, Washington: *Amer. J. Sci.,* v. 254, p. 349–362

———, 1969, *Volcanic hazards in the Cascade Range: Conference on Geologic Hazards and Public Problems,* Office of Emergency Preparedness, May 27–28, 1969, Proceedings, U.S. Govt. Printing Office, p. 5–18

Cucuzza-Silvestri, S., 1968, Temperatura e viscosità delle lave dell'Etna: *Atti Assoc. Geofis. Ital.,* 16th Meeting, p. 261–288

Curtis, G. H., 1954, Mode of origin of pyroclastic debris in the Mehrten Formation of the Sierra Nevada: *Univ. Calif. Berkeley Pub. Geol. Sci.,* v. 29, p. 453–502

———, 1955, Importance of Novarupta during eruption of Mt. Katmai, Alaska, in 1912 (abst.): *Geol. Soc. Amer. Bull.,* v. 66, p. 1547

———, 1968, The stratigraphy of the ejecta from the 1912 eruption of Mount Katmai and Novarupta, Alaska: *Geol. Soc. Amer. Mem. 116,* p. 153–210

Daly, R. A., 1911, The nature of volcanic action: *Amer. Acad. Arts Sci. Proc.,* v. 47, p. 47–122

———, 1968, *Igneous rocks and the depths of the earth,* 598 p.; originally published 1933, McGraw-Hill Book Company; reprinted 1968, Hafner Publishing Co., Inc., New York.

Dawson, J. B., 1964, Carbonatitic volcanic ashes in northern Tanganyika: *Bull. Volcanol.,* ser. 2, v. 27, p. 81–91

Day, A. L., 1939, The hot spring problem: *Geol. Soc. Amer. Bull.,* v. 50, p. 317–336

Day, A. L., and Allen, E. T., 1925, The volcanic activity and hot springs of Lassen Peak: *Carnegie Inst. Washington Pub. 360,* 190 p.

Decker, R. W., and Hadikusumo, D., 1961, Results of the 1960 expedition to Krakatau: *J. Geophys. Res.,* v. 66, p. 3497–3511

Delsemme, A.–H., 1960, Spectroscopie de flammes volcaniques: *Acad. Roy. Sci. Outre-Mer Brussels Bull.,* new ser., v. 6, pt. 3, p. 507–519

————, 1960a, Première contribution à l'étude du debit d'énergie du volcan Nyiragongo: *Acad. Roy. Sci. Outre-Mer Brussels Bull.*, new ser., v. 6, p. 699–707

DeRoever, W. P., and Lodder, W., 1967, Indications of syngenetic origin of gold ore and ignimbrites near Rodalquilar (SE Spain): *Bull. Volcanol.*, ser. 2, v. 30, p. 35–40

Deville, Sainte-Claire, 1857, Memoire sur les emanations volcaniques: *Soc. Geol. France Bull.*, ser. 2, v. 14, p. 254–279

Dickinson, W. R., 1962, Petrogenetic significance of geosynclinal andesitic volcanism along the Pacific margin of North America: *Geol. Soc. Amer. Bull.*, v. 73, p. 1241–1256

Dietz, R. S., 1961, Continent and ocean basin evolution by spreading of the sea floor: *Nature*, v. 190, p. 854–857

Doe, B. R., Lipman, P. W., and Hedge, C. E., 1969, Radiogenic tracers and the source of continental andesites: a beginning at the San Juan volcanic field, Colorado: *Andesite Conf. Proc., Oregon Dept. Geol. Mineral Ind. Bull. 65*, p. 143–149

Durrell, C., 1944, Andesitic breccia dikes near Blairsden, California: *Geol. Soc. Amer. Bull.*, v. 55, p. 255–272

Easton, N. Wing, 1916, Het caldeira-probleem: *Verhandel. Ned. Geol. Mijnbouwk. Genoot. Geol. Ser.*, v. 3, p. 65–77

Eaton, J. P., 1959, A portable water-tube tiltmeter: *Seismol. Soc. Amer. Bull.*, v. 49, p. 301–316

Eaton, J. P., and Murata, K. J., 1960, How volcanoes grow: *Science*, v. 132, no. 3432, p. 925–938

Einarsson, T., 1949, The eruption of Hekla 1947–1948; IV.3 The flowing lava. Studies of its main physical and chemical properties: *Soc. Scientiarum Islandica, Reykjavik*, 70 p.

Ekren, E. B., 1968, Geologic setting of Nevada Test Site and Nellis Air Force Range: *Geol. Soc. Amer. Mem. 110*, p. 11–19

Ellis, A. J., 1957, Chemical equilibrium in magmatic gases: *Amer. J. Sci.*, v. 255, p. 416–431

Elskens, I., Tazieff, H., and Tonani, F., 1964, A new method for volcanic gas analysis in the field: *Bull. Volcanol.*, ser. 2, v. 27, p. 347–350

Engel, A. E. J., Engel, C. G., and Havens, R. G., 1965, Chemical characteristics of oceanic basalts and upper mantle: *Geol. Soc. Amer. Bull.*, v. 76, p 719–734

Enlows, H. E., 1955, Welded tuffs of Chiricahua National Monument, Arizona: *Geol. Soc. Amer. Bull.*, v. 66, p. 1215–1246

Erlich, E. N., 1968, Recent movements and Quaternary volcanic activity within the Kamchatka territory: *Pacific Geol.*, v. 1, Tokyo, p. 23–39

Escher, B. G., 1925, L'éboulement préhistorique de Tasikmalaja et le vulcan Galoungoung (Java): *Leidse Geol. Mededel.*, v. 1, p. 8–21

Evrard, P., 1964, La recherche et la développement de l'énergie géothermique: *Rev. Universelle Mines*, ser. 9, v. 20, no. 11, p. 1–8

Facca, G., and Tonani, F., 1967, The self-sealing geothermal field: *Bull. Volcanol.*, ser. 2, v. 30, p. 271–273

Fenner, C. N., 1920, The Katmai region, Alaska, and the great eruption of 1912: *J. Geol.*, v. 28, p. 569–606

———, 1923, The origin and mode of emplacement of the great tuff deposit in the Valley of Ten Thousand Smokes: *Natl. Geogr. Soc., Contrib. Tech. Papers, Katmai Ser.*, no. 1, 74 p.

Fenton, C. L., and Fenton, M. A., 1952, *Giants of Geology*, rev. ed., Doubleday & Company, Inc., Garden City, N.Y., 333 p.

Finch, R. H., 1930, Mud flow of Lassen Volcano: *Volcano Letter*, no. 266, p. 1–3

———, 1943, Lava surgings in Halemaumau and the explosive eruptions in 1924: *Volcano Letter*, no. 479, p. 1–3

Finch, R. H., and Macdonald, G. A., 1951, Report of the Hawaiian Volcano Observatory for 1948 and 1949: *U.S. Geol. Surv. Bull. 974–D*, p. 103–133

———, 1953, Hawaiian volcanoes during 1950: *U.S. Geol. Surv. Bull. 996–B*, p. 27–89

Fisher, N. H., 1939, Geology and volcanology of Blanche Bay and the surrounding area, New Britain: *New Guinea Geol. Bull.*, no. 1, 53 p.

Fisher, R. V., 1960, Criteria for recognition of laharic breccias, southern Cascade Mountains, Washington: *Geol. Soc. Amer. Bull.*, v. 71, p. 127–132

———, 1961, Proposed classification of volcaniclastic sediments and rocks: *Geol. Soc. Amer. Bull.*, v. 72, p. 1409–1414

———, 1966, Mechanism of deposition from pyroclastic flows: *Amer. J. Sci.*, v. 264, p. 350–363

———, 1968, Puu Hou littoral cones, Hawaii: *Geol. Rundschau*, v. 57, p. 837–864

Fisher, R. V., and Waters, A. C., 1970, Base surge bed forms in maar volcanoes: *Amer. J. Sci.*, v. 268, p. 157–180

———, 1970a, Maar volcanoes: *Second Columbia River Basalt Symposium*, Pullman, Wash., Proc., p. 157–170.

Fiske, R. S., 1963, Subaqueous pyroclastic flows in the Ohanapekosh Formation, Washington: *Geol. Soc. Amer. Bull.*, v. 74, p. 391–406

———, 1969, Recognition and significance of pumice in marine pyroclastic rocks: *Geol. Soc. Amer. Bull.*, v. 80, p. 1–8

Fiske, R. S., and Kinoshita, W. T., 1969, Inflation of Kilauea Volcano prior to its 1967–1968 eruption: *Science*, v. 165, p. 341–349

Fiske, R. S., and Matsuda, T., 1964, Submarine equivalents of ash flows in the Tokiwa Formation, Japan: *Amer. J. Sci.*, v. 262, p. 76–106

Fiske, R. S., Hopson, C. A., and Waters, A. C., 1963, Geology of Mount Rainier National Park, Washington: *U.S. Geol. Surv. Prof. Paper 444*, 93 p.

Foshag, W. F., and Gonzalez, R. J., 1955, Birth and development of Parícutin Volcano: *U.S. Geol. Surv. Bull. 965–D*, p. 355–489

Fouqué, F., 1879, *Santorin et ses éruptions*, G. Masson ed., Paris, 440 p.

Francis, E. H., 1962, Volcanic neck emplacement and subsidence structures at Dunbar, south-east Scotland: *Roy. Soc. Edinburgh Trans.*, v. 65, p. 41–58

———, 1969, Bedding in some Scottish (Fifeshire) tuff pipes and its possible relevance to the formation of maars and calderas: *Intern. Assn. Volcanology and Chem. Earth's Interior, Symposium on Volcanoes and their roots*, Oxford Univ., Abstracts vol., p. 94

Friedlaender, I., 1915, Über vulkanische Verwerfungstäler: *Z. Vulkanol.*, v. 2, p. 186–220

Friedman, I., Long, W., and Smith, R. L., 1963, Viscosity and water content of rhyolite glass: *J. Geophys. Res.*, v. 68, p. 6523–6535

Fries, C., Jr., 1953, Volumes and weights of pyroclastic material, lava, and water erupted by Paricutin Volcano, Michoacan, Mexico: *Amer. Geophys. Union Trans.*, v. 34, p. 603–616

Fuller, R. E., 1927, The closing phase of a fissure eruption: *Amer. J. Sci.*, 5th ser., v. 14, p. 228–230

Furneaux, R., 1964, *Krakatoa*, Prentice-Hall, Inc., Englewood Cliffs, N.J., 224 p.

Furumoto, A. S., Thompson, N. J., and Woollard, G. P., 1965, The structure of Koolau volcano from seismic refraction studies: *Pacific Sci.*, v. 19, p. 306–314

Gass, I. G., and Masson-Smith, D., 1963, The geology and gravity anomalies of the Troodos massif, Cyprus: *Roy. Soc. London Phil. Trans.*, ser. A, v. 255, p. 417–467

Gates, O., 1959, Breccia pipes in the Shoshone Range, Nevada: *Econ. Geol.*, v. 54, p. 790–815

Gedney, L., Matteson, C., and Forbes, R. B., 1970, Seismic refraction profiles of the ash flow in the Valley of Ten Thousand Smokes, Katmai National Monument, Alaska: *J. Geophys. Res.*, v. 75, p. 2619–2624

Geikie, A., 1882, *Geological sketches at home and abroad*, New York, 322 p.

———, 1897, *The founders of geology*, London, 297 p.; reprinted 1962, New York, 486 p.

———, 1897a, *Ancient volcanoes of Great Britain*, 2 vols., Macmillan & Co., London, 969 p.

Gentilli, J., 1948, Present-day volcanicity and climatic change: *Geol. Mag.*, v. 85, p. 172–175

Gibson, I. L., 1969, A comparative account of the flood basalt volcanism of the Columbia Plateau and eastern Iceland: *Bull. Volcanol.*, ser. 2, v. 33, p. 419–437

Gibson, I. L., and Tazieff, H., 1967, Additional theory of origin of fiamme in ignimbrites: *Nature*, v. 215, no. 5109, p. 1473–1474

Gilbert, C. M., 1938, Welded tuff in eastern California: *Geol. Soc. Amer. Bull.*, v. 49, p. 1829–1862

Gilbert, G. K., 1877, *Report on the geology of the Henry Mountains, U.S. Geographical and Geological Survey of the Rocky Mountain Region*, Washington, 160 p.

Gonzalez, R. J., and Foshag, W. F., 1946, The birth of Parícutin: *Smithsonian Inst. Ann. Rept.*, 1946, p. 223–234

Goranson, R. W., 1931, The solubility of water in granite magmas: *Amer. J. Sci.*, 5th ser., v. 22, p. 481–502

———, 1934, A note on the elastic properties of rocks: *Wash. Acad. Sci. J.*, v. 24, p. 419–428

Gorshkov, G. S., 1958, On some theoretical problems of volcanology: *Bull. Volcanol.*, ser. 2, v. 19, p. 103–113

———, 1959, Gigantic eruption of the volcano Bezymianny: *Bull. Volcanol.*, ser. 2, v. 20, p. 77–109

———, 1962, Petrochemical features of volcanism in relation to the types of the earth's crust: *Amer. Geophys. Union Monograph 6*, p. 158–170

———, 1970, *Volcanism and the upper mantle; Investigations in the Kurile Island arc*, Plenum Publishing Corporation, New York, 385 p.

Grange, L. I., 1937, The geology of the Rotorua-Taupo Subdivision, *New Zealand Dept. Sci. Ind. Res. Geol. Surv. Bull. 37*, (n.s.), Wellington, 138 p.

Green, D. H., and Ringwood, A. E., 1967, The genesis of basaltic magmas: *Contrib. Mineral. Petrol.*, v. 15, p. 103–190

Green, J., and Short, N. M., 1971, *Volcanic landforms and surface features, A photographic atlas and glossary*, Springer-Verlag, New York, 522 p.

Green, T. H., and Ringwood, A. E., 1969, High pressure experimental studies on the origin of andesites: Andesite Conference, Proc., *Oregon Dept. Geol. Mineral Ind. Bull. 65*, p. 21–32

Grindley, G. W., 1965, The geology, structure and exploitation of the Wairakei geothermal field, Taupo, New Zealand: *N. Z. Geol. Surv. Bull. 75* (n.s.), 131 p.

Hack, J. T., 1942, Sedimentation and volcanism in the Hopi Buttes, Arizona: *Geol. Soc. Amer. Bull.*, v. 53, p. 335–372

Hamilton, D. L., Burnham, C. W., and Osborn, E. F., 1964, Solubility of water and effects of oxygen fugacity and water content of crystallization in mafic magmas: *J. Petrol.*, v. 5, p. 21–39

Hamilton, W., 1965, Geology and petrogenesis of the Island Park caldera of rhyolite and basalt, eastern Idaho: *U.S. Geol. Surv. Prof. Paper 504–C*, 37 p.

Hamilton, W. M., and Baumgart, I. L., 1959, White Island: *New Zealand Dept. Sci. Ind. Res. Bull. 127*, 84 p.

Hatherton, T., and Dickinson, W. R., 1969, The relationship between andesitic volcanism and seismicity in Indonesia, the Lesser Antilles, and other island arcs: *J. Geophys. Res.*, v. 74, p. 5301–5310

Hay, R. L., 1959, Formation of the crystal-rich glowing avalanche deposits of St. Vincent, B.W.I.: *J. Geol.*, v. 67, p. 540–562

Hay, R. L., and Iijima, A., 1968, Nature and origin of palagonite tuffs of the Honolulu group on Oahu, Hawaii: *Geol. Soc. Amer. Mem. 116*, p. 331–376

Heald, E. F., Naughton, J. J., and Barnes, I. L., Jr., 1963, The chemistry of volcanic gases; 2. Use of equilibrium calculations in the interpretation of volcanic gas samples: *J. Geophys. Res.*, v. 68, p. 545–557

Hearn, B. C., Jr., 1968, Diatremes with kimberlitic affinities in north-central Montana: *Science*, v. 159, no. 3815, p. 622–625

Hentschel, H., 1961, Basischer Magmatismus in der Geosynklinale: *Geol. Rundschau*, v. 50, p. 33–45

Hess, H. H., 1962, History of the ocean basins: *Petrol. Studies Volume Honor A. F. Buddington, Geol. Soc. Amer., 1962*, p. 599–620

Hills, R. C., 1901, Geology of the Spanish Peaks Quadrangle, Colorado: *U.S. Geol. Surv., Geologic Atlas of the United States*, Folio 71

Hodgson, J. H., 1964, *Earthquakes and earth structure*, Prentice-Hall, Inc., Englewood Cliffs, N.J., 166 p.

Holmes, A., 1965, *Principles of physical geology*, 2nd ed., The Ronald Press Company, New York, 1288 p.

Howell, B. F., Jr., 1959, *Introduction to geophysics*, McGraw-Hill Book Company, New York, 399 p.

Humphreys, W. J., 1942, *Ways of the weather, a cultural survey of meteorology*, The Ronald Press Company, New York, 400 p.

Hunt, C. B., 1937, Igneous geology and structure of the Mt. Taylor field: *U.S. Geol. Surv. Prof. Paper 189–B*, p. 51–80

Hunt, C. B., Averill, P., and Miller, R. L., 1953, Geology and geography of the Henry Mountains region, Utah: *U.S. Geol. Surv. Prof. Paper 228*, 234 p.

Imbo, G., 1959, Temperature d'irrigidimento e viscosità magmatica: *Vesuvius Obs. Ann. Rept.*, ser. 6, v. 3, p. 24–38

Isacks, B., Oliver, J., and Sykes, L. R., 1968, Seismology and the new global tectonics: *J. Geophys. Res.*, v. 73, p. 5855–5899

Iwasaki, I., Katsura, T., and Sakato, N., 1955, Geochemical investigations of volcanoes in Japan; part 30, Volatile components of igneous rocks (in Japanese): *Chem. Soc. Japan J. Pure Chem. Sect.*, v. 76, p. 778–782

Izett, G. A., Wilcox, R. E., Powers, H. A., and Desborough, G. A., 1970, The

Bishop ash bed, a Pleistocene marker bed in the western United States: *Quaternary Res.* v. 1, p. 121–132

Jacobson, R. R. E., MacLeod, W. N., and Black, R., 1958, Ring complexes in the younger granite province of northern Nigeria: *Geol. Soc. London Mem. 1*, 71 p.

Jaggar, T. A., 1904, The initial stages of the spine on Pelée: *Amer. J. Sci.*, 4th ser., v. 17, p. 34–40

———, 1908, The evolution of Bogoslof Volcano: *Amer. Geograph. Soc. Bull.*, v. 40, p. 385–400

———, 1917, Lava flow from Mauna Loa, 1916: *Amer. J. Sci.*, 4th ser., v. 43, p. 255–288

———, 1917a, Volcanological investigations at Kilauea: *Amer. J. Sci.*, 4th ser., v. 44, p. 161–220

———, 1917b, Thermal gradient of Kilauea lava lake: *Wash. Acad. Sci. J.*, v. 7, p. 397–405

———, 1931, Preparedness against disaster: *Volcano Letter*, no. 338, p. 2–4

———, 1940, Magmatic gases: *Amer. J. Sci.*, v. 238, p. 313–353

———, 1945, Protection of harbors from lava flow: *Amer. J. Sci.*, v. 243–A, p. 333–351

———, 1947, Origin and development of craters: *Geol. Soc. Amer. Mem. 21*, 508 p.

———, 1949, Steam blast volcanic eruptions: *Hawaiian Volcano Observatory, 4th Special Rept.*, 137 p.

Jaggar, T. A., and Finch, R. H., 1924, The explosive eruption of Kilauea in Hawaii, 1924: *Amer. J. Sci.*, 5th ser., v. 8, p. 353–374

Jensen, H. I., 1907, The geology of Samoa, and the eruptions in Savaii: *Proc. Linnean Soc. N.S. Wales*, v. 31, p. 641–672

Johnson, R. W., 1968, Volcanic globule rock from Mount Suswa, Kenya: *Geol. Soc. Amer. Bull.*, v. 79, p. 647–652

———, 1969, Volcanic geology of Mount Suswa, Kenya: *Roy. Soc. London Phil. Trans.*, v. 265, p. 383–412

Judd, J. W., 1888, The eruption of Krakatoa, and subsequent phenomena; On the volcanic phenomena of the eruption, and on the nature and distribution of the ejected materials, *Roy. Soc. London, Krakatoa Comm. Rept.*, p. 1–56

Katsui, Y., 1963, Evolution and magmatic history of some Krakatoan calderas in Hokkaido, Japan: *J. Fac. Sci. Hokkaido Univ.*, Ser. IV, v. 11, p. 631–650

Kay, G. M., 1951, North American geosynclines: *Geol. Soc. Amer. Mem. 48*, 143 p.

Keegai, V. A., 1966, Tufflavas of the Tetyukhinsk region: in Cook, E. (ed.),

Tufflavas and ignimbrites, American Elsevier Publishing Co., Inc., New York, p. 130–132

Keller, W. D., and Valduga, A., 1946, The natural steam at Larderello, Italy: *J. Geol.*, v. 54, p. 327–334

Kingsley, L., 1931, Cauldron subsidence of the Ossipee Mountains: *Amer. J. Sci.*, 5th ser., v. 22, p. 139–168

Kinoshita, W. T., 1965, A gravity survey of the island of Hawaii: *Pacific Sci.*, v. 19, p. 339–340

Kinoshita, W. T., and Okamura, R. T., 1965, A gravity survey of the island of Maui, Hawaii: *Pacific Sci.*, v. 19, p. 341–342

Kinoshita, W. T., Koyanagi, R. Y., Wright, T. L., and Fiske, R. S., 1969, Kilauea Volcano: The 1967–68 summit eruption: *Science*, v. 166, p. 459–468

Kjartansson G., 1951, The eruption of Hekla 1947–1948, II.4, Water flood and mud flows: *Soc. Scientiarum Islandica, Reykjavik*, 51 p.

————, 1967, *Rummál hraundyngna*, Náttúrufraedingurinn, Reykjavik; cited by Noe-Nygaard, 1968

Knopf, A., 1960, Analysis of some recent geosynclinal theory: *Amer. J. Sci.*, v. 258–A, p. 126–136

Korn, H., and Martin, H., 1954, The Messum igneous complex in South-West Africa: *Geol. Soc. S. Africa Trans.*, v. 57, p. 83–132

Krauskopf, K. B., 1948, Lava movement at Paricutin Volcano, Mexico: *Geol. Soc. Amer. Bull.*, v. 59, p. 1267–1284

Krejci-Graf, K., 1964, Die mittelatlantischen Vulkaninseln: *Geol. Ges. Wien Mitt.*, v. 57, p. 401–431

Krishnan, M. S., 1968, *Geology of India and Burma*, Higginbothams, Ltd., Madras, 536 p.

Kubota, S., and Berg, E., 1967, Evidence for magma in the Katmai Volcanic Range: *Bull. Volcanol.*, ser. 2, v. 31, p. 175–214

Kuenen, Ph. H., 1935, Contributions to the geology of the East Indies from the Snellius Expedition, Part 1, Volcanoes: *Leidse Geol. Mededel.*, v. 7, pt. 2, p. 273–283

Kuno, H., 1959, Origin of Cenozoic petrographic provinces of Japan and surrounding areas: *Bull. Volcanol.*, ser. 2, v. 20, p. 37–76

Kuno, H., Ishikawa, T., Katsui, Y., Yagi, K., Yamasaki, M., and Taneda, S., 1964, Sorting of pumice and lithic fragments as a key to eruptive and emplacement mechanism: *Japan. J. Geol. Geograph.*, v. 35, p. 223–238

Kuno, H., Oki, K., Ogino, K., and Hirota, S., 1969, Structure of Hakone Caldera as revealed by drilling: *Intern. Assn. Volcanology and Chem. Earth's Interior, Symposium on Volcanoes and Their Roots*, Oxford Univ., Abstracts vol., p. 100

Lacroix, A., 1904, *La Montagne Pelée et ses éruptions*, Masson et Cie, Paris, 662 p.

————, 1930, Remarques sur les materiaux de projection des volcans et sur la genèse des roches pyroclastiques qu'ils constituent: *Soc. Geol. France, Centenaire Jubilee Vol.*, p. 431–472.

Lamb, H. H., 1970, Volcanic dust in the atmosphere; with a chronology and assessment of its meterological significance: *Roy. Soc. London Phil. Trans.*, v. A266, p. 425–533

Larsson, W., 1937, Vulkanische Ashe vom Ausbruck des chilenischen Vulkans Quizapu (1932) in Argentina gesammelt: *Geol. Inst. Upsala Bull.*, v. 26, p. 27–52

Lehmann, E., 1952, The significance of the hydrothermal stage in the formation of igneous rocks: *Geol. Mag.*, v. 89, p. 61–69

LeMasurier, W. E., and Wade, F. A., 1968, Fumarolic activity in Marie Byrd Land, Antarctica: *Science*, v. 162, p. 352

Le Pichon, X., and Talwani, M., 1964, Gravity survey of a seamount near 35°N 46°W in the north Atlantic: *Marine Geol.*, v. 2, p. 262–277

Lewis, J. D., 1968, The form and structure of the Loch Ba ring dyke, Isle of Mull, Scotland: *Geol. Soc. London Proc.*, no. 1649, p. 110–111

Lipman, P. E., and Steven, T. A., 1969, Petrologic evolution of the San Juan volcanic field, southwestern Colorado, U.S.A. (abst.): *Intern. Assn. Volcanology and Chem. Earth's Interior, Symposium on Volcanoes and Their Roots*, Oxford Univ., Abstracts vol., p. 254

Locardi, E., and Mittempergher, M., 1965, Study of an uncommon lava sheet in the Bolsena district (Central Italy): *Bull. Volcanol.*, ser. 2, v. 28, p. 75–84

————, 1967, On the genesis of ignimbrites: How ignimbrites and other pyroclastic products originate from a flowing melt: *Bull. Volcanol.*, ser. 2, v. 31, p. 131–152

Loney, R. A., 1968, Structure and composition of the southern coulee, Mono Craters, California: *Geol. Soc. Amer. Mem. 116*, p. 415–440

Luedke, R. G., and Burbank, W. S., 1961, Central vent ash-flow eruption, western San Juan Mountains, Colorado: *U.S. Geol. Surv. Prof. Paper 424–D*, p. 94–96

————, 1968, Volcanism and cauldron development in the western San Juan Mountains, Colorado: *Colo. School Mines Quart.*, v. 63, no. 3, p. 175–208

Lutton, R. J., 1969, Internal structure of the Buckboard Mesa basalt: *Bull. Volcanol.*, ser. 2, v. 33, p. 579–593

Lydon, P. A., 1968, Geology and lahars of the Tuscan Formation, northern California: *Geol. Soc. Amer. Mem. 116*, p. 441–475

Lyell, C., 1855, *Manual of geology*, 5th ed., New York, 647 p.

Macdonald, G. A., 1943, The 1942 eruption of Mauna Loa, Hawaii: *Amer. J. Sci.*, v. 241, p. 241–256; reprinted in *Smithsonian Inst. Ann. Rept.*, 1943, p. 199–212

————, 1951, Beginning of geomagnetic observations at Hawaiian Volcano Observatory: *Volcano Letter*, no. 511, p. 1–3

————, 1953, Pahoehoe, aa, and block lava: *Amer. J. Sci.*, v. 251, p. 169–191

————, 1954, Activity of Hawaiian volcanoes during the years 1940–1950: *Bull. Volcanol.*, ser. 2, v. 15, p. 119–179

————, 1956, The structure of Hawaiian volcanoes: *Koninkl. Ned. Geol. Mijnbouwk. Genoot. Verhandel.*, v. 16, p. 274–295

————, 1958, Barriers to protect Hilo from lava flows: *Pacific Sci.*, v. 12, p. 258–277

————, 1959, The activity of Hawaiian volcanoes during the years 1951–1956: *Bull. Volcanol.*, ser. 2, v. 22, p. 3–70

————, 1961, Volcanology: *Science*, v. 133, no. 3454, p. 673–679

————, 1962, The 1959 and 1960 eruptions of Kilauea Volcano, Hawaii, and the construction of walls to restrict the spread of the lava flows: *Bull. Volcanol.*, ser. 2, v. 24, p. 249–294

————, 1963, Physical properties of erupting Hawaiian magmas: *Geol. Soc. Amer. Bull.*, v. 74, p. 1071–1078

————, 1965, Hawaiian calderas: *Pacific Sci.*, v. 19, p. 320–334

————, 1967, Forms and structures of extrusive basaltic rocks: *Basalts—The Poldervaart treatise on rocks of basaltic composition*, Wiley-Interscience Publishers, New York, v. 1, p. 1–61

————, 1968, Composition and origin of Hawaiian lavas: *Geol. Soc. Amer. Mem. 116*, p. 477–522

————, 1971, Geologic map of the Mauna Loa quadrangle, Hawaii: *U.S. Geol. Surv. Geol. Quad. Map GQ-897.*

Macdonald, G. A., and Abbott, A. T., 1970, *Volcanoes in the sea—The geology of Hawaii*, University of Hawaii Press, Honolulu, 441 p.

Macdonald, G. A., and Alcaraz, A., 1956, Nuées ardentes of the 1948–1953 eruption of Hibok-Hibok: *Bull. Volcanol.*, ser. 2, v. 18, p. 169–178

Macdonald, G. A., and Eaton, J. P., 1955, The 1955 eruption of Kilauea Volcano: *Volcano Letter*, no. 529–530, p. 1–10

————, 1964, Hawaiian volcanoes during 1955: *U.S. Geol. Surv. Bull. 1171*, 170 p.

Macdonald, G. A., and Hubbard, D. H., 1970, *Volcanoes of the National Parks in Hawaii*, 5th ed., Hawaii Nat. Hist. Assn., Hawaii National Park, 56 p.

Macdonald, G. A., and Katsura, T., 1965, Eruption of Lassen Peak, Cascade Range, California, in 1915: Example of mixed magmas: *Geol. Soc. Amer. Bull.*, v. 76, p. 475–482

Macdonald, G. A., and Orr, J. B., 1950, The 1949 summit eruption of Mauna Loa, Hawaii: *U.S. Geol. Surv. Bull. 974–A*, 33 p.

Macdonald, G. A., Davis, D. A., and Cox, D. C., 1960, Geology and ground-water resources of the Island of Kauai, Hawaii: *Hawaii Div. Hydrog., Bull. 13*, 212 p.

MacGregor, A. G., 1952, Eruptive mechanisms: Mt. Pelée, the Soufrière of St. Vincent and the Valley of Ten Thousand Smokes: *Bull. Volcanol.*, ser. 2, v. 12, p. 49–74

Machado, F., 1965, Vulcanismo das Ilhas de Cabo Verde e das outras ilhas Atlântidas: *Junta de Investigações do Ultramar, Estudos, Eusaios, e Documentos*, no. 117, 83 p.

Machado, F., Parsons, W. H., Richards, A. F., and Mulford, J. W., 1962, Capelinhos eruption of Fayal Volcano, Azores, 1957–1958: *J. Geophys. Res.*, v. 67, p. 3519–3529

Mackin, J. H., 1960, Structural significance of Tertiary volcanic rocks in south-western Utah: *Amer. J. Sci.*, v. 258, p. 81–131

Malahoff, A., and Woollard, G. P., 1966, Magnetic surveys over the Hawaiian Islands and their geologic implications: *Pacific Sci.*, v. 20, p. 265–311

Marinelli, G., 1961, Genesi e classificazione delle vulcaniti recenti Toscane: *Soc. Toscan. Sci. Nat.*, ser. A, v. 68, p. 73–116

———, 1963, L'énergie géothermique en Toscane: *Ann. Soc. Geol. Belg. Bull.*, v. 85, no. 10, p. B417–438

Marinelli, G., and Mittempergher, M., 1966, On the genesis of some magmas of typical Mediterranean (potassic) suite: *Bull. Volcanol*, ser. 2, v. 29, p. 113–140

Marshall, P., 1935, Acid rocks of the Taupo-Rotorua district: *Roy. Soc. New Zealand Trans.*, v. 64, p. 323–366

Martin, R. C., 1959, Some field and petrographic features of New Zealand and American ignimbrites: *New Zealand J. Geol. Geophys.*, v. 2, p. 394–411

Mason, A. C., and Foster, H. L., 1953, Diversion of lava flows at O Shima, Japan: *Amer. J. Sci.*, v. 251, p. 249–258

———, 1956, Extruded mudflow hills of Nirasaki, Japan: *J. Geol.*, v. 64, p. 74–83

Matumoto, T., 1943, The four gigantic caldera volcanoes of Kyushu: *Japan. J. Geol. Geogr.*, v. 19, special number, 57 p.

———, 1965, Calderas of Kyushu: *Lunar Geol. Field Conf., Trans.*, Bend, Oregon, p. 15–20

McBirney, A. R., 1959, Factors governing emplacement of volcanic necks: *Amer. J. Sci.*, v. 257, p. 431–448

———, 1963, Breccia pipe near Cameron, Arizona: Discussion: *Geol. Soc. Amer. Bull.*, v. 74, p. 227–232

———, 1963a, Factors governing the nature of submarine volcanism: *Bull. Volcanol.*, ser. 2, v. 26, p. 455–469

————, 1968, Second additional theory of origin of fiamme in ignimbrites: *Nature,* v. 217, no. 5132, p. 938

————, 1969, Compositional variations in Cenozoic calc-alkaline suites of Central America: *Andesite Conf. Proc., Oregon Dept. Geol. Mineral Ind. Bull. 65,* p. 185–189

————, 1970, Some current aspects of volcanology: *Earth-Science Rev.,* v. 6, p. 337–352

McBirney, A. R., and Williams, H., 1965, Volcanic history of Nicaragua: *Univ. Calif. Berkeley Publ. Geol. Sci.,* v. 55, p. 1–65

————, 1969, A new look at the classification of calderas (abst.): *Intern. Assn. Volcanology and Chem. Earth's Interior, Symposium on Volcanoes and Their Roots,* Oxford Univ., supplementary abstracts.

————, 1969a, Geology and petrology of the Galápagos Islands: *Geol. Soc. Amer. Mem. 118,* 197 p.

McCall, G. J. H., 1963, Classification of calderas: 'Krakatoan' and 'Glencoe' types: *Nature,* v. 197, no. 4863, p. 136–138

————, 1964, Froth flows in Kenya: *Geol. Rundschau,* v. 54, p. 1148–1195

McNitt, J. R., 1963, Exploration and development of geothermal power in California: *Calif. Div. Mines Geol. Spec. Rept. 75,* 45 p.

McTaggart, K. C., 1960, The mobility of nuées ardentes: *Amer. J. Sci.,* v. 258, p. 369–382

Meinel, A. B., and Meinel, M. P., 1967, Volcanic sunset-glow stratum: origin: *Science,* v. 155, no. 3759, p. 189

Melson, W. G., and Thompson, G., 1968, Volcanism and metamorphism in the Mid-Atlantic Ridge, 22°N Latitude: *J. Geophys. Res.,* v. 73, p. 5925–5941

Menard, H. W., 1964, *Marine geology of the Pacific,* McGraw-Hill Book Company, New York, 271 p.

Mercalli, G., 1907, *I vulcani attivi della Terra,* Ulrico Hoepli, Milan, 421 p.

Milanovsky, E. E., and Koronovsky, N. V., 1966, Ignimbrite-tufflava formations in the Alpine belt of southwestern Eurasia: in Cook, E. (ed.), *Tufflavas and ignimbrites,* American Elsevier Publishing Co., Inc., New York, p. 54–71

Minakami, T., 1935, Variations in earth-current during the 1935 eruptions of Asama: *Tokyo Univ. Earthquake Res. Inst. Bull.,* v. 13, p. 642–643

————, 1960, Fundamental research for predicting volcanic eruptions. (Part 1) Earthquakes and crustal deformations originating from volcanic activities: *Tokyo Univ. Earthquake Res. Inst. Bull.,* v. 38, p. 497–544

Minakami, T., and Sakuma, S., 1953, Report on volcanic activities and volcanological studies concerning them in Japan during 1948–1951: *Bull. Volcanol.,* ser. 2, v. 14, p. 79–130

Minakami, T., Ishikawa, T., and Yagi, K., 1951, The 1944 eruptions of Volcano Usu in Hokkaido, Japan: *Bull. Volcanol.*, ser. 2, v. 11, p. 45–157

Mohr, E. C. J., 1945, The relationship between soil and population density in the Netherlands Indies: in Honig, P., and Verdoorn, F. (eds), *Science and scientists in the Netherlands Indies*, New York, p. 254–262

Mohr, P. A., 1967, Major volcano-tectonic lineament in the Ethiopian rift system: *Nature*, v. 213, no. 5077, p. 664–665

Moore, J. G., 1965, Petrology of deep-sea basalt near Hawaii: *Amer. J. Sci.*, v. 263, p. 40–52

———, 1967, Base surge in recent volcanic eruptions: *Bull. Volcanol.*, ser. 2, v. 30, p. 337–363

———, 1970, Pillow lava in a historic lava flow from Hualalai Volcano, Hawaii: *J. Geol.*, v. 78, p. 239–243

Moore, J. G., and Melson, W. G., 1969, Nuées ardentes of the 1968 eruption of Mayon Volcano, Philippines: *Bull. Volcanol.*, ser. 2, v. 33, p. 600–620

Moore, J. G., Nakamura, K., and Alcaraz, A., 1966, The 1965 eruption of Taal Volcano: *Science*, v. 151, no. 3713, p. 955–960

Mullineaux, D. R., and Crandell, D. R., 1962, Recent lahars from Mount St. Helens, Washington: *Geol. Soc. Amer. Bull.*, v. 73, p. 855–869

Murai, I., 1960, On the mudflows of the 1926 eruption of Volcano Tokachi-dake, central Hokkaido, Japan: *Tokyo Univ. Earthquake Res. Inst. Bull.*, v. 38, p. 55–70

———, 1960a, Pumice-flow deposits of Komagatake Volcano, southern Hokkaido: *Tokyo Univ. Earthquake Res. Inst. Bull.*, v. 38, p. 451–466

Murata, K. J., Ault, W. U., and White, D. E., 1964, Halogen acids in fumarolic gases of Kilauea Volcano: *Bull. Volcanol.*, ser. 2, v. 27, p. 367–368

Naboko, S. I., 1959, Volcanic exhalations and products of their reactions as exemplified by Kamchatka-Kuriles volcanoes: *Bull. Volcanol.*, ser. 2, v. 20, p. 121–154

Naughton, J. J., Heald, E. F., and Barnes, I. L., Jr., 1963, The chemistry of volcanic gases; I. Collection and analysis of equilibrium mixtures by gas chromatography: *J. Geophys. Res.*, v. 68, p. 539–544

Nayudu, Y. R., 1962, A new hypothesis for origin of guyots and seamount terraces: *Amer. Geophys. Union Geophys. Monograph 6*, p. 171–180

Neumann van Padang, M., 1933, De uitbarsting van den Merapi (Midden Java) in de jaren 1930–1931: *Ned. Indies, Dienst Mijnbouwk. Vulkan. Seism. Mededel.*, no. 12, 135 p. (with English summary)

———, 1939, Über die vielen tausend Hugel im westlichen Vorlande des Raoeng-Vulkans (Ost Java): *Ing. Ned. Indies*, v. 6, no. 4, sec. 4, p. 35–41.

Neumann van Padang, M., Richards, A. F., Machado, F., Bravo, T., Baker, P. E., and LeMaitre, R. W., 1967, *Catalogue of the active volcanoes of the world including solfatara fields Part 21*, Atlantic Ocean, Intern. Assn. of Volcanology, Naples, 128 p.

Noble, D. C., 1968, Kane Springs Wash volcanic center, Lincoln County, Nevada: *Geol. Soc. Amer., Mem. 110*, p. 109–116

Noble, D. C., Sargent, K. A., Mehnert, H. H., Ekren, E. B., and Byers, F. A., Jr., 1968, Silent Canyon volcanic center, Nye County, Nevada: *Geol. Soc. Amer. Mem. 110*, p. 65–75

Nockolds, S. R., 1954, Average chemical compositions of some igneous rocks: *Geol. Soc. Amer. Bull.*, v. 65, p. 1007–1032

Noe-Nygaard, A., 1968, On extrusion forms in plateau basalts; shield volcanoes of "scutulum" type: *Scientia Islandica*, Ann. vol., p. 10–13

Noll, H., 1967, Maare und maar-ähnliche Explosionskrater in Island: *Koln Univ., Geol. Inst., Sonderveröffentlichungen 11*, 117 p.

Oftedahl, C., 1953, Studies on the igneous rock complex of the Oslo region: XIII. The cauldrons: *Skrifter Norske Videnskaps-Akad. Oslo, Mat. Naturn. Kl.*, 3, 108 p.

———, 1960, Permian igneous rocks of the Oslo graben, Norway: *21st Intern. Geol. Congr., Norway, Guide to excursions no. A11 and C7*, 23 p.

Ollier, C. D., 1967, Maars, their characteristics, varieties, and definition: *Bull. Volcanol.*, ser. 2, v. 31, p. 45–73

Omori, F., 1916, The Sakura-jima eruptions and earthquakes, IV. Results of the leveling surveys and the Kagoshima Bay soundings made after the Sakura-jima eruption of 1914: *Imperial Earthquake Invest. Comm. Japan Bull.*, v. 8, no. 4, p. 322–351

Oxburgh, E. R., 1971, Plate tectonics, in *Understanding the Earth*, I. G. Gass, P. J. Smith, and R. C. L. Wilson, editors, Open University Press, Sussex, England, p. 263–285

Palmer, H. S., 1930, The geologic history of Oahu: *B. P. Bishop Mus. Spec. Pub. 16*, p. 4–6

Park, C. F., Jr., 1961, A magnetite "flow" in northern Chile: *Econ. Geol.*, v. 56, p. 431–436

Parsons, W. H., 1939, Volcanic centers in the Sunlight area, Park County, Wyoming: *J. Geol.*, v. 47, p. 1–26

———, 1967, Manner of emplacement of pyroclastic andesitic breccias: *Bull. Volcanol.*, ser. 2, v. 30, p. 177–187

———, 1969, Criteria for the recognition of volcanic breccias: review: *Geol. Soc. Amer. Mem. 115*, p. 263–304

Patterson, E. M., 1955, The Tertiary lava succession in the northern part of the Antrim plateau: *Roy. Irish Acad. Proc.*, v. 57, sec. B, no. 7, p. 79–122

Peck, D. L., Moore, J. G., and Kojima, G., 1964, Temperatures in the crust and melt of the Alae lava lake, Hawaii, after the August 1963 eruption of Kilauea Volcano—a preliminary report: *U.S. Geol. Surv. Prof. Paper 501-D,* p. 1–7

Peck, D. L., Griggs, A. B., Schlicker, H. G., Wells, F. G., and Dole, H. M., 1964, Geology of the central and northern parts of the Western Cascade Range in Oregon: *U.S. Geol. Surv. Prof. Paper 449,* 56 p.

Peck, D. L., Wright, T. L., and Moore, J. G., 1966, Crystallization of tholeiitic basalt in Alae lava lake, Hawaii: *Bull. Volcanol.,* ser. 2, v. 29, p. 629–656

Perret, F. A., 1916, The lava eruption of Stromboli, summer–autumn, 1915: *Amer. J. Sci.,* 4th ser., v. 42, p. 443–463

———, 1924, The Vesuvius eruption of 1906: *Carnegie Inst. Washington Pub. 339,* 151 p.

———, 1935, The eruption of Mt. Pelée 1929–1932: *Carnegie Inst. Washington Pub. 458,* 125 p.

———, 1950, Volcanological observations: *Carnegie Inst. Washington Pub. 549,* 162 p.

Peterson, D. W., 1970, Ash-flow deposits—their character, origin, and significance: *J. Geol. Educ.,* v. 18, p. 66–76

Peterson, N. V., and Groh, E. A., 1961, Hole-in-the-Ground, central Oregon: *Ore-Bin,* v. 23, p. 95–100

Petrov, V. P., 1963, Zoning of lava flows, originating after the extrusion, and formation of "tuffolavas": *Bull. Volcanol.,* ser. 2, v. 25, p. 19–25

Phillips, J., 1869, *Vesuvius,* Oxford, 355 p.

Pirsson, L. V., 1915, The microscopical characters of volcanic tuffs—a study for students: *Amer. J. Sci.,* 4th ser., v. 40, p. 191–211

Popkov, V. F., 1946, On the activity of Biliukai in 1938–1939: *Kamchatka Volcanol. Sta. Bull.,* no. 12, p. 29–33 (in Russian)

Powers, H. A., and Wilcox, R. E., 1964, Volcanic ash from Mount Mazama (Crater Lake) and from Glacier Peak: *Science,* v. 144, no. 3624, p. 1334–1336

Prinz, M., 1970, Idaho rift system, Snake River Plain, Idaho: *Geol. Soc. Amer. Bull.,* v. 81, p. 941–948

Putnam, W. C., 1938, The Mono Craters, California: *Geograph. Rev.,* v. 28, p. 68–82

Ratté, J. C., and Steven, T. A., 1967, Ash flows and related volcanic rocks associated with the Creede caldera, San Juan Mountains, Colorado: *U.S. Geol. Surv. Prof. Paper 524-H,* 58 p.

Reck, H., 1915, Physiographische Studie über vulkanische Bomben: Z. *Vulkanol.* Erganzungsband 1914–1915, 124 p.

Reynolds, D. L., 1956, Calderas and ring complexes: *Koninkl. Ned. Geol. Mijnbouwk. Genoot. Verhandel.*, v. 16, p. 355–379

Richey, J. E., 1961, *Scotland: The Tertiary volcanic districts,* 3rd ed., revised by A. G. MacGregor and F. W. Anderson, Dept. Sci. Ind. Res., Geol. Survey and Museum, Edinburgh, 119 p.

Rikitake, T., Yokoyama, I., Uyeda, S., and Yukutake, T., 1963, Geomagnetic studies on Volcano Mihara: *Bull. Volcanol.,* ser. 2., v. 26, p. 49–55

Rinehart, J. S., 1965, Earth tremors generated by Old Faithful geyser: *Science,* v. 160, no. 3695, p. 494–496

———, 1969, Thermal and seismic indications of Old Faithful geyser's inner workings: *J. Geophys. Res.,* v. 74, p. 566–573

Rittmann, A., 1933, Die geologisch bedingte Evolution und Differentiation des Somma-Vesuvmagmas: *Z. Vulkanol.,* v. 15, p. 8–94

———, 1936, *Vulkane und ihre Tätigkeit,* Ferdinand Enke Verlag, Stuttgart, 188 p.

———, 1958, Cenni sulle colate di ignimbriti: *Atti. Accad. Gioenia Sci. Nat. Catania,* ser. 4, v. 4, p. 524–533

———, 1958a, Geosynclinal volcanism, ophiolites, and Barramya rocks: *Egypt. J. Geol.,* v. 2, p. 61–66

———, 1962, *Volcanoes and their activity,* Wiley-Interscience Publishers, New York, 305 p.

———, 1962a, Erklärungsversuch zum Mechanismus der Ignimbritausbruche: *Geol. Rundschau,* v. 52, p. 853–861

———, 1963, Vulkanismus und Tektonik des Ätna: *Geol. Rundschau,* v. 53, p. 788–800

———, 1963a, *Les volcans et leur activité,* édition Française, Masson et Cie. Paris, 461 p. (Somewhat enlarged from the original second edition in German by H. Tazieff.)

Ross, C. S., and Smith, R. L., 1961, Ash-flow tuffs: Their origin, geologic relations, and identification: *U.S. Geol. Surv. Prof. Paper 366,* 81 p.

Rubey, W. W., 1951, Geologic history of sea water—an attempt to state the problem: *Geol. Soc. Amer. Bull.,* v. 62, p. 1111–1147

Russell, I. C., 1897, *Volcanoes of North America,* The Macmillan Company, New York, 346 p.

———, 1902, Geology and water resources of the Snake River plains of Idaho: *U.S. Geol. Surv. Bull. 199,* 192 p.

Rust, G. W., 1937, Preliminary notes on explosive volcanism in southeastern Missouri: *J. Geol.,* v. 45, p. 48–75

Rutten, M. G., 1964, Formation of a plateaubasalt series (From the example of Iceland): *Bull. Volcanol.,* ser. 2, v. 27, p. 93–111

Sapper, K., 1927, *Vulkankunde*, J. Engelhorns Nachf., Stuttgart, 424 p.

Schmincke, H.-U., 1967, Fused tuff and pépérites in south-central Washington: *Geol. Soc. Amer. Bull.*, v. 78, p. 319–330

Schmincke, H.-U., and Swanson, D. A., 1967, Laminar viscous flowage structures in ash-flow tuffs from Gran Canaria, Canary Islands: *J. Geol.*, v. 75, p. 641–664

Scrope, J. P., 1862, *Volcanoes. The character of their phenomena, their share in the structure and composition of the surface of the globe, and their relation to its internal forces*, 2nd ed., Longman, Green, Longmans, and Roberts, London, 490 p.

Segerstrom, K., 1950, Erosion studies at Parícutin, State of Michoacan, Mexico: *U.S. Geol. Surv. Bull. 965-A*, 164 p.

Sekiya, S., and Kikuchi, Y., 1889, The eruption of Bandai-san: *Coll. Sci. Imp. Univ. Tokyo J.*, v. 3, pt. 2, p. 91–171

Shaw, H. R., 1969, Rheology of basalt in the melting range: *J. Petrol.*, v. 10, p. 510–535

Shaw, H. R., Wright, T. L., Peck, D. L., and Okamura, R., 1968, The viscosity of basaltic magma: an analysis of field measurements in Makaopuhi lava lake, Hawaii: *Amer. J. Sci.*, v. 266, p. 225–264

Shepherd, E. S., 1925, The analysis of gases obtained from volcanoes and from rocks: *J. Geol.*, v. 33, supplement, p. 289–370

———, 1938, The gases in rocks and some related problems: *Amer. J. Sci.*, 5th ser., v. 35-A, p. 311–351

Shepherd, E. S., and Merwin, H. E., 1927, Gases of the Mont Pelée lavas of 1902: *J. Geol.*, v. 35, p. 97–116

Sheridan, M. F., 1970, Fumarolic mounds and ridges of the Bishop Tuff, California: *Geol. Soc. Amer. Bull.*, v. 81, p. 851–868.

Shirinian, K. G., 1963, Ignimbrites and tuffo-lavas: *Bull. Volcanol.*, ser. 2, v. 25, p. 13–18

Shoemaker, E. M., and Moore, H. J., II, 1956, Diatremes on the Navajo and Hopi Reservations: *U.S. Geol. Surv. Trace Elements Invest. Rept. 640*, p. 197–203

Shoemaker, E. M., Roach, C. H., and Byers, F. M., Jr., 1962, Diatremes and uranium deposits in the Hopi Buttes, Arizona: *Petrol. Studies, Volume Honor A. F. Buddington*, Geol. Soc. America, 1962, p. 327–355

Sigvaldason, G. E., 1965, *Surtsey in color*, Myndabókaútgáfan, Reykjavik, 22 p.

Sigvaldason, G. E., and Elísson, G., 1968, Collection and analysis of volcanic gases at Surtsey, Iceland: *Geochim. Cosmochim. Acta*, v. 32, p. 797–805

Simkin, T., and Howard, K. A., 1970, Caldera collapse in the Galápagos Islands, 1968: *Science*, v. 169, no. 3944, p. 429–437

Skelhorn, R. R., MacDougall, J. D. S., and Longland, P. J. N., 1969, The

Tertiary igneous geology of the Island of Mull, Field Excursion Guide to the Tertiary volcanic rocks of Mull: *Intern. Assn. Volcanology and Chem. Earth's Interior, Symposium on Volcanoes and Their Roots*, Oxford Univ., 35 p.

Skinner, B. J., 1970, A sulfur lava flow on Mauna Loa: *Pacific Sci.*, v. 24, p. 144–145

Smith, R. L., 1960, Ash flows: *Geol. Soc. Amer. Bull.*, v. 71, p. 795–842

———, 1960a, Zones and zonal variations in welded ash flows: *U.S. Geol. Surv. Prof. Paper 354-F*, p. 149–159

Smith, R. L., and Bailey, R. A., 1962, Resurgent cauldrons: Their relation to granitic ring complexes and large volume rhyolitic ash flows (abst.): *Intern. Symposium on Volcanology, Tokyo, Sci. Council Japan*, Abstracts, p. 67–68

———, 1966, The Bandelier Tuff: A study of ash-flow eruption cycles from zoned magma chambers: *Bull. Volcanol.*, ser. 2, v. 29, p. 83–104

———, 1968, Resurgent cauldrons: *Geol. Soc. Amer. Mem. 116*, p. 613–662

Smith, R. L., Bailey, R. A., and Ross, C. S., 1961, Structural evolution of the Valles Caldera, New Mexico, and its bearing on the emplacement of ring dikes: *U.S. Geol. Surv. Prof. Paper 424-D*, p. 145–149

———, 1970, Geologic map of the Jemez Mountains, New Mexico: *U.S. Geol. Surv. Misc. Geol. Invest. Map I-571*

Smith, R. L., Friedman, I. I., and Long, W. D., 1958, Welded tuffs, Expt. 1: *Amer. Geophys. Union Trans.*, v. 39, p. 352–353

Smith, S. P., 1887, *The eruption of Tarawera, New Zealand: Rept. to the Surveyor-General, New Zealand*, Govt. Printer, Wellington, 84 p.

Snavely, P. D., Jr., and Wagner, H. G., 1963, Tertiary geologic history of western Oregon and Washington: *Wash. Dept. Conserv. Div. Mines Geol. Rept. Invest. No. 22*, 25 p.

Souther, J. G., 1970, Volcanism and its relation to recent crustal movements in the Canadian cordillera: *Can. J. Earth Sci.*, v. 7, p. 553–568

Speight, R., 1917, The geology of Banks Peninsula: *New Zealand Inst. Trans.*, v. 49, p. 387–392

Sperenskaia, I. M., 1967, Okhotsk ignimbrite province: *Bull. Volcanol.*, ser. 2, v. 30, p. 99–111

Stearns, H. T., 1925, The explosive phase of Kilauea Volcano, Hawaii, in 1924: *Bull. Volcanol.*, 2nd ann., nos. 5–6, p. 193–208

———, 1928, Craters of the Moon National Monument, Idaho: *Idaho Bur. Mines Geol. Bull. 13*, 57 p.

———, 1942, Origin of Haleakala Crater, Island of Maui, Hawaii: *Geol. Soc. Amer. Bull.*, v. 53, p. 1–14

———, 1963, *Geology of the Craters of the Moon National Monument, Idaho*, Craters of the Moon Nat. Hist. Assn., Arco, Idaho, 34 p.

Stearns, H. T., and Clark, W. O., 1930, Geology and water resources of the Kau District, Hawaii: *U.S. Geol. Surv. Water Supply Paper 616,* 194 p.

Stearns, H. T., and Macdonald, G. A., 1942, Geology and ground-water resources of the Island of Maui, Hawaii: *Hawaii Div. Hydrog. Bull. 7,* 344 p.

————, 1946, Geology and ground-water resources of the Island of Hawaii: *Hawaii Div. Hydrog. Bull. 9,* 363 p.

Stearns, H. T., and Vaksvik, K. N., 1935, Geology and ground-water resources of the Island of Oahu, Hawaii: *Hawaii Div. Hydrog. Bull. 1,* 479 p.

Stearns, H. T., Crandall, L., and Steward, W. G., 1938, Geology and ground-water resources of the Snake River Plain in southeastern Idaho: *U.S. Geol. Surv. Water Supply Paper 774,* 268 p.

Stehn, C., 1929, The geology and volcanism of the Krakatau group, *Fourth Pacific Sci. Congr. Guidebook,* Batavia, p. 1–55

Steinberg, G. S., and Rivosh, L. A., 1965, Geophysical study of the Kamchatka volcanoes: *J. Geophys. Res.,* v. 70, p. 3341–3369

Stewart, F. H., 1965, Tertiary igneous activity [in Scotland], in *The Geology of Scotland,* G. Y. Craig (ed.), Oliver and Boyd Limited, Edinburgh, p. 417–465

Stille, H., 1940, *Einführung in den Bau Amerikas,* Gb. Borntraeger, Berlin, 717 p.

Strange, W. E., Machesky, L. F., and Woollard, G. P., 1965, A gravity survey of the Island of Oahu, Hawaii: *Pacific Sci.,* v. 19, p. 350–353

Strong, D. F., and Jacquot, C., 1971, The Karthala Caldera, Grande Comore: *Bull. Volcanol.,* ser. 2, v. 34, p. 663–680

Studt, F. E., 1958, The Wairakei hydrothermal field under exploitation: *New Zealand J. Geol. Geophys.,* v. 1, p. 703–723

Sugimoto, Y., and Namba, M., 1958, Some studies on volcanic activity of volcano Sakurajima, Part 2, On the explosion source "magma reservoir" and the process of volcanic activity: *Kumamoto J. Sci.,* v. 3, no. 4, p. 256–266

Sutherland-Brown, A., 1969, Aiyansh lava flow, British Columbia: *Can. J. Earth Sci.,* v. 6, p. 1460–1468

Taneda, S., 1961, Moving of the magma chamber of the Sakura-jima volcano: *Geol. Soc. Japan J.,* v. 67, p. 593–605

Tanguy, J.-C, and Biquand, D., 1967, Quelques propriétés physiques du magma actuel de l'Etna: *Compt. Rend. Acad. Sci. Paris,* v. 264, p. 699–702

Taubeneck, W. H., 1967, Notes on the Glen Coe cauldron subsidence, Argyllshire, Scotland: *Geol. Soc. Amer. Bull.,* v. 78, p. 1295–1316

Taylor, G. A., 1958, The 1951 eruption of Mount Lamington, Papua: *Australia Bur. Mineral Resources Geol. Geophys. Bull. 38,* 117 p.

————, 1963, Seismic and tilt phenomena preceding a Pelean type eruption from a basaltic volcano: *Bull. Volcanol.,* ser. 2, v. 26, p. 5–11

Tazieff, H. K., 1951, L'éruption du Volcan Gituro (Kivu, Congo Belge) de mars à Juillet 1948: *Congo Belge et Ruanda-Urundi, Serv. Geol. Mem. 1,* 158 p.

————, 1958, L'éruption 1957–1958 et la tectonique de Faial (Açores): *Soc. Belg. Geol. Bull.,* v. 67, p. 13–49

————, 1961, *Les volcans, Encyclopédie essentielle,* Robt. Delpire éd., Paris, 106 p.

————, 1966, État actuel des connaissances sur le volcan Niragongo (République démocratique du Congo): *Soc. Geol. France Bull.,* ser. 7, v. 8, p. 176–200

————, 1969, Investigations of eruptive gases (abst.): *Intern. Assn. Volcanology and Chem. Earth's Interior, Symposium on Volcanoes and Their Roots,* Oxford Univ., Abstracts vol., addendum

Thorarinsson, S., 1951, Laxárgljúfur and Laxárhraun, a tephrochronological study: *Mus. Nat. Hist., Reykjavik, Misc. Papers 2,* 88 p.

————, 1954, The eruption of Hekla, 1947–1948, II.3, The tephra-fall from Hekla on March 29th, 1947: *Societas Sci. Islandica, Reykjavik,* 68 p.

————, 1960, The post-glacial volcanism: On the geology and geophysics of Iceland, *21st Intern. Geol. Congr., Norway, Guide to Excursion A-2,* p. 33–45

————, 1964, *Surtsey, the new island in the north Atlantic,* Almenna Bókafélagid, Reykjavik, 64 p.

————, 1967, The Surtsey eruption and related scientific work: *Polar Record,* v. 13, no. 86, p. 571–578

————, 1967a, The eruption of Hekla, 1947–1948, I. The eruptions of Hekla in historical times, a tephrochronological study, *Societas Sci. Islandica, Reykjavik,* p. 1–170

————, 1970, The Lakagigar eruption of 1783: *Bull. Volcanol.,* ser. 2, v. 33, p. 910–927

Tomkeieff, S. I., 1940, The basalt lavas of the Giant's Causeway district of Northern Ireland: *Bull. Volcanol.,* ser. 2, v. 18, p. 89–143.

Trygvasson, T., 1943, Das Skjaldbreid Gebiet auf Island: *Upsala Univ. Geol. Inst. Bull.,* v. 30, p. 273–320

Tsuya, H., 1939, On the form and structure of volcanic bombs, with special reference to the origin of the basaltic bombs from Volcano Huzi (Fuji) (in Japanese with English abstract): *Tokyo Univ. Earthquake Res. Inst. Bull.,* v. 17, p. 809–825

Turner, F. J., and Verhoogen, J., 1960, *Igneous and metamorphic petrology,* 2nd ed., McGraw-Hill Book Company, New York, 694 p.

Tyrrell, G. W., 1931, *Volcanoes,* Holt, Rinehart and Winston, Inc., New York, 252 p.

————, 1937, Flood basalts and fissure eruption: *Bull. Volcanol.,* ser. 2, v. 1, p. 89–111

————, 1955, Distribution of igneous rocks in space and time: *Geol. Soc. Amer. Bull.*, v. 66, p. 405–426

Upton, B. G., and Wadsworth, W. J., 1965, Geology of Réunion Island, Indian Ocean: *Nature*, v. 207, p. 151–154

Verbeek, R. D. M., 1886, *Krakatau*, Batavia, Java, 495 p.

Verhoogen, J., 1939, New data on volcanic gases: The 1938 eruption of Nyamlagira: *Amer. J. Sci.*, v. 237, p. 656–672

————, 1948, *Les éruptions 1938–1940 du Volcan Nyamuragira: Inst. des Parcs Nationaux du Congo Belge, Exploration du Parc National Albert*, Missions J. Verhoogen, Fasc. 1, Bruxelles, 186 p.

————, 1949, Thermodynamics of a magmatic gas phase: *Univ. Calif. Berkeley Pub. Geol. Sci.*, v. 28, p. 91–136

————, 1951, Mechanics of ash formation: *Amer. J. Sci.*, v. 249, p. 729–739

————, 1960, Temperatures within the earth: *Amer. Scientist*, v. 48, p. 134–159

Verhoogen, J., Turner, F. J., Weiss, L. E., Wahrhaftig, C., and Fyfe, W. S., 1970, The Earth, an introduction to physical geology, Holt, Rinehart and Winston, Inc., New York, 748 p.

Vincent, P., 1960, Les volcans tertiaires et quaternaires du Tibesti occidental et central (Sahara du Tchad): Thesis, Faculty of Sciences, Univ. Paris, ser. A., no. 3617, 307 p.

————, 1963, Le volcanisme ignimbritique du Tibesti (Sahara tchadien). Essai d'interprétation dynamique: *Bull. Volcanol.*, ser. 2, v. 26, p. 259–272

Vine, F. J., 1966, Spreading of the ocean floor: new evidence: *Science*, v. 154, p. 1405–1415

————, 1971, Sea-floor spreading, in *Understanding the Earth*, I. G. Gass, P. J. Smith, and R. C. L. Wilson, editors, Open University Press, Sussex, England, p. 233–249

Vlodavetz, V. I., 1963, Sur la genèse des tufolaves à Kamchatka (à l'est du volcan Maly Sémiatchik): *Bull. Volcanol.*, ser. 2, v. 25, p. 27–30

Vogt, P. R., Schneider, E. D., and Johnson, G. L., 1969, The crust and upper mantle beneath the sea: *Amer. Geophys. Union Geophys. Monograph 13*, p. 556–617

Wager, L. R., and Deer, W. A., 1939, Geological investigations in East Greenland: Part III, The petrology of the Skaergaard intrusion, Kangerdlugssuaq, East Greenland: *Medd. Groenland*, v. 105, no. 4, 352 p.

Wagner, P. A., 1914, *The diamond fields of South Africa*, Johannesburg, 347 p.

Walker, G. P. L., 1962, Tertiary welded tuffs in eastern Iceland: *Geol. Soc. London Quart. J.*, v. 118, p. 275–293

————, 1965, Some aspects of Quaternary volcanism in Iceland: *Leicester Lit. Phil. Soc. Trans.*, v. 59, p. 25–40

————, 1967, Thickness and viscosity of Etnean lavas: *Nature,* v. 213, p. 484–485

Walker, G. P. L., and Blake, D. H., 1966, The formation of a palagonite breccia mass beneath a valley glacier in Iceland: *Geol. Soc. London Quart. J.,* v. 122, p. 45–61

Waltershausen, W. Sartorius von, 1880, *Der Aetna,* prepared posthumously by A. von Lasaulx, Verlag Wilhelm Engelmann, Leipzig, v. 1, 371 p., v. 2, 548 p.

Washington, H. S., 1922, Deccan traps and other plateau basalts: *Geol. Soc. Amer. Bull.,* v. 33, p. 765–803

Watanabe, T., 1940, Eruptions of molten sulphur from the Siretoko-Iôsan Volcano, Hokkaido, Japan: *Japan. J. Geol. Geograph.,* v. 17, p. 289–310

Waters, A. C., 1955, Volcanic rocks and the tectonic cycle: *Geol. Soc. Amer. Spec. Paper 62,* p. 703–722

————, 1960, Determining direction of flow in basalts: *Amer. J. Sci.,* v. 258-A, p. 350–356

Watkins, N. D., and Gunn, B. M., 1969, Major and trace element variation in seventy successive Miocene lavas from southeastern Oregon, U.S.A. (abst.): *Intern. Assn. Volcanology and Chem. Earth's Interior, Symposium on Volcanoes and Their Roots,* Oxford Univ., Abstracts vol., p. 276

Wentworth, C. K., 1926, Pyroclastic geology of Oahu: *B. P. Bishop Mus. Bull. 30,* 121 p.

Wentworth, C. K., and Macdonald, G. A., 1953, Structures and forms of basaltic rocks in Hawaii: *U.S. Geol. Surv. Bull. 994,* 98 p.

Wentworth, C. K., and Williams, H., 1932, The classification and terminology of the pyroclastic rocks: *Natl. Res. Council Bull. 89,* p. 19–53

Wentworth, C. K., Carson, M. H., and Finch, R. H., 1945, Discussion on the viscosity of lava: *J. Geol.,* v. 53, p. 94–104

Wentworth, C. K., Powers, H. A., and Eaton, J. P., 1961, Feasibility of a lava-diverting barrier at Hilo, Hawaii: *Pacific Sci.,* v. 15, p. 352–357

Westerveld, J., 1952, Quaternary volcanism on Sumatra: *Geol. Soc. Amer. Bull.,* v. 63, p. 561–594

————, 1957, Phases of Neogene and Quaternary volcanism in Asia Minor: *20th Intern. Geol. Congr., Mexico, Trans.,* sec. 1, v. 1, p. 103–119

Wexler, H., 1952, Volcanoes and world climate: *Sci. Amer.,* v. 186, no. 4, p. 74–80

White, D. E., 1955, Thermal springs and epithermal ore deposits: *Econ. Geol.,* 50th Anniversary Vol., p. 99–154

————, 1957, Thermal waters of volcanic origin: *Geol. Soc. Amer. Bull.,* v. 68, p. 1637–1658

————, 1967, Some principles of geyser activity, mainly from Steamboat Springs, Nevada: *Amer. J. Sci.,* v. 265, p. 641–684

White, D. E., and Waring, G. A., 1961, A review of the chemical composition of gases from volcanic fumaroles and igneous rocks: *U.S. Geol. Surv. Prof. Paper 424-C*, p. 311–312

———, 1963, Volcanic emanations: Data of Geochemistry, sixth ed., Chapter K, *U.S. Geol. Surv. Prof. Paper 440-K*, 29 p.

Wilcox, R. E., 1944, Rhyolite-basalt complex on Gardiner River, Yellowstone Park, Wyoming: *Geol. Soc. Amer. Bull.*, v. 55, p. 1047–1080

———, 1959, Some effects of recent volcanic ash falls, with especial reference to Alaska: *U.S. Geol. Surv. Bull. 1028-N*, p. 409–476

———, 1965, Volcanic-ash chronology: in *Quaternary of the United States*, Princeton University Press, Princeton, N.J., p. 807–816

Williams, H., 1929, The volcanic domes of Lassen Peak and vicinity, California: *Amer. J. Sci.*, 5th ser., v. 18, p. 313–330

———, 1932, The history and character of volcanic domes: *Univ. Calif. Berkeley Pub. Bull. Dept. Geol. Sci.*, v. 21, p. 51–146

———, 1934, Mount Shasta, California: *Z. Vulkanol.*, v. 15, p. 225–253

———, 1936, Pliocene volcanoes of the Navajo-Hopi country: *Geol. Soc. Amer. Bull.*, v. 47, p. 111–172

———, 1941, *Volcanology: in geology, 1888–1938*, Fiftieth Anniversary Vol., Geol. Soc. America, p. 367–390

———, 1941a, Calderas and their origin: *Univ. Calif. Berkeley Pub. Geol. Sci.*, v. 25, p. 239–346

———, 1941b, *Crater Lake: The story of its origin*, University of California Press, Berkeley, Calif., 97 p.

———, 1942, The geology of Crater Lake National Park, Oregon, with a reconnaissance of the Cascade Range southward to Mount Shasta: *Carnegie Inst. Washington Pub. 540*, 162 p.

———, 1950, Volcanoes of the Paricutin region: *U.S. Geol. Surv. Bull. 965-B*, p. 165–279

———, 1952, The great eruption of Cosegüina, Nicaragua, in 1835, with notes on the Nicaraguan volcanic chain: *Univ. Calif. Berkeley Publ. Geol. Sci.*, v. 29, p. 21–46

———, 1953, *The ancient volcanoes of Oregon*, 2nd ed., Oregon State System of Higher Education, Eugene, 68 p.

———, 1954, Problems and progress in volcanology: *Geol. Soc. London Quart. J.*, v. 109, p. 311–332

———, 1957, Glowing avalanche deposits of the Sudbury Basin: *Ontario Dept. Mines Ann. Rept.*, v. 65, pt. 3, p. 57–89

———, 1960, Volcanic history of the Guatemalan highlands: *Univ. Calif. Berkeley Pub. Geol. Sci.*, v. 38, p. 1–86

Williams, H., and Goles, G., 1968, Volume of the Mazama ash-fall and the origin of Crater Lake caldera, Oregon: *Andesite Conference Guidebook, Oregon Dept. Geol. Mineral Ind. Bull. 62*, p. 37–41

Williams, H., and Meyer-Abich, H., 1955, Volcanism in the southern part of El Salvador, with particular reference to the collapse basins of Lakes Coatepeque and Ilopango: *Univ. Calif. Berkeley Pub. Geol. Sci.*, v. 32, p. 1–64

Williams, H., Curtis, G. H., and Juhle, R. W., 1956, Mount Katmai and the Valley of Ten Thousand Smokes, Alaska (a new interpretation of the great eruptions of 1912): *Eighth Pacific Sci. Congr., Philippines, 1953, Proc.*, v. 2, p. 129

Williams, P. L., 1960, A stained slice method for rapid determination of phenocryst composition of volcanic rocks: *Amer. J. Sci.*, v. 258, p. 148–152

Wright, T. L., Kinoshita, W. T., and Peck, D. L., 1968, March 1965 eruption of Kilauea Volcano and the formation of Makaopuhi lava lake: *J. Geophys. Res.*, v. 73, p. 3181–3205

Yoder, H. S., Jr., and Tilley, C. E., 1962, Origin of basalt magmas: An experimental study of natural and synthetic rock systems: *J. Petrol.*, v. 3, p. 342–532

Yokoyama, I., 1957, Energetics in active volcanoes. 2nd paper: *Tokyo Univ. Earthq. Res. Inst. Bull.*, v. 35, p. 75–97

———, 1963, Structure of caldera and gravity anomaly: *Bull. Volcanol.*, ser. 2, v. 26, p. 67–72

———, 1969, The subsurface structure of Ooshima Volcano, Izu: *J. Phys. Earth*, v. 17, p. 55–68

Zen, M. T., and Hadikusumo, D., 1964, Recent changes in the Anak-Krakatau Volcano: *Bull. Volcanol.*, ser. 2, v. 27, p. 259–268

———, 1965, The future danger of Mt. Kelut (eastern Java—Indonesia): *Bull. Volcanol.*, ser. 2, v. 28, p. 275–282

Zies, E. G., 1924, The fumarolic incrustations in the Valley of Ten Thousand Smokes: *Natl. Geogr. Soc. Contrib. Tech. Papers, Katmai Ser.*, v. 1, no. 3, p. 157–179

———, 1929, The Valley of Ten Thousand Smokes: I. The fumarolic incrustations and their bearing on ore deposition; II. The acid gases contributed to the sea during volcanic activity: *Natl. Geogr. Soc. Contrib. Tech. Papers, Katmai Ser.*, v. 1, no. 4, p. 1–79

———, 1941, Temperatures of volcanoes, fumaroles, and hot springs, in *Temperature: its measurement and control in science and industry*, American Institute of Physics, New York, p. 372–380

Zirkel, F., 1876, *Microscopical petrography, U.S. Geol. Exploration of the 40th Parallel Rept.*, v. 6, 297 p.

Zittel, K. A. von, 1901, *History of geology and paleontology*, translated by M. M. Ogilvie-Gordon, W. Scott, London, 562 p.; reprinted by Hafner Publishing Co., Inc., New York, 1962

Index

(Note: Volcanoes listed in Appendix 1 but not mentioned in the text are not indexed.)

Globular lavas, Suswa Volcano, 168
Glowing avalanches, 142–153, 225, 228
 destruction by, 148, 176, 414
 erosion by, 229
 prediction of, 425
 temperature of, 146, 230
Glowing clouds (*see* Glowing avalanches)
Goles, Gordon, 139, 236, 307
Gonzalez, R. J., 254
Goranson, R. W., 44, 45, 64
Goriachaia Sopka Volcano, Kurile Islands, 112, 439
Gorshkov, G. S., 112, 129, 159, 175, 182, 226, 254, 268, 285, 289, 306, 369, 397, 403, 404, 429, 463
Gough Island, Atlantic, 352
Grabens:
 tectonic, associated with volcanism, 313, 366
 volcanic, 285, 288, 310
Graded bedding:
 in ash, 135, 195
 in cinder, 186
Graham Island (Ile Julia), 35, 253, 449
Grand Canary Island, ignimbrite in, 164
Grande Comore Island, caldera, 298
Grande Ronde dike swarm, 260
Grand Sarcoui dome, France, 117
Grange, L. I., 287, 343
Granitization, 363
Great Basin:
 ignimbrites, 262, 267, 365
 volcanic necks, 383
Great Crack, Hawaii, 201
Great Geyser, Iceland, 332, 333, 337
Great Rift, Idaho, 261
Greek legends of volcanoes, 28
Green, D. H., 404
Green, Jack, xi
Green, T. H., 404
Green, W. L., 102
Greenland, plateau basalts, 257
Greenstones, 363
Gregg, D. R., 312
Gregory, J. W., 36
Griggs, A. B., 364
Griggs, R. F., 154, 241
Grimsvötn Volcano, Iceland, glacier bursts, 174, 175
Groh, E. A., 291
Groundmass, 454
Guam, pillow lavas at, 104
Guettard, Jean Etienne, 31
Gunn, B. M., 258
Guyots, 348

Hack, J. T., 379, 381, 383
Hadikusumo, D., 173, 253, 254
Hakone Volcano, Japan, 321
Haleakala Volcano, Hawaii, 126, 278, 311, 318, 320, 447

Haleakala Volcano (cont.):
 origin of crater of, 319
Halemaumau Crater, Kilauea, Hawaii, 276, 293, 295
 gas collection at, 47
 lava cascade in, 214
 lava lake in, 60, 196, 207, 208
 phreatic eruption at, 243, 244
 temperature measurements at, 55, 57, 58
Hall, James, 33
Hamilton, D. L., 44
Hamilton, Sir William, 31
Hamilton, W. B., 317
Hamilton, W. M., 463
Harker, A., 36
Harris, P. G., 107
Hatherton, T., 406, 407
Havens, R. G., 356
Hawaiian eruption, 206, 210, 211, 213
Hawaiian lava flows, 68, 71
Hawaiian volcanoes, 272, 274, 275, 277, 309, 446–447
 dense masses beneath, 398
 dikes and dike complexes, 374, 377, 378
 explosivity, 354
 history of, 278, 355
 tumescence of, 278
Hawaiian Volcano Observatory, 9, 38
Hawaiian Volcano Research Association, 39
Hawaiite, 356
Hay, R. L., 182, 194
Haystack Butte, Arizona, neck, 384
Heald, E. F., 52, 53, 65
Healy, J., 6
Hearn, B. C., Jr., 386, 387, 408
Hedge, C. E., 407
Hegau volcanoes, Germany, 357, 359
Heiheiahulu cone, Hawaii, 195
Hekla Volcano, Iceland, 30, 63, 64, 93, 96, 137, 206, 281, 448
 carbon dioxide at, 328, 414
 damage by ash from, 412
 water-floods at, 180
Henderson Seamount, 347
Henry Mountains, Utah, 371
Hentschel, H., 369
Herculaneum, destruction of, 234, 413
Hess, H. H., 400
Hesse district, Germany, 357, 359
Hibokhibok Volcano, Philippines, 1, 2, 3, 226, 231, 281, 435
 dome of, 1, 2, 3, 7
 eruption in 1948–1951, 3
 glowing avalanches on, 3–7, 146, 150, 151, 153
 mudflows on, 8
Hills, R. C., 374
Hilo, Hawaii, proposed lava diversion barriers for, 421

208020

DATE DUE

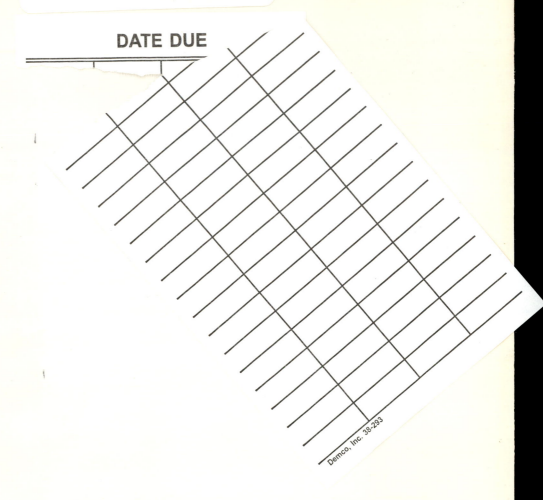

Demco, Inc. 38-293